Praise for
Teaching Everyone: An Introduction to Inclusive Education

"Leaving behind limited categorical labels and concepts, this book does an amazing job of putting disability in its place: as only one of the many ways in which students differ. I can't wait to use this book in my courses."
—**Mara Sapon-Shevin**, Professor of Inclusive Education, Syracuse University

"An important book. Special education as a field needs to move from focusing on student deficits and their remediation to creating learning environments that build on and enhance student strengths. This book is a tool to help special educators truly collaborate in teaching everyone."
—**Michael Peterson**, Director, Whole Schooling Consortium; coauthor, *Inclusive Teaching: The Journey Towards Effective Schools for All Learners*

"The introduction book to special education I have always dreamed about! Informational, progressive, and forward-thinking … promot[es] inclusive practices, differentiation, Universal Design for Learning, and more. Just what the professor ordered!"
—**Patrick Schwarz**, Ph.D., Professor, Diversity in Learning & Teaching Department, National-Louis University, Chicago

"Contributes a fresh, compelling, and comprehensive perspective on the rationales for inclusion, and follows up with general and specific strategies for teaching *all* learners. The thorough attention to the 'why' of inclusion is highly persuasive."
—**Mary Jo Noonan**, Ph.D., Department of Special Education, University of Hawai'i

"Finally we have a textbook for preservice teachers that will introduce them to inclusive education, challenge them think critically, and provide them with practical strategies all at the same time. Rapp and Arndt got it right; they understand that inclusive education isn't about simply offering a visual schedule to a learner with autism or giving extra testing time to a student with learning disabilities, it is about exploring inequities, creating experiences that are appropriately challenging and motivating for all, and building strong communities."
—**Paula Kluth**, Ph.D., author of the *"You're Going to Love This Kid!"* book and professional development DVD

"A comprehensive, user-friendly text … presents best practices in educating all students and offers curriculum-specific teaching and assessment strategies."
—**Cathy Houston-Wilson**, Ph.D., Professor, Associate Chair, Coordinator of Student Teaching, Department of Kinesiology, Sport Studies, & Physical Education

"Packed with rich content … I highly recommend this text for teacher preparation programs that want all of their graduates to *believe* they can teach all students—and to know *how* to teach all students."
—**Rachel E. Janney**, Ph.D., Independent Consultant and Scholar, Lincoln, Virginia

"How refreshing! An introductory text to special education that addresses the process of education rather than focusing predominantly on specific disability labels. This book is an excellent resource for training all K–12 teachers and its widespread use in introductory courses is highly recommended."
—**Jacki L. Anderson**, Ph.D., California State University East Bay

TEACHING EVERYONE

An Introduction to Inclusive Education

TEACHING
EVERYONE

An Introduction to Inclusive Education

by

Whitney H. Rapp, Ph.D.

and

Katrina L. Arndt, Ph.D.
St. John Fisher College
Rochester, New York

Baltimore • London • Sydney

Paul H. Brookes Publishing Co.
Post Office Box 10624
Baltimore, Maryland 21285-0624
USA

www.brookespublishing.com

Typeset by Spearhead Global, Inc., Bear, Delaware.
Manufactured in the United States of America by
Versa Press, Inc., East Peoria, Illinois.

Some individuals described in this book are composites or real people whose situations are masked and are based on the authors' experiences. In some instances, names and identifying details have been changed to protect confidentiality.

Permission to reprint the following is gratefully acknowledged:

Pages 14, 15, 106–107, and 111: Quotations from Widening the circle : the power of inclusive classrooms by Sapon-Shevin, Mara Copyright 2012 Reproduced with permission of BEACON PRESS in the format Textbook via Copyright Clearance Center.

Pages 111–112, 185, 218, and 300: Quotations from *Black Ants and Buddhists* by Mary Cowhey Copyright © 2006. Reproduced by permission from Stenhouse Publishers.

Library of Congress Cataloging-in-Publication Data

Rapp, Whitney H.
   Teaching everyone : an introduction to inclusive education / by Whitney H. Rapp, Ph.D. and Katrina L. Arndt.
     p. cm.
   Includes bibliographical references and index.
   ISBN-13: 978-1-59857-212-4
   ISBN-10: 1-59857-212-1
   1. Special education.   2. Children with disabilities—Education.   I. Arndt, Katrina L.   II. Title.
   LC3965.R36 2012
   371.9—dc23

                                          2012001016

British Library Cataloguing in Publication data are available from the British Library.

2016   2015   2014   2013   2012

10   9   8   7   6   5   4   3   2   1

Contents

About the Online Companion Materials xi
About the Authors xiii
Foreword   *Susan Peters* xv
Foreword   *Douglas Biklen* xvii
Acknowledgments xix
Introduction xxiii

**I   Why Does Teaching Everyone Matter? The History of
     Special Education** 1

1   Construction of Ability and Disability, Intersections of Ability,
    Race, and Gender 3
    Disability Throughout History 5
    How Race, Gender, and Disability Are Socially Constructed 10
    How the Social Construction of Disability Affects Education
        and Schooling 13
    Narrative 1.1. Keith Jones 16
2   History of Special Education 19
    Education in the United States 21
    The Development of Special Education 25
    What We Want to See 29
    Narrative 2.1. Larry Bissonnette 35
3   Special Education Law and Legislation 37
    The Road Traveled 38
    Narrative 3.1. Dr. David Rostetter 47
    Where We Stand 53
    Narrative 3.2. Jeannine Dingus-Eason 54
    Current Context and Issues 55
    The Trip Ahead 57

**II   What Does Teaching Everyone Mean? The Educator's Role
      and Citizenship in the Classroom** 61

4   Early Intervention: Birth Through Preschool   *Martha Mock* 63
    Development of Policy and Practices of Early Intervention 64
    Narrative 4.1. Advice to Professionals Who Must "Conference Cases" ... 67
    Narrative 4.2. Letting Go 69
    Major Principles in Early Intervention and Early Childhood
        Special Education 71
    Summary and Future Directions 79
5   Child and Adolescent Development 81
    Theories of Child and Adolescent Development 82
    Impact of Developmental Theories in Context of School 93

Development in the Context of Disability..98
What Teachers Should Know About Child and
   Adolescent Development...99
Narrative 5.1. Cady Welch 99

6   Classroom Management 105
Building Community..106
Classroom Management 115
Special Education and Classroom Management.................................... 119
Narrative 6.1. Rachel Zindler 124

7   Differentiation... 127
A Conceptual Framework for Successful Differentiation 128
Narrative 7.1. Sam Rapp 133
Differentiation of Instruction... 134
Narrative 7.2. Matt Giordano 135
Considerations and Classroom Cases 139

8   Universal Design for Learning.. 143
Definition of Universal Design for Learning 144
Why Universal Design for Learning? 145
Principles of Universal Design for Learning.. 145
Narrative 8.1. Tina Calabro.. 146
Provide Multiple Means of Representation 146
A Universal Design for Learning Classroom 152

9   Assessment.. 161
Assessment in the Classroom... 163
Evaluation for Special Education... 170
Placement and the Individualized Education Program 175
Narrative 9.1. Laura Whitcomb 177

10   Collaboration 179
Collaboration Best Practices 180
Home–School Collaboration... 184
Collaboration within the School 186
Collaboration Between School and Agencies... 187
Narrative 10.1. Sheri Stanger... 189
Narrative 10.2. Colleen Brown 190

11   Transition from High School to Adult Life... 191
Issues... 192
Legislation and Processes 194
Community Connections... 197
Narrative 11.1. Postsecondary Program Students................................ 199

III   **How Will I Teach Everyone? Instructional Strategies
     by Content Area**..**203**

12   Management Strategies for All Students... 205
Strategies for Management.. 207
Narrative 12.1. Maggie Driscoll 219

13   Reading Strategies for All Students 221
     Reading Instruction and Access to Instruction... 223
     Least Dangerous Assumption 225
     Digital Media, Common Core State Standards, and
         Response to Intervention (RTI) 227
     Strategies for Engagement, Input, Output, and Assessment.................... 229
     Narrative 13.1. Joellen Maples 238

14   Writing Strategies for All Students.. 241
     Components of Writing... 243
     Strategies for Engagement, Input, Output, and Assessment.................... 246

15   Social Studies Strategies for All Students.. 253
     Strategies for Teaching Social Studies to All Students............................. 256

16   Math Strategies for All Students 265
     Strategies for Teaching Math to All Students.. 268
     Narrative 16.1. Michael, High School Math Teacher 277

17   Science Strategies for All Students 279
     Strategies for Teaching Science to All Students 282
     Narrative 17.1. Debra Ortenzi 293

18   Social and Communication Strategies for All Students............................. 295
     Strategies for Teaching Social and Communication Skills
         to All Students 299
     Narrative 18.1. Clara Berg... 308

19   Working with Special Area Teachers and Related Service
         Professionals 311
     Working with Special Area Teachers... 312
     Working with Related Service Professionals... 316
     Narrative 19.1. Susan M. Hildenbrand 319

References.. 321

Appendix: Resources for Comprehensive Teaching....................................... 333

Author Index... 357

Subject Index.. 361

About the Online Companion Materials

Attention Instructors! Free online companion materials are available to help you teach a course using *Teaching Everyone: An Introduction to Inclusive Education*. **Please visit www. brookespublishing.com/rapp to access:**

- Customizable PowerPoint presentations for every chapter, complete with notes for guiding discussions
- Over 20 activities to enhance classes, fostering better student understanding, application, and synthesis of information
- A chapter-by-chapter guide showing how the Council for Exceptional Children (CEC) Initial Content Standards are addressed in the book, highlighting what each chapter offers students as they develop their knowledge of special education

About the Authors

Whitney Rapp, Ph.D., Associate Professor of Inclusive Education, St. John Fisher College, Rochester, New York

Dr. Whitney H. Rapp is an Associate Professor of Inclusive Education at St. John Fisher College in Rochester, New York, where she teaches courses on inclusive education pedagogy, assessment, classroom management, and diversity issues. She is currently serving as Associate Dean of the Ralph C. Wilson, Jr., School of Education. Dr. Rapp holds a B.A. in elementary education and psychology from the State University of New York at Potsdam and an M.A. and a Ph.D. in special education from Michigan State University. Prior to her 14 years of experience in teacher education programs, Whitney taught many different grade levels in a variety of settings, from fully inclusive classrooms to residential special education schools. All of these experiences reinforced her belief that all children can learn and that all children should learn together in inclusive settings. Whitney's current research interests include universal design for learning—particularly strategies to support executive functioning abilities. She presents often at local, state, and national conferences on differentiation of instruction and teacher education. Whitney's spare time is spent with her husband and three children, riding bikes, hiking, gardening, reading, watching movies, and enjoying Owasco Lake.

Katrina L. Arndt, **Ph.D.,** Associate Professor of Inclusive Education, St. John Fisher College, Rochester, New York

Dr. Katrina L. Arndt is an Associate Professor of Inclusive Education at St. John Fisher College. She teaches courses in the undergraduate and graduate programs in inclusive pedagogy, collaboration, assessment, classroom management, and diversity issues, and has supervised student teachers and graduate-field placements. Before entering higher education, she was a preschool teacher, paraprofessional, and special education teacher in Minneapolis, Minnesota, for 10 years. She then worked as secondary English co-teacher in the Rochester, New York, area.

Dr. Arndt holds a B.A. in philosophy from Grinnell College and an M.A. in educational psychology from the University of Minnesota. Her Ph.D. in special education and her Certificate of Advanced Study in disability studies are from Syracuse University. She joined the faculty of St. John Fisher College in 2005, and was a part of the group of faculty who voted to merge the Special Education, Adolescence Education, and Childhood Education Departments to become a single inclusive education department in 2010. Her research interests focus broadly on inclusive practices in schooling and narrowly on sharing the perspectives of children, youth, and adults who are visually impaired, blind, and deafblind. Katrina spends her free time enjoying the outdoors with her partner Lauren, visiting her many nieces and nephews, and hiking in the Adirondacks.

Foreword

At last! A book with a different approach to preparing teachers has become available to the academic mainstream! For over 20 years, education law at the national level has expressed a preference for integrating *all* children into K–12 classes. Yet, teacher education and special education programs have only begun to integrate teacher preparation at the university level. This book bridges that divide by recognizing that all teachers, just as all children and youth, need the knowledge, skills, aptitude, and commitment to teaching and learning in inclusive schools. When we value every student's talents and abilities and look beyond labels to the student underneath who is waiting to be discovered, then our world opens to infinite possibilities.

This book advances our outlook by beginning with a basic premise: Children and youth are not the sources of problems. They are the resources needed to solve our problems. Our sons and daughters, nieces and nephews, and grandchildren, enter school with a wealth of diversity, experiences, curiosity, love of learning, and wish to do well. This book provides a strong foundation to ensure that students succeed by devoting considerable attention in Parts I and II to issues that have long plagued our classrooms and society: issues of equality, fairness, opportunities to learn, attitudinal barriers, and the ways in which our current policies and practices compromise and often impede progress for children—especially those from minority backgrounds. The book provides ample evidence that "at-risk" is not a characteristic of students but a characteristic of the situation students find themselves in when school seems to be more about categorizing, sorting, labeling, and testing students than it is about preparing them for a life of active citizenship and community and family involvement—in short, *life after school*. After all, students are ultimately tested in the experiences of life, not on math or reading scores.

Section III of the book challenges all of us to invest our beliefs, our resources, and our intellectual problem-solving abilities in inclusive education. Students with disabilities and all marginalized youth (whether due to language, religion, race, ethnicity, or gender) do not have to be disadvantaged by their treatment in schools or by exclusion within schools: "If you deny disabled people educational opportunities, then it is the lack of education and not their disabilities that limit their opportunities."[1] Section III recognizes the depth and breadth of approaches needed for opportunities to achieve, not only academic competence, but its necessary complement, social competence in order to live and be in the world.

This book offers us opportunities for social justice in day-to-day tasks undertaken with individual children and youth in classrooms, in schools, and in society. Universal design for learning and social justice are double imperatives and worthy goals in today's global society. This book has made a significant contribution to those goals.

Susan Peters
Associate Professor Emeritus, Michigan State University

---

[1]Judy Heumann, Senior Advisor to the Disability Group, The World Bank, quoted in S.J. Peters. (November 2004). *Inclusive education and EFA strategy for all children*. World Bank.

Foreword

There is much to like about *Teaching Everyone: An Introduction to Inclusive Education*, not the least of which is its clear, didactic style and organization. As I read the book, I never wondered where I was. Each chapter unveils central elements of how educators can conceptualize and implement inclusive education. This begins with a careful description of the disability studies framework, including Kunc and Van der Klift's Credo for Support that explains what assistance looks like when framed from an ally perspective and informed by a critical politics-of-disability understanding. This is a perfect beginning, for it puts forward a strong message of rights, dignity, and educational opportunity along with frameworks that teachers can keep coming back to as a foundational grounding. It is a narrative that needs to be spoken aloud in schools, not only for the benefit of teachers and school leaders, but for students and parents as well.

Teaching Everyone unleashes disability studies on special education or, more accurately, transforms how to think about the intersection of disability and education. Years ago, my colleagues and I published a book entitled *An Alternative Textbook in Special Education*, and while that book began discussions that *Teaching Everyone* takes up, it did not have the benefit of the now well-formed discipline of disability studies. Premises which are evident in the equity-focused discipline of disability studies and also prominent throughout this book include

- A challenge to basic assumptions about disability and normalcy, encouraging educators to understand disability as a part of normal
- An explanation of how ideas about disability shift over time and context, with different effects and outcomes as a child experiences preschool, elementary and middle school, and prepares for life beyond the classroom
- An investigation of the broad theoretical frameworks of disability, from the medical, to the charitable, to the social/political/economic
- An exposure to ways in which certain practices oppress people on the basis of disability, even if said to be done out of concern, such as labeling and tracking in schools
- A call to listen to the narratives of people with disabilities—"nothing about us without us"—for the expertise they can provide
- The requirement that all students have full citizenship, full participation, and agency
- An illustration of how disability can be understood and embraced as an identity, much as occurs with gender, race, and sexual preference

Notions such as these that are identified with disability studies and are reflected throughout the text of *Teaching Everyone* provide the basis for a rich, new conversation about schooling, one that is long overdue.

As the chapters unfold, readers learn about the legal basis for inclusive education, key terms that evoke a sense of possibility in association with difference—notable among these is the idea of *presuming competence*—as well as instructional concepts and practices such as universal design for learning. One of the most difficult hurdles for such a completely new approach to learning about special education is to seamlessly connect clinical knowledge (e.g., about how to teach reading/literacy) with broad social agendas (e.g., equality of educational opportunity for all students or inclusive education for those whose disabilities are most complex). *Teaching Everyone* accomplishes that feat, and it does so without any sense that it might have been a struggle for the authors; it feels natural. That being said, we have to lament that fact that this book has not been around for decades. Happily, it is with us now.

Douglas Biklen
Dean, School of Education, Syracuse University

Acknowledgments

FROM WHITNEY AND KATRINA

Thank you to all our friends and colleagues who helped us conceptualize, write, and revise this textbook. This project evolved from years of discussions and debates with our colleagues, friends, family, and students about the nature of a foundational survey course in special education. Our first thanks goes to our mentors, Dr. Susan Peters and Dr. Douglas Biklen. Our second thanks goes to Rebecca Lazo and Steve Plocher, our wonderful editors. Thank you to Martha Mock for her invaluable expertise in early childhood and her contribution of Chapter 4.

Thanks to our colleagues in the community, including Dr. Deasure Matthews, Dr. Ray Giamartino, Dr. Harold Levy, Don Shuryn, Leslee Mabee, Dr. Tom Hall, and Rob Thomas. We also thank special area teachers and related services professionals who shared their expertise.

Thank you to Danielle Hippert and Tiffany Polino for opening their classrooms to us. Our heartfelt thanks to the amazing and incomparable Ina Vento, Laurie Worthington, Liz Stark, and Beth Jackelen, for sharing the wonderful things they do every day. All are classroom teachers who model exemplary inclusive coteaching.

We thank the people who graciously agreed to add their perspectives to this text, writing narratives that complement our perspective: Clara Berg, Larry Bissonnette, Erin Beyers, Colleen Brown, Tina Calabro, Jeannine Dingus-Eason, Maggie Driscoll, Janice Fialka, Matt Giordano, Dr. Susan Hildenbrand, Keith Jones, Sam Rapp, Dr. David Rostetter, Sheri Stanger, Cady Welch, Laura Whitcomb, Rachel Zindler, all the students in the postsecondary program at St. John Fisher College, and first-year high school math teacher Michael.

Finally, we thank our teacher candidates whose questions keep us learning and researching and whose enthusiasm helps us remember why the hard work is worth every minute.

FROM WHITNEY

I owe great thanks to my husband, Steve Rapp, whose unconditional support is behind all of my accomplishments and whose insight broadens my thinking. I am ever grateful for the encouragement of my family, especially my mother Carol Bailey, for—well, everything. In memory of my grandmother, Reva Abbott, I thank her for teaching all of us that life is about taking care of each other. I am indebted to Dr. Susan Flood, a great teacher, colleague, leader, and friend, for giving me great perspective on the art of wearing many hats. I would also like to express my deep appreciation and admiration to an amazing writing partner, Dr. Katrina Arndt—we wrote a book!

FROM KATRINA

Thanks to Dr. Lauren Lieberman for her constant encouragement and support and to David and Jennifer Arndt for their continuous praxis of acceptance and inclusion. Thanks to Douglas Biklen, Steve Taylor, and Marj DeVault for their guidance and example. Thanks to Dr. Lauren Lieberman and David Arndt for their editing of draft chapters and to Alison Ackerman, Amy Elverum, and Amy Hunt for their thoughtful comments. Thank you to Whitney for writing this text with me—it has been a wonderful, rollicking process to collaborate on this book.

Introduction

This textbook evolved from our years of teaching survey courses in special education to undergraduate and graduate students in our education programs. We both value introducing the background and philosophy of inclusive education to students and framing course content as necessarily critical of a medicalized conceptualization of disability. However, we were frustrated when we tried to find a text that matched our philosophy and grounding in a disability studies perspective.

No textbook on the market had a noncategorical structure. We grew increasingly dismayed at the way disability was presented as individual, immutable fault. We aligned with much of the content of the current introduction to special education textbooks but could not bear to assign a text that used a chapter format of "students with learning disabilities," "students with autism spectrum disorders," and "students with intellectual disabilities." The result of exposure to texts such as these would be major student misconceptions regarding human diversity. Many budding educators leave this type of foundational course with the belief that children are either whole or they are broken, and fixing them entails defining the weak points and labeling them into a disability category. There is not a textbook available today that challenges the ubiquitous focus on labeling and remediation toward "normalcy."

This was disconcerting, as the content of some current introductory texts is exactly what we believe and what we want students to learn. In addition, the content of many textbooks was extremely well researched, well written, and clearly presented. The issue for us is that the structure of chapters divided by disability category presents groups of children as fundamentally similar because of a shared label. This is inaccurate and dangerous, reinforcing a belief in the current structure of special education and labeling that we simply cannot endorse.

In a single semester, we introduce special education to future teachers. Instructors need be more concerned with shaping attitudes and beliefs about disability than about providing a series of teaching strategies that assume that each child with a particular label is more similar than different from other children with the same label. We believe that if you have met one child with autism (or a learning disability, or an emotional disturbance, or another label), you have met *one* child with autism (or a learning disability, or an emotional disturbance, or another label).

Organizing content as though strategies for children with autism are different from strategies for children without autism does not fit for us; we believe that many, many strategies that work for one child will work with many others. And some strategies work for only a few children—a group that includes those with different labels or no label at all. The issue for us is seeing each child as an individual and working to support him or her based on who he or she is—not on a label. We feel so strongly about seeing all children as unique individuals that we stopped using textbooks years ago and instead created course readers of articles, narratives, and web resources that reinforced our resistance to the default of using labels to separate children.

Over many semesters and sections of our survey course, we realized that our goal for this textbook is twofold. First, we want all students in teacher preparation to enter the profession grounded in the belief that all children can learn and that the teacher's role is to support the success of all students. To us, this means helping students understand that a label does not tell teachers very much. Second, we want students to understand the special education system within the context of our American educational system. A label is a way to secure services, to use the system to support children, and a tool for providing supports. Using labels effectively to access supports for students with disabilities is our focus; we actively avoid a focus on labels for the sake of labels.

So our two goals led us to two objectives: teach preservice teachers the educational system we have now so that they can work within it to support children through differentiated instruction and teach teachers what is wrong with relying on labeling to access supports for students who need them.

The primary courses for which this textbook is intended are introductory-level special education survey courses, particularly at the undergraduate level. In such survey courses, preservice educators are introduced to the field of special education and current issues therein. These courses are offered during freshman or sophomore year, at the beginning of their teacher education program. Whether the preservice teacher seeks general and/or special education certification, he or she is highly likely to be required to take an introductory course in special education. This is often the only class that exposes them to issues in special education.

This text is aligned with the Council for Exceptional Children (CEC) Initial Content Standards. In each chapter, there is a list that explains how the content helps students meet several of the 10 standards. In the Online Companion Materials the standards each chapter meets are listed in full with the same information provided for easy reproduction and documentation of alignment. One important note is that throughout the text we used the terms "teachers" and "all students," because we believe that we need to talk about all teachers teaching all students. That means that using language about "special educators" and "students with exceptional learning needs" does not work because all students have some exceptional needs, and all teachers need to understand and respond to that—not just special education teachers.

Specific course titles in current programs include Introduction to Special Education, Critical Issues in Special Education, Study of Elementary and Special Education Teaching, Human Exceptionalities, Teaching Students with Special Needs in the Inclusive Classroom, Social Foundations of Education, and Diverse Learners in Multicultural Perspective.

This book is divided into three parts. Section I includes Chapters 1–3; Section II includes Chapters 4–11, and Section III includes Chapters 12–19. Each section begins with a brief overview of the chapters. In most chapters, there are narratives from people with different perspectives on special education and how disability is socially constructed, including people with disability labels, family members, advocates, and teachers. Each individual was asked to contribute because of his or her ability to share an experience that will support your understanding of the way education works in the United States today.

Section I is titled "Why Does Teaching Everyone Matter? The History of Special Education." The three chapters in this section review a very brief history of formal education in the United States, introduce disability studies as the framework for the text, and discuss how disability is socially constructed. Following that, the history of special education is reviewed, including the laws and legislation that frame special education services in schools today.

Chapter 1, "Construction of Ability and Disability, Intersections of Ability, Race, and Gender," uses disability studies to introduce the ways that people with disabilities have been treated throughout history. How disability, race, and gender are socially constructed is then explored, followed by a consideration of how outcomes might change if we shifted our perspective to think of disability as a form of diversity instead of as something broken that needs to be fixed.

Chapter 2, "History of Special Education," reviews the history of formal education in the United States, including how ideas from the Enlightenment and Progressive eras affected education. How education for students with disabilities developed is explained, including a review of the first law mandating education for all children, The Education for All Handicapped Children Act (EHC). Last, we explain that determining what supports are needed and how teachers are assessed are two factors that have a significant effect on how we think about education for students with disabilities and inclusion.

Chapter 3, "Special Education Laws and Legislation," is focused on special education legislation and laws. Important court cases are summarized, and then the current status of special education is examined. The chapter ends by describing the path we must follow to achieve the equitable education of all children.

Section II is titled "What Does Teaching Everyone Mean? The Educator's Role and Citizenship in the Classroom." The eight chapters in this part are designed to introduce you to child development, how children learn, and your role as an educator. Each chapter has a specific content focus. In order, the chapters include early intervention (by Dr. Martha Mock), child and adolescent development, creating community and classroom management, differentiation and citizenship, universal design for learning (UDL), assessment, collaboration, and transition from high school to adult life.

Chapter 4, "Early Intervention" by Dr. Martha Mock, reviews the history and major principles that guide schooling for young children from birth through age 5 and their families. Next, the Council for Exceptional Children's Division of Early Childhood recommendations for recommended practices from research-based evidence are described.

Chapter 5, "Child and Adolescent Development," discusses different theories about how children and adolescents develop mentally, physically, and socially. How this information affects how schools design the school day and instruction is reviewed, and the chapter ends with a consideration of how typical development guidelines can be mindfully used to support students who develop typically and students who have a different pattern of development.

Chapter 6, "Classroom Management," explores how teachers build community and set up clear routines and expectations for all students. Also in this chapter, positive behavioral interventions and supports (PBIS) and functional behavior assessment (FBA) processes are introduced and explained.

Chapter 7, "Differentiation and Full Citizenship," presents a way of thinking about citizenship based on Kliewer's (1998) work and then describes what differentiation means and how to analyze student needs and plan for teaching a diverse group of students. A case study and examples are used to illustrate what differentiation can be in the classroom.

Chapter 8, "Universal Design for Learning," explores the idea that all aspects of the classroom need to be differentiated so that all students can be successful; this is the definition of universal design for learning (UDL). After explaining the concept of UDL, UDL principles are presented and how to apply those principles to developing curriculum is described. A case study of a fourth-grade teacher using UDL is presented.

Chapter 9, "Assessment," introduces formative and summative assessments and the cycle of planning, assessment, and instruction. Response to intervention (RTI) is described, including why it was developed and how it is used in schools. The chapter ends with a review of the evaluation process for determining if a child is eligible to receive services through our special education system.

Chapter 10, "Collaboration," describes best practices in collaboration, and discusses ways that teachers are expected to collaborate. A focus on the best interests of students helps collaborative relationships. Collaborations between home and school are explained, and then collaboration within the school is explored, ending with a review of collaboration between schools and community agencies.

Chapter 11, "Transition from High School to Adult Life," presents the idea that teaching does not end with high school—it extends into adult life in the work force, higher education, the community, and social life. How to support students transitioning out of school into adult life is essential information for secondary teachers. Legislation that regulates transition planning is reviewed, and then an overview of programs and resources that support community connections is presented.

Section III is titled "How Will I Teach Everyone? Instructional Strategies by Content Area" and includes eight chapters. This section of the book is presented by content area and related skills instead of by disability label, focusing on ways to teach different content and skills to students using the UDL framework. The topics are classroom management, reading strategies, writing strategies, social studies strategies, math strategies, science strategies, social and communication strategies, and working with special area teachers and related service professionals. Our hope is that by the time you reach Section III, you understand that whether a child has a label or not is far less important for day-to-day instructional decisions than strategies to teach content to a diverse group of students. In each chapter, you will find multiple ways to engage students, multiple ways to represent new learning to students, multiple ways for students to express new learning, and multiple ways to assess student progress.

Chapter 12, "Management Strategies for All Students," explores the background of good management and reviews what the American Federation of Teachers (AFT) and the Council for Exceptional Children (CEC) recommend related to managing your classroom. Strategies for management are presented, including how to collect and share data about behavior.

Chapter 13, "Reading Strategies for All Students," introduces reading instruction and the guidelines of the International Reading Association (IRA) and the National Reading Panel. The role of digital media is reviewed, followed by a consideration of how response to intervention (RTI) is being adopted. The last section presents strategies to support all students in reading.

Chapter 14, "Writing Strategies for All Students," describes the kinds of writing students are expected to do in school, and reviews the components of writing and common models of writing instruction. Strategies to help all students with writing are presented in the context of the stages of the writing process, and the chapter ends with a reminder to see and nurture all students' literacy skills.

Chapter 15, "Social Studies Strategies for All Students," explains the standards of the National Council for the Social Studies (NCSS). These standards guide the development of social studies curriculum and provide a framework for organizing instruction. This chapter also reviews significant traditions in social studies teaching over time and explores strategies that are particularly useful in this content area.

Chapter 16, "Math Strategies for All Students," introduces the National Council of Teachers of Mathematics (NCTM) standards in numbers and operations; algebra, geometry, and spatial sense; measurement, data analysis, and probability; and process. The Common Core State Standards for mathematics practice are reviewed as well as strategies for teaching. A key point in this chapter is that math is for everyone: If teachers believe that not everyone is capable in math, research shows that the belief can come true. Students respond to teachers' beliefs about their abilities and rise or fall to the expectations teachers hold.

Chapter 17, "Science Strategies for All Students," introduces the National Committee on Science Education Standards and Assessment (1996) standards and explores ways to make science instruction engaging and accessible for all students, including the need to focus on critical thinking skills instead of memorizing facts. A wide range of resources is provided.

Chapter 18, "Social and Communication Strategies for All Students," explains the components of communication and how to support students' skills in each area. The components reviewed are receptive communication, expressive communication, and social skills. These skills are not traditionally included as a content area and are a part of the hidden curriculum of school—the skills that students need to be successful in school but are not always explicitly taught.

Chapter 19, "Working with Special Area Teachers and Related Service Professionals," emphasizes the importance of planning with other adults in the school who support students, including managing transitions and developing consistent expectations for students. An essential role of all teachers is to work together to serve students and meet each child's unique needs.

The appendix is a list of resources for comprehensive teaching, divided by topic. It includes current web sites, books, and other materials, such as DVDs and films.

Why Does Teaching Everyone Matter?

The History of Special Education

OVERVIEW

Section I includes Chapters 1, 2, and 3 and introduces you to the history of special education. Chapter 1 is titled "Construction of Ability and Disability, Intersections of Ability, Race, and Gender" and has three parts. The first part introduces disability studies and explains how the medical, pity/charity, and social models of disability shape our thinking about people with disabilities. Then we explore how social constructions of race, gender, and disability affect how people are treated. Examining social constructions of race and gender provides an important background in understanding how disability is a social construct, just as race and gender are, and the attitudes and beliefs we have about disability have a significant effect on how we treat people with disabilities. The final part reinforces this last point, detailing the impact of social construction on schooling for students with disabilities.

Chapter 2 is a review of the history of special education. This begins with the development of formal education in the United States, followed by an exploration of the way special education evolved from the civil rights movement through parent advocacy, resulting in the passage of The Education for All Handicapped Children Act (EHC) in 1975. The impact of the use of labels to identify which students receive services through special education is addressed. Then, the way that supports were provided to students with disability labels through the development of a separate system of education—special education—is described, and our concern about the impact of a separate system is presented. The chapter ends with a review of the ways that different children are treated: some (often students without disability labels) as capable learners who deserve to be included, others (often children who have a disability label) as learners who must prove their abilities before being allowed in general education.

Chapter 3 focuses on the court cases and laws that affect special education. The chapter is divided into two sections: 1) a review of significant court cases and laws and 2) a discussion of the benefits and drawbacks to the special education law. In the first section, the connection of the 1954 *Brown v. Board of Education* case to special education is explained, followed by summaries of specific cases. Each case is presented in the same format: the parties bringing the case to court are described, the facts of the case and the ruling are presented, and the significance of the case is explained. We hope this format facilitates your understanding of the legislative details and the reasons why we included each case. In addition to court cases, laws developing and regulating special education are described. Each law's purpose and provisions are detailed, followed by an explanation of the impact of the law on schools. In the second section, the current context and issues are explored. The difference in the spirit and the letter of how the laws are enacted has a strong impact on students. The way laws are interpreted is affected by the attitudes and beliefs that policy makers, school administrators, and teachers have about students with disability labels. The chapter ends with recommendations for future policy and practice.

These three chapters help the preservice teacher understand the context of teaching in the United States today through an exploration of the social constructions that shape attitudes and beliefs about race, gender, and disability and a review of the history of special education. We designed this foundation to stimulate students' critical thinking about general and special education and the profession they are entering.

CHAPTER 1

Construction of Ability and Disability, Intersections of Ability, Race, and Gender

How this chapter prepares you to be an effective inclusive classroom teacher:

- In this chapter, we explain the foundations of disability studies. Through this process, you will see special education as an evolving and changing discipline based on philosophies, evidence-based principles and theories, diverse and historical points of view, and human issues that have historically influenced and continue to influence the field of special education and the education and treatment of individuals with exceptional needs in both school and society. We explain the historically negative treatment of people with disabilities and provide the Credo for Support. We introduce you to three models of looking at disability: the medical, pity/charity, and social models. We explain how the social construction of disability, like the social construction of gender, has changed over time, and we explain the positive effects of such shifts. This background knowledge is a ground upon which to construct your own personal understandings and philosophies of special education. **This helps you meet CEC Standard 1: Foundations.**

- This chapter provides essential grounding in the historical treatment of people with disabilities. It also explains the serious and negative consequences of underestimating students' potential and explains the "least dangerous assumption" philosophy. Reviewing examples of the medical, pity/charity, and social models of disability gives you a context for understanding how your own and others' attitudes and beliefs have effects on students with disabilities. **This helps you meet CEC Standard 9: Professional and Ethical Practice.**

After reading and discussing this chapter, you will be able to

- Explain how some Hollywood films show "better dead than disabled" thinking

- Explain the concept of normal

- Explain the nature/nurture debate

- Explain how industrialization affected the social construction of disability

- Explain the medical, pity/charity, and social models of disability

- Define and explain the concept of social construction

- Explain how race and gender are socially created

- Explain five different ways that disability is constructed and give examples of each construction

- Create and explain a historical time line of the treatment of people with disabilities

- Explain how schooling in the United States is affected by the social construction of disability

- Explain what the least dangerous assumption is and give an example

disability studies   A way of looking at disability that considers how society thinks about disability and how to challenge limits that society puts on people with disabilities

This chapter introduces perspectives about disability throughout history. In the first section, we use **disability studies** to introduce you to ways that people have thought about disability and people with disabilities throughout history. In education, disability studies "examines disability in social and cultural context. Constructions of disability are questioned, and special education assumptions and practices are challenged" (Taylor, 2008, xix). Examining the social construction of ability and disability will give you a new perspective on history. This perspective will help you understand the attitudes and beliefs that are present in today's society. By looking back, we can understand the present and then shape the future. The second section explains how disability, race, and gender are all socially constructed; how different cultures define each one of these characteristics; and who benefits from each social construction. The last section will discuss how the social construction of disability affects education and schooling and how outcomes might change if we shifted our perspective to think of disability as a form of diversity instead of as something broken that needs to be fixed.

Each chapter in this book includes interviews or narratives by people labeled as disabled, their family members, their advocates, and their teachers. Each was carefully chosen to complement the topic of the chapter and to provide insight into the ways families and schools engage in the work of supporting inclusive education for all students. At the end of this chapter, there is an interview with Keith Jones, a disability rights activist who has been featured in the films *Including Samuel* and *Labeled Disabled*.

The appendix includes resources, primarily web sites that we have found to be useful in thinking about disability as a socially constructed status, and we encourage you to check them out. In addition, in the accompanying instructor's materials, we provide activities that your instructor will conduct in class. These activities are ones that we have used in our own classes, and students have reported that these activities are helpful in developing a better understanding of the concepts we discuss.

DISABILITY THROUGHOUT HISTORY

When thinking about disability or a person with a disability, many people first think, "I would hate to have a disability!" or, "Oh, that's so sad!" These two statements capture much of history: that disability is bad, or disability is pitiful, or both. We want to challenge those initial reactions by establishing disability as just another way of being, and not wrong or pitiful. To do that, we look at how people with disabilities have been treated in the past to understand why we might have a reaction that is negative or derisive, pitying, or fearful today.

Photo 1.1. Your attitude is my only handicap. (From Tom Olin, SCW ©1998.)

Throughout history, people with disabilities have been seen as different from people without disabilities. And often, these differences have been seen as negative, and people with disabilities have been characterized as "bad" or "evil." For example, in the Middle Ages some believed that people who are deaf, who have epilepsy, and who have intellectual disabilities were possessed by demons (Braddock, 2002, p. 11). Others believed that having a disability was a punishment from God, and if a person has a disability, it is because he or she did something wrong to deserve the disability. The belief that people who have a disability are evil or strange has been present in film for more than 100 years (Safran, 1998) and continues today. Consider how people with physical disabilities are portrayed in films such as *Edward Scissorhands* (Burton, 1990) and *Hook* (Spielberg, 1991); in both films, the man with a physical disability is considered dangerous and strange. In the Credo for Support (Figure 1.1), Norm Kunc and Emma Van der Klift noted that

> People with physical and mental disabilities have been abandoned at birth, banished from society, used as court jesters, drowned and burned during the Inquisition, gassed in Nazi Germany, and still continue to be segregated, institutionalized, tortured in the name of behavior management, abused, raped, euthanized, and murdered. (Credo for Support)

While this may sound extreme, it is important to know that this is true. Because people with disabilities are not always seen as real people, mistreating them in a range of ways has been accepted. Sometimes, people with disabilities are seen as sick (Charlton, 1998, p. 10), as freaks (Thomson, 1997, p. 11), or as funny and laughable.

A second very old idea, which is still common today, is that having a disability is a terrible fate and that death is better than disability. Throughout history, babies born with disabilities have been abandoned to die. Other children born with disabilities have been institutionalized, and their families counseled that leaving their baby is better than bringing him or her home. In 1974, one mother was told by the doctor "to institutionalize her baby Jason and tell her family and friends the child was stillborn" (Bérubé, 1996, p. 30).

Today, the idea that having a disability is pitiful and people with disabilities are better off dead is still evident. Films such as *Gattaca* (DeVito, Shamberg, Sher, & Lyon,

Throughout history, people with physical and mental disabilities have been abandoned at birth, banished from society, used as court jesters, drowned and burned during the Inquisition, gassed in Nazi Germany, and still continue to be segregated, institutionalized, tortured in the name of behavior management, abused, raped, euthanized, and murdered. Now, for the first time, people with disabilities are taking their rightful place as fully contributing citizens. The danger is that we will respond with remediation and benevolence rather than equity and respect. And so, we offer you a credo for support.

Do not see my disability as a problem. Recognize that my disability is an attribute. Do not see my disability as a deficit. It is you who see me as deviant and helpless. Do not try to fix me because I am not broken. Support me. I can make my contribution to the community in my way. Do not see me as your client. I am your fellow citizen. See me as your neighbor. Remember, none of us can be self-sufficient. Do not try to modify my behavior. Be still and listen. What you define as inappropriate may be my attempt to communicate with you in the only way I can. Do not try to change me; you have no right. Help me learn what I want to know. Do not hide your uncertainty behind "professional" distance. Be a person who listens and does not take my struggle away from me by trying to make it all better. Do not use theories and strategies on me. Be with me. And when we struggle with each other, let that give rise to self-reflection. Do not try to control me. I have a right to my power as a person. What you call non-compliance or manipulation may actually be the only way I can exert control over my life. Do not teach me to be obedient, submissive, and polite. I need to feel entitled to say no if I am to protect myself. Do not be charitable to me. The last thing the world needs is another Jerry Lewis. Be my ally against those who exploit me for their own gratification. Do not try to be my friend. I deserve more than that. Get to know me. We may become friends. Do not help me even if it does make you feel good. Ask me if I need your help. Let me show you how to better assist me. Do not admire me. A desire to live a full life does not warrant adoration. Respect me, for respect presumes equity. Do not tell, correct, and lead. Listen, support, and follow. Do not work on me. Work with me.

Figure 1.1. A Credo for Support. (From Norm Kunc and Emma Van der Klift, Broadreach Training and Resources at http://www.broadreachtraining.com; reprinted by permission.)

1997) and *Million Dollar Baby* (Eastwood, Ruddy, Rosenberg, & Lucchesi, 2004) reinforce this idea. *Gattaca* is set in the future and tells the story of a young scientist who wants to leave planet Earth and immigrate to a new world. He cannot because he is not considered talented enough. A colleague who has a physical disability gives his identity to the able-bodied character so that the younger man can leave Earth. When the identity scam is successful, the colleague incinerates himself, as there is no further purpose or value for his life once he has helped the able-bodied main character. In *Million Dollar Baby* (2004), a young woman fights for the opportunity to train as a boxer. After finding a trainer and developing her skills, she is injured in an accident and becomes quadriplegic. She begs her trainer to kill her so that she does not have to live with quadriplegia. Both endings send the message that it is better to die than to be disabled.

"better dead than disabled" An attitude that having a disability is a terrible fate

Scholars in disability studies resist the **"better dead than disabled"** idea; a good example is Harriet McBryde Johnson's autobiographical book, *Too Late to Die Young* (2005). Strongly opposed to the Jerry Lewis telethon for muscular dystrophy, Johnson wrote,

> I turn on the thon and it's still the dark days before the disability rights movement, when crips exist only to remind others to count their blessings....The telethon suggests we're all doomed and that isn't true. I have one of those diseases. I'm thirty-four and enjoy my life the way it is. (pp. 54, 60)

If we think of people with disabilities as bad or pitiful, we might then move to another idea: That people with disabilities are not the same as "normal" people. And if people with disabilities are not like everyone else, maybe even bad and maybe less than everyone else, then we might say they cannot be members of our society.

How does this happen? In two ways: first, in a belief that over time people will gradually improve to a "perfect person" and second, in the **nature/nurture** debate. The "perfect person" idea—or the "perfectibility of man" idea—is based on the idea that humans can, over generations, gradually improve as a whole species. If this is what we believe, we might want to eliminate people who are seen as holding back progress—and that has included people with disabilities. Second, there is a debate about whether or not humans are biologically determined (the "nature" viewpoint) or environmentally determined (the "nurture" viewpoint) or some combination in between (Carlson, 2001, pp. 9–14). The nature/nurture debate continues today. If we believe that our biology is our destiny, then being born with a disability means being born with flaws and limits—and we are back to thinking that disability is bad.

Furthermore, why we think of disability as either evil or pitiable is related to how people think about difference. Identifying people who are different from most people is connected to our ideas about what normal means. The **concept of normal** sets up categories that had not previously existed. As Baynton noted,

> Normality is a complex concept, with an etiology that includes the rise of the social sciences, the science of statistics, and industrialization with its need for interchangeable parts and interchangeable workers....The natural and the normal both are ways of establishing social hierarchies that justify the denial of legitimacy and certain rights to individuals or groups. Both are constituted in large part by being set in opposition to culturally variable notions of disability. (2001, p. 35)

What does this mean? First, if there is no idea of "normal," then there would be no "abnormal" or "not normal" either. That would be a good thing: Before we thought about one group of people as normal and the rest as not normal, we would consider a range of skills, experiences, and capabilities as merely part of being diverse. Some people are good at reading and writing, others at fixing things and building houses, and others at gardening and farming. But when the social sciences—psychology and sociology—established the idea that being normal was natural and good, and being not normal was bad, society started planting the idea that being normal was something desirable and a good thing, and being different was negative. And society started sorting people into these two categories.

The two categories—normal and abnormal—were affected by the way we work. Davis connected the way we think about disability as negative to industrialization in the late 18th and early 19th centuries (1995, p. 24). **Industrialization** placed a new emphasis on workers' ability to perform jobs in a uniform way, at a uniform speed. Standardization within factory settings of expectations for workers led to an increased interest in making the workforce homogeneous. Disability became apparent when a worker with a disability could not keep up with co-workers. Instead of considering this difference as a valuable part of human society by focusing on other strengths and contributions people with disabilities can make, industrial America shunned any slowdown and perpetrated disability as negative.

At around the same time, the early 1900s, the science of **statistics** established that it is possible to predict, with some certainty, how a group of people will react or perform to a given task or situation. The idea that most people will be fairly competent at a particular task, while some will do exceptionally well and others will not do well at all, emerged. Bogdan and Taylor noted that "Around the turn of the century, early leaders 'discovered' a new class of 'feebleminded' persons and called attention to the presumed menace posed by this class" (1994, p. 9). Industrialization and the need for performing tasks in a routine way added to the idea that there is a bell curve with most people able to do things at a similar pace or skill level, combined to reinforce the idea that disability is bad and that it is better to be in the middle or high end of any bell curve than at the

nature versus nurture　The debate about what traits individuals inherit and what traits are learned. Teachers' beliefs about the degree to which traits are learned have an impact on the way they teach children.

concept of normal　The idea that there are categories of people and being the way most people are is an important goal. The concept sets up people to try to be like each other. This can limit how open people are to those who are different.

industrialization　The change in the United States from mostly farming communities to factories and assembly lines. Industries such as car manufacturing affected how people thought about the need for uniformity, like having car parts on an assembly line all be identical.

statistics　The study of groups represented by quantitative data, which is sometimes used to predict what will happen in the future.

bell curve   The numerical model of a normal distribution. The bell curve has been used to limit opportunities for people who are thought to be less capable than the majority because they fall on the low end of the curve.

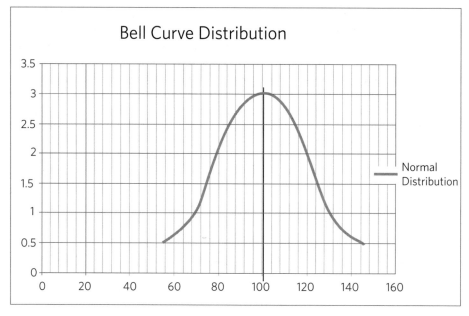

Figure 1.2.   Bell curve—normal distribution.

low end. The problem with this is that we all have a variety of skills and abilities, and we all have various areas of strength and weakness.

Figure 1.2 shows a classic division of people by a score on an intelligence quotient test. The problem with this is that only a single way of being "normal" is measured: performance on an examination that may or may not reflect the skills and abilities of the test-taker and only measures a single set of skills. So we are left thinking that disability is negative and pitiful. How have we managed reactions to that? Historically, freak shows were one way of handling anxiety about disability. Representing people with disabilities as other than human, as freaks, made disability something outside "normal" human experience (see Thomson, 1997; Bogdan, 1988, for discussion on this topic). There were important consequences of pushing disability out of our common experience. Thinking about people with disabilities as **"freaks"** also included being "politically and socially erased" (Garland-Thomson, 2002, p. 56). The ideal of the norm in industrial America made the prospect of disability too frightening to consider.

At the same time that we develop and refine our ideas about the nature of people, and whether or not we agree with nature or nurture arguments, we are also influenced by the models of disability we have adopted, whether or not we realize it. Psychology and sociology have important roles in shaping how we think about disability. Discussions of the medical model, the pity/charity model, and the social model illustrate their impact on how we think about and react to disability.

freaks   A negative term for people who are not considered normal because they look or act differently than most people

The Medical Model

The **medical model** perceives disability as abnormal and sick, as an illness that needs treatment by the medical profession. The field of medicine has been important in diagnosing disorders; in finding cures for diseases; in educating people about health; and in advancing science to support long, healthy lives for people. Immunizations, nutrition, and exercise are all part of our lives because of the field of medicine. At the same time, the field of medicine sometimes overexerts its authority. Sometimes doctors think they

medical model   A way of looking at disability that assumes disability is a physiological flaw inside the person that can be changed. Disability is seen as something wrong that needs to be fixed or cured.

know what someone's life will be like with a disability, and they tell families that there is no hope, or that a child with cerebral palsy will never walk or talk or learn, or that a child with Down syndrome cannot live at home. The problem is that no one—not even a doctor—can predict someone's life. However, the medical profession has sometimes taken control of people's lives without asking because we have created a society that is deferential to medicine. The rationale is that the medical profession is the best equipped field to understand and support people with disabilities. But this can be damaging to people with disabilities.

Linton noted, "The disability studies' and disability rights movement's position is critical of the domination of the medical definition and views it as a major stumbling block to the reinterpretation of *disability* as a political category and to the social changes that could follow such a shift" (1998, p. 11). The field of medicine has said that disability is a medical issue—and the general public should not be involved in deciding how people with disabilities should be treated because they are not equipped to decide what is best.

The medical model is intertwined with ideology that "the norm" is something to strive for. Davis explored the way that the norm was constructed and how the average became desirable (1995, p. 27). Once the norm was established, people with disabilities were seen as undesirable and were rejected. The medical profession, with the development of genetics and eugenics, took on people with disabilities as a population on which to experiment. This was a relief to society; people could marginalize and ignore individuals with disabilities, trusting medicine to "deal" with them. The medical profession was influenced by industrialization and the scientific ideal of the norm, and shaped their practice toward eliminating any experience that fell outside a mythical "normal" part of the bell curve.

The Pity/Charity Model

A second model for thinking about disability is the **pity/charity model**. Jerry Lewis epitomizes the pity model. His telethon to raise funds for the Muscular Dystrophy Association (MDA) includes using terms like "cripple" and referring to a wheelchair as "that steel imprisonment" (Bennetts, 1993, p. 9). The pity/charity model constructs people with disabilities as pitiful because they are sick (Charlton, 1998, pp. 10, 34). It allows people without disabilities to patronize people with disabilities, feeling good about their support and goodwill "charity." In fact, many professionals in rehabilitation and special education are motivated by this pity/charity instinct. This makes relationships between people with disabilities and the professionals who work with (and sometimes for) them, uneasy. The result is a minimum of accessible housing, transportation, employment, and education. The disability rights movement sees these benefits of membership in society not as gifts, but as rights that need to be afforded to every member of society as a matter of course. Reframing the pity/charity model includes educating society that every person has the right to clean, safe, affordable housing, transportation, employment, and education.

The Social Model

A precursor to the **social model**, Bogdan and Biklen identified **"handicapism"** as "a set of assumptions and practices that promote the differential and unequal treatment of people because of apparent or assumed physical, mental, or behavioral differences" (1977, p. 14). Addressing the socially constructed nature of how people with disabilities are treated, they analyze how handicapist attitudes reinforce oppressive practices of labeling and segregation.

pity/charity model A way of looking at disability that assumes having a disability is terrible and limiting. This view is that people without disabilities should feel sorry for people with disabilities and give them money to help them, not because help is their right.

social model A way of looking at disability that assumes disability is part of the diversity of human experience and the way society responds to disability can change to be more supportive.

handicapism Bogdan and Biklen defined this as "assumptions and practices that promote the differential and unequal treatment of people because of apparent or assumed physical, mental, or behavioral differences" (1977, p. 14).

The social model is designed to replace the medical and pity/charity models by thinking about disability in a completely new way. Earlier conceptions of disability tended toward individual, medical, or "personal tragedy" models (Barnes, Oliver, & Barton, 2002, p. 4). The social model of disability proposes that "'disability' is not a product of personal failings, but is socially created....Rather than identifying disability as an individual limitation, the social model identifies society as the problem and looks to fundamental political and cultural changes to generate solutions" (Barnes, Oliver, & Barton, 2002, p. 5). Winter (2003) proposed that the two premises of the social model are that "people with impairments are disabled by society's blatant failure to accommodate to their needs" (p. 2) and that "people with impairments can and should take control of their own lives as much as possible" (p. 8).

HOW RACE, GENDER, AND DISABILITY ARE SOCIALLY CONSTRUCTED

social construction
Assumptions about the world, knowledge, and ourselves that are taken for granted and believed to be universal rather than historically and culturally specific ideas created through social processes and interactions (Adams, Bell, & Griffin, 2007, p. 349).

We have briefly reviewed the history of disability. Now we are going to look at how race, gender, and disability are socially constructed. What is **"social construction"**? Social construction is a way of thinking about something—like disability—that is affected by our attitudes and beliefs. Social constructions can, and do, change over time and from place to place. A social construction is the way a society treats a group of people—any group of people—based on a perceived set of characteristics. Often, social constructions are not very well connected to physical qualities.

Limiting social constructions affect people of color, women, and people with visible disabilities. Baynton noted that "disability has functioned historically to justify inequality for disabled people themselves, but it has also done so for women and minority groups" (2001, p. 33). Hayman agreed, saying "the differences that constitute disability and gender are cultural, social, and ultimately political. We make disability and gender. The same is true of race. Only more so" (1998, p. 125). We will explain what this means in this section.

Race

slavery   People owning other people based on the belief that some humans are not really human and can be owned like property.

Race has tremendous importance in American society. The biological reality is that a White person and an African American person are very similar, but certain differences are believed to be true based on skin color. Figure 1.3 provides some key readings about how race has affected education in the United States.

What we know is that just as disability is affected by social constructions of negativity and pity, race is often socially constructed by the majority—White people—as negative and pitiful. In 1790, the Constitution of the United States allowed only White men who owned property the right to vote. **Slavery** was legal in Southern states and

- 1979—*White Teacher* by Vivian Gussin Paley
- 1994—*Race Matters* by Cornel West
- 1995—*Other People's Children* by Lisa Delpit
- 1996—*The Future of the Race* by Henry Louis Gates Jr. & Cornel West
- 1997—*Why Are All the Black Kids Sitting Together in the Cafeteria?* by Beverly Daniel Tatum
- 1999—*Looking White People in the Eye* by Sherene Razack
- 2001—*Black, White, and Jewish* by Rebecca Walker
- 2002—*This Bridge We Call Home* by Gloria Anzaldua & AnàLouise Keating, Editors
- 2006—*We Can't Teach What We Don't Know* by Gary Howard

Figure 1.3.   Readings about race.

some Northern ones as well, and men and women were legal property. Arguments in the southern United States against freeing the slaves included concern that freed slaves would not be able to live independently, not be able to manage finances or run a household, and would be like children set loose without supervision. The parallels to arguments about people with disabilities not being expected to advocate for themselves or care for themselves are striking.

In 1863 during the American Civil War, President Abraham Lincoln signed the **Emancipation Proclamation**. This was the beginning of the end of slavery: The proclamation freed all slaves in states that had seceded from the Union. In 1866, the 14th Amendment to the Constitution guaranteed equal protection under the law to all citizens, and granted citizenship to all African Americans. Soon after, in 1870, the 15th Amendment was passed, granting African American men the right to vote. This significant shift from being property to being a citizen and voting was groundbreaking.

Emancipation Proclamation   With this document, President Lincoln freed slaves in states that had seceded from the Union.

Throughout the 20th century, American society struggled to understand what race meant. Affirmative action policies emerged in the 1960s, and in 1965 President Lyndon Johnson addressed the graduating class at Howard University, a historically black college and university (HBCU). In his comments, he addressed the negative social construction of African Americans, and the negative effects of this construction. In his speech he said:

> You do not wipe away the scars of centuries by saying: Now you are free to go where you want, and do as you desire, and choose the leaders you please. You do not take a person who, for years, has been hobbled by chains and liberate him, bring him up to the starting line of a race and then say, "You are free to compete with all the others," and still justly believe that you have been completely fair....The Negro, like these others, will have to rely mostly upon his own efforts. But he just cannot do it alone. For they [Whites] did not have the heritage of centuries to overcome, and they did not have a cultural tradition which had been twisted and battered by endless years of hatred and hopelessness, nor were they excluded—these others—because of race or color—a feeling whose dark intensity is matched by no other prejudice in our society. Nor can these differences be understood as isolated infirmities. They are a seamless web. They cause each other. They result from each other. They reinforce each other. Much of the Negro community is buried under **a blanket of history** and circumstance. It is not a lasting solution to lift just one corner of that blanket. We must stand on all sides and we must raise the entire cover if we are to liberate our fellow citizens. (Johnson, 1966)

blanket of history President Johnson's term for the long, oppressive years of slavery in the United States. The negative effects of slavery were felt long after slavery was abolished, and those effects were like a heavy blanket or burden.

In 2002, 30 years after this speech, Shefali Milczarek-Desai wrote that "growing up in Phoenix, I did not know I was different until the girl behind me at the drinking fountain called me a nigger. I was in the fifth grade" (p. 126). Race matters: How to talk about race, think about what race means, and challenge your own beliefs and ideas are such important tasks that it is almost overwhelming. But if we do not address negative and pitiful constructions of race, we miss the opportunity to shape a social construction in positive and liberating ways. There is no more important task in education.

Gender

Being female has been socially constructed to mean many things. Before 1920, women were believed to be incapable of voting, because women were too emotional. In the 1950s in the United States, being a woman meant growing up with the primary end of marrying and raising children. Other roles—businesswoman, doctor, Supreme Court justice, astronaut, athlete—were constructed as inappropriate, unlikely, or impossible. The social construction of women was that women were physically weak, ungifted in math and science, and not rational. All of these constructions were based on ideas and beliefs, not on actual characteristics.

Here are examples of each social construction from the not too distant past in the United States. In 1967, Kathrine Switzer ran in the Boston Marathon. Her web site reviews what happened:

> She was a 20-year-old Syracuse University junior who wanted to prove to herself and her coach she was capable of running 26.2 miles....Switzer never told Boston Athletic Association officials she was a woman, but the race application didn't ask....When the photographers noticed a woman in the race with an official number, the cameras started to click. And something clicked inside a BAA official, Jock Semple, who jumped off the truck and ran at Switzer in an attempt to tear off her number. "Get the hell out of my race and give me that number!"' shouted Semple. (Switzer, n.d.)

Kathrine finished the race, and the Boston Marathon allowed women to run in the race beginning in 1972 (Switzer, n.d.) As attitudes and beliefs about what women's bodies can do have gradually shifted to accept more athleticism, more women participate in athletic activities. The features of a woman's body have not shifted—attitudes have.

Related to achievements in academics, women are not always believed to be as able as men. In engineering and natural science, women are underrepresented. In 1999, women professors were "only 12.5% of associate and full professors in the natural sciences and engineering at all U.S. universities and 4-year colleges" (Lawler, 1999, p. 1272). We believe that this is due, in large part, to the social construction of girls and women as less able in math and science. In 2006, the National Science Foundation reported that

> Data for 2006 show that women continue to constitute a much lower percentage of S&E [science and engineering] full professors than their share of S&E doctorates awarded in that year. Even in psychology, a field heavily dominated by women, women were less than half of all full professors, even though they earned well more than half of doctorates in 2006. (Burrelli, 2008, p. 1)

The fact that women earned more than one half of doctorates but still represent less than one half of full professors in science, engineering, and psychology can be explained at least in part by the beliefs and attitudes that society in the United States has about women and the way women are treated related to intellectual ability.

In a final example, we look at how women have been constructed as emotional and irrational. This way of thinking affected women's suffrage; women were not allowed to vote because they were believed to be "domestic creatures who relied on men for protection" (Field, 2001, p. 115). In her review of the history of women's rights in the antebellum United States, Field noted that at the New York convention in 1821, delegates "treated the idea of White or Black women voting as a joke" (2001, p. 117). Figure 1.4

In 1915, writer Alice Duer Miller wrote:

Why We Don't Want Men to Vote

- Because man's place is in the army.
- Because no really manly man wants to settle any question otherwise than by fighting about it.
- Because if men should adopt peaceable methods women will no longer look up to them.
- Because men will lose their charm if they step out of their natural sphere and interest themselves in other matters than feats of arms, uniforms, and drums.
- Because men are too emotional to vote. Their conduct at baseball games and political conventions shows this, while their innate tendency to appeal to force renders them unfit for government.

Figure 1.4.   Why we don't want men to vote. (From Lewis, J.J. August 26, 1920. The Day the Suffrage Battle Was Won. Retrieved February 14, 2011, from http://womenshistory.about.com/od/suffrage1900/a/august_26_wed.htm.)

presents an alternative view to the belief that women were not able to make decisions and vote by presenting instead a list of reasons why women did not believe men were capable of voting! Switching roles helps highlight how ridiculous it is to make assumptions about a group of people based on beliefs about gender.

This history is a strong contrast to Sandra Day O'Connor, Ruth Bader Ginsburg, and Sonia Sotomayor serving distinguished careers on the Supreme Court. Of course, these ideas, one would hope, seem antiquated and ridiculous now. That is because the social construction of what "woman" means has shifted. The bodily features of being a woman have not changed. Women still have the same kinds of bone structure and reasoning ability that they have always had. What has changed are the features of the society in which we live.

Disability

Disability includes a wide range of impairments, for example, being physically disabled, intellectually disabled, deaf, visually impaired, or emotionally disabled. The range of what falls under the category of "disabled" is broad. We are interested in looking at the ways in which disability is socially constructed. Related to how we think about what it means to be smart, we "make some people smarter than others, by rewarding the smartness of some people and ignoring the smartness of others. We make some people smart, in short, just by choosing to call them that" (Hayman, 1998, p. 26). Put another way, as Bogdan and Taylor explained:

> To suggest that mental retardation is not "real" is not to deny differences among people in terms of intellectual ability. It is to say that the nature and significance of these differences depend on how we view and interpret them. (1994, p. 7)

Society has often assumed that people with disabilities are not able to learn. For example, a common social construction of people who use wheelchairs is that they must be incapable of speaking for themselves. As a result, when we are out with a friend who uses a wheelchair it frequently happens that wait staff will ask, "What does she want?" instead of asking directly. We reply, "I don't know—ask *her*." This social construction—that people who use wheelchairs cannot speak for themselves—results in limiting opportunities for all people who use wheelchairs, whether or not they can speak for themselves.

Children with disabilities were not guaranteed the right to go to school until 1975. Before that time, districts could and did tell parents that their child was not able to benefit from schooling and to keep them at home. After 1975, students with disabilities were guaranteed the right to a free appropriate public education (FAPE), something we have in place still today (U.S. Department of Education, Office of Special Education Programs, 2004).

HOW THE SOCIAL CONSTRUCTION OF DISABILITY AFFECTS EDUCATION AND SCHOOLING

Special education is often viewed from the pity/charity model. A special education teacher is often met with comments like "Oh, I could never do what you do," or "You must be such a special person to help those poor kids." This leads to tension between teachers and people with disabilities.

Linton noted "special education by structure and definition places disability as the major defining variable of learners, the field overemphasizes disability, milking it for explanatory value to justify organizing education into two separate systems" (1998, p. 81). The separate systems of general and special education have become integral parts of our teacher training and educational system. A better option for all children would be preparing all teachers to teach all children and providing teachers with supports to do so.

We have two separate systems because when students with disabilities first entered schools, they were seen as so different from typical students that teachers and legislators believed specialized training must be required before they would feel ready to have children with intellectual or physical disabilities in their classrooms. While it would be hard to find a teacher or principal who would say it this way, the social construction of disability as negative or pitiful is at the heart of the matter. In this section, we review five different ways of thinking about disability, and explain how each social construction limits or supports students with disabilities. The five constructions are that disability is bad, is scary, means inability, is a challenge and opportunity, and is difference.

Disability Is Bad

If we think that disability is bad, we will respond by excluding the student with a disability to avoid negatively affecting other students. Whether or not we say it out loud, many people have an uneasy sense that disability is horrible, they do not want to deal with someone who has a disability, and it would feel more comfortable if people with disabilities were just not around. That unspoken attitude is at the root of a great deal of exclusion in schools. While we are not to blame for the messages we have taken in as we grow up, we are to blame if we do not challenge these messages as teachers.

Disability Is Scary

Something unique about disabilities, unlike gender or race, is that anyone can become disabled at any time. This is frightening, as we know that people with disabilities are not respected or accepted as easily by people without disabilities. A major issue that affects how people with disabilities are perceived is a fear of disability that is uncomfortable and not expressed (Thomson, 1997, p. 12). Most people are afraid of disability, and consequently, interacting with people who have a disability is challenging. Sapon-Shevin noted that

> We assume that there is nothing but sadness and grief in the lives of people with disabilities and their parents and families. We feel pity, we feel fear, and we feel discomfort. None of those feelings encourage us to seek relationships or get closer. (2007, p. 28)

Related to seeking relationships and feeling comfortable, it is often true that the burden of making "normates"—as Thomson (1997) called people without disabilities—comfortable falls on the person with a disability. Otherwise, the person without a disability falls back on medical and pitying models to explain disability, reinforcing oppressive practices. The task is to reconfigure disability as a possible and not necessarily terrible thing—a challenging task given the negative stereotypes we have about disability in American society today.

labeling "Defining a person in terms of a single dimension and then generalizing about that person's overall character on that narrow basis" (Bogdan & Taylor, 1994, p. 13).

Disability Means General Inability

Karuth noted "the hottest place in my personal hell is reserved for...the Special Education Department chairperson who snapped, 'What are you doing in this program if you can't see?'" (1985, p. 52). This dismissive attitude characterizes much of special education; students are not seen as individuals, but as entities to be categorized and expected to perform based on an often limiting and inaccurate label. **Labeling**, as Bogdan and

Taylor explained, "entails defining a person in terms of a single dimension and then generalizing about that person's overall character on that narrow basis" (1994, p. 13). Special education has a long history of labeling—including limiting, paternal constructions of children with disabilities. The label applied to children with disabilities then takes on master status. That is, "once the label is applied, it determines how others relate to you" (Bogdan and Taylor, 1994, p. 217).

Related to intellectual disability, special education does not always presume competence in children with intellectual impairment and does not tend to include children with cognitive delays in inclusive classrooms. In 1995, only two states served more than 50% of students labeled mentally retarded in inclusive classrooms (Kliewer, 1998, p. 42). It is a pervasive belief that children who have Down syndrome are mentally retarded (p. 31), which in fact serves as the cultural model on which Americans base their image of people with intellectual disabilities (p. 50).

Disability Is a Challenge and Opportunity

If we can move away from negative social constructions of disability and see challenge, opportunity, and difference instead of negativity and fear, we can shift how students both with and without disabilities learn. There are benefits for all children to having a classroom of children with a range of needs. One of the most important benefits is that teachers who teach for a range of skills and readiness levels do a better job for all students than teachers who believe there is one right way to instruct. Sapon-Shevin noted that

> No student benefits from rigid, lockstep curricula with no differentiation, a classroom atmosphere that is hostile to individual differences and encourages competition and negative comparison, limited student influence on decision making in classroom processes, and restrictive forms of pedagogy. (2007, p. 114)

If we can see the opportunity for creating learning environments that support all students when a student with a disability is included, we can get to the work of good teaching for all children—and all children will benefit.

Figure 1.5 demonstrates how access to academics increased performance of students with disability labels in New York State on a state math assessment. In 1997, only 5,700 students with disability in the entire state of New York took the math exam. Eleven years later, the total number of students taking the exam had ballooned to 28,000! This enormous increase was a direct result of increased access to high-quality curriculum, and to a rigorous academic program of math content. This increase was not simple and came with a great deal of concern from special education teachers. Special education teachers were afraid that students were too emotionally fragile to attend general education classes and incapable of doing the work. In 2008, almost three times more students *passed* the math exam than *took* the exam in 1997. What changed? The attitudes and beliefs of the teachers. The social construction of disability in New York high schools has shifted a little—disability does not mean inability.

Disability Is Difference

We need to make "the least dangerous assumption" about all students, and assume that everyone can learn and will benefit from education. Sapon-Shevin explained that the "least dangerous assumption states that in the absence of absolute evidence, it is essential to make the assumption that, if proven to be false, would be least dangerous to the individual" (2007, p. 110).

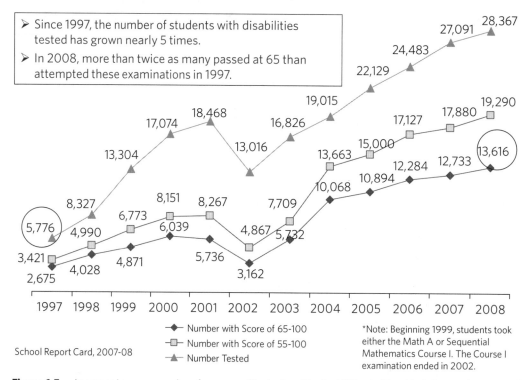

Students with Disabilities Taking Regents Examinations in Sequential Mathematics Course I or Math A

➤ Since 1997, the number of students with disabilities tested has grown nearly 5 times.

➤ In 2008, more than twice as many passed at 65 than attempted these examinations in 1997.

School Report Card, 2007-08

◆ Number with Score of 65-100
□ Number with Score of 55-100
▲ Number Tested

*Note: Beginning 1999, students took either the Math A or Sequential Mathematics Course I. The Course I examination ended in 2002.

Figure 1.5.   Increase in access and performance: Students with disabilities in New York State taking a math exam in high school. (From Cort, R.H. [2009]. *The State of Special Education 2009.* Retrieved November 30, 2011, from http://www.p12.nysed.gov/specialed/techassist/Statewide-Oct09/Oct09statewide.ppt.)

SUMMARY

This chapter used a disability studies perspective to introduce you to the ways in which people have thought about disability throughout history and the effects of that thinking on the education of students with disabilities. We reviewed how industrialization and the concept of the normal limited expectations for people with disabilities and explained the medical, pity/charity, and social models of disability. You learned that race and gender are socially constructed and how those constructions have shifted over time. Finally, we talked about constructions of disability, including beliefs that disability is bad, disability is scary, disability means inability, disability is a challenge and opportunity, and is difference.

NARRATIVE 1.1. | KEITH JONES

Keith Jones is the president and CEO of SoulTouchin' Experiences (http://dasoultoucha.com/PublicMotivationalSpeaking.html). His organization is aimed at addressing issues of access, inclusion, and empowerment—issues that affect him as well as others who are persons with a disability. He has received many awards for his advocacy work, and Mr. Jones is also a performer; he has been featured in two critically acclaimed documentaries: Dan Habib's *Including Samuel* and Maggie Doben's *Labeled Disabled*. He also received critical praise for his role of

Killer P in the independent comedy *Special Needs*. Bill Gibron of Popmatters.com wrote, "The clear breakout star here is someone called Killer P. A bad ass gansta rapper with cerebral palsy, if he's not the future of urban culture, no one is….He's gutbustingly great." We had the chance to interview Keith for this book, and we asked him about his experiences and what he wants teachers to know.

How difficult is it for a person labeled as disabled to be seen as an individual and to find work? You must know the person in order to accept their disability. Even with a disability they can be nasty or nice, or funny or boring. But that is separate and apart from disability. I want to be able to work and buy my food. If you look at the numbers for employment for people with disabilities, it is not motivating. If you have a disability, you can't run out to the store and buy a different body and go back to the job interview. Interviewers are not looking at you as a person; they are seeing themselves and thinking "I could not handle that." There are no expectations for me, because they think "Well if I couldn't live like that, how can he? And how can he work?" Faced with these attitudes, it is very difficult to find work.

What do you think about the way we socially construct gender? I tell men in the room: close your eyes. Can you imagine being a woman? Probably not. If you can't imagine what it is like, then just treat each woman you meet as an individual and take it from there. It is the same with sexual orientation, race, disability. Treat each person as a person, not a stereotype. That seems to be the hardest thing: to not let what is politically correct get in the way of knowing me as an individual.

What do you want teachers to know? The best teacher I ever had was Ms. McMillan in high school, she taught algebra. She was an older Black woman, and she didn't let me slide. She took me aside one day and said, "Listen. I know you can do this. Why you playin'? You need to be counted. You are in school. Your job is to learn. In whatever way you can, your job is to learn." She took an actual interest in why I needed to do the homework. Not just was it correct, but why it was correct. She was one of my best teachers.

If you are in the classroom setting, you want to teach. You want to impart knowledge in a positive way. How are you doing that if you have prejudices, and can't see the child for who they are, which is a child eager to learn? *Teach the student, not the diagnosis*. We get caught up in the technicality of it all. Don't. Flesh, bone, blood, wants, needs, dreams. See those. See the person. Then worry about OK, now how do I reach that individual? Focus on the child—with or without a disability. See the child.

CHAPTER 2

History of
Special Education

How this chapter prepares you to be
an effective inclusive classroom teacher:

- In this chapter we review how formal education was structured and how special education emerged from the civil rights movement. This chapter provides the theoretical foundation for the remainder of the text by positioning special education in a historical perspective. Understanding the ideas that shaped special education helps you reflect on what is effective and ineffective in education and special education today. The dynamic nature of the field is highlighted. **This helps you meet CEC Standard 1: Foundations.**

- All students need access to instruction. The ethical consideration of teacher attitude affecting opportunity for learning is explored in detail so that you will understand how your own attitude can influence your practice. **This helps you meet CEC Standard 9: Professional and Ethical Practice.**

After reading and discussing this chapter, you will be able to

- Explain how formal education developed in the United States

- Define the Enlightenment period and explain the three ideas that emerged from this time

- Explain how the Enlightenment affected how we think about disability

- Explain what the common school is

- Explain how schooling for White and African American and wealthy and poor students differed

- Explain the *Brown v. Board of Education* decision

- Explain the impact of *Brown v. Board of Education* on students with disabilities

- Define hegemony and give an example

- Explain what culturally relevant means and give an example from schooling

- Describe how special education evolved

- Define the EHC and its six provisions

- Explain the impact of labels in schooling on students with disabilities

- Explain both sides of the inclusion debate

- Describe the social construction of special education

- Explain what is meant by "inclusion is an attitude, not a place"

- Explain three orientations to students' capacity for learning and the effect each orientation has on students with disabilities

presuming competence
"A stance, an outlook, a framework for educational engagement" (Biklen & Burke, 2006, p. 168).

least dangerous assumption "In the absence of conclusive data, educational decisions ought to be based on assumptions which, if incorrect, will have the least dangerous effect on the likelihood that students will be able to function independently as adults" (Donnellan, 1984, in Jorgensen, 2005).

In Chapter 1 you learned that the ways in which disability is constructed have a powerful impact on how people with disabilities are treated. The medical, pity/charity, and social models of disability all lead to different ways of thinking about students with disabilities. You learned that if disability is seen as bad or scary, or if disability is seen as inability, opportunities and access to general education are often limited. In contrast, if disability is seen as a challenge and an opportunity, or simply as difference, the results can be positive and powerful.

In this chapter, we review the history of special education by first looking briefly at how formal education developed in the United States. This background is important because special education was not a field of study for many years, before there was legislation requiring schools to consider how to teach students with disabilities, communities relied on families or state institutions as places for children and adults with disabilities to live. You will see benefits and drawbacks to the way that special education has developed in the United States. In the second section, we explore the development of special education and what special education is today. The last part of the chapter discusses what we would like to see in special education in the future.

The narrative for this chapter is from a person with experience with the label autism. Larry Bissonnette lived in an institution before moving into the community. He had experience with the negative and limiting constructions of disability; what he has to teach us about the importance of **presuming competence** and making the **least dangerous assumption** is powerful.

EDUCATION IN THE UNITED STATES

The history of education is far too broad to consider in a single section of a chapter; most education programs have an entire course reviewing the history of education. Our goal in this section is to provide a very brief context for how the formal educational system in the United States evolved.

In what is now the United States, indigenous peoples treated education as a set of skills and knowledge to be mastered before they could be accepted as adults in the tribe (Urban & Wagoner, 2009, p. 3). Children not only learned from their parents, but from their extended family as well as from other members of the community, and education was part of daily living, not something separate from home life, the way most schooling is now.

When Europeans arrived and began colonizing the East Coast, both Native peoples and Europeans changed. However, indigenous people and Europeans did not share mutual respect and equality. Urban and Wagoner noted that "although they themselves were willing teachers, Native Americans found themselves cast in the role of unwilling learners. Although the European colonizers had much to learn, from the outset they assumed the role of master" (2009, p. 11). The consequences of the colonizers assuming the "role of master" are widespread, both in education and government—it is enough to say here that the European adoption of an attitude of mastery has had, and continues to have, profound effects on education.

For example, education was shaped by "deliberate attempts to transplant familiar English customs and institutions to the new world" (Urban & Wagoner, 2009, p. 24)—which included treating education as a private matter. That is, families were expected to hire tutors or teach their children themselves, with no expectation of a public school education. Affluent families who could afford private school or tutors educated their children more formally, while families with fewer resources did not send their children to school. The result was access to academic subject matter for the middle and upper class, and little or no formal education for those in the lower class (Urban & Wagoner, 2009, p. 25).

As colonies of settlers became established, formal education began to take root. In northern colonies, some ministers taught school to supplement their incomes, and in the southern colonies, missionary groups established "charity schools" for poor children, free of charge (Urban & Wagoner, 2009, p. 27). In 1647, Massachusetts passed the Old Deluder Satan Act, designed to ensure that children learned to read and write so that Satan could not prevent them from knowing Bible scripture (Urban & Wagoner, 2009, p. 45). An emphasis on education and literacy based in religious training continued until the **Enlightenment** period.

Enlightenment The time from the 1770s to the 1830s when new ideas about learning emerged: observation is key to understanding the world, progress is inevitable, and people are born as blank slates.

The 1770s to the 1830s was a radical period that shaped how we think today. The Enlightenment period included challenging old ideas, welcoming change, and questioning authority (Urban & Wagoner, 2009, p. 71). Three central ideas that came from this period were 1) the adoption of empirical science—observing the world leads to understanding how things work; 2) the idea that progress is inevitable—people continue to evolve and develop, and the future will be better than the past; and 3) the belief in the goodness of people—people are not naturally evil but are blank slates (Urban & Wagoner, 2009, pp. 74–75). The second idea, that progress is inevitable, is connected to an idea presented in Chapter 1—the perfectibility of man idea. This idea has serious implications for people with disabilities, because if people believe that as humans we are all moving toward a more perfect form, with perfected abilities, then people with disabilities could be seen as incapable and therefore "bad" because people with disabilities do not fit with an ideal perfect human.

The effect of these beliefs on schooling included a change in how teachers presented information. Instead of expecting that good teaching and learning meant that students always sat at desks taking notes while a teacher lectured, good teaching became more about the student being actively involved in learning new things. This more active role included observing events, developing and testing hypotheses, and learning by doing.

The effect of Enlightenment thinking on special education is that some may believe that disabilities impede progress, and a future that is better than the past does not include disability. We disagree with this viewpoint, but we want to be sure you understand how ideas from this time period might affect education today.

common school Ideas about schooling in the 1800s that held that school should be free to families and all White children should attend regardless of status.

As more settlers traveled to the East Coast and developed communities, schools developed as well. By the early 1800s, the term **common school** was heard frequently. The common school is the term used to talk about a set of ideas about schooling: School should be free to parents, should include elementary to high school grades, and should be open to all White children regardless of status (Urban & Wagoner, 2009, pp. 112–113). Notice that at this time African Americans were entering the United States as slaves and were actively prevented from participating in academics for fear that they would rise up and resist.

compulsory attendance laws The requirement that all children of certain ages attend school.

In the late 1800s and early 1900s, laws requiring education were passed in the states. **Compulsory attendance laws** required that all children of a certain age attend some legally recognized school for some period of time and regulated what was taught (Provasnik, 2006, pp. 314–315). At the same time, in the 1890s, people concerned with child labor pushed for enforceable legislation to keep children from working in factories instead of going to school. This led to controversy about the limits of state authority to require school attendance (Provasnik, 2006, p. 319). Controversies surrounding education today, such as testing requirements, the link between teacher pay and student test performance, and inclusive education, are all connected to a long history of debate about who is responsible and has authority to decide what children are taught, how they are tested, and what a good education includes.

Related to the authority of the government, Provasnik noted that "since at least the 1830s, state courts have regularly upheld the power of school authorities to establish and enforce rules and regulations over the admission, attendance, graduation, conduct, suspension, and expulsion of students" (2006, p. 321). This power includes regulating what teachers do—including what they do in their free time—and what they wear. See Figure 2.1 for a list from 1915 regulating what teachers were allowed to do.

It is not possible to talk about schooling in any time period without discussing the different ways that White students and African American students, or middle- or upper-class and poor students, or male and female students were educated. Before the abolition of slavery in 1865, "it was illegal for Blacks to read, write, or attend school. It is important to note that there was no such thing as a public school system for poor Whites" (Lee, 2009, p. 370). So the late 1800s, as we have noted, did not include access to high-quality education for all students. The Declaration of Independence stated that all men are created equal—but in reality, equality was not realized in education; upper-class White boys were most likely to be educated and therefore have access to jobs, advancement, and opportunity.

In 1865, slavery was outlawed with the 13th Amendment, which proclaimed: "Neither slavery nor involuntary servitude, except as a punishment for crime whereof the party shall have been duly convicted, shall exist within the United States, or any place subject to their jurisdiction" (U.S. Constitution). Between 1865 and 1965, education for African Americans was profoundly affected as schools were developed and "the Black community consciously crafted education as a tool for our liberation as a people during the unlikely period between 1860 and 1965" (Lee, 2009, p. 370).

In the late 1800s and early 1900s, schooling continued to evolve, with separate systems for Black and White children. Compulsory attendance laws were passed, and

---

Rules for Teachers — 1915

1. You will not marry during the term of your contract.
2. You are not to keep company with men.
3. You must be home between the hours of 8 PM and 6 AM unless at a school function.
4. You may not loiter downtown in any of the ice cream stores.
5. You may not travel beyond the city limits unless you have permission of the chairman of the school board.
6. You may not ride in carriages or automobiles with any man except your father or brother.
7. You may not smoke cigarettes.
8. You may not dress in bright colors.
9. You may under no circumstances dye your hair.
10. You must wear at least 2 petticoats.
11. Your dresses may not be any shorter than 2 inches above the ankles.
12. To keep the classroom neat and clean you must sweep the floor once a day, scrub the floor with hot soapy water once a week, clean the blackboards once a day and start the fire at 7 AM to have the school warm by 8 AM when the scholars arrive.

School Rules — 1872

1. Will fill lamps, trim wicks and clean chimneys.
2. Each morning teacher will bring bucket of water and a scuttle of coal for the day's session.
3. Make your pens carefully. You may whittle nibs to the individual taste of the pupils.
4. Men teachers may take one evening each week for courting purposes or two evenings a week if they attend church regularly.
5. After 10 hours in school the teachers may spend the remaining time reading the Bible or any other good book.
6. Women teachers who marry or engage in unseemly conduct will be dismissed.
7. Every teacher should lay aside for each pay day a goodly sum of his earnings for his benefit during his declining years so that he will not become a burden on society.
8. Any teacher who smokes, uses liquor in any form, frequents pool or public halls, or gets shaved in a barber shop will give good reason to suspect his worth, intention, integrity and honesty.
9. The teacher who performs his labor faithfully and without fault for five years will be given an increase of $.25 per week in his pay providing the Board of Education approves.

The sources for these "rules" are unknown; thus we cannot attest to their authenticity—only to their verisimilitude and charming quaintness. They have been used for years by the New Hampshire Historical Society Museum as part of its *Going to School* outreach lesson, but they also appear independently on numerous other web sites from Auckland to England.

The rules from 1872 have been variously attributed to an 1872 posting in Monroe County, Iowa; to a one-room school in a small town in Maine; and to an unspecified Arizona schoolhouse. The 1915 rules are attributed to a Sacramento teachers' contract and elsewhere to an unspecified 1915 magazine.

Enjoy.

Figure 2.1. Rules for teachers (1915) and school rules (1872). (From the New Hampshire Historical Society. Retrieved from http://www.nhhistory.org/edu/support/nhgrowingup/teacherrules.pdf; reprinted by permission.)

school systems became more organized and structured. In this **Progressive Era** of education, more children entered school; kindergarten and extracurricular activities were developed; the curriculum was expanded; junior high schools were created; and testing was used to organize students into classes (Urban & Wagoner, 2009).

Education was separate for White and African American children until the landmark desegregation case, *Brown v. Board of Education* (1954). Before 1954, schools for African American and White students were separate. This was legal, as the systems were presumed to be equal in quality and resources. The reality was starkly different: Schools for African American students were underfunded, materials were outdated and

Progressive Era   A period spanning the late 1800s and early 1900s, when most children attended school, curricula and testing were developed, and extracurricular activities began.

Brown v. Board of Education (1954) Supreme Court case that decided that separate schools for African American and White children were not equal.

scarce, and the buildings were often dilapidated. In contrast, schools for White children were newer, cleaner, and better maintained; books were newer; and there were enough materials for all students. This case included the finding that separate schools, materials, and teachers were not equal—and desegregation gradually took place.

The results of desegregation are mixed. After the *Brown v. Board of Education* decision, schools for Blacks changed radically. In segregated schools, Black children were taught primarily by Black teachers, which provided them with authority figures of their own race and knowledge of their culture. But that changed dramatically, as Patterson, Niles, Carlson, and Kelley noted:

> In recent years the high price that African Americans paid for school desegregation has come to light (Bell 2004; Guinier 2004; Shujaa 1996)....Educational researchers have documented that African Americans bore the burden of desegregation and made many sacrifices. These included loss of decision-making authority over their children's education (Morris 2001), loss of teachers and administrators (Cecelski 1994; Karpinski 2006; Tillman 2004), and loss of community when Black schools were closed. Children were bussed out of their neighborhoods (Dempsey and Noblit 1993) to White schools where they and their parents were not welcomed and where teachers were not prepared to teach them (Edwards 1996). (2008, pp. 76–77)

One result of Black schools closing has been that many children go to school for years without seeing a face that looks like a family member. Some children graduate from high school without ever being taught by an African American or Hispanic teacher. This may be your experience. If it is not, can you imagine always looking different from your teachers? This is the reality for many children. Lee reminded us:

hegemonic Assumptions and beliefs that are not often questioned because they benefit the majority.

> The **hegemonic** views that inform our conception of culture are well-known: the idea that Whiteness is superior, that Europe has always represented the pinnacle of human civilizations, and that those who are designated as people of color have some kind of deficits which a good education must overcome. These deficit assumptions to those designated as non-White have a long history in education (Lee, 2009), from the use of IQ tests to argue for differences in abilities based on race compounded with physiological measures (e.g., head size, width of noses, etc.) as further evidence of racial differences; to arguments about cultural deprivation regarding child-rearing practices, and ways of using language that were presumed to interfere with readiness for school. (2009, pp. 374–375)

In fact, some people believe that schools today are more segregated by race than before *Brown v. Board of Education*; although schools with communities that are racially mixed include students of many races, a number of programs are still segregated. For example, fewer students of color take Advanced Placement (AP) classes than White students (Flower, 2008).

culturally relevant Being interesting to a group of people who share a similar background.

So we can see that teaching in ways that are **culturally relevant** is important; if we do not prepare you to teach every child, and work to encourage students from diverse backgrounds to become teachers, we are not serving all children well. Culturally relevant teaching means teaching in ways that understand and respect the values and lives of all students—including those of students from backgrounds that are different from your own. Delpit noted that "by some estimates, the turn of the century will find up to 40% of non-White children in American classrooms. Yet the current number of teachers from non-White groups threatens to fall below 10%" (1995, p. 105). Her estimate was close: Aud, Fox, and KewalRamani reported that "between 1980 and 2008, the racial/ethnic composition of the United States shifted—the White population declined from 80% of the total population to 66%" (2010, p. iii).

Education in the United States has evolved into a complex system, organized by both federal and state laws. More and more, emphasis in education has been focused on testing and determining what students should know and be able to perform on tests. While each state is slightly different in what it requires, all states are connected in some way to federal laws about education.

Another important point is that the role of the schools has expanded from teaching academic subjects to serving children and their families in a range of ways. Schools provide breakfast and lunch for students who cannot afford it, and some schools have programs to send students home with food for their families for the weekend. Schools are often sites for community education and health and wellness information. This can be a problem when schools are not well funded and when school faculty and staff are asked to do more and provide more with limited resources. So we are left with our current educational system: serving all students, with variable success, and facing struggles in funding, achievement, and assessment.

THE DEVELOPMENT OF SPECIAL EDUCATION

In this section, we review how special education developed, including the passage of federal legislation requiring schools to teach children with disabilities. We also discuss the impact of labels and explore the inclusion debate. The history of special education includes wide variation in what schools provided before federal laws required that schools admit students with disabilities.

The fact that children with disabilities are permitted and even required to attend school is a relatively new development in the United States. Until the 1970s, children with disabilities were often excluded from schools. The parental demand for educational opportunities—activism—led the push for children with disabilities being allowed in public schools. It was generally assumed that children with disabilities could not benefit from education in the general education setting, and they typically were in segregated classrooms. Recently, however, education has been shifting to a consideration that all children learn in an inclusive setting—a revelation that is startling to teachers trained to believe that special education includes segregation for the good of the children (Kliewer, 1998, p. 14).

Before schools were required to serve students with disabilities, schools for students who were deaf or blind were created. The first school for students who are deaf, the American School for the Deaf, was founded in 1817 in Connecticut (American School for the Deaf, 2009), and the first school for students who are blind was founded in 1829 in Boston (Perkins School for the Blind, n.d.). The schools were created because of the clear need to support students who are blind or deaf; every state has at least one residential school for students who are blind and one for students who are deaf. Those schools have evolved with changes in education, and while most were residential schools at one time and many continue to have small residential programs, many schools for students who are deaf or blind now serve fewer students due to an increase in inclusive placements. Some have become resource centers, day schools, and regional centers for professionals in the field.

The state schools serving students with sensory impairments (deafness and blindness) were the exception. Most students with disabilities did not attend school in the 1800s and early 1900s. Individual districts, principals, and teachers made arrangements on a case-by-case basis for students, but there was no law requiring that schools teach students with disabilities.

As we noted, in the mid-1950s, some parents of students with disabilities organized and started challenging school districts for the right for their children to go to school. Other parents were concerned about their children with disabilities being in school and wanted to protect them from teasing, bullying, or abuse. The balance between access to education and other children and protecting children from harm is delicate; some parents today are concerned about inclusion because they worry that their child might not be able to tell adults if they are teased or bullied. The important issue to be clear about is that all children deserve the right to an education in a safe environment. Court cases (which you will read about in detail in Chapter 3) led to legislation about children with disabilities and schooling, and in 1975 the first law requiring that all children with disabilities be allowed to go to school was passed. This law included the following statement:

> Congress finds the following: (1) Disability is a natural part of the human experience and in no way diminishes the right of individuals to participate in or contribute to society. Improving educational results for children with disabilities is an essential element of our national policy of ensuring equality of opportunity, full participation, independent living, and economic self-sufficiency for individuals with disabilities. (Education of All Handicapped Children Act, 1975)

free appropriate public education (FAPE) A requirement of Public Law 94-142. Every child in the United States has a right to go to school at no cost to the family.

continuum of services A list of places where a student with a disability might be educated. This includes not only where the student goes to school but is also what services the student receives. Placements range from general education to segregated residential institutions. The law included a list of disability labels.

The Education for All Handicapped Children Act (EHC), also known as PL 94-142, included six major provisions. One of them is that all children have the right to a **free appropriate public education**, also called FAPE. No matter what, every child with a disability has the right to go to school: This is another of EHC's provisions, the *zero reject rule*. Court challenges to this requirement later clarified for schools the full meaning of "all," as you will read about in Chapter 3. Another important part of the way special education is designed is the **continuum of services**. The continuum is a list of schooling options for a child with a disability: in a regular classroom at a regular school, in a separate classroom at a regular school, in a separate school, or in a residential school (such as a state school for the blind or deaf) or hospital.

The use of these labels was new: In the 1950s and 1960s there were not many formal definitions of disabilities (Kleinhammer-Tramill, Tramill, & Brace, 2010). This changed with EHC. The continuum of services was not designed to be directly related to disability labels, but one outcome of having a range of placements has been that children with low-incidence disability labels have typically been placed in more restrictive settings than children with high-incidence disability labels. Information about the percentages of students with different labels and how much time each group of students spends in general education helps us see that schools include students with some disability labels in general education more often than students with other labels. The National Center for Education Statistics (n.d.) noted that

> In 2008–09, some 38 percent of all children and youth receiving special education services had specific learning disabilities, 22 percent had speech or language impairments, and 10 percent had other health impairments. Students with disabilities such as intellectual disabilities, emotional disturbances, developmental delay, and autism each accounted for between 5 and 7 percent of children and youth served under IDEA. Children and youth with multiple disabilities; hearing, orthopedic, and visual impairments; traumatic brain injury; and deaf-blindness each accounted for 2 percent or less of children served under IDEA.
>
> Among all children and youth ages 6–21 who were enrolled in regular schools, the percentage of children and youth who spent most of their school day (more than 80 percent) in general classes was higher in 2008–09 than in any other school year since 1990. For example, in 2008–09, some 58 percent of children and youth spent most of their school day in regular class, compared to 33 percent in 1990–91. In 2008–09, about 86 percent of students with speech or language impairments—the highest percentage of all disability types—spent most of their school day in general classes. Sixty-two percent each of students with developmental delay and of students with visual impairments spent most of their school day in general classes. In contrast, 16 percent of students with intellectual disabilities and 13 percent of students with multiple disabilities spent most of their school day in general classes. (para. 2–3)

We will talk more about this outcome in Part III.

Reports of the percentage of all school-age students receiving services for special education vary. One report claimed that in 2007, the percentage of children who were in school with a disability label was 8.95% (Aud, Fox, & KewalRamani, 2010). The National Center for Education Statistics noted that

> The number of children and youth served under IDEA grew to 6.7 million in 2005–06, or about 14 percent of public school enrollment. By 2008–09, the number of children and youth receiving services declined to 6.5 million, corresponding to about 13 percent of all public school enrollment. (para. 1)

The point we want to make is that all students with a disability label are at some risk of not being taught in general education at least some of the time, and because such a significant percentage of children are labeled with a disability, it is important to pay careful attention to how educational services are described and provided.

All children who are in school who have a disability label have an **individualized education program** or IEP. An IEP is a written document that is designed to help schools provide the support that a child with a disability needs to be successful in school. The IEP is reviewed, and a new one written, at least once each year. Having an IEP means being in special education. What many people know is that having an IEP often leads to a negative stigma—and as a result, some families choose not to pursue an IEP for their child, an indication of how labels have become so negative in special education.

The Impact of Labels

As our educational policies and practices have evolved, so has the way we include and teach students with disabilities. There are benefits and drawbacks to having a whole branch of education called "special": Powell noted that classifying children with labels "requires extensive mediation between its many positive and negative consequences: provision of rights and additional resources but also prevalent stigmatization, even institutionalized discrimination" (2009, p. 164). The creation of special education included listing disabilities that children might have; the list today has 13 categories.

Remember from Chapter 1 that the medical model of disability sees disability as something wrong that needs fixing. This idea had a powerful impact on how special education developed: Disabilities were seen as individual flaws, and special education was designed to remedy a child's "deficits." At the same time, a pity/charity model was in use in the mid-1900s as more and more conversation about the need to help people with disabilities took place. Helping people with disabilities because of their individual weaknesses was praised, and continues to be praised, today. This is a problem because people with disabilities often don't want praise—they want equal rights. In fact, one slogan some disability rights activists use is **"piss on pity"** (Godrej, 2005). See Table 2.1 for other examples of the opposing viewpoints held by people with disabilities and those who evaluate them.

The reason legislation focused on disability labels was well intentioned. Congress was concerned that students with disabilities were not doing well in school; we know that "when P.L. 94-142 [The Education for All Handicapped Children Act (EHC)] was first passed, Congress was especially concerned that many children with disabilities were not succeeding in school because their disabilities had not been identified" (U.S. Department of Education, 2000, p. vii, in Martin, Martin, & Terman, 1996). To address the need to identify students with disabilities, a complex assessment and identification process has been developed (see Chapter 9 for more on assessment). The process for identifying a child as having a disability under special education law is highly detailed;

individualized education program (IEP) Written annual education plan for a student eligible for a disability classification. This document outlines placement, services, accommodations, and modifications necessary to meet the student's individualized needs in the least restrictive environment.

"piss on pity" A reaction by some disabilty activists to people feeling sorry for people with disabilities. Instead of charity, activists work toward people with disabilities having what they need as a right.

Table 2.1.   Language of 'us' and 'them'

We like things.	They fixate on objects.
We try to make friends.	They display attention-seeking behavior.
We take breaks.	They display off-task behavior.
We stand up for ourselves.	They are noncompliant.
We have hobbies.	They self-stimulate.
We choose our friends wisely.	They display poor peer socialization.
We persevere.	They perseverate.
We like people.	They have dependencies on people.
We go for a walk.	They run away.
We insist.	They tantrum.
We change our minds.	They are disoriented and have short attention spans.
We have talents.	They have splinter skills.
We are human.	They are...?

Source: Mayer Shevin, 1989.

there are guidelines that the federal government has established to help ensure that all children with disabilities have the free appropriate public education they are entitled to have.

The EHC has been reauthorized by Congress several times. In 1990 the name of the law was changed to the Individuals with Disabilities Education Act (IDEA), and in 2004 it was changed again to the Individuals with Disabilities Education Improvement Act. Each time, the law was made clearer and explained more about the process of identifying and supporting students with disabilities in school. Annual Reports to Congress (U.S. Department of Education, 2000) about IDEA have noted that

> With each set of amendments to the law, Congress has encouraged the expansion of the professional workforce to support the millions of children served under IDEA. When data were first reported in 1976–77, there were 331,453 teachers and related services personnel providing services to children with disabilities; today there are more than 800,000. Personnel preparation efforts supported under IDEA have helped states staff their classrooms with teachers and paraprofessionals trained in special education and related services fields and have promoted innovation in teacher preparation. (Twenty-Second Annual Report to Congress on the Implementation of the Individuals with Disabilities Education Act, 2000, p. xi)

This report shows the commitment of Congress to support students with disabilities by training teachers and paraprofessionals. This is both great news and bad news. The great news is that Congress supports access to education for students with disabilities. The bad news is that the way this is supported—by creating a special category of teachers and paraprofessionals—helps reinforce the idea that students with disabilities are so different from their typical peers that a completely new branch of education needed to be developed. This is a problem for several reasons. First, some teachers may feel that they do not teach students with disabilities because someone else—a special education person—should do that. Second, some teachers in special education may agree with this division! These two problems are central to the debate about where and how typical students and students with disabilities are taught and who teaches them.

Another factor in how labels impact education is the interplay of federal laws like IDEA and states' rights in how each state implements the law. The interplay is complex, and the result is a wide range in how students with disabilities are educated. Some districts include every student with disabilities in general education classrooms from elementary school through high school; other districts have a combination of services, including resource rooms, self-contained classrooms, separate programs, and separate schools.

The fields of general education and special education assumed that children with disabilities would not benefit as much from learning in a general education setting as in a separate, special education setting, and thus students with disabilities are often taught in segregated classrooms. More recently, education has shifted to a consideration that all children learn best in an inclusive setting—a revelation that is startling to teachers who have been trained to believe that special education includes segregation for the good of children with disabilities (Kliewer, 1998, p. 14).

The Inclusion Debate

Where students are educated has been the source of a great conflict and discussion in education since the passage of EHC. Cole, Waldron, and Majd (2004) explained the two sides of the debate:

> Skeptics charge that efforts to include students with disabilities in general education classrooms may result in the more able students experiencing boredom, while students with disabilities may experience frustration when trying to keep up with the instructional pace....Advocates of inclusion maintain that inclusion is beneficial to all students in terms of academic and social growth. Indeed, many scholars believe inclusion to be an issue of social justice and that the burden of proof should fall upon the shoulders of those who wish to segregate students with disabilities. (pp. 136–137)

How to determine who is included is one part of the debate that we do not want to spend much time on. We believe that all students need to be included, and our colleague David Rostetter said it best: "The more significant a student's disability, the more imperative the need to be included with typical peers." His comment is a response to a general trend of including more students with mild and high-incidence disabilities, such as learning disabilities, while continuing to educate students with severe disabilities in separate classrooms or schools.

A very different way to structure special education would be in place if the social model of disability had been the theory that anchored decisions about how to provide a free appropriate public education for children with disabilities. What do you think that might look like? That is the focus of the next part of this chapter.

WHAT WE WANT TO SEE

Think about your experience in school. Were students with disabilities included in all academic areas? Were special education classrooms and programs separate from other classrooms? Did students and teachers talk openly about the range of ways people understand material, and was needing help accepted and talked about? Were students who used a resource room, test modification, or other academic support ashamed to use those supports?

Now think back to the first part of the chapter. The Enlightenment had three central ideas: that empirical science helps us understand the world, that progress is inevitable, and that people are not inherently bad but are blank slates. Each of these ideas can have wonderful positive effects on how we structure education for students with and without disabilities. First, research (empirical science) tells us that inclusive practices are effective for all students (Cole, Waldron, & Majd, 2004). Related to progress, we have continually improved opportunities for students with disabilities in schooling, both academically and socially. That does not mean we should stop improving; instead, we should push to evolve and change what we do as we learn more about what

social construction of special education Two common ideas about students with disabilities: 1) that students with the same label need the same education and 2) that students with disabilities need education so different from students without disabilities that they must be separated.

is most effective. Finally, a belief that everyone is a blank slate means that everyone—even students with significant behavioral challenges or significant cognitive delays, is a person—not something bad, evil, or broken.

If these are the beliefs we hold, each one impacts what we believe about education and special education. The **social construction of special education** includes thinking about labels, and that has sometimes led to treating individual children who have the same disability label as if they are all the same. The result has been programs that are designed to serve groups of children who may in actuality have very different needs. In the early days of special education, separate programs developed. More recently, there is a growing emphasis on inclusion and inclusive practice. Remember from Chapter 1 that the disability rights movement sees access to housing, school, jobs, and transportation as rights that every member of society should have access to as part of being a citizen. UNICEF, the United Nations Children's Fund, believes that every child has similar rights:

> The Convention on the Rights of the Child was the first instrument to incorporate the complete range of international human rights—including civil, cultural, economic, political, and social rights as well as aspects of humanitarian law. The articles of the Convention may be grouped into four categories of rights and a set of guiding principles.... The guiding principles of the Convention include nondiscrimination; adherence to the best interests of the child; the right to life, survival and development; and the right to participate. (UNICEF, n.d.)

zone of proximal development Psychologist Lev Vygotsky described this: "the child is most successful in solving problems that are closer to those solved independently; then the difficulties grow until, at a certain level of complexity, the child fails, whatever assistance is provided" (1996, p. 187) (see Chapter 5).

We believe that education and special education should not be separate; given appropriate supports, good teachers can teach all students. The two fundamental points of discussion are determining what supports are needed to help teachers teach every student, and how we assess whether or not the teacher has been successful. These two points play a significant role in debates about education and inclusion.

What Supports Are Needed?

response to intervention (RTI) A three-step practice that many schools are using in general education to support students who struggle in academic areas, primarily in reading.

Special education evolved as a separate system because educators, legislators, and administrators believed that children with disabilities are so different from their peers that they must need specially trained teachers. Court cases that you will learn about in Chapter 3 explain this in more detail. Determining what supports a student requires, where that support is provided, and how that support is provided are all complex issues that have been debated since students with disabilities have been in schools.

differentiation "Doing whatever it takes to maximize students' learning instead of relying on a one-size-fits-all, whole class method of instruction" (Wormeli, 2007, p. 9). Differentiation is helpful because students can become independent lifelong learners. If you differentiate and show students many things, they will learn what works for them and know how to ask for what they need (see Chapter 7).

Supports that a student might need may be related to a disability, or not. For every student—whether or not he or she has a disability—we need to consider how to provide a responsive learning environment and a high-quality learning experience. That is, students need to be challenged with lessons that teach to their instructional level, in their **zone of proximal development**. In your teacher preparation program and in this book, you will learn how to do this and how to ensure that every student in an inclusive class (or any classroom) is being challenged appropriately. You will learn about **response to intervention (RTI)** and tiers of support, about **differentiation**, and about making **adaptations and modifications** to your materials and instruction.

Examples of the supports that students might need are small group instruction; modification to the amount of work, the kind of work, or the way the work is done; adaptive equipment to stand or sit, to write or speak, or to read Braille; sign language interpreters; transportation on a bus with a wheelchair lift; and transportation with an adult aide to help get seated and follow directions. Determining what supports are needed gets turned into where education should happen. We believe that inclusive attitudes support students, and that **inclusion is an attitude, not a place**.

For example, a first-grade student named Nate who is frequently overwhelmed by a typical class of 20 children and 1 teacher, and all the noise and bustle of a busy class, may need to be able to leave the classroom and go to a quieter room with fewer children and another teacher. Is this inclusion? Maybe; maybe not. If Nate is a part of the first-grade class, knows his peers and teachers, accesses as much of the curriculum as possible in the first grade, and decides when to leave—that is inclusive. If Nate spends most of his time in the other classroom, visits the typical first grade only occasionally, and is sent out by the staff for any behavior that does not meet a very high standard for any first grader—that may not be inclusive. The quieter classroom might become the place Nate spends most of his time, with little attention or effort on the part of the teachers to support Nate in the first-grade classroom—that is not inclusive. The second major issue—how we determine if a teacher is successful—has a powerful effect on how teachers think about inclusive attitudes, trying new things, and risking new strategies. Where students are educated today is illustrated in Table 2.2.

How Do We Know If a Teacher Is Successful?

Asking teachers to think inclusively, try new things, and risk new strategies is easy if these things are rewarded by the principal and the community. But we live in a time of intense scrutiny over assessment and test scores and major debates about how to evaluate teachers. The result may be less willingness on the part of some teachers to take risks, which we understand—especially because "teachers report that accountability has adversely affected how they teach, impacting curriculum, quality of instruction, and instructional time" (Anderson, 2009, p. 413).

Testing student performance has traditionally been the way that teachers are evaluated. The current climate of accountability in schools has brought attention and a lot of energy to the topic of teacher evaluation. In 2009, the Department of Education developed a competition for education funds called Race to the Top. The American Federation of Teachers commented that this initiative "would simply layer another top-down accountability system on top of the current faulty one" (McNeil, 2009, p. 23). Naturally, if teachers are assessed on whether or not students can perform well on a test, teachers will be very concerned about being sure that the students in the class can perform. But evaluating teachers on just one set of student assessments is not reasonable, and the debate about how to effectively monitor and support teachers to help all students learn continues, which is good news. More good news is that students with disabilities are being expected to learn and demonstrate their learning as our attitudes and beliefs about disabilities shift away from a pity/charity model to more of a social model. Egnor stated that "principals will experience greater pressure from state policy makers to ensure that students with disabilities are exposed to the general education curriculum so they can achieve the statewide general curriculum content standards as required by NCLB [the No Child Left Behind Act]" (2003, p. 12). While the NCLB Act is the source of a great deal of frustration, the silver lining is that everyone is paying attention to all children and how well they are able to demonstrate their learning. That is *great* news.

Supports in Inclusive Settings Leads to Teacher Success

We believe that providing support in inclusive settings leads to improved learning for students—and more success for teachers. Our foundational belief that inclusive attitudes are the way to best teach all children guides us in supporting students and teachers. To put our perspective another way, we believe that **all children can learn**. That belief shapes all of our decisions. What we believe affects what happens in schools in

adaptations and modifications Ways to change what is taught, how material is presented, and how learning is assessed to support all students benefiting from instruction.

inclusion is an attitude, not a place We believe that children are more alike than different, and supporting all students means providing supports in a classroom community where everyone is valued. We do not believe that labels such as "inclusion classroom" are truly inclusive because if there is an "inclusive classroom," that implies that there are other classrooms that are not.

all children can learn Our fundamental belief about children.

Table 2.2. Students with disabilities in general education settings

QUESTION:

What percentage of students with disabilities are educated in regular classrooms?

RESPONSE:

The Individuals with Disabilities Education Act (IDEA), enacted in 1975, mandates that children and youth ages 3 to 21 with disabilities be provided a free appropriate public school education. Data collection activities to monitor compliance with IDEA began in 1976.

In 2008, some 95 percent of students 6 to 21 years old served under IDEA were enrolled in regular school, 3 percent were served in a separate school for students with disabilities, 1 percent were placed in regular private schools by their parents, and less than 1 percent were served in each of the following environments: separate residential facility, homebound or hospital, or a correctional facility.

Percentage distribution of students 6 to 21 years old served under Individuals with Disabilities Education Act, Part B, by educational environment and type of disability: Fall 2006

| Type of disability | All environments | Regular school, time outside regular classroom | | | Separate school for students with disabilities | Separate residential facility | Parentally placed in regular private schools[1] | Home-bound/ hospital placement | Correctional facility |
		Less than 21 %	21–60 %	More than 60 %					
All students with disabilities	100.0	58.0	21.7	15.1	3.0	0.4	1.1	0.4	0.4
Specific learning disabilities	100.0	60.9	28.4	8.6	0.6	0.1	0.9	0.2	0.4
Speech or language impairments	100.0	86.4	5.7	4.7	0.3	#	2.8	#	#
Intellectual disability	100.0	16.2	27.4	48.9	6.0	0.4	0.2	0.5	0.3
Emotional disturbance	100.0	39.2	19.4	23.2	13.1	2.0	0.2	1.1	1.7
Multiple disabilities	100.0	13.2	16.5	46.2	19.1	1.9	0.3	2.6	1.9
Hearing impairments	100.0	53.3	17.2	15.8	8.3	3.9	1.2	0.2	0.2
Orthopedic impairments	100.0	51.3	16.6	24.8	4.9	0.2	0.8	1.4	0.1
Other health impairments[2]	100.0	60.1	24.6	11.3	1.6	0.	1.0	1.0	0.3
Visual impairments	100.0	61.6	13.9	12.0	6.6	4.1	1.2	0.6	0.1
Autism	100.0	36.1	18.3	35.8	8.3	0.6	0.6	0.3	#
Deaf-blindness	100.0	30.0	16.7	29.1	15.5	7.0	0.6	1.3	0.1
Traumatic brain injury	100.0	45.0	23.2	23.0	6.0	0.6	0.6	1.5	0.2
Developmental delay	100.0	61.8	20.6	16.2	0.7	0.1	0.5	0.2	#

Rounds to zero.
[1]Students who are enrolled by their parents or guardians in regular private schools and have their basic education paid through private resources, but receive special education services at public expense. These students are not included under "Regular school, time outside general class."
[2]Other health impairments include having limited strength, vitality, or alertness due to chronic or acute health problems, such as a heart condition, tuberculosis, rheumatic fever, nephritis, asthma, sickle-cell anemia, hemophilia, epilepsy, lead poisoning, leukemia, or diabetes.

NOTE: Data are for the 50 United States, the District of Columbia, and the Bureau of Indian Education schools. Detail may not sum to totals because of rounding.
Source: U.S. Department of Education, National Center for Education Statistics. (2011). *The Digest of Education Statistics, 2011* (NCES 2011-015), Table 46. Retrieved from http://nces.ed.gov/fastfacts/display.asp?id=59

several significant ways. If we believe that some—not all—children can learn, we ignore children we think cannot learn. If we think some children can learn but others have to prove that they are capable of learning, we set up barriers to education for some children. If we believe all children can learn, we prepare teachers to teach all children.

Some Children Can Learn

If we believe that some, not all, children can learn, then that is what will happen. If students with disabilities are denied access to high-quality curriculum, to reading, to interacting with peers who do not have disabilities, we set up self-fulfilling prophecies of failure. The belief that some students cannot learn affects what kinds of classrooms are offered. In the United States, schools have a varied history of including students. In the 1800s, schools were often one room with a single teacher for all grades, and the teacher taught any child able to attend. Today, the belief that some students are so different from other students that they cannot learn similar things leads to segregated placements. The reality of low teacher expectations limiting student success is striking when you look at the data from New York State presented in Figure 2.2.

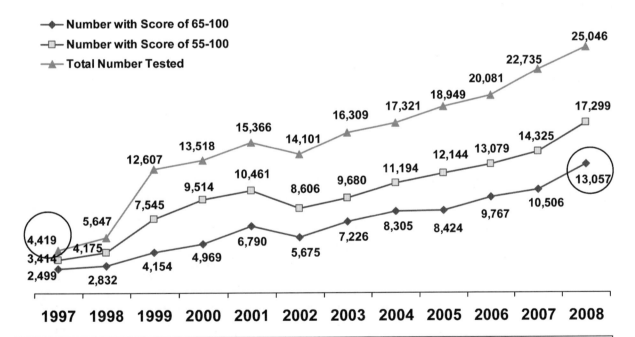

Figure 2.2.   Increase in access and performance: Students with disabilities in New York State taking an English exam in high school. (From Cort, R.H. [2009]. The State of Special Education 2009. Retrieved November 30, 2011, from http://www.p12. nysed.gov/specialed/techassist/Statewide-Oct09/Oct09statewide.ppt.)

Some Children Have to Prove They Can Learn

The belief that students have to "earn their way in" to general education classrooms keeps many students out of the inclusive classroom. If we believe that teachers only have to learn how to teach one way, we limit opportunities for students who learn in a way that is different from that teacher's methods. Determining which children with disabilities must earn their way in is also connected to race. The reauthorization of EHC in 2004 included the following facts:

(B) More minority children continue to be served in special education than would be expected from the percentage of minority students in the general school population.
(C) African-American children are identified as having mental retardation and emotional disturbance at rates greater than their White counterparts.
(D) In the 1998–1999 school year, African-American children represented just 14.8 percent of the population aged 6 through 21, but comprised 20.2 percent of all children with disabilities.
(E) Studies have found that schools with predominately White students and teachers have placed disproportionately high numbers of their minority students into special education. (Individuals with Disabilities Education Act, 2004, p. 118, STAT. 2651)

All Children Can Learn

Historically, we have excluded students with disabilities from general education classrooms, often saying "They are not ready." The readiness model puts the burden of preparation for learning on the child. What we may see in students with disabilities is different ways of showing learning, different rates of learning, and different needs in order to learn—but all children learn.

Students with disabilities are expected to take part in testing. Students with disabilities are expected to have access to high-quality curriculum. Schools expect teachers to be able to differentiate how they teach and to teach every student—not just teach one way. When this belief is present in schools, students do remarkable things.

SUMMARY

In this chapter we reviewed the history of formal education in the United States, including how ideas from the Enlightenment and Progressive Era affected education. Then we examined how education for students with disabilities developed after the first law mandating education for all children, the Education of All Handicapped Children Act (EHC), was passed. Last, we explained that determining what supports are needed and how teachers are assessed are two factors that have a significant effect on how we think about education for students with disabilities and inclusion. We ended with our belief that all children can learn and explained how thinking of inclusion as an attitude that drives all our decisions about teaching can help all students learn.

NARRATIVE 2.1. | LARRY BISSONNETTE

Larry Bissonnette is an advocate and artist who lives in Milton, Vermont, and has had his work exhibited regularly both locally and nationally. Larry is one of the featured artists of the GRACE (Grass Roots Art and Community Effort) project based in Hardwick, Vermont. His work is in the permanent collection of the Musée de l'Art Brut, Lausanne, Switzerland, and in many private collections. His work was most recently featured in the Hobart and William Smith Disability and the Arts Festival in April 2010. He is both the subject and writer of an award-winning film about his life, called *My Classic Life as an Artist: A Portrait of Larry Bissonnette* (2005). In 1991, Larry learned to communicate through typing and began combining words with his art to express his thoughts and ideas. Over the past 15 years, he has been a featured presenter at many educational conferences and has written and spoken on the topics of autism, communication, and art. (Retrieved from http://wretchesandjabberers.org/mobile/larry.php)

What do you want people to know about you?   Taking stock of my personal life story, I make over simplifications in terms of the order of the timeline being one of life living in this real world with my family and life living in the institution. It is more that I normally think of the timeline of my life as living in open water, leaving the land of active participation, sometimes moving ashore to that land, at other times, melding me to participation is my art and typed communication. Most of the time, I make living in my community the center of my universe. Luckily in Milton, Vermont, it's not hard to find the center because it is a slow-moving place with many seen people at church, grocery store, and library sights that you can go to all in one day.

How is life with your sister different than living in the institution?   Opportunities to participate in real community events such as church and right-out-my-backyard parties might make my life satisfactory enough but it is also making my art and typing available to the public that has been important to my growth as a person and advocate for people that can't speak and this has helped others to note my intelligence instead of my disability.

What are the most helpful ways in which people can interact with you?   It's how people gesture understanding about my autism, keeping what is aligned with my intelligence in the start of their interactions with me and what they are conditioned to believe about the lack of interest in the world within people like me. Pushed into the background of forgotten memories.

What do you want teachers to know about supporting students who do not use speech to communicate?   Learning language to express one's ideas is not limited by a lack of ability to speak but by speaking people's lack of estimation of the nonspeaking person's capacity to gain this skill so teachers need to work on watching for intelligence simmering below the surface of a person's outward behavior.

CHAPTER 3

Special Education Law and Legislation

How this chapter prepares you to be an effective inclusive classroom teacher:

- This chapter teaches you about special education laws and the court cases that led to the passing of those laws. You will also learn about historical events that have changed the profession of education. By reading about these events, you will see how they affected families, schools, and students. **This helps you meet CEC Standard 1: Foundations.**

- This chapter teaches you that all students are valuable and have the right to free appropriate public education with equitable learning opportunities. You will also learn definitions of the 13 disability areas according to the law and ways that people are classified depending on their similarities and differences. This chapter will help you think about the impact of classifying people this way and the impact that can have on learning in the classroom. **This helps you meet CEC Standard 2: Development and Characteristics of Learners.**

- This chapter prepares you to be a professional and ethical teacher by teaching you to be sensitive to the many aspects of diversity, to view all students as valuable, and to consider your job as a teacher to fully include all students in all experiences. This chapter shows you what the teacher's responsibilities are under the law as well as ways in which policy will affect your daily practice. This chapter introduces the concept of letter of the law versus spirit of the law and your role of teacher as policy change agent and advocate. **This helps you meet CEC Standard 9: Professional and Ethical Practice.**

After reading and discussing
this chapter, you will be able to

- Describe the components and purpose of IDEA and explain the impact on students and schools

- Describe the etiology of IDEA from PL 94-142 in 1975 to the most recent authorization in 2004 and explain the purpose and impact of the revisions

- Describe the components of ADA and explain the impact on the community

- Explain the concept of "letter versus spirit of the law"

- Explain the connection between the racial desegregation case of *Brown v. Board of Education* and ability desegregation

- Explain the impact of significant court cases on special education and the disability rights movement

- Describe current issues in special education policy and what changes would continue to improve full inclusion of all persons in school and community

This chapter focuses on the legislation and laws significant to the field of special education. The chapter is arranged in three sections. The first section maps the road traveled to date. It tells the story of significant court cases and laws passed. The second section examines where we are now. Building on Chapters 1 and 2, this section describes both benefits and drawbacks of special education laws. The third section describes the path we must follow toward equitable education of all children.

THE ROAD TRAVELED

This section is a chronological review of court cases and major laws affecting students with disabilities (see Figure 3.1). For each court case, we examine the background story that led to the case, recount the facts of the case, provide the ruling, and explain the significance of the case for students with disabilities. For each law, we review the law's purpose, describe its provisions, and explain its impact on the education of all children.

Brown v. Board of Education of Topeka, Kansas (1954)

desegregation
Discontinuing the practice of separating students by race, gender, or disability label so that students with diverse backgrounds and experiences are educated together.

In Chapter 2, you learned about the *Brown v. Board of Education* case and its significance during the Progressive Era of educational history. We return to the case here to illustrate its influence in the fight for inclusion of persons with disabilities in school. *Brown v. Board of Education* concerned racial **desegregation** in public schools. The connection between the inclusion of children with disabilities and African American children was the court's consideration that school segregation, in any form, was unjust (Haskins, 1998).

For many years prior to *Brown v. Board of Education*, African American parents had been challenging the practice of racial segregation in public schools in many states across the country. There were 11 cases in Kansas alone. When Kansas became a state

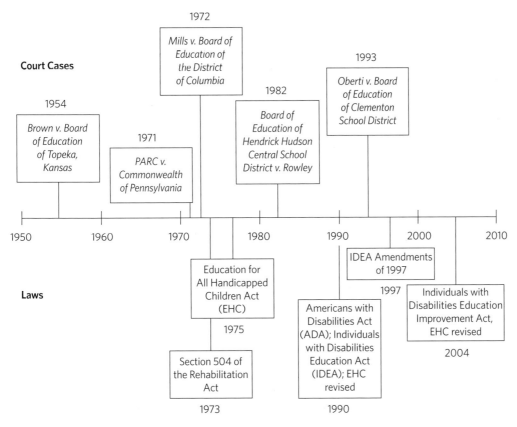

Figure 3.1.   Time line of court cases and laws.

in 1861, it excluded the institution of slavery by law and practice. It was a "free state." Nevertheless, during the 1850s, Kansas was a major battleground among the nation's abolitionists, free-state advocates, and proslavery forces. While some slaveholders tried to settle in Kansas between 1854 and 1861, slavery never took root as part of the state's labor force. However, the state on Kansas's eastern border—Missouri—did enter the Union as a slave state.

For that reason, Kansas vacillated on the issue of racial segregation in public schools. It was not until 1879 that the state legislature passed a law allowing first-class cities (defined as those with populations of 15,000 or more) to operate segregated elementary schools. Kansas did not permit segregated junior high or high schools in any city. As a result, African American children were provided a public school education and were even provided busing, but those in first-class cities were only allowed to attend designated schools based on race (Brown Foundation, 2011). Also, for many years prior to the case, the National Association for the Advancement of Colored People (NAACP) had been preparing to challenge racial segregation in all facets of community life, including schooling. By 1950, the Topeka NAACP had approached several families in the city, asking them to join a class action lawsuit against racially segregated schools. The Reverend Oliver Brown was only one of 13 parents recruited to be plaintiffs in the case. The case was named after the Reverend Brown as a legal strategy because he was the only male (Brown Foundation, 2011). These 13 families, as representatives of so many other African American families in the United States, were affected by segregation because their children were not allowed to attend neighborhood schools that were designated as White schools. African Americans lived in integrated neighborhoods, and yet their children had to travel far away from home every day to attend schools designated as Black schools.

In the fall of 1950, when the children were ready to start the school year, the NAACP encouraged their parents to take them to enroll in White schools. Why should their children endure longer commutes each day when there were schools closer to home? Why should their children have a separate education? When the families were turned away at the schools, the NAACP had the documentation they needed to file a case. In 1951, on behalf of the Browns and 12 other families in Topeka, *Brown v. Board of Education* was launched.

The Case   The locations of the schools and commuting conditions, though significant, were not the only concerns. Of greater concern was the psychological effect of segregation on the children. For 3 long years, the NAACP's chief counsel, Thurgood Marshall, argued several desegregation cases, including *Brown vs. Board of Education*, wrestling against previous rulings such as *Plessy v. Ferguson* of 1896, which upheld "separate but equal" education, and eventually appealing the case to the United States Supreme Court. The Supreme Court of the United States combined five cases all seeking desegregation of public schools—*Belton v. Gebhart (Bulah v. Gebhart)* from Delaware, *Brown v. Board of Education* from Kansas, *Briggs v. Elliott* from South Carolina, *Davis v. County School Board of Prince Edward County* from Virginia, and *Bolling v. Sharpe* from the District of Columbia—all under the heading of *Brown v. Board of Education of Topeka, Kansas* (Brown Foundation, 2011).

The Ruling   The Supreme Court ruled in favor of the families, as quoted here:

> We conclude that, in the field of public education, the doctrine of "separate but equal" has no place. Separate educational facilities are inherently unequal. Therefore, we hold that the plaintiffs and others similarly situated for whom the actions have been brought are, by reason of the segregation complained of, deprived of the equal protection of the laws guaranteed by the Fourteenth Amendment. (*Brown v. Board of Education of Topeka*, 1954, p. 5)

In reaching its decision, the Supreme Court considered documentation by a lower court. The lower court did not rule in favor of the plaintiffs, but the following summary, based on testimony by psychologists, influenced the Supreme Court's decision to overturn the lower court:

> Segregation of White and Colored children in public schools has a detrimental effect upon the Colored children. The impact is greater when it has the sanction of the law; for the policy of separating the races is usually interpreted as denoting the inferiority of the Negro group. A sense of inferiority affects the motivation of a child to learn. Segregation with the sanction of law, therefore, has a tendency to retard the educational and mental development of Negro children and to deprive them of some of the benefits they would receive in a racially integrated school system. (*Brown v. Board of Education of Topeka*, 1954, p. 5)

The Significance   The significance of this case for the inclusion of persons with disabilities in education is easy to demonstrate. Returning to the last quote, we replaced references to race with references to ability:

> Segregation of [nondisabled] and [disabled] children in public schools has a detrimental effect upon the [disabled] children. The impact is greater when it has the sanction of the law; for the policy of separating by [ability] is usually interpreted as denoting

the inferiority of the [disabled] group. A sense of inferiority affects the motivation of a child to learn. Segregation with the sanction of law, therefore, has a tendency to retard the educational and mental development of [disabled] children and to deprive them of some of the benefits they would receive in an integrated school system.

It may seem like a stretch to replace racial inequity with ability inequity. Of course, there are differences between the Black rights movement and the disability rights movement, but both are affected by the social construction of ability. Without knowing members of these groups individually, society has decided what they can and cannot do, based on the social construction of each characteristic.

Photo 3.1. First graders in Baltimore, in a newly integrated class following the *Brown vs. Board of Education* decision, say the pledge to the flag. (Richard Stacks, Copyright © 1955 by The Baltimore Sun; reprinted by permission)

Even more simply, think about it in terms of the motivation of the parents in *Brown vs. Board of Education* and the parents of children with disabilities. The Reverend Oliver Brown, Mrs. Richard Lawton, Mrs. Lucinda Todd, Mrs. Andrew Henderson, Mrs. Vivian Scales, Mrs. Lena Harper, Mrs. Shirley Hodison, Mrs. Marguerite Emmerson, Mrs. Sadie Emmanuel, Mrs. Iona Richardson, Mrs. Alma Lewis, Mrs. Darlene Brown, Mrs. Shirla Fleming, and all of the families from all of the states loved their sons and daughters. When they looked at them, they saw promise. They saw strengths and abilities, hopes and dreams. They saw tenacity to work hard, curiosity to explore new things, and pride in accomplishments hard won. They did not see failure based on outward appearance. They did not see helplessness born of decades of oppression, rejection, and exclusion. They did not see the worthlessness that was assumed by prejudiced, privileged groups. They wanted their children to have opportunities to show society what they could do (see Photo 3.1).

Brown v. Board of Education (1954) laid the foundation for disability rights legislation. It would be 20 more years of inequitable access to appropriate public education for students with disabilities before the first law requiring schools to admit and teach students with disabilities would be passed. However, *Brown vs. Board of Education* (1954) was part of a historic continuum regarding the pursuit of equal opportunity and the pursuit of social justice.

Pennsylvania Association of Retarded Citizens (PARC) v. the Commonwealth of Pennsylvania (1971)

Prior to 1971, there was no legal mandate to provide youth with intellectual disabilities or brain injury access to public education. If those youth were provided the opportunity to attend school with their nondisabled peers, it was based on the school's or district's willingness to do so. Most of the time, schools or districts were not willing to admit students with developmental disabilities because officials believed that they were not able to learn.

The Case   Motivated by the results of *Brown vs. Board of Education* (1954), a group of families in Pennsylvania challenged the exclusion of children with intellectual disabilities. Headed by Nancy Beth Bowman, a citizen with an intellectual disability, members of the Pennsylvania Association of Retarded Citizens (PARC) sued the Commonwealth of Pennsylvania for equal rights to education for children with developmental disabilities. The Commonwealth did not fight to exclude the children; they opted to work with PARC and the court to reach an agreement.

The Ruling   On October 7, 1971, the United States District Court ruled that it is unconstitutional, in any way, to postpone or deny any child with developmental disabilities who is of compulsory school age (from 6 to 21 years old) access to a free public program of education and training, appropriate to his or her learning capabilities. The ruling included preschool services where offered, homebound instruction even if the student did not have a physical disability, and re-evaluation of all plaintiffs who were previously denied (*PARC v. Pennsylvania*, 1971).

The Significance   This case built on the foundation laid by *Brown vs. Board of Education* (1954). It was a start. Now in Pennsylvania, schools could no longer deny those with intellectual disabilities a free appropriate public education. *PARC v. Pennsylvania* addressed one disability classification in one state, but it was the beginning of a shift in what we believe about students with disabilities. Maybe there is not an unbridgeable difference after all. Now there was a path, a bit more clearly defined, for others to follow.

Mills v. Board of Education of District of Columbia (1972)

Peter Mills was a 12-year-old, residing at Junior Village orphanage in the District of Columbia. Because of behavior problems, Peter was removed from school in 1971.

Jerome James was also 12 years old. He lived with his mother and received Aid to Families with Dependent Children (AFDC) benefits. Jerome was considered retarded by the school district and had never been allowed to attend school.

Duane Blacksheare was 13 years old. He resided at Saint Elizabeth's psychiatric hospital and was excluded from public school in 1967 due to behavior problems, even though an evaluation found him to be capable of regular class with support services. For a time, following media attention, Duane attended seventh grade for 2 hours a day without assistance or evaluation of his needs but was later removed from school again.

Janice King, also 13 years old, lived with her father. Due to a childhood illness, Janice had brain damage and cognitive delay with right hemiplegia. Janice's application for public schooling was denied. She had never been provided public-supported education.

Michael Williams was 16 years old. He resided at Saint Elizabeth's psychiatric hospital due to epilepsy and mild cognitive delay. Due to absences and health problems, when he was temporarily hospitalized in 1969, he was denied public education.

George Liddell Jr. was 8 years old. He lived with his mother and received Aid for Families with Dependent Children (AFDC) benefits. George had never attended school. The district excluded him based on his need for a special class for cognitive delay. Evaluations deemed him capable of benefiting from school, but his mother was unable to secure enrollment.

Eight-year-old Steven Gaston lived with his mother and was excluded from his public elementary school in first grade due to slight brain damage, hyperactivity, and a tendency to wander the classroom. Steven was accepted into a private school, but tuition was required in advance. He was on a waiting list for a tuition grant at the time of the court case (*Mills v. Board of Education*, 1972).

By 1972, these seven children and their **advocates** had had enough.

advocates Persons who speak up on behalf of another to obtain rights or services. Advocates work to support people with disabilities because they have a right to what they need in home, school, and community; not through pity or charity.

The Case   The schools of the District of Columbia were not providing publicly supported education and training to children with disabilities. Indeed, it was a problem of major proportions in the district. In 1972, as many as 18,000 of the 22,000 students with disabilities in the District of Columbia were being excluded, suspended, expelled, reassigned, and transferred from regular public schools without due process (*Mills v. Board of Education*, 1972).

These seven plaintiffs sued the Board of Education of the District of Columbia on behalf of other District of Columbia residents of school age who had been unduly excluded from public-supported education. While these families could have applied to private, tuition-based schools, they could not afford to enroll.

The Ruling   The court ordered that the district must by January 3, 1972, enroll Peter, Duane, Steven, and Michael into appropriate programs; adequately review the others to determine appropriate programming; and list for the court all others in the district who had been excluded. On January 27, these mandates had not been accomplished. The court then ordered that a plan be in place for the students by March 1, 1972. When these actions had not been accomplished by March 24, the court ordered the following decree, entitling the plaintiffs to relief:

> All children of the ages hereinafter prescribed who are bona fide residents of the District of Columbia are entitled to admission and free tuition in the Public Schools of the District of Columbia, subject to the rules, regulations, and orders of the Board of Education and the applicable statutes. (*Mills v. Board of Education*, 1972, p. 7)

The Board of Education's argument to this ruling was that it could not afford to admit all students with disabilities unless provided with millions of dollars in federal funds. The court was not persuaded and laid out several specific parameters for service provision and due process hearing procedures to be implemented within 45 days from the final ruling.

The Significance   There are several significant points here. First, this case, as well as *PARC v. Pennsylvania* (1971), is an example of disability rights litigation on behalf of many students. These landmark cases brought attention to the right of all children to have an education that is appropriate for their needs and abilities. Cases such as these spurred advocates to litigation, moving us closer to blanket federal legislation mandating public education for all children of school age.

Second, there is significance in the lengthy resolution of this case. The defendants did not promptly abide by the court's decision. The issue was revisited multiple times before the district was forced to comply. In the meantime, there were students who were not receiving an appropriate education.

Third, it is significant that all plaintiffs in this case were African American, but the written ruling states that the case was about disability, not race. When all of the plaintiffs with disabilities suing for equitable educational opportunities are of color, it makes it clear that **disproportionality** and intersection of race and disability are important considerations.

Section 504 of the Rehabilitation Act of 1973

The Purpose   Shortly after the decision of *PARC v. Pennsylvania* (1971) and *Mills v. the Board of Education* came the Rehabilitation Act of 1973. The Rehabilitation Act was not a direct result of the previous court cases, but it occurred next chronologically and, combined with the significant legislation before it, became an important piece for events later in the time line. The Rehabilitation Act of 1973 required all agencies that accepted federal funding to provide equal opportunities to persons with disabilities. This was enacted primarily in reaction to the number of veterans with disabilities who had been excluded from employment, community services, education, and recreation due to the accommodations required to support them.

The Provisions   Even though this was not an act directly addressing education policy, there was one section with a link to educational services—Section 504, as it has become known in the field of special education. Section 504 states:

disproportionality
When a group of people is over- or underrepresented by percentage in a subset of the whole population. An example is that Native Americans are underrepresented as being gifted and talented—that is, given the percentage of the total population of Native Americans, fewer students than would be expected are placed in programs for gifted students.

No otherwise qualified handicapped individual in the United States, as defined in section 7(6) shall, solely by reason of his handicap, be excluded from the participation in, be denied the benefits of, or be subjected to discrimination under any program or activity receiving Federal financial assistance. (Rehabilitation Act of 1973)

Persons with handicaps were defined as those having physical or mental impairments that substantially limit one or more major life activity, including self-care, walking, seeing, hearing, speaking, breathing, working, and learning (U.S. Department of Health and Human Services, 2000).

The Rehabilitation Act also included provisions for developing and implementing plans for meeting needs and providing services, evaluating persons with impairments, developing methods to ensure persons were assisted in becoming as independent as possible, constructing and improving rehabilitation facilities, developing innovative methods for providing services, providing employment opportunities to previously excluded individuals, and reviewing architectural and transportation barriers. All of these services and options challenged employers, community agencies, and local governments.

The Impact   Since public schools receive federal financial assistance, this allowed persons with impairments limiting their ability to learn to be evaluated and receive plans for supports and services that would maximize their independence.

However, the general nature of the statements in the Rehabilitation Act left the extent and nature of services wide open for interpretation. In other words, the act provided students with disabilities access to schools, but it did not specify what to do with or for them once they were there. Service provision for these students was often representative of society's perception of persons with disabilities at that time—that students with disabilities were less able to learn and their presence in classrooms would hinder the learning of children without disabilities. The result was segregated classrooms and low expectations. Students with disabilities were thus being served in schools in a variety of ways across the country.

Public Law 94-142: The Education of All Handicapped Children Act (EHC) of 1975

The Purpose   In 1975, there were more than 8 million children in the United States with disabilities. More than half of them were receiving poor educational services or were being excluded entirely from schooling. In addition, other students who were in school were not benefiting from their education because of undetected disabilities. Even though training for teachers and teaching methods had advanced so that specialized instruction could be provided, it was not done very consistently (Cheadle, 1987). EHC was passed in response to court cases like *PARC v. Pennsylvania* (1971) and *Mills v. the Board of Education* (1972). It was in the national interest to pass federal legislation that standardized specific procedures to qualify students for specialized services, evaluate their needs, involve families, purposefully plan for and support individualized needs in the least restrictive environment, and provide procedures for grievance. Enter EHC.

The Provisions   In Chapter 2, you were introduced to the ground-breaking provisions established by this law. At the time, it was a huge leap for students who had been left out of schools or inappropriately educated once in the schools. The six significant provisions of EHC are outlined here in more detail. They are free appropriate public education, disability qualifications, nondiscriminatory assessment, least restrictive environment, individualized education programs, parent involvement, and procedural due process.

Autism (added in 1990)
Blindness
Deaf-blindness
Intellectual disabilities (formerly mental retardation)
Emotional disturbance
Hearing impairment
Multiple disabilities
Orthopedic impairment
Other health impairment
Specific learning disability
Speech or language impairment
Traumatic brain injury (added in 1990)
Visual impairment

Figure 3.2. Disability classifications under The Education of All Handicapped Children Act and the Individuals with Disabilities Education Act. (*Source:* Individuals with Disabilities Education Act of 2004.)

Free Appropriate Public Education (FAPE) for Students Ages 6–21 All students considered of compulsory school age must be provided equal access and opportunity in their public, neighborhood school. Embedded in this is the **zero reject rule**, which states that school personnel do not have the right to decide that any student will not benefit from instruction in the public school setting. They cannot reject anyone regardless of their individual needs. However, an exception to this was built into the law. If the school could make a case that the child's disability was too severe to benefit from the services provided, alternative arrangements could be made at another school at no expense to the parents.

Qualification Under Disability Classifications Once the student is evaluated, it may be determined that he or she meets the definition of one or more of the disability **classifications**. All of these categories were given specific definitions and evaluative criteria for qualification. The 11 original categories were outlined in 1975, and 2 more were added in 1990 (see Figure 3.2).

Nondiscriminatory Assessment If a student in the school system, or a child ready to enter the school system, is suspected of having an impairment that will affect learning, the student is entitled to a **nondiscriminatory assessment**. This assessment evaluates the student to see if one of the specified disabilities exists and whether or not the student can be supported in special education. Any discrimination during the evaluation could result in inappropriate education for the student.

First, the evaluation to determine **eligibility** for special education must be conducted in the student's preferred language. Second, the evaluation must include multiple tests. Decisions to place students in special education or label them with a disability cannot be based on the score of one test, particularly an intelligence test. Both formal, standardized and informal, context-based assessments must be conducted to fully evaluate the true performance of a student on various measures. Third, the testing must occur in a manner and environment free of bias and barriers. The tests themselves should be selected for minimal cultural bias in the items and instructions. The testing setting must be physically and emotionally comfortable as to be conducive to best performance by the student, and the student should be familiar with the test administrator. Last, the tests must be conducted and analyzed by a multidisciplinary team of school personnel, so that one person is not solely liable for the resulting decisions.

zero reject rule Schools cannot reject any child from a free appropriate public education. Everyone is allowed to attend school and receive appropriate supports, even students with severe disabilities who do not learn in traditional ways or learn traditional content.

classifications Labels for 13 disability areas under IDEA. Under the current system, special education services are only provided when a student has a disability classification.

nondiscriminatory assessment Evaluation procedures that are as free from cultural and linguistic bias as possible so that an accurate assessment of a child's skills can be measured instead of measuring cultural capital or experience.

eligibility Meeting the stipulated requirements for a disability classification so services can be received. Under IDEA, there are 13 classifications of disability. Eligibility is determined through an evaluation process (see Chapter 9).

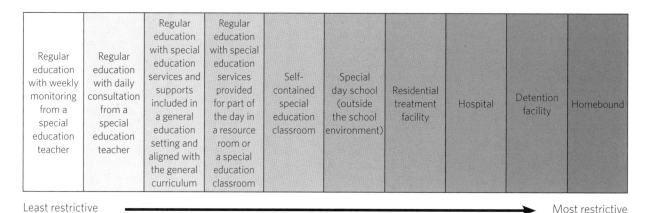

Regular education with weekly monitoring from a special education teacher	Regular education with daily consultation from a special education teacher	Regular education with special education services and supports included in a general education setting and aligned with the general curriculum	Regular education with special education services provided for part of the day in a resource room or a special education classroom	Self-contained special education classroom	Special day school (outside the school environment)	Residential treatment facility	Hospital	Detention facility	Homebound

Least restrictive ⟶ Most restrictive

Figure 3.3. Least restrictive environment (LRE) continuum.

least restrictive environment (LRE) The idea that students with disability classifications should be educated as much as possible with their peers without disability classifications. This does not always happen. There is a continuum of educational settings for students with disabilities, and as a result we believe that students with disabilities are often too segregated from their peers.

individualized education program (IEP) Written annual education plan for a student eligible for a disability classification. This document outlines placement, services, accommodations, and modifications necessary to meet the student's individualized needs in the least restrictive environment.

due process Administration of the law so that no student with a disability is denied his or her rights under the law. Procedures include clear steps for disagreeing and negotiating when the school and family do not agree about a disability label or the way special education services are provided.

Least Restrictive Environment (LRE) The concept of the **least restrictive environment (LRE)** is that each student should be educated with typically developing peers in the general education setting as much as possible. The law provided for a continuum of services, ranging from the general education classroom to various special education classrooms to special education schools to institutionalization or hospitalization (see Figure 3.3).

Individualized Education Program (IEP) For a student with a disability to be educated appropriately, a purposeful plan must be in place. This written plan, the **individualized education program,** is developed by a multidisciplinary team, including parents, and reviewed at least annually. The plan includes present levels of performance; assessment results; goals and objectives for the year; and services, supports, transportation, test accommodations, and assistive technology to be provided.

Parent Participation and Procedural Due Process Parents are to be notified if their child is referred for a special education evaluation. Written, informed consent must be obtained from the parents for the evaluation to occur. If the parents decline, the evaluation for special education will not take place. However, if the parents fail to respond after three proven attempts to obtain written, informed consent, the evaluation can be done. Parents are to be invited to participate in meetings where assessment results are shared, IEPs are developed or reviewed, or mid-year program changes are discussed. If the parents feel that any of the above provisions have not been implemented according to the law, or according to the designated time limits, their voices can be heard. Specific procedures for **due process** are outlined in the law.

The Impact This was huge! Parents nationwide rejoiced! The law says public schools can no longer turn children with disabilities away! They must educate them appropriately! They will be fairly evaluated! There will be a written plan! Parents can be involved! It will be done in a timely manner! If not, parents have a process for bringing complaints!

EHC advanced the field of special education by giving all students access to school. This was great news, but it did not solve all the problems, and it may have created new ones. Some problems we wrestle with today are the reality of disability classifications, the lack of preparation of school personnel to meet individualized needs, the difficulty in developing high-quality IEPs, and the way the least restrictive environment continuum can be used to avoid inclusion.

First of these is the reality of disability classifications. Qualifying students for services by showing they matched predetermined definitions led to a deficit perspective of disability. Students were pigeon-holed into a finite number of categories according to what they could *not* do, how they were *not* developing typically, what they would *not* be able to do as quickly as their typically developing peers. Since instructional programs were also developed according to these categories, it perpetuated the assumption that all students with a particular label learned the same way. Subsequently, much emphasis was placed on labels as a source of information.

Second is the lack of preparation of school personnel to meet a great variety of individual needs. With the passing of EHC millions of school-age children with disabilities nationwide enrolled in public schools. In most cases, school personnel were not prepared for this influx—pedagogically or attitudinally. Not all teachers were educated or felt prepared to meet the needs of all children. General education teachers were trained separately from special education teachers, who were trained separately from specialists in areas such as speech-language, occupational, and physical therapies. Collaboration and coteaching were not common in teacher preparation programs, so these professionals acted separately when working with students.

Related to separate training is the way the individualized education programs (IEPs) were developed. They contained a great deal of information for each student. The variety of programs available was limited, and, in cases of attitudinal unpreparedness, they were kept that way. Program availability drove IEP development, rather than IEP details in a student's best interest driving program development.

Next is the issue of the least restrictive environment (LRE) continuum. Although it was designed to provide several options for educating all students, it came with a message that not everyone belongs in the general education classroom. The hope was that, with the general education classroom at the "top" of the continuum, we would strive to move all students in that direction. The reality is that there is an "out" to inclusive education built right in to the law meant to promote it.

In 1990, EHC was renamed the Individuals with Disabilities Education Act (IDEA). Since then, this law has been reauthorized to provide various provisions as needs arise. Through all of the revisions, it has furthered the rights of students with disabilities, but more work needs to be done on the road to full inclusion. To test the law and understand what it means, many court cases ensued after the passing of EHC to interpret what FAPE and LRE include in classrooms and schools.

NARRATIVE 3.1. | DR. DAVID ROSTETTER

David Rostetter participated in the early design of federal regulations for schools to provide FAPE. He has continued to work in public policy and advocacy issues over the last 35 years. He contributes to a historical perspective about where special education law began and where it will go.

What do teachers need to know about special education law?   Teachers really need to know that, unlike other educational settings, special education really lives at the nexus between law and practice. Teachers need to know about their obligations to students with disability labels, and that knowledge must be tempered with the overriding principle of substantive benefit for children. This period of outcomes and equity has shifted the balance from procedural stuff to substantive benefit for the child. The more serious questions are now: Are your students learning to access information? Are they becoming critical thinkers? Are they learning to read? Instead of "Is their IEP on time?"

At one point in my career as an advocate, I was in a courtroom hearing related to special education services. The judge told the parties that related to special education time lines and forms, "Do not exalt form over substance." The shift is a good one.

Several principles in special education remain relevant: the value of parental involvement, the importance and significance of individualized decision making, and the increasing emphasis and realization that instruction and continued exposure to the regular education curriculum is more than a preference, it is essential.

There have been several reauthorizations, and those principles have remained intact or been strengthened, and in the future will continue to be a part of the law.

Charter schools are a big issue now, as related to equitable access. In California, charter schools were so strong politically that they blew off powerful federal civil rights laws. Fred Weintraub is in Los Angeles. The Los Angeles United School District can charter a school 500 miles away, and it is under LAUSD.

Special education local planning agencies have members of their group 400 miles away because it is assigned to a LEA so far away. Your own school district does not need to be local. Counterintuitive...weird. Fred thinks...wow. This lawsuit just became the whole state...holy crow. Fred checks out charters and sees if they meet the building codes and safety standards for the county of L.A., because that is a condition for granting the charter. It is a complete mess.

I am working on a New Orleans case about charter schools. The case went into court this week because the other side made a motion to dismiss, which was heard a few days ago. The judge began the process of questioning. For that moment in time, the most powerful person in the world is that judge. There is no due process for the judge...they are *powerful*. This judge starts with the defendants, the school-district lawyer. She begins, and he interrupts and says "Explain this 'parental choice' thing to me. Tell me now."

I was working on the case on behalf of 5 students with disability labels, and these parents were denied access by several schools...that is not access. We are not dismissing. The judge ended the hearing by saying to the defendants:

"By May 13 the plaintiffs will give you a series of requests, and you have 45 days. I suggest that you deal with the plaintiffs." The judge's point is that the district would do much better to spend time and energy working with the families than against them in court.

What is the future of special education law?   The line between special education and general education will become more and more blurred in the future. I am concerned that as we push for access to education in charter schools for students with disabilities, laws will pass that say that charter schools do not have to serve students with disabilities—it will be pitched as impossible and not feasible, and that they cannot be expected to serve students with disabilities.

Board of Education of the Hendrick Hudson Central School District, Westchester County, New York v. Amy Rowley (1982)

In 1982, 7 years after EHC passed, the *Rowley* case took place. Amy Rowley was a student at the Furnace Woods Elementary School. She was deaf and was expected to read lips in the classroom. Before she started kindergarten, the school met with Amy's parents to develop a plan to support Amy in the school and classroom. The family was offered placement at the School for the Deaf (which had interpreters) or the local elementary school without an interpreter. Amy's parents felt strongly that Amy should attend her local elementary school. Over the course of the year, she used an FM amplifier. In addition, several school administrators took courses in sign language and a teletype machine was in place in the office for increased family–school communication. The school purported that Amy did very well during her kindergarten year.

For first grade, the school planned for Amy to continue using the FM amplifier and receive tutorial instruction. Her parents agreed with this and also requested that a sign language interpreter be present during all academic instruction. Amy was still missing some of the communication occurring in the classroom during instruction. The school denied this request, because they felt Amy was doing fine academically and socially without an interpreter (*Board of Education v. Rowley*, 1982).

The Case   Amy's parents utilized their due process rights under EHC and requested a hearing to obtain a sign language interpreter for Amy. The hearing examiner found that Amy was indeed entitled to an interpreter. Even though the school felt she was doing fine without one, there was still a discrepancy between her potential with an interpreter and her current performance without one.

The Ruling   The school district brought the case to the District Court. The District Court and the Court of Appeals agreed with the ruling, indicating that the school must look at Amy's potential performance—if it would be greater with the service, then the service was warranted. The Supreme Court, however, overturned the decision. The Supreme Court's final word indicated that "free and appropriate education" under EHC provides for the "basic floor for opportunity," rather than providing for the opportunity to maximize the potential of the child (*Board of Education v. Rowley*, 1982). In other words, the law only provides for the floor, not the ceiling, in supporting a student in the general education classroom.

The Significance   The significance of this court case for students with disabilities was profound. It set a precedent that services need be provided only to the extent that a student benefits from an educational program. Also important to note was the significance for Amy as an individual. In the classroom, Amy was not able to hear everything. A bright student with many strategies of her own, Amy was able to perform academically and to make friends. However, she was still left out of classroom happenings. She was not privy to side conversations, small details during discussions, or comments in the classroom community—all of which can have a ripple effect on the learning of everyone in the setting.

Americans with Disabilities Act of 1990

The Purpose   The passing of the Americans with Disabilities Act (ADA) in 1990 added to the discussion of what makes services "good enough." ADA gave "civil rights protections to individuals with disabilities similar to those provided to individuals on the basis of race, color, sex, national origin, age, and religion" (Disabled World, n.d., p. 1).

The Provisions   ADA guaranteed that persons with disabilities would have equal opportunity in all public accommodations, employment, transportation, telecommunications, and government. It carried the provisions of Section 504 of the Rehabilitation Act over to the private sector, so that even establishments that did not receive federal financial assistance must provide equal opportunity.

The Impact   One important impact is that ADA protects the belief that all persons, regardless of ability, have the right to live independently, make choices, contribute to society, and enjoy full integration in every respect. Providing "equal *opportunity* for all" means providing a fair and level playing field. It was still up to the persons with disabilities to achieve to their own potential and to ensure that rights under the law were afforded to them.

ADA was successful in protecting rights. Persons with disabilities gained equal access to all areas of the community. However, in many cases, it may not have been good enough to ensure inclusion and fairness for all people. Here is a real-life example:

> A store complies with ADA regulations by installing a wheelchair accessible entrance. However, because the front stairs are old and will not withstand modification, the entrance is installed in the back—next to a smelly, overflowing dumpster with the door locked for security reasons. The user must ring a bell and wait in the muck until someone comes to open the door. This is not equitable when compared with a person walking right in the front door, never even seeing (or smelling) the dumpster.

Also in accordance with ADA, persons with disabilities may not be discriminated against in employment. As a result, more and more persons with disabilities are in the workplace, but this does not mean that individuals with disabilities are not treated in a discriminatory way. For instance, Peter, a man with Down syndrome, is employed in the mailroom of a liberal arts college. He has various responsibilities, including delivering mail campus wide. When a call comes to the mailroom regarding problems with delivery, the caller is promptly asked to excuse the problem, because "Well, you know, we have Peter working here now." Two messages are sent loud and clear here: First, any problem must be the fault of the person with the disability. Second, expectations should not be set very high because the person who may have made the error has a disability.

The service system exists in accordance with federal legislation, but many times it is a system without regard to human factors. As Michael Kennedy explained:

> In your home, you choose when and how often you want to use your blankets and what you want to use them for. However, if you are a person with a disability, it's like the service system already has the blanket set out for you. This might not be the one you want or need, especially because you didn't choose it. (1994, p. 74)

Over time, in order to ensure that all parameters of the law and subsequent revisions are met, the service system has become increasingly complex and the delivery processes increasingly cumbersome. By striving to meet the needs of the law that protects the needs of persons with disabilities, we may actually fail to meet the needs of the persons with disabilities. In essence, we no longer see the forest for the trees.

Oberti v. the Board of Education (1993)

Raphael Oberti, a child with Down syndrome, lived in the Clementon School District in New Jersey. Before entering kindergarten, Raphael was evaluated by the district's child study team. The team recommended that Raphael attend kindergarten in a segregated special education school in another district. Raphael's parents visited multiple programs suggested by the district and found them all unacceptable. Raphael's parents and the Clementon School District later agreed that Raphael would attend a developmental kindergarten at Clementon Elementary in the morning and a special education kindergarten in another school district in the afternoon. Raphael's IEP assigned academic goals to the afternoon, special education classroom and social goals to the morning, developmental kindergarten. According to the facts of the case, supports and additional personnel were provided in the afternoon, special education class but not in the morning class in Clementon Elementary School until March when an aide was placed in the classroom.

Over the course of the year, teachers reported that Raphael demonstrated a number of disruptive behaviors in the morning kindergarten class, including temper tantrums, toileting accidents, hiding, hitting, and spitting. Teachers in the afternoon class reported that these behaviors did not occur in their setting. At the end of this school year, the child study team proposed that Raphael attend school the next year in a segregated special education class for students with "educable mental retardation." Since Clementon did not have this setting, Raphael would need to go to another district. Raphael's parents agreed with this placement on the condition that the district would seek a placement in a general education classroom in Clementon Elementary as soon as possible. In December of that school year, Raphael's parents learned that no efforts were being made to find an inclusive setting for Raphael at Clementon Elementary (*Oberti v. Board of Education*, 1993).

The Case   At this point, the Obertis filed a due process complaint against Clementon School District, requesting again that Raphael be placed in a general education kindergarten with appropriate support. The hearing officer ruled in favor of the school district, indicating that, given Raphael's behavior, he was not ready for **mainstream** kindergarten. The Obertis appealed to the district court. Significant testimony in the district court included that of Dr. Lou Brown, an experienced consultant and advocate for students with disabilities, and Amy Goldman, a speech and language therapist. Dr. Brown's evaluation of Raphael in multiple settings indicated that Raphael would be successful in a general education kindergarten, without the previous behavior problems, if appropriate supplementary aids and services were in place. In addition to academic and behavioral success, Raphael would benefit from social interaction with typically developing peers. Ms. Goldman testified that the speech and language therapy that Raphael required would be most effectively provided in the context of the general education classroom (*Oberti v. Board of Education*, 1993).

> **mainstream**   A dated term referring to the general education setting. The connotation is that there is a primary desired setting, and students with disabilities are not always invited to join in it.

The Ruling   In August 1992, the court ruled in favor of Raphael, finding that the school district violated IDEA because the district failed to make reasonable efforts to include Raphael in general education classes with supplementary aids and services, and because the behavioral problems exhibited by Raphael in kindergarten were due to lack of support for his needs. In addition, the court found the school district in violation of Section 504 of the Rehabilitation Act because refusing enrollment in a general education class was an act of discrimination.

The Significance   This case is significant for its application of the "two-part test" that was established in an earlier court case, *Daniel R.R. v. the State Board of Education* (1989). The two-part test is used to determine whether a school is in compliance with IDEA's inclusion requirement. In the first part, the court must determine if education in the general education class, with supplementary aids and services, can be achieved satisfactorily. In the second part, if the court determines that placement outside of a general education class is necessary to benefit the child educationally, the court must decide if the child has been included to the maximum extent possible. Schools must consider three factors for inclusion: the whole range of supplementary aids and services, the benefits of a supplemented general education setting versus the benefits of a segregated special education setting, and the possible negative effects of inclusion on typically developing peers (*Daniel R.R.*, 1989).

Overall, this case had a significant impact on special education. It encourages schools to consider a greater range of inclusive services and settings for students with disabilities before resorting to segregation; essentially, it encourages schools to see the forest *and* the trees. The third factor that schools must consider is the negative impact of inclusion on typically developing peers. This viewpoint reinforces the assumption that interaction with students with disabilities is something negative, rather than positive. If we view disability as a difference, not a deficit, then there is another factor to consider—the possible negative effects of *exclusion* on typically developing peers, because it robs them of an opportunity to learn about diversity.

Cedar Rapids Community School District v. Garret F. (1999)

When Garret F. was 4 years old, his spinal column was severed in an accident. As a result of his injury, Garret had paralysis from the neck down, but his cognitive abilities were unaffected. Garret was able to speak, use a motorized wheelchair with a puff-and-suck straw control, and use a computer with controls on the headrest of his wheelchair. He also required a ventilator at all times to breathe. Garret, an intelligent, creative, friendly boy, attended the Cedar Rapids Community School District in Iowa (*Cedar Rapids v. Garret F.*, 1999).

For 5 years of his schooling, kindergarten through fourth grade, Garret's family paid for full-time, one-to-one nursing services to maintain his ventilation while he was at school. In 1993, Garret's mother, Charlene, requested that the Cedar Rapids School District provide and financially support nursing services for Garret's ventilator so he could continue attending school. The school district denied the request on the grounds that it was not obligated to provide continuous, one-to-one nursing services.

related services
Services provided to students with disabilities beyond the main educational placement. For example, speech-language lessons, physical therapy, occupational therapy, and counseling.

The Case   Garret's mother requested a hearing before the Iowa State Department of Education, using provisions under IDEA that school districts are required to provide free appropriate public education, including "**related services**," to all children. The hearing officer (Administrative Law Judge) ruled in favor of Garret: Because the ventilation required by Garret could be provided by a qualified school nurse and did not require a licensed physician, the school district was obligated to provide it at no cost to the family.

The Cedar Rapids School District appealed this decision to a higher court, the Federal District Court, insisting that the services fall under the category of "medical services" and are thus not required under the heading of "related services." The Federal District Court affirmed the decision of the Administrative Law Judge, finding clearly that Garret needed the ventilation to be able to attend school and that it could be provided without the services of a licensed physician, as was first established in the case of *Irving Independent School District v. Tatro* (1984), in which Amber Tatro was in need of catheterization to attend school. The school district would have to pay a nurse to maintain Garret's ventilation at school. Still not satisfied, the school district appealed to the United States Supreme Court, seeking to establish that the cost of Garret's nurse was an undue burden on the district and should therefore be exempt as a related service (*Cedar Rapids v. Garret F.*, 1999).

The Ruling   While the court maintained that it was expensive and the district may have legitimate financial concerns, it ruled that Garret's services fell under the heading of related services and must be provided by the school district. The ruling quoted *Board of Education v. Rowley* (1982) when it said that under IDEA, "Congress intended 'to open the door of public education' to all qualified children and 'require[d] participating States to educate handicapped children with non-handicapped children whenever possible'" (*Cedar Rapids v. Garret F.*, 1999).

The Significance   This case is significant because it revisits and affirms that meaningful access to free appropriate public education will be ensured for children with disabilities by providing the related services they require, regardless of cost. It ensures that students like Garret will be integrated into the public school system so that they can learn with their peers. Court cases such as these continue to be filed, arguing more specific provisions under IDEA, in an attempt to further define what appropriate truly means.

WHERE WE STAND

This section provides a context for where we are now in terms of special education under the law. This section briefly summarizes changes that have occurred to the Individuals with Disabilities Education Act (IDEA) through multiple reauthorizations, and then details the current provisions of IDEA. In addition, current issues and problems are presented.

Individuals with Disabilities Education Act (IDEA) of 1990 and the Reauthorizations of 1997 and 2004

The Purpose of the Reauthorizations IDEA has been reauthorized three times since it was first passed as Public Law 94-142: The Education for All Handicapped Children Act (EHC) in 1975. Each reauthorization has revised or added components in an attempt to improve educational experiences for students with disabilities and provide more comprehensive, yet standardized, procedures and documentation.

The Provisions In 1990, EHC was renamed the Individuals with Disabilities Education Act. This new title represented the importance of first-person language and the inappropriateness of the term "handicapped." The 1990 reauthorization added autism and traumatic brain injury to the list of disability classifications. It also instituted the individual transition plan (ITP) for students 16 years and older, allowing for the planning and implementation of a coordinated set of interagency services to facilitate successful transition from school to adult life in employment, education, and community living. Last, this reauthorization added social work and rehabilitation counseling to the list of related services that can be provided to students with disabilities on the IEP (Project Ideal, 2008).

In 1997, a provision was added regarding behavior infractions. If a student with a disability engages in unacceptable or dangerous behavior, it must be determined whether the behavior is a manifestation of the student's disability. If so, the student may not be expelled from the school. Instead, a change of placement should be investigated so the student can better be supported toward appropriate behavior. Other provisions added at this time included: Regular educators are part of the IEP team, IEPs must include statements about the student's involvement and progress in the general education curriculum, benchmarks and measurable annual goals are emphasized, assistive technology is considered by the IEP team, orientation and mobility services were added as related services, states must offer mediation services to settle disputes, a variety of assessment tools and strategies must be used, students with disabilities must be included in state and district-wide assessments or be provided with alternative assessments, and transition planning must begin at age 14 (Project Ideal, 2008).

In 2004, the last reauthorization to date, the law was renamed the Individuals with Disabilities Education Improvement Act (IDEA) and added an option for districts to use a response to intervention (RTI) model for determining if a student has a learning disability, rather than a discrepancy model. In short, this means that a district may choose to implement interventions for struggling students to see if the intervention is helpful. If so, the student would continue to receive the intervention due to its success in supporting a specific learning need. The alternative would be to wait until a student is falling behind or failing and therefore demonstrating a discrepancy in performance from peers to determine the need for support. In later chapters, we will explain in much more detail what RTI means and how schools are implementing it in general and special education. Benchmark objectives were no longer required on the IEP unless the student takes alternative assessments (Project Ideal, 2008).

The Impact   The impact of IDEA itself is the same as that of the original EHC: It is the law that provides equal educational opportunity for students with disabilities. The impact of the reauthorizations is a little bit different. The reauthorizations have added new components and revised existing ones, sometimes in contradiction to earlier revisions (e.g., use of benchmark objectives on the IEP). It is often difficult to interpret, let alone remember, all of the changes!

NARRATIVE 3.2. | DR. JEANNINE DINGUS-EASON

Jeannine Dingus-Eason is Caleb's mom. Caleb is a fifth-grade student and has an Individualized Education Program (IEP). Jeannine has worked over the years with Caleb's teams to help them understand who he is and what he needs in school.

What do you want teachers to know?

I want teachers to know that Caleb is smart. Caleb is very opinionated and very strong, and teachers need to be patient with him. Teachers need to figure out how to tap into his strengths. For example, right now he loves current events. Ask him anything about Libya or Charlie Sheen, and he will know! The danger is that teachers sometimes underestimate what he is capable of doing. My concern is that they lower the bar and expect too little from him.

I want teachers to know that grades do not capture who he is. He has high-functioning autism (HFA); we all know he is going to struggle with the social pieces. If it's a topic that does not interest him, he struggles. But I just feel like the report card is such an inaccurate reflection of who he is. At times it is painful to read.

I want teachers to know their narrative makes a difference. What they write on the report card goes straight to my heart. On the report card, there are spaces for teacher narratives. Further down the line, those will make all the difference.

I'm looking at the report card: It's about reading comprehension—all the same things we heard when he was diagnosed with HFA at age 4. He struggles with abstract concepts...he may struggle with word problems in math, with reading comprehension in subjects that do not interest him.

His teacher and I text at least once, twice a week....She was his teacher in third grade. She is amazing. She tries, she is a real advocate for him, and she texts me!!

What do you think about the IEP process?   I have a different perspective now than when we first started. I didn't want to be there initially. I was still reeling from the diagnosis. It was a very dehumanizing process; talking about the person who is not there. My kid was invisible-ized. I also felt like, "Don't let the three letters behind the name fool you," I bring it like Queefa...my alternative personality...the girl who grew up in the hood. If I have to cuss somebody out, I'm not afraid to do it.

It was demoralizing at the beginning. They were talking about phasing out his aide in kinder-garten. Were they really putting a price tag on him? No way...there was an aide hired through a temp agency, which makes no sense with a child with autism who needs consistency. I spent an afternoon walking the halls of central administration and people were unaware that it was happening. I called in a favor, and they took care of it. They were having a going-away party for the aide, and people were shocked...how did that happen?

What got better is that people know who I am now; he's in fifth grade and we've had a few years of IEP meetings. I struggle with that; I feel guilty that not everyone has the cultural and social capital that I have. People know I am a professor, his dad is a dentist. It bothers me that I have access and supports that others do not have. Support from the school related to how the IEP process unfolds becomes a funky mix of social capital, cultural capital, class, and race.

The last meeting I had at central office, it was 15 minutes....They know us as his parents. The social capital piece: I started bringing an advocate whose husband is a lawyer specializing in special education law. Suits filed against the school district for special education have come from him.

I also started bringing Caleb's photograph to the meetings. I wanted everyone to see him. He is not this "thing," he is not an invisible being, he is not an inanimate object. He is a boy. The meetings are now held at the school so I find the atmosphere less toxic.

What do you hope for in the future of education?   That's a huge looming question for us all as parents, educators, and members of a democratic society. It might sound too cliché and even too preachy, but I want policy makers, educators, researchers—the whole lot of us who claim to be invested in public education—to understand that the fate of one is the fate of all. That is, poor educational outcomes for children in one segment of society affect the larger society. That point will continue to be amplified with demographic shifts, growing class gulfs, and the shifting global economy. I think we try far too many Band-Aid solutions or attempts at reform which ultimately will not work because of lack of social understandings—meaning, as whole, we fail to understand the ways in which poverty, race, disability, and gender converge to shape children's educational opportunities. It is tragic. There are pockets of hope in places where people have those understandings of how educational opportunities are shaped by a myriad of factors and those who understand how their roles affect such opportunities.

CURRENT CONTEXT AND ISSUES

The court cases and laws we have reviewed here have brought us to a better place than where we were prior to 1975. However, there is still work to be done, both structurally and attitudinally. Our intention is to instill in teachers a strong belief that all students can learn, that all students are beneficial to the learning community, and that a teacher's role is to advocate for students, focus on their strengths, and create communities where barriers to inclusion are broken down.

To do this, teachers must be familiar with the law and its provisions, as well as problems still facing the advancement of inclusive education. Once aware of these problems, teachers will be most equipped to solve them. Here, we discuss these pervasive problems in the current context of special education: the difference between the letter of the law and the spirit of the law, the perpetuated belief that there are two types of students—normal or disabled, and traditional definitions of intelligence and success.

The Letter of the Law versus the Spirit of the Law

These phrases are used often in the field of education to refer to the way different people comply with laws that have been passed. If a person complies with the "letter of the law," he or she is acting within the literal interpretation of the law as it is written. If a person complies with the "spirit of the law," he or she is acting according to the intent of those who wrote the law. It is possible to act within the letter of the law, but not the spirit of the law, and vice versa.

Under IDEA, Section 504, and ADA, people act within the letter of the law when they follow procedural due process and implement accommodations when mandated. To act within the spirit of these laws means to act according to the intention of those who wrote them. The authors of these laws believed that persons with disabilities deserved equal opportunities, and that they are valuable as citizens in the community, in the workplace, and in the classroom.

Often, when a law is passed, the letter of the law is followed before the spirit of the law. Many people obey the law because they have to, not because they want to. When this is the case, those served under the law still have an uphill battle toward attitudinal equality. Imagine what it must have been like for African American students after 1954. They were allowed to enroll in previously all-White schools, but many teachers and administrators felt forced to have them there. It is not likely that they were welcomed with open arms. More likely, they were tolerated begrudgingly. This would have followed the letter of the law, but not the spirit.

What has it been like for students in the special education system? In the beginning, they may have been tolerated begrudgingly as well. After time, students with disabilities were welcomed into the schools, but they were still often treated as second-class citizens who had to prove their worth and their right to placement in inclusive classrooms: "Laws, rules, regulations, and understandings, may exist between families, courts, schools, businesses, unions, and industries, but who listens to the children?" (Calkins, Lukenbill, & Mateer, 1973, p. 103).

The Belief that There Are Two Types of Students—Normal or Disabled

Under the current system, there is general education and special education. Students receive special education services if they have a disability. This encourages sorting of students into two types—normal or disabled. Rather than considering one type of student with a variety of abilities, we consider one group as able and the other as not as able. Mooney explained this as he reflected on his experiences in special education (and riding a short bus):

> I realized what the short bus is all about: It serves a social function. Our myth of who we are, who we should be, is actually created by categorizing people with disability. Disability is inherently a negation. In our culture, people with disabilities stand more for what they are *not* than what they are—not normal, not whole—a negation calls into being its opposite: the normal. The normal looms over all of our lives, an impossible goal that we are told is possible *if*: if we sit still, if we buy certain consumer goods, if we exercise, if we fix our teeth, if we….The short bus polices that terrain; it patrols a fabricated social boundary demarcating what is healthy and sick, acceptable and broken, enforcing normalcy in all of us. (2007, pp. 27–28)

In addition to sorting students into groups of normal and disabled, we further sort students in the latter group into 13 distinct categories to qualify them for services under the letter of the law. Some students do not fit neatly into one category or another. A student with attention deficit/hyperactivity disorder (ADHD) is often placed in the other health impairment category under IDEA, because ADHD is not its own category. Students with Asperger syndrome are often placed in the autism category, even though Asperger syndrome is not autism. How many categories are necessary so that everyone fits? Does it make sense to fit children into categories?

Traditional Definitions of Intelligence and Success

Historically, students have been considered intelligent based on quantitative measures, such as intelligence quotients, test scores, and grades. They have been considered successful in school if they are neat, organized, compliant, and prompt with homework and provide the correct answers to teachers' questions; if they achieve high grades and learn quickly through traditional **pedagogical methods,** such as readings, lectures, and pen-and-paper tasks; that is, they are "book smart." Howard Gardner, pioneer of the multiple intelligences theory, challenged us to reconsider the notion of intelligence. It is not a matter of how smart students are, but rather how they are smart. Gardner (1991) researched several different intelligences, illustrating the many different kinds of skills, talents, and processing strengths that students have.

pedagogical methods
Teaching or educational methods teachers use to convey content to students and assess what students learned.

THE JOURNEY AHEAD

This section discusses several ways to work toward equitable education for all learners. An important role of all teachers is to advocate for all of their students. There are many ways to do this, from large-scale systemic change to small-scale assistance of individual students toward school success. Here we discuss changes from top-down to bottom-up.

Policy Makers Need to Stop Supporting Segregated Classrooms and Separatist Language

There is a lot of discussion among educational leaders and policy makers regarding support of full inclusion. However, not all policies in place reflect this discussion. Some talk a good talk, but don't always walk the walk. One example is professional development standards of accreditation organizations. Often the standards for preparing teachers to meet the needs of students with exceptional learning needs are separate from standards for preparing teachers to meet the needs of students without disabilities. If teachers and specialists are prepared to serve one group of students separately from another, it perpetuates segregation.

Another example is school building and district leaders enabling the continuation of self-contained special education classes, actively or passively. We hear statements such as, "We like the idea that teachers are being prepared to teach all students in inclusive classrooms. Unfortunately, the reality is we still have self-contained classrooms, so we still need to hire teachers who are able and want to teach in those settings." This practice perpetuates segregation in education.

What can one teacher do? One elementary school teacher asked herself just that. She was the teacher of third, fourth, and fifth graders with disabilities in a self-contained 12:1:2 classroom ratio (12 students with IEPs, 1 teacher, and 2 teacher aides). The teacher (with the support and collaboration of the school principal) investigated what was needed to include all of her students in general education settings with push-in support. This was implemented the following school year. In essence, she disbanded her own classroom. She truly believes that all of the students in the general education classrooms will benefit from inclusion, and she walks the walk. One small classroom. One small school. One big difference.

Teacher Education Programs Need to Prepare Inclusive Education Teachers

Many colleges and schools of education continue to offer single-certification teacher education programs. In these programs, teachers learn how to be general education teachers or they learn how to be special education teachers, depending on which program they choose. Often they may obtain both (dual) certifications if they choose to do so. Nevertheless, the coursework and field experiences for general education preparation are usually separate from the coursework and field experiences for special education preparation.

We Need to Increase Our First-Hand Experiences with Diversity in All Settings

One of the reasons that stereotypes of people with disabilities continue is because most people have few first-hand experiences with diverse learners and abilities. When people meet those with disabilities and learn that they are indeed able, that they indeed have strengths, that they do not fit the stereotyped idea of disability, they change their construction of ability. The more first-hand experiences people have, the wider the definition of what it means to be able.

One of our personal experiences, from elementary school, is representative of many others from the 1970s:

> I attended an urban, public elementary school. I was a good student, academically and behaviorally, so I was often chosen to run errands in the building when I finished my work early. One time, I was delivering a note from the principal to Mrs. Smith, the special education teacher. I had never heard of Mrs. Smith before, so I needed directions to her classroom. I was told to go to the basement, past the art room and the boiler room. The door on the left was Mrs. Smith's room. The door was locked, so I knocked and waited. When she opened the door I was very surprised to see that there were students in there, whom I never knew attended my school. Not being included in classes with these students was not only a missed opportunity for them, it was my loss as well. I grew up not having the opportunity to learn about diverse abilities, different ways to solve problems. I was sheltered because they were segregated in the basement. If I had known them, I would have learned more in elementary school, not less. We need to be with each other to learn about each other, and in doing so learn about ourselves.

We Need to Expect and Embrace Difference and "Imperfection"

stigma Mark or association of disgrace or reproach. Disability has a stigma because many people without a disability do not want to have a disability and may be afraid of or disgusted by people with disabilities.

If we strive for society's idea of "normal," we perpetuate the belief that there is only one way to be acceptable in school. A **stigma** has been associated with disability and receiving special education services, because disability has been thought of as bad and pitiable. If we can embrace disabilities as "different abilities," they would not carry the same negative stigma. The more openly we talk about and embrace differences—strengths and weaknesses—the less power we give to the idea that different is bad. We as teachers can model this just as we model math strategies and good reading habits. We can talk about our strengths and areas where we need help. We can create comfortable, safe classroom spaces where students can feel free to make mistakes, ask questions, and take risks.

Consider the idea that each person is unique, like a fingerprint or a snowflake. Each person is who she is because of her strengths and weaknesses. If you change either one, it is not the same unique individual. Each strength serves a purpose, as does each weakness. If we believe (and celebrate!) that one would not occur without the other, we can view people and their uniqueness in a whole new light. Dr. Temple Grandin, an animal behavioral scientist who has autism, firmly believes that it is her autism that contributes to her gift as an animal behaviorist. A middle school student with neurologically based difficulties in working memory, organization, attention to task, and social skills is a gifted writer and sketch artist. In his own words, "I wouldn't trade a neuron." When people feel comfortable enough with themselves, all of themselves, they enact the change that needs to happen for the trip ahead.

SUMMARY

This chapter covered court cases that significantly affected the disability rights movement as well as legislation that was passed over the last several decades. In addition, future goals for the field of special education and disability rights advocacy were discussed. Reading through this chapter should give you a sense of how much has been accomplished as well as a sense that there is still work to be done. As teachers, it is important to know the letter of the law so you can help spread the spirit of the law. Your role as an activist and advocate will develop over your career so you, too, can impact policy changes—in your school, your district, your community, your state, and your nation.

What Does Teaching Everyone Mean?

The Educator's Role and Citizenship in the Classroom

OVERVIEW

In Section I, we showed a historical progression away from segregated education. From there, we need to work toward successful, fully inclusive educational practices. In Section II, we provide a conceptual framework for what it means to educate *all* students together in an inclusive classroom, school, and community. This part of the book explains that inclusion is an attitude, not a place. It is not enough to simply place students together in a room. There needs to be a belief system in place that all students can and will learn, and that all students should learn together with peers who are diverse in myriad ways.

After reading the chapters in Section II, we hope that you will understand your role as an inclusive educator and that you will understand that regardless of certification title, all teachers can and should be inclusive teachers. This means that your role as a teacher is to be sure that all of your students are successful. To do this, you need to be sensitive to what makes each of your students a unique human being. You need to know their strengths, learning needs, abilities, disabilities, cultural and linguistic diversity, developmental levels, family characteristics, and interests. Effective inclusive educators respond to all of these, and Section II of this text begins to teach you how.

Section II includes Chapters 4 through 11 and is arranged to cover the educational lifespan of the student, from birth through the school years and into adulthood. Chapter 4 describes how early childhood intervention for children with disabilities from birth through preschool was added to the legislation. It covers the issues you need to be aware of to effectively teach this young age group. Chapter 5 teaches you how children and adolescents typically develop, what you can usually expect at each grade level throughout the school years, and how to support students who may develop differently from others along their own unique paths. Chapter 6 introduces you to your role in the development of a nurturing, responsive learning community that celebrates differences and facilitates positive interaction among all members. Chapter 7 covers the theory and practice of differentiation and how to ensure that all students are full citizens in the learning community. Building on Chapter 7, Chapter 8 introduces the concept of universal design for learning (UDL) and teaches you how to make sure your curriculum and classroom support all students. Chapter 9 focuses on assessment and your role in using evaluative methods to recognize each student's unique abilities. Chapter 10 is about collaboration, and addresses your role in working with every stakeholder in a student's education, including the student! Last, Chapter 11 covers the process of transitioning a student from the school years into adult life and the teacher's role in ensuring as high a level of independence as possible.

The chapters in Section II give you just a taste of specific strategies, and you may find yourself wanting more. This is purposeful on our part. Our goal here is to provide you with a theoretical preparation to build your belief system around teaching all students. There are just enough specific strategy ideas to illustrate the concepts we present, but not so many that the theory is pushed aside. Once you have had a chance to absorb this information and collaboratively discuss the related issues, Section III will provide you with the many specific teaching ideas you are seeking.

CHAPTER 4

Early Intervention: Birth Through Preschool

MARTHA MOCK, PH.D.

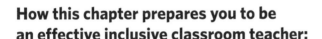

How this chapter prepares you to be an effective inclusive classroom teacher:

- This chapter teaches you about more laws—this time ones that cover children from birth until they enter school in kindergarten. You will learn about issues that are unique to these early childhood years, and how education for this age group was affected by societal, political, and historical events. This chapter also teaches you about issues that families face in learning that their infant has a disability and navigating the process for obtaining services. **This helps you meet CEC Standard 1: Foundations.**

- This chapter teaches you about important considerations that you need to be aware of as a teacher when assessing and instructing infants, toddlers, and preschoolers. **This helps you meet CEC Standard 2: Development and Characteristics of Learners.**

- This chapter teaches you about the importance of collaborating with families of infants and young children and of being sensitive to the many aspects of diversity of the children and their families. **This helps you meet CEC Standard 9: Professional and Ethical Practice.**

Martha Mock, Ph.D., is an assistant professor and directs the early childhood program at the Warner School of Education and Human Development at the University of Rochester. She has worked with and advocated for children with disabilities and their families for over 20 years. She has worked in the area of teacher preparation for over 10 years, as well as been a paraprofessional, teacher, and mentor teacher in a variety of early childhood, special education, and home-based settings. She lives with her husband and daughter in Rochester, NY. She may be contacted at mmock@warner.rochester.edu.

After reading and discussing this chapter, you will be able to

- Identify how historical events have contributed to the development of early intervention and early childhood special education

- Explain how the parents of a young child might find services if they have a concern about their child's development

- Describe the IDEA provisions for birth through age 5, their purpose, and explain the impact on children and their families

- Identify the differences in Part B and Part C of IDEA

- Explain why some states choose to include children at risk of delays in early intervention

- Explain issues that are specific to infants and young children, including early intervention services, assessment in natural environments, family-centered practices, and routine-based interventions

- Explain how family members are an important part of early intervention and early childhood special education

- Explain the importance of service coordination for early childhood special education

- Describe the differences among multidisciplinary, interdisciplinary, and transdisciplinary practices and the importance of striving for transdisciplinary practices

Part B of IDEA The portion of the Individuals with Disabilities Education Act that mandates services to children with disabilities ages 3 to 21 years.

Part C of IDEA The portion of the Individuals with Disabilities Education Act that mandates services to young children who have or who are at risk for developing disabilities or developmental delays from birth to 3 years of age.

This chapter discusses the history, legislation, and major principles in early intervention and early childhood special education. The first section explains the development of policy and practices of early intervention and early childhood special education from a sociohistoric perspective, highlighting key events in the field that have made an impact. The second section focuses on key elements of IDEA as they relate to the provision of services to children from birth to age 5 and their families. **Part B of IDEA** covers services for children age 3 through age 21 and **Part C of IDEA** covers services for children birth through age 3 years. (Part A of IDEA contains the general provisions and definitions used throughout the other parts of the law.) The third section focuses on guiding principles and best practices for services to young children and their families through research in the field that is supported by the key international organization, the Division for Early Childhood, which is a division of the Council for Exceptional Children. The chapter concludes with the narratives of two parents who share their perspective on life with a young child with a disability and their recommendations to other parents and professionals working with families.

DEVELOPMENT OF POLICY AND PRACTICES OF EARLY INTERVENTION

The Post–World War II Era

During the war, a high demand for women in the workforce promoted the development of programs to care for typically developing children under the age of 6 years (Shonkoff & Meisels, 1990). The passage of the Lanham Act of 1940 was the first time the federal government offered financial support for child care (Cohen, 1996). The government valued having young children cared for and educated outside the home. When the war ended, the demand for working women declined and many child care programs closed as women reentered the home to care for their children.

Some groups of school-age children with disabilities were beginning to be educated by private agencies in segregated settings, but there were virtually no services for children with disabilities under the age of 5. Although some research studies conducted with young children with disabilities demonstrated their ability to learn and thrive in an environment that was stimulating (Skeels & Dye, 1938–39), most psychologists, as well as the general public, continued to believe that intelligence was fixed at birth. Earlier in the 20th century, the argument of **"nature versus nurture"** had ensued. Nature refers to the fixed biological and genetic factors that are internal to the child. Nurture refers to variable environmental factors that are external to the child. The belief that nature is the determining factor in a child's development was widely accepted. Theorists such as Arnold Gesell (1880–1961) believed that the course of nature could not be altered and that early intervention to remediate or reduce the impact of a disability on a child's development was impossible (Shonkoff & Meisels, 1990). Therefore, parents were not given much hope by doctors or the community when a child with a disability was born into their family and, unfortunately, were sometimes blamed for their child's disability (Kirk & Gallagher, 1986). Parents began to form groups, such as the National Association for Retarded Citizens, to advocate for their children with disabilities (Kirk & Gallagher, 1986). Although the post–World War II era raised public awareness of people with disabilities due to the return of numerous veterans with physical disabilities and the revelation of the prevalence of disabilities as a result of military screening (Shonkoff & Meisels, 1990), children with disabilities had no right to a public education in the eyes of many Americans.

New hope arose with the election of President John F. Kennedy in 1960. People with disabilities found a close ally in President Kennedy and other advocates in this era of social activism. Children with disabilities and children at risk for educational failure (e.g., those considered poor, disadvantaged) benefited from the heightened social activism and political awareness. Advocacy groups, such as the National Association for Retarded Citizens and the United Cerebral Palsy Association, gathered their voices to bring "attention to the discrepancy between our principles and practices in American society with regard to the exercise of rights and privileges under the law by various subgroups" (Peterson, 1987, p. 99).

nature versus nurture
A philosophical debate focusing on what has a greater impact on a young child's development—a child's in-born characteristics or the interaction a child has with caregivers and the environment.

President's Panel on Mental Retardation   President Kennedy furthered social policy for people with disabilities primarily because of his own personal situation. His sister Rosemary was labeled as having a mental retardation (now known as an intellectual disability). Kennedy established the President's Panel on Mental Retardation (PPMR) that went on to publish *A Proposed Program for National Action to Combat Mental Retardation* in 1962 (Payne & Patton, 1981). The proposal called for research in the area of intellectual disability, establishment of preventative health programs, stronger public and private special education programs, protection of the civil rights of people with intellectual disabilities, and programs to raise public awareness about intellectual disability. This focus on intellectual disability helped to bring children with disabilities into the public eye and forward the movement to serve children with disabilities. In addition, in 1963, 3 weeks prior to his assassination, President Kennedy signed Public Law 88-164. This law embodied many of the recommendations of the PPMR and thereby established the university research, training, and education centers that still exist today. Now known as the University Centers for Excellence in Developmental Disabilities (UCEDD), these 67 centers continue to exist for the purpose of conducting disability research, training, and education as well as improving policy and practice (AUCD, 2011).

Head Start A federally funded early childhood program for preschool-age children focused on families who meet certain income eligibility criteria. The program is designed to serve up to ten percent of students who have disabilities.

Head Start and the War on Poverty

President Lyndon B. Johnson's War on Poverty raised the issue of poverty as a major social concern (Payne & Patton, 1981). The focus on the poor led policy makers to develop new programs, such as **Head Start** in 1964, in an attempt to reverse the perceived effects of poverty. Head Start is a program that provides comprehensive early childhood education, health, nutrition, parental involvement, and family services for economically vulnerable children and their families. Head Start raised public awareness about young children and promoted the idea of early childhood intervention. It is difficult to say where early childhood intervention would be today without the legislation supporting Head Start and the attention it brought to young children at risk and with disabilities.

Handicapped Children's Early Education Assistance Act

In 1968, Public Law 90-538, the Handicapped Children's Early Education Assistance Act (HCEEAA) was enacted. This legislation was the first to bring services for children with disabilities together with early childhood education. It provided 3-year incentive grants for the establishment of First Chance and Handicapped Children's Early Education Programs (HCEEP) to serve children with disabilities from birth to 6 years. HCEEP was significant because it attempted to dispel the common myth that children should begin their education at the age of 6 and recognized the importance of establishing experimental programs for children with disabilities (Peterson, 1987).

Public Law 94-142

As you have learned in previous chapters, in the United States, certain groups of people frequently have been denied access to services and basic human rights until rights are gained through legal or legislative means. Children with disabilities did not have the right to a public education until the landmark legislation of Public Law 94-142 in 1975, which established the rights of children ages 5 to 21 to attend public school and receive an education. This piece of legislation also laid the groundwork for the first educational provisions for children with disabilities under the age of 5. Although great steps have been taken, oppression and violation of rights continue to occur despite efforts within our communities to change this (Kozol, 1991).

Public Law 99-457

In 1975, Public Law 94-142 provided monetary incentives (in the form of federal block grants) to states for serving children ages 3 to 5 years, but did not mandate these services until PL 99-457 in 1986, when children with disabilities across the country, 5 years old and younger, were given the right to early intervention, education, and related services (such as occupational, physical, and speech therapy, to name a few). Public Law 99-457 mandated educational services to preschoolers with disabilities ages 3 to 5 by 1991, and provided monetary incentives to states for planning to serve children with disabilities from birth to 3 years (Florian, 1995). Both PL 94-142 and PL 99-457 sparked major changes in services provided to young children with disabilities. Although PL 99-457 has been enacted for over 2 decades, many theorists, parents, service providers, and politicians still lead the fight to bring the rights of young children with disabilities to the attention of the American public and to the floor of our nation's legislative body (Bronfenbrenner, 1979; Shonkoff & Meisels, 1990; Zigler & Muenchow, 1992).

Significant sociohistorical and political influences on **early childhood intervention** provide a context for understanding how early intervention services developed. One man who had a personal interest in the development and presentation of this legislation was former Senator Lowell Weicker from Connecticut (Florian, 1995). Senator Weicker had a son with Down syndrome who received early intervention services. He believed that every young child with a disability and his or her family should have access to early intervention services. The presentation of PL 99-457 was not only a moral necessity, but

early childhood intervention Practices and services that are designed to assist young children who have delays or disabilities in their development and to assist their families in supporting their child's development.

also a cost-saving measure for society and helped push the bill through Congress (Florian, 1995). Senator Weicker did not do this alone and readily acknowledged the vital role that parent advocates played in the passing of this legislation.

Family-Centered Practices   In the 1970s, professionals expected parents to defer to their opinions and focused services for young children with disabilities on teaching the parents how to conduct intervention with their child. It was not until the 1980s that the voices of families were clearly heard to say "I am the expert on my child." In this decade, early intervention services began to shift away from a "training of parents" model to a more collaborative model. The child was viewed in the context of his or her family as a whole, not simply as the receiver of intervention. This focus has continued to become ingrained within early childhood intervention programs across the nation (Bruder, 2000). More detailed information on **family-centered practices** will be presented later in this chapter. See Narratives 4.1 and 4.2 for a deeper understanding of what life is like for parents who have a child with a disability.

family-centered practices
A set of professional practices in early childhood intervention that ensure that families are an integral part of a young child's services and assessments.

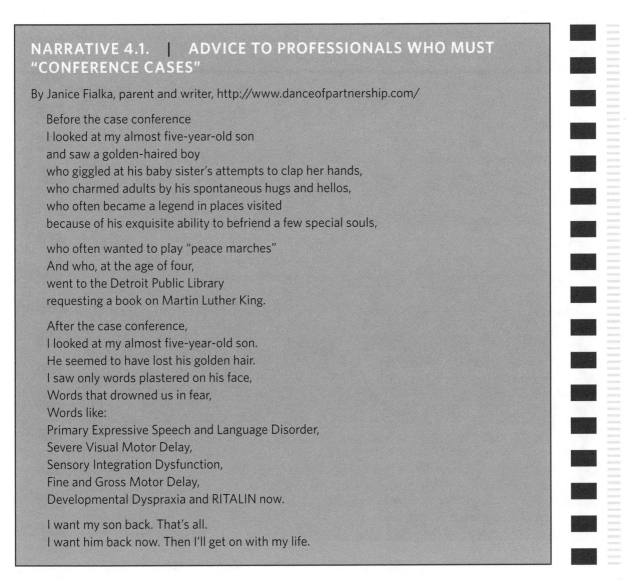

NARRATIVE 4.1. | ADVICE TO PROFESSIONALS WHO MUST "CONFERENCE CASES"

By Janice Fialka, parent and writer, http://www.danceofpartnership.com/

Before the case conference
I looked at my almost five-year-old son
and saw a golden-haired boy
who giggled at his baby sister's attempts to clap her hands,
who charmed adults by his spontaneous hugs and hellos,
who often became a legend in places visited
because of his exquisite ability to befriend a few special souls,

who often wanted to play "peace marches"
And who, at the age of four,
went to the Detroit Public Library
requesting a book on Martin Luther King.

After the case conference,
I looked at my almost five-year-old son.
He seemed to have lost his golden hair.
I saw only words plastered on his face,
Words that drowned us in fear,
Words like:
Primary Expressive Speech and Language Disorder,
Severe Visual Motor Delay,
Sensory Integration Dysfunction,
Fine and Gross Motor Delay,
Developmental Dyspraxia and RITALIN now.

I want my son back. That's all.
I want him back now. Then I'll get on with my life.

(Continued)

If you could see the depth of this pain
If you feel this sadness
Then you would be moved to return
Our almost five-year-old son
who sparkles in sunlight despite his faulty neurons.

Please give us back my son
undamaged and untouched by your labels, test results,
descriptions and categories.
If you can't, if you truly cannot give us back our son
Then just be with us

quietly, gently, softly.

Sit with us and create a stillness
known only in small, empty chapels at sundown.
Be there with us
as our witness and as our friend.

Please do not give us advice, suggestions, comparisons or
another appointment. (That is for later.)

We want only a quiet shoulder upon which to rest our heads.

If you cannot give us back our sweet dream
then comfort us through this evening.
Hold us. Rock us until morning light creeps in.
Then we will rise and begin the work of a new day.

© 1997 Janice Fialka. Reprinted with permission.

A HERO'S POEM: FOR THOSE GIVING LIFE-CHANGING NEWS TO FAMILIES

By Janice Fialka, parent and writer, http://www.danceofpartnership.com/

You have chosen this work.
You must deliver the harsh words to parents
      who pace in the middle of the dark night.

It's a hero's job, but doesn't feel like one.
No one celebrates your achievements,
      or asks you under the bright lights of TV cameras,
      "What does it feel like to be a hero?"

If they ask me, one of the parents who pace
I'd tell them.

You forge into burning buildings
      where scorching flames melt dreams
      and noxious fumes choke back hope.

You extend your hand
>   pulling us out of the blazing heat that consumes who we know and love.
You sit with us in smoke filled rooms that blind us from seeing the child we bore.

You search for gentler ways to say the words that singe our hearts,
And you do this over,
>   and over,
>   and over.

Don't be afraid to touch your lips with the same drops of cool water
>   you tenderly offer to us.

There will be more of us who need you, dear hero.

© 1997 Janice Fialka. Reprinted with permission.

NARRATIVE 4.2. | LETTING GO

By Erin Beyers, parent and blogger

The twins and I headed to one of our favorite "old school" playgrounds made of wooden tunnels and tire swings. Blond curls and pony tails blowing in the breeze—such a beautiful sight. Playground visits inevitably create feelings of tension within me. Most do not offer much play value for William, since he does not sit or stand on his own. He is nearing 50 pounds and too heavy to carry around. Usually, I push him in his jogging stroller and we play chase with his sister Ella. I end up feeling stressed and even guilty that he can't play like the other children. This summer, I am letting go of these feelings that I carry like lead weights; do you want to know why?

I opened my eyes and saw how truly happy William was just to be in the sunshine, listening to the children laughing all around him. He was smiling and vocalizing; I don't think he gives a damn whether or not he is doing exactly what the other children are. It has been *my* sadness and *my* burden that he is not "typical." Most days, we spend hours doing therapies, feeding, managing seizures, stretching tight muscles; so many activities to help him reach his full potential. Everyday, I experience joy mingled with fear and depression. Yet, those sunny playground trips have helped me define what quality of life truly means; enjoying the carefree moments no matter what your abilities allow. Quality of life is so important for William and our entire family. Life is far too short and I am done with unrealistic expectations; my own and those I feel from others. I aim to face challenges with courage and strength and to simply enjoy the sunshine with my twins; free of stress and guilt.

© 2011 Erin Beyers. Read more on the blog: The Road Less Traveled: A Mother's Journey Raising Twins, http://beyerstwins.blogspot.com/; reprinted by permission.

Goals 2000   Programs like Head Start were preserved through the Goals 2000 plan, outlined by President George H.W. Bush and the 50 governors in 1989 at the educational summit (Ysseldyke, Algozzine, & Thurlow, 1992; Zigler & Muenchow, 1992). Goals 2000 were six goals for the American education system to achieve by the year 2000. The first goal established by the summit read as follows: "By the year 2000, all children in America will start school ready to learn" (Ysseldyke, Algozzine, & Thurlow, 1992, p. 145). A new focus on the early years of life in preparation for school became a priority as well as an incentive for setting higher goals and standards for public school systems. This plan was later enacted into law as the Educate America Act by President Bill Clinton in 1994 and is considered the precursor to No Child Left Behind Act of 2001 (U.S. Department of Education, 2001).

Impact of Welfare Reform on Early Intervention   The Personal Responsibility and Work Opportunity Reconciliation Act was signed in August of 1996 (Ohlson, 1998). This ended the entitlement of federal assistance to families and children living in poverty. This act of welfare reform gave states the right to develop welfare programs and guidelines. States have taken this opportunity to reform the welfare process and develop programs that require welfare recipients to participate in job training and/or work for their welfare aid. It is feared that families participating in these programs have fallen deeper into poverty and may have difficulty meeting their children's basic needs (Jesien, 1996; Mock, 2005; Ohlson, 1998).

One group that has been particularly hard hit by welfare reform is parents of young children with disabilities, owing to the special circumstances and the high needs of their young children (Gamel-McCormick, 1998; Jesien, 1996; Mock, 2005; Ohlson, 1998). In Wisconsin and Virginia, parent participation in early intervention programs and activities such as the individualized family service plan (IFSP) has been adversely affected by work provisions and child care issues related to welfare reform work requirements (Gamel-McCormick, 2001; Mock, 2005). In the United States, because only 8% of all child care is considered to be of high quality and 41% of child care is considered harmful to children, finding low-cost, quality child care for a child who has a disability or special health care need is difficult (DeVore & Bowers, 2006; Linehan, 1998), thereby hindering a parent's ability to work or participate in early intervention.

Inclusive Early Childhood Education

Over the past 3 decades, the role of public schools has come to the forefront of special education service delivery and educational reform (Lipsky & Gartner, 2001; Odem, 2000; Stainback, Stainback, & Ayres, 1996). In a 1995 report by the National Center on Educational Restructuring and Inclusion (NCERI), seven factors for the successful inclusion of children with disabilities were identified: visionary leadership; collaboration; refocused use of assessment; support for staff and students; appropriate funding levels and formulas; parental involvement; and effective program models, curriculum adaptations, and instructional practices (Lipsky & Gartner, 1998). Collaboration among Head Start, child care, and early childhood special education (in the public schools) has been a priority for Head Start programs (Linehan, 1998). Strong commitments to collaboration lead to developmentally appropriate, inclusive settings for young children with disabilities to grow and learn.

Reauthorization of IDEA in 1997   The reauthorization of Part C of IDEA established a continued commitment to serving young children at risk for delays in development, and young children with disabilities from birth to 3 years, and resulted in an unprecedented increase in the funding of services to these children. Also included were stronger commitments to: 1) interagency collaboration with Head Start and child care;

2) provision of services in natural environments (e.g., home, child care, play group); and 3) mediation, as outlined in the procedural safeguards of Part B of the legislation (Individuals with Disabilities Education Act Amendments, 1997; LRP, 1997). Other changes in Part B of IDEA included: 1) strengthening language on inclusion for school-age children, 2) creating family-centered opportunities (the option for states to use **individualized family service plans** for children ages 3 to 5), and 3) a commitment to increased funding of preschool services (LRP, 1997).

Also in Part C of IDEA, stronger language regarding serving children in their **natural environments** helped to strengthen the concept that young children need to be served in their natural surroundings, whether in the home or child care, with their typically developing peers (Childress, 2004). Unfortunately, there was no strengthening of language to encourage lead agencies to serve children ages 3 to 5 within preschool environments with typically developing peers. Language pertaining to children with disabilities that requires more explanation of their involvement in the general education curriculum has been added to Part B of the legislation, but because schools do not provide programs for typically developing preschool children ages 3 to 5, it is commonly understood that preschoolers with disabilities are excluded from such provisions.

In recent years, the inclusion of young children with disabilities in preschool and child care settings with typically developing peers has created controversy, as well as discussion (Bricker, 1995). Since the vast majority of preschool children are educated outside the public school system, the inclusion of preschoolers with disabilities becomes a logistical challenge and a financial maze. The community discourse surrounding inclusion involves legal, moral, policy, and financial issues (Crockett & Kauffman, 1998; Yell, 2006). Concerns about cost, as well as concerns about fostering the development of friendships among children with and without disabilities in child care settings, create questions regarding school district philosophy, community resources, children's rights to quality programming, and normalization (Buysse, 1993; Buysse, Wesley, & Keyes, 1998). Securing appropriate supports (e.g., child-to-caregiver ratio, proper staff training) for preschool-age children with disabilities in community child care settings still remains a challenge.

The 1997 reauthorization of IDEA also brought about changes in three areas of the law related to inclusion (although the word inclusion is never used) (Lipsky & Gartner, 1998). These changes encompassed: 1) including a general education teacher on the **individualized education program (IEP)** team, 2) including documented justification of nonparticipation in the general education curriculum, and 3) requiring states to change special education funding formulas to remove incentives for more restrictive placements.

Reauthorization of IDEA in 2004 There were few substantive changes to services for infants, toddlers, and preschoolers with disabilities and delays with the reauthorization of IDEA in 2004. While the regulations (e.g., written document of the legal interpretation of public law that states use to implement laws) for Part B of IDEA 2004 have been in place for years, the regulations for Part C of IDEA 2004 were passed by Congress in 2011. (For a more detailed account of this issue, see http://nichcy.org/laws/idea/partc/). The 1999 Part C regulations remained in place and were utilized until the new regulations were passed (Individuals with Disabilities Education Improvement Act, 2004).

MAJOR PRINCIPLES IN EARLY INTERVENTION AND EARLY CHILDHOOD SPECIAL EDUCATION

Over the past 2 decades, the nature of early intervention for young children with disabilities has shifted from a medical model to a community-based model of service. While appointments and therapies used to be delivered strictly in clinical, hospital, or center-based settings, now early intervention typically occurs in the child's home,

individualized family service plan (IFSP) This plan, mandated by Part C of IDEA was developed for young children (birth to age 3) and their families to receive services.

natural environment Any place where you would find a young child, such as at home, child care, library, pool, or play group.

individualized education program (IEP) This plan, mandated by Part B of IDEA, was developed for preschool and school-age children (3 to 21 years of age) to receive services.

family child care, child care center, or other community-based setting, such as a pre-school. This change has occurred through advocacy by family members, and a movement in the field to ensure the transfer of skills into environments where a young child spends most of his or her time. The major principles of early intervention and early childhood special education are further explained in the sections that follow.

Family-Centered Practices

Infants, toddlers, and preschool-age children are cared for and educated within the context of their family. While both early intervention and early childhood special education systems are mandated to include family members on the individualized family service plan (IFSP) and individualized education program (IEP) teams, the family is to be treated as more than just another partner. With children ages birth to 3 years, families are often providing the majority of direct care to the young child and are carrying out recommendations from the early intervention team (e.g., speech-language pathologists, educators, occupational therapists). IFSPs must include family goals, and services are to be provided in community-based settings and at times in which the family members and primary care providers can be present, such as in the home or a child care center.

In some states, regulations allow families to choose specific providers or agencies that serve their child and family. This model is called a vendor model in early intervention. In other states, there is one county- or city-based agency that provides early intervention and preschool services. Both models have positive and negative aspects. For example, with the vendor model of service, families have a choice of providers, but coordination of those services may be difficult if multiple providers from multiple agencies are working with the same child. With a single-agency model, coordination of services may be easier because interventionists know one another and have a common agency structure, but from the family perspective, there is not a choice of the providers.

Utilization of the principles of family-centered practices is essential when working with young children. The Division for Early Childhood (DEC), the professional organization dedicated to helping professionals and families of young children with disabilities and delays, has identified numerous practices for the delivery of services to families. These practices are based on shared responsibility and collaboration, strengthening family functioning, individualized and flexible practices, and strengths- and asset-based practices (Sandall, Hemmeter, Smith, & McLean, 2005). A thorough understanding of these practices and attention to family–professional communication will ensure that families and young children receive the intervention and services they need (Brady et al., 2004). According to Turnbull, Summers, and others (2007) in the field of early childhood intervention, "the process of delivering family-centered services, such as the way that professionals honor parents' choices, involve multiple family members, build on family strengths, establish partnerships, and collaborate with families in individualized and flexible ways" necessary (pp. 187–188).

Interagency Collaboration

Each state is mandated to have a process in place to identify young children with disabilities and **developmental delays**. This process is called **child find**. Referrals about a child with suspected delays or disabilities may come from multiple agencies or the parents themselves. Community providers, such as doctors or nurses who are in clinics or provide well-child visits, may make a referral to early intervention or early childhood special education. Hospitals that have special care nurseries or neonatal intensive care units (NICUs) have a formalized process by which they refer families directly to early intervention when the child leaves the hospital. Often, hospital personnel will

developmental delay
A chronological delay in the milestones of typical early childhood development, including the areas of physical, cognitive, communicative, adaptive, social, and emotional development. According to Part C of IDEA, each state must establish its own definition of developmental delay.

child find   A process or plan systematically implemented by an early intervention agency to locate children who may need intervention services within the community.

have early interventionists come to the hospital while the child is still there to ease the transition home, and to ensure that the child has access to the services the child and his or her family members need.

Well-child visits provide opportunities for community providers, such as doctors, nurse practitioners, or physician assistants, to discover a child is not meeting the typical developmental milestones and make a referral to early intervention. Community health screenings or health fairs are an additional place where families may receive information about development and may obtain developmental screenings.

Serving At-Risk Children

Philosophically, during the development of the law governing early intervention and preschool children, including young children who appear at risk for developmental delays or disabilities was a priority. Due to the malleable nature of development in very young children, advocates sought to include this group, citing the belief that if intervention is received at an early age, the impact may be the greatest (Bronfenbrenner & Morris, 1998).

In addition to young children with diagnosed disabilities or developmental delays, Part C of IDEA allows for state discretion of whom to serve. Specifically, the law allows states to also include young children from birth through 36 months who are at risk for delay in their definition of developmental delay. Currently, the following states serve at-risk children: California, Hawaii, Massachusetts, New Hampshire, New Mexico, and West Virginia (Shackelford, 2006). But this is subject to change, as no state is mandated to serve this population of young children. With the reauthorization of IDEA 2004, states are required to develop a "rigorous" definition of developmental delay.

Each state also has the ability to choose which state agency is responsible for the oversight of early intervention services; for example, in some states they are administered through the state department of education, while in others they are administered through the state health department or child and family services department. What is most important to remember is that every state must provide services to infants and toddlers with disabilities and delays, as well as to their families. Previously, all early intervention services to young children birth through age 3 were free of charge. States are now allowed to charge small fees and to utilize health insurance payments for some types of services.

Eligibility

Young children must be found eligible for early intervention or preschool services to receive them. This means that, after a screening has occurred or a referral from a doctor (or parent) has been made to an early intervention provider in the community, the child must receive a more comprehensive assessment to decide whether or not he or she "qualifies" to receive early intervention or preschool services.

All states are required by law to use certain categories or diagnosed disabilities for eligibility for services (see Tables 4.1 and 4.2). For young children from birth through 3 years of age (and in some states 2 years of age), the category of developmental delay is also utilized. States may also choose to use the category of developmental delay for children ages 3 through 8. Using this more general category allows professionals to provide needed service to a child with unspecified or more global delays that have not yet been categorized or diagnosed.

Service Coordination

Service coordination is a provision of Part C of IDEA for young children who are eligible to receive early intervention services. Service coordinators are professionals who provide a single point of contact for the family and must organize and coordinate all early intervention services across agencies or providers. They assist the family by identifying their and their child's needs and resources, as well as by developing the individualized family service plan (IFSP). The service coordinator

well-child visit This is an appointment with a pediatrician, nurse, nurse practitioner, or other medical professional, at a scheduled age interval (e.g., 6 weeks, 3 months, 6 months, 1 year), to check up on a young child's health and development.

service coordination Mandated by Part C of IDEA, a method of organizing any IFSP services (e.g., education, speech-language, occupational therapy) a young child and his or her family receive.

Table 4.1.   Overview of early intervention services provided by Part C of IDEA

Who is eligible for services and how does a child qualify?	An infant or toddler under 3 years of age who has a disability or developmental delay. Infants and toddlers with disabilities who need early intervention services because they 1. Are experiencing developmental delays, as measured by appropriate diagnostic instruments and procedures, in one or more of the following areas: Cognitive development Physical development, including vision and hearing Communication development Social or emotional development Adaptive development; or 2. Have a diagnosed physical or mental condition that has a high probability of resulting in developmental delay. The term may also include, at a state's discretion, children from birth through age 2 years who are at risk of having substantial developmental delays if early intervention services are not provided.[1]
What services are provided?	1. Assistive technology 2. Audiology 3. Family training, counseling, and home visits 4. Health services 5. Medical services (only for diagnostic or evaluation purposes) 6. Nursing services 7. Nutrition 8. Occupational therapy 9. Physical therapy 10. Psychological services 11. Service coordination 12. Social work services 13. Special instruction 14. Speech-language pathology 15. Transportation and related travel costs 16. Vision services
What written plan is used to document services and developmental goals?	Individualized family service plan (IFSP) The IFSP must be rewritten at least annually, and reviewed every six months. The IFSP must include information about the child's current levels of development as well as the types and amounts of services the child and family will receive.
What are the mandated time lines?	Once the agency receives a referral, it shall appoint a service coordinator as soon as possible. And within 45 days after it receives a referral, the agency shall complete the evaluation and assessment activities and hold an IFSP meeting.
What is service coordination?	Service coordination (case management) means the activities carried out by a service coordinator to assist and enable a child eligible under this part and the child's family to receive the rights, procedural safeguards, and services that are authorized to be provided under the state's early intervention program. Specific service coordination activities include: 1. Coordinating the performance of evaluations and assessments 2. Facilitating and participating in the development, review, and evaluation of IFSPs 3. Assisting families in identifying available service providers 4. Coordinating and monitoring the delivery of available services 5. Informing families of the availability of advocacy services 6. Coordinating with medical and health providers 7. Facilitating the development of a transition plan to preschool services, if appropriate[2]
Where are services provided?	Natural environments. To the maximum extent appropriate to the needs of the child, early intervention services must be provided in natural environments, including the home and community settings in which children without disabilities participate (Section 303.18 of Part C Federal Regulations of 1999). In addition, with the passage of the Part C Federal Regulations of 2011, if a service is not provided in the natural environment, then a written justification must be made.

(continued)

What rights do parents have?	Parents have the right to both mediation and due process if they believe that their or their child's rights under Part C of IDEA have been violated (e.g., time lines, amounts of services, types of services). In addition, with the passage of the Part C Regulations of 2011, parents have the right to receive access to their child's records within 10 days of the request (which was reduced from the previous 45-day time line).

To review all portions of the Part C Federal Regulations of 2011, visit http://www.nectac.org/partc/303regs.asp
[1]Adapted from Sec. 303.16 of Part C Federal Regulations of 1999.
[2]Section 303.23 of Part C Federal Regulations of 1999.

Table 4.2.   Overview of Part B of IDEA

Who is eligible for services and how does a child qualify?	1. *Child with a disability* means a child evaluated as having an intellectual disability (formerly known as mental retardation), a hearing impairment (including deafness), a speech or language impairment, a visual impairment (including blindness), a serious emotional disturbance, an orthopedic impairment, autism, traumatic brain injury, another health impairment, a specific learning disability, deaf-blindness, or multiple disabilities, and who, by reason thereof, needs special education and related services. (There are detailed definitions of each disability category listed within the IDEA Regulations.) 2. The *developmental delay* label can be used for a child with a disability aged 3 through 9 years (or any subset of that age range, including ages 3 through 5, depending on the state), and may...include a child: 1) who is experiencing developmental delays as defined by the state and as measured by appropriate diagnostic instruments and procedures in one or more of the following areas: physical development, cognitive development, communication development, social or emotional development, or adaptive development; and 2) who, by reason thereof, needs special education and related services.[1]
In addition to special education services, what related services are provided?	Related services means transportation and such developmental, corrective, and other supportive services as are required to assist a child with a disability to benefit from special education. Related services also include the following: 1. Speech-language pathology 2. Audiology services 3. Interpreting services 4. Psychological services 5. Physical and occupational therapy 6. Recreation, including therapeutic recreation 7. Early identification and assessment of disabilities in children 8. Counseling services, including rehabilitation counseling 9. Orientation and mobility services 10. Medical services for diagnostic or evaluation purposes 11. School health services 12. School nurse services 13. Social work services in schools 14. Parent counseling and training[2]
What written plan is used to document services and developmental goals?	The Individualized Education Program (IEP). The IEP must be rewritten at least annually. The IEP must include information about the child's current levels of development and performance, measurable annual goals, how the goals will be measured, as well as the types and amounts of educational and related services the child will receive, and where the child will receive them. (Note: An IFSP may be used if the state allows this for 3- to 5-year-old children. For children ages 16 to 21, a transition plan must also be part of the IEP with measurable postsecondary goals.)
What are the mandated time lines?	Under 34 CFR §300.301(c) (1), an initial evaluation must be conducted within 60 days of receiving parental consent for the evaluation or, if the state establishes a time frame within which the evaluation must be conducted, within that time frame. The IDEA 60-day time line applies only to the initial evaluation.[3]

(continued)

Table 4.2.   Overview of Part B of IDEA *(continued)*

Who may be part of the IEP team?	Under 34 CFR §300.321, the IEP team must consist of: 1. The parents of the child; 2. Not less than one regular education teacher of the child (if the child is, or may be, participating in the regular education environment); 3. Not less than one special education teacher of the child, or where appropriate, not less than one special education provider of the child; 4. A representative of the public agency who... Is qualified to provide, or supervise the provision of, specially designed instruction to meet the unique needs of children with disabilities Is knowledgeable about the general education curriculum Is knowledgeable about the availability of resources of the public agency 5. An individual who can interpret the instructional implications of evaluation results, who may be a member of the team described in paragraphs (2) through (6) of this section 6. At the discretion of the parent or the agency, other individuals who have knowledge or special expertise regarding the child, including related services personnel as appropriate 7. Whenever appropriate, the child with a disability.
What is Section 619 of Part B of IDEA?	This is the section of IDEA that provides states with grants specifically for provision of services to preschoolers (3 to 5 years of age) with disabilities and developmental delays.
Where are services provided?	Services are provided in the least restrictive environment (LRE). Part B also provides students with the right to a free appropriate public education (FAPE).
What rights do parents have?	Parents have the right to be included in any meeting that occurs regarding the educational placement of their child. They also have the right to both mediation and due process if they believe that their or their child's rights under Part B of IDEA have been violated (e.g., time lines, amounts of services, types of services). There are specific time lines for meeting notification, how those notifications are made and other stipulations. [Each state has a Parent Training and Information (PTI) Center mandated by law to provide information and training to parents for this purpose.]

To review all portions of the Part B Regulations, visit http://idea.ed.gov/explore/home.
[1]From IDEA Regulations: 34 CFR §300.8(b) (Adapted from http://www.nichy.org/ and http://idea.ed.gov/).
[2]From IDEA Regulations: 34 CFR §300.34.
[3]From http://idea.ed.gov/.

is responsible for making sure that the family and child receive services within the required time lines, and for establishing and updating the IFSP. Service coordination is not a mandated service under Part B of IDEA, so agencies that provide preschool services to young children ages 3 to 5 do not have to perform the same level of coordination.

Service Provision and Assessment   Providing services from multiple disciplines, such as education, social work, occupational therapy, speech-language therapy, and physical therapy, requires coordination and cooperation. The goals for young children with disabilities often overlap from one area of development to another. In early intervention, many states have moved to a model utilizing a primary service provider. This means that a child may receive services from one provider specifically, who is able to work on multiple areas of development (e.g., motor, language, cognitive development). Multiple professionals may be part of the child's team and may be present for the initial comprehensive assessment, and they may be asked to consult on a monthly basis, but the primary interventionist is responsible for providing direct service to the family and child. The infant or toddler may have multiple appointments or medical needs that the family may have to attend to in addition to early intervention services, so one way to minimize the number of adults a young child must acclimate to and build a relationship with is to utilize a primary interventionist model. There are various models of coordination, service provision, and role release that may occur along a continuum. There are typically three terms used to describe types of service delivery or assessment:

multidisciplinary, interdisciplinary, and **transdisciplinary**. Multidisciplinary means that each professional (e.g., educator, speech-language pathologist, physical therapist) provides intervention only within his or her area of expertise. Interdisciplinary means that professionals from the various disciplines work together to provide services either within their own disciplines, and/or in an area where they have received some instruction from another professional. True transdisciplinary teams rarely exist, as they require extensive training and consistency. Most early intervention teams operate in a multidisciplinary or interdisciplinary way.

Assessment of young children takes place in the home, preschool, child care, community-based and/or center-based setting. All areas of development—cognitive, small-motor (small-muscle groups), large-motor (large-muscle groups), speech and language, adaptive (self-help skills), and social-emotional—are assessed using various types of tests. Assessment tasks can be play-based, routine-based, or activity-based, depending on the type of test and the skill the evaluator is trying to assess.

Natural Environments

As previously mentioned, providing early intervention services to young children in their natural environment became a focus of service provision with the passage of IDEA 1997 and has increased over time. Early interventionists who serve infants, toddlers, and preschoolers may now be found in child care centers, family child care settings, community-based preschools and, of course, a child's home (Childress, 2004). But providing services in an environment where you would find a young child without a disability is only part of the reason. There is another reason to assess or provide services to a child in his or her natural environment. Children behave differently in familiar settings with people they know. When interventionists provide services to a child and family in a natural setting, it is more likely that the child's toys, materials, and even furniture will be utilized. For example, parents and caregivers may ask the physical therapist specific questions about positioning in a high chair or crib that may currently be a problem. Or an occupational therapist who arrives at snack time at child care and observes a child having difficulty spooning food from a bowl may offer a suggestion about a new type of bowl or spoon that will help the child be more successful. Without being in the child's environment, these opportunities for discussion and problem solving would be missed.

Routines-Based Intervention

Routines-based interventions (Jung, 2007; Casey & McWilliam, 2007; McWilliam, Casey, & Sims, 2009) are another meaningful way to engage with family members and caregivers. This type of intervention is as simple as it sounds. During routine-based activities that naturally occur in a young child's life (e.g., feeding, bathing, grocery shopping, riding in the car) interventionists work with parents and caregivers to solve any portions of the child's day where he or she is experiencing a problem, as well as to infuse interventions (e.g., needed stretches, practicing two-step directions) into the daily routines.

McWilliam has also developed an interview technique for interventionists to use specifically around family routines. This type of interview strategy not only helps the family and interventionist identify areas where assistance is needed, but also identifies ways that the family is already solving problems that may be applied to other areas of the day. For example, a family may have taken photographs of the three breakfast choices a child has and laminated them on a placemat for the child to choose from each day but is having trouble with the child acting out when he or she is dressing. Reviewing daily routines carefully and identifying the visual strategy of the photographs and applying it to dressing (by taking photos of clothing pieces and making them into a small laminated book) may assist with this difficult part of the day.

multidisciplinary A team approach to service delivery in which each discipline (e.g., education, occupational therapy, physical therapy) serves a child individually, and is only responsible for implementing their discipline's goals.

interdisciplinary A team approach to service delivery in which a child receives various types of services (e.g., education, occupational therapy, physical therapy) and team members from the different disciplines frequently consult with one another about goals.

transdisciplinary A team approach to service delivery in which a child receives various types of services (e.g., education, occupational therapy, physical therapy) from one or more professionals, who use role release and training among themselves, to address common goals.

routines-based intervention An intervention that is implemented during a young child's daily routine, such as bathing, dressing, or eating.

Transition   Moving from one service system to another may be stressful to families and their children. If a family receives services in a state where two different agencies provide birth to 3 years services (e.g., health department) and 3 to 5 years services (e.g., education department), then transitioning to a new set of providers and perhaps a different environment (e.g., home to school) may be difficult. While Part C of IDEA requires a transition plan for preschool services to be in place, in many states this process is still not adequate. It is the responsibility of the early intervention and early childhood special education providers to clearly communicate with families the differences in eligibility and service provision, as well as their parental rights. The process of transitioning from preschool services to school age (e.g., kindergarten, first grade) tends to be smoother, because in many states the public school system is responsible for implementing preschool special education services, so many of the providers may be the same, although the location of services may be different.

Cultural and Socioeconomic Considerations   When providing services to young children and their families, cultural and socioeconomic considerations must be anticipated and made. Some of the most important considerations are 1) perceptions of disability within the family's culture, 2) family cultural and linguistic practices (Cheatham, Armstrong, & Santos, 2009; Cheatham, Santos, & Ro, 2007), and 3) effects of poverty. Service providers must become aware of their own beliefs about various cultures and understand how these beliefs must not interfere with service provision to families who hold different beliefs. This also holds true for family linguistic practices (e.g., speaking a primary language in the home other than English). Families who have young children with disabilities must be afforded the same rights as other families to practice their culture and language in ways that are meaningful to them. Each family should be treated as a unique family, regardless of previous cultural experiences providers may have had in the past. In families today, various structures (e.g., households made up of two moms or two dads, or a grandparent/extended family member caring for a young child) are the norm; providers who are sensitive to this and maintain a nonjudgmental stance will be the most effective. Socioeconomic status is an additional factor for service providers to consider when working with families.

Poverty   The connection between poverty and a young child's development is overwhelming. Janko-Summers and Joseph cited lack of prenatal care, proper nutrition, and preventative health care as some of the reasons for the strong relationship between disability and poverty: "Children living in poverty are more likely to have disabilities than their peers who live in middle and upper-income families. Children with disabilities are more likely than their typically developing peers to be poor" (Janko-Summers & Joseph, 1998, p. 207). Young children with disabilities frequently require more and different types of care than young children who are typically developing (Jesien, 1996). These issues, as well as barriers that already exist for families who have a child with a disability, forecast dismal outcomes for young children with disabilities who live in poverty (Harbin, 1998; Janko-Summers & Joseph, 1998; Jesien, 1996, Ohlson, 1998; Regnier & Hoffman, 1997).

Parents who have children with disabilities face many special challenges in meeting the needs of their child and the demands of employment. Issues arise such as adequate child care, taking time off for a child's illness, therapy, or physician appointments, locating before- and after-school care, and finding a job with flexible work hours (Jesien, 1996; Ohlson, 1998; Collier-Bolkus, 2000). According to the 2001 National Survey of Children with Special Health Care Needs, conducted by the Maternal and Child Health Bureau (2003), 43% of parents who had children with disabilities and special health care needs had to cut back or stop working due to the care needs of their child. The complexity of this issue and a parent's decision whether or not to work becomes increasingly difficult for those receiving assistance from the welfare system (Ohlson, 1998). Providers who respond in respectful ways to various family values of work and lifestyle will be the most successful.

SUMMARY AND FUTURE DIRECTIONS

Short of all human services becoming a natural and valued part of a community's infrastructure, the sociopolitical sentiments and values of the time will continue to affect the future of early childhood intervention. With this in mind, the field of early childhood intervention must collectively plan for the future and be proactive if all young children at risk and with disabilities are to receive the comprehensive, inclusive array of services that are rightfully theirs. This task will not be an easy one. It calls for radical changes in three institutions of our society: 1) health and human services, 2) Congress, and 3) child care and education.

Currently, funding sources for various federally supported programs in health and human services (including public schools) are separate. Funding for Head Start and IDEA comes from various allocations. Allowing agencies responsible for providing services to young children to combine their funds to support young at-risk children and children with disabilities from birth to 5 years would create a seamless system of early childhood intervention. The difficulty arises when various agencies have differing criteria for qualification. Admittedly, cooperation of this magnitude is almost inconceivable. Such a step would require successful interagency collaboration, bipartisan backing of legislation, and cooperation of professional organizations in the field (such as the National Association for the Education of Young Children and the Division for Early Childhood) to implement this plan.

The second radical change necessary for an increased focus on early intervention and a comprehensive, inclusive array of services is a shift in power and an increased voice for women in Congress. While early intervention and child-related issues are not bound by gender, the influence of women in Congress must not be ignored. A record number of women held positions in Congress in 1992 (Hook, 1993); with this came a focus on family leave and health care legislation. The family leave legislation that was passed in 1993 was due in large part to the hard work of congresswomen. In the 112th Congress, 18% of the House of Representatives and 34% of the Senate are women (Women in Congress, 2011). For continued progress in this arena, it is necessary for more women to hold powerful positions on congressional committees to change policy priorities. Since the congressional system of committee assignments is based on seniority, and many women have not been in congressional positions for a great length of time, they are not assigned the powerful position of chairing a committee. Chairmanships on powerful committees, such as the Committee on Ways and Means, must be obtained for women to have an increased influence on policy in the areas of early childhood intervention, special education, child care, and health care.

Third, within the child care system and public schools, reform must begin with the adoption of a strong policy of inclusion, with appropriate supports for implementation (Bailey et al., 1998; Odem, 2000; Turnbull et al., 2007). With this in mind, quality of programming and family priorities should be maintained. A philosophy that all children from birth through 21 years have the right to be educated with typically developing peers and attend their neighborhood child care centers and school must be adopted and enacted fully. This would mean finding quality, developmentally appropriate community placements for young children from birth through 5 years with disabilities in existing community-based child care, family child care settings, preschools, and Head Start programs. A call for collaboration among child care, public school, and Head Start must be answered. Although this idea may seem extremely radical, it appears to be the only viable solution to inclusion at this age level. It would require continued collaboration and commitment to training on the parts of professionals in child care, early childhood education, early intervention, and early childhood special education. Restructuring of these systems may also be required to meet the needs of young children with disabilities (Bailey et al., 1998; Turnbull et al., 2007). A continued focus on developing policies in the interest of young children with disabilities is the one significant way to forward early childhood intervention.

Last, on an individual level, finding ways to instill a vision of hope in families with young children with disabilities and to open the world of opportunity through community involvement are essential. Families desire hope as a means of looking ahead to a future where their children are valued and perceived as contributing to the world as full members of society.

CHAPTER 5

Child and Adolescent Development

How this chapter prepares you to be an effective inclusive classroom teacher:

- This chapter teaches you about many areas of development for children and adolescents, including cognitive, neurological, identity, social, linguistic, and physical development. You will also learn how children and adolescents typically develop at each grade level in school and what makes each student a unique human being. **This helps you meet CEC Standard 2: Development and Characteristics of Learners.**

- This chapter prepares you to be a professional and ethical teacher by teaching you that developmental milestones are just guidelines and that no two children or adolescents progress through stages or levels the same way. You will also learn that teachers should be sensitive to individualized differences in development and that planning and instruction should reflect developmental levels. **This helps you meet CEC Standard 9: Professional and Ethical Practice.**

After reading and discussing this chapter, you will be able to

- Describe typical development in the following areas: cognitive, neurological, identity, social, linguistic, and physical

- Explain how each area of development affects a student's progress in school

- Explain why teachers should be familiar with the areas of development

- Explain what teachers should know about students who are not developing typically in one or more of the areas

- Explain the concept of multiple intelligences and its impact on inclusion of diverse students

- Explain the concept of mind profile and its impact on inclusion of diverse students

This chapter discusses theories of development in children and adolescents. The chapter is divided into four sections. The first section covers theories of typical child and adolescent development in several areas—cognitive, neurological, identity, social, linguistic, and physical. In the second section, these areas of development are discussed in the context of school and what most children know or do at each grade level. The third section then examines the significance of the theories in the context of development that is different. In the case of disability, ways in which children and adolescents are viewed depend on how typical development is considered. The last section discusses what teachers should know about development and the extent to which typical development should be the yardstick against which students are measured.

The narrative for this chapter is from a person with a disability whose typical development was confused with, or assumed to be, atypical because of her disability. Because people like her have disabilities that result in certain areas of atypical development, it is sometimes overlooked that they also have many areas of typical development.

THEORIES OF CHILD AND ADOLESCENT DEVELOPMENT

Different areas of development include cognitive, social, neurological, emotional, language, physical, and academic development. We need to review these so that we can talk about why teachers need to know this information and how they can apply it to teach all students.

Cognitive Development

Here we discuss two theories: Jean Piaget's theory of cognitive development and Lev Vygotsky's theory of social constructivism. Both have had a significant impact on the understanding of cognitive development of children and adolescents.

Jean Piaget's Theory of Cognitive Development   Jean Piaget was a Swiss psychologist who lived from 1896 to 1980. In 1952, Piaget first published his theory of cognitive development. The premise of his theory is that children and adolescents develop through four different stages in a linear order, meaning that each stage is completed before a child moves on to the next stage. The four stages are:

- Sensorimotor stage (birth to 2 years), characterized by the development of object permanence and motor skills, but a lack of symbolic representation

- Preoperational stage (2 to 7 years), characterized by the development of language and symbolic, yet egocentric, thinking

- Concrete operational stage (7 to 12 years), characterized by the development of conservation and mastery of the concept of reversibility

- Formal operational stage (12 years to adulthood), characterized by the development of logical and abstract thinking (Feldman, 2008)

Completion of each stage depends on the quality of **schemas** that exist in that stage. A schema is a mental representation of the world formed by experiences and interactions with the environment. Piaget's theory tells us that schemas increase in quantity and quality as children develop. At first, infants receive stimuli and react. As learning occurs from these reactions, infants begin to make sense, or form schemas, of what happens. They start thinking about how they can affect the world around them. For example, an infant might kick her foot, bumping a toy that plays a song when it is moved. The infant does not understand at first that kicking the toy made the song play, but after it happens a few times, the infant develops a schema: If I kick my foot, the song plays. I like the song; I'll kick my foot again. In that way, infants become more active in their interactions with the environment. As children impact their environment through physical movement and language, they gain more tools for developing more schemas. That is how children develop more complex ways of seeing and responding to the environment around them. As schemas change and evolve, the child's knowledge of the world changes and evolves, too. The baby in the sensorimotor stage is learning that she can affect her surroundings.

Piaget introduced **assimilation** and **accommodation** as ways for schemas to adapt. Assimilation is the process of fitting a new experience into an existing schema—fitting practice or actions into our theory. Even though the new experience may have unique characteristics, we connect it to similar experiences that are in a schema already. Accommodation is the process of modifying or expanding existing schemas to fit a new experience. When the experience has unique characteristics, the schema must be changed to recognize the new information. Schemas become more complex this way (Atherton, 2009).

Adapting schemas, by assimilation or accommodation, is caused by a mismatch between what the child knows and what he or she needs to know (Novak and Peláez, 2004). This mismatch is known as **disequilibrium**. Its counterpart, equilibrium, occurs only temporarily when the child's existing schemas match the environment. Every time something in the environment poses a new experience, disequilibrium occurs, sparking assimilation or accommodation so that new learning occurs. If the mismatch is too great, no assimilation can occur. If the mismatch is too slight, everything will be assimilated, but accommodation will not occur.

As a child moves through the preoperational stage into the concrete operational stage, he becomes aware of more ways to affect the environment and understand the perspective of others. Think about a boy who learns to play Hide and Seek. At 3 years old, the boy might hide his face under a blanket with his legs sticking out and giggling, thinking that he can't be seen or heard by the seeker. At 6 years old, the boy will ensure that his whole body is hidden and stay still and quiet while hiding. At 9 years old, the boy might try to trick the seeker by stuffing pillows under a blanket in one room to make it look like a hiding body, but then hide himself in another room. He has become more and more sophisticated in his understanding of what hiding means and how to hide effectively from others. His schema of "what is hiding" has become more complex. In addition, the concepts of assimilation and accommodation come into play. Each

schema A term introduced by Piaget to describe the rules or principles that children establish so they can understand new experiences as their cognition develops. In other words, as children learn new things, they organize them into schemas in their mind. Each new experience then fits in some way into an existing schema.

assimilation A term introduced by Piaget to describe one way that cognition develops in children. A child assimilates a new experience by folding it into an existing schema, without modifying the schema. This generally occurs when the new experience agrees with or reinforces existing knowledge.

accommodation A term introduced by Piaget to describe one way that cognition develops in children. A child accommodates new information by modifying an existing schema so that a new experience will fit. This generally occurs when a new experience contradicts existing knowledge.

disequilibrium A term introduced by Piaget to describe what happens when a new experience does not fit an existing schema. In order to make sense of the new experience, accommodation occurs.

time the boy thinks he is well hidden, but another easily spots him, he assimilates these individual experiences until he accommodates the idea that others have a different perspective than he does. In other words, he gathers information from the individual experiences until he has enough evidence to change his thinking. Now he understands what others see is different from what he sees.

Adolescence often brings abilities to analyze and question the perspective of others. This stage is characterized by abstract thinking and awareness of multiple perspectives that lead adolescents to question their parents' or teachers' rules. Once adolescents have greater reasoning and abstract thinking skills, they are more likely to detect inconsistencies in others' reasoning. They are also developing their sense of idealism, so they are often frustrated with flaws in institutions or systems such as school or government (Feldman, 2008).

Piaget was a very influential thinker and many schools and teachers consider his stages of development when planning to teach children. We will look at a problem with his thinking related to disability in the next section.

zone of proximal development A term introduced by Vygotsky that refers to the place in which learning occurs, when a child is challenged but not frustrated.

scaffolding Gradual supports provided to bring a learner to a new level of understanding. To optimize learning, scaffolds should challenge without frustrating the learner.

cultural tools Objects in the environment, such as books or media, that assist learning.

more knowledgeable other A term introduced by Vygotsky that refers to a person with a higher level of understanding who can provide scaffolds to a learner in his or her zone of proximal development in order to further cognitive development.

Lev Vygotsky's Theory of Social Constructivism   Lev Vygotsky was a Russian psychologist whose work was rediscovered long after his death in 1934. Vygotsky put much more emphasis than Piaget on the role the environment and social context plays in cognitive development (Novak and Peláez, 2004). Three main concepts of Vygotsky's theory are the **zone of proximal development**, **scaffolding**, and **cultural tools**.

The zone of proximal development is "the distance between the actual developmental levels as determined by independent problem solving and the level of potential development as determined through problem solving under adult guidance or in collaboration with more capable peers" (Vygotsky, 1978, p. 86). Essentially, it is the edge of the child's independent knowledge where she is ready to take the next step in further learning. With help and social interaction, the child can take what she already knows and add new information and skills: She can change her schemas. Scaffolds are the supports used by teachers to prompt or boost the child to higher understandings. Examples of scaffolds are step-by-step directions, guided questions, or manipulatives to help understand mathematical processes. Cultural tools are physical or intellectual tools in the environment that assist in cognitive development. These include books, media, computers, and most important, oral language.

Vygotsky believed formal education to be influential in promoting cognitive growth at any age, as teachers act as facilitators of learning (Feldman, 2008). Vygotsky's theory also emphasized the importance of culture on learning. According to Vygotsky, learning occurs through social interaction and joint problem solving with **more knowledgeable others**. Thus, the cultural views and traditions of the more knowledgeable others permeate those social interactions and subsequent learning. Consider a scenario where a preteen asks a parent about the crisis of the oil leak on the floor of the Gulf of Mexico. If the cultural context is one that values the environment and conservation of nature, the conversation (which is an important learning experience for the preteen) will focus around ways to contain the oil so that it does not further pollute the water or its inhabitants. If the cultural context is one that values industrial progress and manmade comforts, the conversation will focus on ways to save the oil even it means further damage to the environment. In either context, the preteen is scaffolded to a higher level of understanding through the discussion. If the preteen asks several others the same question, she may be exposed to several different perspectives to consider before forming her own opinion about the topic.

Neurological Development

Researchers have come to know much more about the actual development of a child's brain in recent years. What they have learned is that people are born with brains ready to accept new learning of knowledge and skills. Brotherson (2005) likened the newborn brain to a house that has just been built. The structure of the house is similar to many other houses. There are spaces for particular uses. The wiring may be there, along with fuse boxes and switches, but connections need to be made and secured for the wiring to work. Brotherson noted, "The brain continues to form after birth based on experiences. An infant's mind is primed for learning, but it needs early experiences to wire the neural circuits of the brain that facilitate learning" (2005, p. 3).

Many factors influence the development of the brain throughout childhood. Genetics, nutrition, responsiveness of caregivers, daily experiences, physical activity, and love all play a part in a growing and developing brain. There are genetic factors, but it is the environment that shapes brain development through the five senses of vision, hearing, smell, touch, and taste. Each time a child experiences an environmental stimulus, a connection is made between brain cells. Repeated exposure to the stimulus strengthens the connection. If it is not repeated, the connection is weak and may die out according to a "use it or lose it" principle (Brotherson, 2005). Thinking about the house analogy, the architecture of the brain is in place, and all experiences that lead to learning serve to furnish or decorate the rooms and walls. Thus, the more varied and rich the experiences, the more varied and rich the learning. The following example illustrates this concept. If a baby is exposed to a particular type of food, the "kitchen" will be more receptive to that kind of food. Other babies' kitchens will be different based on the foods they are exposed to.

Brotherson (2005) also outlined critical periods of brain development in youth, as shown in Table 5.1. This chart indicates types of brain development, a description of what children learn in that period, and the "prime time" for the development of those skills.

As you can see in Table 5.1, some of the critical time periods are quite large. This means that some development can occur throughout that time span, but there are smaller windows that are most critical. For example, if a child does not have the opportunity to form attachments to caregivers in the first 18 months of life, she may gain some emotional and social coping skills through age 12, but there will likely always be a deficit in her ability to attach to new people or to maintain meaningful relationships.

Pediatrician Mel Levine's work focused on the neurological development of the mind. Levine (2002) described eight neurodevelopmental systems. Just as the physical health of a body is related to the health of the systems of the body, the learning health of a mind is related to the health of neurodevelopmental systems. That is, if the body systems such as cardiovascular, nervous, and gastrointestinal are healthy, the body will be healthy too. If the systems of learning are all in good shape, then the mind will be healthy and ready to learn.

Levine's (2002) list of the neurodevelopment systems included: the attention control system, the memory system, the language system, the spatial-ordering system, the

Table 5.1. Types of brain development

Type of brain development	Description	Time period
Visual and auditory	Learning to see and hear, understand shapes, colors, distance, movement, and sound variation	Birth to 4 or 5 years of age
Language	Learning to babble, talk, connect words to experiences	Birth to 10 years of age, but most critical in the first few years
Physical and motor	Learning gross-motor skills, such as walking and jumping, and fine-motor skills, such as using a crayon or pencil	Birth to 12 years of age
Emotional and social	Learning capacities such as trust, empathy, happiness, hopefulness, and resiliency, interacting with others, sharing, and nurturing	Birth to 12 years of age. The critical period for forming attachments is birth to 18 months of age.

Source: Brotherson, 2005.

mind profile   A term introduced by Dr. Mel Levine to describe the unique profile of a person's mind, including the strengths and weaknesses in several areas of neurodevelopment. The mind profile is influenced by factors such as genetics, emotion, physical health, peers, family, environment, culture, and education.

plasticity   The ability of a mind to learn a vast amount of information.

sequential-ordering system, the motor system, the higher-thinking system, and the social-thinking system. Each person's mind is a unique combination of strengths and weaknesses in the different systems. This combination is a profile of the mind's functioning. The **mind profile** is shaped by many factors, including genes, family life, stress level, cultural factors, friends, health, emotions, and educational experience.

Additional research indicates that the brain, originally thought to be completely matured by age 10, is not fully developed until the 20s or 30s (Graham, 2008). Since teenagers' brains are still developing, they still have much of their **plasticity**, which means they can learn and remember great amounts of information. The plasticity of female brains peaks at 12 to 14 years and male brains at 14 to 16 years—and this should affect when we expose children of these ages to difficult academic subjects. Gender does matter! The adolescent brain is also affected by sleep cycles. The adolescent brain learns best at least 2 hours after waking. Since junior and senior high school usually start early in the morning, educators should bear in mind that they are asking adolescents to learn when their brains are not working at optimal levels.

Teens' frontal lobes are also not fully mature. The frontal lobe is responsible for judgment, insight, and impulse control. In essence, teens have a discrepancy between being able to come up with an idea and deciding if it's a good one. This has significant impact for adolescents, who are often expected to make adult decisions and carry adult responsibility loads (Graham, 2008).

Identity Development

Erik Erikson was a Danish-German-American developmental psychologist who lived from 1902 to 1994. He offered his theory on the eight stages or psychosocial crises of identity development in 1956. The stages are highly dependent on the parenting that individuals experience throughout childhood, emphasizing a social context of learning. The stages are summarized in Table 5.2.

Another view of the stages of identity development was described by Novak and Peláez (2004) as the way a sense of "self" develops in a person. These include

Table 5.2.   Stages of identity development

Stage	Description	Age
Hope	Learning basic trust versus mistrust; knowing that needs will be met consistently versus insecure and pessimistic about inconsistent care	Birth to 2 years
Will	Learning autonomy versus shame; proud of newfound control, showing initiative, independence, and even stubbornness versus feeling tentative and ashamed of actions or decisions	About 18 months to 3 or 4 years of age
Purpose	Learning initiative versus guilt; learning cooperation, imagination, and leadership versus fear, isolation, dependence, and restricted play	About 3 to 5 years of age
Competence	Learning industry versus inferiority; learning to relate to others according to social rules, and mastering teamwork and academics versus feeling doubt and defeat	About 5 to 12 years of age
Fidelity	Learning identity versus diffusion; moving through a period of self-consciousness and self-doubt with feelings of congruence rather than confusion	About 13 to 20 years of age
Love	Learning intimacy versus isolation; learning to sustain enduring relationships	Young adulthood
Care	Learning generativity (desire to produce something of value to others) versus self-absorption; learning to sustain healthy marriage, parenthood, work productivity, and creativity	Adulthood
Wisdom	Learning integrity versus despair; finding a well-defined role in life	Once the other seven crises have been successfully resolved

Source: Erikson, 1963.

self-recognition, self-awareness and perspective taking, self-statements, self-traits, self-efficacy, self-esteem, and self-control.

Self-recognition is the first step as a child develops a concept of herself as an individual separate from others. Once a child can recognize herself in a photograph or acknowledge that she is looking at her own reflection in a mirror, for example, she is said to have developed self-recognition.

From there, self-awareness and perspective-taking develop. This happens when a child is able to view an experience from his point of view and understand that another person may have a different experience from a different perspective. A good example was offered by Novak and Peláez: A child is shown a coin being put into an empty crayon box. When asked what is in the box, the child with self-awareness of his or her perspective will answer "a coin." Then another person enters who did not see the coin being put in the crayon box. When asked what the other person would think is in the box, a child with a developed sense of perspective-taking will answer "crayons" (2004), because he understands that the person who just entered does not know about the coin. A child who has not yet developed this sense, in contrast, would answer "a coin."

The next piece of identity formation is the development of self-statements. Self-statements are the "I statements" a child makes to explain her thinking to one who does not know her perspective. For this to happen, the child must understand that the other person is not able to know what she is thinking and the child must be able to communicate that thinking in some way so that the other person can understand. Self-statements may be in the form of reason-giving statements that assess the situation (e.g., "I dropped the box because it was too heavy"), or assess one's self (e.g., "I dropped the box because I am not very strong").

Self-traits are related to self-statements. Self-traits can be stable or unstable. It is important to note here the idea of stable versus unstable traits connected to these self-statements. If a child believes an event occurred because of her internal characteristic or stable trait (lack of strength), she will be less likely to try again. If the child believes that an event occurred because of an external characteristic or unstable trait (the box had too many books in it), she is more likely to try again.

Next, self-efficacy, the belief in one's own competence, develops when a child makes self-statements about the ability to accomplish certain tasks. Self-efficacy beliefs take hold when four things are in place: repeated, successful accomplishment of the tasks; observation of a model who is successful in accomplishing the tasks; verbal persuasion or encouragement from others regarding her ability to accomplish the tasks; and emotional arousal of the child. A child with many self-efficacy beliefs will develop positive self-esteem, which is a general belief in her positive attributes.

Last is the idea of self-control. Once a child has developed a positive self-esteem via many experiences of feeling competent, he will be able to exhibit much greater self-control. He will be able to weigh alternatives in order to make appropriate decisions, delay gratification, and better resist the temptation to act impulsively.

As another factor in an individual's development, Feldman (2008) described five personality traits that each person possesses in unique ways. These are openness to experience (levels of independence, imagination, and preference for variety); conscientiousness (levels of carefulness, discipline, and organization); extroversion (levels of talkativeness, sobriety, and sociability); agreeableness (levels of sympathy, kindness, and friendliness); and neuroticism or emotional stability (levels of stability, calmness, and security). Given these variations as well as genetic differences, various expectations, and environmental influences, it should be clear that development may involve patterns but none that are set in stone. Each person is unique and has a unique journey of identity.

Identity development happens in the context of social interaction and in understanding oneself in relation to others. The next section of this chapter discusses social development in children and adolescents, but keep in mind that both types of development are intertwined.

Social Development

To gain an overall picture of social development stages, revisit Erikson's theory in Table 5.2. It provides a general view of how social development occurs along with identity development. That is, each stage of identity development has a social component that is also developing. Here are more specific examples of what that looks like at different age levels:

The social development during the first year of a child's life is considered to revolve around the child's developing a sense that he is a separate being with his own needs and emotions. From birth to about 3 months of age, an infant does not realize that he is a separate person from his parents or other caregivers. His communication is reflexive in nature with the purpose of indicating discomfort, such as hunger, fatigue, or wet pants (Shelov & Altmann, 2009). When reflexive crying or fussing leads to consistent attendance to needs, the infant begins to learn that crying out leads to comfort. At this early age, human faces and sounds are very important and the infant will also connect them with comfort. From 3 to 6 months of age, the infant continues to develop interactions with caregivers in the form of smiles and laughter, but still does not understand that he is a separate person in and of himself. From 6 to 9 months, the infant starts to realize he is separate from other people and shows a preference for his familiar caregivers. At this age, he will also better understand and distinguish his own emotions and needs (e.g., fear versus hunger) and interact toward satisfying them (by reaching for a parent or his bottle). From 9 to 12 months, more complex interaction develops between the infant and his caregivers. He will start to play games such as Peekaboo, and he is able to express his own likes and dislikes. Babbling in early "conversation" emerges during these months (Children, Youth, and Women's Health Service, 2009).

From 1 to 4 years of age, the social development of a child builds on the foundation he has regarding himself as an individual and his needs and wants. At 1 to 2 years old, he is curious about the environment and will begin to explore, but he is still dependent on his caregivers and will often feel most comfortable when they are near. He also notices other children, but generally plays alone. He has not yet begun to develop the concept of sharing. From 2 to 3 years old, he is learning more about his own emotions as well as others' emotions and can connect them to events in the environment, although children this age are still motivated by their own needs and are only aware of their own perspective, so they believe others feel the same way they do. He begins to negotiate how to act as a separate person, which is why this age is often characterized by tantrums and exclamations of "No!" or "Do it myself!" From 3 to 4 years of age, interactive play with others emerges as well as the ability to take turns and wait. Children at this age begin to choose friends and develop the skills in cooperating with them in play (Shelov & Altmann, 2009). At this point, as the child enters the school-age years, each year of a child's development sees intricate changes in his interactions with others.

At 4 to 5 years old, children generally reach the stage where they are interested in and able to play comfortably with other children and understand simple games. Many of the games they play include role-playing such things as "house" or "superheroes." This role-playing provides them with an opportunity to mimic adult roles and activities. Four- or five-year-olds can usually separate from their parents or caregivers without distress. They enjoy the company of friends and need opportunities for practicing social skills while developing relationships with different peers (National Association for School Psychologists, 2011). They may not have a full understanding of the differences between reality and fantasy and may tell stories that seem to be fibs. It is important to note that 4- to 5-year-olds can find the big, wide world scary at times. They need caregivers to provide daily structure and safe limits so they know what to expect (Children, Youth, and Women's Health Service, 2009).

From 6 to 9 years of age, children further develop friendships and independence from the company of family. They begin to feel the need to fit in with their friends and share their values. They need guidance at this point to digest both family and peer values and to come to a compromise that suits them best. Children at this age are more capable of acknowledging others' perspectives and forming true friendships with others (Halliburton & Gable, 2003). During these years, children often like to play with members of the same sex and may express gender stereotypes. Although developmentally typical, they need adult guidance to expose them to examples of both sexes' engaging in any activity they like. They can handle household chores and responsibilities and understand rules and guidelines in various settings (Children, Youth, and Women's Health Service, 2009).

By 10 to 12 years of age (the "tween" years), the social world is becoming a much more complex place. A best friend is common, but all friendships are more complex and changing at this time. Generally, girls are more attuned to who they are with, while boys pay more attention to what they are doing. It is typical at this stage for young adolescents to want to be more independent and to lose some interest in family activities. They truly do feel caught between two worlds during the aptly nicknamed tween years. They need the comfort and structure of family life, while yearning for the freedom and spontaneity of independence (Children, Youth, and Women's Health Service, 2009).

At 12 to 15 years of age, youth are faced with the dwindling of childhood and the nearing of adulthood. It is a stormy and painful process that is dealt with differently by each teenager. Belonging to a group is extremely important at this point, but the family as that group may be too confining. Teens are working out how to be their own person, all their own—not the child that the family has known all along. For that reason, they can become bonded to their friends as tightly as they were attached to parents as toddlers (Feldman, 2008).

At this point in your reading, it shouldn't be surprising to hear that, along with race, gender roles, and disability, adolescence is a social construction. This means that the transition between childhood and adulthood as well as the time frame for the transition is defined within a societal context. Despite specific cultural celebrations, such as the First Communion, confirmation, bar or bat mitzvah, *quinceanera*, or *nen* ordination, American society does not define a specific point of crossover into adulthood. In fact, the transition is prolonged so much that adolescence spans several years with no set path for achieving full independence. Each family may have its own marker of when certain responsibilities or privileges are given. It may be based on age, grade level, maturity, or sudden necessity. The diversity of our society, albeit beautiful, contributes to the vagueness of adolescent roles.

The roles of adolescents may be similar across peers—family member, friend, student—but even these roles are socially constructed and vary according to many variables, such as family structure, socioeconomic status, gender, and geography. Given this level of variation, it is no wonder that the long period of adolescence can be fraught with difficulty in defining who to be, how to act, and what to contribute. "Trying on" different roles is common in adolescence and made easier by a society that offers many choices (Feldman, 2008).

Language Development

Children learn language through an experimental process, in much the same way a linguist would learn about a new language. Infants develop language by being exposed to language; as they hear (or see, for infants who access a signed language) language in use connected to the world around them, they develop an understanding that language is used to communicate. The infant with the toy that plays a song is probably also exposed to language about what she is doing. An adult is probably saying, "Oh, look! You kicked the toy, and now it is playing! Good baby!" or something similar. Infants are immersed in language from the moment they are born. Gradually, they begin to express language as well as receive it. Exposure and repetition have a direct impact on the quantity and quality of language development. The more language input and feedback from adults (particularly the mother) to the child, the more words the child verbalizes and uses correctly in context (Novak and Peláez, 2004).

Saffron, Senghas, and Trueswell likened language development to the discovery of "the internal structure of a system that contains tens of thousands of units, all generated from a small set of materials. These units, in turn, can be assembled into an infinite number of combinations" (2001, p. 1). When learning language, children move from phonemes and morphemes to syntax and semantics. In other words, as infants and children first make sounds, then recognize certain sound sequences as words, then package the words into meaningful units to convey a message (Saffron, Senghas, & Trueswell, 2001). Then, children learn about pragmatics (the appropriate context for words) and how to impact the environment by using certain words in various ways in particular settings. It is a complicated system that takes many years to fully master and appreciate, with many bumps along the way.

At 4 to 5 years old, children can generally speak clearly but may still have trouble with some phonemes, such as saying /th/ for /s/ or /w/ for /r/. Children at this age begin to ask many "why" and "how" questions, knowing that those question words will result in further information about a topic from caregivers. They are able to repeat songs or nursery rhymes and talk about what might happen, not just what has happened or is currently happening. From 6 to 9 years old, vocabulary increases so that children are able to tell complex, lengthy stories or recount happenings. They enjoy jokes and riddles and understand more plays on words. They become more accomplished at conversing on the telephone. Into the tween and teen years, language is another way that adolescents can assert their independence and develop their own style. This may take the form of trying out new words to test their impact in the company of different people, keeping their language to themselves by hardly speaking at all, or practicing their debating skills at every opportunity. This can be frustrating to parents and teachers, but it is important to remember that it is an essential part of their development (Children, Youth, and Women's Health Service, 2009).

Biggle (2005) indicated commonalities in language development between children who are hearing and those who are deaf or hard of hearing. One commonality is that frequent, consistent, and accessible language is the key to development, whether signed or spoken. That said, there are some differences in language development between hearing and deaf children if the parents sign or speak. In cases where language is primarily spoken at home, there can be language delays in the children's development because the child's preferred language is not the dominant language. If American Sign Language (ASL) or Signed English (SE) is used at home by hearing parents who are new at signing, the children may also be exposed to inconsistent or incorrect linguistic input.

Physical Development

During a child's regular check-ups with the pediatrician, a number of things are checked and noted. One is the child's height and weight. This is measured frequently throughout a child's growing years to determine if her growth pattern remains consistent. There is a wide range for how big children are, placed on a percentile scale by age. While being a large or small child does not in itself indicate a problem, pediatricians may raise a red flag if a child's usually consistent growth in height or weight takes a sudden dip or spike on the growth chart (see Figures 5.1 and 5.2), or the percentiles for height and weight vary widely from each other. A child in the 10th percentile for height and 90th percentile for weight would be obese for her age. Conversely, a child in the 90th percentile for height and 10th percentile for weight may be undernourished physically.

Another area to be checked is developmental milestones. There are certain physical and cognitive abilities and characteristics common at various age levels. Children, Youth, and Women's Health Service (2009) outlined the milestones shown in Table 5.3.

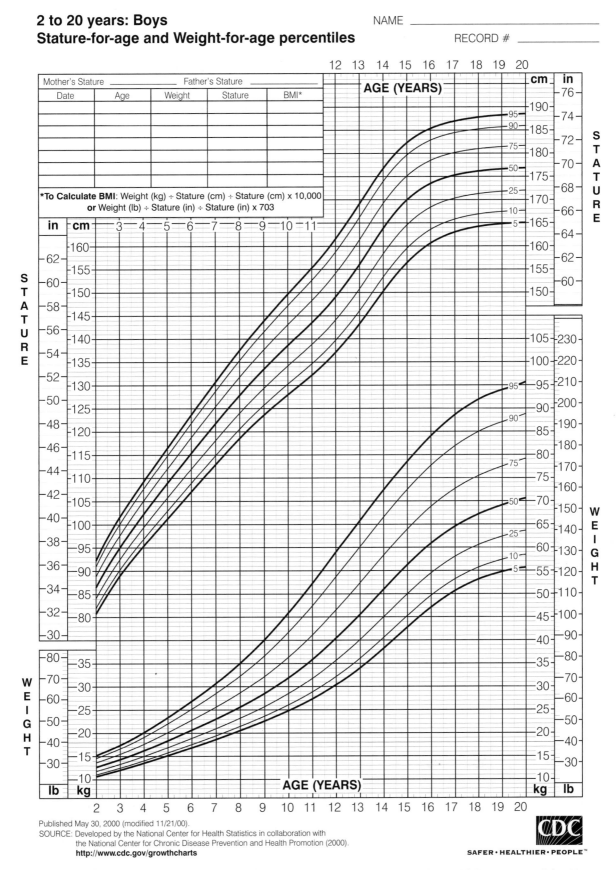

2 to 20 years: Boys
Stature-for-age and Weight-for-age percentiles

NAME _____

RECORD # _____

Mother's Stature _____ Father's Stature _____

Date	Age	Weight	Stature	BMI*

*To Calculate BMI: Weight (kg) ÷ Stature (cm) ÷ Stature (cm) x 10,000
or Weight (lb) ÷ Stature (in) ÷ Stature (in) x 703

AGE (YEARS)

STATURE

WEIGHT

Published May 30, 2000 (modified 11/21/00).
SOURCE: Developed by the National Center for Health Statistics in collaboration with
the National Center for Chronic Disease Prevention and Health Promotion (2000).
http://www.cdc.gov/growthcharts

CDC
SAFER · HEALTHIER · PEOPLE™

Figure 5.1. Growth chart for boys 2–20 years. (*Source:* Developed by the National Center for Health Statistics in collaboration with the National Center for Chronic Disease Prevention and Health Promotion [2000]. http://www.cdc.gov/growthcharts.)

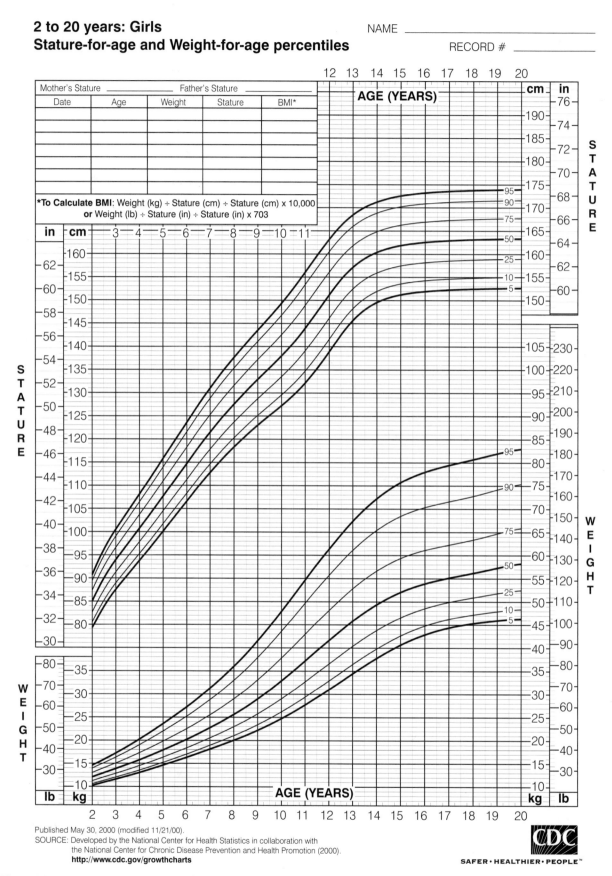

2 to 20 years: Girls
Stature-for-age and Weight-for-age percentiles

NAME _____

RECORD # _____

Published May 30, 2000 (modified 11/21/00).
SOURCE: Developed by the National Center for Health Statistics in collaboration with
the National Center for Chronic Disease Prevention and Health Promotion (2000).
http://www.cdc.gov/growthcharts

SAFER · HEALTHIER · PEOPLE™

Figure 5.2. Growth chart for girls 2–20 years. (*Source:* Developed by the National Center for Health Statistics in collaboration with the National Center for Chronic Disease Prevention and Health Promotion [2000]. http://www.cdc.gov/growthcharts.)

Table 5.3. Developmental milestones

4–5 years of age	• Walk up and down steps, one foot to a step • Throw and catch a ball, use a bat • Stand and walk on tiptoe • Run • Jump over objects • Ride tricycles or bicycles with training wheels • Thread beads on a string • Swing a swing by themselves • Dress and toilet themselves • Draw a person • Count • Write their names, hold a pencil well • Know colors and sort objects
6–9 years of age	• Draw a picture of a house, yard, and sky • Ride a bicycle without training wheels • Climb trees and swim independently • Tell time • Begin to understand money value and use • Know the left hand from the right • Start to make plans
10–12 years of age	• Sexual development of girls includes breast buds, hips taking shape, perhaps menstruation • Sexual development of boys is a bit later than girls at this point, perhaps beginning of nocturnal emissions and voice changes • More able to multitask and take on more responsibilities, interests
12–15 years of age	• Better able to conceptualize broader issues, think abstractly • Sexual development for girls includes full breast development, menstruation, pubic hair, mature facial features • Sexual development for boys includes nocturnal emissions, rapid growth, deepened voice, pubic and facial hair, boosts of testosterone that may make their bodies feel awkward • Growing physical strength and ability in sports

Source: Children, Youth, and Women's Health Service, 2009.

IMPACT OF DEVELOPMENTAL THEORIES IN CONTEXT OF SCHOOL

Progression through school involves all of the areas of development discussed in the first section of this chapter—cognitive or intellectual development, neurological brain development, identity, social and emotional development, language acquisition, and physical development. What students are expected to do at each grade level—kindergarten through high school senior—is typically decided according to where most children are on the developmental scales in each of these areas. Students are expected to start school at a particular age possessing a particular set of skills and then build on each skill year after year.

The Role of Cognitive Development in School

Cognitive development plays a large role in academics and school success. A look at Bloom's Taxonomy of Learning in Table 5.4 shows us the types of cognition that are required of students as well as the complexity of tasks.

One may assume that higher levels of the taxonomy are not reached until students are older, near the end of their schooling. This is not necessarily the case. Students as early as kindergarten are able to perform tasks at the higher levels as well as begin gathering a strong foundation of knowledge and skills. One example is from a first-grade classroom. After story reading and discussion of the characteristics of leprechauns, each student created a leprechaun trap from any materials they wished. *Analyzing* the

Table 5.4.   Bloom's taxonomy

Levels of Bloom's taxonomy	Tasks associated with each level
Knowledge: Finding or remembering information	arrange, define, duplicate, label, list, memorize, name, order, recognize, relate, recall, repeat
Comprehension: Understanding information	classify, describe, discuss, explain, express, restate, review, select, translate
Application: Using information	apply, choose, demonstrate, dramatize, employ, illustrate, interpret, operate, practice, solve, use
Analysis: Taking information apart	analyze, appraise, categorize, compare, contrast, criticize, differentiate, discriminate, distinguish, examine, experiment, question, test
Synthesis: Creating new information	assemble, compose, construct, create, design, develop, formulate, manage, organize, plan, prepare, propose, set up
Evaluation: Making judgments about information	appraise, argue, assess, defend, judge, predict, rate, score, select, support, value

Source: Bloom, 1984.

qualities of various materials, they *synthesized* the information they had learned and created many different kinds of traps and, *applying* their knowledge of leprechaun preferences, loaded them with appropriate bait.

Memory plays an extensive role in academics and learning new information. In addition to the well-known concepts of short-term and long-term memory, Levine included the concept of active, working memory: "The four roles of active, working memory are: 1) holding together parts of ideas/stories while they develop, 2) holding together different parts of a task or activity while doing it, 3) holding together short- and long-term parts of plans, and 4) holding together short- and long-term memory" (2002, p. 102). As you can see, working memory is complex and plays a role in many activities that students are expected to master to be successful in school.

The Role of Neurological Development in School

The neurological development of children and adolescents is complex, and it is integrally related to student performance in school. There is so much more to school than academics or book learning. Success in school depends on mastery of skills in other areas as well, such as social skills, behavior, physical skills, memory, and organization. Let's revisit Dr. Mel Levine's theory on neurodevelopmental systems, and look at how each of the eight systems is related to school performance. Table 5.5 reviews the eight systems. The first column lists the systems, and the second column demonstrates what each system controls. The third column describes possible behaviors of students who are strong in that system, and the fourth column describes possible behaviors of students who have difficulty with that system.

Table 5.5.   Eight systems of school performance

System	This system...	If you are strong in this system, you might...	If you are not so strong in this system, you might...
Attention control	• Distributes mental energy to finish tasks and stay alert. • Regulates thinking to plan and work efficiently. • Resists temptations to let your mind wander; filters out distractions.	• Concentrate on a teacher's lecture for a long time. • Finish lengthy tasks in one sitting. • Put later social plans out of your mind to concentrate on your homework first. • Have consistent work behavior in school.	• Listen to a lecture for a few minutes, then find yourself thinking about something else. • Have difficulty initiating or following through on a task. • Become easily lured away from work by your own mind. • Have excellent days and poor days in school.

System	This system...	If you are strong in this system, you might...	If you are not so strong in this system, you might...
Memory	• Includes three parts—short term, long term, and working memory. • Codes, stores, and retrieves information.	• Easily create and use methods for remembering larger amounts of information.	• Have trouble remembering information because you can't "find where you put it." • Understand what the homework is when the teacher tells you, but later at home you're pretty sure there isn't any because you don't recall it.
Language	Includes: • Automatic (everyday) and literate (academic) language • Concrete and abstract language (e.g., baseball v. sportsmanship). • Basic (practical) and higher (inferential) language. • Receptive (input) and expressive (output) language.	• Easily communicate orally or in writing. • Have an advanced vocabulary. • Easily adjust language use for different environments. • Be a good listener and a good speaker.	• Misinterpret things that are said to you. • Often have that "on the tip of your tongue" feeling. • Get in trouble or teased for saying the wrong thing. • Have trouble inferring things from a story if not spelled out directly.
Spatial ordering	• Deals with or creates information in a gestalt, or visual configuration. • Perceives how things fit together. • Recognizes visual patterns.	• Think in pictures. • Easily visualize dramatic events occurring in a story • Easily discern even the subtlest of patterns. • Have a photographic memory. • Work best with an overall picture of the task to do.	• Often put shoes on the wrong feet or button a shirt incorrectly. • Get lost easily; have a poor sense of direction. • Lose things easily; can't picture where they are.
Sequential ordering	• Processes chains of information. • Orders information in a chronology.	• Easily follow multistep direction in order. • Work best with linear, step-by-step procedures. • Have a great sense of time, always on time.	• Often forget steps in multistep directions. • Often late to class or misjudge a how much time a task will take. • Have difficulty remembering phone numbers or formulas.
Motor	Includes: • Fine motor skills • Gross motor skills • Graphic motor skills (writing) • Oromotor skills (speaking) • Musical motor skills	• Have very good eye-hand coordination. • Fast at typing. • Have good handwriting. • Be athletic and graceful. • Be good at tongue-twisters.	• Have difficulty throwing, catching, or kicking a ball accurately. • Hunt and peck at the keyboard. • Have messy handwriting. • Often move clumsily or awkwardly. • Often misspeak.
Higher thinking	Includes: • Problem solving • Logic reasoning • Forming and using abstract concepts and complicated ideas; symbolism • Critical thinking • Creative thinking • Understanding of rules	• Invent things. • Enjoy learning and concepts such as energy conservation more than facts or dates. • Understand rules and how they apply to situations. • Be able to brainstorm many original ideas.	• Have difficulty with rule-based subjects, such as math or foreign languages. • Be able to remember what you did. before, but have difficulty coming up with new ways. • Rather learn facts and dates than abstract concepts such as irony.
Social thinking	Includes: • Communication and interpretation of feelings • Code-switching • Topic selection and maintenance • Conversational technique • Humor regulation • Requesting skill • Perspective taking • Affective matching • Complimenting • Lingo fluency	• Be comfortable speaking with people in many different types of groups (teachers, peers, younger children). • Understand and appropriately use sarcasm and humor. • Listen and converse easily. • Easily ask for or offer help. • Easily see a situation from another's point-of-view.	• Often say or do the wrong thing in a social situation. • Often misunderstand sarcasm and take it literally. • Speak too informally to teachers or too formally to peers • Have difficulty telling when someone is bored or bothered by your comments • Have difficulty understanding that someone else views the situation differently than you.

Source: Levine, 2002.

It is easy to see how performance in school can be affected by strengths and challenges in each of the systems. Rarely, if ever, is a learner strong across all eight neurodevelopmental systems. It is natural for each learner to be stronger in some systems than in others. Many times, however, learners have to be strong across the board to meet all of the expectations for success in school. Dr. Levine summarized this in the following excerpt from *A Mind at a Time*:

> It's taken for granted in adult society that we cannot all be generalists skilled in every area of learning and mastery. Nevertheless, we apply tremendous pressure on our children to be good at *everything*. Every day they are expected to shine in math, reading, writing, speaking, spelling, memorization, comprehension, problem solving, socialization, athletics, and following verbal directions. Few if any children can master all of these "trades." And none of us adults can. In one way or another, all minds have their specialties and their frailties. (Levine, 2002, p. 23)

The Role of Identity Development in School

Identity and social development, as discussed earlier in this chapter, are intertwined to some extent. They are also highly dependent on the context in which they develop. Look back at Erikson's stages of identity development, and you can see that they are influenced by the actions and reactions of parents and other caregivers surrounding the children during that stage of development. When children are ready to start preschool, they are, according to Erikson's theory, developing a sense of purpose in their surroundings. If caregivers (teachers) allow children to explore their interests, to be creative in how they interact with toys and other children, and gently but consistently guide them in learning skills, children will begin to learn what their purpose is as a young learner and early playmate. If teachers limit exploration and expect that there is only one right way or one right time to play, the children's sense of purpose will be dependent on the adults' sense of purpose for them, rather than their own.

Erikson noted that during the grade-school years, children and young adolescents are developing their sense of competence (Novak and Peláez, 2004). If teachers create a learning community that values diverse ideas, opinions, and strengths, the children will feel a sense of belonging in a context where they are viewed as competent and appreciated. If children are given opportunity to interact and collaborate on projects, with room to disagree and gentle guidance to work through the disagreements, they will feel able to handle situations on their own. In contrast, if during these grade-school years, teachers create a context that values only certain ideas or strengths (e.g., traditional academic strengths), then children who have other talents to offer will not feel a sense of value or competence. If students are not encouraged to interact toward new learning or if disagreements are met quickly by the teacher's intervention and solving the problem for them, children will not feel competent to handle problems on their own. Likely, they will always seek adult help to resolve any issues that come along.

During the high school years and into the young adult years, according to Erikson's theory, adolescents are developing a sense of fidelity. If they are surrounded by adults who understand and appreciate them for who they are and provide them with ways to nurture the strengths, likes, and idiosyncrasies they possess, they will feel self-assured in the unique person that they are growing to be. They will likely find an occupation and hobbies that suit them and fulfill them. If, however, they are made to feel that they fall short of a socially constructed view of success (e.g., straight As, athletic, business-minded), they may spend many hours engaged in activities they do not enjoy, just because they feel like they should be doing them. In this case, we may all lose, because people who think in nontraditional ways may be kept from reaching their full potential in areas that benefit us all (e.g., creating art or organizing nonprofit endeavors).

Overall, the role that identity development plays is whether or not a child or adolescent grows up feeling that school is for him.

The Role of Social Development in School

The importance of social skills plays out in various ways during the school years. In primary and elementary school, younger children may be asked to master skills they are still developing. For example, we often expect youngsters to share well by the time they enter school. The practice of sharing often begins in preschool, but may take years for children to fully master. It is very important to be aware of the developmental milestones before expecting children to act older than they are in social situations.

During middle school, the social aspect, at least in the minds of tweens, is far more important than academics. There is no separating socializing from any bit of the school day, from class to lunch, to extracurricular activities. As Levine so aptly put it:

> Children's social abilities occupy center stage in school. The social spotlights are glaring. They illuminate a galaxy of interpersonal strengths and shortcomings. Interactions with peers yield the bulk of the gratification or humiliation a student experiences in life. Some kids seem to be born with distinct social talents that allow for friendship formation and a solid reputation; others have to be taught to relate….School affords little to no privacy. Those who have stunted functions for social interactions are condemned to feel the pain of exposure and daily humiliation. (2002, p. 35)

During high school, social development plays a role in how independent adolescents are able to be. It is important to provide them with autonomy as well as back-up when they need help. Adults sometimes trap them in the middle by asking them to act grown-up while hovering over them at the same time, micromanaging their studies and social lives. It's a hard balance to strike.

The Role of Linguistic Development in School

Speech and language skills are emphasized in school a great deal. The ability to speak clearly and confidently is called upon in every school context. The bulk of classroom activities and formative assessment involve spontaneous oral response to teacher questions. Classrooms are mostly verbal-linguistic settings (Gardner, 1991). To stay abreast, students are expected to receive and express language swiftly and accurately from a young age.

The Role of Physical Development in School

We mustn't forget how much is asked of children in school that depends on their physical and motor development. Children and adolescents are asked to sit still in their seats for extended amounts of time, without fidgeting.

They are asked to have command over their fine- and gross-motor control skills, to hold pencils, draw, cut, and write in cursive, as well as demonstrate all the different skills asked of them in physical education—running, kicking, throwing, catching, and executing pull-ups, sit-ups, and lay-ups.

Finally, on top of it all, by middle and high school, there is pressure to be fit and attractive and physically mature. Society, via messages in the media, assigns value to certain definitions of physical beauty, strength, and athletic ability.

Welcome to Holland
by Emily Perl Kingsley

I am often asked to describe the experience of raising a child with a disability—to try to help people who have not shared that unique experience to understand it, to imagine how it would feel. It's like this....

When you're going to have a baby, it's like planning a fabulous vacation trip to Italy. You buy a bunch of guide books and make your wonderful plans. The Coliseum. Michelangelo's David. The gondolas in Venice. You may learn some handy phrases in Italian. It's all very exciting.

After months of eager anticipation, the day finally arrives. You pack your bags and off you go. Several hours later, the plane lands. The stewardess comes in and says, "Welcome to Holland."

"Holland?!?" you say. "What do you mean, Holland?? I signed up for Italy! I'm supposed to be in Italy. All my life I've dreamed of going to Italy."

But there's been a change in the flight plan. They've landed in Holland and there you must stay.

The important thing is that they haven't taken you to a horrible, disgusting, filthy place, full of pestilence, famine, and disease. It's just a different place.

So you must go out and buy new guide books. And you must learn a whole new language. And you will meet a whole new group of people you would never have met.

It's just a different place. It's slower paced than Italy, less flashy than Italy. But after you've been there for a while and you catch your breath, you look around...and you begin to notice that Holland has windmills... and Holland has tulips. Holland even has Rembrandts.

But everyone you know is busy coming and going from Italy...and

(continued)

DEVELOPMENT IN THE CONTEXT OF DISABILITY

This section puts the theories and their roles in the school context into a frame of reference. For anyone who works with children, it is important to know about typical development and standard expectations of schools. However, it is even more important to understand that not all children follow the assumed progression.

Think about the theories discussed earlier in this chapter. The developmental stages and expected ages should be used as signposts, steering us in the right direction, rather than used as the only acceptable progression from point A to point B. When reading theories about how children *typically* develop, it is important to be careful not to equate that with *normal* or *acceptable* development. It may be that most children develop a certain way, but not all do, and those who do not, may not be in trouble. They are different or *atypical*, and that is okay.

Picture it this way: Children who are developing atypically are developing off the beaten path. They will probably still get from point A to point B, but it may take longer. The way may not always be clearly visible. There may be obstacles to walk over, around, or move out of the way. They may need to backtrack a bit or rest before moving on. They may need additional equipment or supplies or support along the way, but it still a perfectly travelable path. Once they have reached Point B, they are still at Point B with everyone else. They will have accomplished what others have. In fact, a journey during which one overcomes many challenges along the way while learning about oneself, one's strengths and weaknesses, one's resourcefulness and resolve, and one's persistence and support system, may be the more educational journey. You can see more on the scenic route.

Consider the end of Kingsley's (1987) article (see sidebar) and the important issue it addresses. If parents or teachers get stuck on the fact that children are off the path, they may miss that the new path has value as well. Also, it is important to note the times when children *are* on the typical path. If a child is different in one area, he is not necessarily different in all areas. Not everything he does is due to his disability. For example, the mother of Tim, a ninth-grader with cognitive delays, received a telephone call from her son's special education teacher one day. The teacher indicated a need to add a social skill goal to Tim's IEP concerning his interactions with female peers. When the mother asked why that would be needed, she was told that an incident had occurred in school that day. Tim was seated in one of his classrooms waiting for class to start when a girl he admired entered the room. Tim called out, "Hey, pretty, sit next to me!" Tim's mother was overjoyed! Flirting with a girl, albeit a little awkwardly, is perfectly typical for a 15-year-old boy.

Recall the structure and expectations of school. The benefit of this structure is that it allows school districts and state education agencies to map out a plan—a scope and sequence—for each of the subject areas to be sure everything is covered and that there is not too much discrepancy across schools in curriculum covered in each grade. Subsequent benefits to this planning include: comprehensive coverage of content, teachers know what they will be responsible to teach depending on their grade level and subject-area assignments, students moving from district to district can expect a fairly smooth transition in terms of curriculum content, and benchmarks can be established for student progression "through the ranks."

A drawback to this type of district and state planning is that it establishes a fairly strict expected norm. It assumes there is a single, typical way and standard pace for students to progress through all of the content ahead of them for 13 years. The scope and sequence do not allow for peaks and valleys in performance or learning rate due to diverse processing. If all students are assumed and expected to move through the knowledge and skills as outlined, what happens when a student does not perform as expected? Rather than see this as a difference that warrants attention, patience, and creative problem solving, in this type of system, teachers and administrators unfortunately sometimes see this student as an outlier, a detriment to the flow, and a problem. Students with learning differences or learning challenges can be seen as wrenches in the works, rather than as diverse people who provide opportunities for teachers to embrace as learning experiences for themselves.

WHAT TEACHERS SHOULD KNOW ABOUT CHILD AND ADOLESCENT DEVELOPMENT

So, what to do with all of this information? As teachers, you need to keep an understanding of development in mind and respond accordingly so that all students are supported to reach their full potential. It seems like a daunting task, but it is not so formidable if it is built on a foundation of acceptance and inclusion. Keep these considerations in mind to begin building that foundation. Consider what Cady Welch has to say in Narrative 5.1.

(continued)

they're all bragging about what a wonderful time they had there. And for the rest of your life, you will say, "Yes, that's where I was supposed to go. That's what I had planned."

And the pain of that will never, ever, ever, *ever* go away...because the loss of that dream is a very, *very* significant loss.

But if you spend your life mourning the fact that you didn't get to Italy, you may never be free to enjoy the very special, the very lovely things...about Holland.

NARRATIVE 5.1. | CADY WELCH

My name is Cady Welch, I am 19 years old, and I attend Moss High School and Wes Watkins Technology Center. I live in Hughes County, Oklahoma. I want to live here in my hometown when I am 25. I have a job here at my school. I work as a teacher's aide and a secretary's aide. As a teacher's aide, I laminate papers, cut out circles, make little booklets, make copies, and several other things. As a secretary's aide, I answer the telephone, run errands, file papers, and different things that you do in an office.

My family has always wanted the best for me. They have always encouraged me when I needed their help. They have been with me every step of the way. Furthermore, my friends have supported me when I have needed them. They have always covered for me when something has happened. My friends and I also enjoy going to the movies, shopping, bowling, riding 4-wheelers, fishing, hunting, photography, and cooking.

My future plans are to help my dad, finish at Wes Watkins Technology Center, and to work at a bank. School isn't that difficult, it's just complicated for some students because they have trouble understanding and learning what teachers are teaching or what they are supposed to learn. What would help teachers be good teachers is to let the students take their homework home, because not all of the kids can finish in class or when class is over like the other students.

Some students have trouble finishing homework as fast as the other students. The students who struggle to finish their work are better off if they take homework home. Students want to do their best in school. In order to do that, they need extra time on their work than other kids. School is a good place to be because you can get a good education that helps you achieve and earn your goals, which prepares you for the real world.

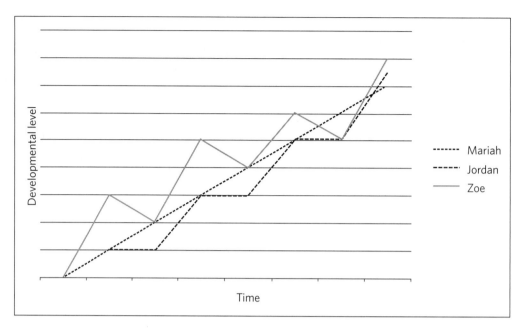

Figure 5.3.   Levels of development over time.

On the Right Path

First and foremost, as you think about the various theories on development, keep in mind that these are *theories*, general rules of thumb. There are always individuals who will progress in ways that do not fit the model described by theorists. Uniqueness in the way that children develop reminds us that they are each highly individual works of art. There are several different paths of development that children might take. Consider the three examples in Figure 5.3.

Mariah progresses steadily and evenly. She gains skills and knowledge a little bit at a time, over time. Each week or month in school, she masters new content and abilities and applies them consistently so that her progress in the future is predictable. Jordan, in contrast, progresses in spurts. He gains a great deal of skills and knowledge all at once, then plateaus for a while, using and applying the abilities he has mastered, but perhaps not taking on anything new for a while. Then, when he is ready, a new set of accomplishments will come in a spurt. Finally, let's look at Zoe. She undeniably progresses in her abilities over time, but in a more unpredictable way. She may have setbacks, so that she is not consistently applying her knowledge and skills. We may see her able to perform a particular skill one week, then not be able to perform it as well the next week. Once she has enough practice, perhaps scaffolded by more knowledgeable others, she is ready to progress once more.

As you can see, all three children progress to the top of the graph over time. In this instance, they arrive at roughly the same time, but in other instances that may not be the case. There is no one right way and no one right time to arrive. Each child does it the right way for him or her. Mariah's way is perfect for Mariah, Jordan's way is perfect for Jordan, and Zoe's way is perfect for Zoe. As teachers, our job is not to change or fix the way students are, but to support their individual paths.

Many Ways to Be Smart

Traditionally, society has defined smart as adept at reading, writing, math, and other school tasks—in other words, "book smart." We must think beyond traditional constructions of what it means to be smart. In *The Unschooled Mind: How Children Think and How Schools Should Teach*, Gardner (1991) fully explained the theory of multiple intelligences as well as the empirical research that supports the theory. In his work, Gardner does not discount the theory of development put forth by Piaget; rather, he goes beyond it, illustrating our growing understanding of the complexity and uniqueness of each child's mind. Rather than anticipating that most children will develop in unison through each Piagetan stage, new theories urge us to see biological, neurological, cultural, and individual differences in each child.

It is a teacher's job to nurture the different ways that students are smart. Gardner (1991) originally described 7 *intelligences* in his theory, ultimately growing the list to include the 11 listed here:

1. Verbal-linguistic

2. Logical-mathematical

3. Musical

4. Bodily-kinesthetic

5. Visual-spatial

6. Interpersonal

7. Intrapersonal

8. Naturalist

9. Spiritual

10. Existentialist

11. Moral

In reviewing this list and thinking of people we know who are truly gifted in these areas, it seems almost absurd to think about book smart as the only way to be smart. Classrooms and schools need to offer different types of learning to students, so they can shine in their own unique ways. This is not easy. Teachers, too, have their own unique intelligences, so it is easiest for them to come up with lessons and activities that reflect those particular areas. It is much harder to come up with ideas that are outside your comfort zone or familiarity. Planning lessons should entail consulting many different resources that provide examples of traditional and nontraditional school activities (see the appendix of this book, Resources for Comprehensive Teaching).

Think of the benefit to all learners to be surrounded by classmates who are talented in so many different ways and are encouraged to share those talents every day in the classroom. It is deceptive to send the message to our students that book smart is the only form of intelligence or that some kids are "good" students and some are not. Like snowflakes and fingerprints, no two mind profiles are alike (Levine, 2002).

Glad You're Here

Classrooms are communities of learners. Everyone belongs in these communities and has the right to full citizenship in the classroom. Kliewer (1998) outlined four elements of full citizenship in the classroom: 1) a belief in one's ability to think, 2) a belief in one's individuality, 3) a belief in the reciprocity of the relationship, and 4) a shared location. A true inclusive community, where all members are full citizens, understands that everyone is competent, that everyone is a thinker. In these communities, everyone is seen as an individual, not automatically the same as others who share their age, grade level, or disability label. In these communities, everyone believes that she benefits from interaction with everyone else—everyone is a teacher and everyone is a learner. Finally, in these communities, everyone shares a location where risks can safely be taken without fear of discouragement, criticism, or failure so that mistakes can lead to growth through encouragement, constructive critique, and success.

As children and adolescents develop their own identities, they need nurturing, supportive learning communities where they are appreciated as valued, contributing members. As they develop social skills, it is important for a teacher to realize that not every student is strong in the area of social thinking and processing. Students do not mess up socially on purpose. They do not bring teasing upon themselves. Everyone wants to fit in and be understood in his or her own way. It is not the same way for everyone. For one student, it may be having lots of friends around a lot of the time. For another, it may be having one or two good friends around some of the time. For another, it may be having lots of alone time, connecting with one friend on occasion. There is no one right way to be socially happy, but everyone is entitled to be happy with her social life.

Some students may need direct instruction in appropriate social interactions. Stephen Hinkle (2010) talked about the hidden social curriculum: Students who have challenges in social thinking and processing need direct instruction in the obvious and subtle nuances of social situations. An example is knowing when to clap your hands as a member of an audience. Those who are able to pick up easily on social cues and are strong in social thinking do not realize all of the small bits of knowledge and skill involved in appropriate interactions. Conducting a task analysis to see all the tiny steps would surprise most teachers.

For Everything There Is a Season

Cooing, babbling, crawling, walking, playing, smiling, laughing, hugging, listening, helping, comforting, and sharing are all part of developing. So are grabbing, lying, stealing, tattling, fighting, rebelling, manipulating, clinging, swearing, and cheating. As children develop, they display the pleasant and the not-so-pleasant aspects of humanity. When they display the not-so-pleasant, they are not broken or wrong. They are still in the process of learning. They need to be taught, not fixed or punished. Alfie Kohn (1996) stated in *Beyond Discipline: From Compliance to Community* that what teachers believe truly matters. If we see students as nasty or brutish, that is how we will respond to them. If we see them as competent, caring individuals who have more to learn, that is how we will respond.

The Right to be Different

All students have the right to a free and appropriate education. All students have the right to a school setting free of violence and drugs. All students have the right to a balanced lunch at school. All students have the right to teach the teacher something. All students have the right to be different.

There will be days when you feel challenged as a teacher. There will be days when you are exhausted and feel like you are running on a treadmill that won't slow down. Expect it so you can prepare for it. It is not fair to tell you that it will be easy and that you can plan a perfect lesson that will go off without a hitch. If that were the case, the first chaotic day or first bombed lesson would chew you up and spit you out. Expect a child to display inappropriate behaviors. Expect a child not to understand the concept you are teaching. Expect a child to throw up in the middle of your lesson. Embrace the opportunity to learn how to prepare for and handle all of these contingencies. Be thankful that these events will improve your teaching every time they happen. You don't want teaching to be boring, do you?

SUMMARY

This chapter discussed several types of development for children and adolescents—cognitive, neurological, identity, social, linguistic, and physical development—in three different contexts. First, an overview of typical development in each area was covered. Second, each area of development was discussed in the context of school and what each student is able to do at each grade level. Third, the areas of development were discussed in terms of difference and what it means when a student does not follow a typical path or rate of development. The chapter concluded with an overview of why it is important for teachers to understand the areas of development, typical student progress, and atypical student progress. Knowing where each student is developmentally is part of knowing all of the diverse aspects of that individual. Good teachers consider all aspects of diversity when planning instruction for their students.

CHAPTER 6

Classroom Management

How this chapter prepares you to be an effective inclusive classroom teacher:

- This chapter emphasizes actively creating inclusive learning environments that support all students, foster cultural understandings, promote safety and emotional well-being, support positive social interactions, and facilitate active engagement of all students. You are introduced to the importance of expecting all students to learn and to providing supports in a way that helps each student be successful. PBIS and the FBA process are introduced. This chapter also provides a brief introduction to how to support students who live in poverty, who are learning English, or who are perceived to be members of the LGBT community. It outlines the PBIS pyramid and is designed to be read by all preservice teachers—including general education teachers—to integrate all students and engage them in meaningful learning activities and interactions. It concludes with a review of the FBA process and provides examples of data collection to help determine why a behavior is happening. **This helps you meet CEC Standard 5: Learning Environments and Social Interactions.**

- The need to support students who are learning English is introduced in this chapter. **This helps you meet CEC Standard 6: Language.**

- In this chapter, we reiterate the importance of high expectations and the provision of opportunity for social and academic success for all students. This aligns with the need for you to be aware of how your own and others' attitudes, behaviors, and ways of communicating can influence your practice as well as the practices of others. **This helps you meet CEC Standard 9: Professional and Ethical Practice.**

After reading and discussing this chapter, you will be able to

- Define classroom community in your own words

- Explain the importance of teachers' beliefs about students related to community building

- Explain how to complete class activities at the beginning of the year to create community

- Explain how to conduct a class meeting

- Explain how to teach students to manage conflicts respectfully

- Explain why it is important to sustain community throughout the year

- Describe the barriers to academic success for students who live in poverty, are learning English, or are perceived to be members of the LGBT community

- Create a pyramid with the 80/15/5 configuration and explain the kinds of support each group of students needs

- Create a list of daily, weekly, monthly, and infrequent routines

- Define differentiated instruction

- Explain what individual routines might look like for a student

- Define PBIS and explain what it means

- Define FBA, explain what it means, and explain the steps in the FBA process

build community   The strategies and activities teachers use to help students feel safe and welcome in the classroom.

In this chapter, we will explore how teachers **build community** and manage their classrooms. The topics are intertwined; a positive and supportive community helps classroom management, and mutual respect, clear routines, and clear expectations help a community flourish. Classroom management is the biggest single concern of new teachers, and this chapter will provide support through information, narratives, and activities. Our focus is on proactive community-building approaches, rather than reactive or punitive approaches.

In the first section of the chapter, classroom communities are described and the teacher's role in creating community is explained. In the second section, classroom management is reviewed, and different approaches are described. The narrative is from Rachel Zindler, an experienced teacher-turned-consultant who describes strategies for developing community and establishing positive classroom management.

Before beginning, please understand that no matter how much you plan, unexpected things will happen—probably every day! Having a strong, nurturing community and good classroom management will help you and your students deal with whatever arises. This is vital, because the one thing you can expect in teaching is the unexpected. We have had field trips cancelled at the last minute, unannounced fire drills, a student throwing up on the teacher's desk, and a bee disrupt a lesson. The trick is to be flexible within a strong community, and we will show you how.

BUILDING COMMUNITY

What is a classroom community, and how do teachers develop it? Mara Sapon-Shevin noted that

Community building is about how adults talk to students, it's about what's on the walls, the books we read, and the songs we sing. And it's about what happens when something goes wrong in class....Community building centers on two things: establishing (proactively) norms of community and responding thoughtfully to challenges to that sense of community. Community building requires thinking—*before* the name calling, the conflict on the playground, or the formation of cliques— about what the culture of the classroom will be and how these norms will be established with students. (2007, pp. 146–147)

Think about your time in elementary and high school. Which of your teachers had the most welcoming, supportive classroom? That did not happen by chance. Teachers think a lot about how to create welcoming spaces, because a student who feels safe and supported learns more easily than a student who feels anxious or afraid. Creating a comfortable classroom where students are expected and encouraged to take risks and make mistakes is an essential skill for teachers, and by building a classroom community you will do just that.

Community begins with the fundamental beliefs that a teacher holds. If a teacher believes that every student is capable of learning and is fundamentally good, all the planning and arrangements that stem from those beliefs reflect that caring and support. If a teacher believes (even if she or he might not say so) that some students are not capable of learning, and that some students are fundamentally bad, the classroom will reflect that, too. The teacher's core beliefs are at the very heart of classroom community (Figure 6.1).

We believe that all students can learn and that all students are fundamentally good. This does not mean that students can do no wrong, but it does mean that when students act in ways that are not acceptable, we work to address the behavior that needs replacing without assuming there is something fundamentally bad about the student. *There is no such thing as a bad child.*

How do you build a community? By interacting with every student, by responding with compassion when students interact with each other, and by setting the tone in your classroom.

You are the model for your students in every interaction: how you speak to other teachers, to other adults, to your own students, and to students from other classes. Your students watch and learn from what you say and how you act. How you handle feeling frustrated and how you manage a conflict or teach problem-solving skills may be as important as the content you teach. Some of the skills you need to know and to teach students include how to get to know each other, how to be respectful, how to manage conflict, how to work in groups, and how to give and receive help. We have divided these skills into two groups: how to build community and how to sustain community. Then, we talk about specific groups of students who may be in your class.

To build community, you must plan deliberately for students to get to know each other; their backgrounds, strengths, and weaknesses are all part of what makes each student unique. At the beginning of the year or semester or quarter, take the time to do getting-to-know you activities with your students. You may think that taking time away from content instruction is impossible, or a waste of time, but we disagree. While teachers

---

I have come to a frightening conclusion. I am the decisive element in the classroom. It is my personal approach that creates the climate. It is my daily mood that makes the weather. As a teacher, I possess tremendous power to make a child's life miserable or joyous. I can be a tool of torture or an instrument of inspiration. I can humiliate or humour, hurt or heal. In all situations, it is my response that decides whether a crisis will be escaped or de-escalated, and a child humanized or dehumanized. —Haim Ginott, Teacher and Child *(1972), p. 13*

Figure 6.1. Excerpt from *Teacher and Child.*

cannot spend days and days on community building, think about this: Part of good teaching is getting to know your students, so that you can teach each group in ways that best suit their needs. If you do not get to know each student and each group of students, you will probably spend some of your instructional time managing the behavior of the group. Instead of losing time later on, reacting to problems, spend some time at the beginning of the year on positive activities. If you are proactive about management early on, you will not have to be reactive later in the year.

Build Community

The beginning of the year is an exciting, nervous time for students and teachers; so much lies ahead, and there is a wealth of possibility. Teachers can use many activities on the first day of school to help students feel welcome and to get to know one another, build community, and communicate expectations.

Some teachers introduce themselves even before the first day of school by mailing a postcard to each student when they get their class lists in August. They may call families or make home visits so that on that on the first day of school, the student and family already feel welcome and valued.

When planning activities to complete with the class, be sure to consider what students might feel comfortable with early in the year and what information may make some of them feel excluded. For example, some students may go on relatively expensive vacations, while others have never left town. Both experiences are important to value, but highlighting the differences early in the year may make the middle- to upper-class student feel bad about having more opportunities, and the less affluent student feel bad for having fewer resources. Both backgrounds deserve value, and over the course of the year, those differences can be explored. On the first day, ask students to share personal and family information that helps everyone get to know each other as individuals.

Here are two examples of class activities—a class puzzle and social bingo (see Table 6.1).

Class Puzzle   Cut poster board into 6-inch puzzle pieces and ask each student to draw or write personal information on one, such as his or her name, age, and family members. Other information varies by grade. First and second graders may report how many teeth they have lost; fourth and fifth graders may include a favorite song, book, or movie; high school students may include future career plans.

If a new student enters the class, redo the class puzzle; the old puzzle will not reflect all members and is no longer complete. The new puzzle gives students a chance to share who they are with the new student, and the new student gets a chance to join the community and feel valued. It also allows students to update their information and gives them a fresh start.

Table 6.1.   Strategies for building community

Class meetings
Class puzzle
Social bingo
Class covenant
Conflict resolution steps
Collaborative group work
Mailboxes for each student, at desks or cubbies
Postcards to send to classmates

Social Bingo   In this popular icebreaker for older students, teachers create a 5×5 grid on a piece of paper. A fact is typed in each box and a signature line is left blank beneath it. The grid's center square has a line for the student's name. When the papers are passed out, each student signs his or her own paper in the center square. Then, students get up and mingle, trying to get a signature from each classmate in a box that describes them. Examples of facts for the board: has more than five siblings, has been to the state capitol, likes pickles and peanut butter sandwiches, has read (a book from the grade level reading list), has slept in a tent, knows how to knit, or has a pet iguana. As with the class puzzle, be careful to include facts that students would be comfortable disclosing to each other, and do not highlight inequities in economic resources. For example, we would not recommend including "has been to Europe" for an icebreaker in the first days of school.

Develop Class Rules or Covenant   After getting-to-know-you activities, the next step is to help students think about your expectations and the class structure. Developing a set of expectations and rules for the group is essential in the first days of school. There is debate about how to do this effectively. If you simply say to students, "These are the rules," students will know what you want. But they may not agree with you and may not think your rules are fair.

An alternate route is to ask students which rules they think the class should have. The opportunity to take part in a process that is grounded in shared decisions and democratic principles is important, and an open discussion about class rules will provide that opportunity. Criticism of this strategy is that it feels faked; really, the teacher knows which rules he or she would like, and asking students for their input might seem inauthentic. If this is a concern for you, you might share with students the issues that you are vested in: for example, emotional and physical safety for everyone, and a way to be organized and clear about what to do. If you share this background before you invite your students to develop rules that are open for revision, you can be authentic about sharing the responsibility.

A balancing act between ensuring a positive, safe learning environment and allowing students input is the goal. In considering the expectations and rules you would like to have in your classroom, remember that you must follow school and district rules. If your principal has a rule against hats in school, you should not change that. This may sound simple, but it matters! The tone you set for your classroom needs to respect the rules of the building and district. If you or the students do not like a school or district rule, talk about it and consider investigating the reasons for it.

A second consideration is to limit the number of rules. There is a lot of advice about the ideal number, but generally having between three and five rules is recommended (Gable, Hester, Rock, & Hughes, 2009). More than that, and students may simply feel regulated and as though they are always going to be caught doing something wrong. Also, it is vital to make rules clear and easy to understand. Finally, try to phrase rules positively. For example, "Use inside voices" is better than "No shouting"; "Use walking feet" is easier to understand and do than "No running." When you say the rule, you are saying what you *want*, and the students can try to meet that expectation. Stating what *not* to do adds a layer of complexity that makes doing what you want more difficult. A student may hear "do not run" and focus only on the word "run."

Class rules can vary from relatively specific to broader ones that encompass many behaviors. Specific rules are those such as, "Use inside voices," while more general ones include "Be respectful" or "Do your best." In one classroom, we saw three posters, each with a heading: Be Safe. Be Kind. Work Hard. Under each heading, students had brainstormed specific examples of what that behavior looked like in their classroom.

Each of your rules will be specific to your situation and can be the focus of discussion in your class. This discussion will sometimes result in rules that you might not have included or have ever thought about. If the list has more than five or six rules, plan to revisit, review, and revise it in 2 weeks. This second meeting is a great way to check in about how things are going and what needs to change or stay the same. It also provides a positive way to talk about the class and may prevent small problems from becoming large ones. Some teachers choose to develop a class creed or covenant instead of a list of class rules; you will decide which strategy helps you connect with your students most effectively and sets a positive tone for learning in your classroom.

Sustain Community

Once the school year begins and students settle into familiar routines, the work of building community becomes the work of sustaining community. Current local and national events and events in the lives of students will provide opportunities to strengthen the community you have built. Class meetings are one strategy that many teachers at all grade levels use to support community. We use them in our college classes and find that the simple act of going around and sharing "something new or good" is an effective tool for learning about each person. A great resource for learning more about class meetings is *Positive Discipline in the Classroom* (Nelsen, Lott, & Glenn, 2000).

Continue Class Meetings   Teachers can sustain the classroom community by continuing to hold class meetings throughout the school year. Class meetings can be varied in many ways, and as the year progresses and students become skilled at participating in class meetings, you can expand their purpose. Instead of asking each student to report something new or good, new prompts can be introduced, or minilessons on a range of topics can be taught while the whole group is together. Examples of topics for minilessons are how to manage conflicts respectfully, how to work in groups, or how to give and receive help. They can be brief morning check-ins to help everyone feel welcomed and heard and they can provide a structure to air conflicts and problems. In an elementary classroom, students may review the contents of a suggestion box and discuss solutions. In secondary classrooms, students can communicate concerns about assignments, seating arrangements, and how to get needed support.

Manage Conflicts Respectfully   If class meetings are used for conflict resolution, it is important to have clear guidelines for participation and taking turns. Teaching strategies for handling emotions and addressing each other respectfully will benefit everyone in the classroom. One common model is to teach steps for conflict resolution, model the steps, and then make a visual aid—in pictures or writing. Here are six steps for teachers to help students who are angry:

1. Approach students calmly, and stop them from hurting each other

2. Acknowledge feelings

3. Gather information (this includes taking turns listening and telling)

4. Restate the problem

5. Ask for ideas to solve the problem and choose a solution together

6. Provide follow-up support (Church, 2007, p. 4).

These steps can be expanded or condensed based on the group you are teaching; some students may need practice identifying feelings, listening to other students, restating the problem, or generating alternatives. Each of these steps is a social skill that needs explicit teaching, practice, and support.

Teach Students to Work Collaboratively and in Groups   Collaborative work is an important part of sustaining community. If you provide competitive games and challenges, there will always be winners and losers. While being a winner can feel great, it is harder to justify any student's feeling like a loser in the classroom. Instead of creating ways to pit students against each other, we believe that students need opportunities to compete against their own performance, improve their skills, and collaborate with each other. Mara Sapon-Shevin wrote extensively about this issue in her book, *Widening the Circle: The Power of Inclusive Classrooms* (2007). She summarized Alfie Kohn's book, *No Contest: The Case Against Competition* (1986) and noted,

> Low achievers are rarely motivated by competition because they do not perceive themselves as having a chance to win. A small number of high achievers may be motivated, but they are generally motivated to "win," rather than to learn….And for all students, competition damages community and students' willingness to help one another. (p. 93)

We agree, and propose that teaching students to work *with* each other instead of *against* each other sustains community. Working in groups includes several skills: identifying what you need or want, being able to listen to others, and being able to talk about and practice compromise. Each skill is an important component of being a group member and these social skills can be taught explicitly to support group work.

Teach Students How to Give and Receive Help   Knowing how to give and receive help is another skill that students need in the classroom. Some students consistently fall into the role of the one being helped, while other students are identified as the helpers. This does not benefit either student. Helpers need to know about and learn from the strengths and gifts of other students, and students who receive help need practice being an expert who can teach others. One way to help everyone know about the strengths that each student has to offer is to make a resource book for the classroom. Every student writes down his or her strengths so that everyone else knows who to ask for help when they need it. Strengths might be linked to interests, such as "knows a lot about Spiderman and superheroes" or to academic skills such as "good at math" or "good at writing detailed paragraphs and peer editing."

Discuss Social Justice   It is important for students to understand how they can be active members of their community beyond the school. *Rethinking Schools*, a helpful resource for teachers, has a belief statement about the role of schools today:

> Schools are integral not only to preparing all children to be full participants in society, but also to be full participants in this country's ever-tenuous experiment in democracy.
>   There are many reasons to be discouraged about the future: School districts nationwide continue to slash budgets; violence in our schools and cities shows no signs of abating; attempts to privatize the schools have not slowed; and the country's productive resources are still used to make zippier shoes, rather than used in less profitable arenas like education and affordable housing. There is a Zulu expression: "If the future doesn't come toward you, you have to go fetch it." We believe teachers, parents, and students are essential to building a movement to go fetch a better future: in our classrooms, in our schools, and in the larger society. There are lots of us out there. Let's make our voices heard. (Rethinking Schools, 2011, para. 8–9)

We agree. An example of teaching students about activism and engagement in the community can be found in *Black Ants and Buddhists*, by Mary Cowhey (2006). She describes how her class of second-grade students learned about voting and the right to vote, and conducted a voter registration drive. Her students studied the civil rights movement, and learned about student activists and the history of the right to vote. Cowhey invited a local attorney to explain voters' rights to her students, and the class learned how to register to vote. Students who were not citizens were interested in knowing how to become citizens, and students and family members had a voter registration drive at the school for 3 days. A family member who is bilingual volunteered, and having a Spanish-speaking person at the table helped many adults get information about voting. Finally, the class took a field trip to city hall to turn in the voter registration cards to the registrar. The mayor asked the students to prepare an exhibit of drawings about their voter registration drive, and the class happily agreed. This is just one way that even young children can be active members of the community. The benefit of this kind of teaching is that, "learning through activism is powerful because the need to use academic skills for social justice motivates their acquisition" (Cowhey, 2006, p. 103).

Who Is in the Classroom?

You are going to have a wide range of students, with a wide range of experiences and needs. Strive to avoid putting children into categories; it is not true that any child who is unlike her peers needs different teaching; all children need high-quality, responsive instruction. You should support the strengths and needs of all children. Some children come from affluent families; others live in poverty. Some students know English because it is spoken at home; other students are fluent in a language that is not English and learn English at school (and are called English Language Learners—ELL). Some children live with two parents; others live with a grandparent, a single parent, with gay parents, in foster care, or with a family friend. Some children are heterosexual, others are lesbian, gay, bisexual, or transgendered (LGBT) or are perceived to be so. Your job is to create a safe, supportive environment for each of your students.

Teachers encounter realities that many others do not. We sometimes see children who do not have access to adequate nutrition, clothing, housing, or medical and dental care. Maslow's hierarchy of need tells us that basic human needs must be met before higher-order needs can be addressed:

> The basis of Maslow's theory of motivation is that human beings are motivated by unsatisfied needs, and that certain lower needs need to be satisfied before higher needs can be addressed. Per the teachings of Abraham Maslow, there are general needs (physiological, safety, love, and esteem) which have to be fulfilled before a person is able to act unselfishly (see Figure 6.2, Maslow's Hierarchy of Needs, 2005).

Practices to sustain community in the face of individual hardship include being sensitive to what students may want to share about their life experiences and being able to help students and their families access supports. Working to meet the basic needs of every child is not your job alone; your school social worker and community agencies will partner with your school and district to support children in getting their needs adequately met. Your role as a teacher is to gather information about resources that can help, and to work with families who would benefit from support.

Students and Poverty   Children who live in poverty may have concerns that other children do not, such as access to clean and safe housing and food security. One measure of poverty is the number of children who are eligible for free or reduced-price lunches at school. Every teacher, in no matter which state or district, needs to be aware that some students and families may need help getting adequate nutrition. This is essential for learning; Alaimo, Olson, and Frongillo (2001) noted that children who live in food-insecure households, where there is limited or uncertain availability of food, are more than twice as likely to have repeated a grade than their peers (p. 46).

The National School Lunch Program serves children whose families live below the level of poverty. In 2007–2008, the percentage of schools reporting that 76–100% of their

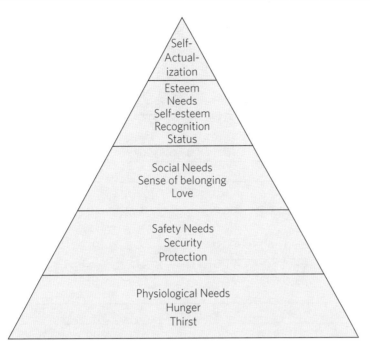

Figure 6.2. From MASLOW, ABRAHAM H.; FRAGER ROBERT D.; FADIMAN, JAMES, MOTIVATION AND PERSONALITY, 3rd Edition, © 1987. Adapted by permission of Pearson Education, Inc., Upper Saddle River, NJ.

White students were eligible for free and reduced lunch were 5.1%; the percentages reported for Black or Hispanic students were 40% and 41.5%, respectively (National Center for Education Statistics; see, Table 6.2).

Providing food for weekends for children and families is one solution. Foodlink Backpack Program and Blessings in a Backpack are examples. Blessings in a Backpack "is designed to feed elementary school children whose families qualify for the federal free and reduced meal program, and may not have any or enough food on the weekends" (Blessings in a Backpack, 2011). Blessings in a Backpack's web site notes that one out of every six children in the U.S. (12.4 million) is at risk of hunger and that the states with highest food insecurity are Mississippi, New Mexico, Texas, Arkansas, Maine, South Carolina, Georgia, Kansas, Oklahoma, and Missouri (Blessings in a Backpack, 2011).

Students Who Are Learning English   Children who are learning English as a second language have challenges that may include frequent moves, poverty, gaps in schooling, and language and cultural barriers (Rodriguez, Ringler, O'Neal, & Bunn, 2009). In the United States, the number of students who are learning English has dramatically increased in the last 10 years. Between the mid-1990s and mid-2000s, the number of students in the United States increased 3.7%, and at the same time, the number of English language learners increased 57% (Teale, 2009, p. 699). Most students learning English have Spanish as their first language.

What we know about students who are learning English as a second language is that they learn English in the same way as their native English-speaking peers. Good teaching includes linked assessment and instruction, clear learning objectives, consistent routines, many opportunities to practice reading and writing, and active student engagement, which are are important components of teaching all students—including those who are learning English (Teale, 2009). Specific strategies to support

Table 6.2. Students in school eligible for free or reduced-price lunch 2007–08

Table A-25-1. Number and percentage of public elementary and secondary students across schools, by percentage of students in school eligible for free or reduced-price lunch and race/ethnicity: School year 2007–08

| Race/ethnicity | Number of students[1] | Percentage of students in school eligible for free or reduced-price lunch | | | | | |
		Total	0–25	26–50	51–75	76–100	Missing/ school does not participate
Elementary							
Total[2]	31,176,444	100.0	25.4	25.6	23.5	19.9	5.5
White	16,713,023	100.0	35.5	32.2	20.3	5.1	6.9
Black	5,270,943	100.0	8.3	16.9	28.5	40.0	6.2
Hispanic	6,950,840	100.0	12.1	16.8	27.9	41.5	1.6
Asian/Pacific Islander	1,494,329	100.0	39.1	24.0	18.8	15.2	2.9
American Indian/ Alaska Native	359,663	100.0	12.2	23.9	31.6	28.1	4.3
Secondary							
Total[2]	16,112,947	100.0	36.2	33.8	17.3	6.5	6.3
White	9,386,497	100.0	47.1	35.4	8.9	1.2	7.4
Black	2,632,525	100.0	15.0	31.6	31.1	15.0	7.3
Hispanic	2,989,287	100.0	19.0	31.9	31.4	15.4	2.3
Asian/Pacific Islander	801,687	100.0	44.9	30.7	15.9	5.3	3.1
American Indian/ Alaska Native	193,173	100.0	23.5	33.0	24.7	14.5	4.3

[1]Includes students enrolled in schools that did not report free or reduced-price lunch eligibility.
[2]Includes students whose racial/ethnic group was not reported.

NOTE: The National School Lunch Program is a federally assisted meal program. To be eligible, a student must be from a household with an income at or below 130 percent of the poverty threshold for free lunch, or between 130 percent and 185 percent of the poverty threshold for reduced-price lunch. Race categories exclude persons of Hispanic ethnicity. For more information on race/ethnicity and poverty, see supplemental note 1. For more information on the Common Core of Data (CCD), see supplemental note 3. Detail may not sum to totals because of rounding.

Source: U.S. Department of Education, National Center for Education Statistics, Common Core of Data (CCD), "Public Elementary/Secondary School Universe Survey," 2007–08. Retrieved from http://nces.ed.gov/programs/coe/2010/section4/table-csp-1.asp

students who are learning English are using cognates (words that have the same origin) in English and another language, choral reading, teaching rhymes, acting out stories, creating individual word libraries, using peer support, and creating "language free" activities (such as a sensory table or dramatic play area) that do not require knowledge of English (Buteau & True, 2009).

Students and Their Families   Some children have families that include a mother and a father living together. But many children have other types of families— a single mother, a single father, a grandmother, gay or lesbian parents, or foster parents. The Census in 2000 showed that two-thirds of children lived in a family group that included a married couple (U. S. Census Bureau, 2004, p. 9). The other third lived in single-parent families (27%) or in a household with neither parent (5%) (U.S. Census Bureau, 2004, p. 9). Creating community includes honoring all types of families.

One way to reflect all families in an elementary school classroom is with a family tree. When one researcher was in an elementary school, she saw that each second grader's locker had a family tree worksheet taped to it. The top half was a picture of a tree with the child's name on the trunk, and the family members listed on its branches. The lower half was lined for the children to write a few sentences explaining who the family members were. This was a great activity that needed one simple change: The tree was labeled with "Mother" and "Father," which does not work for children without this particular family structure. If the tree were left blank, it would be ready for any family grouping.

Students Who Are Lesbian, Gay, Bisexual, or Transgendered   Students who are or are perceived to be lesbian, gay, bisexual, or transgendered often experience bullying. In fact, "the 2009 survey of 7,261 middle and high school students found that nearly 9 out of 10 LGBT students experienced harassment at school in the past year and nearly two-thirds felt unsafe because of their sexual orientation" (The Gay, Lesbian, and Straight Education Network, 2010). It is unacceptable for any student to feel unsafe in school; teachers need to find ways to actively support students who are LGBT. In a study of students and school climate, Diaz and Kosciw noted that "the availability of supportive school staff, Gay-Straight Alliances, LGBT inclusive curricular resources, and the presence of comprehensive anti-harassment school policies were related to improved school climate" (2009, p. 49). In addition to students who understand that they are members of the LGBT community, there are students who are questioning their identity and struggling to understand who they are and what that means for them. All students need access to supportive, caring adults who provide a safe space for listening.

You have now learned about how to build community and how to support all students. Next, you will learn about classroom management and how to be proactive about it.

CLASSROOM MANAGEMENT

There are many approaches to classroom management, and there is no one right way to do it. At a very basic level, if you treat each child with respect and focus on sustaining community, you are off to a good start. We believe that all good classroom management includes clear routines and expectations; high-quality, engaging instruction; supportive feedback; and individual routines and expectations. In this part of the chapter, these strategies will be reviewed.

When you consider your strategies and plans for classroom management, you must remember that you are responsible for the well-being of *every* child in your class; both the child who is bullied and the bully. You must teach and support both the child who acts out and needs a great deal of structure and the child who is quiet and asks for little support or attention. To achieve mutual respect, you must begin by knowing each of your students.

Alfie Kohn wrote that "the practices that flow from a teacher's beliefs tend to elicit certain things from students. Label a particular child a troublemaker and watch him become one" (1996, p. 7). If you expect children to act in a particular way, you will see that happen in your classroom. Your beliefs about children and students shape your classroom practices, and we firmly believe that there is no such thing as a bad child. There may be unacceptable behavior in the classroom and the need for many effective strategies to motivate and engage students, but we think that the child who challenges you the most is your best teacher. That child supports your inquiry and growth as a teacher and classroom manager.

The student who does not follow directions, turn in work, or respectfully communicate with you and others gives you the chance to develop your skills in adjusting the environment, the work, and the support strategies you use. The skills you acquire because of this student will allow you to proceed with more grace and ease the next time

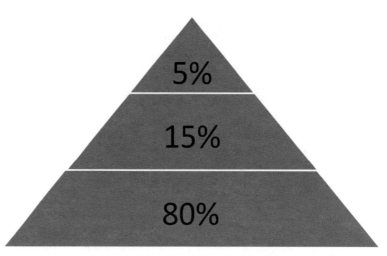

80% of students will respond to a classroom which includes
- Clear routines
- Clear expectations
- High-quality, engaging instruction
- Supportive feedback

15% of students will respond to a classroom which includes
- Clear routines, clear expectations, high-quality, engaging instruction, and supportive feedback
- Proximity
- Individual schedules
- Picture prompts
- Repeated directions

5% of students will respond to a classroom which includes
- Clear routines, clear expectations, high-quality, engaging instruction
- Supportive feedback, proximity, individual schedules, picture prompts, repeated directions
- Individual routines, academic expectations that are attainable for the individual student, behavioral expectations that are attainable for the individual student

Figure 6.3.   Classroom management pyramid.

you have a student who exhibits difficult behaviors. As you learn more about helping all students, you will become more and more skilled at using management strategies, and that range of strategies will increase and make you a better teacher.

The classroom management pyramid in Figure 6.3 illustrates that all students need clear routines; clear expectations; high-quality, engaging instruction; and supportive feedback. Some students need these strategies and in addition may need teacher proximity, individual schedules, pictures prompts, or repeated directions to be successful. A few students need all of these strategies and may also need individualized routines, academic expectations, and behavioral expectations. We have divided the classroom management pyramid into three groups, using an 80/15/5 configuration: approximately 80% of students who respond quite well to these factors, 15% of students who have difficulty doing their best without some additional supports, and approximately 5% of students who need even more intensive supports. The supports required by the middle group are often not particularly time consuming for a teacher to provide and are relatively simple to create or monitor.

Clear Routines and Expectations

Good classroom management begins with clear routines and expectations. If you are not organized, your students will not know what they are supposed to do and will quickly come up with their own ideas about how to use class time. Routines include daily tasks, such as entering the class, turning in homework, completing daily oral reading (DOR) or bell work (a brief academic task that is prominently posted for all students to begin as soon as they come in the room), lining up to leave the room, walking through the hallways quietly, using the restroom, sharpening pencils, completing seat work, and submitting work. Each task needs practice, and many veteran teachers spend the first weeks of school teaching routines as well as academic content. At all grade levels, you cannot expect that students instinctively know how to do these things—especially the exact way you prefer things to be done. You need to explain, role-play, and practice.

Other routines take place less often but are still important. Gathering work for students who are absent is one example; preparing for your own absences is another. Having a system for leaving assignments for absent students reduces the tasks that you need to manage at the beginning of each class. We suggest preparing a folder for each content area or class, and putting materials labeled with absent students' names into the folders each day. When the student returns to school, she or he can check the folder for missed handouts and assignments. The inconvenience of your own absences can be alleviated by keeping a folder for substitutes in your desk at all times. This is often district or building policy; in addition, some principals require that this folder be updated each time a new unit of study is started.

Students also need to be prepared for unexpected situations and emergencies. A fire drill requires a quick and quiet response, which is best taught and practiced as a specific routine. This is typically taught as a buildingwide exercise, but the responsibility for your students lies with you. As you think about your first classroom, consider the other routines that you will want to teach.

Clear daily routines will help you and your students stay focused and interested, and so we recommend writing the agenda on the board for each class. If the lesson goes down a different path than you had planned, you will be aware when the direction changes and have a chance to decide if that is what you want to do. Without an agenda, you will not have a clear sense of whether or not students learned what you had hoped they would or have met your objectives. The analogy we use is of driving someplace new. Without a map, you cannot expect to get anywhere. This is not okay, as you are the teacher driving the group to a destination. With a map, you have options and the chance to choose a detour or stay on your original route. There is no one right way to do any routine; what you decide depends on both you and your students. But no matter which routines you choose, you need to have a reason or rationale for those choices, and you must be able to clearly explain your reasoning to students, to substitute teachers, and to your administrators.

Your expectations need to be as clear as your routines. For each activity, explain what you want students to do, provide a sample, and answer questions about the directions. Provide high-quality, engaging instruction and supportive feedback. Sometimes teachers mistakenly think that if they provide clear expectations, they will be giving something away, but being clear about what you want students to do is good teaching.

High-Quality, Engaging Instruction and Supportive Feedback

All students need access to instruction that is challenging without being frustrating. This is tricky, and takes practice. Learning how to differentiate your instruction is a classroom management tool, because good instruction is engaging, exciting, and reduces off-task behavior.

Differentiated instruction is "a process where educators vary the learning activities, content demands, modes of assessment, and the classroom environment to meet the needs and support the growth of each child" (Thousand, Villa, & Nevin, 2007, p. 9).

Because students learn in different ways and at different rates (as demonstrated in Chapter 5), your teaching must account for these variations. For example, varying learning activities in English could mean that some students read silently, some listen to books on tape, and some read aloud to an adult or peer buddy. The books students read should also vary by reading level, at all grade levels. Many teachers select a topic or theme to study and all students read books related to that topic. In secondary settings, the same book may be reviewed by the whole class or grade level, but the way the content is reviewed may vary, and the product of the reading may vary too: Some students might write five-paragraph essays, while others might create a bulleted list of points.

Supportive feedback is specific, detailed, and informative. We have heard teachers say "Good job!" to work that really is not very good, and we have heard "You can do better" with little advice about how that might be done. Do not give general praise; give praise that tells the student exactly what they did that you noticed. For example, a general "I like your work" does not tell the student what it is that she has done well, but "Your paragraph is well organized with complete sentences, and I see three robust words—well done!" tells her that you have noticed her organization, sentence structure, and vocabulary choices. This is much more useful information.

Supportive feedback also includes telling students when they are making errors—either academically or behaviorally—and how to change what they are doing. Being clear about what you want students to do is important; if they need to change something, you need to let them know what to do instead. For example, "I see papers on the floor right now. Please stop what you are doing to pick up the papers near your desk so that we can all move safely around the room and keep our papers neat." This is a clear direction that describes the problem, what you want students to do about it, and how it helps the community.

Individual Routines and Expectations

The small minority of students who need individual routines and expectations are just as much a part of your class and responsibility as the other 95% of students. Some teachers have difficulty supporting students who have significant needs and feel that they have missed some essential, possibly secret information about what to do. This information is neither secret nor magical. Every teacher needs information about classroom management and how to arrange physical and emotional space to create a safe learning environment for all students. Some excellent support has been developed for students who are not doing what you want them to do.

Individual routines support a single student and meet his or her needs. A student who has difficulty walking in line through the halls might be taught a specific sequence of actions: hear the announcement that it is time to go to lunch, get Social Story from desk about walking in the halls, read Social Story with teacher or another adult as class lines up, get lunch card from desk to hold, join the end of the line, walk with teacher and class in line to lunch. In many ways, this is similar to the routine the other children follow. But this child has specific, explicit supports in place. None of this is babying or giving in to the student; providing individual support for what a few students need is good teaching. See Figure 6.4 for a basic introduction to the sentences used to write a Social Story and to view a sample Social Story

Another student may need support to make the transition from home to school. A junior high school student who has difficulty at the beginning of the day might be scheduled for a study hall in first period to allow him to review his notes, to schedule and gather his materials for each class, and to check in with a teacher or counselor. They might discuss concerns about what happened the previous afternoon or evening and problem solve about what to do.

Carol Gray (2010) writes that a Social Story

Describes a situation, skills, or concept according to ten defining criteria. These criteria guide story development to ensure an overall patient and supportive quality and a format, "voice" and relevant content that is descriptive, meaningful, and physically, socially, and emotionally safe for the audience. (p. xxv)

The 10 criteria for Social Stories are
1. One goal
2. Two-part discovery
3. Three parts and a title
4. FOURmat
5. Five factors define voice and vocabulary
6. Six questions guide story development
7. Seven types of sentences
8. A Gr-eight formula
9. Nine makes it mine
10. Ten guides to editing and implementation (p. xxxvi)

Figure 6.4. The Social Story. (*Source:* Gray, 2010.)

Individual routines can also be designed for academic and classroom routines. If students have difficulty moving from one activity to the next, adding 5-minute and 1-minute alerts can help them know that a transition is coming. Writing a Social Story about what to do in the last 5 minutes and the last minute can help a student know that it is okay for an assignment to be incomplete and that he can move to the next topic because there will be time to complete the work later.

Individual expectations are related to routines and might be related to academic progress, behavior, or both. Some students will not take part in **alternate assessments** that other students are required to take by the **No Child Left Behind Act**. A small percentage of students can complete individual portfolios of work instead, so that teachers can show and measure the student's progress from the beginning to the end of the year. Alternate assessments are covered in more detail in Chapter 9.

SPECIAL EDUCATION AND CLASSROOM MANAGEMENT

The question of how special education fits in with general classroom management is one with many complex answers. You may have heard of **functional behavioral assessments (FBAs)** and **behavioral intervention plans (BIPs)** or **positive behavioral interventions and supports (PBIS).** These processes help teachers and building staff support a positive community and climate as well as teach students communication skills and strategies for solving problems in proactive ways.

Positive Behavioral Interventions and Supports (PBIS)

Positive behavioral interventions and supports is a decision-making framework designed to guide the "selection, integration, and implementation of the best evidence-based academic and behavioral practices for improving important academic and behavior outcomes for all students" (Office of Special Education Programs [OSEP] Technical Assistance Center, 2011). PBIS is a schoolwide program with four main elements: data for making decisions, outcomes that are measurable and supported by data, practices with evidence that the outcomes are achievable, and systems that support implementing the practices (OSEP Technical Assistance Center, 2011). The program often

alternate assessments
Tests and evaluations for students with severe disabilities who will not take the standard tests most children take in reading, math, and other subjects. Alternate assessments are individually designed so that the progress a student makes during the school year can be measured against what the student was able to do at the beginning of the year.

No Child Left Behind Act
The name for the Elementary and Secondary Education Act reauthorized in 2001. It has four main goals for schools: stronger accountability for results, more freedom for states and communities, proven educational methods, and more choices for parents.

functional behavioral assessment (FBA)   A systematic process used to gather information about a student's behavior. Observations, anecdotal records, interviews, and reviewing records are all part of the data collection process that is used in the FBA.

behavioral intervention plan (BIP)   The report made by a team to support changes in the environment and responses to a student who needs to change a behavior. The BIP is written for an individual student.

positive behavioral interventions and supports (PBIS)
Decision-making framework to support academic and behavioral success of all students.

includes three tiers of support, which are often presented in much the same way as the pyramid shown earlier in this chapter. This pyramid is a continuum of interventions, with primary interventions at the bottom that are used for all students, secondary interventions for some students in the middle, and individualized interventions at the top. The same percentages we mentioned before (80%, 15%, and 5%) are expected at each level (Cregor, 2008, p. 33).

More and more schools are using PBIS, because having a consistent, buildingwide approach that all teachers and administrators use to respond to students is useful in many ways. There is a growing research base about the effectiveness of buildingwide models; see the OSEP Technical Assistance Center web site for more information. PBIS is not a mandatory program; the OSEP Technical Assistance Center noted that

> While Congress recognized the potential of PBIS, it was hesitant to dictate any one educational approach to schools. Indeed, Congress was careful to balance the need to promote the education of children with disabilities and the right of states to govern their own educational systems. IDEA's requirements regarding the use of functional assessments and PBIS reflect this balance. IDEA requires:
>
> - The IEP team to consider the use of positive behavioral interventions and supports for any student whose behavior impedes his or her learning or the learning of others (20 U.S.C. §1414(d)(3)(B)(i)).
>
> - A functional behavioral assessment when a child who does not have a behavior intervention plan is removed from his or her current placement for more than 10 school days (e.g. suspension) for behavior that turns out to be a manifestation of the child's disability (20 U.S.C. §1415(k)(1)(F)(i)).
>
> - A functional behavioral assessment, when appropriate, to address any behavior that results in a long-term removal (20 U.S.C. §1415(k)(1)(D)). (OSEP Technical Assistance Center, 2011)

Nevertheless, PBIS is part of many schoolwide plans, and you are certain to encounter it; it is important to be aware of its role as an effective, broad strategy. Also note that OSEP mentions functional behavioral assessment, which is discussed next.

Functional Behavioral Assessment

A functional behavioral assessment (FBA) process is a systematic process used to gather information about a student's behavior. It includes describing a student's behavior, identifying when and where the behavior occurs, how long it lasts, describing the setting, describing any consequences that maintain the behavior, developing a hypothesis for why the behavior happens, and writing a behavioral intervention plan (BIP) or positive behavioral intervention plan (PBIP) that details how the student will be supported in changing a behavior that is not productive or useful.

The FBA process is started when a student does not meet behavioral expectations even when clear routines and expectations, high-quality, engaging instruction, and supportive feedback are being provided, and teacher proximity, individual schedules, picture prompts, or repeated directions have been employed. As illustrated above, the FBA process is also used when a student with a disability label who does not have a BIP is suspended from the classroom for more than 10 days.

Remember that all behavior is communication. For example, saying "I need to use the restroom" communicates exactly that. A young child's shifting her weight from one foot to the other with a worried look may be communicating the same need. The difference is that if someone is able to express what is needed with words, there is little need for others to interpret what is said; the message is clear. In the second case, especially when you do not know the child, you may not understand that shifting weight back and forth and looking worried means "I need the restroom." Instead, you might guess that the child is upset and needs a hug. Or that she is sad and wants to draw a picture about her feelings. Or that she is concerned about something and needs time to think by herself. In the meantime, while you are thinking through what she might need, she *still* needs to use the restroom! With students who are not able to communicate in traditional ways, teachers need to do the detective work to determine what they are trying to say. The FBA process gives you a method for doing so. The goal is to support the student in developing strategies to meet his or her needs in ways that are appropriate for the classroom.

The first step of the FBA process is describing the behavior under review. This needs to be done objectively and descriptively. Saying "she has tantrums all the time" does not tell the reader what is happening. As the reader, you do not have a clear picture in your mind of what goes on. Being clear and descriptive helps everyone share an understanding of what the behavior is. Saying "she throws her body on the floor and yells 'I hate this!' between five and seven times every morning" gives the reader a much better sense of the behavior.

Identifying when and where the behavior occurs, how long it lasts, and in what settings is the next step. This process can take several weeks as you observe, ask others to observe, and keep records. There are many ways to collect **observational data**. One way is by measuring the frequency of a behavior. The behavior chart in Figure 6.5 gives you information about how often a student is out of his or her seat without permission. What patterns do you see in this chart? What else do you want to know? Noticing patterns and raising more questions is an important process to use as you decide what information to gather.

observational data
Information gathered by watching interactions and behaviors of a particular student and the people and things she or he encounters.

Example of behavior chart

Behavior = out of seat without permission
X = 3 or more times   o = 1–2 times

Activity	Time	Mon.	Tues.	Wed.	Thurs.	Fri.
Bellwork	9:00–9:30	o		o		
Reading	9:30–11:00	o				
Math	11:00–12:00	x	x	x	x	x
Lunch	12:00–12:30					
S.S.	12:30–1:30	o		o	o	
Science	12:30–2:00	o				

- What patterns do you see?
- What else would you like to know?

Figure 6.5. Behavior chart sample.

Frequency or event recording is best used for behaviors that have a clear beginning and end. To gather data, use consistent time lengths (such as 15- or 30-minute intervals, or a class session).

Frequency data can be paired with a review of **permanent products**. Permanent products are simply work samples, like a spelling test, written work, or drawings that the student has made. If a student is out of her seat many times in a class session and the permanent product created during that time is of high quality and accuracy, the issue may be that the student is bored. If the permanent product shows that the student started work but then made many erasures, crumpled her paper, and stomped on it, the issue may be that the student was frustrated. Pairing work samples with observational data is crucial to the detective work of the FBA process.

Another essential kind of data to collect is **interview data**. An essential component of any FBA data collection process is interviews with the student, family, and other adults who see the behavior. Interviews should be conducted during a calm break, when everyone is relaxed and able to talk openly about the behavior in question. Questions to ask in an interview include: What does the problem behavior look like? How often does it happen? When does it happen? How disruptive is it? When interviewing someone, the goal is to hear his or her perspective. A student may say things that do not match your experiences; that is okay. The goal is to gather as much information as you can from many perspectives. Something that you find to be disruptive, such as a student lying on the floor screaming "I hate this!" may be perceived by the student as not very disruptive at all. The interview is not the time to discuss that; save sharing your perspective for another time.

Finally, **anecdotal records** are very helpful to determine the **ABCs of behavior**, or Antecedent, Behavior, and Consequence. Anecdotal records are simply written reports about what happened: what was going on before the behavior, the behavior, and what happened afterwards. For example, a brief record might look like this:

Tuesday, May 10, 2011, 8 a.m.–10:30 a.m.

Laura came in this morning with a runny nose and seems to have a cold. After morning meeting, during reading, she put her head on her desk and seemed irritated when I asked her to start her work, but she completed about half of her report. At the end of reading, when it was time to transition to math, she threw herself on the floor yelling "I hate this!" I went to her and rubbed her back and asked her what would help her. She cried and said she felt sick. I sent her to the nurse to rest and to call home.

From this anecdotal report, we see that the antecedent is that Laura does not feel well and that math is about to begin. The behavior is throwing herself on the floor and yelling that she hates this. The consequence is that she is sent to the nurse. If this is something that happened just once, we would probably not be completing the FBA process. But if this happened many times, we might begin to wonder if Laura seems sick and goes to the nurse for reasons other than being ill. That might start us on the path of collecting information to review it. The next step in the process is reviewing all the data and developing a hypothesis about why the behavior occurs, and if we think a consequence of her behavior keeps her doing it again and again.

The teacher or the team reviews the data. The goal is to consider what consequences maintain the behavior. If we see a pattern that Laura is sent to the nurse three times a week and always before math, we might wonder if Laura is avoiding math for some reason. We check the interview and see that Laura does not feel that throwing herself on the floor is disruptive, because she leaves the room fairly quickly to go to the nurse. We wonder if there is something going on with Laura related to math, and review the permanent products. We see that Laura is not doing well in math. She is often lost and

permanent products
Student work, such as reports, tests, essays, worksheets, and drawings.

interview data
Information from talking with a student or adult. Interviews are important for providing a range of perspectives about what is happening.

anecdotal records
Reports written into a narrative of the ABCs of a behavior. These records should give the reader a clear picture of what happened.

ABCs of behavior The Antecedent (what came before a behavior), the Behavior (what happened), and the Consequence (what came after the behavior). Each part needs to be described objectively using clear language so that the reader/listener has a clear picture of what happened.

frustrated and has not done well on the last four quizzes. We decide that missing math is a consequence that maintains the behavior of throwing herself on the floor and yelling "I hate this!"

Now that we have a hypothesis—Laura throws herself on the floor and yells so that she can avoid math—we can develop a Behavior Intervention Plan (BIP) so that we can give Laura tools to ask for a break and experience success in math. We do this because it is not useful for Laura to miss math and throw herself on the floor.

When developing the BIP, we keep some key points in mind, including the philosophy that there is no such thing as a bad child. Laura is not bad; Laura has a need that is not being met, and it is our job to meet it. Here are some key points:

- Behaviors that you want to change are exhibited for a reason.

- You may be able to extinguish the unwanted behavior, but that does not extinguish the need behind it.

- Needs are always appropriate! The need to express needs is always appropriate.

- Some *ways* of expressing needs are not *always* appropriate.

- Teaching the student to express the need in a more appropriate way teaches a replacement behavior.

- Be careful to avoid using words like "always" and "never."

With these points in mind, we develop a plan for Laura. We consider that Laura needs to replace the behavior of throwing herself on the floor and yelling with a new behavior. We remember that replacement behaviors will not be learned right away. They will be learned bit by bit, over time. We consider: What skills does Laura need to acquire for the plan to be successful? What are the prerequisites for these skills? How much should Laura learn at a time? We also consider what we need to change about the environment: What about math needs to change? We consider the difficulty of the work, the amount of work, and the type of support Laura has been getting in math. We decide that we need to do three things: teach Laura that she can ask for a break during math, change the level of difficulty of the math Laura is expected to complete to match her skills, and add more small-group support for teaching new math skills to Laura.

Once we have developed a plan, we implement it and continue collecting data about the behavior in question. We set a date to review the plan in the relatively near future—probably 2 or 3 weeks. When we review the plan, we consider what has worked well, what needs adjusting, and what did not work. Then, we continue the cycle of teaching and monitoring.

SUMMARY

In this chapter, we reviewed how to build and sustain community and how to begin to think about managing a classroom. We introduced the FBA and BIP process, which will come up again in Chapter 12. Remember that our fundamental belief that there is no such thing as a bad child informs all of our decisions about students and their behavior, and we hope the same is true for you when you become a teacher, because you are your students' guide, mentor, and role model for how to respond to each member of the community in good times and during hardship.

NARRATIVE 6.1. | RACHEL ZINDLER

The Value of Community Building in Classrooms   As an education consultant working in New York City public schools, I guide and support teachers in establishing and maintaining best practices in their inclusive classrooms. Over the course of the year, I am lucky to visit dozens of schools and hundreds of classrooms and get to meet with teachers with all levels of experience. We discuss lesson planning for a wide range of learners, strategies for working together as a professional teaching team, and ways to foster independence in students with high needs. These are crucial topics in an integrated classroom, but we always begin our work together with how to construct a comfortable and supportive physical and emotional environment for the kids.

A colleague once said to me that a child should be able walk into his or her classroom on the first day of school and say, "This is a place for me!" The kindergartener who is easily overwhelmed may find a cozy nook to sit in. The third grader who is still learning to read may spy a familiar listening center. The shy student recognizes that the little rug in the corner will be a comfortable place to sit for smaller group lessons, and the active teenager may see raised desks where he knows he will do his best work standing up. The way we design and structure the physical environment speaks volumes about our understanding of students' needs. I often spend the first few weeks of school arranging and rearranging the furniture with teachers until we find just the right balance for the current class.

Beyond the physical environment, children must feel welcomed by the faces around them to take risks and try the new, sometimes difficult, tasks we ask of them every day. The emotional environment involves many things: a smile and a greeting first thing in the morning, a question about the soccer game after recess, clear and reasonable rules agreed to by all members of the community, time and space to discuss social problems when they arise, and a deep respect for different ways of living and learning.

Many teachers rely on community-building activities to establish a sense of belonging and trust within their classrooms during the first weeks of school. Some teachers even devote the entire month of September to setting up routines and getting to know one another, scheduling at least one community-oriented activity per day. Students might draw and interview a partner, write and share stories about their family traditions, work in small groups to master physical challenges collaboratively, or create advertisements to showcase their strengths. A first grader's ad might read "Find me if you need help tying your shoes!" An eighth grader might publicize her computer savvy with a short video. When we encourage kids to share their strengths and personal stories early in the year, we promote self-reflection and respect for diversity, and we communicate the message that all students are valued for the unique abilities they bring to the group.

Although many teachers spend a lot of time on community building in the beginning of the year, by December many complain that their students have begun to push limits more frequently and are having difficulty with certain "behavior problems." At this point, I often ask, "What community-building activities have you been doing?" As the year gets under way, teachers feel pressure to spend precious instructional hours on academics alone. But when students are not able to follow directions or can't get along with each other, we end up trading instructional time for classroom management and redirection. Instead, when we continue to provide regular, scheduled opportunities for guided social interaction and direct teaching of social skills, we leave room for students to learn how to solve conflicts peacefully, to learn appropriate language, and to practice civility toward one another and their surroundings.

As students with language-processing disorders, autism, emotional challenges, and other needs become integrated into most classrooms, it is even more important that we provide direct social instruction and modeling of appropriate behavior *throughout the year*. In many of the successful classrooms I have visited, teachers schedule a "Community Meeting" into their weekly plan, during which they incorporate different activities based on the social climate of the classroom. One week, they might watch a short video, discuss bullying, and brainstorm ways to stand up for a friend. Another week, students might role-play different outcomes for a conflict that has come up repeatedly in the classroom. Yet another week, kids might be assigned secret buddies and practice writing compliments to them, later to be read aloud to the class.

Classrooms founded on mutual respect, where there is ample time and space for problem solving, have fewer behavior "problems." In these classrooms, students take responsibility for their own actions because they recognize the impact on their peers and their environment. In turn, teachers rely less on cumbersome systems for reward or punishment. Schools have a responsibility to teach children the skills they need to be successful outside of school, and while reading, writing, and arithmetic are critical to their success, the greatest asset a child can develop is the ability to socialize—to negotiate, collaborate, and communicate respectfully with their friends, family, and the world at large.

CHAPTER 7

Differentiation and Full Citizenship

How this chapter prepares you to be an effective inclusive classroom teacher:

- This chapter teaches you how students with exceptional learning needs may be marginalized in the classroom and not accepted or respected as full citizens who are valuable contributing members of the learning community. Being aware of this prepares you to individualize instruction so that all students have the opportunity to demonstrate their strengths and abilities. **This helps you meet CEC Standard 3: Individual Learning Differences.**

- This chapter teaches you about differentiated planning that is based on individual learning needs and is modified on an ongoing basis as student needs change. It also starts you out with several examples of areas that may be modified. **This helps you meet CEC Standard 7: Instructional Planning.**

- This chapter prepares you to be a professional and ethical teacher by teaching you that fairness does not always mean that every student receives the same treatment and that the teacher's role is to adjust instruction in consideration of students' needs, not impose instruction upon students. From reading this chapter, you will understand that learning how to differentiate for all learners is a lifelong process, because no two students are alike. It teaches you that your role as a teacher is to actively plan and engage in activities that foster your professional growth and keep you current with evidence-based practices. **This helps you meet CEC Standard 9: Professional and Ethical Practice.**

After reading and discussing this chapter, you will be able to

- Explain the concept of differentiation

- Explain the concepts of alien, squatter, and citizen

- Explain the four components of full citizenship and the role of the teacher in facilitating each component in the classroom

- Explain the concept of marginalization and its impact on the classroom community

- Explain why fair does not always mean equal, and provide examples

- Explain the difference between standardized and individualized assessment and instruction and the impact of each on student learning

- Explain the concept of "ripple effect" in the classroom

- Explain what it means for students in the classroom to have dichotomous needs and the teacher's role in responding to those needs

- Describe how budgetary concerns can be a barrier to differentiation and provide examples of how teachers can overcome that

- Explain how learning to differentiate instruction is a lifelong learning process for a teacher

This chapter is divided into three sections. The first section explains a conceptual framework for supporting the success of all students in the classroom, including a review of Kliewer's alien, squatter, citizen theory. The second section introduces the theory and practice of differentiation of instruction. As a precursor to specific strategies provided in the third section, this part prepares teachers to analyze and plan for a multitude of diverse needs in the inclusive classroom. The third section presents important considerations for effective differentiation and offers case studies and specific examples of successful problem solving by classroom teachers who value the full citizenship of all students.

Narratives include an eighth-grader's marginalization versus citizenship in school and the experiences of a young adult for whom music provided an opportunity to show his unique strengths and talents.

A CONCEPTUAL FRAMEWORK FOR SUCCESSFUL DIFFERENTIATION

conceptual framework
Basis of theory for thinking about a particular topic. A conceptual framework organizes a set of ideas or concepts. Educators who follow the same conceptual framework work together under the same set of values, assumptions, and definitions.

In Chapter 6, you learned that one of the most effective—if not *the* most effective—strategies for managing a classroom of diverse students is the use of engaging instructional activities and learning opportunities. You also know that each student is unique, and the teacher needs to individualize his or her teaching methods and activities to engage each of these learners. At this point, most teachers and teachers-to-be want to get started. They are ready to load up their toolboxes with lesson-plan ideas and strategies for modifying and accommodating different needs. But it is not time yet. There is a **conceptual framework** to be laid before you can build on it with strategies and methods. It is essential to take time to delve deeper into the belief that all children can learn and all children belong together to learn.

What Does It Mean to Be a Full Citizen in the Classroom?

Part of the answer to this question was addressed in Chapter 6. Belonging to a community of learners who value each other's strengths and challenges is an important part of being a citizen in the classroom. In addition to building a classroom community, teachers also must meet the academic needs of all students in the classroom. What does it mean to be a **full citizen** academically as well as socially?

In the book *Schooling Children with Down Syndrome: Toward an Understanding of Possibility*, Kliewer (1998) outlined four elements of citizenship: 1) a belief in one's ability to think, 2) a belief in one's individuality, 3) a belief in the reciprocity of the relationship, and 4) a shared social place. Here each idea is explained:

A Belief in One's Ability to Think
A belief in one's ability to think simply means to believe that everyone is capable of thinking—thinking deeply, thinking creatively, thinking for themselves. To achieve this, you must broaden the way you think about thinking. Traditional definitions regarding the ability to think tend to limit it to those who score highly on intelligence or aptitude tests, those who read and write prolifically and with fluency, and those who are able to comply with didactic teaching methods. This is one way to envision the ability to think, but it is only one way. There are many others. It is restricting to value only the type of thinking that is measured on standardized assessments or traditional classroom assignments. Teachers need to broaden their minds to value many types of intellect and thinking. In that way, the intellect of each and every person becomes apparent. Being able to think of many different ways to solve a problem is intellect. Being able to see the positive in situations and people is a valuable way of thinking. Being able to imagine intricate settings and plots for play is intellect.

Here is an example from a middle-school English class: A nonfiction research paper was assigned. The students could choose any topic they wanted as long as it was nonfictional. The topics ran the gamut; students chose to report on animals, people, inventions, sports, and historic events. One student chose to research the history of dragon lore. He was told that he must choose another topic that was nonfictional. He insisted that his topic was not fictional. Assuming that he did not understand the difference between fiction and nonfiction, the teacher explained it to him and listed a few nonfictional topics to choose from. He did not budge. The teacher finally said, "You may not research that topic. Dragons are not real." In exasperation, the boy replied, "I know dragons are not real. But the legends surrounding dragons are real and they date back hundreds of years. I want to research that." Assuming that students misunderstand without taking the time to discover their own thinking robs teachers of opportunities to learn valuable information about the children, about themselves, and about the world.

Disability and intellect are not mutually exclusive. It is just as likely for a person with a disability to have a particular gift as it is for someone who does not have a disability. Many believe that having a disability is actually what makes it possible to have a gift. Sometimes, unique ways of processing and functioning in the environment are defined as a disability. These unique ways may also open the doors for achievements not accessible to those who process or function in typical ways. Temple Grandin, a doctor of animal science and the leading expert in cattle behavior, believes that her autism allows her to be successful in her field, because she can actually experience sounds, lights, and environmental stimuli the same way cattle do. Other animal handlers are not able to do that because of the way their typical brains work, so they were not able to figure out what made the cattle so distressed. Dr. Grandin studied the facilities, reduced anxiety-provoking stimuli, created enclosures that were more soothing, and subsequently revolutionized the cattle-handling industry to be much more humane.

full citizen A term introduced by Kliewer (1998) to describe a person who fully belongs to a group, and whose presence and contributions are valued.

A Belief in One's Individuality   The belief in one's individuality is the belief that each person has unique characteristics all his or her own. Even though a person may belong to a certain group, it does not mean that he or she is exactly like everyone else in the group. This is where the impact of labels is important to consider. One of the effects of labeling is that a label may serve to define all persons under its umbrella in a particular way. Once we assume that everyone with the same label is generally the same and has the same characteristics and interests, we defeat the belief in individuality.

This is particularly an issue with people who share a disability classification or label. Each person with a disability is a unique person, but labels construct assumptions that everyone who falls under it is alike. Not everyone with an intellectual disability is the same, any more than everyone with brown hair is the same. One parent wisely joked that students could be just as well served in schools if they were classified by height rather than by disability label, because neither really tells you how students learn best or what interests them. To realize each student's full citizenship, it is essential to believe that each student is an individual.

Just as a sign post on a road, a label can point us in a general direction, but we will not know the details of a place until we go there ourselves, spend time, and make our own discoveries. A quote from Kliewer (1998) tells us:

> School citizenship requires that students not be categorized and separated by presumed defect. The phenomenon of categorization at the expense of individual value has been described as a "disability spread in which we extrapolate the characteristics we associate with the notion of disability to the particular individuals we meet." These perceptions are often based on stereotypes and what we think we know about a particular disability. (p. 85)

reciprocity Mutual exchange. According to Kliewer (1998), reciprocity of the relationship means that both parties benefit from the relationship equitably.

A Belief in the Reciprocity of the Relationship   On an individual level, believing in the **reciprocity** of the relationship means that you believe that everyone has something to give and everyone has something to receive; everyone is a teacher and a learner. On a classroom level, it means that no one student or group of students enhances the classroom while another student or group of students drains it. In essence, everyone equally benefits and challenges the community. Working through the challenges benefits everyone.

Some often think of students with disabilities as the receivers and their nondisabled peers as the givers. In fact, one of the loudest arguments against inclusive education is that it might be good for the students with disabilities, but it wouldn't be fair to the other, nondisabled students. Whatever the details—the students with disabilities would take up the teacher's time, there will be more outbursts, the disabled students won't understand the curriculum unless it is watered down—some people have felt that both groups of students will be better off if segregated. We feel exactly the opposite because we believe in the reciprocity of the relationship. Throughout this book, we explain that all people are better off when together, otherwise we are all deprived of experiences and opportunities to learn, make new friends, and grow as people ourselves.

Furthermore, students with disabilities should not have to prove that they are valuable. Those without disabilities have not had to prove their worth. It is assumed that they belong in the classroom, that they will contribute actively and usefully, and that they are pleasant company. This is not a privilege to be granted to a select few. This is a human right to be extended to each and every student.

A Shared Social Place   The idea of the shared place brings together all of the concepts of citizenship. It is a place where each individual belongs and where he or she is valued and can take risks without fear of failure or persecution. When you read Chapter 6, you learned about the importance of building a classroom community as well as some ways to do that. Once you have this in place, you are ready to also learn ways to differentiate lessons and activities to nurture the academic growth of all students. In a differentiated classroom, there is rarely, if ever, one right way to accomplish something. There is no one right way to teach a lesson or to learn it. No one right product of writing, art, music, reading, or socialization. There is no one right way to solve a problem or one right way to be a good student. A differentiated classroom is equipped with various materials, technology, work spaces, and displays. It opens the doors for various learning styles, multiple intelligences, and interests. It welcomes collaboration, group problem solving, and different ways of communicating. It is patient, creative, intriguing, challenging, and individualized.

What Happens When Not All Students Are Full Citizens?

When differentiated classrooms are not realized, there are many scenarios that could take place instead. It may be that students with disabilities are segregated into separate classrooms or separate schools. Students with disabilities who are never seen by their peers are in a group Kliewer called **aliens** (1998). They do not have the same school membership as their typically developing peers; their peers do not know them or see them, and they seem so different from everyone else that they might as well be aliens! Another group of students with disability labels might be in general education classrooms for part of the day, or even the whole day, but the beliefs discussed above are not in place. These students are not exactly aliens, because they are physically included in the classroom. But because they are not truly welcome and do not truly belong, they are **squatters** in their own classroom (Kliewer, 1998). They are marginalized as second-class students.

The **marginalization** can be significant and overt, or mild and subtle, but if it exists, full citizenship will not occur. In turn, effective differentiation toward academic success will not be likely. Here is one instance where the marginalization was subtle, but powerful: Three fifth-grade students were together at a table during a math lesson. One of the students had a learning disability that affected his processing of mathematics as well as social skills. During independent work time, when students were expected to complete their math problems independently and quietly at their tables, the two other boys began whispering and playing with a toy one had brought to class. The teacher's aide, a very compassionate woman who cared a lot for all of the students, approached the table and put her arm around the boy with the learning disability, asking him to settle down and get back to work, when in fact, he was the only one at the table who had not stopped working. The message sent to all of the boys at the table is the disruption was assumed to have been made by the special education student mainstreamed into the math lesson rather than the two others. Whatever had been done to include the student with the learning disability was undone by this brief exchange.

Students who experience this marginalization repeatedly are at risk of developing self-esteem and self-worth problems. They are more likely to become detached from teachers and parents, have behavioral challenges, skip or drop out of school, and become involved in substance abuse. It is important to understand what makes a student a full citizen, but it is also important to know what marginalizes a student, so you can always be working toward a classroom where all students are learning together in a community and where everyone is valued and assumed to be a competent, contributing member.

Are You Ready?

Now that you've thought about full citizenship of all students, consider the "mind-set questions" in Figure 7.1. Take your time and consider each question thoroughly for a few moments. Do you truly believe this of *all* students? Even those with extremely

alien A term introduced by Kliewer (1998) to refer to a person who is excluded entirely from a community. In the school setting, an alien is a student with a disability who does not have the opportunity to learn in the general education setting with typically developing peers.

squatter A term introduced by Kliewer (1998) to describe a person who is physically present in a community or setting, but whose contributions or presence is not valued.

marginalization Pushed to the side of a community or setting. In the school setting, a student who is marginalized may be physically present in the classroom, but does not feel a sense of belonging or his or her contributions are not valued by others.

1. Am I willing to teach in whatever way is necessary for students to learn best, even if the approach does not match my own preference?
2. Do I have the courage to do what works, not just what's easier?
3. Do I actively seek to understand my students' knowledge, skills, and talents so I can provide an appropriate match for their learning needs?
4. Do I continually build a large and diverse repertoire of instructional strategies so I have more than one way to teach?
5. Do I organize my classroom for students' learning or for my teaching?
6. Do I keep up-to-date on the latest research about learning, students' developmental growth, and my content specialty area?
7. Do I ceaselessly self-analyze and reflect on my lessons—including my assessments— searching for ways to improve?
8. Am I open to critique?
9. Do I push students to become their own education advocates and give them the tools to do so?
10. Do I regularly close the gap between knowing what to do and actually doing it?[1]
11. Do I value students with disabilities as much as I value students without disabilities in my school community?
12. Do I believe that students with special learning needs make valuable contributions to the learning community?
13. Do I believe that students with disabilities are smart?
14. Do I believe that students with disabilities can teach others?[2]

[1]Questions 1 through 10 are from Wormeli, R. (2007). *Differentiation: From planning to practice*. Portland, ME: Stenhouse Publishers, pp. 8–9.
[2]Questions 11 through 14 are from Rapp, W. (2010, May 11). *Differentiation: Theory to practice*. Rochester Leadership Academy, St. John Fisher College.

Figure 7.1.   Mind-set reflection questions.

challenging behaviors? Even those with significant intellectual disabilities? Even those with severe physical or health impairments?

Think back to your answers to the questions. For some of them, did you answer yes, but hesitate or feel a pang of nervousness because you are not sure *how* you will do it, even though you truly want to? That is okay! At this point, you may not have sufficient answers to envision how it will play out in the classroom, but if the belief and the willingness are there, the essential foundation of differentiated instruction exists. Having the attitudes and beliefs that you will support all students will help ensure that the strategies and methods you use later will be as effective as possible. Think about it in terms of building a brick house. Imagine each brick in the house is a strategy or a lesson plan activity or an accommodation. These are important to a brick house, of course. However, the foundation that levels the ground and supports the weight, and the mortar that holds the bricks in place, is your belief system about learners—your mind-set. Without a level foundation or consistent mortar, even the best bricks in the world will not build a strong house.

Fair Is Not Equal

fairness   The concept that something is free from bias, dishonesty, or unequal treatment. In education, fairness does not mean that everyone gets the same thing, it means that everyone gets what he or she needs.

There is another concept that is important to add to your conceptual framework before you are fully prepared to learn about differentiation of instruction. That is the misunderstood concept of **fairness**. Many experiences can lead you to think that fairness means that everyone gets the same thing. Do you remember teachers telling you that you cannot have that piece of gum in class unless you have a piece for everyone, or else it wouldn't be fair? Do you remember wanting to get together with a friend and your parents insisting your younger sibling go along too, or it wouldn't be fair?

The definition of fairness in the classroom, however, is not "everyone gets the same." It is "everyone gets what he or she needs." Because everyone has different needs, fairness means that everyone gets something different. This is a huge shift in thinking for most people to make. It is not what we are used to. Richard Lavoie, an expert in strategies for students with learning disabilities, provides an example in his video *How Difficult Can This Be?* that helps explain why fairness as equality is misguided. He asks the audience to imagine that one person among them suddenly fell from her chair to the floor, not breathing, in cardiac arrest. Then he asks them how ridiculous it would be for him to tell the woman that he knows CPR and could help her, but there are many people in the room; if he gave CPR to her, he would have to give it everyone, or it wouldn't be fair, and he can't possibly give it to everyone. In closing, he states that it doesn't have anything to do with everyone else. She needs it, they don't. It is okay to provide a person with something he or she needs without providing it to everyone else. As long as you can look each one in the eye and say that you would do it for him or her if the need were there, then it is fair. As long as you do for each of them what he or she uniquely needs, it is fair. As Sam describes in Narrative 7.1, he often needs something different than the other students to be fully involved in the lesson.

NARRATIVE 7.1. | SAM RAPP

My name is Sam Rapp and I'm an eighth grader with executive functioning disorder who is learning in a district school. In several instances, I have found myself punished for things I've been told I'm allowed to do. Mostly for drawing because it seems I'm not paying attention in class. I consider myself an excellent artist for my age, and have no trouble getting through my classes as long as I'm allowed to draw during class. My IEP shows that I have full reason to draw in class as long as I am still paying attention. Teachers will run continuous, unneeded "checkups" to make sure I'm doing my work. Even after I've shown teachers my IEP and my parents have spoken with them multiple times, I've still sometimes had supplies and even work taken away from me so I can pay attention, even though I can listen and repeat everything the teacher says when I'm not looking. Usually, teachers will avoid calling on me or avoid connecting with me, which is both embarrassing and insulting. In truth, I think that more problems derive from the lack of awareness about a learning disability than from the actual disability itself.

Having EFD makes me unable to concentrate on something for an extended period of time. That way, I can't focus on work for more than one class period, which poses the biggest challenge in school. I also have trouble staying organized, but I have full access to help staying organized in any study hall out of the classroom. Teachers don't usually try to pick me out for having talent in class, but I do have my strengths. I excel at art, reading, and writing more than most of my peers. I was voted "Most Artistic" this year. Most of my strong spots are in creativity and imagination, as opposed to completing a given worksheet or mathematics. How a human learns is hard to understand, but I see it like a scale; when one side is down, the other side is up. Applied to learning it could be: Someone is not good at math, but he is good at reading. We all have our ways of looking at it, but my favorite is "Everyone is good at something, but no one is good at everything."

Many teachers worry that children will not understand and will become upset if they see another student getting accommodations. We believe that children are capable, and often much more willing than adults, of understanding that fair is not always equal. To explain this idea to students, consider using this exercise. Pretend to be a doctor and have each student come to you with a different malady (sore arm, tummy ache, cough, a deep cut). Prescribe cough medicine for each child and send him on his way. When you ask the students if this will work, they will tell you that cough syrup works for a cough, but not for a headache or cut. When asked what the doctor should do instead, they will tell you that each child should get a different treatment because that is what he or she needs. Explaining that teaching is like doctoring will help everyone—teacher included—to feel more comfortable with the idea that different students will receive different accommodations. Now that the foundation of a fair classroom has been reviewed, it is time to consider what differentiation means and how to provide differentiated instruction in the classroom.

DIFFERENTIATION OF INSTRUCTION

Differentiation Is...

differentiation "Doing whatever it takes to maximize students' learning instead of relying on a one-size-fits-all, whole-class method of instruction" (Wormeli, 2007, p. 9). Differentiation is helpful because students become independent lifelong learners. If you differentiate and show students many things, they will learn what works for them and know how to ask for what they need.

Differentiation means knowing each of your students well. The purpose of differentiating for each student is to ensure that students are each being challenged with work that is challenging but not too difficult, and to help each student become an independent learner. Wormeli (2007) stated:

> The two simple charges of differentiation are 1) do whatever it takes to maximize students' learning instead of relying on a one-size-fits-all, whole-class method of instruction and 2) prepare students to handle anything in their current and future lives that is not differentiated, i.e., to become their own learning advocates. (p. 9)

Chapter 6 outlined activities to help the members of the classroom become a community. This is important for the teacher as well as fellow students. The teacher needs to know each student's likes, dislikes, experiences, and dreams. The teacher also needs to know each student's strengths and challenges in academics, behavior, communication, and physical development. In addition to establishing a community from the first day of school, it is important to assess your students both formally and informally to know where they are functioning, so attainable goals are set for everyone. If the student has an Individualized Education Program (IEP), past assessment results and annual updates about her present levels of performance will be reported. Information from the IEP is useful, but remember that students' skills and knowledge change more often than the information on the IEP is updated. In Narrative 7.2, Matt explains how being able to follow his interests and strengths made all the difference to him.

Once you know your students' skill and knowledge levels, interests, and preferred learning styles, you combine that with the essential understandings, skills, and objectives you want them to achieve in planning differentiated lessons. The following figures outline different formats or templates that can be used to frame your planning. This is a first step. It will take a good deal of research and experience to collect a large and varied repertoire for filling in the templates. Part Three of this text offers many strategies in different areas to start building your toolbox.

Figure 7.2 displays a differentiation template from Rutherford (2002, p. 196). This is a simple way to illustrate how instruction can be differentiated in a vast number of ways.

Each box represents something to consider while planning a lesson. The first box encourages you to think of many different sources for your lesson content, many different ways that you can guide the students through the process of learning the content, and

NARRATIVE 7.2. | MATT GIORDANO

My name is Matt Giordano and I'm currently 28 years old. When I was a child in school, I had a severe case of Tourette syndrome along with other related disorders, such as OCD, ADHD, LD, and ODD. Having all of that made school a huge challenge for me, but I got through it successfully with the positive support from my teachers, family, and friends. I am currently the president of an internationally known company, Drum Echoes, Inc. I educate, entertain, and inspire people from all walks of life through the drums: www.drumechoes.com. As a successful person that had many challenges in school, I ask you to teach all of your students in the manner that I was taught by my greatest teachers, who made a huge difference in my life. Teach them with the attitude of knowing that all of your students have the potential of being successful. I was in a general education classroom setting instead of special ed. This was very important in my learning to fit in and to grow up into a successful and independent adult in the real world.

My situation was much different than the rest of my peers, so in order for me to learn, teachers needed to work with me by thinking outside of the box from time to time. My teachers knew that encouraging my strength would help me a great deal in regard to my social life and school work. My greatest strength was drumming. It helped me to overcome my challenges in many ways. I was also permitted to use my gift of drumming for my learning experiences in the classroom. I once had to write a paper on a topic of my choice that was related to the civil war. I chose to write about the drummer boys. We had to present it in front of the entire class and I included a drumming demonstration as a part of the presentation. They allowed me to do a paper that was related to my strengths. That gave me a great deal of motivation and confidence to do the paper and to do it well. That confidence of knowing I could do my school work well continued on throughout the rest of my school years. It also gave me a chance to show my peers that I was an exceptional drummer instead of them seeing me as being unusual. I was well accepted by my peers throughout most of my time in school.

You can effectively teach your students by applying music and drumming activities in the lesson plan. That will make their learning experience a lot more exciting and memorable. A good jingle can be hard for students to get out of their heads, so use that to teach your students. Be creative with it. It can capture their attention, motivate, and inspire them to learn and can be a very effective technique for increasing their academics. This becomes even more true for kids with a variety of learning differences. If you have students that are often excluded from their peers, it can be a good way to get them involved in collaborative group activities. Many young people can have a hard time sitting still at their desks all day, trying to quietly pay attention and learn. This is especially true for kids with ADHD and other learning differences. So why fight it if you don't have to and if it's not necessary? Get them to learn out of their desk through hands on, interactive music and drumming activities. It's fun and effective. You don't have to know how to play the drums to do it. You just have to know how to hit a drum and to be creative with it so it can be applied to your students' lesson plans, which I'm sure you can do.

You can be a great teacher by believing in your students' abilities to learn and to be successful. Teach and inspire them! Encourage their strengths and allow them to shine. Use their strengths to help them overcome their weaknesses. Don't be afraid to be creative and have fun by throwing in some music and beats in your classroom. Everyone with the right tools and the right support can achieve success. A teacher with that attitude and optimism can be the most influential person in children's lives by giving them the opportunity to reach their fullest potential and to achieve the greatest success they can possibly achieve! I will always be grateful to the teachers who did this for me.

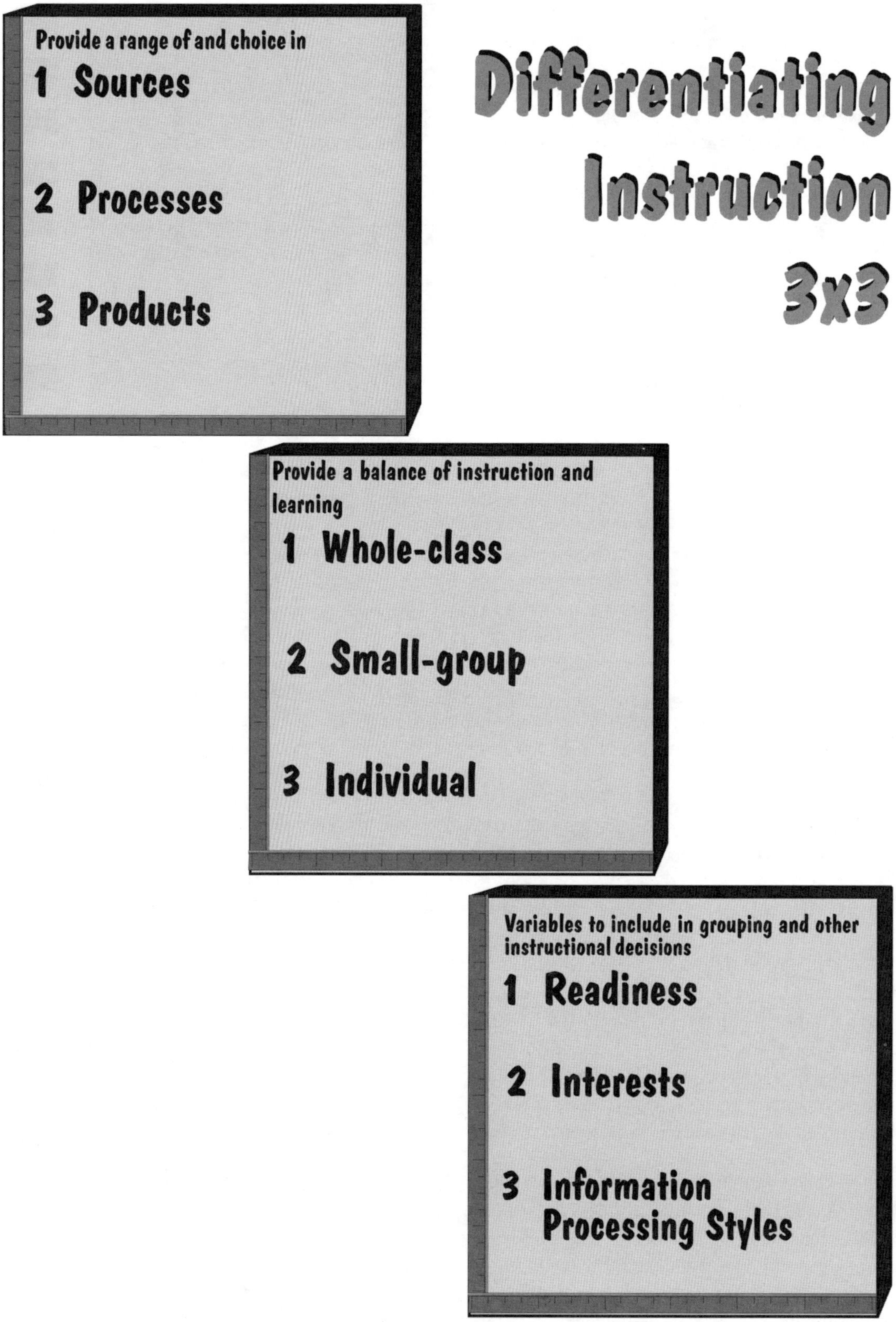

Differentiating Instruction 3x3

Provide a range of and choice in
1 Sources

2 Processes

3 Products

Provide a balance of instruction and learning
1 Whole-class

2 Small-group

3 Individual

Variables to include in grouping and other instructional decisions
1 Readiness

2 Interests

3 Information Processing Styles

Figure 7.2. Differentiating instruction 3 × 3. (Reprinted with permission of the publisher from *Instruction for All Students* by Paula Rutherford. © Copyright 2008. Just ASK Publications, All rights reserved. www.justaskpublications.com)

many different products that can result from the learning so that you are sure the students mastered the content. Just a starter list for sources includes textbooks, trade books, movies, guest speakers, community agencies, newspapers, YouTube videos, and the Internet. Ways to present new information to students and guide them through the process of learning include lectures, class discussions, activities, games, demonstrations, puzzles, and role-playing. Products that show the results of the students learning include tests, quizzes, papers, models, videos, tape recordings, oral or written responses, speeches, illustrations, songs, poems, journal reflections, and demonstrations. By varying these possibilities, you already have dozens of combinations for teaching new content.

The second box in Figure 7.2 reminds you to find a balance in your instruction so that students have opportunities for whole-group instructions, small-group activities, as well as individual work time. Students need to process the information they receive so they can make sense of it and generalize it to situations outside of the classroom. Some students may prefer to work alone, while others may prefer to work in a group. It is important to provide opportunities for their preferred grouping, while also expecting them to sometimes stretch themselves by engaging in a nonpreferred way as well.

The third box in Figure 7.2 indicates the diverse variables you will need to identify in your students so that you can meet everyone's needs. The students in your class will be on different levels of readiness for new content. Some may already have background knowledge and are ready to learn more specific details, while others may need to have some background established first. Some may be independent readers, while others may need some preteaching of vocabulary so they are prepared for the upcoming reading. Some are independent learners and are able to express which of the above variations work best for them, while others may need guidance until they are practiced in selecting the best variations. Topics, materials, and examples you use in lessons should reflect the interests of your students whenever possible. Not only will this help them connect to the new information they are receiving, but also they will know that you are interested in them as people (differentiated instruction and community building in one). Finally, students need to experience lessons in ways that connect to their preferred information-processing styles—whether they are visual, auditory, and/or hands-on learners.

Not only should instruction be differentiated, but assessment needs to be differentiated, too. It is okay to teach students in different ways. It is also okay to require different products from them as a means to assess their understanding and progress. Essentially, students do not all have to do the same homework or take the same tests every day in the classroom setting. Yes, there is a fair amount of **standardized** testing required in our schools. That does not mean all assessment needs to be standardized. As much as possible, it should be customized. Even on the standardized tests, some accommodations can be made, including alternate settings, specialized seating, a scribe or use of computer to record answers, questions read aloud, and extended time to complete the test.

In homework, there are many ways to ensure that all students achieve and practice the same essential understandings and learning objectives without requiring the same products. The following figures illustrate variations of a tool called an assessment menu. Just as in a restaurant, the students have choices in how they are assessed. Simply put, they can choose their homework.

Figure 7.3 is a list menu (Westphal, 2007). The idea is to list several different possibilities for the students to choose from. Each choice would be an effective way for the student to practice a concept and demonstrate understanding.

Each item in the list menu has a point value, and the goal for the student is to complete as many assignments as he or she needs to reach a predetermined sum of points. Example point values are used in the figure with a goal of reaching 100 points, but any values can be used. If a student does not earn full credit on any one assignment, he or she may complete additional activities to reach the goal. Also, the time frame for reaching the goal (e.g., 100 points) may vary depending on the types of activities. The teacher

standardized In conformity with a given standard or rule. In the educational setting, standardized tests are created to assess whether students meet a particular standard of knowledge or skill. Generally, standardized tests are the same test given to a vast number of students across a large demographic area, regardless of the setting in which they learned the material or their diverse learning needs.

✓	Activity/assignment	Possible points	Points earned
	Write spelling words three times each.	**10**	
	Rewrite the list of spelling words in alphabetical order.	**10**	
	Use each spelling word in a sentence.	**10**	
	Create a word search using all spelling words.	**10**	
	Create a crossword puzzle using all spelling words.	**20**	
	Draw an illustration for each of the spelling words. Be sure to label each illustration with the word(s) it depicts.	**20**	
	Create a comic strip using all of the spelling words in the speech bubbles.	**20**	
	Write an acrostic for each spelling word.	**30**	
	Write a song using all of the spelling words.	**30**	
	Write a letter to the principal about a current school issue, using all of the spelling words in the letter.	**40**	

Figure 7.3.   List menu. (Adapted from Westphal, L.E. [2007]. *Differentiating with menus: Language arts.* Waco, TX: Prufrock Press, Inc. http://www.prufrock.com.)

may ask the students to reach 100 points by the end of the week, month, or even marking period. The choice that students have in using an assessment menu has many benefits, including enhanced autonomy; time management; and self-reflection and metacognition regarding their learning needs, styles, and preferences. Time allowed to complete the activities can also vary (3 by the end of the class, 3 by the end of the week, 3 by the end of the marking period) depending on the complexity of the assignments.

Another example is the Tic-Tac-Toe menu (Westphal, 2007) shown in Figure 7.4. This menu allows for nine instructional or assessment variations.

The students have a choice of three in a row (horizontally, vertically, or diagonally). Three tiers or levels of three different variables are represented here. There are three different grouping situations (independently, with a peer partner, and with family members). There are three different information-processing styles (writing, oral communication, and drawing). There are three different curricular areas represented (language arts, mathematics, and social studies). By completing any three in a row, the student will

With a peer partner, construct a time line that includes 10 significant events leading up to the Civil War.	With your family, compare and contrast portraits taken of people/families during the mid 1800s to portraits taken today.	Define and illustrate a list of key words from the readings on the Civil War.
Have a family member quiz you on the spelling and definitions of key words from readings on the Civil War.	Imagining you are a Confederate soldier, write a letter home describing your experiences.	With a peer partner, create a map of the Union and Confederate territories. Indicate important cities and routes.
Write a song or a poem about the Civil War. The words/lyrics should teach someone who has never heard of the war before.	With a peer partner, develop a vocabulary quiz for the rest of the class. Include key words from the readings on the Civil War.	Poll your family members on their opinion about whether women should have been allowed to fight as soldiers in the Civil War.

Figure 7.4.   Tic-Tac-Toe menu. (Adapted from Westphal, L.E. [2007]. *Differentiating with menus: Social studies.* Waco, TX: Prufrock Press, Inc. http://www.prufrock.com.)

experience cross-curricular activities, independent and interdependent learning, connections with families, various learning styles, and social-justice issues. The students can also be given the choice to do more than three. Perhaps they will challenge themselves to do an X or to do the whole grid.

Differentiation Is Not...

It can be very easy to differentiate effectively. It can be just as easy to do it ineffectively. Here are some things that could send you off in the wrong direction:

- Losing sight of the mind-set. It is important to continually return to the mind-set questions and reflect on whether or not you are striving to achieve them in your classroom. Regular sharing of experiences with colleagues is vital.

- Focusing on labels. When you focus on labels, rather than the individual student and his or her strengths, needs, and interests, the strategies you use will become boxed in. You cannot know what a student really needs just by knowing his or her label. Remember, a label is a signpost, not a prescription. Let it point you in the right direction, but not dictate your response.

- Writing 25 different lesson plans for 25 different students. This is not the essence of differentiation. You may have multiple tiers or variations on a lesson, but you will not need as many new versions as you have students. This is due to what is called the **ripple effect**. Any time you come up with a customized strategy for one student, the effects of the strategy will ripple out. It may benefit other students without your planning on it. In addition, the independence the strategy afforded one student will free you up to assist others.

> **ripple effect**   A spreading effect caused by a single action. A ripple effect in the classroom is seen when a teacher implements a strategy to support one particular student's understanding and several more students benefit from the strategy as well.

Differentiation strategies and ideas are often simple: allowing a student to tell a friend the answer rather than writing it down, spelling words in sand or shaving cream rather than on paper, using large writing utensils or a pencil grip on standard-sized utensils, allowing a little more time to finish, and/or providing choices for projects or homework. You do not need a specialist degree to do any of these—just a mind-set, a desire to think out of the box, and flexibility.

CONSIDERATIONS AND CLASSROOM CASES

The more ideas you collect and try in your classroom, the better equipped you will be to meet challenges that come your way. Here are several things to consider in the way of potential challenges:

Dichotomous Needs

We have talked a lot about getting to know the strengths and needs of each individual student. You will almost never teach students individually in isolation from one another. You will have a classroom full of students who are learning together at the same time. You need to be able to meet their needs as they interact. This will be a particular challenge when you have students with **dichotomous** or opposing needs. Perhaps there is a student who needs soft lighting to increase the amount of time he can spend processing written materials, and at the same time another student needs bright overhead lights to better illuminate the classroom space. How can you meet both of these students' needs? Take turns so that only one of them at a time receives the lighting he needs? Of course not. You will need to come up with a solution to this challenge. Take some time now to brainstorm at least three different solutions.

> **dichotomous**   Divided into two sharply distinguished parts. An example of dichotomous needs in the classroom is if one student needs dim lighting and another student needs bright lighting.

Perhaps there is a student in the class who is easily distracted by voices during quiet, independent work time. If she hears others, she finds herself shifting attention to what they are saying and away from the task she is working on. She then has a difficult time refocusing. Also in the classroom is a student who needs to read out loud to best process the text. Often during quiet, independent work time, he reads out loud. Take a few minutes now to brainstorm at least three different solutions for this challenge.

Here is one more example. You have a student in your class who has a large personal bubble. He becomes anxious if others come too close or touch him. There is also a student in your class who regularly wanders around the room and touches objects and classmates. Every time the wandering student comes near, the first student begins to panic. Take a few minutes to brainstorm at least three solutions to this challenge.

We have asked you to brainstorm multiple solutions, because you may need to try several before you find the best one to meet everyone's needs. The solutions should be reasonable in time, effort, and complexity so that you can continue them consistently over time.

Restricted Budget

It would be wonderful if school districts, buildings, and classrooms were allotted as much money as they might need to meet everyone's needs. The reality, however, is that school budgets are tight. Budgets fluctuate between districts and states, but the bottom line is that teachers often use their own money to supply materials for their classrooms. Some have discretionary money for extra things like furniture, carpets, or math manipulatives, but other teachers do not, so they need to supply everything on their own, including paper for the copy machine.

There are paths that teachers can take to solve this challenge. One is to advocate for more funding. This is a long-term solution and will require knowledge of policy making, lobbying, and union negotiations. A second is to apply for grants. This is a somewhat long-term solution and requires quite a bit of time and expertise with funding agencies and proposal writing. These paths should be pursued, but in the meantime, there are students in your classroom waiting for the things they need to learn. So, the short-term solution is to get creative. Think out of the box once again. As Theodore Roosevelt said, "Do what you can, with what you have, where you are." Not having a hefty budget is not an excuse. There is an infinite number of things you can do for free or for very little pocket money. Here are a few examples:

- A desktop easel can promote independence in handwriting, wrist extension, fine-motor skills and hand development, and visual attention to the task as well as proper positioning of the upper extremity. Easels can be purchased online for $50 to $100. An excellent reproduction can be made by gluing a large binder clip and nonslip shelf liner to a three-ring binder for less than $5.

- The following are just five web sites where you can access free stuff for teachers—from worksheets to computer software and hardware to games and toys. You just need the time to look:

  - http://www.scattercreek.com/~zimba/freeforteachers.htm

  - http://www.freakyfreddies.com/teacher.htm

  - http://www.coolfreebielinks.com/Teachers_Freebies/

  - http://www.netrover.com/~kingskid/freestuff.htm

  - http://www.sldirectory.com/teachf/freestuff.html

- Specialty classroom carpets with seating arrangements, letters, and numbers can be purchased for $100 to $300—or you can purchase a warehouse remnant for $20 to $40 and apply any symbols with colored masking tape. Often, home improvement discount stores will give you carpet squares for free rather than throw them out. You just need to be bold enough to ask.

- To cut down on noise and floor damage or to increase stability of classroom chairs, teachers sometimes place tennis balls on the bottom of each chair leg. These balls can be purchased for $1–$2 each ($4–$8 per chair), or you can visit tennis clubs in your area and ask for any "dead" tennis balls they are discarding. As a backup, dollar stores often stock them as well (a can of three balls for $1). They may not be the best tennis balls, but that's okay; they are not for Wimbledon.

Increasing Levels of Independence

The purpose of differentiating for each student is to allow them to become more independent learners. You want to provide them with what they need so they come to know their learning needs and required supports so they can create and use them on their own. This is included in Wormeli's (2007) second charge of differentiation.

Your role is to make sure you are providing supports in a way that scaffolds a student toward independence rather than supporting them in a way that makes them rely on you more and more. If you are doing it right, they will grow to not need you.

Seeking the "Best" Strategy

The challenge is that there is not a "best" strategy. The absolute best thing you come up with for one student may not be very helpful to another, even if they have very similar learning needs and styles. Strategies that are effective in one teacher's classroom may not yield the same results in another classroom. Perhaps the teachers have different mind-sets about students' abilities or their own roles as teachers. Perhaps one scaffolds the students toward independence more than the other. In other words, a strategy is only as good as the context and purpose in which it is applied. In the sidebar, Alan Brightman, founder of Apple Computer's Worldwide Disability Solutions Group, explains software in an excerpt from his book *DisabilityLand.*

The Need to Shift Others' Paradigms

There is one more thing you will be doing while you are teaching your students: You simultaneously will be teaching colleagues, parents, and community members. Part of advocating for your students will be to avoid missing any opportunity to change views on disability. These opportunities will arise in many different situations.

When the teacher down the hall insists that students who are not able to behave appropriately in class should be pulled out so as to eliminate disruptions, an opportunity has arisen to teach the idea that no student needs to earn the right to be included.

From *DisabilityLand*

We were often asked by teachers and by parents, "What's the best special education software?" Or, similarly: "My daughter has a learning disability. What software should I get for her?" Or, similarly: "My son was recently placed in a mainstream class. What software should I get for him?" And so on.

It's an impossible question. I understand why it was asked so much. And, of course, it remains forever unanswerable.

Two reasons.

Software isn't written for a diagnostic label, just as software isn't written for a person's name. You might as well ask for software for a person who wears a size 9 shoe.

More importantly, there is no such thing as special education software. Really. There's good software and there's not-so-good software. There's software that says "special education" on the packaging and there's software that says nothing about any kind of education at all.

How to decide?

Go for the good software and ignore the packaging. Go with what works best for your unique situation. That'll be your best special education software.

But keep one important point always in mind. It doesn't have to be "educational software" to be educational software. Computer programs that help kids draw, to play music, to make up silly sounds...none of these are expressly considered "educational." But in the hands of a good teacher, they might be just what the student needs to reach a particular goal.

Then of course there's the Internet, home of more great software for special education than you'll find anywhere else. And it's all free...at least to try.

So let's review. What's the best education software?

Still unanswerable. For me.

But for you, no longer.

Brightman (2008), p. 77.

When a parent is concerned that her child will not get the attention she needs because there are students with disabilities in the classroom, an opportunity has arisen to teach the idea that everyone in the classroom will benefit and learn from each other and that all children have areas of need.

When the principal denies your request for a piece of assistive technology because it is too much to ask for only one student, an opportunity has arisen to teach the idea that the student who requires it is not the only one, but only one of many, who will benefit.

SUMMARY

This chapter began by building an important foundation or conceptual framework for supporting the success of all students in the classroom. You learned that it is important to support full citizenship in the classroom for all students. You may not always do the same thing for all students to be fair. Rather, you will differentiate both instruction and assessment. In the second section of the chapter, you learned about the theory and practice of differentiation of instruction and specific strategies for both. Last, important considerations were presented for effective differentiation; case studies and specific examples of successful problem solving by classroom teachers who value the full citizenship of all students were presented. In the next chapter, we will describe what happens when every aspect of the classroom is highly and consistently differentiated for all—a universal design of instruction.

CHAPTER 8

Universal Design for Learning

How this chapter prepares you to be an effective inclusive classroom teacher:

- This chapter teaches you the many ways that students are diverse and how that affects their learning in the classroom. It addresses ways for you to be active and resourceful in seeking to understand how primary language, culture, and familial backgrounds interact with the individual's exceptional condition to affect the individual's academic and social abilities, attitudes, values, and interests. **This helps you meet CEC Standard 3: Individual Learning Differences.**

- This chapter teaches you about universal design for learning and how to create a classroom that allows for active engagement, self-motivation, empowerment, self-advocacy, and independence of all students, and that values diverse characteristics and needs. **This helps you meet CEC Standard 5: Learning Environments and Social Influence.**

- In this chapter, you will learn about a case study of a fourth-grade teacher whose classroom is universally designed for learning. This chapter will teach you how she modifies instruction and support strategies based on ongoing evaluation of student needs and progress. The case study shows you how the teacher meets all of her students' individualized education programs when she plans and how she uses appropriate pedagogy and technologies to support student learning. **This helps you meet CEC Standard 7: Instructional Planning.**

- This chapter prepares you to be a professional and ethical teacher by teaching that your role as a teacher is to actively plan and engage in activities that foster your professional growth and keep you current with evidence-based practices. You will learn about many resources and strategies needed to adjust instruction in consideration of students' needs, not impose instruction upon students. You will also learn that knowing how to differentiate for all learners is a lifelong learning process, because no two students are alike. You will keep learning how to do this as long as you keep meeting new students during your career. **This helps you meet CEC Standard 9: Professional and Ethical Practice.**

After reading and discussing this chapter, you will be able to

- Explain the concept of universal design for learning (UDL) and its impact on the full citizenship and inclusion of students

- Explain the principle of multiple means of representation and provide examples

- Explain the principle of multiple means of expression and provide examples

- Explain the principle of multiple means of engagement and provide examples

- Explain the concept and importance of self-regulation

- Explain what executive functions are and how they can be supported by UDL

- Describe the difference between intrinsic and extrinsic motivation

- Explain how universal design of physical space fits into the concept of UDL

- Explain what assistive technology is and how it fits into the concept of UDL

- Provide several examples of high, middle, and low assistive technology

- Explain how Beth, the teacher in the case study, met each principle of UDL

universal design for learning (UDL) Concept that the learning environment, including the space, curriculum and social community, are fully accessible to all persons.

In Chapter 7, you learned about the conceptual framework for ensuring full citizenship of all students in your classroom and received some initial ideas for putting that into practice. This chapter builds on the idea that all aspects of the classroom should be highly differentiated for all students. This is called **universal design for learning (UDL)**. This chapter is divided into four sections. The first section defines the concept of universal design for learning (UDL). The second section discusses the purpose of UDL. The third section covers the three principles of UDL and the application of those principles in developing a UDL curriculum, including instructional goals, methods, materials, and assessment. The fourth section provides a case example of a fourth-grade teacher who strives to provide a classroom space and curriculum according to the principles of UDL.

The narrative is written by Tina Calabro, whose son has cerebral palsy. She tells us about collaboration needed for universal design.

DEFINITION OF UNIVERSAL DESIGN FOR LEARNING

According to the Higher Education Opportunity Act of 2008, universal design for learning

> provides flexibility in the ways information is presented, in the ways students respond or demonstrate knowledge and skills, and in the ways students are engaged; and reduces barriers in instruction, provides appropriate accommodations, supports, and challenges, and maintains high achievement expectations for all students, including students with disabilities and students who are limited English proficient. (p. 11)

Universal design for learning is a set of principles to follow when developing curriculum, so that the curriculum meets the needs of every student, giving all students equal opportunity to learn (National Center on Universal Design for Learning, 2011c).

WHY UNIVERSAL DESIGN FOR LEARNING?

The purpose of UDL is to meet the needs of all students in an inclusive classroom. Students are vastly diverse—in what they learn (what they perceive), how they learn (how they process), and why they learn (what interests and motivates them). If a curriculum is designed with a single "average" student in mind, it will exclude more students than it includes because students learn in many different ways. No two students are alike in their thought processes, learning styles, abilities, or interests.

The National Center on Universal Design for Learning (2011a) described traditional curricula—those designed for the "average" student—as having curricular disabilities. Those curricula are disabled because not every student is "average." They present the content in one or two ways that are typically accessible to an average student but they offer limited instructional options.

A UDL curriculum identifies all the different ways a curriculum needs to be customized so that it can be accessed by all students. Addressing what, how, and why students learn, and understanding what each student would report about what he or she learns, empowers educators to create classrooms where all students are full citizens. It also empowers them to advocate for students so their needs are met in all settings.

An important distinction must be made here. UDL is not the same as retrofitting (making after-the-fact adaptations) a one-size-fits-all curriculum. Rather, UDL is a process by which a curriculum is purposefully and intentionally designed right from the start to address diverse needs (National Center on Universal Design for Learning, 2011c). This is a philosophical distinction as well as a technical one. The practice of retrofitting means that some students (typical students) were thought of first, and other students (those who need adaptations) were thought of later. It sends the message that the classroom is made for only some and others needs to be worked in. This connects to Kliewer's (1998) concepts of full citizens, squatters, and aliens, which were discussed in Chapter 7. That is, full citizenship for all students is difficult with a retrofit model; it is much more possible when UDL is used.

UDL fosters the development of expert learners. Expert learners do not just receive content; they create ways to access content according to their unique needs. These students show that they are resourceful and knowledgeable by activating their own background knowledge to lend it to the learning situation; by identifying and utilizing tools and resources for accessing new learning; and by transforming unfamiliar knowledge into meaningful, useful knowledge. These students show that they are strategic and goal-directed by making plans for learning, organizing effective resources and strategies to be used, and recognizing their own strengths and weaknesses. These students show that they are purposeful and motivated by setting their own challenges, sustaining the effort and persistence needed to achieve the goals, and monitoring their own interest levels and progress toward goals. The way to achieve a classroom that gives every student the chance to be an expert learner is one in which UDL principles are used. Those principles are the described in the next section.

PRINCIPLES OF UNIVERSAL DESIGN FOR LEARNING

There are three primary principles of UDL. The three principles are 1) to provide multiple means of representation, 2) to provide multiple means of action and expression, and 3) to provide multiple means of engagement (National Center on Universal Design for Learning, 2011b).

NARRATIVE 8.1. | TINA CALABRO

My 15-year-old son Mark is in tenth grade at Brashear High School in Pittsburgh, Pennsylvania. He enjoys a fully inclusive education, thanks to the school district's commitment to reaching all students, his parents' involvement, and a well-crafted and implemented IEP.

Mark has athetoid cerebral palsy as a result of asphyxia during birth. He has significant physical disabilities, including quadriplegia and feeding-swallowing disorder. He uses a communication device and an electric wheelchair, both of which he activates with head switches.

When Mark began receiving early intervention services, his therapists introduced a range of assistive technology, such as switches and positioning devices, to enable him to participate in age-appropriate activities. By the time he entered kindergarten, he was using a communication device with a dynamic display, spelling page, and word prediction. The district also provided a one-on-one paraprofessional.

We are fortunate to live in a school district with enthusiastic assistive technology specialists who apply knowledge and effort to the task of ensuring that Mark and other students fully participate in all learning activities. In the primary grades, the school district gave Mark the technological tools he needed to complete "paper" assignments on the computer as well as adaptations and accommodations that allowed him to participate in hands-on activities. In addition, the IEP team met regularly to look ahead in the curriculum to identify barriers to participation and to strategize about how to remove them.

When he entered the intermediate grades, the school district began to provide Mark's textbooks in digital format. The alternative format allowed Mark to move back and forth within a text at his own pace and become a more independent learner. Digital textbooks, wide-ranging computer access, and regular team-planning meetings became the basis for academic success that has extended into Mark's high school years.

PROVIDE MULTIPLE MEANS OF REPRESENTATION

The first principle to follow when designing a curriculum is to provide multiple ways of representing the content to be learned—the "input." If you just provide the content in one way, only the students who can access it that way are going to benefit from it. If you present it in multiple ways, three things happen: 1) more students are going to have access to the new learning, 2) the new information will be reinforced in multiple ways, and 3) students are more likely to be expert learners because they will be familiar with multiple ways to receive information and thus will know what works best for them and can explore a range of ways to learn new information.

To "input" the new learning, three things need to be in place: 1) Students need to be able to perceive the information; 2) students need to be able to understand language, mathematical expressions, and symbols; and 3) students need to be able to comprehend or assign meaning to the information.

Perception   To understand what it means to perceive new learning, we need to make a distinction between sensing and perceiving. Often, senses are confused with

Figure 8.1.   Optical illusion. (From Hill, W.E. [1915]. "My wife and my mother-in-law. They are both in this picture - find them." Illustration in *Puck, 78* [2018], p. 11.)

perceptions. The senses (i.e., sight, hearing, smell, taste, touch) allow us to detect or sense environmental stimuli. **Perception** is what allows us to understand or bring meaning to it once we have sensed it. So, it is possible to sense something, but not be able to perceive it. It is also possible for two different people to sense the same stimuli, but perceive it in different ways. Optical illusions are an example of sight versus visual perception. Look at the image in Figure 8.1. What do you perceive? You may perceive a young woman or you may perceive an old woman. You may even perceive something else entirely, because of the meaning your background knowledge brings to it.

    Perception is needed to learn new information. If teachers present information orally, for instance by lecturing, there are students who will be able to hear the information, but may not be able to make sense of it because they do not perceive auditory input very well. They may need to see it represented visually in words or pictures to process it. Or they may bring a different meaning to the information than the teacher expected, because of their background knowledge and experiences. On the flip side, if teachers present the information visually, by writing on the board or handing out a note packet for example, some students may be able to see and read the information but not be able to make sense of it, because they need to hear an explanation through their preferred auditory modality. In summary, if teachers present information in only one way or assume there is only one way to perceive it, they are excluding many students with differing perceptual abilities.

Understanding Language, Mathematical Expressions, and Symbols

Written information is not only represented in letters and words, it is also represented in numbers and symbols. Not everyone understands these lexicons the same way. Some people are more comfortable with words, while others are more adept at understanding numbers and mathematical symbols. Some have difficulty with both. This depends on the individual's processing style, cultural background, language, and lexical knowledge (National Center on Universal Design for Learning, 2011b).

    There are several ways to make written information more accessible to all students. Vocabulary, numbers, and symbols should be paired with alternative representations of their meaning—photos, illustrations, graphs, or charts. Figure 8.2 contains three different representations of the same information. Which do you prefer? Which helps you

perception Understanding or making meaning from sensory input from the environment.

To-Do List for June

Pay the rent on the 1st.
Haircut at 2:30 p.m. on the 4th.
Take the dog to the vet at 1:00 p.m. on the 8th.
Dentist appointment at 8:45 a.m. on the 9th.
Meet Sarah for lunch at noon on the 10th.
Mom's birthday on the 14th.
Take car for oil change on the 16th.
Visit Grandpa on the 20th.
Bake sale at school on the 24th.
Dance class every Tuesday and Thursday at 6:00 p.m.
Pay the electric bill on the 30th.

Agenda for June

June	Task
1st	Pay the rent.
4th	Haircut at 2:30 p.m.
8th	Dog to vet at 1:00 p.m.
9th	Dentist at 8:45 a.m.
10th	Meet Sarah for lunch at noon.
14th	Mom's birthday
16th	Car for oil change
20th	Visit Grandpa.
24th	Bake sale at school
30th	Pay electric bill.
T/TH	Dance class at 6:00 p.m.

Calendar for June

June						
Sunday	**Monday**	**Tuesday**	**Wednesday**	**Thursday**	**Friday**	**Saturday**
1 Pay the rent	**2**	**3** 6:00 Dance	**4** 2:30 Haircut	**5** 6:00 Dance	**6**	**7**
8 1:00 Vet	**9** 8:45 Dentist	**10** 12:00 Sarah 6:00 Dance	**11**	**12** 6:00 Dance	**13**	**14** Mom's birthday
15	**16** Oil change	**17** 6:00 Dance	**18**	**19** 6:00 Dance	**20** Visit Grandpa	**21**
22	**23**	**24** Bake sale 6:00 Dance	**25**	**26** 6:00 Dance	**27**	**28**
29	**30** Pay electric bill					

Figure 8.2.   Different ways of representing the same information.

understand or keep track of the information more easily? Not everyone will choose the same representation. A curriculum that is universally designed for learning will utilize various representations for all information.

All jargon, slang, and idiomatic expressions should be translated and explained. Structural rules and relationships should be made more explicit, such as the syntax in a sentence or the properties in equations. Make sure everything is available in the person's first language, including American Sign Language for those who sign. This last suggestion is particularly important because students who are learning English as a second language enter classrooms and need access to content presented in Spanish or another first language. In the Rochester City Schools in New York State, some schools have classrooms for first and second graders who speak Spanish that are taught by bilingual teachers—first grade and the first semester of second grade are taught in Spanish. In the second semester of second grade, instruction gradually incorporates both Spanish and English, and in third grade instruction is in English. This very gradual change allows students to perceive information without a language barrier when they are learning to read.

Comprehension   Comprehension occurs when a student takes new information and translates it into useable knowledge. This is an active process that includes attention to select bits of information, integrating new information with existing knowledge, and categorizing the integrated information.

Comprehension can be improved when teachers utilize many different ways to activate existing knowledge. The more connections you can make from what students already know to new information that is learned, the more opportunities you open up for students to comprehend it. The key to comprehension is to connect, connect, connect. Anchor new knowledge to what the students already know. Ask them about their experiences and have them share those experiences with the whole class. Use metaphors and analogies to illustrate concepts. These can also be very powerful in helping students understand how they learn so they can be their own best advocates, a characteristic of expert learners.

For example, a fifth grader was meeting with his teacher and parents following an incident in the classroom. During a particularly chaotic class activity, the student—who has sensory processing difficulties and becomes anxious easily—left the classroom without permission and found a quiet hidden spot in the library to read. When asked why he did that even though he knows it was against the rules, he replied, "Stress for me is like a sieve. When I am stressed, the sieve shakes all of the good decisions out, so when I reach in for a decision, only the bad ones are left." This expression led his teachers to plan a classroom environment that was less stressful for the student.

Another connection to make is between curricular content areas. Working with tessellations (repeated patterns that fill a surface with no gaps, such as a honeycomb or quilt) connects math, art, and science or social studies. Comprehension can also be improved by highlighting patterns or relationships in the information to be learned. Literally using a highlighter to mark the words that rhyme in a poem, the letter combinations in a word family, or the patterns of zero in the multiplication chart can be helpful. Other helpful strategies are providing several examples and nonexamples of a concept and using cues, such as clapping or holding up a hand when new information is used.

PROVIDE MULTIPLE MEANS OF ACTION AND EXPRESSION

The second principle to follow when designing a curriculum is to provide multiple ways for "output"—ways for students to show what they know. The two most common ways that we have students demonstrate their knowledge is through writing (e.g., tests, worksheets, essays) and oral response to teacher-posed questions in class. While these methods should be continued for the students who are well able to demonstrate their learning in these ways, many more options need to be offered as well. To meet the "output" needs of all learners, options for physical expression, options for communication, and options for executive functions (i.e., the functions of organization, planning, and task execution) are essential.

Options for Physical Expression

Some students need to express themselves physically. They need to use their bodies beyond writing and speaking to show what they have learned. Maybe it means tracing letters or words in sand or shaving cream. Maybe it means operating a computer with a joystick, balance board, or eye controls rather than with a traditional mouse. In the narrative by Tina Calabro, we hear that Mark uses head switches to control his wheelchair and communication device. It may mean acting out a concept instead of explaining it. The use of hands-on manipulatives, field trips, and movement around the classroom is essential. Providing options for physical expression also means making sure that everything in the classroom is physically accessible to all students and teachers. Later in this chapter, we will go into more depth about the universal design of classroom space.

Options for Communication

Not everyone is able to express themselves and their knowledge through traditional writing and speaking. It is important to offer many different ways for students to communicate with an audience. Some alternatives for communication include drawing, creating storyboards, film design, music composition, model-making, and sculpture. Assistive technology to help with the writing process may include speech-to-text software, spellcheckers, word-prediction software, and social media such as online discussion forums and blogs.

executive functions
The executive director of the brain's functions. Executive functions make decisions about which skills to use and when, when and how to transition from one skill to the next, and where and how to store the skills when they are not in use. Persons who have executive-function difficulties often struggle with organization, planning, initiating and sustaining tasks, as well as responding to and managing social cues.

scaffolding A way to support a student in new learning. Just like physical scaffolding, instructional scaffolding is made of layers of support that can be removed as the student is able to perform on his or her own.

Options for Executive Functions

Your executive functions are essentially the chief directors of your brain. Another apt metaphor is that they are the "maestro" that conducts your orchestra of skills and abilities (Packer, 2010). **Executive functions** help you decide when and how to use each skill that you have. They are the managers—time managers, material managers, goal setters, planners, task initiators, attention sustainers, and the social skill regulators. Everyone has executive functions, but some people have stronger ones than others.

According to the National Center on Universal Design for Learning, executive abilities are reduced when

> Executive functioning capacity must be devoted to managing "lower level" skills and responses which are not automatic or fluent, thus the capacity for "higher level" functions is taken; and executive capacity is reduced due to some sort of higher-level disability or to lack of fluency with executive strategies. (2011b, p. 5)

UDL responds to stresses on executive functioning by **scaffolding** lower-level skills (such as keeping track of time and materials) so they become more automatic. Once lower-level skills are more automatic, higher-level executive skills (such as long-term goal setting and managing a multistep, complex project) can become more developed (National Center on Universal Design for Learning, 2011b). Skills to be scaffolded are goal-setting, planning, developing strategies that work best for various tasks, managing information to make sense of it, managing all the resources available, and self-monitoring of progress. Scaffolding does not mean doing the work for the students. It means providing a boost or support so the students can accomplish the work themselves. Then, the support is gradually withdrawn or reduced on an individual basis until the student is as independent as possible.

Provide Multiple Means of Engagement

The third principle for designing a curriculum based on UDL is to use many different ways to engage students in learning. Everyone becomes engaged by different types of tasks and different learning situations. Some prefer working alone, while others prefer group work. Some prefer open-ended, highly subjective tasks, while others prefer structured, objective tasks. Each student is unique in his or her learning style and abilities, and in the ways used to engage in various learning opportunities. To increase engagement, teachers need to catch students' interest and help them to sustain effort, to persist toward a goal, and to self-regulate their learning behaviors.

Options for Catching Interest   One of the most effective ways to catch students' interests and encourage them to attend to important information is to provide choice and autonomy. If you have prepared properly, students can choose the process used to accomplish a task, the tools or materials used during the process, and the product they create to show their learning. The differentiated menus in Chapter 7 are an excellent example of offering choice to students. As long as the choices are appropriate—not too easy and not too challenging—providing choice increases interest and engagement.

Another important way to interest students is to offer relevant, valuable, authentic activities. Teaching them to work division problems in math for the purpose of completing a worksheet or test is not authentic. Bringing in a cake and teaching them to work a division problem so that each student receives an equal piece is relevant. Have students bring in real problems from home—how should the vegetable garden be divided, how can I double or halve a recipe, how much tile do I need to cover the bathroom floor—and work the problems to inform their families is valuable. Make sure activities are culturally relevant, as well as socially, developmentally, and individually appropriate.

A final important consideration for increasing interest is to decrease discomfort and distractions. Some students can focus their attention easily on a given task, while others have more difficulty filtering out distractions in the environment, some of which may cause discomfort or distress. There are many factors involved here to make sure the classroom is physically as well as emotionally comfortable. Physically, the temperature should be moderate, the lighting should be adequate, and the furniture appropriate for all students' needs. Emotionally, the classroom should be supportive, free of ridicule and judgment, and encouraging. Each student should be urged to take risks, but not forced out of his or her comfort zone. This comfort zone is unique to each student.

Options for Sustaining Effort and Persistence   Once the teacher has the student's interest, it is important to help the student persevere in his or her efforts. Sustaining effort on a task can be increased by frequently revisiting the goals and steps toward the goal, so the student can "keep an eye on the prize." Varying resources and changing materials can refresh engagement. Fostering collaboration and communication through carefully structured groups helps students guide each other toward task completion. Providing frequent feedback and showing the student how much progress has been made demonstrates how far he or she has come and how much is left to do.

Options for Self-Regulation   For students to self-regulate their learning behaviors, they need to know what those behaviors are and how they can be improved. As a teacher, every time you find an effective strategy for a student, it is important that the student be made aware of the strategy and its positive effect. The more students know about their strengths, needs, and best strategies, the more they will be able to take charge of their own learning, including self-regulating their performance and progress. This is a point that we have made often. Areas in which a student should be self-aware include

self-regulation   The ability to monitor and modify one's own actions as needed.

extrinsic Factors outside or external to a person. They may or may not be tangible. For example, extrinsic rewards are those that are presented from the outside, such as stickers, money, grades, and praise.

intrinsic Factors inside or internal to a person. They are intangible. For example, intrinsic rewards are those a person feels inside, such as pride, a sense of accomplishment, interested engagement, and a sense of joy.

extrinsic (external) and **intrinsic** (internal) motivators, personal coping skills, self-assessment, and self-reflection. Some extrinsic motivators may be grades, prizes, or extra recess. Some intrinsic motivators may be pride in a job well done, excitement about the topic, or a feeling of challenge. Coping skills that help students focus their attention or work through overwhelming situations include drawing or doodling, chewing gum, talking to a peer or counselor, and writing in a journal. Self-assessment and self-reflection are difficult to develop. It is not easy to step back, look at ourselves objectively, and be honest and specific about how we are doing and how we can improve. Teachers can provide scaffolds that help students assess their own performance and reflect on ways to improve.

A UNIVERSAL DESIGN FOR LEARNING CLASSROOM

For a classroom to be universally designed for learning, the three principles and ideas must be applied to both the curriculum and the physical space. Curriculum and space are not the same thing, but they are closely related. Look at Figure 8.3. Universally designed curriculum and universally designed classroom space overlap. They both are steered by the principles guiding multiple inputs, outputs, and kinds of engagement. Remember that a UDL curriculum includes what is learned, how it is learned, and why it is learned. The physical classroom space—including assistive technology—is part of how it is learned. It is the context, the format, the environment where it all takes place.

A space is universally designed if it usable to all people to the greatest extent possible without having to be modified or retrofitted (Connell et al., 1997). Consideration of several elements can help accomplish this. First, the space should be designed so that people with different abilities can all use the space equitably. Equipment should accommodate different physical needs; there should be provisions for privacy and safety for

UNIVERSAL DESIGN FOR LEARNING

Principle 1:

Provide multiple means of representation.

Principle 2:

Provide multiple means of action and expression.

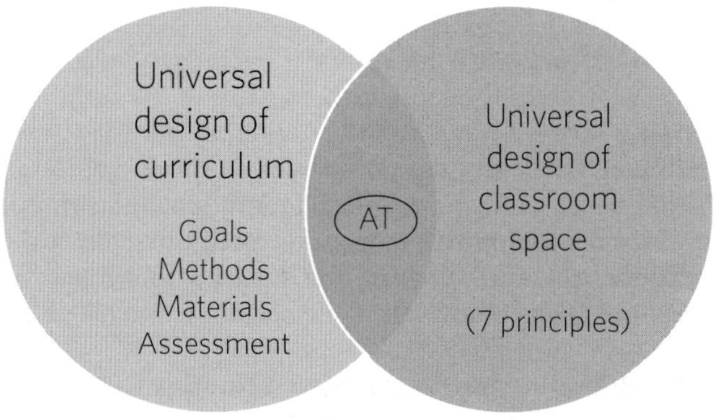

Universal design of curriculum

Goals
Methods
Materials
Assessment

AT

Universal design of classroom space

(7 principles)

Principle 3:

Provide multiple means of engagement.

Figure 8.3. Universal design for learning.

all, so that no one is stigmatized or segregated. Think back to a scenario shared in Chapter 3. The main entrance of a retail store was not wheelchair accessible and the wheelchair entrance was located in the back alley next to a smelly dumpster, where one had to wait until the doorbell was answered. Even though all customers had physical access to the store, it was not equitable. Second, the space should be flexible in use. Choice should be available to all users, equipment should be both right- and left-handed, and adaptability should be provided for each user's pace. An example of this is an ATM with visual, tactile, and auditory feedback, a tapered card slot, and a palm rest. Third, the use of the space should be simple and intuitive. Use should not depend on specialized training or experience, language skills, or concentration level. A good example is a set of instructions with drawings for each step. Fourth, information should be perceptible. Essential information should be presented in visual, auditory, and tactile modes. A good example is a thermostat with visual, tactile, and auditory cues. Fifth, the space should have tolerance for error. Warnings of hazards should be provided and equipment should have fail-safe features. Good examples of this are double-cut car keys that work either way they are inserted, and "undo" features on computer programs. Sixth, the space should require low physical effort. Equipment should allow users to maintain neutral body position and reasonable operating force. Lever handles on doors are an example because they can be operated with minimal force by an open or closed hand. Last, there should be size and space for all to approach and use equipment. Pathways should be roomy, lines of sight should be clear, and equipment should be at heights that allow everyone to use it. When spaces are designed with these elements in mind, they respond to diverse academic, social-emotional, and sensory-physical needs (Peterson & Hittie, 2010).

Assistive Technology

Assistive technology is part of a universally designed space as well as part of universally designed curriculum. **Assistive technology (AT)** can be described as tools, devices, or equipment that helps people accomplish functions or tasks. AT can be mechanical, electronic, electromagnetic, or hydraulic in nature, and the areas supported by AT include seating and positioning, mobility, hearing and sight, speech and communication, prosthetics, academics, daily living tasks, sports, and recreation.

IDEA 2004 requires that AT devices and services be considered for every child when developing his or her IEP. IDEA 2004 defines AT as "any item, piece of equipment, or product system, whether acquired commercially off the shelf, modified, or customized, that is used to increase, maintain, or improve functional capabilities of a child with a disability" (Sec. 602).

assistive technology (AT) Devices or products that allow a person to perform in a way that they would not otherwise be able to do. Areas supported by assistive technology include mobility, communication, computer access, hearing and sight, play and recreation, and seating.

Low-Tech versus High-Tech Assistive Technology

Assistive technology ranges in its complexity from low tech to high tech. Factors considered in deciding the complexity of AT are transparency of purpose, cost, and the time and effort required for its development, training, and use. Low-tech AT is transparent; the purpose or reason for its use is evident. The cost is reasonable, so most people could purchase these items for home or school use without financial assistance. There is little to no training required to use these items. Examples include pencil grips, lever door handles, push-button light switches, and motion-sensor faucets. Medium- or middle-tech AT is a little less transparent in its purposed use. The meaning is guessable, but some training or instruction would be necessary to make full use of it. The cost is a little higher. Examples include DVD or VCR players, digital watches, alarm clocks, and advanced calculators. High-tech AT is the least transparent. Typically, AT of this level is so complex that its use requires specialized training and practice. The cost is high, so that financial assistance is almost always necessary. Examples include augmentative communication devices such as Dynavox or Tango, digital hearing aids, and adapted computer hardware or software.

When Cost Is Prohibitive   The more complex and specialized the assistive technology, the higher the cost. Many teachers would like to outfit their classrooms with many assistive devices, but the cost is prohibitive. Rather than going without, creative teachers have found a way to recreate AT themselves to stretch their budget. Obviously, higher-tech AT cannot be homemade, but much of the low-tech AT can be, so that budget dollars can be used to purchase the high tech. The Oklahoma Assistive Technology Center web site shows several homemade assistive devices, including a desktop display made from a triangular potato chip can, a pencil grip crafted from the handle of a milk jug, and foam core page "fluffers" (2011).

Assistive Technology Is an Investigation, Not Just a Product   The most important thing to remember about AT is that its usefulness is not inherent in the device, but rather in the relationship between device and user; it is only helpful when it matches the person using it. Since a user's needs and abilities are ever-evolving, the best AT for that person should evolve too. It is a lifelong process of investigating the most supportive and liberating devices for individuals.

Assistive Technology Used to Increase Independence   AT can be a wonderful support if it allows a student to perform a task that he or she would otherwise not be able to do. The AT becomes a dependency when a student could increasingly perform a skill, but depends on the AT to do it instead. An example from Rapp (2005) is the use of an FM amplifier in the classroom. A student who is hard of hearing might use the amplifier because he or she is not able to hear all classroom sounds without it. Since the student is not able to improve his hearing, the device allows him to experience the classroom as equitably as possible, rather than impeding the development of a skill. However, if the same FM amplifier is used by a student who has difficulties with auditory processing, she may become overly dependent on the device to filter out background noise, when she could be developing that skill on her own without a device.

Universally designed curriculum and universally designed space—supported by AT—combine as universal design for learning. When these are considered and carefully planned, the result is a classroom proactively created with all students in mind. The following case example highlights a fourth-grade teacher who exemplifies UDL.

Case Example   It is a bright, sunny day in July. School has been out for about a month, and the next school year is still 6 weeks away. The past month has been very relaxing for Beth Jackelen, a fourth-grade teacher at French Road Elementary School in Rochester, New York. She had a great time at her son's high school graduation party. She has been to Boston to visit her daughter, and she has found a lot of time for reading and taking long walks. Even though the summer is only half over, Beth begins to think forward to the new school year. It is time to get to know her students and for them to start to get to know her.

Beth begins with an introductory letter to her students and their families. The letter introduces herself as a teacher, mom, and lifelong learner. It lets them know what to expect the first few days of school and during the whole school year—the friends they will make, field trips they will take, and goals they will accomplish together. Finally, the letter invites the students and their families to visit the classroom in mid-August, before the year begins. Then, Beth makes copies of the letter in every language spoken in the homes of students in her district. She uses Google Translate to make versions in Spanish and Turkish, because she knows that there are students in her building who speak those languages.

Beth knows that some students need to be prepared ahead of time. They need to know what the classroom looks like, what she is like, and where they will sit the first day. Doing her part to relieve that anxiety is just one way that she creates an accessible classroom for all of her students. Plus, those initial visits contribute to the year-long process of gathering valuable information about her students.

Beth takes a look at the roster for the upcoming school year. She has just received it, because a great deal of schoolwide planning has taken place to create each roster. Beth notices she has a diverse class in many ways[1]—10 boys and 11 girls; seven students have IEPs, two have Section 504 plans, four students have two households listed due to joint custody arrangements, one student lives with grandparents, three students have same-sex parents, and one student speaks Russian as her first language with English as her second language. Beth practices saying each name aloud. She gets to Marjika Fields. She is not sure how to pronounce it and makes a note to ask Marjika. The other note she makes is to ask Jameson Claremont if he has a preferred nickname. He is new to the school this year, so one was not listed on the roster.

Next, Beth looks at each student's folder, reading last year's report cards, as well as each IEP and 504 plan. Beth thinks about the mixed feelings other teachers have expressed about this. Some say they like to read as much as they can so they know everything there is to know about the students before they arrive. Others prefer to steer clear of the cumulative files until they have met the students so they aren't tainted by others' opinions. On reflection, Beth agrees they have valid points, but she thinks about it differently. She likes to read the information so she can be prepared, but she does not believe the files could ever tell her everything there is to know about her students. Even after a whole school year of getting to know them, there will be still more to know. This year, the files provide her with enough information to determine an initial classroom arrangement that will respond to many different learning needs. She knows she will need to adjust as needs change and more information comes to light, but what she starts with can be seen in Figure 8.4.

Beth has decided to arrange the student desks into pods of six, in direct line with the Smart Board that she uses for direct instruction. The pods are situated so that no student's back is to the Smart Board. The roster includes 21 students, so three of the pods will start with an empty seat. If she receives a new student during the year, there will be some choice for the best place for the new student. The pods are also conducive to variable grouping. It will be easy for students to work in small groups, individually, or break off into pairs. She has room to converse with each student at his or her desk without disturbing the others in the pod.

Beth thinks about her "wish list" of classroom supplies. When budget allows, the first thing on the list is various seating alternatives. She would love to have a few exercise balls for kids who wiggle while they work, and she can think of a few students who would benefit from swivel chairs so they can see any wall in the classroom without changing how they are seated in the chair. Also, she wishes the desks could be better adjusted for size. The current desks have one or two height settings in the legs, but the width and depth should vary, too.

Beth places the teacher desk near the Smart Board so she can access teaching materials quickly during direct instruction, but it is out of the way of most classroom traffic, because she rarely sits down there when class is in session. There is an extra student

---

[1]Information about Beth's class is not reflective of any one class. It reflects a conglomeration that is representative of a typical roster for any teacher in the school. All student names are fictitious.

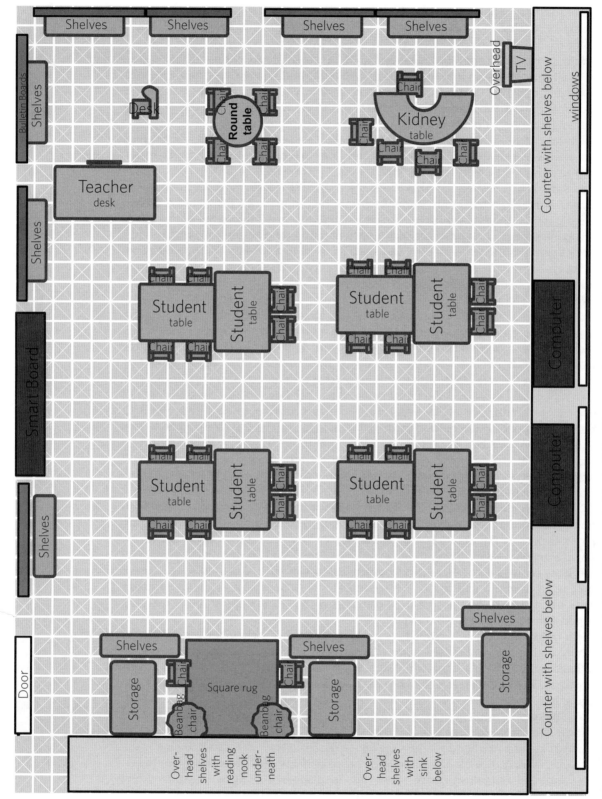

Figure 8.4. Classroom map. (Adapted from Classroom Architect at http://classroom.4teachers.org/.)

desk. Rather than have it returned to storage, she decides to keep it and places it in a light traffic area near her own desk. Along with the round table, it offers another place for students to choose to complete independent work. She knows that some students need to find an isolated spot, while others may need a breakout area to use with a classmate who is not in the same pod. The kidney-shaped table will be used primarily for guided reading groups and is surrounded by teacher and student materials used for this purpose. When guided reading groups are not taking place, it offers yet another breakout workspace.

Beth's favorite spot is the quiet area. Partially nestled in a nook under overhead storage shelves, the quiet area includes a soft rug, giant pillows, beanbag chairs, and upright chairs. The area is surrounded by bookcases that hold a vast range of books and isolate the area from much of the classroom stimuli. There are books at all reading levels. Beth knows it is important for students to have a choice of books that are at, below, and above their current reading levels. She makes sure there are books on many different topics that reflect the interests of her students, as well as culturally relevant books that respond to a range of experiences. Beth arranges a few more storage shelves near the sink and surveys the room from the Smart Board. She can see every area clearly, and has an accessible place for everything she needs during the school day. Beth walks around the classroom several times, taking a different path each time. There is plenty of room among the pods and other furniture for comfortable mobility. This arrangement will certainly change once students enter and Beth sorts out what this particular group of students needs, but this is a great starting point.

Time to think about sensory needs. Because a few of her students have experienced sensory processing difficulties with respect to lighting, over this area and the nearest pod of desks, Beth has the fluorescent light bulbs removed. There is still enough light to read by, but the glare and harsh contrasts are much reduced, as is the hum of the lights. Beth has heard of a product called Classroom Light Filters by Educational Insights. They are flame-retardant, tranquil-colored cloths that stretch over classroom lights and are held in place with Velcro. She adds this to her wish list. Each chair leg in the classroom is already equipped with a tennis ball fitted over the end. She carefully inspects each one. Only a few are worn through or too loose. She pulls out her bin of tennis balls, carefully slits an X on a few with an X-Acto knife, and fits them in place. She makes a note to revisit the nearby tennis club to see if they have another used batch of balls for her. Next, she cleans her box of fidget toys. These are handheld items with many different textures or movements—a sand-filled balloon, a Rubik's Cube, a hacky sack, a golf ball. She has found that many students can sustain attention longer if they handle a fidget toy during class. Some students stick with their favorites and others rotate through them. Funny, she thinks, that some teachers won't use them because of the potential distraction, but she has found that students are less distracted when they are available.

Phew! All ready for the mid-August visits. Beth can't wait to meet her new fourth graders!

Marjika Fields peeks hesitantly around the doorway into her new classroom. Her neighbor had Mrs. Jackelen last year and said she was very nice, but sometimes tough. Excitement and nervousness mix together into a familiar feeling that Marjika associates with the first day of school. Mrs. Jackelen is talking to another boy and his parents, so Marjika and her mom start to look around. Marjika smiles at all the books in the quiet area. She loves to read! It will be fun to lie in a bean bag chair and pick a new book. Next, she sees the sink. Two coffee makers are set up on the counter near a sign that reads, "These pots will always be full of hot water. Be sure to bring in a supply of cocoa or soup mix for a hot treat on cold winter days!" Marjika's mom smiles and pulls out her grocery list to add cocoa mix and soup packets.

Beth bids good-bye to the other student and welcomes the Fields to her classroom. Marjika shakes her hand and says her name (mar-yee'-ka) so Beth is now sure of the pronunciation. Beth shows them around the room, asking Marjika questions about her summer and her favorite things to do in school—important information for getting to know each student. Beth also shows them materials to take home with them. Some of the sheets are school information for them to keep at home and some are questionnaires for them to complete and return the first day of school—"What's the scoop?"—with questions all about themselves and a reading-interest survey. Also, Marjika should bring in a new white t-shirt for their first project—decorating their own class shirt. The last sheet is a list of supplies for the school year. Ms. Fields asks why the folders have to be five different colors, as listed. Beth explains that the students' work will be color-coded to help students who struggle with planning and organization. It is just one way that she has found that helps them remember where everything is and where to keep it when it's done. She also welcomes Marjika to decorate her colored folders if she would like them to be unique. Beth also uses a reminder bulletin board. For the first month, reminders are posted and student work with no name is hung to be claimed. After that, she gradually weans the students off the reminders to help them form planning habits of their own. Although Marjika does not need help in that area, Ms. Fields agrees it is a good idea to have a predictable routine like that for everyone.

The theme of the room is a lily pond. There are lots of frogs and lily pads for decoration. Marjika has written her name on a frog-shaped Post-It note and stuck it to the seat she chose, so she already feels like a frog in the pond. Before she leaves, Marjika takes one more look around the classroom. There are many bulletin boards covered in bright paper ready to be decorated. There are a few things on the walls, but most everything is hanging neatly on a bulletin board within a bold border. Marjika likes this. It is easier to scan everything without feeling overwhelmed or too distracted. Marjika can't wait for fourth grade to start!

After the Fields leave, Beth has a few minutes to herself, so she reviews the test modifications listed on her students' IEPs and 504 plans. She begins to create her "Test Day" chart. She lists all 21 of her students' names down one side and several different testing accommodations across the top. She starts by checking off the accommodations officially listed for students (see Figure 8.5). Having them at-a-glance like this will ensure she doesn't overlook anything for a test or quiz. As the school year progresses and she has an opportunity to get to know her students and observe their performance during assessments, Beth knows she will be checking off additional accommodations for additional students. There is no reason why she can't make all of her students more comfortable during a test. Plus, they will all benefit from the classwide exercises they do on test days—yoga and Brain Gym!

Suddenly, a boy comes bounding into the room. "Hi! I'm Jamie. Jamie Claremont. Jameson Claremont, but I'm Jamie. Just Jamie. Hi! Wow, look at all these frogs. I love frogs!" Beth tells Jamie that she loves frogs too, so they already have something in common. While Jamie travels around the room, checking everything out, Beth speaks to his parents. "As you can see, Jamie is a lot of boy," they begin. "He has been diagnosed ADHD, but we have chosen not to medicate him. We have changed districts, hoping that he can get the support he needs to be successful in school without medication. That just didn't happen in our last district. It's a tall order." Beth has never shied away from tall orders before and doesn't intend to with Jamie, though she does make a mental note that she may need some help with new strategies this year. She spends the next several minutes talking to Jamie's parents about ways to maintain open and frequent communication in addition to the weekly class newsletters that include each student's reflections on the week. They decide right away to set up a journal for Jamie to carry back and forth with updates on home and school happenings, and they set up a date to meet during

	Extra time	Alternate location	Refocus	Short breaks	Stand up and move as needed	Bean bags and clipboard
Jamie	X		X	X		X
Marjika						
Seth					X	
Julie	X	X	X			
Michael	X	X				
Bethany						
Chris	X					
Jose						
Zoe P.	X	X		X		
Zoe R.						
Daniel						X
Gia						
Noel	X	X				
Matt						
Grace	X					X
Heath	X	X	X	X		
Noah						
Lauren						
Svetlana	X					
Li					X	

Figure 8.5. Test day accommodations chart.

the third week of school, right after Meet the Teacher Night. That night, she will have families complete questionnaires about their children and their new school year experiences. It will be helpful to follow up on the Claremonts' responses.

Beth spends the rest of the day meeting several more students and their families. She straightens up the room and heads home. She will do this for the rest of the week so that most, if not all, of the families have a chance to come in. And so begins a new year.

The first few months are fun, but very tiring, as they should be. By November, the community in the classroom has developed. The class has signed a class constitution and engages in several discussions about its implementation, completed buddy projects around the character-education qualities promoted by the whole school, collaboratively built toothpick and marshmallow towers to see how different groups come up with different processes and products, formed bonds with their homework buddies, and put together a time capsule of their favorite things to revisit at year's end.

Also by this time of the year, the students have mastered many different ways of showing what they know. They have given oral reports, written papers and poems, created artifacts, and used various software programs (Jamie likes Raz-Kids the best). All of the students have become comfortable supervising morning business tasks, using the Smart Board for writing and printing notes and running video clips, and making use of the breakout areas in the room. Although some still need support, most of the students are independent in making choices about completing projects, homework menus, and their weekly reflections. They are familiar and comfortable with seating changes, because they know some students need to try different places for learning and it helps them get to know new friends.

Beth has learned a lot, too. In the beginning of the year, she proactively planned for as much as she could, but has remained flexible to try new things as the need arose. She has used many different strategies for several of her students. Jamie is making good use of his desktop checklist so he gets through his work each day. She has added new fidgets, locker checklists, and folder labels for Chris, who is color-blind. Everything in the room is labeled for Svetlana, whose English is growing in leaps and bounds. Music is played at transition time while the Smart Board displays a visual timer. A few minutes of daily yoga has resulted in increased focus and time on-task.

The rest of the school year progresses successfully. All of Beth's lessons have been auditory, visual, and hands-on in some way. Student work groups have changed regularly. Beth's parent-teacher binder grows thicker as she records notes at each meeting. Teaching assistants, push-in special education teachers, autism spectrum–disorder consultants, and college teacher-education students have become important members of the classroom community. The classroom AT repertoire now also includes Fusion laptop computers for students who type instead of write by hand, Flip video cameras for creating motion pictures or capturing field trips, and tape recorders for creating books on tape. Community connections have been established with high school students in a homework club and guest speakers who come to the classroom to talk about the importance of education in various careers. Sometimes problems arose, but Beth always found time to collaborate with teachers, administrators, and families to brainstorm solutions. One example is finding a way to increase travel time through the school for a student with limited mobility.

Beth's classroom is a great example of one that is universally designed for learning. All three principles are exemplified—multiple means of representation, action and expression, and engagement. Many of the things she does apply to more than one of the principles. For example, the use of the Smart Board provides an effective way to represent new learning to the students, provides an effective way for students to express their learning, and provides an effective way to engage students with many different learning styles. Infused throughout all of these is a strong classroom community where students are valued for their uniqueness, strengths, and weaknesses. It is a place where they felt welcome right at the start, where they are safe taking risks and making mistakes, and where they are secure in knowing they have a teacher who is dedicated to finding solutions to problems if they arise.

SUMMARY

This chapter introduced the concept and principles of universal design for learning. The importance of doing this is to make sure that every classroom is designed with every student in mind. UDL encompasses many aspects of the classroom, including space, curriculum, socialization and community building, communication with families, teaching methods, materials, and assessments. The case example of Beth's classroom and the narrative by Tina Calabro illustrate the success students can experience if they are in a setting where they are full citizens.

CHAPTER 9

Assessment

How this chapter prepares you to be an effective inclusive classroom teacher:

- In this chapter, the assessment processes in response to intervention (RTI) and in the eligibility for special education emphasize the importance of gathering information to inform future instruction and decisions about placement and services. The importance of working with families as integral members of the special education team is emphasized. Understanding differences in learning builds the foundation for you to provide meaningful and challenging learning for individuals with exceptional learning needs. **This helps you meet CEC Standard 3: Individual Learning Differences.**

- This chapter reviews the importance of individualized decision making and instruction. The individualized education program (IEP) process and RTI process support teachers' developing long-range individualized instructional plans anchored in both general and special education curricula. The teacher's role in developing clear instructional plans grounded in assessment data is emphasized. **This helps you meet CEC Standard 7: Individual Learning Differences.**

- This chapter carefully reviews the RTI and special education eligibility processes, including the importance of gathering formative data from a range of sources. This review supports your knowledge about the legal policies and ethical principles of measurement and assessment related to referral, eligibility, program planning, instruction, and placement for individuals with exceptional learning needs, including those from culturally and linguistically diverse backgrounds. In this chapter, you are introduced to the importance of using assessment information to identify supports and adaptations for all students. This chapter introduces practices for addressing issues of validity, reliability, norms, bias, and interpretation of formal and informal assessment results toward nonbiased, meaningful evaluation and decision making. **This helps you meet CEC Standard 8: Individual Learning Differences.**

- This chapter explains the role of assessment in special education and reviews the importance of ongoing attention to legal matters, along with serious professional and ethical considerations. This chapter also emphasizes the importance of being a lifelong learner and regularly reflecting on and adjusting your practice. **This helps you meet CEC Standard 9: Professional and Ethical Practice.**

After reading and discussing this chapter, you will be able to

- Define formative and summative assessments

- Describe the cycle of planning, assessment, and instruction

- Explain what a CST is and what it does

- Explain what disproportionality means

- Explain the four components and three tiers of intervention in most RTI models and why RTI is used by many schools

- Create a flowchart of the steps of evaluation for special education

- Explain how the evaluation process for special education includes families

- Describe the continuum of services

- Explain how the IEP is developed

- Explain what is included in the present levels of educational performance and the goals on an IEP

To graduate from high school, you probably took many tests in English, science, social studies, math, and a foreign language. In class, teachers probably asked you to take quizzes, write papers, give oral reports, and work individually, in small groups, and in large groups. To apply to college, you probably took more tests, such as the SAT or ACT. You probably completed an application for college that included writing an essay, providing your grades, and getting references. All of that information assessed your ability in a range of ways and from a variety of perspectives. The goal of all of these assessments was to evaluate your abilities in the areas tested. In this chapter, you will learn about assessment and the assessment process for entering special education. The assessment process for a student who may benefit from having a disability label has detailed steps, and the process of a student's qualifying for special education and having an individualized education program (IEP) is reviewed.

formative assessments
Ways that a teacher checks to see what students are learning to adjust future instruction. Examples include short quizzes, written work, oral review, and reading aloud.

summative assessments
Also called high-stakes tests, these are formal tests given at the end of a unit, semester, or academic year to measure what students learned in a subject area.

For students, formative and summative assessments are routine. **Formative assessments** give teachers information about how students understand the instruction and **summative assessments** give teachers and districts information about how their students compare to other students throughout the state, the country, and the world. Formative assessments are those that the teacher makes and uses as part of a lesson so he or she can adapt the instruction as needed. The assessment is given before the instruction is finished so there is time for the teacher to adjust his or her instruction based on the results. For example, if a group of students are working on geometry proofs, a formative assessment could be a quick quiz about the ways a triangle proof can be completed. The quiz is given and students who do not understand the concept can be retaught. Or, a teacher might meet with small groups of students reading at the same level and talk through how to strengthen their writing by using descriptive words. Listening to what each student says and evaluating students' writing samples are other examples.

Summative assessments are those that give summary information; tests at the end of a unit, quarter, semester, or academic year, such as a fourth-grade reading assessment or high school biology exam at the end of year, are examples. Summative assessments get a great deal of attention because they are one way that schools and teachers are evaluated for their effectiveness with students. There is a great deal of criticism for using only summative assessment data to judge whether or not a teacher or school or district is doing well, and the debate about teacher effectiveness has hinged largely on what we believe about the importance of preparing students for summative assessments. Whatever you believe about summative assessments, they play an important role in schools today.

Formative assessments take place in a range of areas. Students' abilities in academic, social, physical, and behavioral areas are routinely observed and monitored by all teachers. Written tests given regularly, such as weekly spelling tests, are one example of academic assessment. Other assessments are provided to the class as formative preassessments. Afterwards, instruction is designed based on what students know. Another assessment is then given to evaluate what students have learned. Social assessments may include observations of students, or interviews with students to determine how each student feels about his or her social relationships in school. Physical assessments might take place in collaboration with the physical education teacher and include flexibility and strength measures. Behavioral assessments are often conducted when a student has difficulty meeting expectations in the classroom and include observations, interviews, and data collection to determine what happens before and after a challenging behavior occurs.

All assessments are part of a cycle of preassessment, planning, instruction, assessment, and planning. The process is a continuous one that helps teachers create positive, supportive learning environments for all students. For students with disabilities, the same cycle applies, but it may be applied more individually and may be more frequent.

First, you will explore the way that assessment is used in the classroom for students with and without disability labels. Next, you will review the assessment and evaluation process, including the steps teachers and teams take to determine if a student meets the eligibility criteria for special education. Then you'll learn how the assessment results are used for placement and developing a high-quality IEP. The narrative in this chapter is from Laura Whitcomb, the director of Special Education in the Hilton Central School District in western New York State.

ASSESSMENT IN THE CLASSROOM

From Chapter 7, you learned that assessment needs to be differentiated. That is, it is acceptable—and even essential—that you give students a range of ways to show their understanding and progress. Standardized testing is one part of academic assessment, but the best teachers do not spend too much time focusing on those kinds of tests, because high-quality, differentiated instruction is the best test preparation there is. Many teachers, principals, and districts make the mistake of thinking that learning how to complete a standardized test is the most important part of learning. But the focus of good teaching should be on good instruction informed by frequent assessments, and adjusting the teaching methods, processes, and products to meet students' needs. The cycle of assessment, planning, and instruction is the focus of this section. Related to this cycle is **response to intervention (RTI)**. First, we talk about the cycle, and then explain what RTI means in today's schools.

response to intervention (RTI) One way that schools can effectively and systematically monitor student progress and adjust instruction when the students are not mastering what is being taught.

The Planning-Assessment-Instruction Cycle

The cycle of preassessment, planning, instruction, assessment, and planning is one that all teachers use every day, over and over (see Figure 9.1). This is key to teaching because without careful thought, instruction may not be connected to students' background knowledge, how students learn, and how students show what they learned.

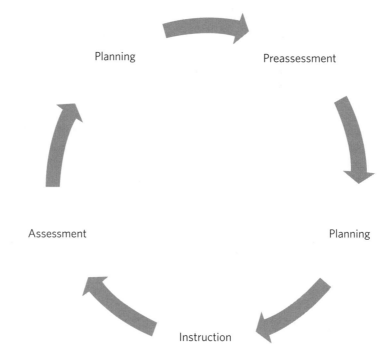

Figure 9.1. Planning-assessment-instruction cycle.

Preassessments begin the cycle. Preassessing knowledge and skills that students already have helps the teacher plan a lesson that meets the students exactly where they are as a group. For example, if a middle school teacher is beginning a unit in social studies about World War II, a preassessment might be a simple 10-question quiz about the basic facts: the dates, countries involved, reasons for the war, and outcomes. If students respond and it is clear that the class already has good background knowledge about the war, the lesson the teacher plans will be different than if the class has very little information.

After the teacher plans and delivers lessons about World War II, another assessment can be given. This may be the preassessment given a second time. If the preassessment is used as an assessment after teaching, it is easy to compare what students learned through the lesson. After the lesson has been taught and students have learned the material, the cycle begins again with new material. This example and ones like it happen every day as teachers reflect on student performance and adjust their instruction based on assessment of student learning.

Assessing a group of students is not very different from assessing an individual student. If a student struggles with some academic, social, physical, or behavioral area, the teacher will devote some time and attention to developing hypotheses about what is happening and why. The teacher may return to Chapter 6 and review the pyramid of support, and consider how the child learns best. The teacher will try strategies to improve student learning and change factors that she believes may have a role in the student's performance.

For example, if a student in elementary school is not recognizing letter/sound relationships in kindergarten, the teacher may review how that information is presented and realize that using a Smart Board to present letters while saying sounds is effective for most students, but a few are not mastering the information. She may decide to present information in a new way to a small group, or to the whole class by using a sand tray to trace letters, using shaving cream on the table to trace in, or using large cutouts of letters to practice writing the letter on an easel. Changing her instruction to meet the needs of students who learn best through movement is a change in her instruction based on her use of the formative assessment that not all of her students are recognizing letter/sound relationships.

A teacher monitors all students continuously. If she realizes that she still has a student who struggles with the letter/sound relationships, even after changing her instruction, she may try a new strategy. If the new strategy is not effective, the teacher will consider bringing her concern to a building team.

Asking others in the building for support is a common strategy and not a special education service, although there will probably be special education teachers in the group. Most schools have some form of **child support team (CST)** or building level team (BLT) to support teachers in their assessment and instruction. Teams often meet weekly to review teacher concerns about individual students. The team meeting typically begins with updates about students who were discussed in previous meetings and then attention is brought to new concerns. Typically, there is a form for teachers to complete when submitting a concern, including the specific concern, the strategies the teacher has already tried to address her concern, and the kinds of support the teacher would like to have. The teacher may or may not attend the meeting—the important thing is that teachers access a team of people who may have ideas they have not considered.

Deciding what strategies to try and how to modify instruction has been a point of contention in the field of education. A few teachers believe that the way they teach is not open for revision, and if a student cannot learn that way, it is the student's responsibility to adjust how they learn to be successful in the classroom. We do not agree with this perspective. We believe that high-quality, responsive instruction is the responsibility of the teacher, who has had years of training and is being paid to be in school and provide instruction. If students are not successful, we place responsibility for that squarely on the teacher's shoulders.

The complexity of how to assess what a student is capable of learning is significant, because variables connected to academics, demographics, and economic status all affect which students enter special education (Hosp & Reschly, 2004).

Disproportionality is the result. Disproportionality is "the extent to which membership in a given group affects the probability of being placed in a specific disability category" (Oswald, Coutinho, Best, & Singh, 1999, p. 198). That is, being a member of a particular race increases the risk of being identified as having a disability. Black students have been consistently labeled as mentally retarded or as having emotional disabilities more often than would be expected (Sullivan et al., 2009, p. 14). That is, students who are African American are being labeled as having disabilities when they probably do not have those disabilities. Remember that disability is socially constructed, and the result can be overlabeling or underlabeling because of the beliefs of the people in power.

Response to Intervention

Response to intervention, or RTI, is a practice that many schools are using in general education. The No Child Left Behind Act (NCLB) requires schools to focus on accountability, school improvement, and students' making adequate yearly progress. IDEA requires schools to provide effective instruction, progress monitoring, and early intervention services (IDEA Partnership, 2007, slide 6). Both laws emphasize the importance of closing achievement gaps between students who are White and students of color, providing high-quality, scientifically based instruction and interventions, and holding schools accountable for all students' meeting grade level standards (IDEA Partnership, 2007, slide 7). The similarities in IDEA and NCLB provide an opportunity for general education and special education to collaborate in supporting all students—not through labels, or having a general education/special education division, but by working together to support all students, whether or not they have a disability label. Figure 9.2

child support team (CST) A building-based team of teachers and professionals who help teachers with strategies to support students when the teacher needs resources. CSTs may have other names but the idea is always to support teachers in meeting the needs of particular students.

disproportionality When students of a particular ethnicity are labeled too often or too rarely based on the percentage of that ethnicity in the general population.

RᴛI

RESPONSE TO INTERVENTION
A FAMILY GUIDE

COMMUNITY CONSOLIDATED SCHOOL DISTRICT 59

RTI Introduction

CHANGES IN FEDERAL AND STATE LAWS HAVE DIRECTED SCHOOLS TO FOCUS MORE ON HELPING ALL CHILDREN LEARN BY ADDRESSING PROBLEMS EARLY WITHIN THE GENERAL EDUCATION SETTING.

THESE NEW LAWS EMPHASIZE THE IMPORTANCE OF PROVIDING HIGH QUALITY, SCIENTIFICALLY-BASED INSTRUCTION AND INTERVENTIONS, AND HOLD SCHOOLS ACCOUNTABLE FOR THE ADEQUATE YEARLY PROGRESS OF ALL STUDENTS.

Questions Parents Can Ask the Teacher

❋ WHAT SHOULD MY CHILD BE LEARNING IN HIS/HER CLASSROOM?

❋ HOW ARE LESSONS DESIGNED TO MEET MY CHILD'S NEEDS?

❋ WHAT ARE THE TEACHING STRATEGIES THAT MY CHILD'S SCHOOL IS USING IF HE/SHE IS STRUGGLING IN THE CLASSROOM?

❋ HOW CAN I HELP MY CHILD WITH LEARNING AT HOME?

❋ HOW WILL I LEARN ABOUT MY CHILD'S PROGRESS SO I KNOW MORE ABOUT HIS/HER SKILLS AND NOT JUST GRADES?

❋ WHAT HAPPENS IF MY CHILD CONTINUES TO STRUGGLE AND THE TEACHING STRATEGY IS NOT WORKING?

FOR MORE INFORMATION ABOUT SPECIAL EDUCATION, YOUR RIGHTS IN THIS PROCESS, AND HOW RTI MAY BE USED TO INFORM ENTITLEMENT PLEASE CONTACT:

VALERIE GUDGEON

EXECUTIVE DIRECTOR OF EDUCATION SERVICES
(847) 593-4335

POTENTIAL BENEFITS OF RTI

☑ IMPROVES EDUCATION FOR ALL STUDENTS.

☑ ELIMINATES THE "WAIT TO FAIL" SITUATION THAT PREVENTS AT-RISK STUDENTS FROM RECEIVING SERVICES EARLIER RATHER THAN LATER.

☑ PROGRESS-MONITORING TECHNIQUES PROVIDE MORE INSTRUCTIONALLY RELEVANT, EASILY UNDERSTOOD INFORMATION VERSUS TRADITIONAL EVALUATIONS.

☑ ALLOWS TEACHERS TO KNOW WHAT WORKS NOW TO IMPROVE STUDENTS' SKILLS.

Figure 9.2. Response to intervention (RTI) family guide brochure. (From Community Consolidated School District 59, Arlington Heights, Illinois; reprinted by permission.) (continued)

District 59 is committed to "improving students' life chances"

WHAT IS RTI?

RTI IS A WAY TO PROVIDE SUPPORT AND INSTRUCTION FOR CHILDREN WHO ARE STRUGGLING TO LEARN. FORTUNATELY, MOST STUDENTS THRIVE IN GENERAL EDUCATION CLASSROOMS.

FOR THOSE WHO DON'T THRIVE, TEACHERS PROVIDE A SECOND TIER OR LEVEL OF SUPPORT THAT FOCUSES ON THE AREA(S) IN WHICH THE CHILD STRUGGLES. A CHILD'S PROGRESS IS STUDIED AND FINDINGS ARE USED TO MAKE DECISIONS ABOUT TEACHING AND OTHER LEARNING SUPPORTS.

A THIRD MORE INTENSIVE TIER OF SUPPORT IS PROVIDED IF THE STUDENT DOES NOT MAKE PROGRESS IN THE SECOND TIER.

WHAT DOES THE DISTRICT 59 RTI CONTINUUM OF SUPPORT LOOK LIKE?

FEW STUDENTS   Tier III
Intensive Interventions
Delivered explicitly in small groups (5 or less) using specialized materials and monitored weekly.

SOME STUDENTS   Tier II
Supplementary Interventions
May occur in classroom or pull-out program, in small groups (8 or less), using targeted interventions systematically applied and monitored bi-weekly, in addition to the core curriculum

ALL STUDENTS   Tier I
Core Curriculum
Occurs in the regular classroom, uses core curriculum. Student progress is universally monitored 3 times per year.

ACADEMIC AND/OR BEHAVIOR

WHAT ARE THE KEY COMPONENTS OF AN RTI FRAMEWORK?

♣ UNIVERSAL SCREENING OF ALL STUDENTS TO HELP IDENTIFY STUDENTS WHO NEED EXTRA SUPPORT.

♣ INTEGRATED DATA COLLECTION THAT INFORMS INSTRUCTION.

♣ THREE TIERS OF INCREASINGLY INTENSIVE AND INDIVIDUALIZED INSTRUCTION AND INTERVENTION.

♣ PROBLEM-SOLVING BY A TEAM TO FIND SOLUTIONS FOR STUDENTS NEEDS.

FAMILIES PLAY A CRITICAL ROLE IN SUPPORTING WHAT THEIR CHILDREN ARE LEARNING IN SCHOOL.

RESEARCH SHOWS THAT THE MORE PARENTS ARE ACTIVELY INVOLVED IN LEARNING, THE MORE LEARNING, THE STUDENTS' STUDENT' ACHIEVEMENT. THERE ARE MANY WAYS FAMILIES CAN SUPPORT THEIR CHILD'S LEARNING AT HOME. ASK YOUR CHILD'S TEACHER HOW YOU CAN HELP.

Figure 9.2.   Response to intervention (RTI) family guide brochure. (From Community Consolidated School District 59, Arlington Heights, Illinois; reprinted by permission.)

167

represents the resource the Community Consolidated School District 59 in Arlington Heights, Illinois, developed to explain RTI to families.

The National Center on Response to Intervention web site explains that RTI, like PBIS, has four components. First, there is a schoolwide instructional and behavioral system (which could be PBIS); second, a screening system to identify students who are struggling; and third, a way to monitor the progress of those struggling students; and fourth, decision making that is based on data (National Center on Response to Intervention, n.d.). The National Center on Response to Intervention defines RTI this way:

> Response to intervention integrates assessment and intervention within a multilevel prevention system to maximize student achievement and to reduce behavior problems. With RTI, schools identify students at risk for poor learning outcomes, monitor student progress, provide evidence-based interventions and adjust the intensity and nature of those interventions depending on a student's responsiveness, and identify students with learning disabilities. (n.d., para. 25)

RTI is defined by the IDEA Partnership as "the practice of providing high-quality instruction/intervention matched to student needs *and* using learning rate over time and level of performance *to* inform educational decisions" (2007, slide 8). It is one way that schools can effectively and systematically monitor student progress and adjust instruction when the students are not mastering what is being taught. More and more districts are adopting RTI as a model for reading and writing instruction. Figure 9.3 is a referral form teachers in Syracuse, New York, use when they are concerned that a student is at risk because of academic, behavioral, emotional, or medical needs.

RTI helps teachers support students by monitoring their progress carefully and changing how they teach based on the results of frequent assessments. RTI is frequently discussed related to reading instruction but is also used in other academic subject areas.

RTI includes tiers of interventions, most often three tiers. A pyramid with three sections—just like the one used in Chapter 6 to talk about supporting students' behavior —is the most frequent way RTI is shown. Typically, Tier 1 includes instruction for all students, with good differentiated teaching. Tier 1 typically meets the needs of about 80% of all students. Tier 2 typically includes some focused support for a small group of students, usually about 15% of the class. This focused support includes designing interventions to support academic needs, taking data to see whether or not the intervention is effective, and changing the intervention if the data show that the student is not making progress. Interventions for academic instruction often include small-group teaching and focused instruction on specific skills for a period of several weeks. Tier 2 strategies are often provided by general and special education teachers in collaboration with each other.

Tier 3 interventions are designed to support students who have not been successful with Tier 1 and Tier 2 strategies. This small group—at the small top of the pyramid (see Figure 9.4)—typically includes about 5% of students. A debate in education today is whether or not Tier 3 means special education. We do not think it should always mean special education, but we believe that providing intensive supports is more than a single teacher on her or his own can be expected to provide while also meeting the needs of the other students in the classroom. Getting the support you need to teach effectively using a cycle of assessment and instruction is the essential part; whether it is RTI or another strategy in your district is not as important.

Next, we look at what happens when a student is not making progress, even after you have tried a range of strategies to support his or her learning.

Student At-Risk Referral Form

General Information	**To be completed at meeting**

General Information

Student name: _____

Referring teacher(s): _____

_____

Parent/Guardian: _____

How and when was parent notified of referral: _____

To be completed at meeting

ID number: _____ DOB: _____

Referral date: _____

Address: _____

Phone: _____

Reason for Referral (Primary Concern):

_____Academic   _____Behavioral   _____Emotional   _____Medical

Please describe the specific concerns prompting this referral. What makes this student difficult to teach? List any academic, social, emotional or medical factors that negatively impact the student's performance.

_____

_____

_____

_____

How do this student's academic skills compare to those of an average student in your classroom?

_____

_____

_____

*In what settings/situations does the problem occur **most** often?*

_____

*In what settings/situations does the problem occur **least** often?*

_____

What are the student's strengths, talents or specific interests?

1. _____

2. _____

3. _____

Parent/Guardian Contact Prior to Referral

_____Phone call   _____ Note home   _____Conference   _____Home visit

Interventions

1. Begin date _____   End date _____   Person(s) responsible _____

What have you tried to do to resolve this problem?

_____

_____

How did it work? _____

_____

2. Begin date _____   End date _____   Person(s) responsible _____

What have you tried to do to resolve this problem?

_____

_____

How did it work? _____

_____

3. Begin date _____   End date _____   Person(s) responsible _____

What have you tried to do to resolve this problem?

_____

_____

How did it work? _____

_____

_____

Please provide additional information such as this student's most current report card, schedule and attendance record and return with referral.

Figure 9.3.   Student at-risk referral form. (From the Syracuse City School District, Syracuse, New York; reprinted by permission.)

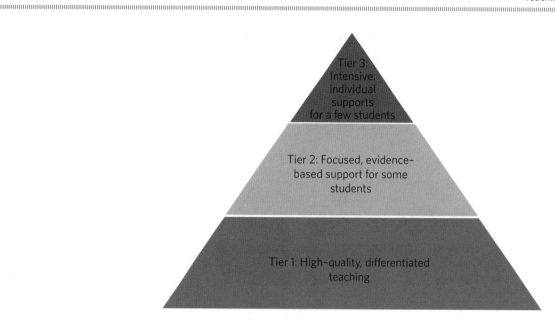

Figure 9.4. Response to intervention (RTI) pyramid.

EVALUATION FOR SPECIAL EDUCATION

In this section, we review what happens if a student is not successful with general education instruction after instruction has been monitored and a range of teaching styles and ways of collecting information have been tried, perhaps with the RTI model. If a student continues to struggle, it may be that he or she has a disability, and figuring out if that is the case through a formal assessment is the way that a disability is identified.

There is a clear, detailed process to determine if a student has a disability that affects learning; that process is the focus of this section. A student qualifies for special education after a referral for evaluation, evaluation, and determining his or her eligibility for special education services. Remember that the Individuals with Disabilities Education Improvement Act (IDEA, 2004) has six provisions for serving student with disabilities: a free appropriate public education (FAPE); qualification for services because of a disability; assessment that is nondiscriminatory; education in the least restrictive environment (LRE); individualized education programs; and the guarantee of parent involvement and procedural due process. This chapter focuses on the evaluation process, which includes qualification for services because of a disability and how the guarantee of parent involvement and procedural due process is met.

Every state follows the regulations set out in IDEA 2004. The way meetings are conducted or education plans are formatted may vary, but all states are held to the same federal requirements. Many states prepare materials for families to explain the assessment process. The National Dissemination Center for Children with Disabilities (NICHCY) is a fantastic national resource that provides information for educators and families about special education. A NICHCY resource is the basis for this section, because it is a national clearinghouse for information.

The steps in Table 9.1 are the way a student with a disability is identified and provided with special education services. But before an initial referral to special education is completed, there are prereferral interventions. Prereferral interventions cover a wide range of instructional and behavioral strategies, such as the ones we talked about in Chapters 6, 7, and 8.

Table 9.1.   Steps in the special education process

	Basic steps in special education	
Step	This step includes	Time line for completing the step
1	Parent permission is requested and granted. Child is identified as possibly needing special education.	
2	Child is evaluated.	60 days from parent consent OR state time line
3	Eligibility is decided.	
4	Child is found eligible.	
5	IEP meeting is scheduled.	Within 30 calendar days from eligibility decision
6	IEP meeting is held; IEP is written.	
7	Services are provided.	
8	Progress is measured and reported to parents.	At least as often as reports are provided to parents of children without disability labels
9	IEP is reviewed.	At least once a year
10	Child is reevaluated.	At least once every 3 years

Source: NICHCY, 2010a.

In addition, strategies from the chapters in Part 3 are essential tools for teachers to try as prereferral interventions before assuming that a child may need special education services. High-quality instruction that includes frequent assessments is key to good teaching. In some cases, poor teaching that is not responsive to individual student needs is the reason for student failure—not a disability. In this section, we assume that the building team has tried a range of teaching strategies and worked closely with a variety of other professionals before determining that the student may need special education.

Step 1: Child Is Identified as Possibly Needing Special Education

There are two ways that children are identified: Child Find or a referral for evaluation from the school or parents. Child Find is part of IDEA and is the requirement that every state have a way to identify, locate, and evaluate all children who might need special education (NICHCY, Basic Steps, n.d., p. 1). Schools collaborate with hospitals and pediatricians, and early intervention services are available in all states. A baby or toddler can receive special education services at home or in a preschool through early intervention before he or she transitions to kindergarten. The second way is a referral from the school or parents because there is a concern about the child's progress. In either case, the parents must agree that the evaluation process takes place.

Written consent for the evaluation to continue is mandatory; if the family does not allow the evaluation, it does not take place. Some families have strong feelings about why they choose not to have their child evaluated. They may be concerned about their student having a disability label, and families may refuse to allow the evaluation process for special education because of their concerns. Concerns families may have include low expectations, segregation from the general education classroom, teasing, and a negative impact on self-esteem. Given what you have learned about how disability is constructed, why do you think some families feel this way?

Step 2: Child Is Evaluated

If the family provides the written consent for evaluation, the team of school personnel can begin observations and testing. The team of people includes a general education teacher, a special education teacher, a school psychologist, a social worker, and a Committee on Special Education Chair. The chair is most often a district employee, and his or her job is to facilitate and monitor students' evaluations and IEP meetings. Other people who may be involved include a speech-language pathologist, an occupational therapist, a physical therapist, and behavior specialists. Some districts have developed autism teams in the last few years as more students are being identified as having an autism spectrum disorder. The key is that the people involved are chosen according to the individual student and his or her needs.

Evaluations must take place within a certain amount of time. The rule under IDEA is 60 days, but each state has the right to make its own time line. Evaluation is designed to answer three questions:

1. Does the child have a disability that requires the provision of special education and related services?

2. What are the child's specific educational needs?

3. What special education services and related services are appropriate to address those needs? (NICHCY, Basic Steps, n.d., para. 10).

The evaluation process needs to be "full and individual" (NICHCY, Evaluating Children, n.d.)—that is, the evaluation is focused only on the child in question. The evaluation must consider functional, developmental, and academic information, and evaluate the child's health, vision, hearing, social and emotional status, general intelligence, academic performance, communication, and motor abilities (NICHCY, Evaluating Children, n.d).

Evaluating how a student is doing includes formal and informal assessments. Informal assessments are observing the student in class, noting how well she completes work in different subjects, how well she is able to do what is asked, and how she connects with her classmates. A range of formal tests is selected and given related to the areas of possible need. The special education teacher, school psychologist, and other team members will review and choose tests based on their experience with standardized tests. A big issue is being sure that the assessments are valid and reliable. An assessment is valid if it provides an accurate measurement of what it is designed to measure. That may sound simple, but it is very complex.

Step 3: Eligibility Is Decided

Deciding whether or not a child has a disability under IDEA entails the team of school professionals and the parents reviewing the evaluation results. The categories of disability are autism, deafness, deaf-blindness, developmental delay, emotional disturbance, hearing impairment, intellectual disability (formerly mental retardation), multiple disabilities, orthopedic impairment, other health impaired, specific learning disability, speech or language impairment, traumatic brain injury, and visual impairment/blindness (NICHCY, Evaluating Children, n.d., para. 3).

If a child seems to have a disability but does not fit neatly into one of these categories, the team is faced with determining how to best provide for the student within the current system of labeling. We believe that the important issue is that the student receives what supports he or she needs to be successful in school, and the labeling process can be a tool for getting those supports. Teachers need to understand this system so they can use it to support students, but they should not be overly focused on a label. Labels are best for jars—not people. Using the label to help get students what they need is a far better position than allowing the labels to drive discussion about what is possible. So, for example, if a student has needs in school because attention deficit disorder impacts his learning, how can we use this system to get supports for him? In the short term, that can be accomplished by using the label "other health impaired" to get services that might not be available without the label. In the long term, work to change how students are supported so that a label is not needed to give each student what she or he needs to do well in school.

Step 4: Child Is Found Eligible for Services

If a child is not found eligible, she continues in school with support that all children access, such as response to intervention monitoring and differentiated instruction. If a child is found to have a disability as defined by IDEA, the team of school professionals and parents have 30 calendar days to write the first **individualized education program (IEP)** for the child. Ideally, this process includes the student's input and ideas because it is about his education.

individualized education program (IEP) Written report of a student's disability label, levels of performance, goals for the year, and placement and services to be provided in school. The IEP is the cornerstone of special education programs.

Most of the services provided by teachers and professionals, such as occupational therapists, physical therapists, and speech and language pathologists, are through special education. That is, students who have gone through the assessment process and have IEPs are the majority of students these professionals see. There is some variation— for example, the Rochester City School District in Rochester, New York, has a speech-language pathologist go to every kindergarten class as part of the job, to support all children. But the primary service of special education professionals is for students with IEPs.

Step 5: IEP Meeting Is Scheduled

This step sounds basic, but it is important. Parents must have enough advance notice to attend if they would like to attend, and the meeting must be at a time and place that are agreeable to everyone. In actual practice, this does not always happen; often meetings are scheduled at the convenience of the school, and parents have to take time off work to come to school during the day. We believe schools should be much more responsive to families and hold meetings in the late afternoon, and consider community sites for meetings instead of always meeting in the school.

The IEP meeting will include the assessment team and the parents, and ideally the student will attend as well. For young children, or others who might not be able to sit in a long meeting, conducting an interview in advance about what she or he would like to learn and would like to do in school is a useful way to bring the child's perspective to the meeting.

Step 6: IEP Meeting Is Held and IEP Is Written

At the meeting, it is very important that everyone be open to a range of options. Sometimes the IEP meeting feels overwhelming to the family, especially the first time. Learning that your child has a disability and needs additional supports can be discouraging and scary. The IEP includes a review of the student's "present levels of performance" in academics, social development, physical development, and behavior (called management). How the student is doing is determined by a review of the assessments, which took place before the meeting.

The team sets goals for the student for the year in four areas and decides where the child will be in school. This meeting is critically important; what happens in this meeting can be changed, but is typically the plan for a whole year. Placement is part of the IEP meeting, and this is often a central concern. Districts are required by IDEA (in Sec.

General education classroom full time	General education classroom and special education classroom mix—more general education	General education classroom and special education classroom mix—more special education	Special education classroom full time	Separate (special) school	Residential school (institution) or hospital

Figure 9.5. Continuum of services. (*Source:* U.S. Department of Education, 2006.)

300.115—Continuum of alternative placements) to have a range of placements along a continuum of services (see Figure 9.5).

The continuum must include two things. It must include the placements that are listed as part of the definition of special education (in Section 300.38 of IDEA). Those placements are instruction in regular classes, special classes, special schools, home instruction, and instruction in hospitals and institutions. The continuum must also "make provision for supplementary services (such as a resource room or itinerant instruction) to be provided in conjunction with regular class placement" (Individuals with Disabilities Education Act, 20 U.S.C. 1412(a)(5)).

Step 7: Services Are Provided

Service provision is simply the classroom instruction and related services that the student experiences every day in school. In Chapter 7, you learned about differentiation and citizenship. In Chapter 8, you learned about universal design for learning (UDL). In the first section of this chapter, you learned about the planning-assessment-instruction cycle and RTI. These services are provided for all students, including those with an IEP. In addition, related services, such as assistive technology support, speech-language, adapted physical education, physical therapy, occupational therapy, or some other service that is needed for a particular student to be successful, are provided. Because we feel strongly about inclusion, we believe that most services can and should be provided in the general education classroom.

Step 8: Progress Is Measured and Reported to Parents

Students with IEPs have progress reports about how they are doing related to their individual goals, and this information is reported to the parents at least as often as students without IEPs have reports. Most students get report cards of some kind at least every semester, and sometimes each quarter. As often as the district sends grades home for all students, students with IEPs also need their progress reviewed. The progress report does not typically include a meeting—simply a report mailed home, just as grades are mailed home.

Step 9: IEP Is Reviewed

At least once a year, the IEP is reviewed and the goals that were set are discussed and new goals are developed. Some districts hold the annual review on the anniversary of the first IEP meeting, which means that special education teachers who case manage or supervise the IEPs of 10 to 20 children have 10 to 20 IEP meetings throughout the year, each one on the anniversary date of the initial IEP for each student. Other districts hold all IEP meetings at a particular time, often in the spring, so that placements for the fall can be discussed for the next grade.

Step 10: Child Is Reevaluated

Reevaluation happens every 3 years and is often called the "triennial" for this reason. Parents can ask that their student be evaluated more frequently if there is a significant change, but that is not always supported by the school district. The first evaluation for a student suspected of having a disability is typically fairly comprehensive, because the team is trying to determine what needs the student has. As a child gets older and has a history of school experiences, the next triennials can be focused specifically on what the student needs. Often, triennials after the first one refine what was done in the past.

Now that you have reviewed the steps that are included in evaluations for special education, you will see what happens when the IEP is written.

PLACEMENT AND THE INDIVIDUALIZED EDUCATION PROGRAM

Once the team has determined that a student has a disability and will receive special education services, the individualized education program, or IEP, is written. This process should not take place without the input of the student and should be very student-centered. In fact, students should be facilitating their own IEP meetings as early as middle school, because the student is the one most affected by what the IEP includes. Families are similarly important to the process; just as teachers are expert in pedagogy, or how to teach effectively, families are experts about their child. No one knows the student better than the family who love, support, and care for him or her the majority of the time. The IEP form includes information about the student and his or her learning needs in several areas.

Background Information

This brief initial section typically gives the student's name, address, ethnicity, disability label, grade and age, and date of annual IEP and 3-year reevaluation. This information may appear in different places on different forms.

Present Levels of Performance

The first major part of the IEP is the *present levels of performance*. This section is the place where all the assessment results are described and interpreted. The assessments that were used are named and the results are explained in clear language, because while the school personnel who are reading the IEP are probably familiar with the process and the tests used, the family may have never even heard of the term IEP before this process began. In New York State, the present levels of performance section is divided into four areas: academic achievement, social development, physical development, and management needs. Next, there is a short section that asks if there are special factors to consider, such as positive behavioral interventions or services to address language needs, or assistive technology for communication needs (New York State Education Department, 2010).

The next major section of the IEP is the goals. **Goals** are developed for the student in all areas where needs were identified. This makes sense: If the student has a need in one of the areas, the team must decide what goals are reasonable to achieve in one year.

goals What a student hopes to accomplish. Goals can be short term or long term.

Recommended Programs and Services

This section of the IEP tells where the student will be educated. The continuum of services described in Chapter 1 is under consideration here. When IEP teams reach this portion of the IEP, ideally the needs of the students are considered, and the best combination of placements is structured to meet those needs. However, it is more common that teams hear things like "Well, we don't have that program, so here are the two options" or "Our EB/D program is located in the other elementary school, so he will need to take the bus even though his home school is 2 blocks away." IEP meeting directors sometimes try very hard to fit the student into existing programs instead of fitting the programs to meet the student's needs. This is not acceptable practice, and we encourage you to help the IEP team stay focused on the individual student. Some families bring a photograph of their child to the meeting, as a visible reminder that the topic of the discussion is a person with needs and feelings. Remember Jeannine Dingus-Eason's comments about her son from Chapter 3? She brings a photograph and expects the team to see Caleb as an individual. Her experience is a valuable one to learn from.

On the New York State IEP form, programs are described by the recommendations for a staff-to-student ratio, group or individual services, and direct or indirect services from a special education teacher. Related services and supplementary aids services are also listed.

SUMMARY

In this chapter, you were introduced to formative and summative assessments. Next, you reviewed the cycle of planning, assessment, and instruction. You learned a bit about the child support team's role in assisting teachers with the cycle, and the way that disproportionality has affected who is labeled with a disability. In the next section, you learned what RTI includes, why it was developed, and how it is used in schools today. The chapter ended with a review of the way a student who may have a disability is evaluated for special education.

NARRATIVE 9.1. | LAURA WHITCOMB

Director of Special Education, Hilton Central School District, New York

Teacher Input Is Vital to the CSE Process   When a teacher comes to the Committee on Special Education (CSE) ready to contribute and participate, the whole process is enhanced. I urge teachers new to the assessment process of special education to familiarize themselves with their school's unique way of doing things. Because the assessment process for entering special education is prescribed by state and federal laws and regulations, one would expect that the process would look very similar from state to state, school district to school district, and child to child. That is not the case. The building-level process of prereferral and the district-level process of bringing a child's case to the CSE will have many steps, and it is very important that the teacher understand and be involved all along the way.

To understand fully the process used to identify a student as having a disability, it is important for new teachers entering the field of special education to understand the different types of assessment that occur *prior* to a CSE referral and how those assessments can affect decisions about whether to investigate the possibility that a disability is present. Whether we call those assessments prereferral information or RTI progress monitoring is not important. What is important is that ongoing formative assessment is used by teachers to elicit evidence of student learning so that instructional or management adjustments can be made when a child struggles. It is very likely that an adjustment in instructional methods, classroom environment, management strategies, or a combination of all three can significantly improve a child's learning and success in the classroom.

When instruction is differentiated in response to formative assessment, many students who just need "something different" will begin to succeed and will not need further assessment to investigate a disability. When this basic classroom level of formative assessment and differentiated instruction is not in place, children who do not respond to the "one-size-fits-all" approach (Tomlinson) erroneously may be thought to have a disability. This process of assessment-intervention-ongoing assessment-intervention is best practice for teaching in general and is necessary to make decisions about a child as a learner.

I see that teachers and other staff members are sometimes frustrated by this expectation, feeling like "others" are second guessing their hunches about students. Yet, from the CSE standpoint, we are required to rule out other factors before considering that a child may have a disability. For the classroom teacher or special education teacher supporting a "preferral assessment/intervention" process, your best efforts to assess and implement adjustments in instruction or interventions *with fidelity* is very important!

When a child does not respond to the differentiation of instruction and/or environment in the classroom, one would hope that there is another level of interventions (tier 2) available, although this varies greatly from school to school. Some schools have many general education interventions built into their programs to meet the needs of the more at-risk student. Interventions such as small group or individual reading and math services that supplement classroom instruction can remediate weaknesses and get a child back on track without needing special education services. Even in the related services areas, such as speech and language, occupational or physical therapy, some schools will provide prereferral/RTI services to children who may just need a boost in a certain skill—which again will prevent the need for special education. This is less common, but a great resource to have, especially when young children may just lag behind developmentally and will respond when and if they receive the right intervention at the right time.

If a child continues to lag behind despite the use of varied instructional approaches, most would agree that it is time to investigate whether a disability is present. Once a referral is made to special education, then another level of assessment begins and teacher input continues to be important. A range of assessments must be completed to determine a student's academic level, cognitive ability, adaptive behavior, motor skills, and language-processing abilities. The design of the assessment process varies by child, depending on the suspected area of disability. Input from parents and from teachers who know the student can help evaluators determine the most appropriate assessments to conduct. Once all the assessments are complete and the CSE meets, teacher and parent input continue to be vital to the process.

When I chair a committee on special education meeting, I rely on the teacher's input to inform the committee about the student's classroom performance, strengths, and needs that may not be revealed by formal testing. The CSE is working to identify the root cause of a child's learning difficulties and the teacher has a unique perspective that is essential to the process. Teacher input helps the CSE take all the information into consideration and then design a plan of special education programming that is individualized to meet the needs of that child.

CHAPTER 10

Collaboration

How this chapter prepares you to be an effective inclusive classroom teacher:

- This chapter emphasizes the importance of valuing all family groupings and being sensitive to the many aspects of diversity. This chapter also emphasizes the importance of asking for help when it is needed—a direct connection to being a lifelong learner. **This helps you meet CEC Standard 9: Professional and Ethical Practice.**

- This chapter teaches the components of collaboration and the importance of having good collaborative skills. The relationships special education teachers have with other teachers, related service providers, teaching assistants, and community agencies are reviewed. This chapter addresses that teachers are viewed as specialists by myriad people who actively seek their help to effectively include and teach all students. You will also learn that teachers are a resource to their colleagues in understanding the laws and policies relevant to all students. **This helps you meet CEC Standard 10: Collaboration.**

After reading and discussing this chapter, you will be able to

- Define collaboration

- Explain the components of best practice in collaboration

- Review and choose a tool to support self-awareness about learning styles and preferences

- Explain how good communication occurs

- Understand the importance of asking for help when needed

- Define and give examples of subversive pedagogy

- Explain what cultural consciousness means and give examples

- Understand how to identify and nurture families' strengths

- Create a resource to use when explaining the components of coteaching

- Explain ways that teachers collaborate with related service personnel and teaching assistants

- Understand the importance of collaborating with community agencies that may serve students

This chapter reviews best practices in collaboration and discusses ways that teachers are expected to collaborate. In the first part, collaboration is defined and best practices are described. Next, collaboration between home and school is explained and then collaboration within the school is examined. Finally, we review collaboration between schools and agencies. Each relationship must be framed as one that shares a focus on supporting what is best for the student. When this is the case, the discussions and collaborations can work through what each party believes is best, and how to make that happen.

Collaboration is a skill all teachers need. The days of teachers going into their own classrooms and teaching all day without other adults present are gone. Today, it is more likely that a teacher interacts with other adults in and out of the classroom. For this reason, it is essential that new teachers understand the component skills of effective collaboration and the range of people with whom they will work to support students.

Narratives in this chapter come from Sheri Stanger, Megan Stanger's mother, and Colleen Brown, Zack's mother. Megan's needs are complex, and over the years Sheri has worked with hundreds of educational professionals to support Megan effectively. Colleen has the perspective of a parent and an advocate; she works for The Advocacy Center in Rochester, New York, and in that capacity helps families and individuals with disabilities collaborate in a range of ways with a wide range of services and service providers.

COLLABORATION BEST PRACTICES

What is collaboration? How does collaboration happen? Fundamentally, collaboration is working with others. Collaboration happens when two or more people talk to each other and work to meet a common goal. In schools, collaboration happens all the time, every day. Teachers work with each other—general education teachers collaborate with special education teachers, content area teachers collaborate within and across content areas, special education teachers work with each other. Teachers also collaborate with a range of other adults in the school: teaching assistants, speech-language pathologists, occupational therapists, physical therapists, school psychologists, social workers, counselors, librarians, custodial staff, cafeteria staff, administrators, administrative assistants, coaches, and bus drivers.

Beyond the school walls, teachers also work with communities and families. Teachers work with community agencies to support students beyond the school day. As you will learn in Chapter 11, the IEP process in high school includes transition planning. Transition planning should ideally include making connections with colleges and agencies that provide services for adults. From Chapter 4, remember that for students younger than kindergarten age, early intervention services are often provided through an agency, and a significant transition takes place from early intervention into kindergarten. At a very fundamental level, everyone is working to serve students. Problems can pop up when members of a team do not agree about what is best for an individual student or a group of students. The rest of this section is divided into components of best practices in collaboration: knowing your strengths and the strengths of others, communication skills, knowing when to ask for help, sharing a common goal, being flexible, and taking risks.

Knowing Your Strengths and the Strengths of Others

To work well with others, it is important to first know yourself. There are a range of tools to help you learn about your preferences related to planning, teaching, and communicating with others. For example, the Myers-Briggs test is one tool that gives information about individual styles in four areas: if you prefer your own inner world or the outside world (introverted or extroverted), how you manage information (sensing or intuition), how you make decisions (thinking or feeling), and what kind of structure you prefer when dealing with others (judging or perceiving) (The Myers Briggs Foundation, n.d.). Many districts use the Myers-Briggs Type Inventory to help teachers and other professionals understand their personality types, so that they are aware of their own preferences and can be sensitive to the preferences of others, which may be very different.

Another rating scale that is useful in helping professionals learn about their own styles and preferences is the Kaleidoscope, a learning styles inventory that has forms for educators and students (Performance Learning Systems, 2011). The Kaleidoscope inventory gives insights into how you learn best, how you like to work, your personality, and how you view the world (Performance Learning Systems, 2011). There are many other rating scales; these are just two examples (see Table 10.1). Rating scales can be a good way to know yourself and learn about the strengths of others. The discussion can then become one of finding complementary strengths instead of focusing on differences as something negative. For example, when we coteach, we laugh about the way one author types each lesson plan with starting and ending times next to each item, while the other arrives with a creative, interactive lesson fully mapped out in her head—and a few scribbled notes on a half sheet of paper. Both ways have value and we have learned to value the organization and creativity we each bring to our shared lessons.

Communication Skills Sometimes it feels like all we do as teachers is talk to each other! Because this is the nature of teaching, having good communication skills is essential. This includes receiving and expressing information. Receiving information is listening with an open mind, reviewing materials with a receptive attitude, and being open to new ideas. Expressing information means speaking respectfully and persuasively, providing materials in ways that are accessible to all, and being open to new ideas.

Table 10.1. Learning preferences and styles

Rating scale	Measures
Myers-Briggs Type Inventory (Myers Briggs Foundation)	Introvert/extrovert Sensing/intuition Thinking/feeling Judging/perceiving
The Kaleidoscope Profile (Performance Learning Systems)	Sensory preferences—How you learn best Organizational preferences—How you like to work Perceptual preferences—How you view the world Personality temperaments—Who you are

Kolb Learning Style Inventory (Experience-Based Learning Systems, Inc.)	Learning style typology (9 types):
	  Initiating
	  Experiencing
	  Imagining
	  Reflecting
	  Analyzing
	  Thinking
	  Deciding
	  Acting
	  Balancing

VARK Learning Profile Questionnaire (*VARK, A Guide to Learning Styles*—Neil Fleming)	Visual Aural Read/write Kinesthetic
Gardner's Multiple Intelligences (Howard Gardner)	Spatial Linguistic Logical-mathematical Bodily-kinesthetic Musical Interpersonal Intrapersonal Naturalistic

Receiving information with an open mind is one of the single biggest keys to collaboration. We have often been in meetings where the faculty seemed disconnected and resistant to any message the administration was trying to convey. This may be because veteran teachers have been in the same district or building through multiple administrative changes, and feeling jaded or cynical about the next new innovation or plan is one response to feeling that time in meetings is wasted, with no real change or improvement. This response may be based on past experiences, but it can be ultimately harmful to students because that same teacher is often one who does not want to hear new things or stretch himself in new ways to become a better instructor. While you shouldn't adopt every new idea you hear wholeheartedly without careful analysis of the possible benefit, neither should you reject something new simply because it is new. Part of being an effective teacher and advocate means carefully reflecting on everything you do and connecting meaningfully with colleagues so you can make educated decisions about your practice.

Expressing information includes two important components. First, speaking respectfully and persuasively includes knowing your audience. You might have a fantastic idea, but if you cannot communicate what it is and why it should be given a trial run, it will never get off the ground. Having persuasive speaking skills is part of being a good teacher; it is not in addition to being a good teacher. To effectively advocate for your students, your school, and your district, you must be able to identify the points you want to make and make them clearly and simply.

Second, providing materials in ways that are accessible to everyone means thinking carefully about your audience. If materials are prepared in English but many people in the audience read Spanish, you are not communicating effectively. For example, an Open House flyer needs to be accessible to all families, which means that you need to count on spending the time necessary to have the flyer available in every language used by households in your classroom. If you do not, then you are not welcoming all families. Another consideration is the reading level of the flyer. If you have families that do not have strong literacy backgrounds, you need to consider how to communicate the information on the flyer clearly and simply so that those who are not strong readers can access the content. Finally, if you have students or family members who are blind, you must think about ways to have the material available in Braille or electronically (so that a text-to-speech program can read it aloud). Only when everyone in your intended audience can access your message is your job of being a good communicator complete.

Knowing When to Ask for Help   Collaborating includes knowing that more than one perspective is a good thing. A synergistic outcome that is greater than the sum of the parts is often the result. Sometimes teachers fall into the mistake of thinking that not knowing all the answers means that they are not good teachers. This is not true. Good teachers are always learning new things and know that it is not only okay to need help sometimes, it is an important skill to know when to ask for help when it is needed.

Share a Common Goal   Having common goals may sound simplistic. Teachers are all concerned with supporting student success, but knowing what that includes, and deciding what short-term goals to set to meet the goal of supporting all students, can lead to major differences in how individual teachers believe they should teach.

In addition, pressure to meet testing goals exists in American schools today. Determining if teachers are effective is a current and controversial debate, and that means that teachers are under enormous duress to perform well. So the common goal of helping students succeed is a challenging one.

Determining what the goals are for a particular team is essential; if two individuals do not share the same goal, the result may be conflict and misunderstanding. This can be directly connected to the goals on a student's IEP. For example, if a student with a reading level far below grade level is included in her ninth-grade English class, the English teacher may have the goal of supporting the student so that she can read one to two grade levels higher by the end of the year. The special education teacher may have a goal for the student related to her social connections and relationships outside of class. When the two goals—one academic and the other social—are not shared and discussed, both teachers may end up frustrated with each other. Instead, it is important to articulate the goals, so that everyone can agree on the focus for the year.

Goals may be broader than a single student's IEP; teams and whole buildings often set goals for the year related to the building climate, to overall academic achievement, or to professional development. A common goal is a commitment to inclusive practice. Inclusion is an attitude, not a place, and the goal should be to support students in inclusive ways. With that shared understanding, decisions can come from the same place and the team will be able to work through the many details of implementing plans with that knowledge and shared commitment.

Be Flexible   Be willing to try new things, or to give someone else the chance to try their idea first. Be prepared for the give-and-take of collaborative practice, and be prepared for the opportunity to practice not always getting your way. Working as a member of a team means that every person has valuable input, and your ideas are important, but so are others' ideas. Practice bending without breaking.

Take Risks   The secret to good teaching is knowing that there is always more to learn, and there is always something new to try. Trying something new, or something that you are not sure will work, is risky, but the best way to learn is to be open to new methods and ideas. Staying open might include coteaching, learning a new course to teach in your content area, or implementing a different way to teach your content.

Taking risks might also include following your instincts when your administration asks something of you that does not feel right, or acts in ways that do not support what you believe is good practice. Paula Kluth (2003) called this **subversive pedagogy** and gave several examples of this in her book *You're Going to Love This Kid!* She talked about going to an IEP meeting and seeing the administration refuse to consider an inclusive placement for a boy with disabilities. She talked with the administrator after the meeting about it, but it was clear that the decision had been made. So she secretly got a copy of a "parent's rights in special education" booklet and highlighted the sections that were important for the family to know. She mailed it to the family anonymously. The family hired a parent advocate, and another meeting was scheduled to discuss the family's interest in inclusive placements.

HOME–SCHOOL COLLABORATION

The National Association of School Psychologists said that home–school collaboration "involves families and educators actively working together to develop shared goals and plans that support the success of all students" (2005, para. 1). Actively working together means that all parties are focused on what is best for the student and are striving to provide those services.

Today, the majority of teachers are White women. Demographically, today's schools have a growing population of African American and Hispanic students, and it is likely that many students of color will never be taught by someone who looks like them or has the same cultural background. Gloria Ladson-Billings addressed this in her article on culturally relevant teaching (1995) and explained that it is essential for teachers to do three things in their classrooms: ensure that students are academically successful, ensure that students develop and maintain a **cultural consciousness**, and ensure that students develop a critical consciousness (p. 160). You might be wondering how this connects with home–school collaboration. The answer is in the second point. For teachers to ensure that students feel welcome in school, and that school is a place that will help them learn and be successful, they must feel that who they are and where they come from is valued. Too often, students do not feel this way. Your task is to address this by getting to know students and their families.

Getting to know students and their families means accepting and embracing extended family as part of the family. Some children are raised by a community of family: parents, grandparents, aunts, uncles, and cousins. We would like you to consider that it can be a wonderful thing for a child to have many adults who love and care for them, not a sad and deplorable situation when a child lives with more than one family member at different times. In Table 10.2, a range of ideas is listed to help you try to connect with families. Feel free to add your own ideas to the list!

In the rest of this section, you will review how you can share the expertise that you have as a teacher, and how you can learn from families, who are the experts about

subversive pedagogy
"Rejecting common institutional practices in favor of those that are humane and appropriate" (Kluth, 2010, p. 52).

cultural consciousness
An awareness that students' cultures must be used as a vehicle for learning (Ladson-Billings, 1995, p. 161).

Table 10.2. Ways to connect with families

- Send a postcard home before the start of the school year, welcoming each student.
- Greet families outside the school as they come in.
- Meet students at the door and ask how the afternoon went the day before.
- Write a class newsletter each week, and translate it into every language used by families in the class (check out Google Translate).
- For Open House night, send personalized invitations to each family.
- Start a math-games night every quarter to teach families about the games you use for math.
- Ask family members how they would like to be a part of the classroom community.
- Be open and welcoming of family visitors: Have different jobs ready for different kinds of volunteers. Ideas include reading to the class, preparing materials for an activity, teaching a small group or the whole class about an area of expertise, or typing the class newsletter.

their children. Remember that you are with students about 6.5 hours each school day; families are with their children the other 17.5 hours of each school day, all weekends, and all vacation days; families are the ones who really know the students you see during the school day.

Share Your Expertise

Sharing expertise is how to connect useful ideas and strategies with families. When you are considering connecting with families, realize that there is probably diversity in families' experience with schooling. Some parents and family members enjoyed school, were successful in school, and expect to have a strong connection to their child's classroom. Other family members may not have finished school, or did not enjoy schooling for a variety of reasons. Your job is to support the success of all students, and one integral part of that is to welcome and support the families that send the students to school each day.

Learn from Families' Expertise

Families are a source of expertise on a wide range of topics. First, families are the experts in the students they send to school. They know more about the student than you do; they live with them, watch them grow, help them build skills, and stay with them through good and tough times. Some teachers lament that they could do their jobs so much better if only the parents or families would do their parts. But who are teachers to decide what families should do? Complaining about what families do not do is not productive. Finding the strengths that families have is productive. Mary Cowhey noted that she consciously makes time to connect with every family outside of school before the school year begins. She explains why this is important:

> Home visits are a good way to learn about and understand the diversity of my students' families, but they also give families an opportunity to talk with me about other issues in their family's life. These may include issues such as the serious illness of the child or a family member, recent or impending death, birth/adoption, marriage, separation, divorce, custody dispute, incarceration, addiction, rehabilitation, unemployment, disability, or other family issues. It is important to know how these things might affect a child's moods, schedule, and energy level. It is often a relief for a parent or guardian to explain the context of family issues before they manifest themselves as anxiety or inappropriate behavior in the classroom. (2006, p. 198)

Like Cowhey, we believe that getting to know families is essential to being a good teacher.

COLLABORATION WITHIN THE SCHOOL

In schools, there is a great deal of collaboration that must take place if students are going to get what they need. Remember response to intervention (RTI) from Chapter 9? Implementing RTI requires significant collaboration between teachers and other professionals to determine what interventions work best, how to implement new strategies, and to provide enough adults to effectively teach and collect data for improving performance. In this section, we review three kinds of collaborative relationships: teacher–teacher, teacher–related service professional, and teacher–teaching assistant.

Teacher–Teacher

Teachers have a long history of working by themselves. Some say teachers want to teach so that they can be the queen or king of their own kingdom. They are the ruler, and there is no discussion about who is in charge in a teacher's classroom. In a recent article about teacher collaboration, DuFour said that a study in 1983 reported that teachers "view their classrooms as their personal domains, have little access to the ideas and strategies of their colleagues, and prefer to be left alone rather than engage with their colleagues or principals" (2011, p. 57). DuFour went on to say that since then, not very much has changed because the profession of teaching has not required collaboration as an essential skill. He asked us to imagine: What if an airline pilot were told to proceed to a certain runway, but instead of guiding the plane to the assigned runway, she just said "No, I'd rather have a different runway, and I don't want to wait." That would not be acceptable! But the history of teaching has not always included clear expectations that teachers collaborate. We believe that teachers should collaborate routinely, as hearing other opinions and sharing strategies supports everyone's professional growth.

Teachers collaborate in many ways: planning, sharing materials and resources, problem solving, serving on committees, serving on building-support teams, and coteaching. In the next paragraphs, we review the ways that teachers support each other informally and then explain what coteaching is about.

Teachers today often may be alone in the classroom, or rarely alone, depending on whom they are teaching and what the district and building administration believes about collaborative practice. But all teachers should talk to each other, sharing ideas, problems, and finding solutions. Having strong communication skills to listen and explain what you mean respectfully is an important part of using the strategies. Take opportunities to connect with your colleagues when you are a new teacher, and continue to do so once you are veteran. You will continue to learn throughout your career. Having colleagues to share with and learn from will support your professional growth and help you be the best teacher you can be.

Coteaching is made up of four components. It involves two or more certified teachers jointly delivering instruction in diverse classrooms within a shared physical space (Conderman, Bresnahan, & Pedersen, 2009, pp. 2–3). The certified teachers may be a general education and a special education teacher working together, or two general education teachers, or two special education teachers. Most traditionally, coteaching has been a general and special education teacher together, each sharing their expertise to serve a group of students with a variety of needs (and with a range of labels or no labels) in a classroom.

Teacher–Related Service Professional

Teachers work with other professionals in many ways. School counselors and social workers are probably the most common professionals teachers see regularly, for numerous reasons. Counselors handle school schedules in junior high and high school and may also coordinate and lead groups for small groups of students related to areas of need. Groups might be organized for students dealing with grief and loss, divorce, homelessness, a family member in the military, or some other common stressor. In elementary settings, counselors typically spend less time with scheduling and more time providing services to small groups or individual students.

Teacher–Teaching Assistant

Teaching assistants are an integral part of education teams. How you collaborate with a teaching assistant depends on the needs of the students in the classroom, your own style, the style of the teaching assistant, and the way the job is structured. The first factor, the needs of the students in the classroom, is the most important. Some students have teaching assistants on the IEP to provide individual support. In recent history in special education, students with the label autism were sometimes automatically assigned a teaching assistant. Now it is more common that teaching assistants are assigned to individual students on their IEPs under related services, based on a more thorough review of individual student needs. Some schools have teaching assistants in the classroom to support the teacher instead of being assigned to a particular student. In both cases, the teaching assistant is an integral part of the educational team and should be invited to team meetings, asked for input, and treated as a valuable source of information. Teaching assistants are often the team members with the most information about students' daily lives, including student opinions, struggles, and achievement.

Your style and the style of the teaching assistant play a role in how you decide to work together. When one author was a teaching assistant for 3 years, the teachers she worked well with were directive about what needed to be done. Directions such as, "At this hour, this is my list for you, in priority order. I need these copies made, I have a set of quizzes for you to grade, and if there is time I have a small group lesson to preteach the next concepts coming up in science" were much appreciated: the author knew what was expected and in which order to complete tasks. It was much more difficult to work with a teacher who was less clear. Many teachers were afraid to sound bossy, and would say things like, "Well, what do you want to do in class today?" The author would think to herself, "How should I know? I'm not a teacher and I do not know what needs doing!" Being clear about what you want done is important.

Along with being clear about what you need done, be supportive and aware of your teaching assistant's strengths and preferences. If you do not know your teaching assistants, set up activities to get to know them and let them get to know you. Do ice-breaker activities and teaming activities to develop rapport so that you can work together to benefit students. Ask your administrators for a scheduled meeting time to convene with teaching assistants and review how things are going. Be sure that teaching assistants are invited and attend team meetings and trainings.

Attending meetings relates to how the job is structured. Many teaching assistants are paid hourly, and only for the hours that students are in school. Meetings before or after school may be the only time that you and your teaching assistants can meet, but be aware that they may not be paid for their time and may not be able to be at school beyond their paid hours. If this is the case, advocate with administrators for scheduled meetings that are paid for teaching assistants. Expecting them to work without pay is not reasonable.

COLLABORATION BETWEEN SCHOOL AND AGENCIES

Schools and agencies need to collaborate with each other, especially during the transitions from preschool to kindergarten and from high school to adult life. Schools are required by IDEA 2004 to work with other service providers, including early childhood intervention agencies and adult service agencies. IDEA 2004 stated that:

> If a purpose of a child's IEP Team meeting will be the consideration of postsecondary goals for the child and the transition services needed to assist the child in reaching those goals, the LEA, to the extent appropriate, and with consent, must invite a representative of any participating agency that is likely to be responsible for providing or paying for transition services to attend the child's IEP Team meeting. However, if the participating agency does not attend the meeting, the LEA is no longer required to take other steps to obtain participation of an agency in the planning of any transition services. (U.S. Department of Education, 2006)

What is positive about this statement is that the LEA, or local educational agency, is required to invite representatives of any agency that will be serving the young adult with a disability after they transition out of high school. What is a problem is that the school's responsibility is complete once the invitation has been extended. After the student graduates from high school, he or she faces a new system for services and support and we believe that it is essential for schools and adult service agencies to work together with young adults. At the same time, we appreciate that the schools cannot force agencies to attend meetings of young adults, and that agencies have their own systems for supporting young adults. In Chapter 11, you will read that there are many kinds of adult service agencies and that the type of services varies by location. The most important parts of collaboration related to transition-age students are to complete person-centered planning and help students develop self-advocacy skills so that they leave high school knowing what their goals are and what supports they need to accomplish them.

SUMMARY

In this chapter, you learned about best practices in collaboration and reviewed school-home collaboration strategies. Then you learned about collaboration in school between teachers, and ended with a review of collaboration between schools and agencies. The key to successful collaboration is sustaining a focus on the best interests of the student; when everyone works to understand and provide what is best for the student, the discussions can be rich, collaborative, and supportive.

NARRATIVE 10.1. | SHERI STANGER

My daughter Megan is 17 years old and has CHARGE syndrome—a rare congenital disorder that occurs in about one in every 10,000 births and is the leading cause of congenital deaf-blindness in the USA. Megan has both vision and hearing loss along with developmental delays, behavioral challenges, and a history of medical issues. And she is a fantastic young adult with many positive attributes and skills.

I am a certified school counselor and prior to the birth of my daughter had worked with children and young adults who were blind and deaf-blind. No training in the world prepares you to parent a child with complex health, developmental, and sensory needs. If there's one thing I have learned, you can't do it alone. The old adage, "it takes a village" is true. Serious collaboration among parents/guardians, school personnel, therapists, agencies, and recreational programs is imperative to ensure the success of a child.

Over the years, I learned to be informed, assertive, and proactive. I learned to include everyone in the educational decision-making process. There should be no surprises at the annual review if all parties involved have communicated effectively throughout the year.

Intense collaboration with our small school district, along with the assistance from our state deaf-blind project, supported Megan's various transitions and moves through multiple school settings. Involvement with our state deaf-blind family organization—the New York Parent Network—and my involvement with the National Family Association for Deaf-Blind and the CHARGE Syndrome Foundation, connected me to other parents and taught me to be an effective advocate for a child with deaf-blindness. The skills that I developed over the years, along with my contacts in the field, helped me become a better collaborator. I consider my husband and myself to be a part of the educational team. Everyone comes to the table with their area of expertise and the parents are no different. We know our child's history, development, likes and dislikes because we are with her most of the time. Some of my daughter's most successful school years occurred when her teachers were willing to learn about her syndrome and participate in trainings given by the deaf-blind project or the Perkins School for the Blind. I truly respect the teacher who tells me he or she doesn't know an answer but is willing to research and learn.

Megan's success in life as a student, friend, athlete, worker, and family member depends on the collaboration of many. Though she presents with many challenges, she has been successful on many fronts including foreign languages, sports, and vocational tasks. Opportunities outside the classroom through special recreation programs, camps, religious school, Girl Scouts, music, and art helped her to discover her interests and develop her talents, which in turn helped to improve the quality of her IEP goals and her success as a student. This was accomplished through a collaborative process called Person Centered Planning with a facilitator, Megan, and the people in Megan's life. This involves a positive discussion of the student's interests, likes, and dislikes, and the circles of people in her life. This process teaches everyone involved new things about Megan. It helped generate her IEP goals and transition plan, which helped to ensure her success rather than failure in school. Once her interests were discussed, the team developed strategies to make them a reality.

I wear many hats to ensure my daughter's success in life, but the hat of the collaborator is sometimes a tough fit. We should all work on getting the right fit and wear that hat proudly.

NARRATIVE 10.2. | COLLEEN BROWN

I am one of seven children. Being included in the family was always a must. Now my children are part of a 40-member extended family unit consisting of grandparents, aunts, uncles, and cousins. Inclusion is a mainstay in our family and exclusion is never considered. I needed to begin with this background, because until teachers and school administrators take the time to understand the family unit, discussions of resource rooms, self-contained classrooms, or segregated schooling cannot be recommended at an individualized education program (IEP) meeting.

Effective collaboration between school and family can only begin when the school has had discussions and knowledge of the *vision* the family has for the child (as the child ages, this will change to the child's *vision* along with family support). Many barriers and bad meetings could have been avoided if the school had only asked why we were against a self-contained classroom for our child. Once I had done research on the rights of my child and knew about least restrictive environment (LRE), I became an informed parent with laws backing our *vision* for my son. *Never* go into an IEP meeting when you don't know the family vision for that child. Nothing good ever comes of it.

Once the school knew we would go to war with them for inclusion, the principal provided an inclusive environment for my son in the fourth grade. This environment consisted of a volunteer general education teacher, a volunteer general education teacher for ELA and math, and a teaching assistant for science and social studies. I mention the word volunteer, because at the IEP meeting my husband and I said we only wanted teachers who believed inclusion would work for our son: this was a nonnegotiable.

Fourth grade was a success, and then for fifth grade the team of teachers looked at the students who had been included and determined what would best meet their needs. They created a blended classroom of students with high performance along with students having more educational needs. Throughout the school year, they always had an open forum at the beginning of the day, and then a student meeting that provided peer modeling for my son and others. After unit tests, depending on how they did on the tests, students would get pulled for support—whether or not the student had an IEP. Throughout the year, they would work with me, and worked through the transition to middle school. It was a joint effort to best meet his needs and the *vision*. One of the most memorable comments they said to me was "you know your child best." I really felt supported. During the IEP meeting addressing the transition to middle school, they recommended services we knew our son needed and it was a collaborative decision before even going to the middle school IEP meeting: Wow, what a change!

As a professional, you have to have an open mind about all children and what they can achieve. Do not put up barriers to success, life will do that on its own. Ask yourself, how am I going to be remembered by that student and his or her family? My best memories of Zack's life come from the teachers who believed and cared enough to think outside the box.

CHAPTER 11

Transition from High School to Adult Life

How this chapter prepares you to be an effective inclusive classroom teacher:

- This chapter teaches you about planning in a collaborative context for a student's transition to adulthood in nine critical life areas. **This helps you meet CEC Standard 7: Instructional Planning.**

- This chapter teaches you about assessment that takes place in a student's educational program to evaluate progress and needs as the student prepares to transition to adult life. You will also learn about the importance of meaningful assessment that involves the student and is results-oriented (i.e., geared toward identifying supports and adaptations needed for independent adult living). **This helps you meet CEC Standard 8: Assessment.**

- This chapter teaches you about your legal responsibility as a teacher in planning for the student's transition to adult life. You will learn that professional and ethical teachers involve the student as much as possible in decision making, begin the planning early to maximize learning and independence, are aware of community agencies that provide adult services, and are sensitive to the diversity of individual students. **This helps you meet CEC Standard 9: Professional and Ethical Practice.**

- This chapter teaches you about many types of adult service agencies and the services they provide. You will also learn about your role as a teacher in collaborating with agencies, other school personnel, families, and students to plan and implement a comprehensive transition plan that meets all legal provisions. **This helps you meet CEC Standard 10: Collaboration.**

After reading and discussing
this chapter, you will be able to

- Explain why early planning is important for a student's transition to adult life

- Explain what it means for a student to be an active participant in transition planning and the impact on the student's transition

- Explain the concepts of advocacy and the teacher's role in facilitating them

- Describe the role of IDEA in transition to adult life

- Explain coordinated set of activities and their significance in transition planning

- Explain person-centered planning and its significance in transition planning

- Explain the nine critical life areas and their significance in transition planning

- Explain long-term adult outcomes and the factors to consider in planning them

- Provide examples of adult service agencies in the community and their roles in transition to adult life

||||||||||||||||||||||||||||||||||||||||||||||||||||||||||||||||||||||||||||||||||||||||||||

This chapter, the last in Part II, concludes the discussion regarding what teaching everyone means. Teaching everyone does not end with high school; it extends into adult life in the work force, higher education, the community, and social life. Transition planning is of utmost importance in the lives of persons with disabilities. This chapter is divided into three sections. The first section discusses important overarching issues regarding transition to adult life. The second section reviews legislation that regulates transition planning at the state and federal levels and covers the processes to follow that ensure purposeful, inclusive planning for all individuals. The third section provides an overview of programs and resources that support community connections.

The narrative for this chapter is from a group of students attending a postsecondary program on a college campus.

ISSUES

Early Planning

As mentioned above, transition planning is extremely important, but there is often a risk that it will not be given the time and attention it needs early enough. Planning for adult life cannot start at the beginning of adult life. This is true of everyone. Imagine not thinking about college until the day after high school graduation. You would have missed the boat on several important steps. As high school students, you would have missed PSATs, SATs, college visits, entrance applications, scholarship applications, and financial aid statements. The next step in your life after high school takes purposeful thought and planning at least 2 years in advance. It often takes the help of parents, older siblings, and friends to help support your transition. For students with disabilities who may need support services outside of high school, this planning needs to start even earlier. It may take some students longer to master skills for independent living, so the earlier the preparation starts, the better. Also, agencies that provide services for young adults with disabilities may have a waiting list. Planning early on for the transition will help everything fall into place when the time comes.

In addition to the help of parents, older siblings and friends, some young adults may also need specialized support that is provided by **community service agencies**. These agencies offer services such as assisted living, job coaching, mobility training, and therapies. One cannot walk in the door and immediately receive services. Many have waiting lists of several months to years, with complex pathways to travel for evaluation and qualification for services. So, planning must start early—for some, even before high school. The next section will go into more detail regarding legally mandated time lines for starting the planning process.

Nothing About Me without Me

In Chapter 9, you learned about the importance of including students in IEP planning. This is particularly important for transition planning. Not only should students be present for planning meetings, they should be **active participants**—speaking for themselves, asking questions, and requesting clarification. Not asking students to attend a planning meeting is like providing clothes for a student without including her in the shopping. Asking if it is okay after the fact is not the same as including the student as an active participant. While advice and support may always be welcome, students need to be able to go shopping on their own and make their own educated decisions about what to buy and wear.

Advocacy to Self-Advocacy

The earlier multidisciplinary teams live by the credo "nothing about me without me," the more prepared students will be as active participants or **self-advocates**. It starts with the role of the teacher as advocate and is handed over to the student step by step, just as any academic skill would be. When we want to effectively teach a new math concept to a group of students, we explain, then demonstrate an example, then guide students through a few examples, then have the students try a few on their own. All the while, we utilize tools and resources, such as number lines, manipulatives, or drawings. Advocacy skills can be scaffolded in the same way.

At first, the teacher has the skill and the student is not yet involved. Next, the teacher remains the more knowledgeable other but offers the student opportunities to practice the skill with guidance. Halfway through, the teacher and student are equal partners. The student is grasping the skill quite nicely, but still relies on the teacher to monitor progress or offer new opportunities for practice. Next, the teacher begins to fade out, offering minimal assistance when needed while the student performs independently. Last, the student is completely independent in the skill. It may be some students do not ever complete a particular skill independently, but it is important that students are as involved as possible in each process, including transition planning.

In her book, *You're Going to Love This Kid!* Kluth (2010) discussed the role of the teacher in supporting inclusive schooling. One way that teachers can support inclusion is to serve as advocates and teach advocacy skills to students with disability labels. Teachers can model advocacy and scaffold involvement of students by teaching other educators about inclusive education or specific disabilities and answering questions the local community may have about disabilities. The most effective teachers also remain aware of the law as it relates to inclusive education. They become involved with advocacy groups such as TASH, The Arc; the National Disability Rights Network (NDRN); the National Dissemination Center for Children with Disabilities (NICHCY); and the National Organization on Disability (NOD).

Teachers also need to study the school community and question their own practices to establish and sustain processes and systems that respect and value all students.

community service agencies Agencies in the community that are federal-, state-, county-, or grant-funded and that provide services to persons with disabilities. Services may include support with employment, education, living arrangements, community use, and recreation.

active participant One who is directly and personally involved in his or her own program planning, service implementation, and assessment.

self-advocates Those who are able to indicate their own strengths, needs, likes, dislikes, and future plans and goals. This includes educating others about themselves, breaking down stereotypes, and clarifying misconceptions.

For example, teachers can present information on specific disabilities at professional development venues and provide students with opportunities to make choices and voice opinions about their educational and transitional planning (Kluth, 2010, p. 50).

LEGISLATION AND PROCESSES

Transition Services Under IDEA

Transition services under the law have grown since they were first mandated by IDEA in 1990, then further defined by the 1997 and IDEA 2004 reauthorizations. The necessity of transition planning has led to thorough descriptions of the steps to be taken at specified times in a student's education, as well as processes to be followed with the intent of maximizing each student's potential for success and full inclusion in adult life after school.

First, IDEA defines transition services as a **coordinated set of activities** for a child with a disability. This means that a multidisciplinary team will plan a whole set of services during the school years that will carefully and purposefully prepare students with disabilities to transition into many different types of areas of adult life (2004, Section 602). Each student will require a differentiated set of services, depending on his or her needs. The services related to transition might be many of the same ones that are provided on the IEP already, and they are mentioned during transition planning because those needs will continue as the student becomes an adult. Services may include speech pathology and audiology, occupational therapy, physical therapy, transportation, social work, counseling, orientation and mobility training, academic coursework, community-based instruction, job training or shadowing, work experience, and social skill instruction.

Second, IDEA stipulates that the coordinated set of activities must be based on the student's needs, taking into account the student's strengths, preferences, and interests. This **person-centered planning** relates to the idea of "nothing about me without me."

The planning that is done for the high school years is centered on the person and includes the person in every planning step. It is not based on the programs that are available, nor is it based solely on parents' or teachers' goals for the student. In one program, students create collages to illustrate their dreams and goals in each area of independent adult living. Some collages show cars or images of driver's licenses. Other collages show wedding and baby pictures. Some show pictures or drawings of workers in various careers.

Last, the coordinated set of activities should be results-oriented so that each student is prepared for adult life. This means that students' goals should be assessed and attended to so they are prepared for nine **critical life areas** as outlined in IDEA (see sidebar). These areas are vocational training and employment, continuing education, living arrangements, getting around the community, socializing and networking, financial independence, leisure and recreation, sexuality and self-esteem, and personal health and medical care.

In reviewing this list, imagine everything that you needed to be able to do to go away to college and/or live in your own apartment. If you were going to live off-campus at college or in your own apartment after high school while you worked, you had to grocery shop and cook for yourself. If you lived on campus at college, you needed to know what is healthy for you and what is not. Everyone, no matter where he or she lives, needs to know about drugs and alcohol, and to make educated decisions about staying well.

Once your family has stopped paying bills related to your care, you need to be able to earn and manage money so that you have enough to pay the bills

coordinated set of activities A set of activities, programs, and experiences that make up the high school education of a student with a disability. The set of activities is based on long-term adult outcomes and its planning directly involves the student as an active participant.

person-centered planning When the coordinated set of activities is created, the person for whom it is created is considered at all times. The activities should be based on that person's strengths, needs, interests, and goals. The activities should not be based on others' goals for that person or merely which programs happen to be available.

critical life areas Nine areas listed in IDEA as critical to a full, independent adult life. These are listed in the sidebar below.

Critical life areas

- Vocational training and employment
- Continuing education
- Living arrangement
- Getting around the community
- Socializing and networking
- Financial independence
- Leisure and recreation
- Sexuality and self-esteem
- Personal health and medical care

on time and have some left over for fun. You need to be able to do your laundry and clean your living space. You need to be able to find a doctor or dentist, make appointments, travel to them, and follow through with medications and self-care instructions when needed.

You need to be able to find things to do for fun, make and keep friends, have romantic relationships if desired, and know about how to be intimate with a partner without being exposed to unwanted pregnancy or sexually transmitted diseases. You need to be self-aware about who you are attracted to and know how to choose a romantic partner who will treat you respectfully. On top of it all, you have a job to perform—either in the workplace or in higher education.

Think about how you learned those skills. Who taught you to do all that? Did you take classes? Did you go to workshops or have a tutor? Did you pick it up by watching others or trying it on your own a couple times? Transition services as mandated by IDEA were put in place to make sure that students with disabilities receive well-planned, person-centered, direct instruction in these areas so that they can be as independent as possible and fully included in the community.

Now think about something else. Did you ever mess up at any of those things? Have you ever eaten chips for dinner because you forgot to grocery shop or didn't feel like cooking? Have you ever made a mistake in your checkbook and bounced a check? Have you ever ruined a load of laundry, gone over 6 months without having your teeth cleaned, or gotten into a big fight with a friend? If you have, you most likely were able to chalk it up as a learning experience and moved on. Everyone makes mistakes sometimes. Full inclusion in the community—full citizenship as adults—means that everyone has the opportunity to make mistakes on occasion. We need to make sure that there is not a double standard for people with disabilities. A laundry faux pas that leaves a person's wardrobe completely pink is a mistake, not a reason to believe they cannot be independent. If a person, any person, makes the same mistake over and over, then support may be needed. Until then, let everyone live and learn. Sometimes young adults with disabilities are held to an unreasonably high standard and that is not okay, because it is not equitable with the standard for their typically developing peers.

When Should Planning for Transition to Adulthood Start?

IDEA mandates that official transition planning begin by the time the student is 16 years old. At this point, a new version of the IEP, called the transition IEP, must be completed at each annual review meeting. The transition IEP includes **long-term adult outcomes**: vocational, continuing education, living arrangement, community living, and recreation goals. It also includes adult services that will need to be in place to support the student in reaching and maintaining these goals once he or she graduates from high school. The last section of this chapter discusses some adult service agencies in more detail.

long-term adult outcomes Outcomes for independent adult life that are set by the beginning of the high school years and strived for throughout the educational program of a student with a disability.

Even though the legally mandated starting point is 16 years of age, transition planning may start earlier. The transition IEP may not be completed until the start of high school, but preparing students for adulthood goals begins many years earlier by giving students a wide range of experiences. The multidisciplinary team collaborates to decide the best use of instructional time for each individual student in an inclusive context. This collaboration should always include the student. Engaging students in discussions about their interests, strengths, and needs better prepares them to make decisions about their future. The more they know about themselves as learners and contributors to the community, the more they will be able to advocate for themselves.

What Is the Process to Follow for Successful Transition to Adulthood?

The process for a successful transition to adulthood encompasses all of the issues and components discussed above: person-centered planning toward a coordinated set of

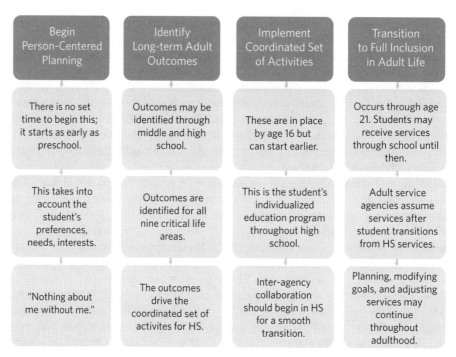

Figure 11.1.   Transitioning to adulthood.

activities with long-term adult outcomes in the nine critical life areas. There are four phases of the process that begin as early as kindergarten and continue throughout adulthood. Figure 11.1 shows a summary of the four phases. We will discuss each of them here in more detail.

Begin Person-Centered Planning   Planning for a person's livelihood beyond the school years begins as early as formal schooling begins. As mentioned above, as soon as kindergarten, all students should be exposed to various career paths, recreational interests, and living arrangement choices in inclusive settings with typical peers. Throughout the elementary school years, more purposeful exposure to these experiences helps each student match them to his or her performance levels cognitively, socially, physically, and behaviorally.

During the middle school years, purposeful planning takes place to explore further who the student is. Questionnaires may be completed by the student and the family outlining what they envision for postsecondary education, living arrangements, vocation, and recreational activities. There are also formal, standardized assessments, such as the Transition Planning Inventory by Pro-Ed, used to identify students' preferences, needs, and interests in the nine critical life areas. Also, vocational assessments, interest inventories, and aptitude assessments provide more information about a student's career development and necessary skills. Details about the student that are revealed by these assessments include how they acquire, organize, process, and apply information; understand the use of time, money, materials, and facilities; select, use, and maintain technology and technological equipment; interact with others; understand systems in the workplace and monitor or correct their performance in that system; read, write, use basic math, listen, and speak; problem solve and think creatively; and demonstrate personal qualities, such as responsibility, self-management, self-esteem, and social skills.

Throughout this process of gathering information, it is important to consider the student's strengths and abilities as well as need areas and disabilities, the student's concerns and his or her family's concerns about adult life, progress that has occurred in the past year, and what supports have worked for the student as well as supports that have not worked in terms of building skills.

Identify Long-Term Adult Outcomes   After gathering detailed information about the student's strengths, preferences, needs, and interests, long-term adult outcomes are developed. Those outcomes are developed by the end of the middle school years in order for them to be in place on the IEP by age 16. Outcomes are completed for each of the nine critical life areas. Where does the student want to be by age 21 in each of the nine areas? What support will the student need to get there by age 21? Will the student need the continuing support of an adult service agency after age 21 to fulfill this goal? All of this is summarized into long-term adult outcome statements. There is often more than one outcome for each area. The outcomes can, and often do, change over time—maybe each year as the student develops.

Implement the Coordinated Set of Activities   The coordinated set of activities is driven by the long-term adult outcome statements. Once it is known what outcomes the student is striving for and the team considers the support and skill-building necessary to achieve those outcomes, a coordinated program can be developed. The IEP is now the plan for these coordinated services. At each annual review meeting for students 16 and older, the transition IEP is completed to prepare the student for lifelong adult outcomes. Special education programs and related services, testing accommodations, transportation and assistive technology needs, and support personnel all prepare the student for adulthood.

Transition to Full Inclusion in Adult Life   The individualized program discussed above is part of the IEP and is reviewed each year through the end of high school, or until the student turns 22 years old, whichever is later. IDEA provides services for students with disabilities in a school setting through age 21. Then, adult service agencies take over.

Adult service agencies provide supports throughout adulthood in many different areas. It is extremely important that interagency collaboration occurs among the school and all of the adult service agencies so that there is not an interruption in support services and all services are relevant, appropriate, and individualized. The next section introduces specific types of adult service agencies and their provisions.

COMMUNITY CONNECTIONS

Connections to the community begin during the school years as part of each student's transition IEP, when the school and appropriate adult service agencies collaborate about services for young adults. There are different types of agencies depending on the support needed and the critical life area of focus. Each state has its own agencies, so it is important to know which are available in your state. A great resource for this is the National Dissemination Center for Children with Disabilities. The web site provides information regarding adult services—what they are and where they are. The State Resource Sheets link lists many types of agencies and their contact information in your state (NICHCY, 2011). Below are overviews of several categories of adult service agencies: vocational rehabilitation agencies, service agencies for individuals with intellectual disabilities or mental health concerns, independent living centers (advocacy centers), Social Security Administration (SSA), and postsecondary education program providers.

Vocational Rehabilitation Agencies

Each state has its own vocational rehabilitation agency, with regional or local offices. The purpose of vocational rehabilitation agencies is to support individuals with disabilities in finding gainful employment, postsecondary education, and living arrangements for financial independence and personal fulfillment. Vocational rehabilitation agencies receive both federal and state funding. Counselors for the agencies work with individuals with disabilities (as well as with IEP teams if the individual is still school age) to develop a rehabilitation plan to reach employment goals. The plan is typically for a limited amount of time, but a subsequent plan can be developed and implemented for further goals. Employment services may include vocational guidance and counseling (teaching what certain jobs entail and determining if they are a match for the individual), assessment and evaluation to determine skill levels, job placement, technological services, and adaptive tools. Postsecondary education services may include college programs, apprenticeship programs, and job training. Independent living services may include housing placement, transportation services, interpreter services, and orientation and mobility training (NICHCY, 2011).

Service Agencies for Individuals with Intellectual Disabilities or Mental Health Concerns

Each state may have multiple agencies with regional offices that provide comprehensive support in the areas of employment, independent living, and adult services. The agencies receive federal, state, and local funds. Case managers assigned to each individual provide access to local services that may include supported or sheltered employment, competitive employment, therapeutic recreation, day activities, respite care, and placement in group homes and supervised apartments. These are general examples. Services provided by each agency and the opportunities available in each state or locality vary greatly (NICHCY, 2011).

Independent-Living Centers (Advocacy Centers)

Independent-living or advocacy centers are typically run by individuals with disabilities for individuals with disabilities. The purpose of independent-living centers is to help people reach high levels of self-sufficiency and independence in the community. The centers receive local funds and serve particular areas, so the services vary greatly. In general, they provide classes and programs for further education and information, as well as advocacy support so individuals can be more fully included in the community. A large part of the educational outreach is to teach disability awareness (NICHCY, 2011).

Social Security Administration (SSA)

The Social Security Administration is a federal agency that provides financial assistance and employment services to individuals whose severe disabilities compromise their capacity to work enough to support themselves. Financial assistance programs include Social Security Disability Insurance (SSDI), Supplemental Security Income (SSI), Plans to Achieve Self-Support (PASS), Medicaid, and Medicare. Employment services available through work-incentive programs may include cash benefits while working, Medicaid or Medicare benefits while working, financial assistance with work-related expenses due to disability issues, or assistance in changing employment. Sometimes, medical and housing benefits are also available (NICHCY, 2011).

Postecondary Education Program Providers

Postsecondary education, particularly college attendance, has not historically been an option for students with disabilities, especially those with intellectual or pervasive developmental disabilities. In recent years, however, more and more postsecondary education programs have been established. Traditionally, college was designed to support a small percentage of the community in education beyond high school. The perception, based in real outcomes, was that getting a college degree was a guarantee of a better job and more opportunities than were possible with a high school degree alone. College is increasingly seen as something most students are expected to do, and that shift, along with an increased awareness of the rights of people with disabilities, means that college seems like the natural setting for students with disabilities who are between 18 and 22. The result is more and more partnerships between school districts and college campuses.

The film *Through the Same Door* features Micah Fialka-Feldman, a young man with a cognitive disability who attends college. Micah receives support to attend college classes, hold a part-time job on campus, and engage in social activities with his college peers.

In Massachusetts, the Inclusive Current Enrollment Initiative was started in 2007. This partnership between public high schools and seven community colleges supports individuals with intellectual disabilities, ages 18 to 22, in achieving their goal of attending college. Students supported by the initiative take classes tailored to their interests and career goals so they leave with competitive skills for the work force.

In New York, St. John Fisher College hosts another type of postsecondary education program, described in Narrative 11.1. Students, ages 18 to 21, attend class taught by their high school teachers, but are on the college campus. This environment provides

NARRATIVE 11.1. | POSTSECONDARY PROGRAM STUDENTS

"Everyone has a right to choose his or her own destiny, to work toward making his or her dreams a reality" (Thoma, Bartholomew, & Scott, p. 31). By adhering to these standards, the Webster-West Irondequoit Postsecondary Program at St. John Fisher College assists developmentally disabled young adults between the ages of 18 and 21 in making such choices. The program is designed to develop young adults' skills, strengths, and talents while at the same time providing mutually beneficial outcomes for both the students and the St. John Fisher campus at large. The main areas on which the program focuses are independent living skills, occupational guidance, and personal-social skills as dictated by the Life-Centered Career Education Curriculum (LCCE). The campus provides the many opportunities indicated below, which are accompanied by comments from the young adults themselves.

Vocational Exploration Experiences   "Working on campus helped me become more comfortable with the interview process. I was a hard worker and I went from a volunteer to a paid position. I feel very proud and good about myself." — Sasha

Travel Training   "St. John Fisher has given me more experience in riding on the RTS (Rochester Transportation System) bus. Since I've been working on getting my license, my teachers have shown me a company called VESID. I talked to a representative and now I take driving sessions with Morgan School of Driving." — John

Community Connections   "We went to the YMCA, Wegman's, PCC (Project Community Convergence), and other places for field trips while we were not taking advantage of activities on campus. When we were at the Heart Walk and the PCC I felt proud. I felt proud because I understand that the things I did there helped people. The Heart Walk raised money to help people who have heart diseases and the PCC let us clean up their school. I felt special because I found out doing those things helped people in need." —Mike

"I was able to volunteer to help paint a city school. I was glad to be part of the St. John Fisher College SWAV (Students With A Vision) group and help in my community. It made me feel good inside. I would definitely do it again." —Emery

Fitness and Health   "Health and fitness is very important. We all love to be healthy by staying active on campus. Sometimes we use the SLC (Student Life Center)." —John

Self-Advocacy   "The program has helped me realize advocating for myself is easier than I thought. My job at the St. John Fisher library allowed me to ask my boss if I could have more responsibilities." —Holly

Communication and Interpersonal Skills   "This program has allowed me to learn how to ask for what I need in the right way. I used to get picked on a lot and that made me angry so now I'm working on not being so angry and asking for needs in an appropriate way. Being a part of the program is helping me do this."—Emery

Social Opportunities on Campus (Peers)   "While at the program, I was able to take part in the Teddi Dance. The Teddi Dance is a 24-hour dance to raise money for families and kids that are affected by cancer. It is a great time to get to know new people on campus and just have fun!" —Sasha

"We have had the chance to hang out with SWAV members and other students on campus. I was able to go see my friend's dorm room."—Katie

Independent Living Skills   "In my class, we learn what independent living skills are and how we can strengthen them. The class really helps because it makes it so much easier for when you do have a place of your own. In high school, I didn't think much of my life after it, but when I came into this class it showed me that there's a lot in life and that you make your future." —John

St. John Fisher College Benefits Received from the Program's Presence:

- Increased levels of campus diversity
- Providing student observation hours for undergraduate and graduate students
- St. John Fisher student-teaching experiences (School of Education)
- St. John Fisher student-internship experiences (Graduate School of Counseling)
- Program-led discussion panel about disability awareness to teacher candidates
- Numerous on-campus volunteer hours
- Volunteer work experiences (Lavery Library, Campus Bookstore, Child Care Center, Lackmann Foodservice)
- Various social gatherings with campus professors, campus personnel, students

greater work, recreation, and age-appropriate social opportunities for young adults who are ready for life beyond high school but are still working toward their critical life area goals. Students in the program independently navigate the campus, take part in student clubs and events, utilize campus services, such as the dining halls, library, and athletic center, and engage in volunteer work positions for training experience. In addition, the students often serve as guest panelists in education courses to speak to future teachers about transition to adulthood and effective differentiation of instruction.

Also in New York is the Institute for Innovative Transition. The Institute provides support to community members to effectively address transition issues for individuals with developmental disabilities, ages 14 to 25. Target service areas include information and dissemination, technical assistance, workshops and programs, training and professional development, and policy initiatives (The Institute for Innovative Transition, n.d.).

Programs such as these offer benefits to all involved. The students in the program gain skills and experiences unique to college campus life. The members of the college campuses (i.e., students, faculty, staff) are part of a diverse learning community. Everyone expands their idea about the purpose of college.

SUMMARY

This chapter introduced important considerations regarding transition from school to adulthood for students with disabilities: starting planning as early as possible, including the student in all planning, and preparing individuals to be self-advocates. Legally mandated components of transition planning under IDEA were delineated to show how the law is responding to the relevant issues for young adults leaving school. Four phases of transition planning and service implementation were provided in detail, and specific adult service agencies and postsecondary programs were described. The teacher's role in transition planning is the same as the teacher's role in differentiated classroom instruction: get to know the individual and coordinate several supports that focus on the student's strengths and interests so that the student's fullest potential can be reached.

How Will I Teach Everyone?

Instructional Strategies by Content Area

OVERVIEW

Section III includes Chapters 12 through 19. In Chapters 12 through 18, we revisit the principles of universal design for learning (UDL) introduced in Section II in the context of each area of the curriculum: management, reading, writing, social studies, math, science, and communication. These chapters provide specific examples of differentiated activities that can be found in a universally designed classroom like Beth's classroom case study in Chapter 8. Chapter 19 includes strategies for connecting with special area teachers (i.e., art, music, physical education) and related service personnel (i.e., speech, occupational, and physical therapists) regarding student needs.

Chapters 12 through 18 have three sections: 1) an introduction that covers national learning standards and discusses important considerations for the curricular area, 2) specific strategies for teaching each curricular area, and 3) a summary. In each chapter, you will find multiple ways to engage students, to represent new learning to them and allow them to express it, and to assess their progress. Here, we review information from Chapter 8 regarding each of the UDL principles you will see addressed in Chapters 12 through 18. The four areas are engagement, input, output, and assessment.

ENGAGEMENT

To engage students, we first need to recruit their interest. This means we need to find ways to make learning relevant, authentic, and valuable in their lives. We need to provide students with activities that fit their learning styles and personality types and allow them to make choices about which activities they participate in. We also need to make sure that we remove any barriers to participating, such as distractions or situations that the student may find threatening, including intense competition or on-the-spot performances in front of peers.

After students are interested, teachers need to sustain student engagement and effort in a learning task or activity. To do this, students should be included in setting salient goals that provide the right amount of challenge, which we determine through knowing each student's skills, abilities, strengths, and areas of need. Students should be provided with many opportunities to collaborate and communicate with peers and teachers. We should also find ways to give students specific feedback as to how they are mastering knowledge and skills.

Last, engaging students includes supporting them in self-regulation. We can do this by optimizing their motivation for reaching the goal, providing them with many skills and strategies for learning and managing frustration, and offering opportunities for self-assessment and reflection.

INPUT OF NEW INFORMATION

To effectively teach new information to students, teachers need to present it in several different ways so that students with various perceptual abilities can perceive the information. Display information in print and digital media so that it can be changed to meet different students' needs. You also need to present information in ways that meet the needs of students with preferences in auditory, visual, and tactile/kinesthetic learning styles.

Another way to help students input new information is to make sure they understand language, vocabulary, expressions, and symbols. We need to provide information in multiple forms of media so we can vary the syntax and structure of new information. We also need to ensure that students understand all forms of communication.

Once we have supported students in accessing new information, we need to find multiple ways for them to make connections and comprehend it. We can do this through activities that activate their existing background knowledge. This entails highlighting patterns, critical features, big ideas, and relationships. Comprehension is facilitated by providing for various styles of information processing, providing different ways to visualize concepts, and by helping students transfer or generalize new learning to other situations.

OUTPUT OF STUDENT LEARNING

The first way to differentiate for student expression of new learning is to provide multiple options to which students can physically respond and/or navigate through problem solving with hands-on activities and manipulatives. We need to allow students to use tools and assistive technologies to express knowledge and perform skills.

Another way to universally design output is to provide many ways for students to express and communicate their learning. This entails allowing students to use multiple media and a variety of tools and technology to construct and compose their responses. We also need to provide graduated levels of support as they practice and gain fluency as well as provide options of response for all of the multiple intelligences.

Last, student output is facilitated by supporting the executive functions. This means we need to provide multiple ways for students to set appropriate goals, plan, develop strategies, manage information and resources, and monitor their own progress.

ASSESSMENT

Assessment that is universally designed considers a variety of evidence for skill and knowledge mastery. Differentiated assessment goes beyond traditional pen-and-paper assessment or direct oral questioning by teachers to include performance assessment, portfolio assessment, and student self-assessment.

Finally, Part III wraps up with Chapter 19, "Working with Special Area Teachers and Related Service Professionals." This is an important chapter because these professionals are essential to the educational programs of all students. Most of the strategies presented are the result of surveying these educators regarding what new teachers should know about their areas and how to connect and collaborate with them.

CHAPTER 12

Management Strategies for All Students

How this chapter prepares you to be an effective inclusive classroom teacher:

- This chapter provides examples of evidence-based instructional strategies for behavioral expectations. Then, strategies are provided for multiple ways of engaging students according to the principles of universal design for learning (UDL). Emphasis is on multiple ways for students to access new information and express their understanding of what is expected. **This helps you meet CEC Standard 4: Instructional Strategies.**

- This chapter explains how to create learning environments that support student safety and well-being. It also addresses the importance of acknowledging and supporting diverse perspectives in a supportive environment. It describes how to support students with motivational interventions to support behavioral success. Stimulating interest in proactive behavior is addressed. Ways to safely intervene with students in crisis are also covered. **This helps you meet CEC Standard 5: Learning Environments and Social Interactions.**

- This chapter describes effective conflict-resolution steps that support effective communication skills between students. **This helps you meet CEC Standard 6: Language.**

- In this chapter, using data to inform decisions is explained. How to use observational data and communicate what is found is reviewed. **This helps you meet CEC Standard 8: Individual Learning Differences.**

- This chapter helps you understand the importance of articulating your expectations clearly so that all students are able to meet behavioral standards that are appropriate for them. **This helps you meet CEC Standard 9: Professional and Ethical Practice.**

After reading and discussing
this chapter, you will be able to

- Explain why behavioral skills need to be taught

- Explain how PBIS relates to classroom management

- Describe how to establish a safe and caring classroom community that engages students

- Explain routines that are used in classrooms and give examples

- Explain how to communicate behavioral expectations to all students

- Define self-monitoring

- Describe how to teach conflict-resolution skills

- Define and explain how to address bullying

- Describe how to collect and communicate data about individual or group behavior

In this chapter, we explore how teachers manage their classrooms. A positive and supportive community helps classroom management, and mutual respect, clear routines, and clear expectations help a community flourish. Classroom management is the biggest single concern of new teachers, and this chapter provides information, narratives, and activities to support them. The focus is on proactive approaches, rather than reactive, punitive approaches.

Chapter 6, Classroom Management, was an introduction to this topic. You learned about the importance of building and sustaining community. This includes knowing and valuing all students, initiating activities that help students get to know each other, and using class meetings. Then, you learned what FBAs, BIPs, and PBIS mean and how those processes are used in schools. You also learned about a three-tiered pyramid that explains how management strategies support students who need little, some, or significant support to sustain appropriate classroom behavior. The pyramid base includes about 80% of students, the middle tier about 15% of students, and the top about 5% of students.

In this chapter, you will learn strategies that will support you as an effective classroom manager for all of your students. Strategies include both those designed for all students and those for individual students. This first section reviews the background of good management and what is recommended by the American Federation of Teachers and the Council for Exceptional Children related to managing your classroom. It then provides strategies for management using the four headings: Engagement, Input, Output, and Assessment. Maggie Driscoll, who just finished her first year of teaching, shares a narrative about her experiences. There is a brief summary at the end of the chapter.

The first point we want to emphasize is that teachers are powerful forces in students' lives and how we think about students affects how we treat them. Remember from Chapter 6 that "making the weather" (Ginott) is something we do every time we begin class. We can support or suppress students simply by changing the attitude and beliefs we hold about students. Remember that Alfie Kohn (1996) told us that if we believe that a child will be a troublemaker, then that is what will happen. That is, if we expect that a student will get into trouble, we interpret everything he or she does through that lens of "troublemaker." Instead, Kohn encouraged teachers to see every child as doing his or her best. That does not always happen, but if we approach students with the assumption that they are doing the best they can, we respond with the attitude that we can support their learning. Sonia Nieto wrote, "the teachers whose classes I was eager to get to and in whose classes I excelled were the ones who treated and nurtured me as an individual, a special person" (2003, p. 28).

Student behavior management includes skills that need to be taught. When a student struggles in math, you do not send him out of the room with no materials and take away his opportunity to learn math. In the same way, when a student has a conflict with another student or talks back to the teacher, sending her out of the room takes away her opportunity to learn how to resolve conflict and talk respectfully to adults. For a student who struggles in math, you should identify what skills are needed, decide how to teach those skills, and provide opportunities for practice. For a student who struggles with social relationships, or task persistence, or conflict management, you need to do the same things: identify what skills are needed, decide how to teach those skills, and provide opportunities for practice.

The American Federation of Teachers (AFT) noted that "many behavior problems can be prevented or corrected using effective behavior-management strategies" and that one key aspect of preventing problems is to reward positive behavior (American Federation of Teachers, Defining consequences, n.d., para. 1). The underlying assumption of rewarding positive behavior is that if you spend time and energy on what students are doing well and give little attention to students who are not doing what they should, there is little incentive for students to misbehave. Another resource is the Council for Exceptional Children (CEC), which has a range of resources related to classroom management and supporting positive student behavior.

Resources for good classroom management often include many connections to **positive behavioral interventions and supports (PBIS).** Remember from Chapter 6 that PBIS is not a mandatory program, but many districts are adopting its four elements: data for making decisions, outcomes that are measurable and supported by data, practices with evidence that the outcomes are achievable, and systems that support implementing the practices (OSEP Technical Assistance Center, 2011). What this means is that, throughout the school, everyone shares the same language about expectations for behavior and uses the same kind of reinforcement for good behavior.

The rest of the chapter presents strategies for management in the categories from Chapter 8: engagement, input, output, and assessment. In each area, strategies to support general classroom management as well as strategies to support individual students will be considered (see Figure 12.1).

positive behavioral interventions and supports (PBIS)
A decision-making framework to support academic and behavioral success of all students.

STRATEGIES FOR MANAGEMENT

Remember that engagement, input, output, and assessment work with each other. These strategies have been divided into categories to help you see how universal design for learning (UDL) helps teachers think about all four facets of instruction. However, if you see a strategy under "output" and think "Hmm…that seems more like assessment to me" you are probably right! The categories are a way to help teachers consider all students and their needs related to knowing what behavior is expected and developing the skills to meet those expectations.

Engagement

Engagement with classroom management means communicating to students why a safe, supportive environment is better than the alternative. Spending time teaching routines, having class meetings, and managing the environment in a supportive and caring

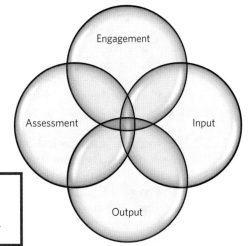

- Establish community.
- Teach routines.
- Stimulate interest in proactive behavior.

- Model the practices you want to see.
- Teach character.
- Teach self-monitoring.
- Teach conflict resolution.
- Address bullying.

- Observe interactions.
- Collect data.
- Communicate the data.

Figure 12.1.   Management strategies.

manner are the best ways to demonstrate your commitment. You also need to engage all students by being sure that students are all welcomed into the community. This means having materials that represent a diverse range of ethnic backgrounds, genders, and abilities; showcasing student work in ways that celebrates achievement without competition; and sharing responsibility with students for a safe and supportive class environment. Start lessons by connecting to students' lives; making instruction relevant is an integral part of good instruction, which supports good management. Strategies are grouped into three headings: establish community, teach routines, and stimulate interest in proactive behavior.

Establish Community   Community is created through the physical space and the way people treat each other. The physical arrangement of the furniture and materials can have a major effect on how well students are able to relax and learn. Arrange the room so that there are places for individual, small-, and large-group work. This probably sounds familiar when thinking about elementary school; be sure to consider how older students can work in groups as well. When you enter your classroom at the beginning of the school year, take a good look at it. Is it arranged to permit the best environment for learning? Can you and your students live and learn with the configuration of furniture, equipment, and accessories in the classroom? Educational researchers who studied the practices of effective teachers concluded that classroom designs greatly enhance opportunities for student progress. The American Federation of Teachers recommends that when you arrange your room, you think about these things:

- What are high-traffic areas? How can you avoid congestion near those?

- What are potential distractions?

- Do you have a clear view of students?

- Do students have a clear view of you, the board, and posted information?

- Are you using the walls and bulletin boards effectively? Consider displaying rules, assigned duties, a calendar, schedule, student work, and extra-credit activities.

- Do students have room to move around without disrupting each other? (American Federation of Teachers, Arranging your classroom, n.d., para. 1)

Once you have considered these things, you will work with the room, furniture, and resources available to you. Examples of classroom arrangements from the American Federation of Teachers show many variations on the general theme of providing areas for different kinds of work, room to move around freely, and a way for students to work together or separately. In your own classroom arrangements, consider what kinds of work the arrangements would facilitate and what kinds of work would be more challenging in these arrangements.

For students who have sensory sensitivities, consider how you can change environmental factors such as lighting, acoustics, need for personal space, and supportive responses to fascinations. Lighting can be adapted by requesting that fluorescent bulbs be shielded or used at a low setting. Many children prefer natural lighting from windows or localized soft lighting from lamps.

For students who are sensitive to sound, be sure that you are aware of their sensitivities and provide them with strategies to manage them. Some students wear earmuffs or earplugs at various times during the day—for example, during Drop Everything and Read time, or while working independently. What you will find is that your students all vary in the amount of noise they like while working. Some work better with soft music; others prefer absolute silence. Your job is to accommodate all of your students' needs so that everyone can do his or her best work and show his or her best behavior.

The amount of personal space students need also varies. Some students need reminders to avoid moving into others' personal space. Clear visual boundaries, such as tape on the floor around a desk or a square made of tape borders to sit in on the carpet can help remind students to give each other the room they need to learn best. Some students may ask that they have a desk placed off to the side of the room instead of in a group.

Some students have strong interests, and those interests can be seen in two ways: as a distraction from the academic work or as an entry point to academic work. For example, if a little girl seems almost obsessed with ponies and unicorns, one reaction might be to forbid her from talking about ponies and unicorns during school. But we do not support this; not being able to talk about what you like is not supportive or useful. Instead, the teacher should support talking about ponies and unicorns and incorporate that interest into academic areas. In this way, the student is supported and valued and will be able to show her best work. At the same time, any difficulty in classroom management has been circumvented, because there is no need for the student to feel frustrated or upset.

Teach Routines   Routines are good for everyone. Knowing what lies ahead helps everyone anticipate how the day will go and prepare for the day's lessons. You might want to post the **agenda** for the hour or the day in clear, plain language in the same place each day so that students know where to look. You could also review the agenda out loud with the class. The agenda review can be done in several ways that support students. Students who benefit from movement can be asked to come to the board and use a pointer to show each agenda item as the teacher discusses it. Students who benefit from a check of comprehension can be asked to restate the day's activities (that may include what the special is that day, what the activity is at lunch recess, and what after-school clubs are meeting) (see Table 12.1).

agenda Schedule of events or activities. Agendas can be individual or for the whole class.

Table 12.1.   Sample class agenda—Elementary and secondary

Elementary
Morning work
Reading
Special (Physical Education)
Snack
Math
Lunch/Recess
Social Studies
Writing
Clean up

Secondary (English)
Class meeting
Poem of the day (Giovanni's "Cotton Candy on a Rainy Day")
Literature Circles—*Romeo and Juliet*, Act 2

scaffolding   Providing support to help a student perform a skill he or she is not able to complete independently. Scaffolding can be done for an individual student, a small group, or the whole class. Different students have different scaffolding needs.

Stimulate Interest in Proactive Behavior   Every student comes to the classroom with his or her own history, feelings, and ideas about school. Students who struggle to meet behavioral expectations may believe that there is no point in trying to do well, because they will fail. For these students, you need to provide supports so that they experience success. Strategies to help students experience success include working with interests, contracts for trying new things (see Figure 12.4 for a contract template), and working in the way that best suits the student. When considering how the student works best, consider both the student's needs and the skills he or she must develop: if a student strongly prefers working alone but you believe it would be good for him to learn to compromise and work with another student, consider a contract that includes some time for working alone and some time for working with a partner. Then, give the student options for who he would like to work with, and limit that time so that the experience is successful. By **scaffolding** the experience, you can gradually build the student's skills while sustaining his or her positive feeling about school. Using the FBA processes from Chapter 6 informally will help you consider what scaffolds would be useful.

Input

exit ticket   Brief question, rating scale, or sentence starter given at the end of class for students to complete and hand to the teacher as they leave the class.

Input for management means considering how students understand what is expected. It also includes ensuring student understanding of vocabulary and symbols and helping students make connections between the directions and what they actually do. For example, saying "get ready for lunch" can mean many different things, depending on the class. In a secondary classroom, it might mean putting away individual materials in backpacks, returning books to the class bookshelf, and completing an **exit ticket**. In an elementary classroom, it might mean getting a coat or jacket, cleaning scraps off the floor, and clearing off desktops in preparation for the first activity after lunch. In both cases, it is important to be specific about what students are to do.

Teach behavioral expectations as you would academic expectations. Remember that how to act in the classroom may include skills that some students do not have. Acting appropriately in the classroom may require that students have strong self-regulation skills, are able to understand social cues from the teachers and other students, and are genuinely interested in performing well in that setting. If any of these components are missing, it is easy to understand why some students do not do what is asked. We need to understand the skills required to meet the expectations.

Visual strategies include posting general information (e.g., class rules, daily agenda, schedule of specials, lunch menu choices) and individual information (e.g., schedules for push-in or pull-out services, individual calendars on student desks). There are many ways to do this, and it is important to strike a balance between too much and too little information. Students can be overwhelmed by too much visual information, but too little may not feel welcoming or warm. When you plan your bulletin boards and displays, you might want to include a solid border in a contrasting color around the edges, so that students can easily see the content and know where it begins and ends. For example, if you have a word wall that extends the length of the room, use a border to create the long box that all the words will fit into along the wall. A second tip is to post a clear, descriptive heading that tells what information is being conveyed.

Some students have difficulty making sense of spoken directions. Being sure that students are giving their attention (which can look different for different students) before beginning directions is one strategy. Another is to stand near the student who needs support to understand oral directions. A third strategy is to consider using a microphone that is linked to classroom speaker, although this may be confusing for students who have difficulty making the connection between the voice and the person speaking.

The remainder of this section covers strategies for input in five areas: model the practices you want to see, teach character, teach self-monitoring, teach conflict resolution, and address bullying.

Model The Practices You Want to See   Modeling the behaviors that you want students to use sounds simple and is simple. If you want students to take turns and be respectful of each other, model listening carefully to students and speaking with respect. For example, if a student is speaking and another teacher comes to your room, give the student your attention until he is finished speaking before shifting your attention to the other adult. If you want students to deal with minor irritants graciously, model managing small annoyances graciously. For example, if students are putting homework in the take-home bin instead of the homework bin, manage that by talking about it during morning announcements or a class meeting; do not scream at the whole class. In other words, "Do not put out a match with a fire hose" (see Figure 12.2). For something small, have a small reaction. Save the big reaction for true emergencies.

Strong reaction   Small problem

Figure 12.2.   Do not put out a match with a fire hose.

Table 12.2. Six character-building behaviors students should learn

Caring—Kind, compassionate behavior, expressing gratitude, forgiving others, and helping people in need

Citizenship—Helping to make school and community better, staying informed, obeying rules and laws, respecting authority, and protecting the environment

Fairness—Playing by the rules, taking turns and sharing, being open-minded, listening to others, not taking advantage of others, and not blaming others

Respect—Being tolerant of differences; using good manners and appropriate language; not threatening, hitting, or hurting anyone; and dealing peacefully with anger, insults, and disagreements

Responsibility—Doing what one is supposed to do, persevering, doing one's best, maintaining self-control, thinking before acting, and being accountable for one's choices.

Trustworthiness—Being honest, doing what you say you'll do; doing the right thing, building a good reputation; being loyal to family, friends, and country; and not deceiving, cheating, or stealing.

Source: © 2011 Josephson Institute. The definitions of the Six Pillars of Character are reprinted with permission. www.charactercounts.org.

Teach Character   This may sound controversial. There is debate about the role of public schools related to character education. We think everyone would agree that it is important for students to be treated with respect and to treat others with respect. The National Education Association (NEA) web site has a section on classroom management, and within that section is information about six character traits students should learn (see Table 12.2).

These six character traits—caring, citizenship, fairness, respect, responsibility, and trustworthiness—are components of classroom management because they teach the fundamental principles of being a good citizen and student. Each trait is important for good citizenship and membership in the school community and in the community at large. We do not think anyone would disagree that helping students develop skills of caring, fairness, respect for others, and being trustworthy is an important part of teaching.

In her book about reading, Kylene Beers (2003) explained how one teacher used a bell to help students see how mean they were being to each other. She described what happened when the teacher came in with the bell for the first time:

> She placed it on her desk and said, "Every time one of you says something mean, you're acting like a real ding-a-ling. You do it so much and so often, you don't even hear it. In this class, we will treat each other with respect. Every time you make a statement or do something that makes you sound like a ding-a-ling, I'm going to ring this bell. The first day you go all class period with no ding-a-lings, you get to go to lunch 5 minutes early. The first time you go all week with no ding-a-lings, you all earn a hundred for a major test grade. When we've gone a month with no ding-a-lings, we'll have a pizza party with a movie." These eleventh graders just moaned. That day, she must have rung the bell more than 50 times. Kids were testing her— hard. She didn't flinch but just kept ringing the bell….Students were beginning to tell each other, "Oh man, don't say that; she's going to ring that bell." And she would….over time, the negative behavior slowly went away. One day, after about four days in a row of no bell ringing, the class talked about what was happening. One student remarked, "Ding-a-lings [now the class term for negative comments or gestures] become so common that you don't even hear them. Now, I hear them so much in my other classes that I'm amazed how awful they really are." (pp. 266–267)

Changing the culture of this classroom helped students see how entrenched their unkind comments were and created a safe space in which students could focus on the academic content of the class. This is important for all students and may be especially valuable for students who are marginalized in other settings because of a perceived difference or weakness.

Teach Self-Monitoring   Self-monitoring means being aware of your own behavior. Monitoring is often used to reduce a behavior that is disruptive in some way or to increase a behavior that is positive. Simply being more aware of the behavior by monitoring often reduces how often it happens. Examples of behavior that might need to be reduced are calling out answers, touching other people, and wandering around the room. Examples of positive behaviors are taking turns, giving positive feedback, and working cooperatively. Giving students control over the data collection process engages them in the monitoring and can be so effective that simply recording data reduces the amount of unproductive behavior. According to Peterson and Hittie (2010), the five steps of self-monitoring are ensuring that the students can accurately describe the behavior, developing a method for tallying the data, implementing self-monitoring, meeting with the adult, and providing reinforcement (pp. 380–382).

self-monitoring Being aware of your own behavior and knowing how to ask for what you need to do your best work.

Describing behavior can be difficult for students, which is why this first step is essential. Behaviors that a teacher may want to reduce for a group include students talking during quiet work time, being out of their seats too much, taking a long time to transition between activities, or leaving papers and trash on the floor. Behavior that an individual student might need to change includes calling out answers without being called on, daydreaming, leaving the classroom, or talking back to the teacher. The key is that students understand what behavior is under scrutiny. Discuss the behavior with students and ask for volunteers to demonstrate the behavior in question. Once you are confident that everyone understands what the behavior is, move to the next step.

Developing a method for tallying the data typically means making a simple record sheet for the student or students that is easy to use, clear, and reproducible. See the sample in Figure 12.3 for a student who is monitoring how often she raises her hand to be called on and how often she talks out. There is room for a simple tally mark next to each class, and room for notes. Tally sheets should be simple enough for the student to use easily. When you are teaching a whole class to self-monitor, privacy will probably not be an issue, but if you are working with an individual student, he or she may want some privacy about the process.

Implement the self-monitoring for a period of time. You may collect data along with students for the first day or two to confirm that you agree about the behavior. If the student does not accurately record data, you have several options. You can reteach the first step, because the issue may be that the student does not understand the behavior

Name: Sarah			
Date: Tuesday, May 24, 2011			
I am monitoring: How many times I am called on before talking and how many times I talk out.			
Class	I raised my hand before talking	I talked out	Notes
Math			
Physical Education			
English			
U.S. History			
Spanish			
Resource Lab			

Figure 12.3.   Tally sheet—Data collection for self-monitoring talking in class.

being tallied. You can talk through a specific instance where you recorded the behavior and the student did not (or the reverse), trying to understand why one person thought the behavior had happened and one did not. You can plan to collect data again for a shorter interval: instead of a full day, try a half-day or single period, or even a portion of a class period. This process may mean that the behavior in question actually declines to the point that you no longer feel the need to collect data.

If you decide to continue, choose a period of time for collection. The period of time should be relatively short—a school week or less—so that you and the student or students can review what is happening and check in about what patterns are emerging in the data.

Finally, meet again with the student and provide reinforcement. The reinforcement may be a secondary issue. This process is often satisfying and rewarding on its own, and the only reinforcement needed may be the opportunity to talk with an adult about what has changed. If you decide to provide reinforcement, consider using specific praise and reinforcement that the student selects. This may be the point when you and the student decide to arrange a formal contract based on a new behavior being established and an unproductive behavior being reduced (see Figure 12.4 for a contract template).

If you decide to develop a **behavior contract**, be sure it includes the behavior you want to see, what the student will do, and what the teacher will do. Also include the date and the way the contract will be reviewed. Keep the time span relatively brief—no more than a week—for the first contract. A behavior contract is successful only if you follow through.

Teach Conflict Resolution   An important skill for all students is managing conflict. Conflict is not something to fear; healthy conflict can lead to new learning. In Chapter 6,

behavior contract
Written agreement about what the two parties will do, including a clear description of the behavior and date for review. Contracts are typically between a teacher and student.

conflict resolution
Solving problems between people in a way that allows both parties to be heard and respected.

Contract Template

Date: _____

This contract is between _____ and _____ .
                                                         (student)   (teacher)

I, _____ , agree to
          (student)
_____

_____

_____

I, _____ , agree to
          (teacher)
_____

_____

_____

This contract will be reviewed on _____ .
                                                                  (date)

_____   _____
          (signature)   (signature)

Figure 12.4.   Student–teacher contract template.

you learned about the importance of teaching students how to manage conflicts, and reviewed six steps for resolving conflict:

- Approach students calmly, and stop them from hurting each other

- Acknowledge feelings

- Gather information (this includes taking turns listening and telling)

- Restate the problem

- Ask for ideas to solve the problem and choose a solution together

- Provide follow-up support (Church, 2007, p. 4)

There are strategies for conflict resolution related to these six steps. The first step, approaching calmly, may be more challenging than it sounds: When students are angry and may be trying to hurt each other, you need to keep yourself safe and stay calm because if you are incapacitated or upset yourself, you are not able to be a good manager of the classroom for all students. There are differing opinions about whether or not a teacher should risk being hurt by breaking up a fight.

One strategy we advocate in all instances is to remove the audience from students who are fighting. This maintains the safety of students who are not involved, reduces the effects of a group of students standing around, sometimes egging on a student, and minimizes the need for the students fighting to save face in front of their friends.

Strategies to help students acknowledge their feelings can be incorporated into class meetings or direct instruction. For elementary-age students, using pictures clearly labeled with different feelings can help students understand what they are feeling. This is an important skill; some students need help to understand the difference between feelings such as being hungry, tired, anxious, frustrated, jealous, or embarrassed. Teaching young students about feelings can be as simple as telling them what they might be feeling and acknowledging why they might have that feeling. When a young child is frustrated with work that seems too difficult, the teacher might say, "I think you might be feeling frustrated. It looks to me like the work you are doing seems hard, and your body seems tense and you seem like you are stressed. Let's take a break and talk about it." With adolescents, some students are able to identify and manage their emotions with little support and others need assistance to identify feelings and manage them. For students who need instruction in knowing how to sort out what they are feeling, a small group with age-appropriate examples can be a supportive place to learn about what they might be feeling and why. See Table 12.3 for resources to teach

Table 12.3.   Resources to teach students about feelings

Resource	Where to find it	Notes
A 5 Is Against the Law!	Author: Kari Dunn Baron Publisher: Autism Asperger Publishing Company, Overland Park, KS.	Designed for young adolescents with clear explanations and figures
Feeling face cards	Sandbox Learning http://www.sandbox-learning. com/Default.asp?Page=146	These cards can be personalized by changing the child's gender, hair color, hair style, eye color, glasses/no glasses, and skin tone
Feeling face cards	Confident Kids Support Groups http://www.confidentkids. com/other_resources. htm#Feelings%20Faces	Many resources to explain and express emotions through pictures of faces. Thirty emotions are included.
Feeling face cards	http://www.feelingfacescards. com/	These faces are colorful and exaggerated, and may be overwhelming for some students

Table 12.4. Bullying: Tips for students from Teaching Tolerance

If you are being bullied...	If you witness bullying...	If you are the bully...
• Reach out • Be cool in the moment • Change the school community	• Interrupt it • Get help	• Make a commitment to change • Focus on empathy and responsibility • Change your behavior

From Teaching Tolerance. http://www.tolerance.org; adapted by permission.

students about feelings and how to manage them. The feeling face cards are listed three separate times because there are so many options; check out each site for slightly different versions.

bullying   Victimizing another person or using a power imbalance to make someone else feel bad on purpose.

Address Bullying   How we treat each other is an essential part of engaging students in management. One strategy to support all students is to treat each other as complex, interesting people with strengths and weaknesses. Seeing each other as competent and valuable is an intangible and essential part of engaging all students in a supportive environment. Treating each other respectfully also includes creating a climate that does not tolerate bullying. Bullying is a real issue in schools; the American Academy of Child and Adolescent Psychiatry reports that "as many as half of all children are bullied at some time during their school years, and at least ten percent are bullied on a regular basis" (2008, para. 1). The Teaching Tolerance web site has tips for students being bullied, those who witness bullying, and those who are bullies (see Table 12.4).

These tips remind us that our role includes supporting every student, including the bully. There are extensive resources available about bullying at the Teaching Tolerance web site, including data about incidence and how to teach different age groups about reducing bullying.

OUTPUT AND ASSESSMENT

The output and assessment sections are combined in the chapter, because classroom-management output is intertwined with the assessment of that information. The output of classroom management is most easily measured in the data you collect about your classroom. This may include the number of times you send a student to the office or detention, the observational data you have asked other teachers or teaching assistants to collect for you, and the data you have collected from students about their ability to learn in your class. Output about management is also the results you see in academic performance; if students are in a class that is well organized, supportive, and has clear routines, they will be able to learn and you will be able to teach and concentrate your energies on differentiated, interesting teaching. The output is, partly, your students' test scores. Other output of classroom management is less tangible.

The output of classroom management can be described by reviewing what students do, how they feel about school and the class, and how they behave in the classroom and in other settings, such as lunch, music, physical education, and assemblies.

Observe Interactions

To gauge how students are feeling and acting in the classroom, observe. When observing in your own classroom, arrange to have another teacher come to your classroom for a period, and simply sit out of the way and watch: Who is getting along? Who is completing their work?

Collect Data

Collecting information, or data, is the key to management. There are several strategies for collecting data about the class. Remember from Chapter 6 that there are all kinds of charts and methods to record behaviors of individual students, groups of students, or adults. What data you collect depends on what is happening in your classroom. As a teacher, you will quickly learn to gauge student engagement and interest by how the room feels and to adjust your instruction accordingly. Remember the teacher who set up the ding-a-ling bell—she did not spend time charting the number of mean comments students made before deciding to bring in the bell; she just did it. This is great! She noticed an issue in her classroom and addressed it—she was responsive to her classroom and changed the climate for the better.

However, there may be times when you are not sure what is happening, or want more information before deciding whether or not to act. This is where collecting data comes in, just as it does with conducting a functional behavioral assessment. Collecting data does not have to be done through a formal process or include the building-support team. The data you will collect when determining what is going on in the classroom will probably include observational data, where you observe the class for a period of time. For example, you may be concerned about how well students transition from working in groups to returning to their seats. You could make a simple chart to record when this kind of transition happens and then watch the time and report that information to students. Then, you can set a goal with the class to reduce that baseline time.

Other observational data you might want includes seeing what happens when your students are in other settings. Observing students in art, music, physical education, or library time gives you the chance to see how students act with other teachers and with each other when they are not with you. You get to see other adults responding to your students and can sometimes step back and see how others solve problems in ways that have not occurred to you. If you are in a coteaching class, taking turns with direct instruction gives each teacher the opportunity to see another teacher work with students, and this can be very useful.

Another form of data that you may decide would be helpful is self-assessments. You may be curious about what students like to do in their free play time, or what strengths students bring to the class. You might want to poll students about the kind of tests they prefer, or ask how they prefer to work when in an independent work session. Gathering data about student preferences can guide your instruction and help you group students based on their learning style or preferred multiple intelligence.

Finally, data that are routinely collected can be reviewed. Attendance, visits to the nurse, behavior referrals, and positive behavior commendations are all regularly available. Many teachers also have very visible reminders about how students are doing on particular class goals. Some teachers keep track of how many compliments they hear students giving each other throughout the day, or tally how often groups complete work with a single reminder to get started. Permanent products are also data that can give insight into why a student may struggle at certain times of day.

Communicate the Data

Once you have all this information, it is important that you communicate appropriately to students. Some teachers make the mistake of keeping their rationale for what they do a secret from students, assuming that it is not the students' right to know why teachers make the decisions they do. We agree that students should not be part of all decisions, and some things are best left to the discretion of the teacher—after all, that is why the teacher is responsible for the class. However, we believe that a management strategy that is often overlooked is simply telling students what you are doing and why. For example, if you have been frustrated with the way the room is messy at the end of the day and have instituted a 5-minute clean-up time at the end of the period, telling students why you are frustrated and what you want to do about it will be much more productive if you are clear about the issue and why it matters. In *Black Ants and Buddhists* (2006), Mary Cowhey did not spend much time teaching her first-grade students how to move quietly in the halls. It became an issue, because her class was noisy when moving through the school. Once she was aware of the issue, Cowhey wrote:

> I could understand that a classroom closer to the center of the school might feel annoyed or distracted if they had to put up with noisy hallway traffic interrupting their lessons. I discussed this criticism with my class. They agreed it was true and hadn't considered that it might be annoying and distracting to students and adults who were trying to concentrate on their work. (p. 215)

Cowhey brought the issue to the class as a shared responsibility to address; as a class, they agreed that walking with silent dignity—as they had learned from their lessons related to the civil rights march in Selma, Alabama—was a good solution. It worked, and there were no more issues with being noisy in the hallways. If Cowhey had not explained the issue and why it might be a problem to her young students, she might have lectured them about their bad behavior, warned them to act better, or even shamed them that they were being babyish. None of those responses models respect and caring in the classroom community; communicating the information while asking students to be partners in solving the issue is a more respectful strategy.

A potential outcome of sharing data with your students is that you may find that something you thought was a significant issue may be less serious than you believed before gathering data. Knowing that you need to be able to explain what you are asking students to do prevents creating rules for the sake of creating rules. When the things you do make sense, it is much more likely that students will respond positively to your directions.

SUMMARY

In this chapter, we reviewed the background of management from Chapter 6 and made two important points. First, teachers have a powerful effect on students, and how we think about students and what motivates their action has a similarly powerful effect on how we react when students do not do what we expected or what we wanted. Second, how students behave in school is a subject that needs direct instruction, just as academic content areas need direct instruction. Students who do not act the way we hope they will need support and teaching, not punitive measures that do not help them develop skills they need to act in ways that are expected in school. Strategies for management were presented in the areas of engagement, input, output, and assessment. In engagement, we reviewed how to establish community, teach routines, and stimulate interest in proactive behavior. You then learned about input strategies, including how to model the practices you want to see, teach character, teach self-monitoring, teach conflict resolution, and address bullying. The chapter concluded with output and assessment—reviewing strategies to observe, collect data, and communicate the data to students.

NARRATIVE 12.1. | MAGGIE DRISCOLL

Maggie is a first-year teacher working in the Washington, D.C., schools.

A teacher is someone who provides instruction to children. But what is it that we instruct, actually? Given my professional and personal experience, I think the question should be as teachers, "What don't we instruct?" With credits accrued, courses completed, degree earned, and certificates granted —all of these things did not prepare me for the experience of my first classroom. One can only fully understand this concept when faced with a first year of teaching.

Postgraduation, in the midst of a failing economy and lean job market, many of my peers went immediately to grad school. Although grim, I chose to face the job market. After count-less applications and interviews, I finally found myself accepting a job in our nation's capital, Washington, D.C.

I was assigned to a Special Education LD (Learning Disabled) self-contained classroom. I began my year with seven students—all boys ranging from grades 1 to 3—and one teaching assistant. I had a limited number of books, no air conditioning, and absolutely no supplies, such as paper, crayons, and markers. More important, I found out that I was walking into a classroom of stu-dents who had had no teacher for the past 2 months. These boys had already had two teachers the previous year, then another at the beginning of the current school year. Students were not supposed to be forgotten like this. So there I was, the fourth teacher these boys have had in the past 2 years. I had to try and teach them something, anything, in the remaining 4 months of school. This was not what I pictured when dreaming about my first teaching job.

I quickly found out that almost all of my students were at a kindergarten or below reading level. They struggled equally with math. Although they were behind academically, they were significantly behind socially, which concerned me. Basic social skills are necessary and play an integral role in learning.

I decided right away to focus on my students' social skills. I wanted them to learn about one another, and to socialize appropriately. In college, Dr. Rapp taught us the concept of "Classroom Meetings." I decided to attempt to do these with my students. These boys had been disap-pointed and let down by adults for most of their lives. I wanted them to know that there are people who care about them; that they were too significant for anyone to forget. They would only understand that by building meaningful relationships with both peers and adults.

By the end of the year, my students were openly complimenting one another. They were making eye contact with each other, asking each other questions, sharing supplies, and playing together at recess. They even sometimes complimented one another and resolved conflicts without my help.

I'll admit that most of my students still could not read by the end of the school year. They did not know how to add or subtract numbers higher than ten. Yet, more important, I can say that I did teach them something: how to communicate with one another. For me, that was a small victory.

CHAPTER 13

Reading Strategies for All Students

How this chapter prepares you to be an effective inclusive classroom teacher:

- This chapter provides evidence-based strategies in each of the five components of reading: phonics, phonemic and phonological awareness, comprehension, vocabulary, and fluency. This chapter explains the importance of understanding each student's reading level so that appropriate materials can be provided and you can develop differentiated instruction for each student's needs. In differentiated instruction, all students have the opportunity to demonstrate their strengths and abilities and develop their reading skills. **This helps you meet CEC Standard 4: Instructional Strategies.**

- This chapter teaches you about formal and informal reading assessments and introduces running reading records and informal reading inventories (IRIs). This information teaches you how to use multiple types of assessment for reading. **This helps you meet CEC Standard 8: Assessment.**

- This chapter draws significant attention to the many aspects of diversity—especially supporting students who are learning English and providing culturally relevant materials and instruction. This chapter emphasizes the importance of access to reading and the ways that teachers can foster a positive attitude about reading and success in reading for all students. **This helps you meet CEC Standard 9: Professional and Ethical Practice.**

After reading and discussing this chapter, you will be able to

• Understand the skills students need to have to read

• Explain the connection between the least dangerous assumption and access to reading instruction

• Explain why considering the language load of instruction is important for students learning English

• Explain why culturally relevant pedagogy is essential in reading instruction

• Define digital literacy and give examples

• Report what the Common Core State Standards are designed to do

• Explain the connection between RTI and reading instruction

• Explain the National Council of Teachers of English (NCTE) research-based teaching practices for reading

• Understand strategies for each component of reading and explain how to use them

• Explain formal and informal reading-assessment strategies

R eading is given extensive attention in school. Our society is based on literacy, and schools have not done a good job of ensuring that all students can read. In 1998, the National Assessment of Educational Progress report showed that 23% of twelfth-grade students and 26% of eighth-grade students did not have basic reading skills, and the average African American twelfth grader read about as well as the average White eighth grader (Robinson, McKenna, & Wedman, 2004, p. 157). In 2007, the U.S. Department of Education, National Center for Education Statistics, found that only 23% of eighth graders scored at a proficient level in reading.

The debate about the reasons for this poor performance is heated, and educators are working to support all students' reading; poor performance is not due to lack of attention to the subject. Many elementary schools have long blocks of time dedicated to English Language Arts and scheduled times for Drop Everything And Read (DEAR), or Sustained Silent Reading (SSR). During DEAR or SSR, everyone in the building—from students to teachers to custodians and lunch personnel—is expected to stop what they are doing to read for a period of time. In middle and high school, reading is integrated into almost every class, and being able to read at grade level is a prerequisite for many subjects. For example, math-story problems, directions in science lab, and readings in U.S. history all include literacy skills.

least dangerous assumption   The assumption that will do the least damage, or restrict the fewest opportunities, for students who cannot tell us what they are learning.

In this chapter, reading instruction and reading strategies are introduced in four sections. First, you'll learn about reading instruction and access to reading instruction. We discuss the **least dangerous assumption** and explore how some students—including students with disabilities and students of color—have not had access to good reading instruction. Students who speak a second language at home are another group who provides opportunities for teachers to consider how to best support their reading proficiency. Next, you'll examine the rise of digital media, the Common Core State Standards, and response to intervention. Third, you will learn strategies for engaging all students in reading by using the same four sections found in every strategy chapter: engagement, input, output, and assessment.

> • Tovani, C. (2000). *I Read It, but I Don't Get It: Comprehension Strategies for Adolescent Readers.* Portland, ME: Stenhouse Publishers.
> • Atwell, N. (2007). *The Reading Zone.* New York: Scholastic.
> • Galda, L., & Graves, M. (2007). *Reading and Responding in the Middle Grades: Approaches for All Classrooms.* Boston: Allyn & Bacon.
> • Beers, K. (2003). *When Kids Can't Read: What Teachers Can Do. A Guide for Teachers 6-12.* Portsmouth, NH: Heinemann.
> • McGregor, T. (2007). *Comprehension Connections: Bridges to Strategic Reading.* Portsmouth, NH: Heinemann.

Figure 13.1.   Resources for reading instruction.

READING INSTRUCTION AND ACCESS TO INSTRUCTION

The goal of reading is to make meaning from print (Haager & Klingner, 2005). How this happens is the topic of a great deal of debate. In 1998, the National Reading Panel defined reading as a process that includes five components: **phonics**, **phonemic and phonological awareness**, **comprehension**, **vocabulary**, and **fluency**. Within each of these components are specific skills that students need to make meaning from text. There are many resources for teaching the skills of reading, and it is easy to be overwhelmed by the amount of information available to you. A resource list for reading instruction is provided in Figure 13.1 as a starting point.

In addition to the five components the National Reading Panel identified, a new component has emerged: **digital literacy**. Bruce notes that "one consequence of the growing access to the Internet is that students are increasingly using e-mail, instant messaging, web resource sites, essay sites, online reference tools, online tutoring, and ask-an-expert sites as an integral part of their school work" (2007, p. 4). This shift to digital resources means that

> Teachers have a key responsibility to scaffold multimodal literacies and model new technical proficiencies. They can lead students to engage in sophisticated, mature forms of communication that are unattainable for many students without intervention and expert guidance. In discussions about the multimodal literacy practices of youth, what is being missed is that many adolescents, particularly those who are not of the dominant, middle class culture, are still novices. (Mills, 2010, p. 41)

Teachers need to consider the five components of reading and digital literacy. One way to think about reading instruction is to consider the skills students need to read. To read, a student must have three skills: an understanding of how the alphabet works, understanding that reading is about meaning, and fluency in reading (Daniel, Clarke, & Ouellette, 2004, p. 45). In Table 13.1, you can see how the components of reading

phonics   Associating letters and letter combinations with sounds.

phonemic and phonological awareness   Understanding that words can be divided into parts by their sound and meaning.

comprehension   Understanding what was read.

vocabulary   Words.

fluency   Ease or smoothness; in reading, "a combination of word reading accuracy and automaticity, reading rate, and prosody" (Lane, Pullen, Hudson, & Konold, 2009, p. 280).

digital literacy   The ability to gather and use information from a range of sources, including print and electronic media.

Table 13.1.   Components and skills needed to read

Components of reading	Skills needed to read
Phonics	Understanding how the alphabet works
Phonemic and phonological awareness	
Comprehension	Understanding that reading is about meaning
Vocabulary	
Fluency	Fluency in reading

Sources: National Reading Panel (1998) and Daniel, Clarke, & Ouellette (2004).

align with the skills readers need. Helping students develop these skills is the task of elementary-school teachers, especially in kindergarten through third grade. Students who struggle with reading are often struggling because of a problem related to one of these skills: They are not able to decode the letters and understand the words; or they are able to sound out the letters but do not know what the words they are reading mean; or they are able to sound out the letters, and know what individual words mean, but read with difficulty and as a result lose track of the meaning.

whole-language approach A way of thinking about reading instruction that considers both phonics instruction and meaning.

One theory about learning to read is that reading starts with the text, and the brain's information-processing system makes sense of the words (Haager & Klingner, 2005, pp. 199–200). Reading instruction from this theory emphasizes building skills, such as phonics and fluency, and was common in the 1960s, 1970s, and 1980s (Haager & Klingner, 2005). A second theory is that reading starts with the reader and his or her search for meaning. Reading instruction that emerged from this way of thinking was a **whole-language approach** designed to teach students how to use clues in the reading to help understand the meaning. New theories about how reading takes place have focused on the connection between the reader and text, and most assume that there is an interaction between the reader and the text (Haager & Klingner, 2005). A whole-language approach is what you probably experienced in school and is the approach still used in schools today.

The current climate of reading instruction in schools emphasizes learning the five skills plus digital literacy needed for reading by using a wide range of strategies, programs, and supports. There is an overwhelming amount of information about how to best support readers in each grade, and teachers must remain well informed about trends in literacy education. The International Reading Association (IRA), with a web site at http://www.reading.org/General/Default.aspx, is a great resource and starting point for learning about literacy. A second resource is the National Reading Panel, which has a web site at http://www.nationalreadingpanel.org/. Many different reading programs are available for teachers, and many books about reading for all grade levels and all types of readers are available. As part of your teacher training, you will probably take more than one class in how to teach reading.

The National Reading Panel made recommendations for reading instruction in 2000. However, the panel was criticized for not including skills needed in a technological age. Collaboration, critical thinking, and presentation skills are all now needed as well. These are the skills included in digital literacy.

In 2000, the International Reading Association (IRA) Commission on Adolescent Literacy developed seven principles to support adolescent reading. See Table 13.2 to

Table 13.2.   Principles to support adolescent reading

RESOLVED, that, because of the expanding literacy demands placed upon adolescents, the International Reading Association believes they deserve

- Access to a wide variety of reading material that they can and want to read;
- Instruction that builds both the skill and the desire to read increasingly complex materials;
- Assessment that shows them their strengths as well as their needs, and that guides their teachers to design instruction that will best help them grow as readers;
- Qualified teachers who model and provide explicit instruction in reading comprehension, critical reading, and studying strategies across the curriculum;
- Reading specialists who assist individual students having difficulty learning how to read;
- Qualified teachers who understand the complexities of individual adolescent readers, respect their differences, and respond to their unique characteristics; and
- Homes, communities, and a nation that will not only support their efforts to achieve advanced levels of literacy, but also provide the resources necessary for them to succeed.

From the International Reading Association. (1999). On Adolescent Literacy (Resolution). Newark, DE: Author. Reprinted with permission of the International Reading Association.

review them. The principles they recommend are valid not only for adolescents but for all readers. Briefly, the principles include access to engaging material, instruction to build skills and desire, assessment that guides expert teaching, access to reading specialists, and a community that supports student efforts in reading.

Notice that some of the principles are things that teachers can work toward in their buildings using resources at hand: providing a range of reading materials, instruction that supports student skills and desire to read, expert instruction that models and teaches comprehension, and teachers who understand the complexity of students. Other factors—such as access to reading specialists and homes, communities and a nation that supports student efforts—are more complex and long term. You can work in your communities to develop these factors in small and large ways through book drives, collaborations with public libraries, and reading events. In each case, your responsibility is to help students and your community value reading and literacy.

What a student is expected to do at each grade level through high school graduation related to reading changes from state to state. For example, in New York State there are four broad standards for English Language Arts, and the state identifies what students in different grades should be able to do for each standard. Students must be able to use language for social interaction, for critical analysis and evaluation, for literary response and expression, and for information and understanding (New York State Academy for Teaching and Learning, n.d.). In California, three broad topics are used to organize the guidelines for what children should be able to do at each grade related to reading. The topics are Word Analysis, Fluency, and Systematic Vocabulary Development; Reading Comprehension; and Literary Response and Analysis (California Department of Education, 1998). What is similar about the guidelines and standards? They all deal with being able to use language to communicate and to comprehend and evaluate text in a range of ways.

LEAST DANGEROUS ASSUMPTION

Remember from Chapter 1 that the least dangerous assumption is one that will do the least damage, or restrict the fewest opportunities, for a student who cannot communicate what he is learning. In the past, students with communication and speech disabilities were often relegated to segregated classrooms and offered limited access to reading instruction. This was the case because students with disabilities were considered unable to read and teachers believed that it was a waste of time to try to teach them reading. The danger, of course, is denying opportunity to students.

In his book *Schooling Children with Down Syndrome* (1998), Chris Kliewer wrote about a student named Ruth who was considered to be completely illiterate and severely retarded. Ruth was not deemed capable of reading, and therefore could not read. But when she changed schools, her new teacher was clear that Ruth would be treated as capable. First, she was connected to her school community, which allowed her opportunities to engage in literacy and express literacy in ways that her first teachers had thought was impossible. After 3 years, she learned to read and write. Ruth had not changed; her context had changed. Your job as a teacher is to make the assumption that will do the least damage if you are wrong. Ruth's first teachers made a dangerous and limiting decision by denying her access to reading instruction; do not make the same mistake.

Engaging All Students

Engaging all students includes finding material that all students can get excited about reading. Some students are interested in reading and need little support from teachers to dive in. Other students, though, will need carefully planned activities and materials to find reading exciting and enjoyable. In *Just Give Him the Whale!* (2008), Kluth and Schwarz explained the importance of working with student interests instead of against them. In writing about students with autism, they comment that many students who have an autism spectrum disorder have very strong interests—like whales! Or trains, fans, baseball statistics, airplanes, bugs, and dinosaurs. A responsive approach is to use a strong interest to support reading, instead of prohibiting the student from reading and writing or talking about his or her interest.

language load How challenging a test is based on the amount of new or specific vocabulary that is needed to read fluently.

Students who speak a language other than English are a diverse group, but overall they do not do well in school. Hadaway (2011) recommended that teachers think about the **language load** of instruction for students who are not fluent in English. That is, think about the amount of specialized vocabulary that is used in the classroom and in lessons (pp. 38–39). Reducing the language load of new vocabulary for students with limited vocabularies is one strategy to support students learning English. A second strategy is to limit reading to a single area. This may not sound quite right; often, we hear teachers talk about the need for students to read across genres and read widely to experience a range of styles, be introduced to new vocabulary in context, and practice other strategies, such as comparing and contrasting and making connections. But for students who are learning English, focusing on one topic or theme may support students' familiarity and comfort with reading (Hadaway, 2011).

There is an enormous body of literature related to culturally responsive teaching and engaging all students. Being culturally responsive means that you consider who your students are, what experiences they have had, and what cultural norms they embrace, and you value those experiences. Choose textbooks and books that represent a range of experiences and authors. In elementary and high school, introduce readings by men and women; Whites, Blacks, and Latinas; and straight and gay authors. Choose your literature explicitly around considerations of both reflecting student experiences and exposing them to new ideas. A good resource is the Teaching Tolerance web site (http://www.tolerance.org/), which tells us that

> Good teaching requires that teachers build on their students' prior knowledge. Moreover, students learn best when they feel recognized and acknowledged for the aspects of their identity they deem important. When students feel that their identities are ignored, they often disengage from learning and adopt a stance of outsider among strangers. (n.d.)

Acknowledging student identity can mean one of two things: the author and experiences are directly similar to the reader or the teacher presents readings that are not entirely the same at first glance and explains how the content is related.

Culturally relevant reading instruction may sound overwhelming. It sounds professional and as if there is only one right way to provide it. But the reality of teaching is that we must always be learning new things and must always remember that there is no shame in asking questions. We must also remember that we don't know what we don't know, so it is imperative that we learn to ask questions about what is missing. Cultural diversity is a topic that is often sidestepped, but it cannot be if we are going to support all students becoming good readers in our classrooms. Geneva Gay (2002) said that we must work to be culturally responsive teachers if we are going to improve the success of ethnically diverse students. And as we saw at the beginning of the chapter, on average, students who are African American read at a much lower level than White students. This is unacceptable, and addressing culturally responsive reading is one way to remedy this issue.

DIGITAL MEDIA, COMMON CORE STATE STANDARDS, AND RESPONSE TO INTERVENTION (RTI)

In this section, we review three significant trends in literacy education: the rise of digital media, the formation of the Common Core State Standards (CCSS), and the development of response to intervention (RTI).

Digital Media: M.02, 2G2BT (My Two Cents, Too Good to Be True)

A renowned literacy professor claims that literacy is the ability to solve problems in the context of the modern age (C. Ikpeze, personal communication, 2011). Our modern age includes digital media that are increasingly popular and available. Text, pictures, video, music, and links to related content are available online in ways that are impossible with a printed book. There is debate in the field of reading instruction about how to effectively harness the interest students have in digital media to help them become strong readers. Gee and Levine believed that "digital media offer a largely untapped but essential resource for students to develop basic reading skills" (2009, p. 49).

A tension between printed media and online media is the way that readers engage with the content. Wolf and Barzillai (2009) explained the difference, saying that with a printed book,

> Little is given to the reader outside the text. For that reason, readers must engage in an active construction of meaning, in which they grapple with the text and apply their earlier knowledge as they question, analyze, and probe. In the process, they learn and build knowledge and go beyond the wisdom of the author to think their own thoughts. (p. 34)

So reading print media requires the reader to do a great deal of work on her own. The contrast to this kind of reading is what happens when reading digital text. Wolf and Barzillai (2009) gave an example: When reading a Shakespeare play, going online

> can drive a discovery process that links the reader not only to the text of the play and various comprehension supports, but also to relevant historical information, videos of the play, discussion groups, articles from noted literary critics, and artistic interpretations that may drive deeper reflection. (p. 35)

The two types of media require different skills; with print media, the reader is alone with the text and has only his or her own thinking processes to create meaning. With digital text, the reader has extensive resources to sift, weigh, and assess. In the first case, a reader may need supports for comprehension and to make connections, and in the second case a reader may need supports to effectively judge and use the many available resources. What is clear is that literacy is more than reading static print, and the sixth component of reading is facility with digital media.

Common Core State Standards

A new conversation in education is whether or not we can compare state standards. The answer right now is that we cannot; each state has developed its own standards and guidelines, and the result is an unclear picture of what children are required to do. The result has been the development of the CCSS. The CCSS were created using evidence from a variety of states and are designed to be the academic goals for K-12 schools to meet by the time a student graduates from high school (Hill, 2011). The CCSS for Math and English Language Arts have been adopted by more than 40 states, territories, and the District of Columbia; this means that each will strive for a consistent end result (In the States, 2010). This shift to CCSS will help educators across the country have conversations about reading skills that were difficult in the past because of the lack of shared expectations.

So what do the CCSS for reading require? The expectation is that students who meet these standards are ready for a career or college. Related to reading, students need to be able to comprehend complex texts—and this is a challenge, because in 2005, only 51% of students taking the ACT test were ready for college level reading (Hill, 2011).

Response to Intervention (RTI)

Remember from Chapter 9 that RTI is the integration of assessment and intervention in instruction so that all students can maximize their potential. RTI often includes three levels of support, and if students are not reading successfully with classroom instruction, they are offered more support and are monitored carefully. If the more intensive teaching does not result in reading improvement, the teaching is changed. The cycle of assessment and instruction puts responsibility for students' reading success on the teacher.

RTI is a strategy many states are adopting to support reading instruction. The goal of RTI is to help struggling readers before they fail and to provide research-based, data-driven instruction, so that when a particular reading strategy is working, it can be continued, and when it is not working, it can be changed. This is a positive development in reading instruction for two reasons: first, students who have not been doing well in reading are supported quickly; second, the emphasis on reading instruction is on how to help the student become a better reader. RTI models require teachers to keep data and review it frequently, and if a student is not doing well, the teacher is expected to determine if the reading program needs adjustment or if other strategies need to be tried. When a new strategy is tried, data are collected about that strategy, too. This is vital, because a reader who does not feel good about reading may quickly become frustrated and stop trying to improve. If teachers are quick to see that a student struggles and can determine why she is struggling and how to help her do better, the student can gain the skills to become a better reader. This sounds simple, but the reality is that we are not getting better at reading instruction for all students. The Nation's Report Card: Reading 2007 found that "significant score gaps persisted between White and minority eighth-graders" (Lee, Grigg, & Donahue, 2007, p. 29).

The second reason that the use of RTI in reading instruction is a positive development is that the emphasis on struggling readers shifts from a focus on whether or not the student has a learning disability or other disability to how to help the student be a better reader. Any program is positive if it helps turn teacher time and attention to the business of refining and improving instruction instead of choosing a label. Years of data in education have proved that labeling a student with a learning disability and sending them to special education almost guarantees failure in reading. This may sound harsh, but it is true.

Noted reading expert Richard Allington (2006) wrote about the three-tier model (see Figure 13.3) and cautions that the tiers will be effective only if the instruction is based on research. His concern with the way some schools are using a tier model is that schools are buying three different reading programs—one for each tier. He notes that a student receiving service in all three tiers "would encounter three different commercial reading programs every day! That seems like a good plan if you wanted to confuse a struggling reader" (p. 20). Instead, he recommends using research to design instruction that is tailored to the individual student (see Table 13.3).

Table 13.3. Allington's three-tier model

Tier 1—High-quality, comprehensive classroom reading instruction

Tier 2—Small-group (five students or fewer) supplemental instructional support

Tier 3—Intensive, very small groups (two or three students) or one-to-one tutorial instruction (extended day school model)

From Allington, R.L. (2006). Research and the three tier model. *Reading Today, 23*(5), 20. Copyright © 2006 by the International Reading Association (www.reading.org); reprinted by permission.

Allington noted that RTI initiatives have allowed school districts to use up to 15% of their budget for special education to support RTI processes (2011). He went on to say that this is good news, but

> This legislation makes it clear that RTI is a general education initiative; this funding is turned over to a general education team to fund the general education effort to teach everyone to read—in other words, to fund the three tiers of the RTI intervention. (Allington, 2011, p. 41)

RTI helps general education teachers see all students—without and with labels—as readers. The strategies that teachers learn to support readers are sometimes presented as "strategies for students with Asperger syndrome" or "strategies for students with learning disabilities." We strongly disagree with this stance: Every student is unique, and knowing one student with a learning disability means that you know *one* student with a learning disability. However, it is more than likely that once you skip over that social construction of disability you may find great strategies that work for many students. Try to find those strategies and relate them to the four areas of UDL: engagement, input, output, and assessment.

STRATEGIES FOR ENGAGEMENT, INPUT, OUTPUT, AND ASSESSMENT

In this section, we are going to review strategies to help readers. Kylene Beers believed that the difference between independent and struggling readers is the number of strategies readers have and know how to use when faced with difficult reading. Struggling readers have problems in three areas: poor reading skills, a negative attitude about reading, and not knowing what they like to read (2003, p. 17). Your task is to teach students the strategies they need so that they can become fluent readers. Remember that the strategy you choose must fit the student; do not try to force a student into a using strategy that does not work for him or her. The trick is to develop a mental filing cabinet of many strategies, so that for each student you teach you have a range of strategies to choose from and can find the right strategy for that student at that point in their development.

Reading instruction has ranged from directive and repetitive drilling to more student-centered, guided inquiries. There has also been a shift away from literature-based instruction in which the whole class reads the same novel at the same time to an emphasis on strategy instruction (Senechal, 2011). There are strong advocates for each method for teaching reading, and many teachers believe that the important thing in choosing a model of reading instruction is to match the model to the child, not the child to the model. Many districts buy reading programs and require all teachers to use them. This can be useful as students move from grade to grade because teachers have common language to describe students' strengths and weaknesses in reading. The caution is that using a reading program without being thoughtful about each student may result in some students' not responding well to that model and falling behind.

In Figure 13.2, you will see that strategies for reading are organized into the engagement, input, output, and assessment areas. In each category, strategies specifically for

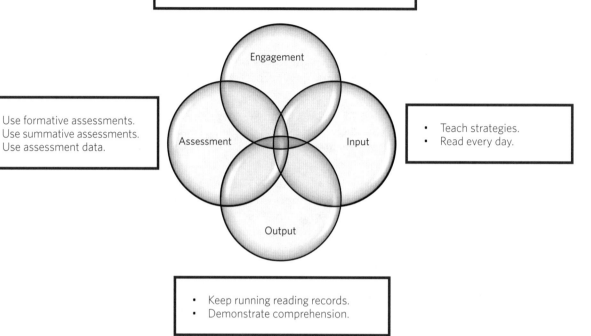

- See all students' literacy skills.
- Provide access to independent reading level.
- Provide access to culturally relevant material.
- Support a positive attitude about reading.

- Use formative assessments.
- Use summative assessments.
- Use assessment data.

- Teach strategies.
- Read every day.

- Keep running reading records.
- Demonstrate comprehension.

Figure 13.2. Strategies for engagement, input, output, and assessment in reading.

reading are introduced. These examples are just the tip of the iceberg; there are many, many strategies in each area.

Engagement

This section is divided into four subheadings: seeing all students' literacy skills, access to students' independent reading level, access to culturally relevant material, and support a positive attitude about reading. There are so many subheadings here because it is very easy for students to disengage. Finding reading material that is engaging means knowing what each student is interested in and is able to read easily. Tanny McGregor believed that engaging students in reading is best started by meeting students where they are and using teacher modeling and guided practice (2007, p. 4). She believed that when you plan to teach a new strategy, it is important to follow a consistent pattern of providing a concrete experience and a sensory experience, using wordless books, and giving time for text.

See All Students' Literacy Skills   All students have the capacity to learn. Seeing how students are literate is sometimes a challenge, as some students have been labeled with a disability and are considered incapable of learning. Using the least dangerous assumption means that you will be assuming that all children are learning literacy skills when they are routinely taught reading, even if they are not able to show what they know. An important factor in teaching reading is to think about reading and reading skills as a web, instead of a ladder (see Figure 13.3). Traditionally, educators believed that the

Literacy Ladder or Literacy Web

Figure 13.3. Models of literacy.

second rung of reading skills could not be reached until the first rung was mastered. This is limiting: If there are skills on the first rung that are not possible for a student, other skills will never be introduced because the teacher believes that those skills are impossible for that student. Examples of skills on the first rung are things like "says letters and sounds out loud" or "tracks text with eyes and traces letters from left to right when someone reads aloud." But these skills may not be possible.

If, instead, we consider literacy as a web of interconnected skills, when a student is not able to say letters and sounds or track print with his eyes or fingers, we can continue to expose him to opportunities to develop those skills and at the same time shift to another set of skills on the reading web and introduce other tasks, such as "summarizes stories through acting out" or "makes connections between the story and other books."

Access to Independent Reading Level   Students must have access to reading materials at their independent reading level, or they will not engage and remain engaged with the material. Fluent readers given material that is beyond their abilities quickly become struggling readers, and struggling readers often give up reading altogether because struggling with material that is too difficult is frustrating, makes students feel stupid, and makes the effort seem pointless. Richard Allington noted that

> The current situation in many schools is that struggling readers participate in 30–60 minutes of appropriate supplemental reading instruction and then spend the remaining five hours a day sitting in classrooms with texts they cannot read, and that cannot contribute to learning to read. (2007, p. 7)

Allington explained that to support struggling readers, focusing on evidence-based principles is essential. He recommends collecting data on the number of struggling readers in the building who have "books in their hands that they can read, books that allow struggling readers to learn science and social studies content and that also foster reading growth" (2007, p. 9). If students are not provided with materials they can read independently, we cannot expect them to become fluent readers able to comprehend the information we want them to access.

Access to Culturally Relevant Material   Engaging students includes providing reading materials that hooks them—that are interesting and worth spending time on because in some way the text speaks to the student. One group of strategies to engage readers is to provide material that allows the reader to see him- or herself in the story—to make text-to-self connections. This means reading widely yourself and providing books from varied authors on a range of topics.

Table 13.4. Checklist for books

Book	No Mirrors in My Nana's House	Number the Stars	Holes	The Dark Is Rising
Author	Ysaye M. Barnwell	Lois Lowry	Louis Sachar	Susan Cooper
Main Character	Little girl	Annemarie Johannesen	Stanley Yelnats	Will Stanton
Setting	Grandmother's house	Denmark and Sweden	Camp Green Lake, a juvenile detention facility in a dry desert lake bed	England—Will's home and countryside
Plot	Little girl dances through her grandmother's house	Annemarie is a young Jewish girl smuggled out of Denmark in 1943 to safety in Sweden.	Stanley goes to Camp Green Lake after a wrongful conviction and challenges the corrupt warden, eventually freeing himself and his friend	Eleven-year-old Will is an "Old One," and must save the world by collecting and guarding emblems of power.

Source: Harper & Brand, 2010.

Valuing many perspectives is essential because "students who do not find representations of their own cultures in texts are likely to lose interest in school-based literacies" (National Council of Teachers of English, n.d., p. 5). Students can complete brief reading-interest surveys to help you learn what they are interested in reading, and including biographical information about authors can help students understand authors' experiences and perspective.

Students also need opportunities to read material that introduces them to new perspectives. Harper and Brand believe that "when multicultural literature and literature-related activities are infused into the curriculum in developmentally appropriate ways, children uncover commonalities and differences within and among diverse groups of people. They learn to value both the differences and the commonalities" (2010, p. 224). Harper and Brand have developed a checklist for picture books that includes eight parameters to consider: author, story, character, setting, plot, theme, illustrations, and developmental appropriateness (2010, p. 226) (see Table 13.4).

Support a Positive Attitude About Reading   Find books that reflect students' interests—for students with strong fascinations, providing readings about their interests is a wonderful way to engage their attention and concentration for reading (see Table 13.5).

Table 13.5. Supporting a positive attitude about reading

Student	Reading profile	Interests	Reading material
3rd grader	Avoids reading, says "It is stupid" Grade-level fluency Poor comprehension	Space travel Dinosaurs	Picture books about space and dinosaurs Second-grade reading materials about space and dinosaurs
6th grader	Likes reading children's picture books Poor fluency Struggles with retelling	Horses Ballerinas Fairies	Picture books about horses, ballerinas, and fairies Books at independent reading level about horses, ballerinas, and fairies
11th grader	Avoids all reading Seems defeated by all reading tasks Low tolerance for any errors	Cars Dirt bikes Basketball	Car magazines Dirt bike catalogs *Sports Illustrated* Children's books about cars, dirt bikes, and basketball as part of program to read aloud to elementary school children

A second consideration to support a positive attitude about reading is to be sure that students know how to choose reading that is at their level. Reading teachers talk about three levels of reading: independent, instructional, and frustrational (Beers, 2003, p. 205). Giving students materials that are too difficult will not engage them, and we must provide students with opportunities for high-success reading (Allington, 2011). Engagement might begin with wordless books. That is, the story is told completely through illustrations. For example, Mercer Mayer has a series of books about a boy and a frog (as well as many other children's books) at his web site, http://www.littlecritter.com/index.htm. High-success reading for students in middle- and high- school grades—which may be far below the grade level they are in—can be designed respectfully by having students read at their reading level and be peer tutors for younger students at the same reading level. In that way, older students' dignity is preserved as they read what might be called "babyish" or "low" books.

Engagement with reading can be supported by providing text using technology. Reading on a computer screen can be more interesting, and have many more options, than a print book. Computer technology has advanced to the point of highlighting each word as the text is spoken aloud, and this kind of reading can help new readers follow along. Some elementary schools subscribe to educational web sites, such as Tumblebooks, Starfall, Brainpop, and Brainpop Jr. Brainpop has free activities whether or not the school subscribes to the site. Nettrekker is another site that children may access at home. Scholastic.com has Magic Schoolbus and Word Girl, and PBS Kids has educational games for elementary school-age children. Finally, some children like Dr. Seuss books.

Input

Students need to be exposed to a wide range of perspectives and genres. The exposure begins in elementary school and should continue throughout a student's academic career. It is essential that you introduce students to a range of materials from a variety of authors, and introduce students to culturally relevant, engaging literature. The National Council of Teachers of English (NCTE) notes that six research-based teaching practices to promote adolescent literacy are

1. Demystify content-specific literacy practices

2. Motivate through meaningful practice

3. Engage students with real-world literacy practices

4. Affirm multiple literacies

5. Support learner-centered classroom environments

6. Foster social responsibility through multicultural literacy (NCTE, n.d., p. 4)

These six recommendations help teachers in middle school and high school recognize and support the many literacies students use in upper grades and build on early reading skills.

Writing about the process of reading, Beers believes that reading instruction includes teaching students to use skills such as seeing cause-and-effect relationships; making connections, inferences and generalizations; predicting, summarizing, and sequencing events; comparing and contrasting; pulling out the main ideas; and analyzing. She notes that "I came to understand that *reading skills* are simply *thinking skills* applied to a reading situation" (Kylene Beers and Reading Strategies, n.d.).

What students get from reading is tied closely to the skills and strategies they have in their possession. A common saying in elementary school is that students learn to read until fourth grade, and then they read to learn. That is, the expectation of formal reading instruction through third grade is fairly typical. After third grade, students who are not able to read are often separated from their peers for reading instruction, fall behind in academic areas other than reading, and are on a path of repeated failures in most academic areas. This is because from fourth grade on, students are expected to have grade-level reading ability and be able to use their reading skills for not only reading and writing, but for social studies, math, and science as well. The result for many students who do not read well is repeated failure, shame, embarrassment, and disconnection from school. Students in junior high and high school who do not do well and yet continue to attend school are making a strong statement: "I am not good at this, and I need your help. Please give that to me." The sad reality is that many teachers are not able to answer that request with good teaching of reading.

The list of skills Beers created above addresses one part of the skills needed for reading: the understanding that reading is about meaning. The other two components are understanding how the alphabet works and fluency in reading. In the remainder of this section, you will learn strategies to support students as they develop those skills.

Teach Strategies   Strategies are presented for the five components of reading: phonics, phonemic and phonological awareness, comprehension, vocabulary, and fluency. Strategies for phonics and phonemic and phonological awareness help students learn the connection between letters and sounds, understand the sounds letters and letter combinations make, and teach skills for attacking new words. Spelling words in shaving cream or on a sand tray can help students use their kinesthetic awareness to remember how to create letters and words. Tracing cutouts of letters and drawing letters in the air are two more ways to help students with making letters. Pairing writing tasks with the sounds that letters make can also help.

Esmé Codell taught fifth grade, and many of her students struggled with reading. She noted

> They can't really comprehend what they are reading because they are preoccupied with guessing the sound each letter is supposed to make. It was sometimes painful to see these big kids struggling, reading from books they chose, books they felt good about. So I told them we are making an alphabet museum…for the kindergarteners….My fifth graders are getting their needed alphabet practice without having to feel ashamed. After all, it's not their fault. (1999, p. 28–29)

Esmé's practical idea helped her students learn the sound/letter combinations they needed to become better readers. *Words Their Way*, 3rd Edition (Bear, Invernizzi, Templeton, & Johnston, 2004) gives detailed directions for teaching spelling and word knowledge. Sorting and organizing lists of words can help students understand the relationships between sounds and letters or words. When planning to teach words and sounds, use the 10 principles of word study (see Table 13.6) to help you choose activities for your students that will introduce them to new words, reinforce the words they know, and help them become automatic readers.

Other word-attack strategies include teaching students about similarities between words and identifying the parts of words. Understanding that work, working, worker, and worked are all forms of the root word "work" is an example of this kind of reading activity. Another example is taking a list of words and dividing them into groups based on combinations of consonant-vowel-consonant or consonant-vowel-vowel within the word, or dividing a group of words into categories by the sound the vowel or vowel cluster makes within a word. These word-attack strategies help students manage new vocabulary in reading and know what to do when they encounter an unfamiliar word.

Strategies for comprehension help students explain cause-and-effect relationships; make connections, inferences, and generalizations about the content; predict,

Table 13.6.   Ten principles for word study

Remember: Teaching is not telling.

1. Look for what students use but confuse.
2. Contrast what is new with what is already known.
3. Use words students can read.
4. Compare words "that do" with words "that don't."
5. Sort by sound and sight.
6. Begin with obvious contrasts.
7. Do not hide exceptions.
8. Avoid rules.
9. Work for automaticity.
10. Return to meaningful texts.

From BEAR, DONALD R.; INVERNIZZI, MARCIA; TEMPLETON, SHANE; JOHNSTON, FRANCINE, WORDS THEIR WAY, 3rd Edition, © 2004. Adapted by permission of Pearson Education, Inc., Upper Saddle River, NJ.

summarize, and put events in a sequence; and compare and contrast information within the story. To support these skills, use Wikki Stix or highlighters to mark text. Depending on the comprehension skill you are emphasizing, you can change how text is marked in many different ways. You might ask students to mark characters' names in different colors to see the pattern of conversation, mark unfamiliar words to learn new vocabulary, or mark transition words, such as "first," "next," and "then," to sequence events.

A strategy to pair readers of different abilities is Peer-Assisted Learning Strategies (PALS). This is an important strategy because often students are grouped for reading by ability, and it can be discouraging to be a lower reader. While it is important to have reading instruction that meets student needs—and this is usually most easily managed through ability groups—it is also important to help all students see themselves and each other as competent with text by mixing up groups and providing reading activities that allow students of different abilities to work together. PALS pairs an average or high reader with a lower-level reader for about four weeks. This strategy works well in classes that have students reading at a range of levels. Students do activities and take turns being the reader and the coach. The activities include partner reading, retelling, paragraph shrinking, and prediction relays (Haager & Klingner, 2005, p. 225). PALS supports fluency and comprehension.

A strategy used by Laurie Worthington and Ina Vento, teachers in a cotaught third grade, is "click or clunk." A student reads a page in a book and at the end of the page reflects: Did it make sense? Can I summarize what happened? If the answer is yes, that is a click—I got it. If not, the student rereads the page and asks the same questions. If the answer is yes, something clicked, and then the student knows she is able to understand the story. If the answer is no, that is a clunk—I do not understand it. That tells the student that the book may be too difficult to read independently.

Strategies for vocabulary help students figure the meaning of new words. The literature in reading instruction is clear that an important way to build vocabulary is to read books that are slightly above the student's current reading level so that new words are encountered. Many elementary teachers use the five-finger strategy to help students choose reading that will be interesting without being too difficult. With this strategy, students choose a book they would like to try. The student chooses a page to read and holds up his hand with all four fingers and thumb open. When the student gets to a word he or she does not recognize, one finger is folded down, and the student keeps reading. For each word that is unfamiliar, another finger or the thumb is put down. At the end of the page, if all four fingers and the thumb are down, the student knows the book is probably too difficult to read independently. If all five are still up, the book is an easy read.

Strategies for fluency include those that help students know what they are able to read independently. Fluency is "a combination of word reading, accuracy and automaticity, reading rate, and prosody" (Lane, Pullen, Hudson, & Konold, 2009, p. 280). That is, how smoothly a student can read. Without that knowledge, students can become frustrated and give up if they consistently choose reading that is in their frustration level.

Read Every Day   It is important that students read every day. They need to be reading material that is at independent or instructional levels. Reader's Workshop is one model to ensure regular reading: Nancie Atwell's *In the Middle* (1998) was the classic text that explained how to structure reading time, and her ideas have been adopted in many schools at all grade levels. It is difficult to dedicate time to silent reading, but this is an essential part of reading instruction because the way to become a better reader is to read. The caveat is that students only become better readers through reading when they are reading material that is at their independent level and engages their interest. The problem for many struggling middle- and high-school readers is that the material they have is far too difficult, and the material they are able to read is deadly dull. We suggest strategies such as the one Esmé Codell developed for her struggling fifth graders; provide a safe way for students to access material that is at their independent reading level without feeling embarrassed or ashamed about their reading skills.

Output

The output of reading is what a student is able to do with the content they have read and is what is assessed. Chapter 14—Writing Strategies for All Students is closely tied to the output of reading because reading and writing are so closely related. In addition to writing, there are other ways that a student can show you what she has learned, what connections she has made, and what the reading means to her. The output of reading may include retelling the story verbally, acting out scenes, or drawing a series of pictures for a picture walk using skills such as summarizing, inferencing, connecting, and predicting.

Running Reading Records   Running reading records are used to evaluate how fluently and quickly students can read aloud. Many districts require that reading rates be recorded for all students at the beginning and end of the year to show progress. Typically, a running reading record is a timed reading that is unfamiliar and at the student's independent reading level. The student is given the text and asked to read aloud. The teacher records on a score sheet the errors the student makes and reviews them to see what skills the student needs help with. For example, word substitutions may indicate that the student is rushing and filling in what sounds right without considering meaning or may be sounding out the first part of words but skipping the endings. Hearing students' reading gives teachers insight into the strategies the student uses and guides future instruction.

Demonstrate Comprehension   Comprehension in reading is assessed by writing summaries, making connections between the text and other texts, the world, or the self, and by interpreting the text for meaning. Graphic organizers are common for output beginning in elementary grades. In lower elementary grades, picture walks are a common way to retell a story. The student is given a worksheet with blank boxes in a row and asked to draw the main events and add captions. In upper-elementary grades, students are often asked to complete a graphic organizer that includes prompts, such as sentence starters: first, then, next, and last. These sentence starters help students sequence events. In middle and high school, retelling stories is often the first activity, which is followed by extensions from the text into analysis through different perspectives.

There are many rubrics available online to assess how well a student retells a story; one is available at the Reading A-Z web site at http://www.readinga-z.com/. The site recommends that when asking a student to retell, assess how well he or she can provide the main idea and supporting detail, the sequence of events, who the characters are, the setting and plot, as well as the problem and solution.

Assessment

Assessing reading focuses on the five components of reading: phonics, phonemic awareness, comprehension, vocabulary, and fluency. Assessments can be formative or summative. Formative assessments are those that inform instruction; these assessments are given before, during, and after instruction to help teachers know what skills students possess and what skills need to be taught. Summative assessments give summary information; these assessments are generally the ones given at the beginning and end of the school year and are the source of a great deal of debate. The debates include whether or not a single assessment gives a clear picture of what a student is able to do, whether or not the tests measure what they are designed to measure, whether the tests are culturally relevant, whether the tests are fair, and whether or not summative test scores should be used to evaluate teachers and be linked to teacher pay.

There is debate about whether or not teacher pay should be linked to how well students perform on statewide assessments, including reading assessment. We feel strongly that teachers need to provide good instruction that meets the needs of all students, and we feel just as strongly that teacher pay should *not* be linked to how well students perform on state assessments. We believe that student growth should be measured individually. If a student was two grades below his grade level in reading in the fall but advanced a grade level, that growth should be indicated. But large-scale assessments do not typically allow for this kind of detail; the student will still be one grade below grade level and will be considered a failure for the teacher, when the reality is that the teacher taught the student well enough that he progressed a full grade in reading.

For students who are learning English, you may want to assess reading ability in the language they use at home. Assessments are being made in more languages today. For example, there is a Spanish informal reading inventory (Flippo, Holland, McCarthy, & Swinning, 2009) called the English-Español Reading Inventory for the Classroom by Flynt and Cooter (1999).

Formative Assessments   Formative reading assessments include informal reading inventories, vocabulary and spelling tests, and reading comprehension information. **Informal reading inventories (IRIs)** have emerged in the field of reading instruction as a good tool to use to test what students are able to do. Flippo et al. (2009) suggested that when choosing an IRI, teachers ask themselves questions related to the content; how comprehension is measured; how easy the IRI is to give; the criteria used to determine independent, instructional, and frustration level; and how much information is provided about interpreting the results.

To select an informal reading inventory, you need to consider how suitable it is for three key things: what you want to assess for your students, the best way to assess that skill, and how helpful the IRI will be in giving you insights to help you design instruction for each student (Flippo, Holland, McCarthy, & Swinning, 2009).

Summative Assessments   Formal reading tests include oral reading, reading comprehension, work recognition, and word-attack skills (Pierangelo & Giuliani, 2009). One test that many schools use is the Dynamic Indicators of Basic Early Literacy Skills, or DIBELS. DIBELS is often used in kindergarten through fifth grade to predict how the

informal reading inventories (IRIs)
Formative reading tests that tell a teacher how well a student is completing a reading task. There are many kinds of IRIs.

student will perform in different reading tasks, such as phonological awareness, alphabetic principle, and fluency with connected text (Haager & Klingner, 2005, p. 233).

Using Assessment Data   One district we know requires that teachers maintain a literacy binder for each student, and it is passed along as the student moves through the grades. The binder contains writing samples and a reading level from the beginning and end of each academic year. In May and June, most elementary students are being tested on their reading and that performance is compared to their reading level from the fall. The goal for every student is that he or she advances at least one grade level each academic year.

SUMMARY

In this chapter, we reviewed what reading includes and how to support all students in accessing engaging materials, how to support a range of inputs and outputs, and how to assess student reading. Being a responsive teacher means that you will always be watching how each student reads, what he or she prefers to read, and what he or she is able to tell you—in writing, speaking, drawing, or acting—about what was read.

NARRATIVE 13.1. | JOELLEN MAPLES

Joellen Maples is an assistant professor in the Literacy Department at St. John Fisher College in Rochester, New York, who has 11 years' experience teaching eighth-grade reading in an inclusive middle school:

Back when I was an idealistic, young English teacher, I was bursting with ideas about how I would share Shakespeare with my students. As an English major, I naively believed that they would share my love of reading. However, much to my dismay, they did not. I taught in an inclusive setting and was not prepared for the various reading levels represented in one classroom. I was shocked to learn that some of my eighth graders were nonreaders, while the rest ranged from third-, fourth-, and fifth-grade reading levels. Gone were my dreams of inspiring my students with the classics. Paradoxically, the basal texts, required for use in the classroom, were "on grade level," which meant eighth grade. To compound matters, the stories were not relatable when viewed through the lens of my students' urban background. To achieve success in the reading classroom, reading materials must be interesting, highly relatable, and appropriate for the students' reading levels. I remember looking in disbelief at my students as they would put their heads on their desks in boredom. I could not comprehend simply choosing not to read.

At the perfect moment, I discovered young adult literature, and I immediately recognized its potential as an avenue to promote interest in reading. I was determined to get my students hooked with materials that covered their specific interests. By inundating them with appealing literature, I laid the groundwork needed to support my long-term goals of increasing literacy among my students. My approach was to operate in stealth, honing their reading skills without them realizing it. Initially, I was skeptical. As a literature snob, I wanted them to read the books that I wanted them to read. I had to quickly learn, with some profound and simple advice from my mentor, that the goal was to get them to read. Period. I was desperate, but willing to give young adult literature a try.

I started with *Holes*, a young adult text by Louis Sachar. In *Holes,* Stanley Yelnats is accused of stealing a pair of shoes. As his punishment, he must choose between jail and Camp Green Lake. Stanley chooses camp, where he is forced to dig holes all day. However, in that summer, he learns more about life than he could ever imagine. My students were instantly hooked. I would read aloud to them daily, and eventually, I had some of them reading aloud as well. Every time class would start, they would ask, "Can we read today?" To have them request to read was my sweetest reward.

One day, there was a fight in the hallway that the math teacher and I had to break up. Dealing with the discipline issues prevented me from getting back to class on time, and my students kept popping their heads out saying, "Mrs. Maples, when are you coming to class? We want to finish the book!" In the midst of the excitement, I failed to recognize that my students were begging me to read. As I was headed back to my classroom, I noticed that an eerie silence was emanating from my room and immediately felt a sense of dread thinking, "Oh no! What have they done?" Any teacher knows that, when you are out of the classroom, students can find all kinds of trouble to get themselves into.

Unable to imagine what they could be doing, I raced to my door and I will never forget what I saw. Robert, my best reader, was sitting at my podium reading the ending of *Holes* to his classmates. I surveyed the room and saw that all of my students were on task and following along. They could not wait to find out what happened. It was in that moment that the power of young adult literature availed itself to me. Through this medium, readers, struggling or not, could develop a love for literacy. New teachers interested in learning more about young adult literature in all content areas can check out ALAN (Assembly on Literature for Adolescents of the National Council of Teachers of English) at www.Alan-ya.org. ALAN holds an annual conference in November where attendees learn how to integrate young adult literature into their teaching. Young adult authors also provide sessions, giving away copies of their latest books to start classroom libraries. Students deserve rich, high-interest texts to which they can relate and it is our job, as teachers, to provide them.

CHAPTER 14

Writing Strategies for All Students

How this chapter prepares you to be an effective inclusive classroom teacher:

- This chapter introduces you to evidence-based strategies for building vocabulary, improving spelling, and teaching the components of the writing process. The importance of engaging students in writing in a range of ways, including teaching code-switching, is introduced. This is important for supporting the performance of all students in writing. Knowing how to encourage students to be engaged in writing and producing writing will help you modify materials and curricula to meet each student's needs. **This helps you meet CEC Standard 4: Instructional Strategies.**

- This chapter reviews formal and informal writing assessments. This information teaches you how to use different types of assessments for writing. **This helps you meet CEC Standard 8: Assessment.**

- This chapter draws attention to providing culturally relevant materials and instruction, including the importance of teaching code-switching skills. This chapter emphasizes the importance of opportunities to write and the ways that teachers can help all students be engaged in writing. **This helps you meet CEC Standard 9: Professional and Ethical Practice.**

After reading and discussing this chapter, you will be able to

- Understand the Common Core State Standards for writing

- Explain the ways formative and summative assessments drive writing instruction

- Explain and give examples of the kinds of writing expected in school

- Explain the steps of the writing process

- Explain the impact of technology on writing and the production of writing

- Describe three models of writing instruction

- Define code-switching

- Explain how to engage students in writing

- Understand strategies for spelling, for building vocabulary, and for each stage of the writing process

- Explain how to assess writing

When one of us was a high school teacher coteaching 11th-grade English, we had the opportunity to review student essays every other week as we worked from September until June to prepare students for the New York State Regents Exam in English. The exam was given in two 4-hour blocks on consecutive days; students answered reading comprehension questions, wrote short-answer responses, and wrote four essays. The range of skills students needed to have ready was impressive: reading and comprehending, interpreting, making connections, understanding cause-and-effect relationships, making inferences and generalizations, predicting, summarizing, sequencing events, comparing and contrasting, pulling out the main ideas, and analyzing—all the skills we reviewed in the previous chapter about reading—*and* being able to express these skills in writing. The goal of this chapter is to explore the writing tasks students are expected to complete in school. One author's experience with writing assessment for high school students illustrates the complexity of writing and the numerous skills that students must master to be effective writers.

During that academic year our school's emphasis on teaching the skills of writing included many of the strategies you will find in this chapter. But regardless of the writing task facing students at the end of a particular academic year, all students need to have the skills to produce clear writing as adults. The goal of writing instruction is to help students express their ideas clearly, because our society is based in literacy, and basic reading and writing skills are expected of adults. Adults are expected to write for a range of reasons: to fill out forms, to apply for jobs, to make lists, to write letters and e-mails, to Tweet and text, to blog, to journal, and maybe to write for an audience. The difficulties many students have with writing may prevent them from seeing the value in being able to clearly express themselves in a permanent format for others to see.

Writing assessment, like reading assessment, has received a great deal of scrutiny in the last few decades. The Common Core State Standards Initiative that you read about in Chapter 13 has guidelines for writing assessment:

> Each year in their writing, students should demonstrate increasing sophistication in all aspects of language use, from vocabulary and syntax to the development and organization of ideas, and they should address increasingly demanding content and sources.

Students advancing through the grades are expected to meet each year's grade-specific standards and retain or further develop skills and understandings mastered in preceding grades. (2010)

This statement drives how states consider what students should be able to write at each grade level. In 2011, the National Assessment of Education Progress (NAEP) tested students nationwide in grades four, seven, and eleven in writing. Students completed writing tasks in three areas: **narrative writing**, **informative writing**, and **persuasive writing** (National Center for Educational Statistics, More About NAEP Writing, n.d.).

Information from the NAEP tests, which are given to samples of students in various subjects, is considered quite important by policy makers and school personnel because the tests are the "common yardstick" for student performance. Results showed that "the writing skills of eighth- and twelfth-graders improved in 2007 compared to earlier assessment years, with gains across many student groups" (Salahu-Din, Persky, & Miller, 2008, para. 1). This is good news, but how useful this information is and how writing assessments may constrain what teachers and students feel they can do in the classroom with writing is debatable.

In 2004, Thomas criticized the weight we place on writing assessments, noting "we should be highly critical of what shapes curriculum, instruction, and assessment in our classrooms" (p. 76). He explained that "our test mania has made testing an act of sorting instead of a means to more effective teaching and learning" (p. 78), and he gave the example of a score report that tells the teacher very little about how to change his or her instruction for a particular student. In contrast, feedback that describes the writing—"Jessica's personal narrative includes a number of specific verbs—such as 'peppered,' tossed,' and 'mumbled'—that give her most recent piece a stronger voice than her earlier works" (p. 78)—gives the teacher information about how best to design future instruction for this student.

What Thomas was describing in the second example was the value of formative assessment, which we explored in Chapter 9. Remember that formative assessments inform instruction, while summative assessments (such as the NAEP tests) give information about what was learned. As a teacher, you may be evaluated in part on how well your students perform on summative assessments. Your task is to recognize that good formative assessment, high-quality responsive instruction, and instruction that engages all students is the best test preparation you can provide. This holds true in all subjects, including writing.

In the first part of this chapter, we review the components of writing and common models of writing instruction. Then we return to the universal design for learning structure and present information on strategies for writing in areas of engagement, input, output, and assessment. We conclude with a brief summary. In a single chapter of a textbook, it is very difficult to adequately address the field of writing, but we will give an overall review of the field and give you a taste of strategies that have been successful for many students.

COMPONENTS OF WRITING

Literacy expert Joellen Maples noted that the types of writing taught in schools today include narrative writing, informative writing, persuasive writing, and **expository writing**. Narrative writing focuses on telling a story—either factual or fictional—and includes short stories, biography, autobiography, novellas, and novels. Informative writing is a broad category that communicates facts, opinions, or a combination. Examples of informative writing include the traditional five-paragraph essay that you might remember writing in school; it included an introductory paragraph, three body

narrative writing   The production of stories or personal essays (National Center for Educational Statistics, More About NAEP Writing, n.d.).

informative writing
Sharing knowledge or conveying messages, instructions, and ideas (National Center for Educational Statistics, More About NAEP Writing, n.d.).

persuasive writing
Seeks to influence the reader to take some action or bring about change (National Center for Educational Statistics, More About NAEP Writing, n.d.).

expository writing
Writing that shares information or explains something.

paragraphs with supporting details, and a concluding paragraph. Comparing and contrasting, explaining a sequence of events, or presenting a problem and solution are all techniques that can be used in informative writing. Expository writing is writing that shares information or explains something; the writer's opinion is not shared. This kind of writing is often sequential, and uses terms such as "first," "then," and "last" to order events or steps of a process. Newspaper and magazine articles, journal articles, and nonfiction books are examples. Persuasive writing is writing that tries to convince or persuade the reader. Examples of persuasive writing include creative writing and essays that express an opinion and provide support for it.

Within each kind of writing, there are many genres used at the teacher's discretion based on what she or he wants to focus on. Each is introduced in elementary grades, and as students move through middle school into high school, the complexity and length of each kind of writing increases. In this section, we review writing instruction and the role of digital literacy.

In the last 30 years, there have been several significant changes in writing instruction in schools. Four areas have received attention: the process of writing, the effects of writing on learning, the reading-writing connection, and the use of software and word processers to write (Robinson, McKenna, & Wedman, 2004). The generally accepted steps of the writing process are drafting, revising, editing, proofing, and publishing (Robinson, McKenna, & Wedman, 2004). There are variations: Some models identify prewriting as the first step (Tompkins, 2008), others models have four steps, and still others have up to seven (see Table 14.1).

The important thing is that the way writing is taught in all grades includes identifying the topic to write about, revision and rewriting, and publication of the finished piece. Many students struggle with revision and redrafting. Teaching students that rewriting, correcting, and editing are part of writing is an important component of instruction.

The second area that has received attention in recent years is the way that writing can help the knowledge students have become organized and coherent (Robinson, McKenna, & Wedman, 2004). That is, writing can be a tool to help students make sense of what they know. This can be especially true for students who have difficulty organizing their thoughts verbally; getting ideas on paper and seeing them can help visual learners engage with ideas and develop their thinking by seeing ideas in text. Graphic organizers and outlines can be utilized to support students' organization.

The third area is the strong connection between reading and writing. It used to be thought that reading and writing were essentially opposite processes; reading takes information in, while writing puts information out (Robinson, McKenna, & Wedman, 2004). Seeing reading and writing as complementary has resulted in writing being introduced to young children as a way to help them with reading. Jones, Reutzel, and Fargo said that "the concrete task of creating written text serves as a bridge to the more

Table 14.1. The writing process

Discover a subject	Conceive	Draft	Prewrite
Sense an audience	Craft	Revise	Draft
Search for specifics	Correct	Edit	Revise
Create a design		Proof	Edit
Write		Publish	Publish
Develop a critical eye			
Rewrite			
Moore, 2004, p. 204	*Fletcher & Portalupi, 2007*	*Robinson, McKenna, & Wedman, 2004*	*Tompkins, 2008*

abstract task of reading" (2010, p. 327). The strong connection means that how we teach writing affects reading; teaching students that they are good writers can help students see that they are also capable of being good readers. One strategy to support this perspective is the "author's chair": In lower elementary classrooms, teachers may use an "author's chair" for students to explain their writing pieces to their peers. The emphasis on being able to communicate ideas in writing helps students see themselves as competent communicators, and that confidence can be used to extend the focus into reading.

The fourth area—software and word processors—is addressed briefly here and again in the next section. Being able to produce writing through typing instead of handwriting can defuse barriers to writing that emerge for students who do not have good fine-motor control for writing in pen or pencil. A mechanical barrier such as this should not be a barrier to communicating ideas in writing. The advent of such assistive technologies as the **Neo2** and the **iPad2** has made technological adaptations affordable and accessible to many students who may have lacked access to writing in the past.

BTW, IMHO, Digital Media Is Gr8 :)

Digital media and writing are a match made in heaven; students using the Neo2 and iPad are able to complete writing assignments that would take significantly longer if written out in longhand. Beyond typing, students write all the time using digital media. But education has not completely accepted instant messaging, text messaging, and other forms of digital communication. Teachers are concerned about the rules of writing and the conventions of grammar, but Baron (2009) said that we do not need to worry about the use of texting and shorthand spelling ruining the way students use the English language:

> Before we despair that language is going to hell in a handcart, we should remember two lessons. First, normativeness in language goes through cycles, much like taste in music and politics. All is not lost. And second, regardless of the swings that language goes through, there is room for individual schools or teachers to set their own standards. (p. 46)

Instead of shying away from digital media, we need to learn about it, use it, and help our students use it well. Word processing programs can help students

> Merge notes, drafts, and outlines seamlessly; edit as they go; retrieve deleted passages; reorder entire paragraphs; change selected words; incorporate tables and visual images to back up one's point; and even customize formats and self-publish....This increased ability to write and edit fluently has freed students to focus more on expressing what they want to say. (Weigel & Gardner, 2009, p. 39)

Of course, this is all predicated on the availability of the technology and access to skilled users to gain competence. Remember that not all students will have access to a computer outside of school, and not all students will be fluent users of technology without direct instruction. Your role is to advocate for equitable use of technology in all schools and remain fluent in using emerging digital technologies. This means continuing your training once you are a teacher, and remembering that the best teachers are always learning.

Models of Writing Instruction

The model of writing instruction you use in your classroom may be determined by the school district. There are many writing curricula, and two frequently used in schools today are **balanced literacy** (Fountas & Pinnell, 1996) and the **six traits of writing** by Education Northwest (6+1 Trait Rubrics, 2011). A third model that is used in conjunction with both of the other two models is **writer's workshop** (Atwell, 1998). Each model is designed to support strong writing skills in all students, although balanced literacy is

Neo2   Assistive technology: small, portable keyboard and display for typing text. Web site at http://www.renlearn.com/neo/NEO2/default.aspx

iPad2   Assistive technology: a small, lightweight portable computer. Web site at http://www.apple.com/ipad/

balanced literacy
Model of writing instruction that includes shared writing, interactive writing, writer's workshop, and independent writing (Fountas & Pinnell, 1996).

six traits of writing
A model of writing instruction that teaches ideas and content, voice, sentence fluency, word choice, organization, conventions, and visual representation using rubrics for different developmental levels (Writing Assessment Rubric, n.d.).

writer's workshop
Model of writing instruction that includes minilessons, independent writing time, and individual writing conferences (Atwell, 1998).

most commonly an elementary program. The 6+1 Trait model and Weriters' workshop are used in all grades.

Balanced literacy is organized around guided reading and writing groups, and uses different tasks. In writing, tasks include shared writing, interactive writing, writer's workshop, and independent writing (Fountas & Pinnell, 1996, p. 23). The 6+1 Trait model has been adopted by many districts; it provides rubrics for each trait at different grade levels, and many districts use it throughout a student's education. The seven traits are: ideas and content, voice, sentence fluency, word choice, organization, conventions, and visual representation (Writing Assessment Rubric, n.d.).

Writer's workshop—a component of balanced literacy—is a model that emphasizes using class time for a brief minilesson on a topic of use to the majority of the class, independent writing time, and individual writing conferences with the teacher every few days to check progress on a writing project. Students are taught how to draft, write, revise, and publish their work. This model is very effective for students who have strong intrapersonal skills and are able to work relatively independently. For students who need more support, a writing conference may be scheduled daily to provide guidance. A strength of the workshop model is how well it aligns with differentiated instruction; each student writes at his or her own pace, at his or her own level. This allows students above and below grade level to be challenged as writers and to work within their zone of proximal development.

Now that you have briefly reviewed the kinds of writing expected in school, the writing process, and some common models of writing instruction, you will learn some strategies to support all students' writing.

STRATEGIES FOR ENGAGEMENT, INPUT, OUTPUT, AND ASSESSMENT

Many students struggle with writing, and the strategies in this section are the tip of a very large iceberg of supports that are available (see Figure 14.1). Strategies to help writers can be grouped into two categories: those that help the writer through the thinking process and those that help the writer with the production of the text. For more information on detailed, concrete strategies to support writers, check out the books listed in the Writing Resources in Figure 14.2.

Engagement

There are several major considerations for engaging students in writing. First, just as with reading, it is important that all students are seen as literate and capable of expressing themselves through writing. Second, teach code-switching.

See All Students' Literacy Skills   As we said in Chapter 13, all students have the capacity to learn, and we expect you to use the least dangerous assumption about all students. Engaging students in writing means providing many and varied opportunities for typing and writing to express ideas. Strategies to engage students include trying different writing utensils, different writing grips, weighted writing utensils, and assistive technology for typing. Experiment with many ways to interest students in writing and persist in expecting that students will produce symbolic language to express ideas.

Related to the expectation of writing, an important strategy is to accept a wide range of behaviors as writing. Beginning a pencil stroke on the top left side of the page and moving to the right and down is a beginning writing skill; so is forming letters with spaces between them from left to right. For beginning writers, single letters may represent complete words, spacing may be inconsistent, and there may be no punctuation.

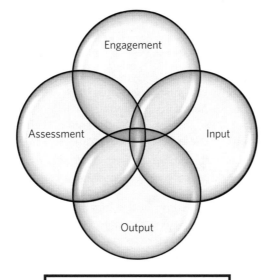

Figure 14.1. Strategies for engagement, input, output, and assessment in writing.

See all engagement with producing lines, scribbles, or shapes as writing, and provide opportunities to both write and type consistently.

Finally, because the least dangerous assumption is essential, never assume that when a student is not writing or typing that he is not able to do so; assume instead that you have not yet found the way for that student to write effectively and persevere with new ideas, opportunities, and strategies. In the documentary *Autism is a World*, Sue Rubin noted that as a person with autism, she had great difficulty expressing herself through speaking, writing, or typing. When her educational team introduced her to facilitated communication, she initially resisted, rebelling against the challenge of focusing her attention on choosing keys to type into words. But her team persisted, and she is now able to express her keen intellect through a keyboard because of that persistence (Wurzburg & Rubin, 2005).

Teach Code-Switching   **Code-switching** from slang to conventional English is an important skill, and students who speak a version of English that is not recognized in school need to have their usage honored, but also need to be taught the conventions of

code-switching Being able to use two forms of English fluently; typically between Standard English and Ebonics/Black Vernacular English (White, 2011).

- Daniels, H., Zemelman, S., & Steineke, N. (2007). *Content-Area Writing: Every Teacher's Guide*. Portsmouth, NH: Heinemann.
- Vopat, J. (2007). *Micro Lessons in Writing*. Portsmouth, NH: Heinemann.

Figure 14.2. Writing resources.

English that are accepted at school. An English teacher explained how he supports all students in his classroom through using code-switching:

> Though we should teach the conventions of Standard English, we should also acknowledge and even celebrate the unique and highly effective forms of discourse that students bring with them into the classroom. I was proposing that not only does a broader view of what counts as appropriate classroom discourse promote an inclusive English classroom, it creates a culturally responsive and inclusive foundation from which to teach students code-switching to Standard English. (White, 2011, p. 44)

Learning how to use both fluently gives students the cultural capital they need to navigate school and society. The mistake schools have often made is to tell students that the only right way to talk and write is conventional English—anything else is wrong and unacceptable. Instead, we should teach students that there is a time and a place for all language usage, what those times and places are, and how to switch back and forth.

Input

How students feel about writing and what they are able to write are connected. The input of writing is the "discover a subject" (Moore, 2004), "conceive" (Fletcher & Portalupi, 2007) or "prewrite" (Tompkins, 2008) step of the writing process. The writing prompts students use can be integrally tied to their experiences and culture, or be stilted packaged prompts that limit creativity because the topic does not relate to them. Students must be able to write from their own experiences and who they are to produce their best work. How you talk about writing and what students write can have a significant effect on the quality of what students produce.

Philip Done (2005) is a third-grade teacher, and in an essay about writing he explained how he engaged students and gave them the tools to see the world around them as good material for writing. He wrote:

> "Boys and girls," I announced, "today we are going to learn how to write." Justin groaned. Then I said, "Now put your coats and hats on. We are going outside." "Yeah!" they all screamed. "But there is one rule," I said. "You may not say one word when we go outside. Got it?" They smiled and nodded with their mouths closed....It began to drizzle. They all looked at me, expecting me to say it's time to go back inside. We didn't. The children looked at each other with wide eyes. We took our hats off instead and tried to catch raindrops in our mouths. They were dying to speak, but no one did. For they knew it would break the spell....Finally we walked inside, took off our coats, wiped our feet, and hung up our hats...." Yes, Peter?" I said. "You may speak now."..."Mr. Done," he asked, "when are we going to learn how to write?" I smiled. "You just did, Peter. You just did." (pp. 75–76)

Done's example shows how the teacher can set the stage for strong writing by engaging students and focusing their attention on the details, saving those for a writing task after returning to the classroom. Other input for strong student writing is also grounded in student experience.

Teach Strategies   Strategies help students understand and use the stages of writing, practice spelling and build vocabulary, and become skilled at writing in different ways. As shown in Table 14.1, the writing process includes prewriting activities. Murray includes discovering a subject, sensing the audience, searching for specifics, and creating a design before writing. These steps are similar to the conceiving or prewriting stages others have suggested.

Strategies for prewriting include brainstorming, clustering or mind mapping, free writing, and asking the six questions of journalism (i.e., who, what, when, where, why, how) (University of Kansas Writing Center, n.d.). Brainstorming can be done alone or with a partner and includes writing all the ideas about the topic without judgment; the goal is to generate a lot of possibilities. Mind mapping means taking blank paper and writing the main idea in the center. Then, each idea that relates to the topic is written (or drawn) around the topic, each idea in its own space. In this way, the student sees how each idea relates to the main idea and to other ideas. This strategy is useful for organizing the writing task. The six journalism questions can be made into a worksheet to record the answers. This can be especially useful for informative or expository writing.

Once students have completed prewriting and are settled into the actual writing, provide strategies for getting the words on the page. Laman (2011) suggested encouraging students to talk to each other during a writer's workshop. A strategy for writing a research paper is the I-Search Paper (Assaf, Ash, Saunders, & Johnson, 2011). In an I-Search paper, students write four sections: what I knew, why I am writing this paper, the search, and what I learned.

Strategies to practice spelling and build vocabulary relate to helping students make the connections between the sounds and the letters and words, and understanding the meaning of unfamiliar words. For spelling, focus on strategies that help students see patterns in words, such as sorting words by beginning sounds, end combinations (e.g., –ck, –ed, –ing), or vowel clusters. Also, help students hear rhyming words and explore how words sound the same and different by reading words and listening. A second strategy for spelling that supports kinesthetic learners is to write spelling words in shaving cream or a sand tray (as mentioned in Chapter 13). Spelling City (with many different games for spelling lists that teachers can upload) is a site that some schools subscribe to for weekly spelling lists.

Strategies for building vocabulary include teaching new words and helping students incorporate richer words into their writing. A second strategy is to have students create personal dictionaries for new vocabulary encountered in reading to include in later writing.

To introduce a new kind of writing, such as biography, provide grade-level models from a range of authors and backgrounds and discuss the way the writer structured his or her narrative. Provide explicit information about what is included in that kind of writing, and compare and contrast the new way with what students already know. Completing KWL charts—what we Know, Want to know, and what we Learned—can be a good way to help students see what they have learned about a new style.

Choose a Writing Goal and Communicate It   When students begin a writing task, each student needs a clear understanding of what you expect and how you are going to assess it. It may be that you do not have a clear sense of how to assign a writing grade, which means that you and your students may be frustrated when it comes time for you to assign a writing task and assess it. We bring this up in the input section because as students begin to write, they need to know what is expected; the rubric or guidelines become the roadmap for their destination. Without a clear goal, students will not know what to do.

Output

The output of writing is text. The text may be printed, written, or typed. It may have been spoken and converted into text by computer software. Giving students options in how they produce writing and the formats they use to create it is good practice. The format for writing is increasingly based in typed text. The strategies in this section are grouped into two headings: support stages of writing and help students.

Support Stages of Writing   Drafts look different than published work, and how teachers approach and read drafts in different stages affects how students feel about their writing. Thompson (2011) found that when she required that students develop a beginning, middle, and end to their stories from the outset, her students struggled. When students were allowed to let their writing develop more naturally, their writing improved.

graphic organizers
Worksheets with blank lines or shapes (in many variations) to help students record information.

In prewriting, use strategies that help students find the story they want to tell without stifling their voice or doing the work for them. Thompson (2011) believed that using **graphic organizers** to help students begin the prewriting process is useful only when used sparingly. Too much emphasis on the graphic organizer was not useful for her fifth-grade class.

In the editing stage, strategies must scaffold skills toward independent editing. Teachers sometimes fall into the mistake of doing all the editing for students, who then simply recopy or retype the work without thinking about the changes that are required. This is not useful for the student, who is not learning to edit effectively. Instead, we recommend strategies that help students learn to see errors and identify places to strengthen word choice, sentence structure, and mechanics. Thompson (2011) recommended reviewing your state standards for ELA and developing a checklist for students to use when editing. A checklist can be tailored to the needs of your particular class. One way to structure a checklist is to review the 6+1 Trait model and focus on one at a time, gradually introducing new traits throughout the year. In one school district, first and second graders are introduced to the first two traits, and then in third grade the next three traits are introduced. In fourth grade, all seven are used.

Publishing student work can be formal or informal. Some principals ask that all students have work displayed in the classroom, while others ask that only the best work be displayed. We believe that all students need to be valued, which includes valuing the work he or she creates. Strategies for publishing include dedicating a bulletin board to writing samples, publishing a weekly or monthly newsletter, writing letters to the local newspaper, or scanning work and posting it electronically on a school web site.

Help Students Revise   Many students struggle with the revision process. After a first draft is on paper, teaching strategies for revision will help students see editing and revision as an integral part of writing. Students need strategies to manipulate the text without feeling overwhelmed. Story surgery is one strategy to add revisions. In story surgery, students take a hard copy of the draft and read it over. Then, they cut the story into sections based on where material needs to be added or edited. The strip of text is taped on a new sheet of paper, and new text added in exactly the right place. This process continues, with the transfer of drafted text onto a new page and additions where information is needed. Material that is not needed is discarded (Fletcher & Portalupi, 2007, p. 58). A second strategy is pruning the draft by reading each sentence and asking "Do I need this?" If the answer is no, the sentence is pruned (Fletcher & Portalupi, 2007, p. 96).

Assessment

Assessment in writing evaluates how well the writer organized and expressed their thoughts. The 6+1 Trait model is one example of how to evaluate writing in seven key areas: ideas, organization, voice, word choice, sentence fluency, conventions, and presentation (Education Northwest, 2011).

There are many ways to assess writing; the essential point to take away is that you must clearly teach the steps required to develop the skill in question, and must have a clear way to assess the result. Saying "I can just tell" if an essay or piece of writing is good is not acceptable. You must be able to explain to the writer the strengths and weaknesses in the writing. Developing and using rubrics that are clear and detailed is the beginning of assessing writing effectively. Many school districts will assign grade-level teams or the English department to review Common Core Standards or state standards and use that information for assessment.

When assessing writing, it is important to consider why students make the errors they do. Crovitz noted that "teachers must be aware of the complexity and sophistication that underlie a writer's development while resisting behaviorist notions of rote learning that assign negative implications to error-making, all the while considering the real-world impact of errors on particular audiences" (2011, p. 32).

Give Feedback to Fit Students' Needs   When giving feedback to students, remember that the goal is to help them improve in writing. If your feedback feels critical or punitive, students may be discouraged and resist writing. If your feedback is too general to be useful, students will not have the information they need to improve. Strategies to give feedback in ways that help students become better writer include limiting parameters of feedback to one to four areas (remember that the traits of writing many districts use include ideas and content, voice, sentence fluency, word choice, organization, conventions and visual representation), asking students what they would like feedback about, and giving feedback several times on different parameters each time.

SUMMARY

In this chapter, we reviewed the kinds of writing students are expected to do and the components of writing. Digital media play an increasingly significant role in writing, because technology allows students who cannot hold writing utensils the opportunity to type or speak to produce text. The most common models of writing instruction in schools include balanced literacy, the 6+1 Trait model, and writer's workshops; you are probably familiar with at least one of these models. Strategies to support all students in writing were presented in the stages of the writing process. Please remember to use the least dangerous assumption about all students, and to provide all students with access to literacy experiences and opportunities.

CHAPTER 15

Social Studies Strategies for All Students

How this chapter prepares you to be an effective inclusive classroom teacher:

- This chapter provides evidence-based strategies for making local-global connections and making instruction interactive. How to design thematic units is reviewed. This chapter explains the importance of focusing on enduring understandings and seeing multiple perspectives. Teaching critical thinking skills is emphasized throughout. **This helps you meet CEC Standard 4: Instructional Strategies.**

- This chapter explains the importance of using multiple types of assessments. It connects to material from Chapter 7. **This helps you meet CEC Standard 8: Assessment.**

- This chapter draws significant attention to the importance of seeing multiple perspectives and using a range of materials. It reviews how to gently challenge students when teaching about the many aspects of diversity. **This helps you meet CEC Standard 9: Professional and Ethical Practice.**

After reading and discussing
this chapter, you will be able to

- Explain the National Council for the Social Studies themes

- Explain why using multiple sources is essential in teaching social studies

- Explain how teaching social studies includes teaching critical thinking skills

- Define enduring understandings

- Describe strategies for making local-global connections

- Describe strategies for making instruction interactive

- Explain how to teach social justice concepts

- Explain where to find primary and digital sources and why these sources are important

- Explain how to design a thematic unit

- Describe how to provide multiple ways to assess student learning

What do you think of when you hear "social studies"? You might think of studying wars and historical events, learning about government, and taking economics. That is right, in part. But social studies is more than these few topics. Social studies instruction has typically included history, geography, civics, economics, sociology, anthropology, and psychology (Social Science Education Consortium, 1996, p. 15). There have been significant traditions in social studies teaching, and each has informed curriculum development and implementation. Three of the traditions are 1) social studies as a vehicle for cultural or citizenship transmission, 2) as the study of social sciences (including history), and 3) as reflective inquiry (Social Science Education Consortium, 1996, p. 15). Those three traditions guide how curriculum develops and is taught and shape how teachers consider the major themes in human history. Think about what you learned in your social studies classes from kindergarten through high school. What tradition was most evident?

The recent emphasis on reflective inquiry informed the development of instructional strands. The National Council for the Social Studies (NCSS) guides instruction around 10 topics or themes. Those 10 themes inform the development of curriculum for social studies (see Figure 15.1).

The National Council for the Social Studies explained how the themes should inform instruction:

> The themes represent strands that should thread through a social studies program, from grades pre-K through 12, as appropriate at each level. While at some grades and for some courses, specific themes will be more dominant than others, all the themes are highly interrelated. To understand culture (Theme 1), for example, students also need to understand the theme of time, continuity, and change (Theme 2); the relationships between people, places, and environments (Theme 3); and the role of civic ideals and practices (Theme 10). (National Curriculum Standards for Social Studies: Introduction, n.d.)

Clearly, the Council expects and supports connections between these broad themes, which raises a critical question: Why is it that some of us remember feeling rushed through U.S. history and global history without remembering any of it? Or feeling

Figure 15.1.   Social studies themes. (*Source:* National Curriculum for the Social Studies, n.d.)

bored by a teacher lecturing about events in the past that seemed disconnected from our own lives?

How you answer is based in the way you were taught. Ideally, you had engaging instruction that introduced you to many ways of thinking about events and patterns in history. If this was not your experience, you are not alone. In many classrooms, teachers use a single source. This is problem, because a single textbook—even one that strives to present multiple perspectives—should not be the only resource used in social studies. Howard Zinn noted a significant flaw in most textbooks: They "do not acknowledge their biases" (Bigelow, 2008, p. 2). The result is "a winner's history"—one that tells the stories of those on the top, such as presidents, diplomats, and generals. What is left out is the rest of the people, all of whom are affected by major events. The people missed are those who still experience disparity in society today: women, communities of color, those with disabilities, English Language Learners, and the LGBT community. Without hearing those perspectives, students miss important lessons.

Bigelow explained the importance of shifting how we teach history:

> When we look at history from the standpoint of the workers and not just the owners, the soldiers and not just the generals, the invaded and not just the invaders, we can begin to see society more fully, more accurately. (2008, p. 2)

It may be that the social studies you were taught included many perspectives. If it is not the case, do not despair; you can teach differently and provide insight into a range of experiences. The way you engage your students includes helping them see the effects of events on different people. A renowned social studies teacher, Jeffrey Liles, an associate professor in inclusive education with significant expertise in the foundations of education, explained that the way to do this is to use the textbook as a resource without letting the textbook drive the decisions you make about what perspectives and events to include in your curriculum. We will touch on this again in the input section.

Some people may think that it is not possible to teach with a focus on critical thinking; local, national, and global communities; sweeping themes; and a sense of responsibility to the community because the standards rely too heavily on testing factual information. We disagree. It is true that major historical events and trends are integral to social studies, but if you look closely at the standards, there is no mention of specific events or dates; the emphasis is on broad themes —which include global connections (Theme 9); time, continuity and change (Theme 2); culture (Theme 1); and individuals,

> 1. Critical thinking
> 2. Local, national, and global communities
> 3. Sweeping themes in human history
> 4. Sense of responsibility for their surrounding culture

Figure 15.2.   Key elements in teaching social studies.

groups and institutions (Theme 5). Clearly, the NCSS supports teaching in ways that help students think critically about their role in society and the trends that affect all people.

Cornbleth stated:

> Meaningful social studies teaching refers to teaching for learning and critical thinking that incorporates diverse perspectives and students. This means taking students beyond memorization to comprehension and coherence. It means connecting pieces or chunks of information both with each other (e.g., a diagram or web rather than a list) and with what one already knows (i.e., elaborating or extending mental schema). (2010, p. 215)

Critical thinking is a key element of teaching social studies. A second essential component of social studies education is teaching students about local, national, and global communities. Two other elements are teaching students how events reflect sweeping themes in human history and helping students develop a sense of responsibility for their surrounding culture. How to teach students these elements while meeting state and national standards is the focus of this section.

In 2003, Seif said that "students need to understand key historical ideas and events, major economic and social forces, the effect of geography on people's lives, political forces in a democratic society, and a variety of global issues and challenges" (2003, p. 54). These big topics are what drive social studies education, and there are many ways to introduce these ideas, forces, and events to students (see Figure 15.2).

enduring understandings
The significant points we want students to know, understand, and appreciate (Horton & Barnett, 2008).

How can teachers effectively teach everything that is included in the 10 themes? Seif (2004) recommended curriculum that focuses in big ideas, or **enduring understandings**. A strategy for curriculum development called Understanding by Design can help teachers focus on big ideas to teach about significant events in history. For example, Seif described teaching about the signing of the Magna Carta as an event that helps students develop an understanding of the rule of law. The concept of enduring understandings becomes an important strategy to connect world events to the classroom community, and we will review this in the next section.

In this chapter, we review strategies for teaching all students in the four areas of Universal Design for Learning: engagement, input, output, and assessment. In the section on engagement, you will learn how to make connections between local and global events, present multiple perspectives, be interactive, and gently challenge students. In the input section, we review using resources beyond the textbook, talk about primary sources and digital sources, and introduce thematic units. We combine output and assessment and examine strategies to show mastery in multiple ways and incorporate critical thinking (see Figure 15.3).

STRATEGIES FOR TEACHING SOCIAL STUDIES TO ALL STUDENTS

Engagement

Engaging students in social studies is complex. Students have a range of background experiences and bring those to the classroom. Those experiences might include being

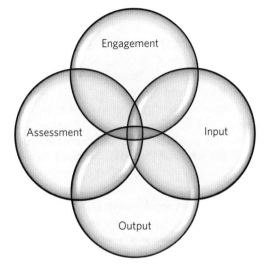

Figure 15.3. Strategies for engagement, input, output, and assessment in social studies.

taught from a variety of perspectives, being taught to think critically, or being taught to connect social studies to their own lives. In contrast, some students' previous social studies instruction may have been lecture and worksheet based and seen as boring. In both cases, it is your task to bring social studies to students in engaging ways. Four strategies to do this are to be aware of local-global connections, present multiple perspectives, be interactive, and gently challenge students.

Local-Global   When considering how to teach social studies, Howard Zinn suggested that "one important thing is not to concentrate on chronological order, but to go back and forth and find similarities and analogies" (Bigelow, 2008, p. 9). This makes sense to us, but many teachers struggle to fit what they know to be good practices into a course structure and design that feels limiting. That is, culturally relevant teaching that connects material to students' lives and allows for deep exploration of topics might seem impossible when teachers feel pressured to get through a certain amount of material each quarter or semester.

The solution is to review the standards for social studies. While there is probably going to be some amount of information that you need to communicate to your students, the larger picture of the 10 themes is a framework that allows for a great deal of creative teaching. For example, consider the NCSS theme of global connections and the topic of global warming. Introduce students to the topic of global warming, and support student research into local perspectives and responses to the idea that humanity is changing the world we live on in a significant way through our actions. A good resource for local-global connections is *Rethinking Globalization* (Bigelow & Peterson, 2002).

Other strategies to make local-global connections are to use print and online media to gather information about a universal topic, such as water management, unions, or immigrant policies. Move back and forth from the local to the global, helping students make connections between their daily lives and the lives of people affected by events around the world. Recent tsunamis around the world and flooding in the United States are examples of a way to engage students in this kind of critical thinking. Juxtaposing how the United States responded after Hurricane Katrina in New Orleans in 2005 and how the Japanese responded to the tsunami in March 2011 is an example of a global-local parallel.

Present Multiple Perspectives   This recommendation can be carried out with many strategies. One that is widely used is RAFT: Role, Audience, Form, and Time or Topic (Rutherford, 2008). In RAFT, students design scenarios about the content. Rutherford explains that students "rethink, rewrite, and discuss an event or concept in another place or time or through the eyes or voice of the famous or familiar" (2008, p. 135). A similar strategy is Flip Side, in which a student chooses an issue, interviews six peers for their opinions, and explains the similarities or differences among their views (Rutherford, 2008). Rutherford's books include many strategies and are included on the resources list.

Interactive   To engage students in social studies, you should design lessons that are interactive. For example, plan lessons that incorporate multiple intelligences. The Delaware Social Studies Education Project (DSSEP) has a wonderful web page at http://www.udel.edu/dssep/index.html. Once at the site, follow the pedagogy link to the strategies for teaching social studies page.
     Suggested strategies to investigate include:

> Case study, concept formation, double exposure, dueling documents, fishbowl, gallery walk, inquiry, KWL, mock trials, model United Nations, moot court, post it poll, problem based learning, stay or stand, synectics, take a stand, and cooperative learning strategies: graffiti groups, teams-games-tournaments, think pair share, and jigsaw (Strategies for Teaching Social Studies, 2008).

Each strategy is a starting point for interactive lessons that engage students readily, and each strategy link offers ideas for different grade levels and for different content. A second great resource is the Georgetown Independent School District in Texas, which has an Instructional Strategies for Social Studies site (see the Appendix at the end of the book for the link). From this site, you can download Word documents and PowerPoint slides to use in your classroom. For example, one resource is a concept diagram, with two versions. Each graphic organizer includes boxes or lines to record information; one has picture cues to support organization and sequencing the task; the other has no picture cues. The variation is a great example of differentiated work (see Figure 15.4).
     When selecting a strategy, consider each group of students and individual student needs for each class. Some classes, by the nature of the particular class composition, will do well with activities that require respectful debate and challenging ideas. Other groups of students will need direct instruction about maintaining a class community that is respectful before being able to try such activities. The key to selecting strategies for any group is to first consider the needs and abilities of the students; as we have said before, begin with the students and select the activities that best support the learning the group needs.

Challenge Gently   Engaging students who are privileged in discussion of social justice must be a balance between exposure to unfamiliar content and nuance and

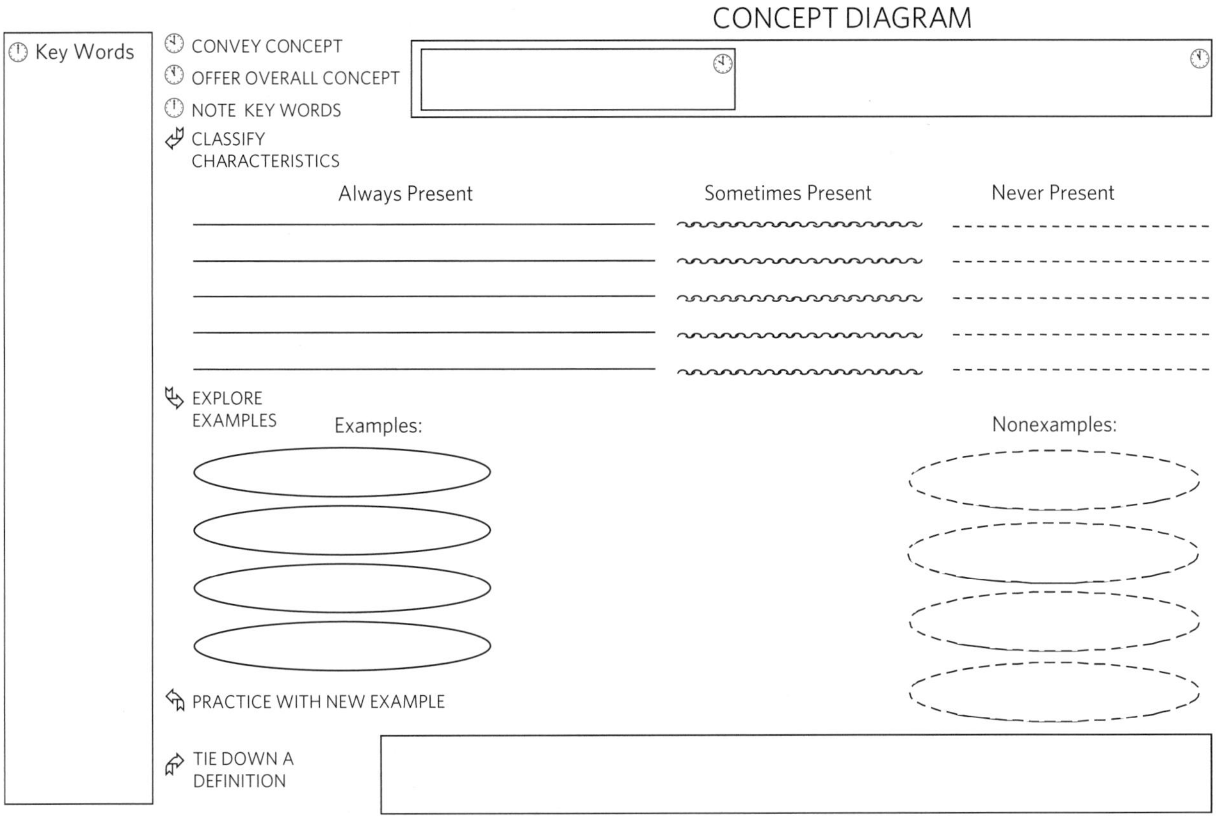

CONCEPT DIAGRAM

Key Words

- CONVEY CONCEPT
- OFFER OVERALL CONCEPT
- NOTE KEY WORDS
- CLASSIFY CHARACTERISTICS

| Always Present | Sometimes Present | Never Present |

EXPLORE EXAMPLES

Examples:

Nonexamples:

PRACTICE WITH NEW EXAMPLE

TIE DOWN A DEFINITION

Figure 15.4. Concept diagram. (From Georgetown Independent School District, Texas; reprinted by permission.)

support. Seider (2009) studied a group of privileged high school students in a Boston suburb and learned three lessons. First, knowledge can be overwhelming (p. 55). The size and scope of social problems, such as malnutrition and global poverty, immobilized rather than empowered students. He suggested that you consider how to develop positive emotions, such as hope and inspiration, by presenting information about solutions and innovations as well as sobering facts and figures. Second, Seider found that after students had been taught about poverty, students were afraid of experiencing it themselves. To address this, he recommends formal perspective-taking exercises and introducing students to the work of visionaries. Third, students responded negatively to radical arguments. He had students read Peter Singer's essay about solving world poverty and found that students responded to Singer's ideas with scorn. In his essay, Singer said:

> I can see no escape from the conclusion that each one of us with wealth surplus to his or her essential needs should be giving most of it to help people suffering from poverty so dire as to be life-threatening. That's right: I'm saying that you shouldn't buy that new car, take that cruise, redecorate the house or get that pricey new suit. (Singer, 1999)

Students responded to the essay with suspicion, resentment, and trivialization (Seider, 2009, p. 57). Seider proposed that, instead of just radical readings, you present radical readings as well as more balanced perspectives to help students reconcile many viewpoints.

Input

Howard Zinn said that a problem in teaching history has been "the emphasis in teaching American history through the eyes of the important and powerful people, through the presidents, the Congress, the Supreme Court, the generals, the industrialists" (Bigelow, 2008, p. 8). The problem is not that this information is not important; the problem is that so much important information is omitted. In this section, we review strategies for providing input for all students: use resources beyond the textbook, design thematic units, use primary sources, and use digital resources.

Use Resources Beyond the Textbook   Jeffrey Liles noted that one of the most important things to remember when teaching social studies is that you are the teacher, and you can design a curriculum (or work with a team to design a curriculum). That is, do not allow a textbook to constrain the lessons, activities, information sources, and assessments you plan. A textbook may be a good starting point but should never be the only source of information for students. We are emphasizing this because we know that teachers do not always feel as though they have input or authority related to choosing what materials students use. In fact, Alter noted that "educators often support the use of standardized textbooks because they believe they have no other choice" (Sapp, 2009, p. 74). As we said in the Input section, teachers need to advocate for materials that help engage all students—and using many sources is an integral strategy to do this.

primary sources
Original material.

Use Primary Sources   An excellent resource beyond the textbook is primary sources. **Primary sources** are original documents, files, audiotapes, and videotapes. The advent of the Internet and scanned documents has made an enormous range of primary documents available online. One example is the Library of Congress at http://www. loc.gov/index.html. The Library of Congress is "the nation's oldest federal cultural institution and serves as the research arm of Congress. It is also the largest library in the world, with millions of books, recordings, photographs, maps and manuscripts in its collections" (About the Library, 2011, para. 1). The resources available mean that students with access to computers at school should always be able to use primary sources in their research and review of materials.

For example, Martin Luther King's "I Have a Dream" speech is a primary source. Reviews or critiques of Dr. King's speech that refer to it are secondary sources. In social studies, it is essential that primary sources be valued and used. A textbook is a secondary source that tells students about primary sources. The danger in using a secondary source is the interpretation of what is important in the primary sources. Two secondary sources about Dr. King's speech may interpret it very differently. In Figure 15.5, look at the two perspectives on Dr. King's speech.

San Diego State University faculty were interested in using Dr. King's speech to help students understand Dr. King's background, the times, and the way he used a diverse range of references to reach a broad audience. Faculty were also vested in having students listen to the entire speech instead of reading it silently. *Presentation Magazine* was interested in analyzing what made the speech memorable. Both critiques are valuable resources, but the primary source—the speech itself—is an essential beginning of the lesson so that students have access to the same material as the sources that critique it.

Educating students about the way history can be interpreted differently by different people is important, and if you are not providing students with access to primary sources and teaching them how to evaluate secondary sources, you are not preparing them to think critically.

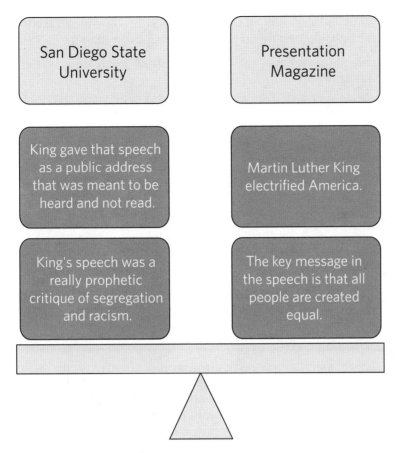

Figure 15.5. "I Have a Dream" critiques. (*Sources:* Coartney, 2007; Edwards, 2010.)

Use Digital Resources   We have talked about the importance of moving beyond a single text and using primary documents, and both dovetail neatly with using digital resources. Engagement with materials can be dramatically improved by changing the format in which material is presented. For example, YouTube or TeacherTube can bring content into your classroom in a way that is far more interesting than reading from a text. Review all content you plan to use for appropriateness and length.

An important consideration for any media you use is how accessible it is to students who do not see or hear. A solution that is universally designed is the Universal eLearner, which provides two tiers of captioning and two tiers of audio description (Sapp, 2009). Captioning and audio description provide universal access to media that is inaccessible to some students, and also support the learning of students who are learning English, who struggle with visual or auditory input, or who benefit from support with organization.

The Indiana Board of Education was willing to consider alternatives to traditional textbooks in social studies, and a group of teachers took advantage of the opportunity. These teachers used Universal Design for Learning to support their search for new materials, and in the process used a resource called netTrekker (Thinkronize, Inc.) as their database for digital resources (Nelson, Arthur, Jensen, & Van Horn, 2011).

Design Thematic Units   **Thematic units** are a series of lessons focused around a central idea or enduring understanding. Thematic units can last 1 to 6 weeks, and are

thematic units   A series of lessons focused around a central idea or enduring understanding. Thematic units can last 1 to 6 weeks, and are organized around a place, event, era, phenomena, entity, or people (Horton & Barnett, 2008).

organized around a place, event, era, phenomena, entity, or people (Horton & Barnett, 2008). Thematic units are best designed by following these six steps:

1.   Limit the scope—accept that you cannot and *should* not teach everything there is to know about the topic.

2.   Identify what is important—ask yourself: "What is the point of teaching this topic to students?"

3.   Create the enduring understanding—the big idea we want students to know, understand, and appreciate.

4.   Plan the conclusion—working backward from the end will help you design the summative assessment. Remember that the assessment must evaluate students' knowledge and comprehension of the enduring understanding.

5.   Plan the introduction—which includes telling students three things: 1) how learning will be assessed, 2) the criteria for evaluation, and 3) the enduring understanding statement. Be sure the enduring understanding is in grade-appropriate language.

6.   Develop the body—beginning from the introduction, scaffold lessons in sequence. A way to evaluate whether or not to include an activity is to ask: Does it contribute to a greater awareness of the enduring understanding? If not, do not include it (Horton & Barnett, 2008).

Using these steps or a similar process of planning is well suited to considering the needs of all students in the classroom. For example, if you have students who are learning English or who struggle with reading for another reason, you will be able to see where you can provide alternatives that lead toward the enduring understanding while meeting student needs and providing appropriate challenges.

Output and Assessment

Output and assessment strategies to support all students include providing choice. The output of social studies instruction can vary from multiple-choice tests, to essays, to oral presentations, to poster sessions, and mixed-media displays. The best strategy with output is to establish the goals and objectives for the unit and communicate those goals to students so they know what they are expected to learn. Once students know what they need to be able to do, you can provide a range of options for how they demonstrate that learning.

Incorporate Multiple Ways to Show Mastery   Writing, presenting, and preparing artwork in a single medium or multiple media are all possible outputs. In Chapter 13, Reading Strategies for All Students, you learned that teaching with only the summative assessment in mind is not useful. Instead, providing many ways for students to demonstrate mastery of content gives students with different learning styles and needs ways to reach high standards.

Some teachers offer a menu of options (as in Chapter 7) and ask students to select the product that they are most comfortable developing. For example, in a thematic unit about the Civil War, one middle-school student might decide to show what she has learned through a report on five different documents, another student creates a 3-minute movie reenacting two perspectives of a single battle, and a third creates a collage that incorporates 10 significant facts from the Civil War that have connections to our lives in the 21st century. Finally, a group of students asks for a traditional pencil-and-paper exam that covers the content of the textbook and additional resources that everyone accesses. If you have prepared a list of objectives for the theme and students know what they need to show you, all of these options can develop the skills we want to see students use in social studies.

Incorporate Critical Thinking   Teaching students how to think deeply about what they are learning is one of the single most important tasks of social studies. In each strategy option, there are opportunities to challenge students to think deeply about their perspective, why they hold it, and to support their opinion with information and insight.

When developing units and the enduring understandings you want students to learn, use Bloom's taxonomy (introduced in Chapter 5) to prepare assessments that require students not only to know and comprehend the content, but also to apply, analyze, synthesize, and evaluate it. Table 15.1 is an example for a thematic unit on gender roles for a ninth-grade class.

Table 15.1.   Critical thinking skills from a thematic unit on gender roles

Enduring understanding: Gender roles have a pervasive effect on opportunities for girls and women throughout the world

Levels of Bloom's taxonomy	Tasks associated with each level	Sample assessment tasks for the unit
Knowledge: Finding or remembering information	arrange, define, duplicate, label, list, memorize, name, order, recognize, relate, recall, repeat	Local: arrange a list of elected officials for the town by gender Global: arrange a list of presidents of 20 countries by gender
Comprehension: Understanding information	classify, describe, discuss, explain, express, restate, review, select, translate	Local: discuss leadership opportunities for women in the home town and state Global: express the percentage of female presidents in the world through line and pie graphs
Application: Using information	apply, choose, demonstrate, dramatize, employ, illustrate, interpret, operate, practice, solve, use	Local: interpret what the number of leadership opportunities for women means for male and female students and the community Global: use information about the percentage of female presidents in the world to illustrate the balance of power men and women have in the world
Analysis: Taking information apart	analyze, appraise, categorize, compare, contrast, criticize, differentiate, discriminate, distinguish, examine, experiment, question, test	Local: look at degrees held by women leaders in the community to determine preparation and experience needed for these roles Global: compare the number of female presidents to the number of male presidents in the world from 1950 to today and relate to views on gender in those countries
Synthesis: Creating new information	assemble, compose, construct, create, design, develop, formulate, manage, organize, plan, prepare, propose, set up	Local: develop a plan for the community to increase or sustain the current number of female elected officials Global: assemble a binder of materials about leadership opportunities for girls and women in countries with female presidents
Evaluation: Making judgments about information	appraise, argue, assess, defend, judge, predict, rate, score, select, support, value	Local: appraise the community related to opportunities for women to be elected into office Global: select a country with a high percentage of female elected officials and assess factors that support female leadership

SUMMARY

In this chapter, we introduced the National Council for the Social Studies standards and emphasized the importance of teaching critical thinking skills, connections between local and global communities, sweeping themes, and a sense of responsibility to the community. We reviewed strategies to support all students in engagement, input, output, and assessment, including using thematic units and primary documents to develop responsive differentiated lessons that meet the needs of every student.

CHAPTER 16

Math Strategies
for All Students

How this chapter prepares you to be
an effective inclusive classroom teacher:

- This chapter gives you several examples of evidence-based instructional strategies for math. According to the principles of universal design for learning (UDL), you will learn about strategies for multiple ways of engaging students, multiple ways for students to access new information, and multiple ways for students to express their understanding of mathematical knowledge and concepts. You will also learn about culturally and linguistically responsive teaching in the area of mathematics. **This helps you meet CEC Standard 4: Instructional Strategies.**

- This chapter teaches you multiple ways of assessing mathematical understanding and gives you examples of formal and informal math assessments. You will also learn about using assessment results to plan future instruction. **This helps you meet CEC Standard 8: Assessment.**

- This chapter prepares you to be a professional and ethical teacher by teaching you the importance of being sensitive to the diversity of students. It also teaches you that no two students learn math the same way. You will learn that your role as teacher is to individualize all aspects of teaching to meets students' needs and that learning how to do this is a lifelong learning process. **This helps you meet CEC Standard 9: Professional and Ethical Practice.**

After reading and discussing this chapter, you will be able to

- Explain the significance of the National Council of Teachers of Mathematics (NCTM) and the Common Core State Standards (CCSS) on the teaching of mathematics

- Explain the importance of culturally relevant teaching of mathematics

- Explain gender issues in the context of teaching mathematics

- Describe multiple ways to engage diverse students in mathematics and provide several examples

- Describe the importance of literature, music, art, emotion, choice, and self-regulation for engaging students in mathematics

- Describe multiple ways to represent mathematical concepts and language to students and provide several examples

- Describe multiple ways that students can express their mathematical understanding and provide several examples

- Explain the difference between formal and informal math assessments and the significance of each

The following account is one of our personal experiences:

About 12 years ago, I was observing a student teacher as she taught a math lesson dividing fractions to an inclusive fifth-grade class. She was using transparent Cuisinaire rods on an overhead projector (well before the Smart Board's time). Each pair of students had a set of the manipulatives as well. As she demonstrated with hands-on visuals how dividing a fraction of the whole would result in even smaller pieces of the whole, and how that led to a quotient with a greater denominator, I broke my usual subtle presence as an observer in the classroom to exclaim, "OHHHH!!!" It was the first time I had ever understood the concept behind division of fractions. Thirty years old, with a Ph.D., observing a student teacher, I finally truly understood that part of my fourth-grade math. In school, I was considered good in math. That is, I always earned good grades in math, because I was able to memorize the steps I was taught to follow to arrive at the correct answer on homework and tests. I never enjoyed math, though. I did not always understand the concepts behind the steps or know exactly why I was doing those steps. I simply went through the motions. So, when dividing fractions, I just flipped the second fraction and multiplied. It was a student teacher more than 20 years later who taught me why.

This account provides two lessons. First, a student who does not seem to be struggling in math needs differentiated math instruction. Memorizing the steps to follow in one prescribed way to arrive at one correct answer is not always enough to engage the student in math enough to truly understand it, enjoy it, and want to learn more. Second, a student who *is* struggling in math and/or has trouble remembering the steps of an algorithm needs differentiated math instruction to become engaged enough to understand it, enjoy it, and want to learn more.

There is a growing need in our work force for problem-solving and critical-thinking skills. Procedural or rule-driven knowledge is not paramount anymore (Gargiulo and Metcalf, 2010). Silverman (2002) said, "The left hemispheric curriculum of reading, handwriting, and calculating, which dominated schools for centuries, is obsolete. Instead of worshipping the printing press, schools will need to prepare students for the computer-based, visually-oriented careers that await them" (pp. iii–iv).

What this means for you as a teacher is that you need to be prepared to teach mathematical reasoning and thinking, how to use technology, and how to use visual skills regularly.

Two national organizations have set forth standards for mathematics instruction in the 21st century. The **National Council of Teachers of Mathematics (NCTM)** outlined these essential standards for students in grades K–12:

- Numbers and Operations: understand numbers, meaning of operations, and have computer fluency

- Algebra: understand patterns, relations and functions; represent and analyze mathematical situations; use mathematical models; and analyze change

- Geometry and Spatial Sense: analyze characteristics and properties of geometric shapes; specify locations and describe spatial relationships; apply transformations; and use visualization, spatial relations, and modeling to solve problems

- Measurement: understand measurable attributes and apply appropriate techniques and tools

- Data Analysis and Probability: formulate questions and display relevant data to answer them, select and use appropriate methods to analyze data, develop and evaluate inferences and predictions, understand and apply basic concepts of probability

- Process: problem solving, reasoning and proof, communication, connections, and representation.

The **Common Core State Standards (CCSS)** for mathematics practice are as follows:

- Make sense of problems and persevere in solving them.

- Reason abstractly and quantitatively.

- Construct viable arguments and critique the reasoning of others.

- Model with mathematics.

- Use appropriate tools strategically.

- Attend to precision.

- Look for and make use of structure.

- Look for and express regularity in repeated reasoning. (Common Core State Standards Initiative, n.d.)

These standards are in place to ensure that students are college-ready or prepared for the workplace. The NCCC standards focus on teaching reading in all curricular content areas so that in all subject areas, math included, students will be able to access and understand complex texts. Texts will not just be books but may include online journal articles and digital materials (Hill, 2011). So, if students are expected to access a variety of resources, we as teachers must understand and be competent in their use, too.

An important issue in achieving this goal is the consideration of **culturally relevant teaching**. For mathematics, this means ensuring that concepts are presented in such a way that students of all cultures and genders and speakers of all languages are engaged and see how the concepts apply to them in daily life; can access and comprehend the concepts, vocabulary, and symbol systems of mathematics; and are given a variety of opportunities and tools to express multiple ways of solving mathematical problems, and those expressions are assessed equitably. To do this, teachers must know their students.

National Council of Teachers of Mathematics (NCTM) A national organization that works to provide standards and guidelines for equitable, high-quality math instruction for all students.

Common Core State Standards (CCSS) A national curriculum that outlines a consistent, clear understanding of what students are expected to learn, so teachers and parents know what they need to do to help them.

culturally relevant teaching Pedagogy that responds to all students' cultural backgrounds, learning needs, and interests so that they can be successful academically.

Just as there is no one set of strategies for math that is effective for all students with a certain disability label, there is no one set of strategies for math that is effective for all students from a certain race, ethnic background, or gender. For any student, if she is valued for who she is and respected and responded to for the various supports and creative ideas needed to help her grasp concepts, the teaching is responsive and relevant. The conceptual framework underlying differentiation that we discussed in Chapter 7 is synonymous with the belief system of culturally relevant teaching. Culturally relevant teachers believe that all children can be competent regardless of race or social class. They scaffold students between what they know and what they do not know, focus on engaging instruction rather than behavior management, extend students' thinking, and demonstrate extensive knowledge of students and of the subject matter (Ladson-Billings, 1995). Culturally diverse students can be successful in math if their teacher believes they can be and creates a curriculum that is universally designed for learning.

This is also true of gender. Recent studies indicate that there is not a gap in mathematics ability between boys and girls, as once thought (Burkley, Parker, Stermer, & Burkley, 2010; Else-Quest, 2010; Hyde & Mertz, 2009). Rather, cultural influences and societal expectations contribute to girls' beliefs about their math abilities and their interest in the subject. If teachers believe that both girls and boys are competent in math and provide a multitude of strategies for mastering the concepts, the performance gap will continue to decrease.

mathematical language
Systems, vocabulary, symbols and numbers used to communicate mathematical ideas and concepts.

For students who are English Language Learners (ELL), there has been a myth that mathematics would be the easiest content area for them to master because it can be taken out of the context of language. After all, it's just numbers and symbols, right? Irujo (2007) reminded us that the answer is no. There is a significant language base to mathematics that can be difficult for ELL students because the words and phrases do not translate perfectly from one language to the next. There are many concepts that rely on positional, relational, and syntactical understandings that come across differently in different languages. It is not enough to remove the concepts from language. Teachers must find ways for ELL students to make sense of **mathematical language.**

The strategies described in Figure 16.1 and in the second section respond to these issues. The strategies are presented by engagement, input, output, and assessment.

STRATEGIES FOR TEACHING MATH TO ALL STUDENTS

Engagement

There are many strategies and lesson ideas you can employ to engage students in math. Here, we present many different engagement strategies in four categories: literature, music and art; connections to real life and emotion; choice; and self-regulation strategies.

Literature, Music, and Art   The first category of engagement strategies is about literature, music, and art. Incorporating these into math instruction is important. It makes each lesson a cross-curricular lesson. Also, age-appropriate literature, poetry, music, and art forms that incorporate math concepts show students math in context.

There are many children's and young-adult books with math themes. Here is a list of web sites where you can find dozens for various age levels:

- Aurora University—Books about math and numbers at http://libguides.aurora.edu/content.php?pid=48714&sid=693429. This web site lists many books about math concepts, many of them with nature themes.

- Children's Picture Books at http://www.childrenspicturebooks.info/math_picture_books.htm. Here you will find a long list of picture books about math by many authors and illustrators.

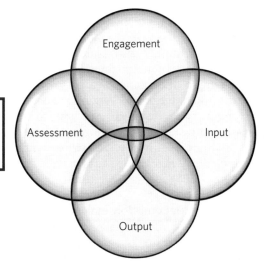

Figure 16.1. Engagement strategies.

- Greg Tang's web site at http://www.gregtang.com/. Greg Tang writes many different picture books about math. This web site includes all of his titles as well as math-centered kits and puzzles.

- Math Cats' Math and Literature Idea Bank at http://www.mathcats.com/grown upcats/ideabankmathandliterature.html. This web site will show you many different ways of using literature in math lessons.

- National Association for the Education of Young Children—Math Related Children's Books at http://tyc.naeyc.org/articles/pdf/MathbookslistSchickedanzexcerpt.pdf. This is the link to an annotated bibliography of picture books.

- Oklahoma Panhandle State University's Math Fiction at http://www.opsu.edu/www/education/Math%20Fiction.htm. This web site lists and summarizes several young adult fiction books that emphasize math concepts.

Music is an effective way to engage learners in math lessons. Schoolhouse Rock provides many music videos about multiplication. The entire collection is on DVD. Also, the web site Songs for Teaching: Using Music to Promote Learning at http://www.songsforteaching.com/mathsongs.htm offers several math ditties.

Another way to increase engagement in math is to use art. Seeing math concepts in artwork and photography shows a different side of the subject area. Paula Kluth and Sheila Danaher show us one way to do this in their book *From Tutor Scripts to Talking Sticks: 100 Ways to Differentiate Instruction in K–12 Inclusive Classrooms*. Their idea is to take or find photos that illustrate concepts being introduced (2010, p. 78). For example, a photograph of a bicycle wheel can be used to illustrate radius, diameter, and circumference of a circle. Rather than just asking students to think of a wheel, actually showing a large photograph of a bicycle wheel is much more engaging.

Connection to Real Life and Emotion   The second category of engagement strategies includes those that help students make connections between the math concepts and their daily lives. This helps math "come to life" for them and helps them realize how math concepts can be important to them beyond the classroom and school performance. Also, an emotional connection to information makes it more meaningful and accessible.

Math in Daily Life at http://www.learner.org/interactives/dailymath/is a web site that describes how mastery of math concepts can help you in daily life situations, from leasing a car to playing at the casino. Geared toward middle and high school, this can help answer the oft-asked question, "When am I ever going to use this?"

Another strategy is to tie math concepts to important societal problems that need to be solved. Some students have a raised awareness of and sensitivity to global issues. Students are more readily engaged when taught math concepts in the context of social justice (Rapp, 2009). *Rethinking Mathematics: Teaching Social Justice by the Numbers* (Gutstein & Peterson, 2005) is an excellent resource for showing students how math is valuable and authentic.

Fitzell (2005) wrote that emotion makes curriculum meaningful, and this applies to math as well. Her advice was to make examples a story, to read with dramatization, and to use a gripping picture. Just one example could be to tell the story of a family who lost their home in a tornado or flood and show a news clipping and photo of damaged property. The class can then set to work planning what the family needs and how much money it will cost to rebuild or replace what was lost. Allowing students to share their own similar stories is an important part of engaging them.

Math centers that you can set up to mimic real-life situations will encourage students to engage in math practice. A classroom market with money, coupons, produce scales, and recipes is one idea. A quilting station, where students measure fabric and patch together patterns of cloth, is another idea.

Choice   The third category of engagement strategies is choice. Any time that a student can make his or her own choice about learning, engagement is increased. The homework menus presented in Chapter 7 are a great example. Figure 16.2 shows a menu for math.

In addition to menus, tiered math problems provide choices with just the right amount of challenge for individual students. For any math problem, provide options of increasing difficulty from an introductory level to a more sophisticated level. Wormeli (2007) provided an example for finding the surface area of three-dimensional solids. From least to most sophisticated, the tiers could be: determine the surface area of a cube; determine the surface area of a rectangular prism; determine the amount of wrapping paper needed to cover a rectangular box; determine how many cans of paint you'll need to buy to paint a house with given dimensions, if one can of paint covers 46 square feet (p. 84). Once students choose a starting point, the teacher can guide them through increasing levels of mastery.

Another way to offer choice to students is to allow them to work in different group sizes. Activities can be done by the whole class or half the class, in small groups or teams of various size, partners, triads, or by individual study (Wormeli, 2007). Fitzell (2005) offered some examples of ways to collaborate on math problems:

- Solve problems with a partner; one solves while one explains

- Solve complex story problems in a small group; make sure everyone contributes

- Have teams construct problems linking many math operations, then solve them (p. 158).

Choose and complete three activities in a row.

There are 25 students in the class. To complete a craft project, each student needs 3 pipe cleaners. Write an equation to show how many pipe cleaners are needed in all. Draw a picture model to go with it.	Your teacher is correcting math homework. A student multiplied 32×5 and wrote the answer as 150. If you were the teacher, how would you explain to the student how to correctly solve the problem?	Solve the problem 48×4 two different ways
Create a "caterpillar" that has seven body parts: OOOOOO(58) Place prime numbers in each body part so that the sum of the numbers equals 58.	Which product do you think will be greater? Why? $38 \times 9 =$ $3 \times 89 =$	Your brother has 15 stuffed animals. Your friend has twice as many as your brother. You have a third as many as your friend. Write an equation to show how you figured out how many you have.
Make a collage of items that can be divided into equal parts or fractions.	Interview a classmate about ways that multiplication and division are used in daily life.	You are bringing a birthday treat to school. There are 24 people including yourself and the teacher. You buy a bag of 72 candies. Write an equation to show how each person received equal amounts and how many are left over.

Figure 16.2.   Math menu. (Adapted from Westphal, L.E. [2007]. *Differentiating with menus: Math.* Waco, TX: Prufrock Press, Inc. http://www.prufrock.com.)

Self-Regulation Strategies   The last category of engagement strategies is ways to help students regulate and monitor their own understanding and work. The first part of this is to make sure that students are working in a setting that is free of as many distractions and threats as possible. By threats, we mean anything that might make the student feel uncomfortable—physically or emotionally—frustrated, or insecure. The case of Beth's fourth-grade classroom in Chapter 8 included many strategies for keeping discomfort and distraction to a minimum. The quiet area where students can choose between various seating options or use a clipboard under softer lighting is just one example. Allowing students the opportunity to share their thinking can be engaging, but demanding that they present orally to the class unexpectedly can be threatening.

Gargiulo & Metcalf (2010) shared examples of strategies that increase engagement because they help students regulate their own learning. Teachers can provide **graphic organizers** to fill out, **mnemonics** to rehearse, and strategy posters to review. Silverman (2002) also encouraged the use of mnemonics. OnlineMathLearning.Com at http://www.onlinemathlearning.com/math-mnemonics.html includes several mnemonics for many different math concepts. LINCS is a research-based mnemonic strategy to assist in remembering new vocabulary: list the parts; imagine a picture; note a reminding word; construct a story; and self-test your memory.

Input

There are many different ways that you can represent math concepts to students to increase their understanding. This section covers multiple representations of math concepts in three categories: visual, auditory, and tactile input; teaching math language; and anchoring activities.

Visual, Auditory, and Tactile Input   The first category of representation or input strategies includes ways that make math visual, auditory, and tactile so that different

graphic organizers
Visual representations of knowledge, ideas, or concepts. They can come in many different formats, including webs or charts.

mnemonic   A memory aid. An example of a mnemonic is the acronym ROY G. BIV to denote the colors in a rainbow—red, orange, yellow, green, blue, indigo, and violet.

modality A mode of sensing and processing information, such as visual, auditory, and tactile modalities.

types of learners can experience new information through their preferred **modality**, while also being exposed to math in other ways.

Improving input includes presenting text in print as well as digital media that can be changed (read aloud, written in Braille, highlighted, enlarged, bordered) as needed. Accessible Instructional Materials (AIM) Navigator at http://aim.cast.org/experience/decision-making_tools/aim_navigator provides alternatives to print-based textbooks in all content areas.

A visual strategy is called Math in Sight (Kluth & Danaher, 2010). This is a way to illustrate math concepts visually and three-dimensionally. This might include taping the digital time equivalents (:05, :10, :15) around the face of an analog clock; breaking down and labeling the classroom schedule into halves or thirds; and marking length measurements around the classroom walls in feet, yards, and meters (p. 204).

Auditory strategies include using a tape recorder during lessons for the student to listen to afterward; class discussions about each new concept; having students restate new information to themselves or a partner; say important things three times with the saying "this is triple important"; assign strong note-takers to take notes with carbon paper underneath their paper so there are instantly copies for the students who need to focus on just listening; have students read their texts, notes and tests out loud (speaking into a u-shaped tube will limit distractions for others); have students explain the new concepts to someone else (even a pet); and change the volume or tone of your voice for new words or phrases (Arem, 2009).

Some learners need to touch and feel things to learn best. A program called Touch Math at http://www.touchmath.com provides a way to teach numeration, addition, subtraction, multiplication, and division by using the "TouchPoints" of each number. Kluth and Danaher (2010) showed how tactile numbers made with yarn, glue, pipe cleaners, sandpaper, or adapted rulers created with raised dots or marks can increase comprehension of numbers for tactile learners. Other helpful ideas include using real coins and paper dollars to teach money, working problems in shaving cream on the desk, and writing on different surfaces with different writing utensils (e.g., Smart Board and stylus pens, white board and dry erase markers) to vary tactile input. Stewart Dickinson has created three-dimensional Braille models of math concepts (http://emsh.calarts.edu/~mathart/Tactile_Math.html)

Teaching Math Language   The vocabulary and symbols of math can be difficult to learn for some students. Words and phrases introduced are specialized to mathematics and are not typically used in daily life. Some symbols such as +, –, and % are common, but others are not, such as the Greek letters for certain concepts or functions. It is important to find different ways to help students learn this language.

The Mathematics Glossary at http://www.learnalberta.ca/content/memg/index.html is a great resource to help students reinforce the meaning of words and phrases. Each vocabulary term is described and illustrated. Coded and cued assignments (Kluth & Danaher, 2010) can bring attention to keywords and symbols so students are aware of the language each time it is used in context. This simply entails circling or drawing a box around the key information in bright colors.

Gargiulo and Metcalf (2010) indicated strategies to increase mathematic communication. One way is to create math dictionaries. Each time a math lesson will include new vocabulary, the terms can be pretaught, using flash cards with the term, its definition, and a visual representation. Then all the cards can be hole-punched and kept on a ring for easy access during the subsequent lessons. All words should be shown through pictures and sign language to provide multimodal input.

Anchor Activities   Anchor activities are those that make comprehension connections for students. One way to anchor the concept of square root is to illustrate numbers with perfect squares on graph paper (Wormeli, 2007). For example, the number 9 would be illustrated as a square that is 3 boxes high and 3 boxes wide. Numbers that don't have perfect squares would have partial boxes on each side, but they would still be the same amount high as wide. To anchor the concept of simple interest, conduct a **simulation** where students invest paper money in your "bank" for a few days (Wormeli, 2007). Allow them to choose from different investment options that yield different results. Each school day could represent a calendar month or year, so they can see the return on their investment after a certain amount of time.

Charts and graphs are an excellent way of representing information or data in many different ways so that students can make sense of it (Bryant-Mole, 1994). A pie chart can show how much money is spent on each part of a budget or how time is spent on various activities. This is a more effective way for some students to understand relative amounts than to see numbers in a list. **Pictographs** can help a student remember information because the symbols or icons used can attach significance through the visual representation.

simulation An imitation of a real thing or process.

pictograph A visual representation that conveys meaning through its pictorial resemblance to the real thing.

Output

Once students have learned new information, they need to express it in some way so their progress can be assessed and further teaching can take place if necessary. Here are several ways that students can express what they know in three categories: tools, toys, and movement; multiple intelligences; and supports.

Tools, Toys, and Movement Math is a great content area for tools and toys. There are endless possibilities for things that can be used as counters or **manipulatives**: beads, blocks, bottle caps, LEGOs, erasers, candies, buttons, balls, tokens, and straws. Anything that can be collected, counted, grouped, or stacked provides alternative ways for students to express their knowledge of math concepts such as numeration, ordering, addition, subtraction, multiplication, division, and fractions. Kluth and Danaher (2010) added to this with their idea of a Manipulative Box (p. 201). Stacking trays or boxes can keep many different manipulatives sorted for student use whenever they need them. Variety is important. Individual students will prefer different items; plus, variety and choice are engaging. Cuisinaire (1995) offered a way to present fraction concepts with a product called Fraction Circles. Several disks—each a different color and each split into different fractions (whole, halves, thirds, fourths, sixths, and eighths)—stack to show fraction equivalents.

manipulatives Objects that can be touched, held, and manipulated to aid in the learning of a concept.

Assistive technology must also be considered for supporting student expression of learning. Assistive technology for math—ranging from low tech to high tech—includes all of the manipulatives mentioned above, plus abacuses, number lines, enlarged math worksheets, calculators (talking, large display, special features), talking clocks, alternative keyboards, and math software (Technology and Media Division of the Council for Exceptional Children & Wisconsin Assistive Technology Initiative, n.d.).

Games are an engaging way for students to practice math concepts independently, with a partner, or in a small group. Silverman (2002) shared that the board game Stratego© by Milton Bradley can be modified to practice multiplication facts during play. Place a fact on each piece. In an attack, the higher product wins the square. Math Sphere Board Games at http://www.mathsphere.co.uk/resources/MathSphereFreeResources Boardgames.htm offers several board games as well. Interactive online math games can be found at:

- Cool Math 4 Kids, http://www.coolmath-games.com/

- Math Playground. http://www.mathplayground.com/games.html

- Math Arcade on Fun Brain, http://www.funbrain.com/brain/MathBrain/Math Brain.html

- Multiplication.Com, http://www.multiplication.com/interactive_games.htm

- Woodland Maths Zone, http://www.woodlands-junior.kent.sch.uk/maths/

reproducibles
Templates, worksheets, and visual displays that can be copied or reproduced as needed by teachers for lessons.

Last, a fun way for students to do math individually at their desks—perhaps if they finish a task early—is Take It To Your Seat Math Centers by Evan-Moor (Norris, 2002). Books of templates can be purchased for various age levels. Each template contains all of the visuals, materials, and **reproducibles** needed to create a small math kit that fits in a shoebox or pocket folder or hangs on a clothes hanger. The pieces can be laminated to withstand wear and tear.

Multiple Intelligences   The next category of expression or output strategies is multiple intelligences. Here are examples of activities for students to do that appeal to various intelligences. Activities such as those in in Table 16.1 should be provided for all areas—both for students who find comfort in their preferred area as well as for students who are ready for a challenge in their nonpreferred area.

Table 16.1.   Activities for multiple intelligences

Multiple intelligences	Activities for students
Verbal-linguistic	• Write and perform fairytales that incorporate math concepts in the resolutions of their conflicts (Wormeli, 2007). • Respond to nonfiction writing prompts (LePatner et al., 2005). • Write a series of story problems for others to solve (Fitzell, 2005). • Make up puns using math vocabulary (Fitzell, 2005). • Create poems telling when to use different math operations (Fitzell, 2005).
Logical-mathematical	• Create charts and graphs (Bryant-Mole, 1994). • Create number sequences and have others find the pattern (Fitzell, 2005).
Bodily-kinesthetic	• Work through math equations on a Human Calculator (Kluth & Danaher, 2010, p. 212). • Estimate measures by touch (Fitzell, 2005). • Use bodies to show addition, subtraction, multiplication, and division. • Use geoboards and rubber bands to illustrate geometric shapes.
Musical-rhythmic	• Explain mathematical operations through songs or jingles (Fitzell, 2005). • Make up sounds for different math operations (Fitzell, 2005).
Visual-spatial	• Express math concepts in a comic strip. See *Comic Strip Math* (Greenberg, 1998) • Create art. See *Math Art* (Brunetto, 1997). • Create charts and graphs (Bryant-Mole, 1994). • Mind map proofs for geometry theorems (Fitzell, 2005). • Draw posters depicting math processes.
Interpersonal	• Explain how to work through a problem to others while they follow (Fitzell, 2005). • Solve problems with a partner, one solves and one explains (Fitzell, 2005). • Teach others how to use a calculator (Fitzell, 2005).
Intrapersonal	• Complete independent skill games. • Use the computer to practice skills or play online math games. • Self-test with flash cards. • Use classroom response systems (clickers) to gather student responses to math problems.
Naturalist	• Design classification charts for math formulas and operations (Fitzell, 2005).
Existentialist	• Solve social justice math problems from *Rethinking Mathematics: Social Justice by the Numbers* (Gutstein & Peterson, 2005).

Supports The last category for expression strategies includes supports to scaffold students who need additional support to show what they know. Sometimes students have difficulty managing all of the information they have learned and expressing it in a comprehensive way. Frayer Model concept cards can help with this (Gargiulo & Metcalf, 2010). Each card is split into four quadrants. Different information is written or illustrated in each quadrant—definition, facts and characteristics, examples and nonexamples.

Kluth and Danaher (2010) shared two examples of math support—the Math Helper Binder and the Preprinted Notebook. The Math Helper Binder contains reference materials for students to refer to while completing homework or other assessments. The contents are personalized and may include number lines, addition/subtraction or multiplication charts, place-value chart, list of common formulas, math vocabulary words with definitions, conversion tables, money-value equivalents, and key words or phrases used in word problems. The Preprinted Notebook is simply a notebook with all of the independent practice and homework problems written out for the student. For students who struggle with copying the problems correctly, this support allows them to use their effort toward solving the problem rather than copying. Fitzell (2005) offered a similar strategy for students who have trouble copying or lining up the place columns correctly—turn the loose-leaf paper sideways—instant columns!

Assessment

There are, as with all other content areas, formal and informal assessments for assessing performance in students. Formal assessments include district-, state- and nationwide assessments that determine whether particular standards have been met. The National Assessment of Educational Progress (NAEP) math assessment is an example of this. It is administered nationwide in grades four, eight, and twelve. The results tell us broadly what students in the United States can do in math at those three levels. Formal assessments can also be used to determine if a student has a particular weakness or disability in math. These diagnostic tests are administered individually and provide a detailed look at the particular knowledge and skills a student has or does not have. The Test of Mathematical Abilities—Second Edition (TOMA-2) is an example.

Informal assessments in daily classroom practice give us different, yet equally important, information about students' math abilities. Jarrett (1999) found that informal, formative assessment before, during and after instruction is critical for diverse learners because they need many opportunities to demonstrate their ideas and progress. These assessments also help teachers reflect on ways to improve instruction for struggling students and meet varied needs as they arise. The next section discusses many different ways that teachers can accomplish formative assessment.

Assessment Ideas

Learning contracts were one idea put forth by Tomlinson (2003). A learning contract provides practice for an individual student in his or her areas of need. Contracts can be constructed in a variety of formats but are most effective if they have certain components: clarification of goals for a particular unit of study; indication of the student's current proficiency; a set of tasks, activities, and teaching sessions that prompt students toward the clarified goals; and expectations for work time and organization.

Jarrett (1999) listed several assessments that are effective in evaluating progress in math: portfolio assessments, concept maps, performance assessments, and rubrics. A portfolio assessment is a collection of evidence that demonstrates a student's ability to

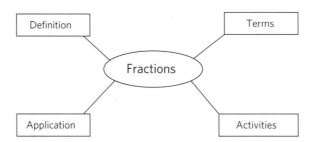

Figure 16.3.   Concept map.

reflect on conceptual understanding, solve through problems, and communicate about math. An example of an entry in a portfolio assessment may be the graph that a student created depicting data gathered through a classroom survey. The student's explanation of his or her work can be written by the student or scribed by the teacher and attached to the graph. Concept maps, or webs, can be used to assess how a student organizes his or her thoughts about a particular math concept. An example of a completed concept map is shown in Figure 16.3.

authentic With a real-life purpose or application. An authentic activity in the classroom is one that connects the activity to daily life to increase the likelihood that the students will be engaged in the activity and apply it in other contexts.

Performance assessments entail the teacher's evaluating the student's skills by observing her performing a task or applying a task in context. The more realistic and **authentic** the performance, the better. Observing a student measure the classroom and calculate how much carpet is needed or observing the student cook while halving or doubling a recipe is authentic. Two different types of rubrics can then be used to assess the student's performance. Holistic rubrics evaluate the final product, and analytical rubrics evaluate the process used to reach the end product. For students struggling with new math concepts, analytical rubrics are preferred because they can determine specifically where the student is having the most trouble along the way.

Grading Alternatives

An effective way to differentiate assessment for diverse learners is to provide alternatives to traditional letter or number grades. Fitzell (2005) indicated that it is fair and responsive to offer alternatives. Some ways to do this include varying the weights on different parts of an assignment; grade based on improvement or change in performance rather than final product; base the grade on process rather than product; base the grade on progress toward achieving IEP goals; or base the grade on criteria defined previously on a learning contract.

SUMMARY

Many of the strategies discussed in the sections above fit more than one area of the UDL components—engagement, input, output, and assessment. For example, Math Snapshots are engaging and a great way to provide visual input. If students collect or take photographs, this simple idea can be used for output and assessment.

Also, these strategies are just a start. We certainly do not intend this to be a comprehensive list. It is a jump start to get you thinking about all the creative ways you can teach and assess math skills and knowledge. Keep searching for and collecting different ideas for all types of learners. Communication with colleagues is an important way to gather as well as to develop brand new strategies.

Remember that math is for everyone. Research tells us that there are still expectations for some students to perform lower than others in math because of societal beliefs and influences. In some contexts, girls do better in math than boys because the social construction of math ability is that boys are not capable at math; the reverse is the social construction in the United States. Both constructions are limiting and need to be challenged.

Believe that all of your students are mathematicians and it is your job to bring that out in them. Make math real for all of your students so they see the value and authenticity of its use.

NARRATIVE 16.1. | MICHAEL, HIGH SCHOOL MATH TEACHER

They say teaching is a calling. They say you have to *want* it, *love* it, because otherwise you'll never survive it.

I think a lot of that sentiment is due to advocacy. As a teacher, you have to advocate for a huge variety of students—kids you're not related to, kids you never knew before they show up in a desk chair or on a piece of paper in your mailbox, kids you see for a mere hour every weekday for 18 or 36 weeks, and then maybe once or twice in the years that follow but in all likelihood never again, and certainly never in the same way. Kids who don't even care that you're trying to advocate on their behalf. Kids who might not even *have* an advocate besides you.

The new semester brought an opportunity for class switching—and with it, an opportunity to push for changes that I know will bring my students success.

There were some obstacles. It seems the counselors and the math department will forever be at odds over what happens when a student gets a D. The counselors are under the impression that a D first semester and a C second semester show enough improvement to move a student along to the next class in the math sequence, while the math department adamantly maintains that students must earn at least a C in *both* semesters to move on. At least it will be solved next year—we're officially getting rid of Ds. Anything below a 69.5% is an E.

I have a student in algebra 1 who works hard and generally stays pretty well focused but had a pretty consistent D all semester long—and ended up with a D+ for his overall semester grade. Thinking that this meant he would have to retake that first semester eventually anyway, I immediately recommended him for the algebra-loop class, which would really help him cement his algebra skills and get him really ready for algebra 1B next year. He's only a freshman this year, so he could take algebra 1B next year, geometry the year after that, and algebra 2 in his senior year to finish off his requirements with ease. His counselor recommended I run this by his parents so that they can make an informed decision, and when I sent his mother a long e-mail explaining his options, she responded positively to my recommendation of the loop. She told me she hadn't been sure at the beginning of the year if this was the right class for her son, thanked me for recognizing that he did put in a good amount of effort (I *always* find a positive for the parents—it's common courtesy and also an inevitable by-product of caring about your students), and asked whether the loop would fit into his schedule.

So I e-mailed the counselor back, armed with a formidable arsenal of genuine parental support and a perfect plan for minor changes to my student's schedule that would fit the loop nicely into place. I thought we were good to go, setting this student up for success and making sure he wouldn't have to go back and redo that first semester sometime later to get the C he needs to move on. It's at this point in our story that along comes a spider. The counselor asks me to remind the parent that a passing grade in the second semester will allow her son to move onto geometry (which is news to me), just in case that influences her decision. I pass along the information, and reiterate my recommendation that the loop class is still the best place for the student to gain really solid algebra skills to help him be successful in future math classes.

This last piece happened on the eve of the new semester. He arrived in my first-hour algebra class, thanked me on behalf of himself and his mom for all of my e-mails, and told me they'd decided he will stay in my regular algebra 1 class.

CHAPTER 17 Science Strategies for All Students

How this chapter prepares you to be an effective inclusive classroom teacher:

- This chapter gives you several examples of instructional strategies for science. According to the principles of universal design for learning, you will learn about strategies for multiple ways of engaging students, multiple ways for students to access new information, and multiple ways for students to express their understanding of scientific knowledge and concepts, critical thinking, and problem solving. You will also learn about culturally and linguistically responsive teaching in the area of science. **This helps you meet CEC Standard 4: Instructional Strategies.**

- This chapter teaches you multiple ways of assessing scientific understanding and gives you examples of formal and informal science assessments. You will also learn about using assessment results to plan future instruction. **This helps you meet CEC Standard 8: Assessment.**

- This chapter prepares you to be a professional and ethical teacher by teaching you the importance of being sensitive to the diversity of students. It also teaches you that no two students learn science the same way. You will learn that your role as teacher is to individualize all aspects of teaching to meets students' needs, and that learning how to do that is a lifelong learning process **This helps you meet CEC Standard 9: Professional and Ethical Practice.**

After reading and discussing this chapter, you will be able to

- Explain the significance of the National Committee on Science Education Standards and Assessment to the teaching of science

- Explain the importance of culturally relevant teaching of science

- Explain the difference among formal, symbolic, and societal curriculum and the teacher's role in each

- Describe multiple ways to engage diverse students in science and provide several examples

- Describe the importance of literature, music, art, connection to real life, and choice for engaging students in science

- Describe multiple ways to represent science concepts and language to students and provide several examples

- Describe multiple ways that students can express their scientific understanding and provide several examples

- Explain the difference among structured, guided, and student-directed inquiry and provide examples of each

- Explain the difference between performance-based and product-based science assessments and the significance of each

---

National Committee on Science Education Standards and Assessment A national organization that strives to define what it means to be scientifically literate and what all students—regardless of background or circumstance—should understand and be able to do at different grade levels in various science categories.

inquiry Process used to further knowledge or solve a problem.

The current state of affairs regarding U.S. students and science competency is a call for high-quality science education. Eicher (2007) stated that the 2005 National Assessment for Educational Performance (NAEP) indicates that only 29% of fourth and eighth graders and 18% of twelfth graders are at or above the proficiency level in science.

The **National Committee on Science Education Standards and Assessment** (1996) put forth eight categories of content standards:

1. Unifying concepts and processes in science

   - Systems, order, and organization

   - Evidence, models, and explanation

   - Change, constancy, and measurement

   - Evolution and equilibrium

   - Form and function

2. Science as **inquiry**

   - Understanding of scientific concepts

   - An appreciation of "how we know" what we know in science

   - Understanding of the nature of science

   - Skills necessary to become independent inquirers about the natural world

   - The dispositions to use the skills, abilities, and attitudes associated with science

3. Physical science

4. Life science

5. Earth and space science

6. Science and technology

7. Science in personal and social perspective

8. History and nature of science

An important aspect of the National Science Education Standards is the intent to work toward a change in what is emphasized as students learn science. The standards place less emphasis on knowing scientific facts and information, studying subject matter for its own sake, separating science knowledge and science process, covering many science topics, and implementing inquiry as a set of processes. What this means for you when teaching science is that balancing the realities of formative assessment that may give attention to this kind of information with the knowledge that those assessments are misguided. The standards place more emphasis on understanding scientific concepts and developing abilities of inquiry; learning subject matter in the context of inquiry, technology, and science in personal and social perspectives; integrating all aspects of science content; studying a few fundamental science concepts; and implementing inquiry as ideas to be explored and learned rather than as a set of processes to follow.

This is good news for a universal design for learning (UDL) science curriculum. An emphasis on inquiry can mean use of **active processes** and hands-on learning opportunities. There are great benefits for all students when they have opportunities to talk about processes and discoveries, engage all of their senses, and question and interact with each other, the materials, and the instructors. One thing to be aware of, however, is that science instruction may still rely heavily on textbooks and other **expository texts** that may disengage students who struggle with reading and/or need alternative representations of the information for optimal learning.

Gallard (2011) reminded us that it is vital for science teachers to be aware of and respond to the diverse perspectives and experiences that students bring to the classroom. The learning process is all about negotiating meaning from what is presented. If a student's base for making meaning is significantly different from others in the classroom, he or she will struggle. This base could rise from racial, ethnic, linguistic, or ability differences. In any case, a classroom where students have multiple, varied opportunities to engage, receive, and express learning is a culturally relevant and responsive classroom that meets the needs of all students.

Science is not free of cultural influence; science textbooks are not free of racism; and the history and development of science should not be solely attributed to European cultures (Gallard, 2011, p. 4). Because of this, students need to learn science in an environment that addresses these issues and consistently helps students see themselves as scientists.

Gay (2002) discussed three types of curricula and ways in which culturally responsive teachers address them. The first is **formal curriculum**, which is the official instruction and adopted textbooks approved by the governing bodies of the school system. Though improving over time, these methods and materials may still carry cultural bias. Culturally responsive teachers analyze the formal curriculum for these biases and adapt whenever needed to improve the quality. For science, this means making sure that lessons, activities, and assignments that accompany the curriculum incorporate all students' needs and backgrounds. The second type is **symbolic curriculum**, such as bulletin board decorations, trade books in the classroom, rules and regulations for the school or classroom, and tokens of achievement. Culturally responsive science teachers

active processes Ways in which students are actively involved in learning.

expository texts Type of writing where the purpose is to inform, explain, or describe how to do something.

formal curriculum The official instruction and adopted textbooks approved by the governing bodies of the school system.

symbolic curriculum What students learn from the ways in which cultural groups are displayed in classroom materials other than official instruction and textbooks, such as trade books, bulletin boards, awards, and certificates.

societal curriculum
What students learn from
the ways in which cultural
groups are displayed in
mass media.

know that these symbols are powerful and make sure that images displayed represent diversity of age, gender, social class, cultural background, ability, and learning style. The third type is **societal curriculum**—ways in which cultural groups are displayed in mass media. Culturally relevant teachers include their students in critical discussions about how cultural groups and experiences with science are portrayed in the media (Gay, 2002).

STRATEGIES FOR TEACHING SCIENCE TO ALL STUDENTS

In this section, we review strategies for teaching science to all students in the four areas of universal design for learning: engagement, input, output, and assessment, as illustrated in Figure 17.1.

Engagement

The strategies for engagement are presented in four categories: literature, music, and art; connections to real life and emotions; choice; and self-regulation strategies.

Literature, Music, and Art   Lessons that combine science, literature, music, and art are engaging and present scientific concepts in context. Also, as mentioned above,

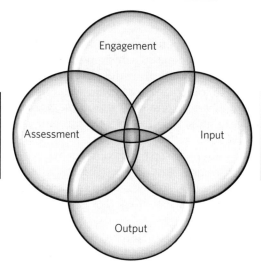

- Literature, music, and art
- Connection to real life
- Choice
- Self-regulation strategies

- Considerations for science
- Assessment ideas
- Grading alternatives

Engagement

Assessment   Input

Output

- Visual, auditory, tactile
- Teaching science language
- Anchoring activities

- Tools, toys, and movement
- Multiple intelligences
- Lesson-planning ideas
- Support strategies

Figure 17.1.   Strategies for teaching science.

expository texts may disengage students, and trade books may provide a greater chance for students to relate to the content. An example of a trade book for science is *Science Verse* by Jon Scieszka and Lane Smith (2004). This picture book contains fun, engaging poems about many scientific concepts, such as evolution, the water cycle, and the food chain. While the poems do not include all of the details the students need to learn about each concept, they do make great attention-grabbers at the beginning of a new lesson.

There are many children's and young adult books with science themes that provide more detail about various topics. The following web sites offer a range of titles for grades K-12:

- National Science Teachers Association—Outstanding Science Trade Books for Students K-12 at http://www.nsta.org/publications/ostb/

- Children's Picture Books at http://www.childrenspicturebooks.info/science_picture_books.htm

In addition, the Mediterranean Association of International Schools web site at http://www.scilitlinks.org/index.htm offers several activity ideas for linking science and literature in the elementary school grades. For example, the activity "All in the balance" pairs *Mirette on the High Wire* by Emily Arnold McCully (1992) with a lesson on measurement with balance scales. The National High Magnetic Field Laboratory's Magnet Lab web site at http://www.magnet.fsu.edu/education/community/scienceinliterature/ offers the equivalent for older students and adults.

Another effective way of engaging students in the concepts of science is to incorporate music and art. Beginning any lesson with a rock song about nature or displaying pottery with bird-track imprints is sure to grab attention. Acorn Naturalists at http://www.acornnaturalists.com/store/index.aspx is full of fun links to science art and songs about science and nature. The rock band, They Might Be Giants, has a 2-disc DVD set of science songs entitled *Here Comes Science*. Topics include the periodic table of elements, paleontology, blood, and the solar system.

Schmidt (2005) described a lesson in a senior elective physics class where the student teacher used drums, guitars, and vocal cords to illustrate properties of sound. Students were enthusiastic about participating and learning new vocabulary words, such as oscilloscope, resonance, natural frequency, amplitude, and sound waves, because they were interested in the musical context.

As a way to incorporate art and cultural background knowledge, Boutte, Kelly-Jackson, and Johnson (2010) shared a science project called Cell Analogies Collage. Students were required to choose 10 vocabulary words from a new unit on cell biology and display the definition/context of those words in a collage depicting an analogy of their own. One student's project entitled *Let the Cells Say Amen*, compared parts of the cell to roles in her church (nucleus = God, chloroplast = pastor, microvilli = congregation). The opportunity to bring a piece of who they are to the assignment and to create a visual representation engages the students in meaningful learning of detailed scientific content.

Connections to Real Life   The second category of engagement strategies for science includes ways to connect science to real life. To engage students in learning science, it is important for them to see how it applies to their daily lives outside of school. Centers in the classroom that connect with home and community activities that are familiar to the students will help make these connections. For example, the market center described in Chapter 16 that teaches math concepts of money, weight, and fractions, can also teach about the food pyramid and nutrition.

Part of connecting science with real life is to move students away from the stereotypical image of a scientist and expose them to the reality of what scientists do and how they work. Sally Ride Science at https://www.sallyridescience.com/node/243 presents diverse role models so students can see the range of possibilities science has to offer and see themselves as scientists so they are encouraged to pursue those interests (Eicher, 2007). Sally Ride Science classroom kits prepare teachers to teach science in a way that dispels the stereotype of the mad male scientist in a laboratory surrounded by bubbling beakers and shows them that scientists are anything from astrobiologists and medical illustrators to earthquake seismologists and wildlife officers (Eicher, 2007).

A seemingly small touch, but potentially very engaging, is to provide the materials necessary for students to dress the part. Lab coats or their own field kits, clipboards with data entry sheets (instead of loose-leaf paper), and safety goggles go a long way in helping students feel like scientists and seeing themselves in that role (Rapp, 1997).

Choice   The third category of engagement strategies for science is choice. There are many ways that students can be given autonomy to make choices about their own learning. Activity menus are a great strategy to support choice. Figure 17.2 shows an example of a list menu for science.

Complete activities so the sum of points equals at least the boiling point of water in degrees Fahrenheit.

✓	Activity/assignment	Possible points	Points earned
	Make flashcards for the new science vocabulary words. Be sure to include a meaningful visual.	10	
	Make a poster about the conversion of Fahrenheit to Celsius.	10	
	Teach a classmate how a thermometer works. Be sure the classmate learns enough so that he/she can teach someone else.	10	
	List five reasons why it is important to know how to read a thermometer and to know both Celsius and Fahrenheit.	10	
	Write a meteorology script for the morning weather report. Include the temperature in both Celsius and Fahrenheit and include advice about weather-related activities and dress.	20	
	Write a story about a farmer during a year when the temperatures were unseasonably cold for the the spring planting season. Be sure to write about everyone who is affected by this scenario and what the ideal conditions would be.	20	
	Create a time line of equipment used over the past 100 years to predict weather conditions. For each entry on the time line, explain how the new technology affected weather reporting.	20	
	Interview a meteorologist about how he or she is able to predict upcoming temperatures.	30	
	Record daily temperature and barometric pressure readings every day for 10 days. Plot the results on a line graph, and write a summary about the pattern of changes. Explain whether this is typical for the time of year.	30	
	Build a working thermometer that can be demonstrated for the class. Display the apparatus with a poster explaining how it works and how you built it.	40	

Figure 17.2.   List menu for science. (Adapted from Westphal, L.E. [2007]. *Differentiating with menus: Science*. Waco, TX: Prufrock Press, Inc. http://www.prufrock.com.)

Flexible grouping is an important way to offer choice to students (Wormeli, 2007). Some ways for students to collaborate in different group sizes are suggested by Fitzell (2005):

- Use lab teams for science experiments and exercises

- Discuss controversial health topics and form debate teams

- Play science vocabulary games with classmates

It is important for students to be grouped with different classmates for different activities. Discussions expose students to different ways of thinking about concepts and creative ways to explore them. If always given the choice, students will often partner or form small groups with the same classmates over and over. To avoid this, there are strategies for varying student groups that can be planned ahead of time so as not to use up valuable instruction time during a lesson. For partners, a popular method is clock buddies (Rutherford, 2002). Each student receives a template of an analog clock. For each number on the clock, each student finds a partner and they write each other's name by that number. For the 12 numbers, each student should have 12 different clock buddies. At the beginning of any activity for partners, the teacher need only pick a number—for example, 10—and instruct the students to pair up with their 10 o'clock buddy. While this may not mix each student with everyone else in the class, at least there will be much greater variety when partners are called for. For larger grouping varieties, popsicle sticks come in handy. Label a popsicle stick for each student in the class. Purposefully arrange your class in groups of three and label their sticks accordingly—one group will have green dots, one group blue, one group pink, and so forth. Now, rearrange the sticks in groups of four so students are with new classmates, and label each group with a different indicator—this time shapes. One group has triangles, one group squares, and so on. You can do this for as many different group sizes that you think you will need—five, six, or more. Now, when you start a lesson that needs groups of four, you just need to say "everyone get into your shape groups." If you have places in the classroom labeled to match, they will know just where to go.

Tiered science activities provide choices with just the right amount of challenge for individual students. For any science topic, provide options of increasing difficulty from an introductory level to a more sophisticated level. Wormeli (2007) provided an example for cellular biology. From least to most sophisticated for a lesson about the cell, the tiers could be: identify the parts of a cell, explain the systems within a cell and what functions they perform, explain how a cell is part of a larger system of cells that form a tissue, demonstrate how a cell replicates itself, identify what can go wrong in mitosis, list what we know about how cells learn to specialize in the body, and explain how knowledge of cells helps us understand other physiology (p. 85). Once students choose a starting point, the teacher can then gradually guide them through increasing levels of mastery.

Self-Regulation Strategies   The last category of engagement strategies for science is self-regulation strategies. Gargiulo and Metcalf (2010) suggested that opportunities for rehearsing responses can increase engagement. It is a self-regulation strategy that may help students gain confidence in the concept they are rehearsing. Rather than calling on a student on the spot, provide them with a question card in advance with the instructions to write the answer on the card. During the lesson, when the student is called on, he or she can use the question card as a resource to answer the question and contribute to the discussion.

Another self-monitoring idea is to provide the students with a checklist or Bingo board of concepts to be learned. Once they feel they have a solid understanding of the concept, they mark if off. After the list or board is complete, they are ready to be evaluated on their learning.

Input

Strategies for input are provided in three areas: Visual, auditory, and tactile strategies; teaching science language; and anchor activities.

Visual, Auditory, and Tactile Inputs   The first category of representation or input strategies provides students with multiple versions of the information, including visual, auditory, and tactile. In science, though the national standards speak to a greater emphasis on inquiry, there is still significant reliance on textbooks (Gargiulo & Metcalf, 2010). One of the best ways to facilitate input of information for students is to make text more accessible for various learning needs. As with math, Accessible Instructional Materials (AIM) Navigator at http://aim.cast.org/experience/decision-making_tools/aim_navigator provides alternatives to print-based textbooks in science. Another alternative to print-based text is Beyond Penguins and Polar Bears at http://beyond penguins.nsdl.org/. This web site is an online magazine utilizing podcasts, photographs, and digital books to present lessons and activities integrating science, literacy, and the polar region.

Other media for representing information through various modalities include computers with extralarge monitors, interactive whiteboards, Internet-accessed virtual field trips to science museums or landforms, computer-software simulation programs (for example, the mummification simulation at http://oi.uchicago.edu/OI/MUS/ED/mummy.html), and human resources, such as museum curators and science experts from the community (Garguilo & Metcalf, 2010, p. 380).

Teaching Science Language   The second category of input strategies offers multiple ways for students to learn the vocabulary or language of science. Some students struggle with the acquisition of essential science vocabulary that may impede their ability to share experiences and contribute to valuable class discussions (Jarrett, 1999). With science, one school of thought is that preteaching vocabulary may not be as effective as waiting to introduce the new words until the students have explored and been involved in a relevant activity. Once the students have worked intimately with equipment and formed questions to ask about various phenomena, the vocabulary will be more meaningful to them and thus more readily learned. For example, "Remember when you pushed the brick across the sandpaper? Well, that push is called a 'force'" (Jarrett, 1999, p. 18).

Mnemonics are useful for remembering the many different sets of information in science units, especially when paired with a meaningful visual image. *ROY G. BIV* is a colorful guy. He tells us the colors in the spectrum are red, orange, yellow, green, blue, indigo, and violet. Another, *King Penguins Congregate on Frozen Ground Sometimes,* helps us remember that the zoology classifications in order are kingdom, phylum, class, order, family, genus, and species.

Fitzell (2005) shared the Three-Card Match Review. Choose three colors of index cards (e.g., pink, blue, yellow). Make a set of cards for each new term to learn—a pink card for the vocabulary word, a blue card with a photo or drawing, and a yellow card with the definition or essential fact. Mark each set with matching numbers or symbols so the student can self-check. Shuffle the cards and have the student practice by finding the word and its corresponding picture and definition (pp. 75–76). Another idea from Fitzell (2005) is Draw It So You'll Know It. After teaching for 10 minutes, stop the lesson for 3 minutes and have the students draw a picture of what they just heard or

Word	nocturnal

Definition	(adj.) active at night or occurring at night

Synonyms	Ways/places the word is used	Antonyms
Nighttime	Animals Flowers	Diurnal Daytime

Memory sentence/Sounds like...

Night–turn–all. The nocturnal coyote slept all day but at night turned all on.

Mind picture

Figure 17.3.   Word map.

read about. Converting thoughts to this visual imagery helps reinforce new language through multiple modalities.

The word-map technique, as shown in Figure 17.3, may also support language acquisition. A graphic organizer is used to map out a word or phrase several different ways—definition, synonyms, antonyms, applications, in a memory sentence, and as a mind picture (Gargiulo & Metcalf, 2010).

Anchor Activities   The third category of input strategies are activities that make connections for students or anchor new information to previous knowledge. Wormeli (2007) anchored the concept of Newton's Law to students' familiarity with a playground ball. Place a playground ball on a cafeteria tray and set it on a level desk for several minutes (or even overnight) to show that it doesn't move, and ask the students to draw conclusions about whether or not it will move if the current conditions stay the same. Then ask them what would have to happen for the ball to move. Experiment with each of their suggestions (tilt the tray, move the desk, create a breeze). Once the ball moves, have the students observe it until it stops and ask them what made it stop. Describing

Table 17.1.   Anchoring activities

Book	Example of anchor activity
Bingham, J. (1991). *The Usborne Book of Science Experiments.* London, England: Usborne Publishing Ltd.	*Sounds interesting*: Investigate how sounds reach your ear and how sounds travel using a radio, balloon, 2-liter bottle, plastic wrap, rubber band, and candle.
Edom, H. (1990). *Science with Water.* London, England: Usborne Publishing Ltd.	*Water power*: Learn how water and gravity can power machinery using egg cartons, paper plates, spools, a pencil, two rulers, and tape.
Edom, H., & Butterfield, M. (1991). *Science with Air.* London, England: Usborne Publishing Ltd.	*Rising air*: Investigate how temperature affects air movement using paper, a paper plate, crayons, and a needle and thread.
Robinson, T. (2001). *The Everything Kids' Science Experiments Book.* Avon, MA: Adams Media Corporation.	*Balance*: Learn about levers, gravity, and fulcrums using a ruler, pencil and a handful of pennies.
Smith, A. (Ed.). (1996). *The Usborne Big Book of Experiments.* London, England: Usborne Publishing Ltd.	*How your eyes work*: Investigate this concept using a yogurt cup, black paint, dishwashing liquid, a thumb tack, rubber band, tracing paper, candle, and a ruler.

what they see with familiar materials walks them meaningfully though a complex scientific concept.

The books in Table 17.1 hold dozens of ideas for anchoring activities that use household objects to illustrate science concepts.

Output

Strategies for output are provided in four areas: toys, tools, and movement; multiple intelligences; lesson-planning ideas; and support strategies.

Tools, Toys, and Movement   The first category of expression or output strategies is tools, toys, and movement. Hands-on exploration is an extremely effective way for students to grasp complex phenomena in science. Reading about inertia and potential and kinetic energy will introduce the ideas to students, but they may need a hands-on activity to better understand the concepts. One way to do this is to race MatchBox cars down an inclined track and describe the processes that occur, while reinforcing the newly introduced vocabulary.

Have as many tools and materials as possible available for student use, and incorporate them into your science lessons and science centers: microscopes; batteries and wires; magnifying lenses; magnets; plastic tubing; rulers (some with Braille and large print); measuring wheels; terrariums and aquariums; portable keyboards, felt boards, magnet boards, and tape recorders for taking field notes; and digital cameras, iPods, stickers, foam dots, rubber stamps, and raised-line graph paper for collecting and recording data (Gargiulo & Metcalf, 2010, p. 380).

Find fun and affordable science toys at Steve Spangler's Science Toys web site at http://www.stevespanglerscience.com/category/science-toys. Having science toys available at recess or incorporating them into lessons will provide engaging ways for students to demonstrate their science-language acquisition, inquiry skills, and concept knowledge.

Multiple Intelligences   Table 17.2 gives examples of activities for students to do that appeal to various intelligences. Activities should be provided for all areas—both for students who find comfort in their preferred area as well as for students who are ready for a challenge in their nonpreferred area.

Table 17.2. Activities for students

Multiple intelligences	Activities for students
Verbal-linguistic	• Respond to nonfiction writing prompts for science (LePatner et al., 2005) • Write a humorous story using science vocabulary (Fitzell, 2005) • Write steps used in an experiment so someone else can do it (Fitzell, 2005)
Logical-mathematical	• Illustrate patterns in successful and reliable scientific experiments (Fitzell, 2005)
Bodily-kinesthetic	• Incorporate drama and movement by having students perform a soap-opera love story among electrons as they attach and reattach to one another and create molecules (Wormeli, 2007) • Use concrete models to demonstrate science concepts (Fitzell, 2005)
Musical-rhythmic	• Musical molecules (Chapman, 1993, p. 145)
Visual-spatial	• Use the symbols of the Periodic Table of Elements in a comic strip • Create montages/collages on science topics (Fitzell, 2005) • Web attributes of various systems in the body (Fitzell, 2005) • Draw pictures of things seen under a microscope (Fitzell, 2005)
Interpersonal	• Design group research projects and implement plans (Fitzell, 2005) • Use lab teams for science experiments (Fitzell, 2005) • Debate controversial health topics (Fitzell, 2005)
Intrapersonal	• Create a diary on "The Life of a Red Blood Cell" (Fitzell, 2005) • Write an imaginary conversation between body parts (Fitzell, 2005)
Naturalist	• Create a creature classification lab (Chapman, 1993, p. 124) • Find five ways to classify a collection of leaves (Fitzell, 2005)
Existentialist	• Solve environmental science problems such as species extinction or water pollution. See Harvard University's River City Project at http://muve.gse.harvard.edu/rivercityproject/ • Debate controversial health topics (Fitzell, 2005)

Lesson Planning Ideas   This section covers additional ideas for providing multiple opportunities for students to express their science knowledge and skills.

Opportunities to share observations, compare findings, and brainstorm inquiry questions are extremely important for students who learn through interaction. Offer ways for this to happen in various-size groups and with various people. A science journal between teacher and student allows the student to share what she is thinking by writing, drawing, or scrapbooking clippings and also to receive feedback from someone with a higher level of expertise. The teacher may also ask the student if the journal can be shared with other teachers in the school who have a greater knowledge base about a particular subject. Receiving feedback from multiple reviewers is an authentic exercise in the world of science.

Arrange book talks for small groups of students. Provide a number of readings to choose from. They may be expository texts or trade books. Perhaps even a video series. Assign a structured meeting time and roles that the group members will rotate through. Some roles may be discussion director, vocabulary definer, illustrator, and fact finder.

Another way for students to express their learning to an audience is to create a large hallway mural of a science concept, such as the water cycle. Accompanying the mural can be a pocket of feedback forms for passersby (i.e., other students and teachers) to complete and return to the scientists. In addition to murals, models, dioramas, Power Point presentations, posters, and videos can be displayed, or reports can be published in school newsletters.

Support Strategies   Sometimes students have difficulty managing all of the information they have learned and expressing it in a comprehensive way.

Think VAKT—visual, auditory, kinesthetic, tactile (Gargiulo & Metcalf, 2010). Each lesson needs to have visual images (guided notes with pictures), auditory discourse (oral presentation and discussion), movement (demonstration), and hands-on materials (models, tools and assistive technology). Then, students with different learning and response styles will have an opportunity to demonstrate knowledge and skills. Here is just one example of an effective lesson on atomic structure:

- Start with a KWL chart. This is a chart with three columns labeled, "what we Know," "what we Want to know," and "what we Learned." Open the lesson by asking students what they know about atoms and atomic structure. This is brainstorming, so any student's response goes on the list. It should be a list of what they currently know. If a student offers something that someone believes is inaccurate (including the teacher), a notation should be made in the second column: "We want to know if everything we know so far is accurate." Then continue with other questions the students have about atoms. The teacher can also contribute to the list if there are important questions to be asked that the students have not mentioned. This is good modeling and supportive pedagogy. The last column is revisited at the end of the lesson or unit.

- Provide a visual representation (e.g., poster, diagram on the Smart Board, teacher model) of the atomic structure and a packet of guided notes about atomic structure. Include word-map templates for new vocabulary. Also provide hands-on materials, such as atom-model kits or clay with toothpicks. The visual, packet, and hands-on materials will accompany the auditory instruction by the teacher, class discussion, and question-and-answer sessions. The auditory instruction should be done in several increments (maximum of 10 minutes) with other activities in between. The activities can be brief (even just 2 minutes), but the break is needed for students to process what they just learned. This is called the 10-2 theory (Rutherford, 2002, p. 77). Here are some things you can say to prompt kids to learn during these breaks:

  - Turn to Your Neighbor (TTYN) and ask for his or her opinion about this or explain to him or her what I just said.

  - Draw it so you know it! (Fitzell, 2005).

  - Numbered Heads Together (Rutherford, 2002). Get into your triangle groups of four, number yourselves one through four, and make sure everyone knows the answer to my question. In 1 minute I will call out a number one through four and those folks will enlighten us.

  - Complete a word map for the vocabulary word electron.

  - Make a model of the helium atom just like mine up here. You may work alone, with a partner, or in groups of three. Make sure everyone has a role.

- Have the students complete a self-assessment rubric. There should be categories on understanding the new concepts and vocabulary, participation in class discussion, contributions to small-group or partner work, and level of engagement. The students can evaluate themselves on a rating scale (e.g., Exemplary, Proficient, Developing, Not Yet Acceptable) or with symbols (e.g., smiley face, neutral face, frown face).

- Close by returning to the KWL chart to complete the last column—what we Learned. This column contains clarification of inaccuracies in the first column, new knowledge and skills, as well as thoughts from the self-assessment (e.g., "I learned I work better with a partner than in a group of four"). This is all important science learning.

Here are additional ways to support students during the lesson above:

- Allow extra processing time. Follow the 10-second rule before calling on students (Fitzell, 2005). If we want to move students away from memorizing science facts and move them toward science inquiry, we need to remember that a response or idea will take time to bubble up.

- Make sure students have a chance to move often. Some will need this more than others. Those who need to move a lot can help pass out papers, come to the board to scribe, come to the table to help with the model, and move across the room to meet with a partner. Everyone will benefit from 30-second stretches every 15 to 20 minutes: "Everyone take 30 seconds to stretch while I organize my materials up here." Some will stretch and some will put their heads down. Their choice.

- Provide fidget toys. Allow them to roll the clay or plastic atoms in their hands while listening.

- Vary your tone of voice when introducing key words, phrases, and information. Say it thrice. Use hand signals (e.g., flashing jazz hands) to indicate a new word coming up.

- Provide headsets or u-shaped plastic tubes (commercially bought or made out of white plumbing pipe from a hardware store) for students who need to talk out loud while processing their word maps or models.

- Check frequently to see who is with you. Ask for a thumbs up (they have it) or thumbs down (explain it again). Ask for hands up to show you on a scale of five (they totally have it) to one (they are completely lost). Provide red, yellow, and green cards to each student and ask for a card check: green (keep going), yellow (slow down), or red (stop for a break).

Last, Jarrett (1999) shared levels of scientific inquiry to support diverse students. The three levels of the inquiry continuum are structured inquiry, guided inquiry, and student-directed inquiry. In **structured inquiry**, students have opportunities to interact with visual, auditory, and hands-on materials but follow a prescribed set of procedures or instructions from the teacher. In **guided inquiry**, the teacher supplies the question or concept to be investigated and may outline some parameters, but the students determine the procedures to follow to arrive at an answer or solution. In **student-directed inquiry**, students independently generate the concept to explore and design their own investigation (pp. 15–16).

ASSESSMENT

In addition to standards for the instruction of science, the National Science Education Standards put forth standards for assessment. Based on exemplary assessment practices, the standards serve as a guide to developing assessment tasks, practices, and policies for evaluating not only student progress, but teacher, program, and assessment effectiveness as well. If applied well, feedback from assessments can help change policies in science education, guide professional development of science educators, and encourage students to improve their knowledge and understanding of science (National Committee on Science Education Standards and Assessment, 1996).

structured inquiry A process of inquiry where students have opportunities to interact with visual, auditory, and hands-on materials but follow a prescribed set of procedures or instructions from the teacher.

guided inquiry A process of inquiry where the teacher supplies the question or concept to be investigated and may outline some parameters, but the students determine the procedures to follow to arrive at an answer or solution.

student-directed inquiry A process of inquiry where students independently generate the concept to explore and design their own investigation.

Five standards outline important considerations for authentic and valid science assessment:

1.   Assessment Standard A: Assessments must be consistent with the decisions they are designed to inform.

2.   Assessment Standard B: Achievement and opportunity to learn science must be assessed.

3.   Assessment Standard C: The technical quality of the data collected is well matched to the decisions and actions taken on the basis of their interpretation: assessments evaluate what they claim to, tasks are authentic, and students have ample opportunities to perform.

4.   Assessment Standard D: Assessment practices must be fair, including free of cultural and linguistic bias, set in a variety of contexts, and modified for students with disabilities.

5.   Assessment Standard E: The inferences made from assessments about student achievement and opportunity to learn must be sound (National Committee on Science Education Standards and Assessment, 1996).

performance-based assessments Assessments that evaluate the process a student uses to arrive at the solution or answer.

product-based assessments Assessments that evaluate the product put forth by the student, regardless of the process used.

It is important to measure all aspects of science learning, including knowledge of the natural world, understanding of the impact of scientific study, and the ability to inquire. To assess knowledge and understanding of the natural world, both **performance-based** and **product-based assessments** that include opportunities for communication about science are necessary. Some examples of performance-based assessments are public presentations, peer discussions, and conducting laboratory procedures. Some examples of product-based assessments are exams, journals, written papers or reports, physical models, and collection of objects. In order to assess the ability to inquire, we need to observe and collect evidence of students' ability to identify a worthwhile and researchable question, plan an investigation, execute the plan, present findings, and draft a research report (National Committee on Science Education Standards and Assessment, 1996).

As with the content standards, the assessment standards strive to shift emphases of assessment in science. Less emphasis should be placed on assessing what is easily measured, which includes assessing discrete knowledge; assessing scientific knowledge; assessing to learn what students do not know; assessing only achievement; end-of-term assessment by teachers; and development of external assessments by measurement experts alone. More emphasis should be placed on assessing what is most highly valued: rich, well-structured knowledge; scientific understanding and reasoning; and what students do understand. In addition, emphasis should be placed on achievement and opportunity to learn, engaging students in ongoing self- and peer-assessment, and involving teachers in the development of external assessments (National Committee on Science Education Standards and Assessment, 1996, p. 100).

SUMMARY

In this chapter, we reviewed what high-quality science education includes and reviewed the disconnect that sometimes happens in classrooms. Too much focus on knowing scientific facts can lead to less emphasis on critical thinking skills in science. Finding the balance between a foundation of knowledge and opportunities for critical thinking and inquiry is the challenge for teachers. We presented strategies in the areas of engagement, input, output, and assessment and provided a range of web site and book resources for you as a starting point. The chapter ended with a reminder to give attention to assessments that evaluate what students understand and that include students in ongoing self-evaluation.

NARRATIVE 17.1. | DEBRA ORTENZI

James Watson, discoverer of the DNA molecule, said, "I think people are born curious and they have it pounded out of them." This is so true! Students everywhere are curious souls, and a great teacher will help them discover their questions and teach them how to find the answers.

Teaching science involves opportunities for discovery and exploration. Students should be given materials and allowed to manipulate them, generating their own thoughts, questions, and ideas. These experiences grab the attention and creative thinking of all people, no matter their native language, background, or previous knowledge. Teachers can then shape a unit around the student-generated questions, referring back to them again and again.

Visual aids, silent teachers posted around the room, and repetition are essential for students to retain new concepts. Using personal stories, pictures, and real-life examples help students relate to new information. Graphic organizers are helpful for many students as they make sense of new facts and ideas.

The bottom line is, kids are kids. Whether you teach in the city or the suburbs, you must get to know your students and form relationships. Engage them in the lessons. Capture their natural curiosity and value their ideas. Respect them as individuals and as important members of your classroom community. Everyone has something they are good at; find your students' strengths and help them thrive. Join them on a learning adventure, showing them what you have done recently to learn more about each topic. Model what it means to be a lifelong learner; that is the most important gift you could ever give anyone.

CHAPTER 18

Social and Communication Strategies for All Students

How this chapter prepares you to be an effective inclusive classroom teacher:

- This chapter gives you several examples of evidence-based instructional strategies for social skills and communication. According to the principles of universal design for learning (UDL), you will learn about strategies for multiple ways of engaging students; multiple ways for students to access new information; and multiple ways for students to express their understanding of social skills, speech, and language. **This helps you meet CEC Standard 4: Instructional Strategies.**

- This chapter teaches you about the hidden curriculum within learning environments, and that individuals with exceptional learning needs may need direct instruction for unspoken aspects of social skills. The chapter also gives you examples of direct instructional interventions to teach students to respond effectively to current social expectations **This helps you meet CEC Standard 5: Learning Environments and Social Interactions.**

- This chapter teaches you about typical and atypical speech, language, and social skill development. It gives you examples of individualized strategies to enhance language development and teach social and communication skills, as well as augmentative, alternative, and assistive technologies. You will learn about culturally and linguistically responsive teaching in the area of social skills and communication. **This helps you meet CEC Standard 6: Language.**

- This chapter teaches you multiple ways of assessing social understanding and gives you examples of formal and informal speech and language assessments. You will also learn about using assessment results to plan future instruction. **This helps you meet CEC Standard 8: Assessment.**

- This chapter prepares you to be a professional and ethical teacher by teaching you the importance of being sensitive to the diversity of students. It also teaches you that no two students learn social and communication skills the same way. You will learn that your role as teacher is to highly individualize all aspects of teaching to meet students' needs and that learning how to do this is a lifelong learning process. **This helps you meet CEC Standard 9: Professional and Ethical Practice.**

After reading and discussing this chapter, you will be able to

- Explain the differences among receptive communication, expressive communication, and pragmatic language and the impact that difficulties in these areas may have

- Explain what the SCANS Skills and Competencies list is and its connection to teaching social and communication skills

- Explain components of language other than speech and their significance in social skills

- Describe the hidden curriculum and the impact on students who have difficulty with this

- Provide several examples of ways teachers can support students in learning the hidden curriculum

- Describe multiple ways to engage diverse students in learning social and communication skills, and provide several examples

- Describe multiple ways to support receptive communication skills and provide several examples

- Describe multiple ways to support expressive language skills and provide several examples

- Explain augmentative and alternative communication and provide examples

- Explain the difference between formal and informal receptive language, expressive language, and social skill assessments, and the significance of each

receptive communication Receiving and understanding what is being communicated to you.

expressive communication Expressing language to communicate to someone else.

social skills Understanding and appropriately communicating in various situations.

pragmatic language Another phrase for appropriate social skills.

There are many components to communication. For this chapter, we will break it into three areas: receptive communication, expressive communication, and social skills. **Receptive communication** is receiving and understanding what is being communicated to you, and **expressive communication** is expressing language to communicate to someone else. Communication occurs in various contexts, so not only do students need to know how to receive and express messages, they need to know how to adjust those skills depending on the context. **Social skills** are understanding and appropriately communicating in various situations. This is also called **pragmatic language**.

The SCANS Skills and Competencies is a list of skills young people need to be successful in the work world today. Put forth by the Secretary's Commission on Necessary Skills (SCANS), the list includes three parts: Basic Skills, Thinking Skills, and Personal Skills. Basic Skills entail reading, writing, arithmetic/mathematics, listening, and speaking. Thinking Skills entail creative thinking, decision making, problem solving, seeing things in the mind's eye, knowing how to learn, and reasoning. Personal Skills entail responsibility, self-esteem, sociability, self-management, and integrity/honesty. SCANS also lists five workplace competencies: 1) identifies, organizes, plans, and allocates resources; 2) works with others; 3) acquires and uses information; 4) understands complex interrelationships; and 5) works with a variety of technologies (U.S. Department of Labor, 1999). Many of the skills listed here directly or indirectly rely on strong receptive communication, expressive communication, and social skills. Along with academic knowledge and skills, we must ensure students gain social knowledge and skills to be independent, contributing members of today's work force.

As Clara Berg writes in her narrative, "communication is the exchange of thoughts, ideas, and/or actions between two or more people." There are many different ways for that exchange to occur. Consider this from *DisabilityLand* by Alan Brightman (2008):

A wonderful poster was put out some years ago by [Scope] of Great Britain. In it, a fourth- or fifth-grade child is sitting at a computer that he's operating with a head wand. He looks proud and serious. The monitor screen is covered with lines of text. Across the top of the poster a bold caption reads:

"Just because I couldn't speak, they thought I had nothing to say."

Lots of nonvocal people have much to say and with access to a computer are, for the first time, being heard: across a room, over a phone, even on public assembly stages. For anyone willing to listen, nonvocal individuals will give you an earful. (p. 110)

In this chapter, we provide numerous strategies for engagement, input, output, and assessment of receptive and expressive communication (see Figure 18.1).

Students who are able to receive and express language may still have difficulty using it appropriately in various situations and contexts. There are so many subtleties, variations, exceptions, and nuances to navigate and keep track of. Some students are adept in this area. They are able to manage all of the complexities with ease without being directly instructed how to do so. They pick up clues from watching their parents, teachers, and peers. They notice the subtle differences in someone's mannerisms, inflection, and formality of speech as the context changes. Other students are not able to pick this up on their own and will need direct instruction about the social cues happening around them, and what to do about each cue.

In *A Mind at a Time*, Mel Levine (2002) described eight neurodevelopmental systems: the attention control system, the memory system, the language system, the

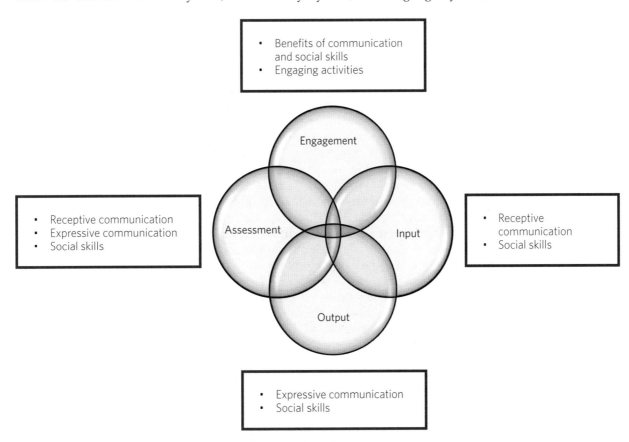

Figure 18.1. Strategies for communication.

spatial-ordering system, the sequential-ordering system, the motor system, the higher-thinking system, and the social-thinking system. In this view, the language system is not the same as the social-thinking system. Many students may be strong at receiving and expressing communication but have significant difficulty regulating the social behaviors surrounding that communication. Important social behaviors include the ability to resolve conflicts without aggression, the ability to monitor your own interactions, the ability to self-market ("sell yourself") and maintain a good public image, the ability to collaborate and cooperate with others, and the ability to read and act on social incidents and people's actions and gestures to build relationships and friendships (Levine, 2002).

It is important to provide responsive instruction and learning opportunities to help all students develop these essential social behaviors. Lavoie (2005) offered several reasons to purposefully teach social skills. Social difficulty affects the whole community—whether that is the family or the classroom. If one person is experiencing difficulty, it ripples out to everyone. In school, there are many social parameters to follow. Outside of school, social abilities are still highlighted—at the dinner table, playing with peers or siblings, and interacting with community members. Even students who would rather be alone are expected to express that intention appropriately without offending or alienating others. It is hard to compensate for social-skill difficulties. Short of a parent or teacher following the students everywhere to prompt social interactions, the student is on his own. Social skills are a significant factor in a student's future success, happiness, and acceptance. This does not mean that a person needs to be a social butterfly to be happy. This means that no matter what the person's social preference, the skill to communicate one's needs and preferences appropriately and an understanding of certain societal expectations are needed.

There are several reasons why social difficulties may occur even for students who have strong language skills. First, the student may be visually or aurally misperceiving their environment. Some social problems that occur due to misperception are poor observation skills (such as failing to recognize a peer's clothing or appearance), poor response to visual input (such as figuring out what is going on in a movie or demonstration), underdeveloped sense of direction, taking a much longer time to become oriented to a new setting, difficulty judging distance or speed (which makes it challenging to participate in sports or backyard games), and difficulty modifying the volume of voice (which can lead to inappropriate volume in conversation) (Lavoie, 2005).

Second, the student may have difficulty inhibiting behaviors. They do not stop themselves from expressing thoughts or impulses, even when they may be offensive, hurtful, or dangerous (Lavoie, 2005). Without realizing it, many of us inhibit inappropriate impulses hundreds of times each day—feelings, observations, and physical impulses. Students who have trouble inhibiting impulses might mention that they are bored in your class, or tell a peer her new hair cut is ugly, or scratch themselves in public.

Third, the student may not be able to plan or predict very well. Social behaviors occurring when this is the cause might be the inability to internalize language or self-talk to monitor upcoming actions; poor problem-solving skills; poor emotional control, so that their frustration level rises very easily; poor recall and working memory, so that it is difficult to hold the threads of multiperson conversations in the mind and respond effectively; poor activation skills, so that they do not initiate social interactions; or reduced arousal and persistence, so that they cannot sustain attention to social interactions very long (Lavoie, 2005).

Fourth, some students are inflexible. Not in the sense that they are stubborn, but in the sense that they have a hard time bending to changes, or "going with the flow." It is difficult for these students to shift gears form one situation to another. These students become easily overwhelmed and anxious in new settings, with fast-paced schedules, or in complex social situations. They can become agitated or even aggressive in an attempt to cope. Often this difficulty results in a "meltdown" in response to a seemingly simple and routine situation (Lavoie, 2005).

There are also several areas of **paralinguistics**, or nonverbal language, that contribute to what we communicate during interactions. These are vocalics, eye contact, hygiene, artifactual systems, and proximics. **Vocalics** refers to tone of voice. In addition to knowing what to say, students need to know how to regulate the way that they say it. Changing the volume, pitch, and tempo of the voice can significantly change the meaning of a message. Eye contact is another important aspect of communication. Typically, it denotes caring and sincerity during an interaction. It can also help the speaker read the audience's reactions. We will discuss eye contact more during this chapter. Some people believe eye contact to be a necessary part of social competence, but there are students who are not able to make eye contact as expected. Luke Jackson writes in his user guide to adolescence, *Freaks, Geeks, and Asperger Syndrome*, "Poor or no eye contact is seen to be a problem with social interaction, though I would dispute that. It is only a problem for those who want to be looked at" (2002, pp. 22–23). Hygiene can affect interactions as it makes a statement about a person's self-esteem, self-respect, and confidence. **Artifactual systems** refer to what we wear that expresses ourselves to others. This includes clothing, hairstyles, jewelry, makeup, and other accessories. It is important for students to know that signals can be sent by their appearance and what they choose to wear. Last, **proximics** refers to the distance between people during social interactions. Sometimes it is referred to as personal space or personal bubble. There are unwritten rules that regulate the appropriate amount of distance during various interactions (Lavoie, 2005).

The answer to supporting students who have trouble with any of these social skills is to directly teach them "the hidden curriculum." The **hidden curriculum** is a set of rules or guidelines for social interaction that are not typically directly taught because it is assumed that students already know them or that they will pick them up or learn them simply through observation as they develop. The hidden curriculum underlies social interactions, school performance, and even safety (Myles, Trautman, & Schelvan, 2004). It is complex and ever-developing. A great many social interactions and the skills needed to manage it can be predicted, but there will always be unique situations that pop up for individuals. In addition, the hidden curriculum varies by age, gender, culture, and audience. Teaching about the hidden curriculum can affect a student's well-being in school, at home, in the community, in the workplace, and even with the legal system.

The following sections address how to teach students the knowledge and skills needed to manage the complexity of social skills by making them aware of the hidden curriculum as well as by providing the supports for learning how to communicate clearly and process paralinguistics and how to make and maintain friendships when desired.

STRATEGIES FOR TEACHING SOCIAL AND COMMUNICATION SKILLS TO ALL STUDENTS

Engagement

One important way that communication and social skills are engaging is that, when effective, they lead to positive connections with others, reduction in conflicts and misunderstandings, better advocacy for self and others, the achievement of goals, and friendship. Friendship, a mutually beneficial relationship, is a source of enjoyment and sense of belonging. Everyone deserves the right to form friendships if they desire, and to feel joy and a sense of belonging. Positive connections and friendship cannot be forced. They depend on opportunity to choose interactions and on chemistry. For everyone to have equitable opportunity for this, the community must be based on the

paralinguistics Nonverbal language, including proximics, vocalics, and artifactual systems.

vocalics Tone of voice.

artifactual systems What we wear that expresses ourselves to others, such as clothing, hairstyles, jewelry, makeup, and other accessories.

proximics The distance between people during social interactions.

hidden curriculum The unspoken rules to follow in given social situations. For a student with typical social skill development, these rules do not need to be directly taught. For a student struggling with social skill development, differentiated instruction may be needed.

belief that everyone is valued and is able to contribute meaningfully to a relationship (Kliewer, 1998). When a teacher creates a classroom community where students want to know one another, he or she has created a setting where communication and social interaction are inherently engaging.

In *Black Ants and Buddhists*, Mary Cowhey (2006) talked about how she learned how important it is to create a setting like this for English language learners:

> About half of my first graders were bilingual Spanish speakers, learning English as a second language. During class discussions, I was often frustrated by some of my impulsive English-speaking students' habit of calling out answers after I had called on an English language learner. I knew from having participated in community meetings in Spanish (my second language) that it took a lot of concentration for me to follow the gist of the discussion and a lot of courage for me to think I might be able to add something to it. I then organized my thoughts into my "baby talk" Spanish and raised my hand. It was hard for me to continue to follow the discussion while I continued to rehearse my Spanish sentence in my head as I waited to be called on. If I were not called on soon, the window of opportunity for my comment to be relevant would shut. If I were interrupted once I started to speak, I would lose my carefully rehearsed sentence and sit there with an open mouth.
>
> My first graders soon developed our first class rule, "You can't step on someone else's words" (p. 62).

Regardless of the diversity of the students in the classroom—language, ethnicity, gender, ability—it is important to help students realize the many diverse ways they and their peers communicate and interact to establish a community of patience, understanding, and desire to know and support each other.

Mary Cowhey, not thinking about how it fit into the curriculum, invited to their classroom adults who were learning English and needed to tell their story in ways other than conventional speech. In doing so, she created engaging interactions for her students, who likely did not realize they were practicing oral-language development or social skills. There are many more activities that are engaging and fun, without seeming like communication and social-skill instruction.

One example is Inside-Outside Circles (Rutherford, 2002). This is an activity that uses communication skills to practice new content knowledge. Divide the class in half. Each half forms a circle—one circle on the inside facing out, and the other circle around them facing in. If there is an odd number of students, the teacher should join the group so everyone has a partner. Instruct the students to share with the person facing them one thing they learned from the recent lesson. Then the outer circle rotates one person clockwise and repeats the direction. Benefits to this activity include repetition of material learned, practicing one-on-one communication with many different peers who have diverse communication skills and styles, and movement at the end of a lesson!

Another example involves road maps. Use a map web site, such as Google Maps at http://maps.google.com/or MapQuest at http://www.mapquest.com/to print copies of a town or city map. Be sure that it is zoomed in close enough to see the names of several streets and intersections. Pair students up and provide them each with an identical map. Instruct one partner to choose a starting location and an ending location, and give the other student directions to find the way from point to point. Then, they switch roles. The students can self-check by determining if the partner found his or her way to the previously chosen destination. This activity reinforces receptive and expressive communication, map skills, directionality, and geography. An extension of this activity is to have the pairs write or tell a story about why the person needed directions and what happened when he or she found (or didn't find!) the destination.

Another engaging activity is to make photocopies of newspaper comic strips after whiting out the words in the speech bubbles. Then have students work individually, in pairs, or in small groups to complete a comic strip conversation about a newly learned concept. Then, they may choose to act out the scene.

Dramatic activities are fun and effective for reinforcing communication skills, particularly paralinguistics. Any time you incorporate theater or role-playing into a lesson, the students have an opportunity to build their expressive communication. Drama Kids International at http://www.dramakids.com/x_index.php offer classes and camps all year long for students 5 to 17 years old. There are locations in many countries and in many states in the U.S. The program has been proven to build confidence, self-esteem, and communication skills for kids of all learning styles and abilities. They are fully inclusive and welcome opportunities to bring students together who communicate in different ways.

Other hands-on and role-playing activities can be done in the classroom setting. The Strong National Museum of Play in Rochester, New York, has a large section devoted to communication activities. Many of them can easily be recreated in the classroom:

- Any type of theater, with dress-up costumes and props, allows students to freely express themselves and communicate a story with or without reading and writing

- Puppet theaters (with ready-made puppets or materials for puppet making) combine communication skills and art

- Pattern Talk consists of a magnetic easel, each side of which is equipped with identical sets of magnetic shapes. On one side, a student creates a design and describes it so that a student on the other side can recreate it

- Coding and decoding messages (e.g., Morse code, alphanumeric codes, symbol codes, or other ciphers) builds language-usage skills.

- Patterned flags, as used by ship crews on the high seas, can be held in different positions to communicate a message. This is a nonverbal, bodily kinesthetic communication activity.

- Whisper tubes (various lengths and shapes of white plumbing pipes) are a fun way to get students talking to one another.

- Playing store, post office, or telemarketer.

Kluth and Danaher (2010) share three engaging ideas for encouraging students to express themselves. One is called the Personal Portfolio. This is essentially a book or album of things that represent who the student is. He or she can then share it with peers to start conversations or find things they have in common. Another idea is the Question Jar. A jar or other container is filled with questions written on paper strips and can be used by the teacher any time he or she needs to fill a few minutes between lessons or classes. The questions can be on any topic ("What did you learn in history today?" or "If you could be an animal, what would you be?") and submitted by the students so they are engaged in learning their classmates' responses. A third idea is the Talking Spinner. This works similarly to the Question Jar, but there are a fixed number of questions on the spinner and the students can see what they are ahead of time. This works well to scaffold the participation of students who need time to prepare their answers.

Last, board games are a fun and effective way for students to build many communication and friendship skills, including negotiating, taking turns, following rules, being gracious when winning or losing, sharing, having patience, and strategizing (Lavoie, 2005). Stocking your classroom with well-chosen board games is a great way to use indoor recess or if-you-finish-early-time as skill-building time. See Table 18.1 for board games matched to the multiple intelligences.

Table 18.1. Board games for multiple intelligences

Multiple intelligence	Board games and other social indoor toys
Verbal-linguistic	• Scrabble • Trivial Pursuit • Perquacky • Boggle
Logical-mathematical	• Backgammon • Blokus • Clue • Othello • Monopoly • Any card game • Yahtzee • Dominoes
Bodily-kinesthetic	• Twister • Pick-up Sticks • Jacks • Jenga • Dominoes • Maptangle • Mousetrap
Musical-rhythmic	• Musical Squares • Pop the Question • Fiddlesticks • Quartet • Classical Snap
Visual-spatial	• Blokus • Chess • Connect Four • Stratego • Pictionary • Win, Lose, or Draw • Kaboodle • Jigsaw puzzles
Interpersonal	• Any game played with peers!
Intrapersonal	• Scruples • Ungame • Charades
Naturalist	• Clue • Mah Jongg • Any card game • Jumanji • Petcha Didn't Know • Dominant Species
Existentialist	• Passport to Culture • Dominant Species • Perspective • The Game of Life
All	• Cranium • Cadoo • Zigity

Input

There are many things that teachers can do to help students receive and understand messages and improve social skills.

Receptive Communication   To help students receive and understand the meaning of messages, the most important thing to remember is to reach multiple modalities each time you communicate. Pair verbal messages with visual and/or tactile input as much as possible. Visual input to accompany verbal descriptions may include pictures, icons, or photographs; public signs and symbols, such as those for danger or a restroom; and checklists, marked buttons, calendars, and lists. Tactile input can include an object cue, gesture, or touch. Object cues are small items that you use to represent different events or tasks. For example, a small plastic apple may represent lunchtime, a hacky sack might mean physical education, and a paintbrush means art. Gestures are simply movements you make that students can see and copy when they receive the message. Saying "It's time for lunch" could be paired with the sign for lunch (putting the gathered fingers of one hand to the mouth), "It's time for physical education" could be paired with an imaginary jump shot, and "It's time for art" could be paired with an imaginary sweep of paintbrush on canvas. A touch cue could be a simple touch on the shoulder to be sure the student knows it is time to pay attention to the message you are giving. Another touch cue could be touching the part of the body that needs to move first. For example, touching the hand to indicate that it is time for the student to move his hand to his lunchbox and pick it up to go to lunch.

The Austin, Texas, Independent School District practices the following response to intervention (RTI) strategies for receptive language concerns:

- Emphasize cue words for sequence (first, second, next, before, after, last) and cue words for signaling answers (who, which, because).

- Model the use of "think time."

- Model note-taking, especially visual methods of organizing information, such as bullets, graphic organizers, highlighting.

- Model visualizing information or making a mind picture.

- Model self-questioning.

- Teach vocabulary in context, make associations, and describe similarities and differences (2009).

The Northamptonshire County Council Autistic Spectrum Team (2009) listed additional ideas: preface communication with the student's name to gain attention; when giving instructions, list the tasks in the same order the student would use to complete them; make sure your instructions are not really questions (e.g., say "Please push your chair in," rather than, "Why don't you push your chair in?"); tell the student what *to* do instead of what *not* to do; provide each student with a listening partner; avoid or correct confusion over nonliteral or ambiguous expressions, such as "I'm dying to go to lunch,"; explain context for words that have multiple meanings; and avoid sarcasm.

The Colorado Services to Children with Deafblindness offers a fact sheet on receptive communication (Wilson, 2009). When a teacher is sending a verbal or visual message to a student who is deaf-blind, it may not be received. It is up to the teacher to work with the signing aide, interpreter, or support service provider (SSP) to develop ways for the student to receive the message, and then expand his or her understanding. There are several levels of communication cues that facilitate reception and understanding of a message. From most to least concrete, they are: natural context cues, movement cues, or touch cues; object cues, gesture; miniature objects, associated objects, pictures, line drawings, or other tangible symbols; and visual sign cues, tactile sign cues, speech, written words, or Braille. All of these are used in combination with speech to reach multiple senses. Natural context cues are things that occur naturally when a routine activity is taking place. For example, a school bell ringing when it is time for class to start or the smell of food when it is time to eat. Motion cues move the student through a representative portion of the activity that is about to start, such as moving the student's hand to his mouth to eat. Touch cues are used by touching the part of the student's body that is needed to perform a task, such as touching the shoulder to indicate you have approached to communicate with the student. Object cues are the actual objects to be used in the activity to cue the student to start, such as a computer keyboard or sports equipment. Gesture cues are slightly more abstract because an association between the gesture and activity must be made before they hold meaning, such as waving good-bye or shaking the head for "no." Once the student understands the meanings of object cues (i.e., the actual object for the activity), other symbols can be used instead: miniature or associated objects, pictures, line drawings, icons, or symbols. Most abstract are visual/tactile cues that require an understanding of symbolic language, such as visual and tactile sign cues, speech, written words, or Braille.

Assistive technology (AT) can also be used to improve or facilitate receptive communication. Low-tech AT includes many of the things mentioned above: line drawing, pictures, Braille, and objects. It also includes things like a visual schedule or calendar created with symbols or icons of each activity arranged in sequence on a board. It can also be as simple as the international symbol for "No"—a red circle with a line through it (Stokes, n.d.). Mid-tech options for language comprehension include the Talk Pad and the Language Master. The Talk Pad is a device that can be programmed with multistep directions. The student pushes the button after completing each step to receive the next direction. The Language Master is a device that reads preprinted cards. For a similar activity with multistep directions, the student can pass one card at a time through the reader. High-tech AT to support receptive language could include videotaping a demonstration of instructions, or any computer software that provides multimodal input of language: words, pictures, and sounds.

Social Skills   As discussed in the introduction to this chapter, even when students do not have difficulty receiving or expressing language, they may have difficulty applying the communication appropriately in various social contexts. In this section, we provide specific strategies teachers can use to help students navigate the complex social arena.

The first is the social story, developed by Carol Gray. As you learned in Chapter 6, a social story is one that shares accurate, meaningful information to help a student understand what is happening and how to respond in a given situation, particularly one that is unexpected or not routine. Each story is specially written based on several criteria regarding the goal of the story, the type of story needed, and the audience. *The New Social Story Book* (Gray, 2010) is an excellent resource for prewritten social stories as well as instructions for writing your own to use with a student. For example, here is a story entitled "When my teacher is somewhere else":

> My name is Andrea. My teacher's name is Mrs. Smith. Most school days, Mrs. Smith teaches the class. Sometimes she has to be somewhere else. Teachers get sick. Mrs. Smith may be sick. She may need to stay home. Teachers go to teacher workshops. Mrs. Smith may go to a teacher workshop. Many teachers have children, and their children get sick. Mrs. Smith has triplets. One of her triplets may be sick, so she needs to stay home. We have a substitute teacher when Mrs. Smith needs to be somewhere else for the day. This is okay. Mrs. Smith will return to our class as soon as she can. (p. 171)

The Hidden Curriculum by Brenda Smith Myles, Melissa Trautman, and Ronda Schelvan is also a wonderful resource for teaching students the unstated rules of a multitude of social situations. These are subtleties that are easily overlooked by anyone who does not have difficulty with social-skill development, because they learn them more naturally without having to think much about them. This book includes strategies for helping students think through ways to stay safe, reflect on past events, approach upcoming events, and avoid embarrassment or offending someone. It also defines figurative speech, idioms, and slang. One example is the Power Card (p. 30). This is the size of a business card and summarizes the solution or list of possible solutions to employ if overwhelmed in a particular situation. The card can be carried in a pocket or wallet, or taped in a notebook or locker.

Two similar resources are *The Incredible 5-Point Scale* by Kari Dunn Buron and Mitzi Curtis and *A 5 Is Against the Law* by Kari Dunn Buron. Both feature the use of a five-point scale to support students in understanding intensity. You can use a five-point scale to teach about appropriate voice volume: 1) silent, 2) whisper, 3) conversation, 4) loud, and 5) yelling (Buron & Curtis, 2003, p. 39). You can use a five-point scale to help students with obsessive-compulsive difficulties realize the extent to which they are affected by their obsessions: 1) It is a great day! My obsessional personality is a neurological work of art; 2) I am feeling pretty relaxed today. I can probably think about my obsessions but still do well in the classroom; 3) I am thinking about my obsessions, but I may need to talk to someone about it. I think I have some control; 4) I am feeling pretty nervous and will probably need some support; and 5) I can't control it. I will need lots of support (Buron & Curtis, 2003, p. 16). Last, you can use a five-point scale to help adolescents understand appropriate behavior for dating and romantic relationships: 1) Just looking at the girl you like briefly and smiling; 2) Talking to a safe person about the girl you like; 3) Staring at the girl that you like without ever talking to her; 4) Going out of your way to follow a girl in the hallway; 5) Against the law: Making comments about a girls' body, touching or kissing a girl without her permission (Buron, 2007, p. 25). Both of these books include templates for scaffolding students through the five-point thought process of specific situations.

Some students may need direct instruction in recognizing when others are no longer interested in the topic of conversation. Provide specific examples of what people may do or say when no longer interested: facial expressions, body language, and turning away the eyes or body (Cooper-Kahn & Dietzel, 2008). Demonstrate what this looks like and point out examples you see. In general, remember that students with social-skill difficulties will not just pick up on subtle cues or unspoken responses. It is important to be direct and to address faux pas right away.

Additional ways to improve social language are to model appropriate grammar, tone of voice, and volume of voice, rather than repeatedly scold or correct students; provide prompts to support a student telling a story (next, then); ask specific questions ("What do you have planned after school today?") rather than vague or general questions ("What's up?"); explicitly state expectations ("We will go to the store when you have finished your homework and have fed the dog" instead of "We will go to the store when you are ready") (Lavoie, 2005).

Output

Expressive Communication   Typically, students are expected to make their needs known and to respond to questions through speech. When this is not possible as a sole means of communicating, **augmentative or alternative communication** (AAC) is used. AAC is not a replacement for speech but offers alternatives (perhaps in addition to speech) to support an individual's communication for full participation in social

augmentative or alternative communication Modes of communication other than conventional reading, writing, speaking, and listening, such as sign language or assistive technology.

interactions, school, home, community, workplace, and recreational settings. AAC may include gestures; sign language; finger-spelling oral symbols; writing; facial and body movements; language representatives, such as pictures or icons; and the use of electronic/technological devices (American Speech-Language-Hearing Association, 2011).

multimodal communication
Communicating in multiple ways, such as a combination of speech, sign, and assistive technology.

YAACK (AAC Connecting Young Kids) indicates that AAC interventions can be used in conjunction with speech therapy. For many students, developing their speech is desired and appropriate, but they should not be left unable to communicate in the meantime. Assessments are conducted to determine the best AAC for each individual student, depending on age, ability, needs, goals, and the environments in which the communication will occur. AAC should be introduced as early as possible so students make the transition into school with a means of communicating already in place. AAC facilitates inclusive education for students with communication difficulties, particularly if it allows **multimodal communication** or communication via multiple means, including speech, gestures, and AT.

AT is also used to support expressive communication. Low-tech AT for expression includes picture-point communication board systems. PECS (Picture Exchange Communication System) is one example. Icons or symbols are used to represent objects, people, places, and activities in the student's daily life. They are placed on a board, on pages in a book, or as cards on a ring so that the student can sort through and point to the symbols needed to communicate a message (Stokes, n.d.). Another low-tech example is cards for many different situations: break cards, choice cards, "all done" cards, and "I need help" cards. The student holds up the card to indicate his or her need to the teacher or classmates. Kluth and Danaher (2010) offered low-tech alternatives for writing without a pencil: rubber stamps, sticky words and phrases, and letter tiles. Mid-tech AT for expressive communication includes Voice Output Communication Aids (VOCAs). There are several on the market that can be programmed with words or phrases in the student's vocabulary to voice messages for the nonverbal student. Some of these are the Big Mack, the Talk Pad, Voice in the Box, Dynavox, and Tango. High-tech AT for expressive communication includes computer equipment that can be used to write or speak and that may be operated through customized means, such as a touch window, trackballs, head switch, wand, joystick, straw, or even eye movement (Stokes, n.d.).

Social Skills   Lavoie (2005) offered several strategies to model and to teach to students that help reduce anxiety and work through a social situation: exercise, deep breathing, the 6-second quieting response (i.e., smile, inhale, exhale, tell yourself your body is calm, return to what you were doing or saying), and tightening and relaxing muscles. Another way to help is the six-step ASSERT process to help students assert themselves when they feel mistreated by a peer (Lavoie, 2005, p. 322):

A = Attention. Be certain that you have the person's focused attention before you begin.

S = Soon, short, simple. Speak to the person soon after the incident; be brief and succinct.

S = Specific. Explain exactly the behavior that concerns you.

E = Effect. Explain the impact that the behavior has on you.

R = Response. Explain what you want the person to do.

T = Terms. Come to an agreement on each person's responsibility.

Essentially, students need many opportunities to engage in various social situations. Rather than wait until they are ready, provide them with a safe place to make mistakes and learn from them, just as you do with academic skills. Provide them with varied contexts and group sizes, so their practice is scaffolded. Start with interaction with the student one-on-one, then have him interact with a partner, then in groups of three and larger.

Assessment

Receptive and Expressive Communication There are several formal assessments that can be used by speech and language pathologists to determine a student's skills and needs in various areas of receptive and expressive speech and language. Table 18.2 lists assessments and their descriptions and purposes.

Social Skills There are several types of assessments available for the evaluation of social skills. **Sociometric devices** are designed to assess an individual's relative popularity within a group, by polling students in terms of their peers' social traits. This can

sociometric devices
Informal assessment, such as a survey, designed to assess an individual's relative popularity within a group.

Table 18.2. Assessing communication

Assessment	Description	Purpose
Peabody Picture Vocabulary Test—3rd Edition (PPVT-III)	Items consist of pictures in a multiple-choice format. The evaluator names a stimulus, and the student points to the corresponding picture.	Measures receptive language. Ages 2 to adult.
Test of Auditory Comprehension of Language—3rd Edition (TACL-3)	Three subtests contain items on vocabulary, grammatical morphemes, and elaborated phrases and sentences.	Measures receptive language. Ages 3 to 9.
Goldman Fristoe Test of Articulation—2nd Edition (GFTA-2)	Three subtests contain items on sounds in words, sounds in sentences, and stimulabilty (reproducing misarticulated sounds).	Measures expressive language, particularly articulation. Ages 2 to 21.
Boehm Test of Basic Concepts—3rd Edition (BTBC-3)	Items ask students to effectively identify concepts of size, direction, quantity, time, and classification.	Measures language concepts. Grades K to 2.
Comprehensive Receptive and Expressive Vocabulary Test—2nd Edition (CREVT-2)	Two subtests contain items on receptive vocabulary and expressive vocabulary.	Measures receptive and expressive language, particularly vocabulary. Ages 4 to adult.
Test of Adolescent and Adult Language—3rd Edition (TOAL-3)	Ten subtests contain items on listening, speaking, reading, writing, spoken language, written language, vocabulary, grammar, perceptive language, and expressive language.	Measures all areas of receptive and expressive communication. Ages 12 to 24.
Test of Early Language Development—3rd Edition (TELD-3)	Two subtests contain items on receptive language and expressive language.	Measures both receptive and expressive language. Ages 2 to 7.
Photo Articulation Test—3rd Edition (PAT-3)	Items consist of color photographs and asks the student to articulate the subject in the photos.	Measures expressive language, particularly articulation. Ages 3-$\frac{1}{2}$ to 9.
Test of Language Development—3rd Edition (TOLD-3)	Nine subtests contain items on picture vocabulary, oral vocabulary, grammatic understanding, sentence imitation, grammatic completion, relational vocabulary, word discrimination, word articulation, and phonemic analysis.	Measures receptive and expressive language, particularly phonology, syntax, and semantics. Ages 4 to 8.

Source: Pierangelo and Guiliani, 2009.

teacher-ranking systems
Teacher's tally of how many times students interact with each other.

behavior-rating scales
More formalized assessment that rates on a graduated scale a student's ability to perform certain social functions in a variety of settings: home, school, and community.

interviews Personal interaction with a student to gain the student's perspective on his or her social skills and needs.

observation checklists
More formalized measure that entails checking the occurrence or absence of social behaviors in various settings.

provide information to teachers about who is interacting with whom and who may need support to find friends or interact with a wider range of peers. **Teacher-ranking systems** entail a teacher's tallying how many times students interact with each other. This does not collect data on the quality of the interactions, only the quantity. **Behavior-rating scales** are more formalized assessments, with versions to be completed by parents, teachers, or peers. These scales rate a student's ability to perform certain social functions in a variety of settings: home, school, and community. **Interviews** with the student provide information about the student's perspective on his or her social skills and needs. **Observation checklists** are more formalized measures that entail checking the occurrence or absence of social behaviors in various settings. These can be valuable in determining if certain behaviors are situation-specific (Lavoie, 2005).

SUMMARY

Communication skills include receptive and expressive speech and language skills. Social skills entail the situational or pragmatic use of speech and language. Students may struggle in one or more of these areas and require specific support to be fully included in home, school, and community settings. It is important for teachers to be aware of the particular difficulties a student is having so appropriate support can be provided. The hidden curriculum of school needs to be taught directly to some students so they can develop appropriate social skills.

NARRATIVE 18.1. | CLARA BERG

Communication is the exchange of thoughts, ideas, and/or actions between two or more people. As parents, we become our child's first teachers and it is our responsibility to help them learn how to communicate and develop social skills.

However, as we all know, it's easier said than done! But with the right tools, parents and teachers have the power to encourage social interaction among children, and thus strengthen their ability to communicate, which in turn will develop their social skills in a natural environment.

As we watch our children develop, we encourage them to have their own opinions and make personal choices in the distinct hope that it will allow them to become self-sufficient and independent. Our intention is to help them become independent thinkers and develop their own way of processing information.

One of the most important skills we need to help our children develop is to learn how to "listen." We do so by listening to our children as an example. Their messages are often conveyed in many ways other than spoken words. So we listen when they express themselves by voice, American Sign Language (ASL), gestures, body motions, or through technology. The important thing here is to make sure we listen.

Depending on how well we listen, and how we express our understanding of their attempt to communicate, our responses might facilitate a dialogue and continue expanding on a preferred subject. In contrast, a lack of response can have a detrimental effect. It can make the other person feel as though he has not been understood or heard. That would undeniably make that person lose interest in initializing communication in the future. He might see it as a failed attempt and not want to try again.

For the children who are not incidental learners, we must open the world to them. We should allow them to explore different environments and situations, which in turn will expand their horizon and create new sources of curiosity, increasing their knowledge of the world around them.

Our generation grew up hearing our teachers and parents bark orders without explanations. If a child dared to ask why she had to do something, the expected response was usually, "Because I said so." That position has changed dramatically.

Since I consider myself a "seasoned parent" of typically and specially-able developed young adults, I want to share what worked with my children as they were growing up:

- Allow and motivate children to question and explore the little mysteries of life.

- Stimulate their imagination as they develop new words and knowledge.

- Respect children's interests! It's easier for them to learn words and communicate when they are around things that interest them.

- Honor their choices and requests (as much as possible and as long as they are safe) so that they can see that their opinions are valid and respected.

- Teach through play! Nobody wants the fun to end, so if they are learning *and* having fun, they will want to spend more time with the selected activity.

- Create opportunities for young children to interact with other children to stimulate their social skills. Children imitate and learn from each other.

My sincere advice is to enjoy and have fun with the children; they grow up faster than you can imagine!

CHAPTER 19

Working with Special Area Teachers and Related Service Professionals

How this chapter prepares you to be an effective inclusive classroom teacher:

- This chapter teaches you about the roles and responsibilities of many different special area teachers and related service professionals. It also outlines the ways in which you as a classroom teacher can plan instruction with these professionals to maximize learning of cross-curricular content to meet goals of students' individualized educational programs. **This helps you meet CEC Standard 7: Instructional Planning.**

- This chapter prepares you to be a professional and ethical teacher by teaching you to appreciate and respect the roles and expertise of all professionals in the educational setting and to strive to collaborate with all stakeholders to support students. **This helps you meet CEC Standard 9: Professional and Ethical Practice.**

- This chapter teaches you ways in which classroom teachers, special area teachers, and related service providers can collaborate to maximize learning and engaged time in all settings. **This helps you meet CEC Standard 10: Collaboration.**

After reading and discussing
this chapter, you will be able to

- Explain the roles of special area teachers and their significance in the education of students

- Explain the role of occupational therapists and their significance in the education of students

- Explain the role of physical therapists and their significance in the education of students

- Explain the role of speech and language pathologists and their significance in the education of students

- Explain the role of ESOL teachers and their significance in the education of students

- Explain why adapted physical education teachers are not related service professionals

- Provide examples of adapted physical education supports

- Explain the importance and several benefits of collaboration between classroom teachers and special teachers

- Explain the importance and several benefits of collaboration between classroom teachers and related service professionals

- Provide examples of ways to increase and improve communication with special area teachers and related service professionals

special area classes
Nonacademic content area classes that are part of the required curriculum for all students, such as physical education, adapted physical education, music, art, technology, health, and library skills.

related service professionals Professionals who provide services for students with special needs, such as occupational therapists, physical therapists, speech and language pathologists, and English for Speakers of Other Languages (ESOL) teachers.

This book has covered many issues and topics to help prepare you to be a classroom teacher who creates a learning community of full citizens, universally designs curriculum and classroom space, and improves your practice for all students. This is only a beginning, but one that we hope you will build on to become an effective inclusive educator. However, students are not with one teacher all day long. In fact, they are with several different teachers throughout the school day. In high and middle school, students probably change rooms and teachers for each class they take. In elementary school, even though students have a homeroom, they leave that room for **special area classes**: physical education or adapted physical education, music, art, technology, health, and library. In addition, some students receive additional, specialized support from **related service professionals**: speech and language pathologists, occupational therapists, physical therapists, counselors, and English for Speakers of Other Languages (ESOL) instructors.

This chapter discusses the importance of strategies for branching out beyond the four walls of your classroom to connect with all teachers and professionals in the school building to ensure that students are supported every minute of the school day. All professionals in the school building strive to fully support the students they work with, and it is important to plan for consistency across settings and transitions from class to class.

WORKING WITH SPECIAL AREA TEACHERS

While requirements vary by state, most states require that elementary-, middle-, and high-school students complete a certain number of hours of physical education or adapted physical education, music education, visual arts education, technology education, health education, and library instruction. Adaptive physical education (APE) teachers are direct service providers rather than related service professionals, because physical education is mandated for all students, as opposed to related services, which are only provided if students need them. All students receive physical education for the development of physical and motor skills as well as patterns, such as throwing, catching, walking, and running. These classes also develop skills in aquatics, dance, and individual or group sports. APE teachers can modify or adapt all of these areas so they are appropriate for students with disabilities. APE teachers provide services in planning, assessment of individuals and assessment of ecosystems or environments, prescription and placement as outlined as a direct service on the IEP, teaching, counseling, coaching, evaluation of APE services provided to a student, coordination of APE with other resources, and advocacy (Adapted Physical Education National Standards, 2008a).

APE has been practiced since the 19th century. Ongoing research and application since that time have developed the field into a body of knowledge for specialists who practice according to 15 standards (Adapted Physical Education National Standards, 2008b):

1. Human development

2. Motor behavior

3. Exercise science

4. Measurement and evaluation

5. History and philosophy

6. Unique attributes of learners

7. Curriculum theory and development

8. Assessment

9. Instructional design and planning

10. Teaching

11. Consultation and staff development

12. Student and program evaluation

13. Continuing education

14. Ethics

15. Communication

More specifically, areas of physical education that are differentiated for students by APE teachers include: adapted equipment, such as a lighter bat, a larger goal, or a scoop for catching; modified rules, prompts, and cues, such as seating for a batter, using an oral prompt, or modified time limits; modified boundary and playing field, such as decreased distances or simplified patterns of play; adapted actions, such as grasps, modified body positions, or using other parts of body for play; and modified time, such as providing frequent rests or varying the tempo of activity (PE Central, 2011). A fantastic resource for learning more about APE and differentiation of physical education is the book *Strategies for Inclusion by* Lauren Lieberman and Cathy Houston-Wilson.

As a classroom teacher, it is important for you to connect with all of these special area teachers for several reasons:

- You should be well aware of the content taught in the special area classes. If you know what the students are learning in physical education, music, art, technology, health, and the library, you can reinforce those concepts in your lessons. Cross-curricular connections are effective ways of reinforcing new knowledge. Also, knowing details about your students' entire school day is a way to connect with students and build a strong learning community.

- The provisions on students' individualized education programs (IEPs) apply to the entire school experience, not to just one class or classroom. Connecting with special area teachers facilitates continuity of support for students with disabilities. For example, if a student receives extended time on tests, this applies to tests or quizzes in health class as well as quizzes in all other subjects. If a student receives counseling services "as needed," all teachers who work with the student should be aware of the behaviors that indicate that service is needed. Special area teachers are not always able to attend IEP meetings or parent-teacher conferences. This should not be presumed to be a lack of interest or investment in the success of students. Special area teachers have very large case loads. In some instances, their roster may include every student in the school! You should know their feedback and concerns to relay to families at conference time if the special area teachers are not able to attend.

- Students with IEPs and 504 plans are not the only ones who have special needs. As we have discussed throughout this book, all students have strengths and needs when it comes to their learning. These needs may be consistent or may be temporary on a bad day or following a particular event (e.g., an intense argument with a friend right before art class). Connecting with all teachers about students who need support facilitates success for all.

- As a classroom teacher who sees your students for longer periods of time at a stretch than do special area teachers, you have more time to explore various grouping arrangements. You are likely able to figure out sooner who works well with whom and who needs support to work with others. Passing your findings along to special area teachers is very helpful so they can maximize what instructional time they have with the students.

- Some students need to be closely observed for behavior patterns in various settings across the school day. For example, a functional behavioral assessment (FBA) may be conducted for a student, and one of the behaviors exhibited is refusal to participate in class discussions. If data are collected and communicated across all settings, the intervention plan following the FBA can be used by all to support the student.

- Last, communication is important so all teachers know about other issues, such as class absences, illnesses, or injuries.

It is important to connect regularly and meaningfully with all of these teachers. How can you do that when daily school schedules barely allow for you to pass like ships in the night? In this next section, we share some feedback that special area teachers would like new teachers to know about their areas, as well as strategies for facilitating effective communication and collaboration with each other.

What They Would Like You to Know

cross-curricular

Applying to more than one area of the curriculum.

First and foremost, special area subjects are not extra or tacked-on subjects. They are integral, **cross-curricular** areas of student learning that directly reinforce knowledge and skills being learned in academic classes. For example, instrumental music instruction also reinforces reading skills, math skills (e.g., spatial relationship and counting skills), history, group dynamics, and time management (Lois Michalko, elementary school instrumental music teacher). Art and music can reinforce study of various cultures in social studies by introducing songs or visual arts from historical time periods (Laura Baldwin, elementary school music teacher; Eileen, high school visual art teacher; Amanda Kirkebye, elementary school art teacher). In technology class, research and problem-solving skills are used in conjunction with knowledge about different areas of technology to create a product or derive a solution to an issue (William Morris, high school technology teacher). Physical education allows students to expend energy that is built up while seated at desks, provides time to work with others and learn about teamwork, and develops understanding about the importance and impact of being physically active (Robin, elementary school physical education teacher).

Second, special area teachers have curriculum to follow. They are required to meet state standards and core curriculum goals, depending on their district. They give tests, assess grades, complete report cards, and give assignments (William Morris, high school technology teacher). They have a lot of content to cover in a finite amount of time. They are dedicated to folding their subject area in with other academic content areas, but they need to plan to do that (Laura Baldwin, elementary school music teacher).

Third, it is important to know strategies that work for individual students to help with reading or written expression, social skills, and attention. Using the same vocabulary can reinforce expectations and facilitate learning. Knowing what has been tried before and whether it was successful can reduce frustration and increase engaged time (Laura Baldwin, elementary school music teacher; Eileen, high school visual art teacher; Lois Michalko, elementary school instrumental music teacher).

Last, special area subjects may be areas of great strength for students. Some students who struggle in academic subjects may shine through special areas. Sometimes art, music, or physical education teachers can connect with a student in a way that other teachers cannot because the students are particularly drawn to expression via those modalities (Amanda Kirkebye, elementary school art teacher). In art, there are so many ways to express oneself, and no wrong answer, so that success is almost guaranteed (Eileen, high school visual art teacher). Multiple intelligences theory by Howard Gardner and brain research by Eric Jensen are important to know so that teachers can understand which students need music, art, or physical movement to learn effectively in any classroom, regardless of the topic (Marla Graff-Mathis, elementary school vocal music teacher).

Ways to Connect

Essentially, you will need to find as much time as possible to connect with special area teachers so everyone is made aware of student needs and consistent support can occur across settings. Here are some ideas for stretching the school-day schedule:

- E-mail! This seems too obvious even to mention, but it is one of the best ways to connect with other teachers when it is not possible to meet face to face. A shared commitment to checking e-mail [almost] daily must be in place. Perhaps it means getting up early every other morning or staying a little late every other day to catch up on messages. The best thing about e-mail is that it can be checked at your convenience.

- You might also schedule a time for a telephone conference. Maybe you will be at your daughter's soccer practice later and have plenty of time to connect with another teacher for a 10-minute telephone call. Be sure to move to a private area for your conversation to protect the confidentiality of students.

- Carving out a niche for one-on-one meetings. This can be done a number of ways. Classroom teachers can devote the same day each week to arrive earlier or stay later so that special area teachers know when they can seek them out regarding a particular student and vice versa. If your schedules do line up, appointments can be made during the day. Perhaps you have the same lunch period, so you can talk privately over lunch.

- One creative way for elementary-school teachers to find a few minutes together is to have "entry" tasks (i.e., bellwork) for students to do at transition times. For example, when the classroom teacher brings the class to music, the music teacher has them find seats and complete bellwork for 3 minutes, giving the two teachers time to relay pertinent information. The same would occur when the music teacher brings the class back. This is only 3 minutes of the special area class time, but it provides a calm activity for the class to settle into the new setting, and it reviews knowledge and skills being learned. Some bellwork ideas:

  - Sentence starters: "In the last music class, I learned...."

  - Provide worksheets (for individuals) or decks of cards (for partners) that match art vocabulary words with photos of art.

  - Have students find their preassigned place in the gym and start warm-up exercises, or ask one student to lead a game of Simon Says.

  - In the computer lab, allow students to log in and play an educational game for 3 to 5 minutes.

- One simple but effective way to find time together is for the classroom teacher to stay and participate in the special area class occasionally, perhaps once a month. This is a great way for the classroom teacher to learn the routines of the special area class, for the special area teacher to observe effective strategies used with individual students, for both teachers to work together to form cooperative groups, and for both teachers to share cross-curricular ideas. It will also maximize meeting time that may occur between the two teachers at a later time.

- Finding time to meet as a team with several teachers is even trickier, but not impossible. Time can be reserved at staff meetings or professional development sessions for teams to meet. With all teachers present in one location and an open agenda, a lot can be accomplished in a brief time.

- One elementary school has a creative solution. During the week, grade-level teams or "families" meet regularly. At least one special area teacher who is free at that time attends the meeting. Then the special area teacher reports back to all special area teachers during their one weekly meeting. That way, all special area teachers can find out about thematic units being studied, IEP meetings coming up, and current student needs and concerns even if they are not available during the team meeting time.

Administrative support is very important. Scheduling common lunch or planning times is one of the best things a principal can do to increase staff collaboration. Also, a principal or vice principal who is willing to step into a classroom to "sub" for 15 to 20 minutes creates an impromptu common planning time. All of this ensures that there are no holes in the net (Marla Graff-Mathis, elementary school vocal music teacher).

WORKING WITH RELATED SERVICE PROFESSIONALS

Related service professionals—speech and language pathologists, physical therapists, occupational therapists, and ESOL instructors—are different from special area teachers because not all students receive services from related service professionals. All students attend physical education or adapted physical education, music, art, technology, health, and library when these classes are required in the school district. Related services are obtained through evaluation that demonstrates qualification for the service under IDEA if the students need the services to benefit from instruction in school. These professionals are invited to attend IEP meetings, though their attendance is not required by law. Dr. Susan Hildenbrand addresses the impact of this in Narrative 19.1.

What They Would Like You to Know

Each related service professional has a unique role and is specially prepared to fill it. You should know what each related service is about. There are ways that the therapies can be supported in your classroom so that students can make advancements rather than have setbacks between therapy sessions.

Speech and Language Pathologists (SLPs)   Speech and language pathologists (SLPs) provide services to students with a wide range of difficulties, including articulation, fluency of speech, voice or resonance, swallowing, receptive language, expressive language, and pragmatic language. If these difficulties significantly affect the educational progress of a student, the student qualifies for speech and language therapy under IDEA. SLPs are involved with students at the first sign of difficulty. They utilize response to intervention (RTI) initiatives to prevent school failure and to determine the level of services a student might need in a range of areas, including articulation, voice, fluency, receptive language, expressive language, and pragmatics (Suzanne Frame, speech pathologist). If a student continues to struggle and a disability is suspected, SLPs conduct assessments as part of the multidisciplinary evaluation team. They then select appropriate, culturally responsive interventions to be included on the IEP. SLPs collaborate with classroom teachers and other professionals in the school to provide comprehensive services to individual students. They may pull students out of the classroom for individual or small-group therapy sessions, or they may "push-in" to the classroom to coteach a large group lesson with the classroom teacher (American Speech-Language-Hearing Association, 2011).

Occupational Therapists   Occupational therapists (OTs) support students with a wide variety of skills designed to prepare them for making a living. OTs conduct lessons in many different learning environments: classrooms, playgrounds, lunchrooms, and bathrooms. OTs observe and assess students in the school environment so they can come up with supports and strategies that facilitate the student's full participation in all activities. This may include teaching motor skills, social skills, or coping mechanisms for overstimulation. Observing the environment also allows the OT to reduce barriers that may impede a student's full participation. OTs may rearrange a physical setting to improve mobility or sensory input. OTs utilize a wide variety of assistive technology to increase independence. OTs collaborate with other professionals and are involved in assessment and development of the IEP (American Occupational Therapy Association, 2011).

Physical Therapists   Physical therapists (PTs) are medical professionals who have knowledge of anatomy, physiology, pharmacology, and neurology. PTs evaluate students to determine a need for physical therapy services under IDEA. If a student requires services, the PT provides support in gross-motor and reflex development, movement, pain reduction, restorative function, and prevention of further disability. Physical therapists can connect families with orthotic (i.e., bracing) specialists, orthopedic surgeons or neurologists. PTs are also an integral part of IEP development and implementation (American Physical Therapy Association, 2011; Dr. Susan Griffen, physical therapist; Catherine Klinkbeil, physical therapist)

ESOL Instructors   English for Speakers of Other Languages (ESOL) is not a service mandated under IDEA because it is not a service for students with disabilities. It is a service for students who do not speak English fluently enough to benefit from instruction in that language. However, the role goes far beyond that. Teachers of English to Speakers of Other Languages (TESOL), Inc., a global educational association, values professionalism in language instruction, advancing individual language rights, providing accessible high-quality education, interaction of research and reflective practice for educational improvement, and respect for diversity and multiculturalism (TESOL, 2007). ESOL instructors strive to meet the TESOL standards by developing listening, speaking, reading, and writing through several proficiency levels (i.e., starting, emerging, developing, expanding, and bridging). The standards state that English Language Learners should be able to communicate for social, intercultural, and instructional purposes in the school setting and should be able to communicate information, ideas, and concepts necessary for academic success in language arts, mathematics, science, and social studies (TESOL, 2007).

Crandall (1998) said this about the role of ESOL teachers:

> Today, elementary ESL teachers may be required to teach initial literacy, provide the major language arts instruction, introduce academic concepts, promote academic and social language development, and help students make up for missed prior schooling, as well as serve as counselor, interpreter, and community and school liaison. While attempting to accomplish these many objectives, elementary ESL teachers may also find that the 30-minute pull-out ESL class has given way to 90- or 120-minute ESL/language arts blocks or even full-day assignments in which ESL teachers "plug-in" and work collaboratively with classroom teachers in the mainstream classroom. Whatever the context, elementary ESL teachers are likely to find themselves teaching not only language but also the academic concepts and strategies to help English-language learners use their new language more effectively for learning. (p. 24)

Ways to Connect

As with special area teachers, it is important to find time to connect one-on-one with all of the related service professionals who also work with your students. You need to know what they are working on, and related service professionals need to know as much about the individual students and their school day as possible. Here are some ideas for effective and efficient sharing of information:

- Find time to connect. Even when schedules are difficult to coordinate, it is important to find times to touch base (Jessica Warner, elementary school ESOL teacher). If possible, make plans to have lunch together once each month. If lunchtime is not an option, carve out a time before or after school. In between meetings, be sure to make use of e-mail!

- Keep a journal for each student. In the beginning of the year, use a small notebook and start by journaling as much as you know about the student's strengths, needs, interests, likes, dislikes, and so on. Throughout the year, the student carries the notebook during the school day so it can be used by anyone who works with him or her. It only takes a moment to jot down what the student is working on, any new or ongoing concerns, progress to look for, or skill reinforcement that can be done in other settings.

- Complete checklists or observational evaluations. Over the course of the year, the related service professionals need to know which skills each student is generalizing to other settings where they are not present. You can be most helpful by carefully and thoroughly completing any checklist or observational evaluation that comes your way. Sending the evaluations home and following up with parents will increase the quality of data collected regarding the student's progress.

- Participate in lesson plan exchanges. One great idea is to send copies of lesson plans to the related service professionals. It will provide them with information about topics being studied in the classroom so they can reinforce them in therapy sessions. In addition, the related service professionals can provide ideas for supporting students in the classroom during the lesson, such as visual schedules, checklists, and supports for following routines (Monica St. Croix, speech-language pathologist).

- Under IDEA any professional who is providing a related service to a student should be invited to the annual IEP meeting for that student. Their attendance is not mandatory, but the invitation is. If they are not able to attend, they may send a report for the team to consider. However, there are many more meetings that take place throughout the school year that related service professionals should be invited to: IEP preplanning meetings, grade-level team meetings, and parent-teacher conferences. Even if they are not able to attend, the invitation starts the ball rolling for follow-up conversations or notes to be shared regarding student progress.

SUMMARY

Special area teachers and related service professionals are integral parts of students' school experience and educational growth. Many cross-curricular opportunities exist if planning occurs. A commitment to finding time to connect with other teachers in the building is essential in creating a fully inclusive, fully responsive education program for all students. Part of your job as a teacher and an advocate is to know what other teachers do and to find out ways that you can support students together.

NARRATIVE 19.1. | DR. SUSAN M. HILDENBRAND

Assistant Professor, Inclusive Education Department, St. John Fisher College

I have been a teacher for 23 years and have played many different roles in the classroom: general educator, special educator, and teacher educator! During this educational journey, I have also been a part of many individualized education program (IEP) meetings, and sadly, many have not been the collaborative, student-centered processes that I envision they were designed to be. I have participated in these meetings as a classroom teacher seeking help for a challenging student, as a special educator promoting inclusion for all learners, and as a parent advocate helping parents find their voice to guarantee that their child does not fall between the cracks of a complex special education system. I have always respected the guidelines that IDEA has in place to support students with disabilities, but perhaps the law designed to protect students with special needs is actually putting a roadblock in the way of team problem solving, which creates the most effective learning environment for the students.

If the IEP is a joint endeavor, all parties involved with the carrying out of the plan should be involved in the planning-and-writing meetings so that all of the stakeholders are equal and full participants in the process. However, it is now legal, due to the reauthorization of IDEA in 2004, for any member of the planning team—including the general education teacher or related service professionals—to be excused from any IEP meetings if the parents and the team agree to the absence prior to the meeting and a report is provided to the team.

Simply by allowing any important member of the educational team to choose not to attend a disabilities educational planning meeting negates the worth of that student as a member of the general education classroom. This action may reflect the teacher's attitude about ownership over a student with disabilities that is governed under special education law, not general education law. When certain teachers choose not to attend, either because of lack of interest or lack of release time, what could be a unique and creative perspective about ways to support a student's success is missing.

Real-time problem solving can produce a dynamic dialogue that leads to new and innovative strategies to follow the student throughout his whole day and entire repertoire of classroom situations and teachers. It is vital that we bring all stakeholders to the table so that the student benefits from the wisdom of different minds and solutions. In addition, participation in the writing of IEP goals and strategies will encourage buy-in from all of the service providers who work with the student and should increase understanding of the IEP itself.

Although the letter of the law does not encourage this full participation, it is very important that we follow the spirit of the law and push for collaboration no matter what the cost! Search for creative and unusual meeting times so that all of the student's teachers and support staff can attend, and let them know their presence is requested and needed! Seek out administrative support for release time for teachers so they can attend. Far too many times, I have seen general education and specials teachers defer to the special education teacher to create and provide the interventions and IEP goals, but by law, everyone who attends the IEP meeting has an equal role in the results. Therefore, it is vital to get everyone to the table to find the most effective ways to build an educational program that leads to student success.

References

CHAPTER 1

Adams, M., Bell, L.A., & Griffin, P. (2007). *Teaching for diversity and social justice.* (2nd Ed.). New York: Routledge.

Barnes, C., Oliver, M., & Barton, L. (Eds.). (2002). *Disability studies today.* Oxford, UK: Polity Press.

Baynton, D.C. (2001). Disability and the justification of inequality in American history. In P.K. Longmore & L. Umansky (Eds.), *The new disability history* (pp. 33–57). New York: New York University Press.

Bennetts, L. (1993, September). Letter from Las Vegas: Jerry vs. the kids. *Vanity Fair.*

Bérubé, M. (1996). *Life as we know it.* New York: Random House, Inc.

Bogdan, R. (1988). *Freak show.* Chicago: The University of Chicago Press.

Bogdan, R., & Biklen, D. (1977, March/April). Handicapism. *Social Policy, 7,* 14–19.

Bogdan, R., & Taylor, S. (1994). *The social meaning of mental retardation.* New York: Teachers College Press.

Braddock, D. (Ed.). (2002). *Disability at the dawn of the 21st century and the state of the states.* Washington, DC: American Association on Mental Retardation.

Burrelli, J. (2008, July). Thirty-three years of women in S&E faculty positions. *National Science Foundation Info Brief, NSF 08-308.*

Burton, T. (Director) (1991). *Edward Scissorhands* [Motion picture]. USA: 20th Century Fox.

Carlson, E.A. (2001). *The unfit: A history of a bad idea.* Cold Spring Harbor, NY: Cold Spring Harbor Laboratory Press.

Charlton, J.I. (1998). *Nothing about us without us.* Berkeley, CA: University of California Press.

Credo for Support. (n.d.). Retrieved from http://www.normemma.com/dvds.htm

Davis, L.J. (1995). Constructing normalcy. In L.J. Davis (Ed.), *The disability studies reader* (pp. 9–28). New York: Routledge.

DeVito, D., Shamberg, M., Sher, S., Lyon, G. (Producers), & Niccol, A. (Director). (1997). *Gattaca* [Motion picture]. USA: Jersey Films.

Eastwood, C., Ruddy, A.S., Rosenberg, T., & Lucchesi, G. (Producers), & Eastwood, C. (Director). (2004). *Million dollar baby* [Motion picture]. USA: Warner Brothers.

Field, C.T. (2001). "Are women…all minors?": Women's rights and the politics of aging in the antebellum United States. *Journal of Women's History, 12*(4), 113–137.

Garland-Thomson, R. (2002). The politics of staring: Visual rhetorics of disability in popular photography. In S.L. Snyder, B.J. Brueggemann, & R. Garland-Thomson (Eds.), *Disability studies: Enabling the humanities* (pp. 56–75). New York: The Modern Language Society of America.

Hayman, R.L., Jr. (1998). *The smart culture: Society, intelligence, and law.* New York: New York University Press.

Johnson, H.M. (2005). *Too late to die young.* New York: Henry Holt and Company.

Johnson, L.B. (1966). Commencement Address at Howard University: "To Fulfill These Rights." In *Public Papers of the Presidents of the United States: Lyndon B. Johnson, 1965* (Vol. II, entry 301, pp. 635–640). Washington, DC: Government Printing Office. Retrieved from http://www.lbjlib.utexas.edu/johnson/archives.hom/speeches.hom/650604.asp

Kliewer, C. (1998). *Schooling children with Down syndrome.* New York: Teachers College Press.

Karuth, D. (1985). If I were a car, I'd be a lemon. In A.J. Brightman (Ed.), *Ordinary moments: The disabled experience* (pp. 9–31). Syracuse, NY: Human Policy Press.

Lawler, A. (1999). Tenured women battle to make it less lonely at the top. *Science, 286,* 1272–1278.

Linton, S. (1998). *Claiming disability.* New York: New York University Press.

Milczarek-Desai, S. (2002). Living with and within differences: My search for identity beyond categories and contradictions. In G. Anzaldúa & A. Keating (Eds.), *This bridge we call home* (pp. 126–135). New York: Routledge.

Safran, S.P. (1998). The first century of disability portrayal in film: An analysis of the literature. *The Journal of Special Education, 31*(4), 467–479.

Sapon-Shevin, M. (2007). *Widening the circle: The power of inclusive classrooms.* Boston: Beacon Press.

Spielberg, S. (Director) (1991). *Hook* [Motion picture]. USA: Amblin Entertainment.

Switzer, K. (n.d.). The 1967 Boston Marathon. Retrieved May 24, 2009, from http://www.katherineswitzer.com/boston.html

Taylor, S. (2008). Foreword: Before it had a name: Exploring the historical roots of disability studies in education. In S. Danforth & S.L. Gabel (Eds.), *Vital questions facing disability studies in education* (pp. xiii–xxiii). New York: Peter Lang.

Thomson, R.G. (1997). *Extraordinary bodies.* New York: Columbia University Press.

U.S. Department of Education, Office of Special Education Programs (OSEP). (2004). Individuals with Disabilities Education Act. Retrieved from http://idea.ed.gov/explore/home

U.S. Department of Education. (2000). Twenty-second annual report to congress on the implementation of the Individuals with Disabilities Education Act. Retrieved from http://www2.ed.gov/about/reports/annual/osep/2000/index.html

Winter, J.A. (2003). The development of the disability rights movement as a social problem solver. *Disability Studies Quarterly, 23*(1), 33–61.

CHAPTER 2

27th Annual Report to Congress on the Implementation of the Individuals with Disabilities Education Act, 2005 (Vol. 1). Retrieved from http://www2.ed.gov/about/reports/annual/osep/2005/parts-b-c/27th-vol-1.pdf

American School for the Deaf (2009). A brief history of ASD. Retrieved from http://www.asd-1817.org/page.cfm?p=429

Anderson, L.W. (2009). Upper elementary grades bear the brunt of accountability. *Phi Delta Kappan, 90*(6), 413–419.

Anonymous. (2010). Continued drop in children with IEPs is good news, observers say. *Special Education Report, 36*(5), 7.

Aud, S., Fox, M., & KewalRamani, A. (2010). *Status and trends in the education of racial and ethnic groups* (NCES 2010-15). U.S. Department of Education, National Center for Education Statistics. Washington, DC: U.S. Government Printing Office.

Biklen, D., & Burke, J. (2006). Presuming competence. *Equity & Excellence in Education, 39*, 166–175.

Brown Foundation. (n.d.). Retrieved from http://brownvboard.org/

Cole, C., Waldron, N., & Majd, M. (2004). Academic progress of students across inclusive and traditional settings. *Mental Retardation, 42*(2), 136–144.

Delpit, L. (1995). *Other people's children: Cultural conflict in the classroom.* New York: The New Press.

Education of All Handicapped Children Act. (1975). PL 94-142, 20 U.S.C. § 1401.

Egnor, D. (2003). Implications for special education policy and practice. *Principal Leadership, 3*(7), 10–13.

Flower, L.A. (2008). Racial differences in the impact of participating in Advanced Placement programs on educational and labor market outcomes. *Educational Foundations, 22*(1 & 2), 121–132.

Godrej, D. (2005). Stuff pity! *New Internationalist,* November 2005. Retrieved from http://www.newint.org/issue384/keynote.htm

Individuals with Disabilities Education Improvement Act of 2004, PL 108–446, 20 U.S.C. §§ 1400 *et seq.*

Jorgensen, C. (2005). The least dangerous assumption: A challenge to create a new paradigm. *Disability Solutions, 6*(3), 1, 5–9, 10.

Klienhammer-Tramill, A., Tramill, J., & Brace, H. (2010). Contexts, funding history, and implications for evaluating the Office of Special Education Program's investment in personnel preparation. *The Journal of Special Education, 43*(4), 195–205.

Kliewer, C. (1998). *Schooling children with Down syndrome: Toward an understanding of possibility.* New York: Teachers College Press.

Lee, C.D. (2009). From Du Bois to Obama: The education of peoples of African descent in the United States in the 21st century. *The Journal of Negro Education, 78*(4), 367–384.

Martin, E.W., Martin, R., & Terman, D.L. (1996). The legislative and litigation history of special education. *The Future of Children, 6*, 25–39. (Used by the U.S. Department of Education in its 22nd report to Congress.)

McNeil, M. (2009). Criteria seen as too restrictive in quest for "Race to Top" funds. *Education Week, 29*(3), 23.

National Center for Education Statistics. (n.d.). The condition of education: Children and youth with disabilities. Retrieved from http://nces.ed.gov/programs/coe/indicator_cwd.asp

Patterson, J.A., Niles, R., Carlson, C., & Kelley, W.L. (2008). The consequences of school desegregation in a Kansas town 50 years after *Brown. The Urban Review, 40*, 76–95. doi: 10.1007/s11256-007-0074-6

Perkins School for the Blind. (n.d.). Perkins history. Retrieved from http://www.perkins.org/about-us/history/

Powell, J. (2009). To segregate or to separate? Special education expansion and divergence in the United States and Germany. *Comparative Education Review, 53*(2), 161–187.

Provasnik, S. (2006). Judicial activism and the origins of parental choice: The court's role in the institutionalization of compulsory education in the United States, 1891–1925. *History of Education Quarterly, 46*(3), 311–347.

UNICEF. (2008). Retrieved from http://www.unicef.org/index.php

Urban, W.J., & Wagoner, J.L., Jr. (2009). *American education: A history* (4th Ed.). New York: Routledge Taylor and Francis Group.

U.S. Constitution. Amendment 13.

U.S. Department of Education. (2000). Twenty-second annual report to congress on the implementation of the Individuals with Disabilities Education Act. Retrieved from http://www2.ed.gov/about/reports/annual/osep/2000/preface.pdf

U.S. Department of Education, National Center for Education Statistics. (2009). *The Digest of Education Statistics 2008* (NCES 2009-020), Table 51. Retrieved from http://nces.ed.gov/fastfacts/display.asp?id=59

Vygotsky, L. (1934/1996). *Thought and language.* Kozulin, A. (Ed). Cambridge, MA: The MIT Press.

Wormeli, R. (2007). *Differentiation: From planning to practice grades 6–12.* Portland, ME: Stenhouse Publishers.

CHAPTER 3

Americans with Disabilities Act of 1990, PL 101-336, 42 U.S.C. §§ 12101 *et seq.*

Board of Education of Hendrick Hudson Central School District v. Amy Rowley, 458 U.S. 176 (1982).

Brown Foundation. (n.d.). Retrieved from http://brownvboard.org/

Brown v. Board of Education of Topeka, 347 U.S. 483 (1954).

Calkins, C.F., Lukenbill, R.W., & Mateer, W.J. (1973). Children's rights: An introductory sociological overview. *Peabody Journal of Education, 50*(2), 89–109.

Cedar Rapids Community School District v. Garret F., 526 U.S. 66 (1999).

Cheadle, B. (1987). PL 94-142: What does is really say? *Future Reflections, 6*(1). Retrieved from http://www.nfb.org/images/nfb/Publications/fr/fr6/Issue1/f060113.html

Daniel R.R. v. State Board of Education, 874 F. 2d 1036 (5th Cir. 1989).

Disabled World. (n.d.). Americans Disability Act (ADA). Retrieved April 14, 2010, from http://www.disabled-world.com/disability/ada/

Education for All Handicapped Children Act, PL 94-142 (1975).

Gardner, H. (1991). *The unschooled mind: How children think and how schools should teach.* New York: Basic Books.

Haskins, J. (1998). *The dream and the struggle: Separate but not equal.* New York: Scholastic.

Irving Independent School District v. Tatro 468 U.S. 883 (1984).

Kennedy, M.J. (1994). The disability blanket. *Mental Retardation, 32,* 74–76.

Mills v. Board of Education of the District of Columbia, 343 F. Supp. 866 (1972).

Mooney, J. (2007). *The short bus: A journey beyond normal.* New York: Henry Holt and Company.

Oberti v. Board of Education of Borough of Clementon School District, 995 F. 2d 1204 (1993).

PARC v. Pennsylvania, 334 F.Supp. 1257 (1972).

Project Ideal. (2008). Major components of the amendments to PL 94-142. Retrieved April 14, 2010, from http://www.projectidealonline.org/publicPolicy.php

Rehabilitation Act of 1973, PL 93-112, U.S.C. §§ 504 *et seq.*

U.S. Department of Health and Human Services. (2000). Your rights under Section 504 of the Rehabilitation Act. Retrieved April 14, 2010, from http://www.hhs.gov/ocr/civilrights/resources/factsheets/504.pdf

CHAPTER 4

Association of University Centers on Disability. (2011). AUCD history. Retrieved from http://www.aucd.org/template/page.cfm?id=156

Bailey, D., McWilliam, R., Buysse, V., & Wesley, P. (1998). Inclusion in the context of competing values in early childhood education. *Early Childhood Research Quarterly, 13*(1), 27–47.

Brady, S., Peters, D., Gamel-McCormick, M., & Venuto, N. (2004). Types and patterns of professional-family talk in home-based early intervention. *Journal of Early Intervention, 26*(2), 146–159.

Bricker, D. (1995). The challenge of inclusion. *Journal of Early Intervention, 19*(3), 179–194.

Bronfenbrenner, U. (1979). *The ecology of human development: Experiments by nature and design.* Cambridge, MA: Harvard University Press.

Bronfenbrenner, U., & Morris, P. (1998). The ecology of developmental processes. In W. Damon (Series Ed.) & R. Lerner (Vol. Ed.), *Handbook of child psychology: Vol. 1. Theoretical models of human development* (5th Ed., pp. 993–1028). New York: Wiley & Sons.

Bruder, M.B. (2000). Family-centered early intervention: Clarifying our values for the new millennium. *Topics in Early Childhood Special Education, 20*(2), 105–115.

Buysse, V. (1993). Friendships of preschoolers with disabilities in community-based child care settings. *Journal of Early Intervention, 17*(4), 380–395.

Buysse, V., Wesley, P., & Keyes, L. (1998). Implementing early childhood inclusion: Barrier and support factors. *Early Childhood Research Quarterly, 13*(1), 169–184.

Casey, A., & McWilliam, R.A. (2007). The STARE: The Scale for Teachers' Assessment of Routines Engagement. *Young Exceptional Children, 11*(1), 2–15.

Cheatham, G., Armstrong, J., & Santos, R.M. (2009). "Ya'll Listenin?" Accessing children's dialects in preschool. *Young Exceptional Children, 12*(4), 2–14.

Cheatham, G., Santos, R.M., & Ro, Y.E. (2007). Home language acquisition and retention for young children with special needs. *Young Exceptional Children, 11*(1), 27–39.

Childress, D. (2004). Special instruction and natural environments: Best practices in early intervention. *Infants & Young Children, 17*(2), 162–170.

Cohen, A.J. (1996). A brief history of federal financing for child care in the United States. *The Future of Children, 6*(2), 26–40.

Collier-Bolkus, W.P. (2000). The impact of the welfare reform law on families with disabled children that need child care. *Dissertation Abstracts International, 61*(5), 1795 (UMI No. 9973938).

Crockett, J., & Kauffman, J. (1998). Taking inclusion back to its roots. *Educational Leadership, 56*(2), 74–77.

DeVore, S., & Bowers, B. (2006). Childcare for children with disabilities: Families search for specialized care and cooperative childcare partnerships. *Infants & Young Children, 19*(3), 203–212.

Florian, L. (1995). Part H early intervention program: Legislative history and intent of the law. *Topics in Early Childhood Special Education, 15*(3), 247–262.

Gamel-McCormick, M. (1998). Welfare reform and parent participation: Effects on IFSP and IEP participation. Paper presented at the 14th Annual Division for Early Childhood Conference on Children with Special Needs, Chicago, IL.

Gesell, A. (1943). *Infant and child in the culture of today.* Harper & Brothers: London.

Harbin, G. (1998). Welfare reform and its effects on the system of early intervention. *Journal of Early Intervention, 21*(3), 211–215.

Hook, J. (1993, October 9). Women remain on periphery despite electoral gains. *Congressional Quarterly Weekly Report.*

Individuals with Disabilities Education Act Amendments of 1997, 20 U.S.C. §§1401 *et seq.*

Individuals with Disabilities Education Improvement Act of 2004, 20 U.S.C. §§1401 *et seq.*

Janko-Summers, S., & Joseph, G. (1998). Making sense of early intervention in the context of welfare to work. *Journal of Early Intervention, 21*(3), 207–210.

Jesien, G. (1996, November). Potential effects of Wisconsin Welfare Reform (W-2) on families who have very young children with disabilities and special health care needs. Paper presented at the Conference on Evaluating Comprehensive State Welfare Reforms, Madison, WI.

Jung, L.A. (2007). Writing Individualized Family Service Plan strategies that fit into the ROUTINE. *Young Exceptional Children, 10*(3), 2–9.

Kirk, S., & Gallagher, J. (1986). *Educating exceptional children* (5th Ed.). Boston: Houghton Mifflin Company.

Kozol, J. (1991). *Savage inequalities: Children in America's schools.* New York: Harper Perennial.

Linehan, A. (1998, December). Together we can: Head Start, child care, special education partnerships. Paper presented at the 14th Annual Division for Early Childhood Conference on Children with Special Needs, Chicago, IL.

Lipsky, D.K., & Gartner, A. (1998). Taking inclusion into the future. *Educational Leadership, 56*(2), 78–81.

Lipsky, D.K., & Gartner, A. (2001). Education reform and early childhood inclusion. In M.J. Guralnick (Ed.), *Early childhood inclusion: Focus on change* (pp. 39–48). Baltimore: Paul H. Brookes Publishing Co.

LRP Publications. (1997). *1997 IDEA Amendments: An overview of key changes.* Horsham, PA: Author.

Maternal and Child Health Bureau. (2003). Children with special health care needs: Findings from the National Survey of Children with Special Health Care Needs. Paper presented at the Maternal and Child Health Bureau Data Speak virtual conference. Retrieved from http://mchb.hrsa.gov/mchirc/dataspeak/events/may_03/presenter.htm

McWilliam, R.A., Casey, A., & Sims, J. (2009). The Routines-Based Interview: A method for gathering information and assessing needs. *Infants & Young Children, 22*(3), 224–233.

Mock, M. (2005). Women who have young children with disabilities and their experiences with welfare reform. *Dissertation Abstracts International, I*(08), 2951 (UMI No. 3143215).

Odem, S. (2000). Preschool inclusion: What we know and where we go from here. *Topics in Early Childhood Special Education, 20*(1), 20–27.

Ohlson, C. (1998). Welfare reform: Implications for young children with disabilities, their families, and service providers. *Journal of Early Intervention, 21*(3), 191–206.

Payne, J., & Patton, J. (1981). *Mental retardation.* Columbus, OH: Merrill Publishing Company.

Peterson, N. (1987). *Early intervention for handicapped and at-risk children: An introduction to early childhood-special education.* Denver, CO: Love Publishing Company.

Regnier, M., & Hoffman, C. (1997). *Caring for a child with a disability: Daily challenges, barriers to work, and the unintended consequences of welfare reform.* Madison, WI: Wisconsin Council on Developmental Disabilities.

Sandall, S., Hemmeter, M.L., Smith B.J., & McLean, M.E. (Eds.) (2005). *DEC recommended practices: A comprehensive guide for practical application in early intervention/ early childhood special education.* Missoula, MT: Division for Early Childhood.

Shackelford, J. (2006). *State and jurisdictional eligibility definitions for infants and toddlers with disabilities under IDEA.* National Early Childhood Technical Assistance Center, Washington, DC.

Shonkoff, J., & Meisels, S. (1990). Early childhood intervention: The evolution of a concept. In S. Meisels & J. Shonkoff (Eds.), *Handbook of early childhood intervention* (pp. 3–32). Cambridge: Cambridge University Press.

Skeels, H., & Dye, H. (1938–39). A study of the effects of differential stimulation on mentally retarded children. *Journal of Psycho-Asthenics, 44*, 114–136.

Stainback, S., Stainback, W., & Ayres, B. (1996). Schools as inclusive communities. In W. Stainback & S. Stainback (Eds.), *Controversial issues confronting special education: Divergent perspectives* (pp. 31–43). Boston: Allyn and Bacon.

Turnbull, A.P., Summers, J.A., Turnbull, R., Brotherson, M.J., Winton, P., Roberts, R.,… & Stroup-Rentier, V. (2007). Family supports and services in early intervention: A bold vision. *Journal of Early Intervention, 29*(3), 187–205.

U.S. Department of Education. (2001). Goals 2000: Educate America Act. Retrieved from http://www2.ed.gov/G2K/g2k-fact.html

Women in Congress. (2011). Historical data: Women representatives and senators by Congress, 1917–present. Retrieved from http://womenincongress.house.gov/historical-data/representatives-senators-by-congress.html?congress=112

Yell, M.L. (2006). *The law and special education* (2nd Ed.). Old Tappan, NJ: Merrill/Prentice Hall, Inc.

Ysseldyke, J., Algozzine, R., & Thurlow, M. (1992). *Critical issues in special education.* Boston: Houghton Mifflin.

Zigler, E., & Muenchow, S. (1992). *Head Start: The inside story of America's most successful educational experiment.* New York: Basic Books.

CHAPTER 5

Atherton, J.S. (2009). Assimilation and accommodation. *Learning and Teaching.* Retrieved from http://www.learningandteaching.info/learning/assimacc.htm

Biggle, S.J. (2005). Language and literacy development in children who are deaf or hearing impaired. *Kappa Delta Pi Record, 41*(2), 68–71.

Bloom, B.S. (1984). *Taxonomy of Educational Objectives Book 1: Cognitive Domain* (2nd Ed.). Boston: Addison Wesley Publishing Company.

Brotherson, S.E. (2005, April). Understanding brain development in young children. *Extension Bulletin FS-609.* NDSU Extension Service, North Dakota State University, Fargo, ND.

Children, Youth, and Women's Health Service. (2009). Parenting and child health. *Child development.* Retrieved from http://www.cyh.com/HealthTopics/HealthTopicDetails. aspx?p=114&np=122&id=1870

Erikson, E.H. (1963). *Childhood and society.* London: Vintage Books.

Feldman, R.S. (2008). *Adolescence.* Upper Saddle River, NJ: Pearson Education, Inc.

Gardner, H. (1991). *The unschooled mind: How children think and how schools should teach.* New York: Basic Books.

Graham, E. (2008). The teenage brain. *Dream online.* Retrieved from http://www.childrenshospital.org/dream/summer08/the_teenage_brain.html

Halliburton, A., & Gable, S. (2003, September). *Development during the school-age years of 6 through 11.* University of Missouri Extension. Retrieved from http://extension.missouri.edu/PIGH6235

Hinkle, S. (2010, December). Dissecting the hidden curriculum: A different approach to social skills. Presentation at the annual meeting of TASH, Denver, CO.

Kingsley, E.P. (1987). *Welcome to Holland*. Retrieved from http://www.our-kids.org/Archives/Holland.html

Kliewer, C. (1998). *Schooling children with Down syndrome: Toward an understanding of possibility*. New York: Teachers College Press.

Kohn, A. (1996). *Beyond discipline: From compliance to community*. Alexandria, VA: Association for Supervision and Curriculum Development.

Levine, M. (2002). *A mind at a time*. New York: Simon & Schuster.

National Association for School Psychologists. (2011). *Development in social skills in young children*. Retrieved from http://www.teachersandfamilies.com/open/parent/socialskills4.efm

Novak, G., & Peláez, M. (2004). *Child and adolescent development: A behavioral systems approach*. Thousand Oaks, CA: Sage Publications.

Saffran, J.R., Senghas, A., & Trueswell, J.C. (2001). The acquisition of language by children. *Proceedings of the National Academy of Sciences, 98*(23), 12874–12875.

Shelov, S. P., & Altmann, T. R. (Eds.). (2009). *Caring for your baby and young child: Birth to age 5*. American Academy of Pediatrics.

Vygotsky, L.S. (1978). *Mind in society*. Cambridge, MA: Harvard University Press.

CHAPTER 6

Alaimo, K., Olson, C.M., & Frongillo, E.A. (2001). Food insufficiency and American school-aged children's cognitive, academic, and psychosocial development. *Pediatrics, 108*(1), 44–53.

Blessings in a Backpack. (2007–2011). Hunger statistics. Retrieved from http://www.blessingsinabackpack.org/WHOWEARE/HUNGERSTATISTICS.aspx and http://www.blessingsinabackpack.org/WHOWEARE.aspx

Buteau, G., & True, M. (2009). Differentiating instructional strategies to support English language learners. *New England Reading Association Journal, 44*(2), 23–25.

Church, E.B. (2007). Resolving conflicts. *Scholastic Early Childhood Today, 21*(5), 4.

Cowhey, M. (2006). *Black ants and Buddhists*. Portland, ME: Stenhouse Publishers.

Cregor, M. (2008). The building blocks of positive behavior. *Teaching Tolerance, 34*, 18–21.

Diaz, E.M., & Kosciw, J.G. (2009). *Shared differences: The experiences of lesbian, gay, bisexual, and transgender students of color in our nation's schools*. New York: GLSEN.

Gable, R.A., Hester, P.H., Rock, M.L., & Hughes, K.G. (2009). Back to basics: Rules, praise, ignoring, and reprimands revisited. *Intervention in School and Clinic, 44*(4), 195–205. doi: 10.1177/1053451208328831

Gay, Lesbian, and Straight Education Network (GLSEN). (2010). 2009 National School Climate Survey: Nearly 9 out of 10 LGBT Students Experience Harassment in School. Retrieved from http://www.glsen.org/cgi-bin/iowa/all/news/record/2624.html

Ginott, H. (1972). *Teacher and child*. New York: Avon Books.

Gray, C. (2010). *The new social story book, 10th anniversary edition*. Arlington, TX: Future Horizons, Inc.

Kohn, A. (1996). *Beyond discipline: From compliance to community*. Alexandria, VA: Association for Supervision and Curriculum Development.

Kohn, A. (1986). *No contest: The case against competition*. New York: Houghton Mifflin Company.

Maslow, A.H., Frager, R.D., & Fadiman, J. (1987). *Motivation and personality* (3rd Ed.). Upper Saddle River, NJ: Pearson Education, Inc.

National Center for Education Statistics. (n.d.). Special Analysis 2010: High poverty public schools. Retrieved from http://nces.ed.gov/programs/coe/2010/analysis/note.asp

Nelsen, J., Lott, L., & Glenn, H.S. (2000). *Positive discipline in the classroom* (3rd Ed.). New York: Three Rivers Press.

OSEP Technical Assistance Center on Positive Behavioral Interventions and Supports. (2011). What is schoolwide positive behavioral interventions & supports? Retrieved from http://www.pbis.org/school/what_is_swpbs.aspx

Rethinking Schools. (2011). About rethinking schools. Retrieved from http://www.rethinkingschools.org/about/index.shtml

Rodriguez, D., Ringler, M., O'Neal, D., & Bunn, K. (2009). English language learners' perceptions of school environment. *Journal of Research in Childhood Education, 23*(4), 513–526.

Sapon-Shevin, M. (2007). *Widening the circle: The power of inclusive classrooms*. Boston: Beacon Press.

Teale, W.H. (2009). Students learning English and their literacy instruction in urban schools. *The Reading Teacher, 62*(8), 699–703.

Thousand, J.S., Villa, R.A., & Nevin, A.I. (2007). *Differentiating instruction: Collaborative planning and teaching for universally designed learning*. Thousand Oaks, CA: Corwin Press.

U.S. Census Bureau. (2004). Children and the households they live in: Census 2000 special reports. Retrieved from http://www.census.gov/prod/2004pubs/censr-14.pdf

CHAPTER 7

Brightman, A. (2008). *DisabilityLand*. New York: Select Books, Inc.

Kliewer, C. (1998). *Schooling children with Down syndrome: Toward an understanding of possibility*. New York: Teachers College Press.

Rosen, P. (Producer), Lavoie, R. (Writer). (1989). *How difficult can this be?: Understanding learning disabilities: Frustration, anxiety, tension, the F.A.T. city workshop* [Motion picture]. Alexandria,VA: Artwork PBS.

Rutherford, P. (2002). *Instruction for all students*. Alexandria, VA: Just ASK Publications, Inc.

Westphal, L.E. (2007). *Differentiating with menus*. Waco, TX: Prufrock Press, Inc.

Wormeli, R. (2007). *Differentiation: From planning to practice grades 6–12*. Portland, ME: Stenhouse Publishers.

CHAPTER 8

Connell, B.R., Jones, M., Mace, R., Mueller, J., Mulick, A., Ostroff, E., & Vanderheiden, G. (1997). The principles of universal design. Retrieved April 6, 2011, from http://www.ncsu.edu/www/ncsu/design/sod5/cud/about_ud/udprinciplestext.htm

Higher Education Opportunity Act, PL No. 110-315 (2008).

Individuals with Disabilities Education Improvement Act of 2004, 20 U.S.C. 1400 *et seq.*

Kliewer, C. (1998). *Schooling children with Down syndrome: Toward an understanding of possibility.* New York: Teachers College Press.

National Center on Universal Design for Learning. (2011a). The concept of UDL. Retrieved February 15, 2011, from http://www.udlcenter.org/aboutudl/whatisudl/conceptofudl

National Center on Universal Design for Learning. (2011b). UDL guidelines. Retrieved February 15, 2011, from http://www.udlcenter.org/aboutudl/udlguidelines

National Center on Universal Design for Learning. (2011c). What is UDL? Retrieved February 15, 2011, from http://www.udlcenter.org/aboutudl/whatisudl

Oklahoma Assistive Technology Center. (2011). Homemade AT. Retrieved April 11, 2011, from http://www.theoatc.org/resources/HomemadeAssistiveTechnology.asp

Packer, L.E. (2010). Overview of executive dysfunction. *Schoolbehavior.com.* Retrieved March 10, 2011, from http://www.schoolbehavior.com/index.php?s=executive+functions

Peterson, J.M., & Hittie, M.M. (2010). *Inclusive teaching: The journey towards effective schools for all learners* (2nd Ed.). Boston: Pearson.

Rapp, W.H. (2005). Using assistive technology with students with exceptional learning needs: When does an aid become a crutch? *Reading and Writing Quarterly, 21*(2), 193–196.

CHAPTER 9

Hosp, J.L., & Reschly, D.J. (2004). Disproportionate representation of minority students in special education: Academic, demographic, and economic predictors. *Exceptional Children, 70*(2), 185–199.

IDEA Partnership. (2007). Leaving no child behind [PowerPoint slides]. Retrieved from: from http://www.google.com/search?q=NCLB+RTI+connection&rls=com.microsoft:en-us&ie=UTF-8&oe=UTF-8&startIndex=&startPage=1

Individuals with Disabilities Education Act of 2004. 20 U.S.C. 1412(a)(5).

National Center on Response to Intervention. (n.d.). What is RTI? Retrieved from http://www.rti4success.org/

NICHCY (National Dissemination Center for Children with Disabilities). (2010a). 10 basic steps in special education. Retrieved from http://www.nichcy.org/EducateChildren/Steps/Pages/default.aspx

NICHCY (National Dissemination Center for Children with Disabilities). (2010b). Evaluating children for disability. Retrieved from http://www.nichcy.org/EducateChildren/evaluation/Pages/default.aspx

New York State Education Department. (2010). Model forms: Student information summary and individual-

ized education program (IEP). Retrieved from http://www.p12.nysed.gov/specialed/formsnotices/IEP/memo-Jan10.htm

Oswald, D.P., Coutinho, M.J., Best, A.M., & Singh, N.N. (1999). Ethnic representation in special education: The influence of school-related economic and demographic variables. *The Journal of Special Education, 32*(4), 194–206.

Sullivan, A.L., A'Vant, E., Baker, J., Chandler, D., Graves, S., McKinney, E., & Sayles, T. (2009). Confronting inequality in special education, Part 1: Understanding the problem of disproportionality. *Communiqué: The Newspaper of the National Association of School Psychologists, 38*(1), 1, 14–15.

CHAPTER 10

Conderman, G., Bresnahan, V., & Pedersen, T. (2009). *Purposeful co-teaching: Real cases and effective strategies.* Thousand Oaks, CA: Sage Publications.

Cowhey, M. (2006). *Black ants and Buddhists.* Portland, ME: Stenhouse Publishers.

DuFour, R. (2011). Work together but only if you want to. *Phi Delta Kappan, 92*(5), 57–61.

Kluth, P. (2010). *You're going to love this kid! Teaching students with autism in the inclusive classroom.* Baltimore: Paul H. Brookes Publishing Co.

Ladson-Billings, G. (1995). But that's just good teaching! The case for culturally relevant pedagogy. *Theory into Practice, 34*(3), 159–165.

The Myers Briggs Foundation. (n.d.). MBTI Basics. Retrieved from http://www.myersbriggs.org/my-mbti-personality-type/mbti-basics/

National Association of School Psychologists. (2005). *Position statement on collaboration.* Retrieved from http://www.nasponline.org/about_nasp/pospaper_hsc.aspx

Performance Learning Systems. (2011). Learning styles inventory. Retrieved from http://www.plsweb.com/Products-Resources/Learning-Styles-Inventory

U.S. Department of Education (2006). 34 CFR Parts 300 and 301: Assistance to States for the Education of Children With Disabilities and Preschool Grants for Children With Disabilities; Final Rule. *Federal Register, 71* (156), p. 46765.

CHAPTER 11

Individuals with Disabilities Education Improvement Act of 2004, 20 U.S.C. 1400 *et seq.*

The Institute for Innovative Transition. Transforming Transitions through Programs, Policy, and Practice. (n.d.). Retrieved April 15, 2011, from http://www.ny-transition.org/

Kluth, P. (2010). *"You're going to love this kid!" Teaching students with autism in the inclusive classroom.* Baltimore: Paul H. Brookes Publishing Co.

NICHCY (National Dissemination Center for Children with Disabilities). (2011). Adult services: What are they? Where are they? Retrieved March 3, 2011, from http://www.nichcy.org/EducateChildren/transition_adulthood/Pages/adultservices.aspx#vr

Thoma, C., Bartholomew, C., & Scott, L. (2009). *Universal design for transition: A roadmap for planning and instruction*. Baltimore, MD: Paul H. Brookes Publishing Co.

CHAPTER 12

American Academy of Child and Adolescent Psychiatry. (2008). Bullying. *Facts for Families, 80*. Retrieved from http://www.aacap.org/galleries/FactsForFamilies/80_bullying.pdf

American Federation of Teachers. (n.d.). Arranging your classroom. Retrieved from http://www.aft.org/yourwork/tools4teachers/classmgt/arranging.cfm

American Federation of Teachers. (n.d.). Defining consequences. Retrieved from http://www.aft.org/yourwork/tools4teachers/classmgt/consequences.cfm

Beers, K. (2003). *When kids can't read: A guide for teachers 6-12*. Portsmouth, NH: Heinemann.

Church, E.B. (2007). Resolving conflicts. *Scholastic Early Childhood Today, 21*(5), 4.

Cowhey, M. (2006). *Black ants and Buddhists*. Portland, ME: Stenhouse Publishers.

Kohn, A. (1996). *Beyond discipline: From compliance to community*. Alexandria, VA: Association for Supervision and Curriculum Development.

National Education Association. (2011). *Six character-building behaviors students should learn*. Retrieved from http://www.nea.org/home/ns/29672.htm

Nieto, S. (2003). *What keeps teachers going?* New York: Teachers College Press.

OSEP Technical Assistance Center on Positive Behavioral Interventions and Supports. (2011). What is school-wide positive behavioral interventions & supports? Retrieved from http://www.pbis.org/school/what_is_swpbs.aspx

Peterson, J.M., & Hittie, M.M. (2010). *Inclusive teaching: The journey towards effective schools for all learners*. New York: Pearson.

Teaching Tolerance. (n.d.). *Bullying: Tips for students*. Retrieved from http://www.tolerance.org/activity/bullying-tips-students

CHAPTER 13

Allington, R.L. (2006). Research and the three-tier model. *Reading Today, 23*(5), 20.

Allington, R.L. (2007). Intervention all day long: New hope for struggling readers. *Voices from the Middle, 14*(4), 7–14.

Allington, R.L. (2011). What at-risk readers need. *Educational Leadership, 68*(6), 40–45. Atwell, N. (1998). *In the middle: New understandings about writing, reading, and learning*. Portsmouth, NH: Boynton/Cook Publishers.

Bear, D.R., Invernizzi, M., Templeton, S., & Johnston, F. (2004). *Words their way: Word study for phonics, vocabulary, and spelling instruction* (3rd Ed.). Upper Saddle River, NJ: Pearson Merrill Prentice Hall.

Beers, K. (2003). *When kids can't read: A guide for teachers 6-12*. Portsmouth, NH: Heinemann.

Bruce, B.C. (2007). Diversity and critical social engagement: How changing technologies enable new modes of literacy in changing circumstances. In D.E. Alvermann (Ed.), *Adolescents and literacies in a digital world* (pp. 1–18). New York: Peter Lang.

California Department of Education. (1998). English–Language arts content standards for California public schools: Kindergarten through grade twelve. Retrieved from http://www.cde.ca.gov/be/st/ss/documents/elacontentstnds.pdf

Codell, E.R. (1999). *Educating Esmé*. New York: Workman Publishing.

Daniel, J., Clarke, T., & Ouellette, M. (2004). Developing and supporting literacy-rich environments for children. In R.D. Robinson, M.C. McKenna, & J.M. Wedman (Eds.), *Issues and trends in literacy education* (3rd Ed., pp. 45–52). New York: Pearson.

Flippo, R.F., Holland, D.D., McCarthy, M.T., & Swinning, E.A. (2009). Asking the right questions: How to select an informal reading inventory. *The Reading Teacher, 63*(1), 79–83.

Galda, L., & Graves, M. (2007). *Reading and responding in the middle grades: Approaches for all classrooms*. Boston: Allyn & Bacon.

Gay, G. (2002). Preparing for culturally responsive teaching. *Journal of Teacher Education, 53*(2), 106–116.

Gee, J.P., & Levine, M.H. (2009). Welcome to our virtual worlds. *Educational Leadership, 66*(6), 49–52.

Haager, D., & Klingner, J.K. (2005). *Differentiating instruction in inclusive classrooms: The special educator's guide*. New York: Pearson Allyn & Bacon.

Hadaway, N.L. (2011). A narrow bridge to academic reading. *Educational Leadership, 66*(7), 38–41.

Harper, L.J., & Brand, S.T. (2010). More alike than different: Promoting respect through multicultural books and literacy strategies. *Childhood Education, 86*(4), 224–233.

Hill, R. (2011). Common core curriculum and complex texts. *Teacher Librarian, 38*(3), 42–46.

In the States. (2010). *Common Core State Standards Initiative*. Retrieved from http://www.corestandards.org/in-the-states

Kliewer, C. (1998). *Schooling children with Down syndrome*. New York: Teacher's College Press.

Kluth, P., & Schwarz, P. (2008). *Just give him the whale!* Baltimore: Paul H. Brookes Publishing Co.

Kylene Beers and Reading Strategies (n.d.). All America Reads Program Info. Retrieved from http://www.allamericareads.org/program/strategies.htm

Lane, H.B., Pullen, P.C., Hudson, R.F., & Konold, T.R. (2009). Identifying essential instructional components of literacy tutoring for struggling beginning readers. *Literacy Research and Instruction, 48*(4), 277–297.

Lee, J., Grigg, W., & Donahue, P. (2007). *The Nation's report card: Reading 2007* (NCES 2007-496). Washington, DC: National Center for Education Statistics, Institute of Education Sciences, U.S. Department of Education.

McGregor, T. (2007). *Comprehension connections: Bridges to strategic reading*. Portsmouth, NH: Heinemann.

Mills, K.A. (2010). Shrek meets Vygotsky: Rethinking adolescents' multimodal literacy practices in schools. *Journal of Adolescent & Adult Literacy, 54*(1), 35–45.

National Council of Teachers of English. (n.d.). Adolescent literacy: A policy research brief produced by the

National Council of Teachers of English, Urbana, IL: NCTE.

New York State Academy for Teaching and Learning. (n.d.). English Language Arts. Retrieved from http://www.p12.nysed.gov/nysatl/engstand.html

Pierangelo, R., & Guiliani, G. A. (2009). *Assessment in special education: A practical approach* (3rd Ed.). Upper Saddle River, NJ: Pearson.

Robinson, R.D., McKenna, M.C., & Wedman, J.M. (Eds.) (2004). *Issues and trends in literacy education* (3rd Ed.). New York: Pearson.

Senechal, D. (2011). Let strategies serve literature. *Educational Leadership, 68*(6), 52–56.

Teaching Tolerance. (n.d.). Mythtakes—Working with racially and ethnically diverse students. Retrieved from http://www.tolerance.org/sites/default/files/general/tt_discussion.pdf

Tovani, C. (2000). *I read it, but I don't get it: Comprehension strategies for adolescent readers.* Portland, ME: Stenhouse Publishers.

U.S. Department of Education, National Center for Education Statistics. (2007). Table 121. Average reading scale score and percentage of 8th-graders in public schools attaining reading achievement levels, by locale and state or jurisdiction: Selected years, 1998 through 2207. Retrieved from http://nces.ed.gov/programs/digest/d09/tables/dt09_121.asp

Wolf, M., & Barzillai, M. (2009). The importance of deep reading. *Educational Leadership, 66*(6), 33–37.

CHAPTER 14

6+1 Trait Rubrics. (2011). *Education Northwest.* Retrieved from http://educationnorthwest.org/resource/464

Assaf, L.C., Ash, G.E., Saunders, J., & Johnson, J. (2011). Renewing two seminal literacy practices: I-Charts and I-Search papers. *Voices from the Middle, 18*(4), 31–42.

Atwell, N. (1998). *In the middle: New understandings about writing, reading, and learning.* (2nd Ed.). Portsmouth, NH: Heinemann.

Baron, N.S. (2009). Are digital media changing language? *Educational Leadership, 66*(6), 42–46.

Common Core State Standards Initiative. (2010). English language arts standards—Writing—Introduction. Retrieved from http://www.corestandards.org/the-standards/english-language-arts-standards/writing/introduction/

Crovitz, D. (2011). Sudden possibilities: Porpoises, eggcorns, and error. *English Journal, 100*(4), 31–38.

Done, P. (2005). *Thirty-two third graders and one class bunny: Life lessons from teaching.* New York: Touchstone.

Fletcher, R., & Portalupi, J. (2007). *Craft lessons: Teaching writing K-8* (2nd Ed.).York, ME: Stenhouse Publishers.

Fountas, I.C., & Pinnell, G.S. (1996). *Guided reading: Good first teaching for all children.* Portsmouth, NH: Portsmouth.

Jones, C.D., Reutzel, D.R., & Fargo, J.D. (2010). Comparing two methods of writing instruction: Effects on kindergarten students' reading skills. *The Journal of Educational Research, 103,* 327–341.

Laman, T.T. (2011). The functions of talk within a 4th-grade writing workshop: Insights into understand- ing. *Journal of Research in Childhood Education, 25,* 133–144.

Moore, M.T. (2004). Issues and trends in writing instruction. In R.D. Robinson, M.C. McKenna, & J.M. Wedman (Eds.), *Issues and trends in literacy education* (3rd Ed., pp. 201–210). New York: Pearson Education, Inc.

National Center for Educational Statistics. (n.d.). More About NAEP Writing. Retrieved from http://nces.ed.gov/nationsreportcard/writing/moreabout.asp

Robinson, R.D., McKenna, M.C., & Wedman, J.M. (2004). *Issues and trends in literacy education.* (3rd Ed.). New York: Pearson Education, Inc.

Salahu-Din, D., Persky, H., & Miller, J. (2008). The nation's report card: writing 2007. Retrieved from http://nces.ed.gov/nationsreportcard/pubs/main2007/2008468.asp

Thomas, P. (2004). The negative impact of testing writing skills. *Educational Leadership, 62*(2), 76–79.

Thompson, C.L. (2011). A dose of writing reality: Helping students become better writers. *Phi Delta Kappan, 92*(7), 57–61.

Tompkins, G.E. (2008). *Teaching writing: Balancing process and product.* (5th Ed.). Upper Saddle River, NJ: Pearson.

University of Kansas Writing Center. (n.d.). Prewriting Strategies. Retrieved from http://www.writing.ku.edu/~writing/guides/prewriting.shtml

Weigel, M., & Gardner, H. (2009). The best of both literacies. *Educational Leadership, 66*(6), 38–41.

White, J.W. (2011). De-centering English: Highlighting the dynamic nature of the English language to promote the teaching of code-switching. *English Journal, 100*(4), 44–49.

Writing Assessment Rubric. (n.d.). Six traits writing assessment. Retrieved from http://6traits.cyberspaces.net/rubric2.html

Wurzburg, G. (Producer), Rubin, S. (Writer). (2005). *Autism is a World* [motion picture]. United States: State of the Art, Inc.

CHAPTER 15

Alter, G.T. (2009). Challenging the textbook. *Educational Leadership, 66*(8), 72–75.

Bigelow, B. (2008). *A people's history for the classroom.* Washington, DC: The Zinn Education Project.

Bigelow, B., & Peterson, B. (2002). *Rethinking globalization.* Milwaukee, WI: Rethinking Schools Press.

Coartney, L. (2007). King in the Classroom. San Diego: San Diego State University. Retrieved from http://advancement.sdsu.edu/marcomm/features/2007/mlk.html

Cornbleth, C. (2010). What constrains meaningful social studies teaching? In Parker, W.C. (Ed.). *Social studies today: Research and practice* (pp. 215–223). New York: Routledge.

The Delaware Social Studies Education Project. (2008). Strategies for Teaching Social Studies. Retrieved from http://www.udel.edu/dssep/strategies.htm

Edwards, S. (2010). Analysis of Martin Luther King's I Have a Dream speech. *Presentation Magazine.* Retrieved from http://www.presentationmagazine.com/martin-luther-king-i-have-a-dream-speech.htm

Horton, T.A., & Barnett, J.A. (2008). Thematic unit planning in social studies: Make it focused and meaningful. *Canadian Social Studies, 41*(1). Retrieved from http://www2.education.ualberta.ca/css/Css_41_1/index41_1.htm

Library of Congress. (2011). About the Library. Retrieved from http://www.loc.gov/about/National Archives. (n.d.). Teachers' Resources. Retrieved from http://www.archives.gov/education/

National Council for the Social Studies. (n.d.). National curriculum standards for social studies: Introduction. Retrieved from http://www.socialstudies.org/standards/introduction

Nelson, L.L., Arthur, E.J., Jensen, W.R., & Van Horn, G. (2011). Trading textbooks for technology: New opportunities for learning. *Phi Delta Kappan, 92*(7), 46–50.

Rutherford, P. (2008). *Instruction for all students.* (2nd Ed.). Alexandria, VA: Just Ask Publications.

Sapp, W. (2009). Universal design: Online educational media for students with disabilities. *Journal of Visual Impairment & Blindness, 103*(8), 495–500.

Seider, S. (2009). Social justice in the suburbs. *Educational Leadership, 66*(8), 54–58.

Seif, E. (2003/2004). Social studies revived. *Educational Leadership, 61*(4), 54–59.

Singer, P. (1999). The Singer Solution to World Poverty. *The New York Times Magazine.* Retrieved from http://www.nytimes.com/library/magazine/home/19990905mag-poverty-singer.html

Social Science Education Consortium. (1996). *Teaching the social sciences and history in secondary schools: A methods handbook.* Long Grove, IL: Waveland Press, Inc.

CHAPTER 16

Arem, C.A. (2009). *Conquering math anxiety: A self-help workbook.* Belmont, CA: Brooks/Cole Publishing Company.

Brunetto, C.F. (1997). *MathArt projects and activities: Dozens of creative projects to explore math concepts and build essential skills.* New York: Scholastic, Inc.

Bryant-Mole, K. (1994). *Charts and graphs.* London: Usborne Publishing Ltd.

Burkley, M., Parker, J., Stermer, P.S., & Burkley, E. (2010). Trait beliefs that make women vulnerable to math disengagement. *Personality and Individual Differences, 48,* 234–238.

Common Core State Standards Initiative. (n.d.). Standards for mathematical practice. Retrieved May 13, 2011, from http://www.corestandards.org/the-standards/mathematics/introduction/standards-for-mathematical-practice/

Cuisinaire Company of America (1995). *Learning with fraction circles.* White Plains, NY: Cuisinaire Company of America, Inc.

Dacey, L., & Lynch, J.B. (2007). *Math for all: Differentiating instruction, grades 3–5.* Sausalito, CA: Math Solutions Publications.

Else-Quest, N.M. (2010). Cross-national patterns of gender differences in mathematics: A meta-analysis. *Psychological Bulletin, 136*(1), 103–127.

Fitzell, S. (2005). *Successful inclusion strategies and techniques for differentiating curriculum to meet IEP requirements for students with mild to moderate special needs (grades 6–12)* [Resource handbook]. Bellevue, WA: Bureau of Education & Research.

Gargiulo, R.M., & Metcalf, D. (2010). *Teaching in today's inclusive classrooms: A universal design for learning approach.* Belmont, CA: Wadsworth.

Greenberg, D. (1998). *Comic-strip math: 40 reproducible cartoons with dozens of funny story problems that build essential math skills.* New York: Scholastic, Inc.

Gutstein, E., & Peterson, B. (Eds.). (2005). *Rethinking mathematics: Teaching social justice by the numbers.* Milwaukee, WI: Rethinking Schools.

Hill, R. (2011). Common core curriculum and complex texts. *Teacher Librarian, 38*(3), 42–46.

Hyde, J.S., & Mertz, J.E. (2009). Gender, culture, and mathematics performance. *Proceedings of the National Academy of Sciences, 106,* 8801–8807.

Irujo, S. (2007). Teaching math to English language learners: Can research help? *The ELL Outlook.* Retrieved April 16, 2011, from http://www.coursecrafters.com/ELL-Outlook/2007/mar_apr/ELLOutlookITIArticle1.htm

Jarrett, D. (1999). *Mathematics and science instruction for students with learning disabilities.* Portland, OR: Northwest Regional Educational Laboratory.

Kluth, P., & Danaher, S. (2010). *From tutor scripts to talking sticks: 100 ways to differentiate instruction in K-12 inclusive classrooms.* Baltimore: Paul H. Brookes Publishing Co.

Ladson-Billings, G. (1995). Making mathematics meaningful in a multicultural context. In W.G. Secada, E. Fennema, & L. Byrd (Eds.), *New directions for equity in mathematics education* (pp. 126–145). Cambridge: Cambridge University Press.

LePatner, M., Matuk, F.N., & Ruthven, R. (2005). *Nonfiction writing prompts for math, science, and social studies.* Englewood, CO: Advanced Learning Press.

National Council of Teachers of Mathematics. (n.d.). Math standards and expectations. Retrieved May 13, 2011, from http://www.nctm.org/standards/content.aspx?id=4294967312

Norris, J. (2002). *Math centers—Take it to your seat, grades 1-3.* Monterey, CA: Evan-Moor Corporation.

Rapp, W.H. (2009). Avoiding math taboos: Effective math strategies for visual spatial learners. *Teaching Exceptional Children Plus, 6*(2). Retrieved May 13, 2011, from http://escholarship.bc.edu/education/tecplus/vol6/iss2/art4

Silverman, L.K. (2002). *Upside-down brilliance: The visual-spatial learner.* Denver, CO: DeLeon Publishing.

Technology and Media Division of the Council for Exceptional Children & Wisconsin Assistive Technology Initiative. (n.d.). *Assistive technology consideration quick wheel.* U.S. Office of Special Education.

Tomlinson, C.A. (2003). *Fulfilling the promise of the differentiated classroom: Strategies and tools for responsive teaching.* Alexandria, VA: Association for Supervision and Curriculum Development.

Wormeli, R. (2007). *Differentiation: From planning to practice, grades 6–12.* Portland, ME: Stenhouse Publishers.

CHAPTER 17

Boutte, G., Kelly-Jackson, C., & Johnson, G.L. (2010). Culturally relevant teaching in science classrooms: Addressing academic achievement, cultural competence, and critical consciousness. *International Journal of Multicultural Education, 12*(2), 1–20.

Chapman, C. (1993). *If the shoe fits…: How to develop multiple intelligences in the classroom.* Palatine, IL: IRI/Skylight Publishing Inc.

Eicher, L. (2007). Real-life role models engage students in science and open the door to exploration in class and beyond. *Sally Ride Science.* Retrieved April 26, 2011, from https://www.sallyridescience.com/node/243

Fitzell, S. (2005). *Successful inclusion strategies and techniques for differentiating curriculum to meet IEP requirements for students with mild to moderate special needs (grades 6–12). Resource handbook.* Bellevue, WA: Bureau of Education & Research.

Gallard, A.J. (2011). Creating a multicultural learning environment in science classrooms. *National Association for Research in Science Teaching.* Retrieved April 27, 2011, from http://www.narst.org/publications/research/multicultural.cfm

Gargiulo, R.M., & Metcalf, D. (2010). *Teaching in today's inclusive classrooms: A universal design for learning approach.* Belmont, CA: Wadsworth.

Gay, G. (2002). Preparing for culturally responsive teaching. *Journal of Teacher Education, 53*(2), 106–116.

Jarrett, D. (1999). *Mathematics and science instruction for students with learning disabilities.* Portland, OR: Northwest Regional Educational Laboratory.

LePatner, M., Matuk, F.N., & Ruthven, R. (2005). *Nonfiction writing prompts for math, science, and social studies.* Englewood, CO: Advanced Learning Press.

McCully, E.A. (1992). *Mirette on the high wire.* New York: Penguin and Putnam Books for Young Readers.

National Committee on Science Education Standards and Assessment. (1996). National science education standards. Retrieved April 26, 2011, from http://www.kids4research.org/frog_dvd/NSE_Standards.pdf

Rapp, W.H. (1997). I hear, and I forget; I see, and I remember; I do, and I understand: An exploration of children's museums as successful learning environments for students with and without disabilities. Unpublished doctoral dissertation, Michigan State University.

Rutherford, P. (2002). *Instruction for all students.* Alexandria, VA: Just ASK Publications, Inc.

Schmidt, P.R. (2005). *Culturally responsive instruction: Promoting literacy in secondary content areas* (Report No. ED-01-CO-0011). Retrieved from the Learning Points Associates web site http://www.learningpt.org/literacy/adolescent/cri.pdf

Scieszka, J., & Smith, L. (2004). *Science verse.* New York: Viking.

Wormeli, R. (2007). *Differentiation: From planning to practice, grades 6–12.* Portland, ME: Stenhouse Publishers.

CHAPTER 18

American Speech-Language-Hearing Association (ASHA). (2011). Augmentative communication: A glossary. Retrieved May 4, 2011, from http://www/asha.org/public/speech/disorders/accPrimer.htm

Austin Independent School District Speech Language Services. (2009). *RTI strategies for receptive language concerns.* Retrieved May 25, 2011, from http://turnaroundleadershipacademy.net/speechlang/docs/meetings_materials/09_10/Dec09/RtIStrategies_Receptive.pdf

Brightman, A. (2008). *DisabilityLand.* New York: Select Books, Inc.

Buron, K.D. (2007). *A 5 is against the law: Social boundaries: Straight up! An honest guide for teens and young adults.* Shawnee Mission, KS: Autism Asperger Publishing Co.

Buron, K.D., & Curtis, M. (2003). *The incredible 5-point scale: Assisting students with autism spectrum disorders in understanding social interactions and controlling their emotional responses.* Shawnee Mission, KS: Autism Asperger Publishing Co.

Cooper-Kahn, J., & Dietzel, L. (2008). *Late, lost, and unprepared: A parents' guide to helping children with executive functioning.* Bethesda, MD: Woodbine House.

Cowhey, M. (2006). *Black ants and Buddhists: Thinking critically and teaching differently in the primary grades.* Portland, ME: Stenhouse Publishers.

Gray, C. (2010). *The new social story book.* Arlington, TX: Future Horizons.

Jackson, L. (2002). *Freaks, geeks, & Asperger syndrome: A user guide to adolescence.* London: Jessica Kingsley Publishers.

Kliewer, C. (1998). *Schooling children with Down syndrome: Toward an understanding of possibility.* New York: Teachers College Press.

Kluth, P., & Danaher, S. (2010). *From tutor scripts to talking sticks: 100 ways to differentiate instruction in K-12 inclusive classrooms.* Baltimore: Paul H. Brookes Publishing Co.

Lavoie, R. (2005). *It's so much work to be your friend: Helping the child with learning disabilities find social success.* New York: Touchstone.

Levine, M. (2002). *A mind at a time.* New York: Simon & Schuster.

Myles, B.S., Trautman, M L., & Schelvan, R.L. (2004). *The hidden curriculum: Practical solutions for understanding unstated rules in social situations.* Shawnee Mission, KS: Autism Asperger Publishing Co.

Northamptonshire County Council Autism Team. (2009). Autistic spectrum team. Retrieved May 16, 2011, from http://www.northamptonshire.gov.uk/autismteam

Rutherford, P. (2008). *Instruction for all students.* (2nd Ed.). Alexandria, VA: Just Ask Publications.

Stokes, S. (n.d.). Assistive technology for children with autism. Retrieved May 4, 2011, from http://www.specialed.us/autism/assist/asst10.htm

U.S. Department of Labor. (June, 1999). *What work requires of schools: A SCANS report for America 2000.* Washington,

DC: U.S. Government Printing Office. Retrieved from http://wdr.doleta.gov/opr/fulltext/document.cfm?docn=6140

Wilson, R. (2009). Fact sheet: Receptive communication. Colorado Services to Children with Deafblindness. Retrieved May 16, 2011, from http://www.cde.state.co.us/cdesped/download/pdf/dbReceptiveCommunication.pdf

YAACK. (1999). Does AAC impede natural speech?—and other fears. *YAACK: AAC Connecting Young Kids.* Retrieved May 4, 2011, from http://aac.unl.edu/yaack/b2.html

CHAPTER 19

Adapted Physical Education National Standards. (2008a). What is adapted physical education? Retrieved May 13, 2011, from http://www.apens.org/whatisape.html

Adapted Physical Education National Standards. (2008b). Why a national standard for adapted physical education? Retrieved May 13, 2011, from http://www.apens.org/national_standard.html

American Occupational Therapy Association. (2011). About occupational therapy. Retrieved May 13, 2011, from http://aota.org/Consumers.aspx?css=print

American Physical Therapy Association. (2011). Who are physical therapists? Retrieved May 13, 2011, from http://www.apta.org/AboutPTs/

American Speech-Language-Hearing Association. (2010). Roles and responsibilities of speech-language pathologists in schools [Professional issues statement]. Retrieved May 13, 2011, from http://www.asha.org/policy

Crandall, J. (1998). The expanding role of the elementary ESL teacher: Doing more than teaching language. *ESL Magazine, 1*(4), 10–14.

Lieberman, L.J., & Houston-Wilson, C. (2009). *Strategies for inclusion* (2nd Ed.). Champaign, IL: Human Kinetics.

PE Central. (2011). Differentiating instruction for students with disabilities. Retrieved May 13, 2011, from http//www.pecentral.org/adapted/adaptedactivities.html

TESOL. (2007). TESOL's mission and values. Retrieved May 14, 2011, from http://www.tesol.org/s_tesol/sec_document.asp?CID=3&DID=220

Resources for Comprehensive Teaching

NATIONAL AND INTERNATIONAL GOVERNMENT AGENCIES

Web Sites

Convention on the Rights of the Child (from UNICEF):
http://www.unicef.org/crc/index_30177.html

- The Convention on the Rights of the Child was the first instrument to incorporate the complete range of international human rights—including civil, cultural, economic, political, and social rights, as well as aspects of humanitarian law. The articles of the Convention may be grouped into four categories of rights and a set of guiding principles. By clicking on any of the categories on the web page, you can link to a plain language explanation of the applicable articles in the Convention. Additional provisions of the Convention (articles 43 to 54) discuss implementation measures for the Convention, explaining how governments and international organizations like UNICEF will work to ensure that children are protected in their rights. You can see the full text of the Convention at the above link.

Division for Early Childhood (DEC): http://www.dec-sped.org/

- Official web site for DEC, a nonprofit organization advocating for individuals who work with or on behalf of children with special needs—from birth through age 8—and their families.

Institute of Education Sciences (IES) of the U.S. Department of Education:
http://ies.ed.gov/

- Web site of IES, which provides rigorous and relevant evidence to inform education practice and policy and shares this information broadly. By identifying what works, what doesn't, and why, IES aims to improve educational outcomes for all students, particularly those at risk of failure. It is the research arm of the U.S. Department of Education, and by law its activities must be free of partisan political influence.

National Center for Education Statistics (NCES) of the U.S. Department of Education:
http://nces.ed.gov/

- The purpose of the NCES web site is to provide clear, complete information about NCES' mission and activities and to serve researchers, educators, and communities. NCES is the primary federal entity for collecting and analyzing data related to education in the United States and other nations. NCES is located within the U.S. Department of Education and the Institute of Education Sciences.

U.S. Office of Special Education Programs (OSEP):
http://www2.ed.gov/about/offices/list/osers/osep/index.html

- Official web site for OSEP, which is a federal government agency dedicated to improving results for infants, children, and youth with disabilities from birth through age 21 by providing leadership and financial support to assist states and local districts.

World Health Organization: http://www.who.int/en/

- Official web site for WHO, which is the directing and coordinating authority for health within the United Nations system. It is responsible for providing leadership on global health matters, shaping the health research agenda, setting norms and standards, articulating evidence-based policy options, providing technical support to countries, and monitoring and assessing health trends.

Books/Materials

National Center on Educational Outcomes. (2006). *NCLB and IDEA: What Parents of Students with Disabilities Need to Know and Do.* Washington, D.C.: U.S. Office of Special Education Programs (OSEP).

- A reader-friendly document that is useful to parents who need answers to frequently asked questions as well as teachers who need to answer parents' questions or point them in the right direction.

DISABILITY AWARENESS, ADVOCACY, INCLUSION

Web Sites

ALLIANCE National Parent Technical Assistance Center (NPTAC):
http://www.parentcenternetwork.org/national/aboutus.html

- The ALLIANCE National Parent Technical Assistance Center (NPTAC)provides Parent Centers, Parent Training and Information Center (PTIs), and Community Parent Resource Centers (CPRCs) with innovative technical assistance, up-to-date information, and high-quality resources and materials. A major goal of the ALLIANCE National PTAC is to build the capacity of Parent Centers to improve results for children with disabilities from birth to age 26 in rural, urban, and suburban areas and from underrepresented and underserved populations. populations.

Association of University Centers on Disabilities: http://www.aucd.org/

- The AUCD is a membership organization that supports and promotes a national network of university-based interdisciplinary programs. It provides information on resources, policies, events, and councils for local, state, national, and international agencies, organizations, and policy makers concerned about people living with developmental and other disabilities and their families.

Center for Early Literacy Learning (CELL): http://www.earlyliteracylearning.org/

- CELL provides resources (videos, tools, posters, etc.) for early childhood intervention practitioners, parents, and other caregivers of children, birth to five years of age, with identified disabilities, developmental delays, and those at risk for poor outcomes. Spanish resources are also available.

Center on Human Policy: http://thechp.syr.edu/

- The Center on Human Policy (CHP) is a Syracuse University–based policy, research, and advocacy organization involved in the national movement to ensure the rights of people with disabilities. Since its founding, the Center has been involved in the study and promotion of open settings (i.e., inclusive community opportunities) for people with disabilities.

Community for All Toolkit (from the Center on Human Policy): http://thechp.syr.edu/toolkit/

- This toolkit was developed at the request of volunteers, advocates, self-advocates, and professionals concerned that the remarkable progress made toward the inclusion of people with cognitive, intellectual, and developmental disabilities into the fabric and mainstream of community life in America was at risk. In some places in the United States, there are those who would not only continue to deny people currently in public and private institutions freedom and opportunity through continued institutionalization, but who also want to expand the role of these institutions.

CONNECT: The Center to Mobilize Early Childhood Knowledge: http://community.fpg.unc.edu/connect

- CONNECT routinely hosts online discussions and provides resources for early childhood practitioners, researchers and families. Resources include the CONNECT Modules: free, web-based modules and resources for early childhood instructors and learners.

Disability History Museum: http://www.disabilitymuseum.org/

- An online museum that aims to provide all site visitors, people with and without disabilities, researchers, teachers, and students with a wide array of tools to help deepen their understanding of human variation and difference, and to expand appreciation of how vital to our common life the experiences of people with disabilities have always been.

Disability Studies Web Ring: http://www.webring.com/hub?ring=disstudies

- This web ring brings together web sites that contain articles, essays, papers, and/or other information in support of disability rights, the independent living movement, and community living.

Division for Early Childhood (DEC): http://www.dec-sped.org/

- The DEC web site provides information on conferences, policy, advocacy, research, and events based on best practice for children with disabilities.

Division for Early Childhood (DEC) Family Resources: http://www.dec-sped.org/Families/Resources_for_Families

- Family Resources provides links to state programs and resources for families.

Division for Early Childhood (DEC) Tools You Can Use:
http://www.dec-sped.org/About_DEC/Recommended_Practices/Tools_You_Can_Use

- The DEC provides tool for parents, administrators, and teachers for working with young children with disabilities.

Family Support Center on Disabilities: Knowledge & Involvement Network (KIN):
http://familysupportclearinghouse.org/

- The Center offers a centralized resource on the full range of options available to individuals with disabilities and their families.

National Association for the Education of Young Children (NAEYC):
http://www.naeyc.org/

- NAEYC provides publications, conferences, resources, and information on public policy for educators of children with disabilities. They also provide information for families on accredited programs.

National Association of Councils on Developmental Disability (NACDD):
http://nacdd.org/site/home.aspx

- NACDD provides information on public policy, research and news. They are a membership organization and offer meeting and newsletters to their members, but also provide information on meetings for other related organizations as well as links to other sites.

National Disability Rights Network (NDRN): http://www.napas.org/

- Official web site of NDRN, whose vision is of a society where people with disaibilities have equality of opportunity and are able to participate fully in community life by exercising choice and self-determination. This is an excellent resource for those involved in the transition to adult life.

National Dissemination Center for Children with Disabilities (NICHCY):
http://www.nichcy.org/Pages/Home.aspx

- The official web site of NICHCY, a national information center that provides information on disabilities and disability-related issues, focusing on children and youth, from birth to age 22.

National Early Childhood Technical Assistance Center (NECTAC): http://www.nectac.org/

- NECTAC focuses on programs for infant and toddlers with disabilities as well as preschool programs for children with disabilities. The web page provides links to related research, events, and publications.

National Head Start Association (NHSA): http://www.nhsa.org/

- The NHSA provides links to current news on early intervention, including legislature, as well as research and services, such as professional development.

National Organization on Disability (NOD): http://www.nod.org/

- The official web site of NOD, an organization that promotes employment and the full participation of America's 54 million people with disabilities in all aspects of life.

Natural Environments: http://naturalenvironments.blogspot.com/

- Natural Environments is an early childhood intervention blog by Robin McWilliam, Endowed Siskin Chair of Research in Early Education, Development, and Intervention. The blog focuses on early interventions within natural environments.

NECTAC Research and Reference Portal:
http://www.nectac.org/portal/portal.asp

- This web page provides access to a variety of research and reference materials for administrators, researchers, policy makers, practitioners, families and advocates for young children with special needs.

NICHCY Early Intervention Providers:
http://www.nichcy.org/EarlyInterventionProviders/Pages/Default.aspx

- This part of NICHCY is specifically for early intervention providers. It provides information on Part C of IDEA, different disabilities, and effective practices for children from birth to age 3.

NICHCY IDEA Law: http://www.nichcy.org/Laws/IDEA/Pages/Default.aspx

- This part of NICHCY's web site is full of information about IDEA, including summaries of requirements, a full copy of the law, guidance on IDEA from the Office of Special Education Programs at the U.S. Department of Education, training material, and more.

NICHCY State Specific Information:
http://www.nichcy.org/Pages/StateSpecificInfo.aspx

- This part of the NICHCY's web site provides a search database for state agencies, disability-specific organizations, organizations for parents, and other organizations by state.

Parent to Parent: http://www.p2pusa.org/

- Online community that provides emotional and informational support for families of children with special needs.

Routines-Based Interview: http://ectc.education.ne.gov/rbi/rbi.htm

- The Routines-Based Interview (RBI) is a clinical, semistructured interview designed to establish a positive relationship with the family, obtain a rich and thick description of child and family functioning, and result in a list of outcomes/goals chosen by the interviewee.

TASH—Equity, Opportunity, and Inclusion for People with Disabilities:
http://www.tash.org/index.html

- TASH strives for a world in which people with disabilities are included and fully participating members of their communities, with no obstacles preventing equity, diversity, and quality of life.

Technical Assistance Alliance Acronyms:
http://www.taalliance.org/publications/pdfs/all49.pdf

- The Technical Assistance Alliance Acronyms web site lists acronyms related to early intervention, education, special education, and other laws important to individuals with disabilities and their families.

Technical Assistance Center on Social Emotional Intervention for Young Children (TACSEI):
http://www.challengingbehavior.org/

- TACSEI uses research on young children with, or at risk for, delays or disabilities and creates free products and resources to help decision makers, caregivers, and service providers apply best practices.

Books/Materials

Bridges, R. (1999). *Through My Eyes.* New York: Scholastic, Inc.

- A photo documentary written at upper-elementary reading level that chronicles Ruby Bridge's firsthand experience at William Frantz Public School.

Haskins, J. (1998). *The Dream and the Struggle: Separate but not Equal.* New York: Scholastic, Inc.

- A young adult trade book that documents the experiences of youth in racially segregated schools.

Sapon-Shevin, M. (2007). *Widening the Circle: The Power of Inclusive Classrooms.* Boston: Beacon Press.

- This is a great resource for discussions on issues of inclusion, the celebration of diversity, and the benefit to all members of the classroom.

Schwarz, P. (2006). *From Disability to Possibility: The Power of Inclusive Classrooms.* Portsmouth, NH: Heinemann.

- Like Sapon-Shevin (2007), this text discusses issues of inclusion and diversity with several specific examples from classroom settings.

Thomas, J.C. (2003). *Linda Brown, You Are Not Alone: The Brown v. Board of Education decision.* New York: Hyperion Books for Children.

- A picture book that shows the impact of the spirit of the *Brown v. Board* decision.

Films

Feldman, R., Fialka, J., & Rossen, P. (Producers). (2011). *Through the Same Door.* Dance of Partnership Publications.

- Documentary of Micah Fialka-Feldman's experience in a postsecondary college program. Includes powerful interviews with Mikah, his family, friends, teachers, and coworkers.

"Only a Teacher"—3-hour documentary series from the Public Broadcasting System (PBS) about teachers from 1830s to the present. Retrieved from: http://www.pbs.org/onlyateacher/timeline.html

- The documentary series "Only a Teacher" explores the diverse faces and many roles of the American teacher from the 1830s to the present. In three 1-hour episodes, "Only a Teacher" presents historical background about the profession and how it developed, while giving voice to contemporary teachers and their concerns. The series plays out as a dialogue between past and present as teachers from different eras describe their dreams and setbacks, challenges, and achievements.

We Can Shine: From Institutions to Independence. Documentary available from: http://espocinema.wordpress.com/

- A documentary about the state of institutions for the developmentally disabled in New York State from the 1900s onward. The film chronicles the events that led to the Willowbrook Consent Decree. The film's message is to show that with the proper supports, guidance, and love, people diagnosed with developmental disabilities can achieve—surpassing the expectations of most. With this in mind, the documentary showcases people with developmental disabilities who are achieving—many through the help of the Office for Persons with Developmental Disabilities (OPWDD)'s Self-Determination program.

PROFESSIONAL ORGANIZATIONS

Web Sites

Adapted Physical Education National Standards: http://www.apens.org/

- Comprehensive resource on the roles and profession of adapted physical education teachers and programs.

ALLIANCE National Parent Technical Assistance Center (NPTAC): http://www.parentcenternetwork.org/national/aboutus.html

- The ALLIANCE National Parent Technical Assistance Center (NPTAC) provides Parent Centers, Parent Training and Information Centers (PTIs), and Community Parent Resource Centers (CPRCs) with innovative technical assistance, up-to-date information, and high-quality resources and materials. A major goal of the ALLIANCE National PTAC is to build the capacity of Parent Centers to improve results for children with disabilities from birth to age 26 in rural, urban, and suburban areas and from underrepresented and underserved populations.

American Federation of Teachers (AFT): http://www.aft.org/

- Union of professionals whose mission is to improve the lives of members and their families; to give voice to their legitimate professional, economic, and social aspirations; to strengthen the institutions in which they work; to improve the quality of the services provided; to bring together all members to assist and support one another; and to promote democracy, human rights, and freedom.

American Occupational Therapy Association: http://aota.org/

- Comprehensive resource on the roles and preparation of occupational therapists.

American Physical Therapy Association: http://www.apta.org/

- Comprehensive resource on the roles and preparation of physical therapists.

American Speech-Language-Hearing Association: http://www.asha.org/

- Comprehensive resource on the roles and preparation of speech-language pathologists.

Center for Early Literacy Learning (CELL): http://www.earlyliteracylearning.org/

- This site has resources for early childhood intervention practitioners, parents, and other caregivers of children, birth to 5 years of age, with identified disabilities, developmental delays, and those at risk for poor outcomes.

Common Core State Standards Initiative: http://www.corestandards.org/

- The Common Core State Standards provide a consistent, clear understanding of what students are expected to learn, so teachers and parents know what they need to do to help them. The standards are designed to be robust and relevant to the real world, reflecting the knowledge and skills that young people need for success in college and careers.

CONNECT: The Center to Mobilize Early Childhood Knowledge:
http://community.fpg.unc.edu/connect /

- CONNECT develops web-based, instructional resources for faculty and other professional development providers that focus on and respond to the challenges faced each day by those working with young children and their families in a variety of learning environments and inclusive settings. The practice-based modules are designed to build early childhood practitioners' abilities to make evidence-based decisions. They emphasize a decision-making process, realistic problems to solve, the importance of integrating multiple perspectives and sources of evidence, the relevance and quality of content, and feedback.

Council for Exceptional Children: http://www.cec.sped.org/

- Official web site of CEC, the largest international professional organization dedicated to improving the educational success of individuals with disabilities and/or gifts and talents. CEC advocates for appropriate governmental policies, sets professional standards, provides professional development, advocates for individuals with exceptionalities, and helps professionals obtain conditions and resources necessary for effective professional practice.

Institute for Innovative Transition: Transforming Transitions Through Programs,
Policy, and Practice: http://www.nytransition.org/

- The Institute for Innovative Transition works to improve the quality of life for people with developmental disabilities and their families as they transition from school age to adulthood.

International Reading Association (IRA): http://www.reading.org/General/Default.aspx

- IRA is a nonprofit, global network of individuals and institutions committed to worldwide literacy. More than 70,000 members strong, the Association supports literacy professionals through a wide range of resources, advocacy efforts, volunteerism, and professional-development activities. Members promote high levels of literacy for all by improving the quality of reading instruction, disseminating research and information about reading, and encouraging lifetime reading habits.

National Association for the Education of Young Children:
http://www.naeyc.org/

- The National Association for the Education of Young Children (NAEYC) is the largest nonprofit association in the United States representing early childhood education teachers, experts, and advocates in center-based and family child care. NAEYC is dedicated to improving the well-being of all young children, with particular focus on the quality of educational and developmental services for all children from birth through age 8. NAEYC is committed to becoming an increasingly high-performing and inclusive organization.

National Association of Councils on Developmental Disability:
http://nacdd.org/site/home.aspx

- The National Association of Councils on Developmental Disabilities (NACDD) is a national membership organization representing the 55 state and territorial councils on developmental disabilities. NACDD is a 501(c)3 organization with the purpose of promoting and enhancing the outcomes of member councils in developing and sustaining inclusive communities and self-directed services and supports for individuals with developmental disabilities.

National Council of Teachers of English (NCTE): http://www.ncte.org/

- The National Council of Teachers of English is a professional organization devoted to improving the teaching and learning of English and the language arts at all levels of education. The Council promotes the development of literacy, the use of language to construct personal and public worlds, and the achievement of full participation in society, through the learning and teaching of English and the related arts and sciences of language.

National Early Childhood Technical Assistance Center (NECTAC): http://www.nectac.org/

- NECTAC is the national early childhood technical assistance center supported by the U.S. Department of Education's Office of Special Education Programs (OSEP) under the provisions of the Individuals with Disabilities Education Act (IDEA). NECTAC serves Part C—Infant and Toddlers with Disabilities Programs and Part B—Section 619 Preschool Programs for Children with Disabilities in all 50 states and 10 jurisdictions to improve service systems and outcomes for children and families.

National Education Association (NEA): http://www.nea.org/

- The web site of NEA, a national professional organization that believes every student in America—regardless of family income or place of residence—deserves a quality education. In pursuing its mission, NEA has determined that it will focus the energy and resources of its 3.2 million members on improving the quality of teaching, increasing student achievement, and making schools safer, better places to learn.

PACER Center: http://www.pacer.org/

- This is the web site of the PACER Center (Parent Advocacy Coalition for Educational Rights), the mission of which is to expand opportunities and enhance the quality of life of children and young adults with disabilities and their families, based on the concept of parents helping parents. Founded in 1977, PACER Center was created by parents of children and youth with disabilities to help other parents and families facing similar challenges. Today, PACER Center expands opportunities and enhances the quality of life of children and young adults with disabilities and their families. PACER is staffed primarily by parents of children with disabilities and works in coalition with 18 disability organizations.

Technical Assistance Center on Social Emotional Intervention for Young Children (TACSEI): http://www.challengingbehavior.org/

- The Technical Assistance Center on Social Emotional Intervention for Young Children (TACSEI) assembles the research that shows which practices improve the social-emotional outcomes for young children with, or at risk for, delays or disabilities and creates free products and resources to help decision makers, caregivers, and service providers apply these best practices in the work they do every day.

DIFFERENTIATION RESOURCES AND STRATEGIES

Web Sites

Accessible Instructional Materials (AIM) Navigator: http://aim.cast.org/experience/decision-making_tools/aim_navigator

- The AIM Navigator is an interactive tool that facilitates the process of decision making about accessible instructional materials for an individual student. The four major decision points in the process include: 1) determination of need, 2) selection of format(s), 3) acquisition of format(s), and 4) selection of supports for use. The AIM Navigator also includes a robust set of guiding questions and useful references and resources specifically related to each decision point.

All Kinds of Minds: http://www.allkindsofminds.org/

- All Kinds of Minds is a group that recognizes each student has a unique learning profile that reflects his or her particular learning strengths, weaknesses, and affinities. The web site provides many links and forums dedicated to building expertise about learning in schools, so that educators can consider how students learn and why they might be struggling.

Brain Gym: http://www.braingym.org/

- Official web site of Brain Gym International. Brain Gym describes a specific set of movements, processes, programs, materials, and educational philosophies that emphasize how moving with intention leads to optimal learning.

CAST UDL Book Builder: http://bookbuilder.cast.org/

- Use this site to create, share, publish, and read digital books that engage and support diverse learners according to their individual needs, interests, and skills.

Cool Freebie Links: http://www.coolfreebielinks.com/Teachers_Freebies/

- Free goodies, samples, and resources for teachers, educators, and home schoolers.

Education World: http://www.education-world.com/index.shtml

- An online resource that includes: original content—including lesson plans—practical information for educators, information on how to integrate technology in the classroom, and articles written by education experts; web site reviews; special features and columns; and employment listings.

Educational Insights: http://www.educationalinsights.com/

- Web site of Educational Insights, a leading manufacturer of learning toys and innovative, hands-on educational materials for classrooms. Products include games, puzzles, classroom kits, electronics, reading and math manipulatives, pocket charts, activity books, science kits, teacher resources, and classroom organizational tools.

Free Primary Teaching Resources: http://www.netrover.com/~kingskid/freestuff.htm

- Lots of free teaching resources for primary teachers. These teacher resources have free lessons and programs for the primary teacher. Everything an elementary teacher needs to teach great lessons to children.

Fulfilling the Promise of Differentiation: http://caroltomlinson.com/

- Carol Tomlinson's web site is devoted to responding to the needs of all learners. This site connects teachers with information on presentations, books, articles, and other resources.

Google Maps: http://maps.google.com/ and MapQuest: http://www.mapquest.com/

- Online resources for printing maps and directions.

Internet Magic!: http://www.scattercreek.com/~zimba/freeforteachers.htm

- Free stuff for educators, including computers, software, arts and crafts, posters, awards, puzzles, graphic organizers, curriculum, maps, magazines, newspapers, worksheets, printables, lessons ideas, technical support, test prep, and study-skill materials.

Paula Kluth: Toward Inclusive Classrooms and Communities: http://www.paulakluth.com/

- This web site is dedicated to promoting inclusive schooling and exploring positive ways of supporting students with autism and other disabilities. Most of Paula's work involves collaborating with schools to create environments, lessons, and experiences that are inclusive, respectful, and accessible for all learners.

Pro Teacher: http://www.proteacher.com/

- A professional community and web directory for elementary school teachers from pre-K to grade 8.

Rethinking Schools: http://www.rethinkingschools.org/index.shtml

- Rethinking Schools has tried to balance classroom practice and educational theory. It is an activist publication, with articles written by and for teachers, parents, and students. It also addresses key policy issues, such as vouchers and marketplace-oriented reforms, funding equity, and school-to-work.

School Behaviors: http://www.SchoolBehaviors.com/

- Online resource for educators about neurological disorders in children and teens, with practical tips for accommodations and classroom management.

Strong National Museum of Play in Rochester, New York: http://www.museumofplay.org/

- The National Museum of Play is the only collections-based museum in the world devoted solely to play. The museum blends the best features of both history museums (extensive collections) and children's museums (high interactivity) and provides families, children, adults, students, teachers, scholars, collectors, and others a multitude of offerings, including hands-on exhibits, educational programs, preschool for children ages 3 to 4, a circulating library, standards-based school lessons, and teacher development opportunities.

Teachers Free Stuff: http://www.freakyfreddies.com/teacher.htm

- Web site for free samples and school supplies.

Teaching and Learning Center of the Council for Exceptional Children: http://www.cec.sped.org/Content/NavigationMenu/NewsIssues/TeachingLearning Center/default.htm

- The Teaching and Learning Center of CEC is a comprehensive resource for special educators and others who work with children and youth with disabilities and/or gifts and talents. It includes information about the different exceptionality areas; instructional strategies; professional practice topics such as assessment, diversity, and behavior management; strategies for teaching subject-area content; evidence-based practices, and current special education topics. It also contains information on professional roles, professional standards, accreditation and licensure, and financial aid.

TeachNet: http://www.teachnet.com/how-to/manage/

- A web site where teachers can post ideas and communicate with each other. The purpose of the web site is to connect teachers and give them a voice.

Tools for Teachers (from American Federation of Teachers):
http://www.aft.org/yourwork/tools4teachers/index.cfm

- Online resource that provides teachers with information about classroom management, working together, teaching careers, classroom materials, special populations, funding opportunities, and professional development.

Transition Planning Inventory—Updated Version (TPI-U):
http://www.proedinc.com/customer/productView.aspx?ID=875

- The Transition Planning Inventory (TPI) is an instrument for identifying and planning for the comprehensive transitional needs of students. It is designed to provide school personnel a systematic way to address critical transition-planning areas that are mandated by the Individuals with Disabilities Education Act (IDEA) of 2004 and that take into account an individual student's needs, preferences, interests, and strengths.

Universal eLearner (UeL): http://www.tfaconsulting.com/universal_elearner.html

- The UeL system is intended to be an online learning application designed to present educational material to students K to 12. The system is intended to be fully accessible to students with visual impairments, auditory impairments, motor impairments, cognitive impairments, and students who are learning English as a second language. The web-based system presents separate user interfaces and workflows for students, teachers, and parents.

Virtual Middle School Library: http://www.sldirectory.com/teachf/freestuff.html

- Online resources for free stuff for classroom use, including worksheets, printables, crafts, maps, clip art, calendars, and materials.

Books/Materials

Kluth, P. (2010). *"You're Going to Love this Kid!": Teaching Students with Autism in the Inclusive Classroom* (2nd Edition). Baltimore: Paul H. Brookes Publishing Co.

- Autism expert Paula Kluth targeted this second edition to the specific needs of today's primary and secondary school educators. The book is still packed with the ready-to-use tips and strategies that teachers are looking for. Readers will also get updates on all of the other topics covered in the first edition, including fostering friendships, building communication skills, planning challenging and multidimensional lessons, and adapting the curriculum and the physical environment. And with the new first-person stories from people with autism and their teachers and parents, readers will have a better understanding of students on the spectrum and how to include them successfully.

Kluth, P., & Danaher, S. (2010). *From Tutor Scripts to Talking Sticks: 100 Ways to Differentiate Instruction in K-12 Inclusive Classrooms.* Baltimore: Paul H. Brookes Publishing Co.

- This one-of-a-kind book proves that designing differentiated instruction can be simple and fun! Packed with creative adaptation ideas like fidget bags, doodle notes, and choice boards, this book offers 100 teacher-designed, kid-tested strategies for K-12 educators to meet the needs of all students in inclusive classrooms. This is an ideal resource for helping students who need extra support, scaffolding, reminders, organization, or enrichment.

Kluth, P., & Schwarz, P. (2008). *Just Give Him the Whale: 20 Ways to Use Fascinations, Areas of Expertise, and Strengths to Support Students with Autism.* Baltimore: Paul H. Brookes Publishing Co.

- This concise, highly practical guidebook gives educators across grade levels a powerful new way to think about students' "obsessions": as positive teaching tools that calm, motivate, and improve learning. Written by top autism experts and nationally renowned speakers Paula Kluth and Patrick Schwarz, this guide is brimming with easy tips and strategies for folding students' special interests, strengths, and areas of expertise into classroom lessons and routines.

Lieberman, L.J., & Houston-Wilson, C. (2009). *Strategies for Inclusion* (2nd Edition). Champaign, IL: Human Kinetics.

- Excellent resource regarding differentiated physical education activities and strategies.

Rutherford, P. (2008). *Instruction for All Students* (2nd Edition). Alexandria, VA: Just Ask Publications.

- This book reflects current research about best practice in teaching and learning in standards-based classrooms. In addition to resources for actively engaging students and multiple approaches to lesson and unit design, this text includes information on technology integration, formative assessment, 21st-century thinking skills that promote rigor and relevance, and formats for job-embedded learning.

Rutherford, P. (2009). *Why Didn't I Learn This in College?* (2nd Edition). Alexandria, VA: Just Ask Publications.

- This book includes updated tools and procedures for teaching and learning in the 21st century. It is based on the construct that the best management program is a good instructional program.

Rutherford, P. (2011). *Meeting the Needs of Diverse Learners.* Alexandria, VA: Just Ask Publications.

- This book is designed to help teachers build skillfulness in recognizing, respecting, and responding to the needs of the wide range of diverse students in today's classrooms. This book provides an array of strategies for use with gifted students, English Language Learners, and students with special needs.

Peterson, J.M., & Hittie, M.M. (2010). *Inclusive Teaching: The Journey Towards Effective Schools for All Learners.* Boston: Pearson.

- This textbook synthesizes a vast array of strategies from many different sources, including workshop approaches to learning, differentiated instruction, universal design for learning, multicultural education, positive behavioral support, antibullying practices, reducing the learning gap between minority and majority groups, and more.

Technology and Media Division of the Council for Exceptional Children & Wisconsin Assistive Technology Initiative. (n.d.). *Assistive Technology Consideration Quick Wheel.* U.S. Department of Education, Office of Special Education Programs.

- This tool is a hands-on device (a wheel that spins) that offers quick suggestions for low- to high-assistive technology for various need areas.

Westphal, L.E. (2007). *Differentiating with Menus.* Waco, TX: Prufrock Press, Inc.

- This book offers several suggestions and examples for creating homework menus for various grade levels and content areas.

Wormeli, R. (2006). *Fair Isn't Always Equal: Assessing and Grading in the Differentiated Classroom.* Portland, ME: Stenhouse Publishers.

- This book offers the latest research and common sense thinking that teachers and administrators seek when it comes to assessment and grading in differentiated classes. Filled with real examples and "gray" areas that middle- and high-school educators will easily recognize, the text tackles important and sometimes controversial assessment and grading issues constructively. The book covers high-level concepts, ranging from "rationale for differentiating assessment and grading" to "understanding mastery," as well as the nitty-gritty details of grading and assessment.

Wormeli, R. (2007). *Differentiation: From Planning to Practice Grades 6-12.* Portland, ME: Stenhouse Publishers.

- This book takes readers step-by-step from the blank page to a fully crafted differentiation lesson. Along the way, the author shows middle- and high-school teachers the behind-the-scenes planning that goes into effective lesson design for diverse classrooms.

Films

Schoolhouse Rock DVD:
http://disneydvd.disney.go.com/schoolhouse-rock-election-collection.html#15039

- This two-disc set contains all of the songs from the PBS series Schoolhouse Rock. The songs have catchy tunes and lyrics that reinforce concepts in literacy, math, and science.

MANAGEMENT RESOURCES AND STRATEGIES

Web Sites

Association for Positive Behavior Support: http://www.apbs.org

- APBS is an international organization dedicated to promoting research-based strategies that combine applied behavior analysis and biomedical science with person-centered values and systems change to increase quality of life and decrease problem behaviors.

Center on Positive Behavioral Interventions and Support: http://www.pbis.org/

- The Center on Positive Behavioral Interventions and Supports has been established by the Office of Special Education Programs, U.S. Department of Education, to give schools capacity-building information and technical assistance for identifying, adapting, and sustaining effective schoolwide disciplinary practices.

National Center on Response to Intervention: http://www.rti4success.org/

- The National Center on Response to Intervention is housed at the American Institutes for Research and works in conjunction with researchers from Vanderbilt University and the University of Kansas. It is funded by the U.S. Department of Education's Office of Special Education Programs (OSEP). The Center's mission is to provide technical assistance to states and districts and build the capacity of states to assist districts in implementing proven models for RTI.

Teaching Tolerance: http://www.tolerance.org/

- An organization dedicated to reducing prejudice, improving intergroup relations, and supporting equitable school experiences for the nation's children. It provides free educational materials to teachers and other school practitioners in the U.S. and abroad.

Books/Materials

Cushman, K. (2003). *Fires in the Bathroom: Advice for Teachers from High School Students.* New York: The New Press.

- The author, an education journalist working in conjunction with the nonprofit organization What Kids Can Do, extensively interviewed high school students in several urban areas about every aspect of school, producing this compendium of their advice here.

Wong, H.K., & Wong, R.T. (2009). *The First Days of School: How to Be an Effective Teacher.* Mountain View, CA: Harry K. Wong Publications.

- This book walks a teacher—either novice or veteran—through structuring and organizing a classroom for success in ways that can be applied at any time of the year at any grade level, preK through college.

Wormeli, R. (2001). *Meet Me in the Middle.* Portland, ME: Stenhouse Publishers.

- This book provides successful strategies for addressing key middle-level teaching challenges, including: differentiating instruction, motivating early adolescents, teaming, teaching in block-length classes, using authentic and alternative assessment effectively, writing in all subjects, holding students and teachers accountable, involving parents, mentoring teachers, using games in the classroom, applying the latest in brain research, the National Board Certification process, and understanding the young adolescent.

Wormeli, R. (2003). *Day One and Beyond.* Portland, ME: Stenhouse Publishers.

- This book offers advice on practical survival matters, such as what to do the first day and week, setting up the grade book and other record keeping, and what to do if you only have one computer in the classroom; classroom management, including discipline, getting students' attention, and roving classrooms; social issues, like the unique nature of middle-level students, relating to students, and positive relations with parents; and professional concerns, from collegiality with teammates to professional resources all middle-level teachers should have.

LITERACY RESOURCES AND STRATEGIES

Web Sites

Brainpop: http://www.brainpop.com/

- Web site with animated science, health, technology, math, social studies, arts & music and English movies, quizzes, activity pages and school homework help for K-12 kids.

Brainpop Jr.: http://www.brainpopjr.com/

- Provides educational movies for students from kindergarten to grade 3. Homework Help, leveled quizzes, games and activities for kids. Exceptional resource for teachers and home schools.

Mercer Mayer—Little Critter: http://www.littlecritter.com/index.htm

- This is an interactive web site with literacy activities, all based on Mercer Mayer's Little Critter book characters.

Middle School Writing Activities:
http://www.education.com/activity/middle-school/writing/

- This web site provides Middle School writing activities from easy middle school writing activities to more advanced ones.

National Reading Panel: http://www.nationalreadingpanel.org/

- This web site of the NRP offers research assessment of reading instruction approaches.

Raz-Kids: http://www.raz-kids.com/

- Raz-Kids online provides leveled books and reading quizzes and gives educators choices. Students listen to books read aloud, read with vocabulary and pronunciation support, and read without support. Students may browse and read freely in the bookroom, or teachers can easily limit students to appropriate reading levels and specific books, and track student reading progress. Students can practice reading to improve reading comprehension and reading fluency anywhere with Internet access.

Reading A-Z.com: http://www.readinga-z.com/

- This web site offers thousands of printable teacher materials to teach leveled reading, phonemic awareness, reading comprehension, reading fluency, alphabet, and vocabulary.

ReadWriteThink.org: http://readwritethink.org

- This web site offers free reading and English Language Arts materials.

Spelling City: http://www.spellingcity.com/

- An interactive web site to help students independently practice spelling and vocabulary skills.

Starfall: http://www.starfall.com/

- A free web site to teach children to read. Perfect for kindergarten, first grade, and second grade. Contains exciting interactive books and phonics games.

Tumblebooks: http://www.tumblebooks.com/library/asp/customer_login.asp?
accessdenied=%2Flibrary%2Fasp%2Fhome%5Ftumblebooks%2Easp

- An online collection of animated, talking picture books that teach young children the joys of reading in an engaging format.

SOCIAL STUDIES RESOURCES AND STRATEGIES

Web Sites

American Indians in Children's Literature (AICL):
http://americanindiansinchildrensliterature.blogspot.com/

- American Indians in Children's Literature (AICL) provides critical perspectives and analysis of indigenous peoples in children's and young adult books, the school curriculum, popular culture, and society. This web site provides links to book reviews, media about Native Americans, and more.

Center for Global Studies:
http://cgs.illinois.edu/k-12-educational-resources/lesson-plans/

- The Center for Global Studies globalizes the research, teaching, and outreach missions of the University of Illinois at Urbana-Champaign. The Center is a National Resource Center in Global Studies designated by the U.S. Department of Education.

Delaware Social Studies Education Project: http://www.udel.edu/dssep/index.html

- The Delaware Social Studies Education Project is a social studies initiative, launched in 1999, by the Delaware Center for Teacher Education at the University of Delaware. Its goals are to advance the status and quality of social studies education, locate and develop resources for teachers, identify and disseminate instructional materials aligned with Delaware content standards, deliver quality professional development, and keep educators informed about the latest developments in social studies.

Georgetown Independent School District in Texas: Instructional Strategies for Social Studies: http://www.georgetownisd.org/ccorner/socstudies/Instructional StrategiesforSocialStudies.asp

- This site provides instructional strategies for social studies to help teachers effectively engage students with difficult content in their classes using reading and writing strategies.

Library of Congress: http://www.loc.gov/index.html

- The Library of Congress is the nation's oldest federal cultural institution and serves as the research arm of Congress. Using key words such as "special education" or "disability studies" or "disability" results in listings of many useful documents and artifacts.

NetTrekker from Thinkronize, Inc.: http://www.nettrekker.com/us/

- NetTrekker is a leader in the organization and delivery of digital K-12 educational content and is dedicated to enhancing education with highly effective technologies.

Teaching for Change: http://www.teachingforchange.org/

- This organization provides teachers and parents with the tools to transform schools into centers of justice where students learn to read, write, and change the world. It operates from the belief that schools can provide students the skills, knowledge, and inspiration to be citizens and architects of a better world—or they can fortify the status quo.

Books/Materials

Bigelow, B., & Peterson, B. (2002). *Rethinking Globalization*. Milwaukee, WI: Rethinking Schools Press.

- This is a resource for teaching strategies that will help students make sense of an increasingly complicated and scary world. *Rethinking Globalization* alerts readers to the challenges we face—from child labor to sweatshops, global warming to the destruction of the rainforests—and also spotlights the enormous courage and creativity of people working to set things right. It includes role plays, interviews, poetry, stories, background readings, and hands-on teaching tools.

MATH RESOURCES AND STRATEGIES

Web Sites

Aurora University—Books About Math and Numbers:
http://libguides.aurora.edu/content.php?pid=48714&sid=693429

- This guide will help you locate children's and young adult books about math concepts.

Children's Picture Books:
http://www.childrenspicturebooks.info/math_picture_books.htm

- This web site has information and reviews to help parents and teachers select the perfect picture book about math for any child.

Cool Math 4 Kids: http://www.coolmath-games.com/

- An interactive site for students, Cool Math 4 Kids has games, fun math lessons, puzzles and brain benders, and flash cards for addition, subtraction, multiplication and division, geometry, fractals, and polyhedra.

Greg Tang's web site: http://www.gregtang.com/

- Official site of children's book author Greg Tang, who has written several fun and intriguing books about math concepts. The web site also includes links to math games he has created.

Math Arcade on Fun Brain: http://www.funbrain.com/brain/MathBrain/MathBrain.html

- Several interactive online math games for varying levels of skill.

Math Cats' Math and Literature Idea Bank:
http://www.mathcats.com/grownupcats/ideabankmathandliterature.html

- This site has many good ideas for integrating math and literature, shared by teachers.

Mathematics Glossary: http://www.learnalberta.ca/content/memg/index.html

- On this site, after choosing a grade level and mathematical term, a written and illustrated definition of the term appears.

Math in Daily Life:
http://www.learner.org/interactives/dailymath/

- This site helps students explore how math can help us in our daily lives. In this exhibit, they look at the language of numbers through common situations, such as playing games or cooking, and use decision-making skills.

Math Playground: http://www.mathplayground.com/games.html

- This site has action-packed activities for elementary and middle-school students, featuring math games, math word problems, math worksheets, logic puzzles, and math videos.

Math Sphere Board Games:
http://www.mathsphere.co.uk/resources/MathSphereFreeResourcesBoardgames.htm

- A superb free collection of board, counter, and dice games—including instructions, equipment needed, and colored layouts. These are ideal for printing out in color and laminating, making a long-lasting resource.

Multiplication.Com: http://www.multiplication.com/interactive_games.htm

- This site has activities, games, and worksheets to help students with multiplication facts.

National Association for the Education of Young Children—Math-Related Children's Books: http://tyc.naeyc.org/articles/pdf/MathbookslistSchickedanzexcerpt.pdf

- This site lists many excellent children's books with math-related themes and content.

Oklahoma Panhandle State University's Math Fiction: http://www.opsu.edu/www/education/Math%20Fiction.htm

- This site provides an annotated bibliography of children's and young adult books about math concepts.

OnlineMathLearning.Com: http://www.onlinemathlearning.com/math-mnemonics.html

- This site features plenty of online math help, math fun, and other useful resources. Find interesting quizzes, practice, homework help, and other materials; or fun facts, games, puzzles, and other cool stuff to make this subject something to be enjoyed rather than dreaded.

Songs for Teaching: Using Music to Promote Learning: http://www.songsforteaching.com/mathsongs.htm

- A fantastic online resource that lists a plethora of songs about many different math concepts, compiled from various albums. Click on the song title to play the song online or purchase a CD for the classroom.

Tactile Math by Stewart Dickinson: http://emsh.calarts.edu/~mathart/Tactile_Math.html

- This web site displays and explains how Stewart Dickinson created three-dimensional models of complicated mathematical concepts for students who are blind or have visual impairments.

Touch Math: http://www.touchmath.com

- Official web site of the Touch Math program, a multisensory teaching and learning math program for preschoolers, elementary, middle, and high school students.

Woodland Maths Zone: http://www.woodlands-junior.kent.sch.uk/maths/

- This site provides free interactive math games and puzzles that teach addition, subtraction, multiplication and division, and geometry.

Books/Materials

Brunetto, C.F. (1997). *MathArt Projects and Activities: Dozens of Creative Projects to Explore Math Concepts and Build Essential Skills.* New York: Scholastic, Inc.

- In this unique book, there are dozens of creative projects that make a natural connection between math and art. Projects involve number sense, measurement, patterns, symmetry, statistics, and more. The projects are geared to the NCTM standards for use with grades 3 to 5.

Bryant-Mole, K. (1994). *Charts and Graphs.* London: Usborne Publishing Ltd.

- This is an activity book for 7- to 11-year-olds that introduces basic concepts of mathematics, using the "prehistoric" Og family to bring math into amusing everyday situations.

Cuisinaire Company of America (1995). *Learning with Fraction Circles.* **White Plains, NY: Cuisinaire Company of America, Inc.**

- This book is the user guide that accompanies a set of math manipulatives for teaching fractions. The guide explains how to teach hands-on lessons on fractions.

Greenberg, D. (1998). *Comic-Strip Math: 40 Reproducible Cartoons with Dozens of Funny Story Problems that Build Essential Math Skills.* **New York: Scholastic, Inc.**

- This book has many skill-building story problems that reinforce specific key math skills, such as multiplication, division, fractions, measurement, geometry, and more. Each reproducible page features a 4-panel comic strip and 10 fun-to-solve problems.

LePatner, M., Matuk, F.N., & Ruthven, R. (2005). *Nonfiction Writing Prompts for Math, Science, and Social Studies.* **Englewood, CO: Advanced Learning Press.**

- This book provides several writing prompts based on math concepts. It is based on the idea that writing is a cognitive process that allows teachers not only to assess students, but to plan appropriate instructional strategies that will most benefit that student. There are several books available for various grade levels.

Norris, J. (2002). *Math Centers—Take It to Your Seat, Grades 1–3.* **Monterey, CA: Evan-Moor Corporation.**

- This book has 15 self-contained Math Centers for grades 1 to 3, presented in a hanging pocket, shoebox, or folder. The skills practiced include skip counting, counting puzzles, computation, number families, telling time, word problems, calculator puzzles, patterning, linear measure, number names, geometric shapes, math challenges, money, fractions, and ordinal numbers. Additional books are available for higher grades as well.

SCIENCE RESOURCES AND STRATEGIES

Web Sites

Acorn Naturalists: http://www.acornnaturalists.com/store/index.aspx

- This web site is full of fun links to art and songs about science and nature.

Beyond Penguins and Polar Bears: http://beyondpenguins.nsdl.org/

- *Beyond Penguins and Polar Bears* is an online magazine integrating science, literacy, and the polar regions. In each thematic issue, students can explore the Arctic and Antarctica; learn science concepts and literacy strategies; read about misconceptions, equity, and technology; listen to podcasts and electronic books; or browse the photo gallery. The web site also includes lessons and unit plans aligned to national standards for teachers.

Children's Picture Books: http://www.childrenspicturebooks.info/science_picture_books.htm

- This web site has information and reviews to help parents and teachers select the perfect picture book about science for any child.

Harvard University's River City Project: http://muve.gse.harvard.edu/rivercityproject/

- With funding from the National Science Foundation, Harvard University has developed an interactive computer simulation for middle-grades science students to learn scientific inquiry and what the site terms "21st-Century Skills." River City has the look and feel of a video game but contains content developed from National Science Education Standards, National Educational Technology Standards, and 21st Century Skills. For more information about 21st Century Skills, visit http://p21.org/

Mediterranean Association of International Schools: http://www.scilitlinks.org/index.htm

• This web site enhances science and reading in grades K through 6 by connecting hands-on science activities to children's literature.

Mummification Simulation: http://oi.uchicago.edu/OI/MUS/ED/mummy.html

• An interactive web site that simulates the mummification process by ancient Egyptians. Each step describes the historical context and beliefs about the process and defines related vocabulary.

National High Magnetic Field Laboratory's Magnet Lab web site: http://www.magnet.fsu.edu/education/community/scienceinliterature/

• This web site provides links to fiction and nonfiction books for children, youth, and teens that integrate science and literature.

National Science Teachers Association—Outstanding Science Trade Books for Students K–12: http://www.nsta.org/publications/ostb/

• The books that appear in these online lists were selected as outstanding children's science trade books. They were chosen by a book review panel appointed by the National Science Teachers Association (NSTA) and assembled in cooperation with the Children's Book Council (CBC).

Sally Ride Science: https://www.sallyridescience.com/node/243

• To dispel stereotypes and fuel student interest in science, America's first woman in space, Dr. Sally Ride, founded a company that provides cutting-edge programs and content on science careers, presenting science—and scientists—in a whole new light. In addition, the Sally Ride Science programs help teachers answer one of the most challenging questions students ask: "Why do I need to learn this?"

Steve Spangler's Science Toys: http://www.stevespanglerscience.com/category/science-toys

• This is an online store for easy, hands-on science experiments, science toys, and teacher resources.

Books/Materials

Bingham, J. (1991). *The Usborne Book of Science Experiments.* London: Usborne Publishing Ltd.

• This book provides clear instructions for many simple science experiments that can be conducted with household objects.

Edom, H. (1990). *Science with Water.* London: Usborne Publishing Ltd.

• This is an illustrated exploration of the properties and basic scientific principles of water, with simple but safe experiments and games.

Edom, H., & Butterfield, M. (1991). *Science with Air.* London: Usborne Publishing Ltd.

• These experiments and tricks are all carefully designed to help young scientists explore the intriguing properties of air, using only ordinary household equipment.

The text and illustrations are clear and simple, so children can enjoy using the books by themselves.

LePatner, M., Matuk, F.N., & Ruthven, R. (2005). *Nonfiction Writing Prompts for Science.* **Englewood, CO: Advanced Learning Press.**

- This book provides several writing prompts based on science concepts. It is based on the idea that writing is a cognitive process that allows teachers not only to assess students but to plan appropriate instructional strategies that will most benefit that student. There are several books available for various grade levels.

McCully, E.A. (1992). *Mirette on the High Wire.* **New York: Penguin and Putnam Books for Young Readers.**

- This picture book incorporates science concepts into a story about Mirette and the "Great Bellini," who traverses the Paris skyline on a high wire in the climactic scene of this story about conquering fear.

Robinson, T. (2001). *The Everything Kids' Science Experiments Book.* **Avon, MA: Adams Media Corporation.**

- With this book, all you need to do is gather a few household items and you can recreate dozens of mind-blowing, kid-tested science experiments. High school science teacher Tom Robinson shows you how to expand your scientific horizons— from biology to chemistry to physics to outer space.

Scieszka, J., & Smith, L. (2004). *Science Verse.* **New York: Viking.**

- This is a collection of clever, funny poems about science concepts.

Smith, A. (Ed.). (1996). *The Usborne Big Book of Experiments.* **London: Usborne Publishing Ltd.**

- This is an introduction to science activities, showing how to set up and carry out dozens of investigations using everyday objects. The book is split into themed sections that show a range of activities, including chemical reactions, nature projects, and sensory tests. All the activities are accompanied by a list of facts and a quick quiz question. A section at the back of the book explains the scientific terms that are used during the experiments. Step-by-step instructions ensure that each project is easy to follow.

Films

They Might Be Giants & Dillet, P. (Producers). (2009). *Here Comes Science.* **Idlewild.**

- This 2 disc CD+DVD set from the band They Might Be Giants creates a new, creative way for kids to learn; with songs like Electric Car, Photosynthesis, and Solid Liquid Gas (among others)—kids will learn about science while having fun. The album features 19 songs and 19 entertaining videos.

SOCIAL SKILLS AND COMMUNICATION RESOURCES AND STRATEGIES

Web Sites

Drama Kids International: http://www.dramakids.com/x_index.php

- Drama Kids offers acting classes and drama programs for teens, kids, and toddlers.

Books/Materials

Buron, K.D. (2007). *A 5 Is Against the Law! Social Boundaries: Straight Up! An Honest Guide for Teens and Young Adults.* Shawnee Mission, KS: Autism Asperger Publishing Co.

- This book takes a narrower look at challenging behavior with a particular focus on behaviors that can spell trouble for adolescents and young adults who have difficulty understanding and maintaining social boundaries. Using a direct and simple style with lots of examples and hands-on activities, *A 5 Is Against the Law!* speaks directly to adolescents and young adults.

Buron, K.D., & Curtis, M. (2003). *The Incredible 5-Point Scale: Assisting Students with Autism Spectrum Disorders in Understanding Social Interactions and Controlling Their Emotional Responses.* Shawnee Mission, KS: Autism Asperger Publishing Co.

- This book shows how the use of a simple 5-point scale can help students understand and control their emotional reactions to everyday events. This book shows how to break down a given behavior and, with the student's active participation, develop a scale that identifies the problem and suggests alternative, positive behaviors at each level of the scale.

Cooper-Kahn, J., & Dietzel, L. (2008). *Late, Lost, and Unprepared: A Parents' Guide to Helping Children with Executive Functioning.* Bethesda, MD: Woodbine House.

- A book for parents and teachers of children from primary school through high school who struggle with impulse control, cognitive flexibility, initiation, working memory, planning and organizing, and self-monitoring.

Gray, C. (2010). *The New Social Story Book.* Arlington, TX: Future Horizons.

- This book offers more than 150 social stories, each one professionally written by Carol Gray. It also teaches how to write social stories.

Myles, B.S., Trautman, M.L., & Schelvan, R.L. (2004). *The Hidden Curriculum: Practical Solutions for Understanding Unstated Rules in Social Situations.* Shawnee Mission, KS: Autism Asperger Publishing Co.

- This book offers practical suggestions and advice for how to teach and learn those subtle messages that most people seem to pick up almost automatically but that have to be directly taught to individuals with social-cognitive challenges.

Author Index

Algozzine, R., 70
Allington, R., 228, 231
Anderson, L.W., 31
Arem, C.A., 272
Armstrong, J., 77
Arthur, E.J., 261
Ash, G.E., 249
Assaf, L.C., 249
Atherton, J.S., 83
Atwell, N., 245
Ayres, B., 70

Bailey, D., 79, 80
Baldwin, L., 314
Barnes, C., 10
Barnett, J.A., 262
Baron, N.S., 245
Bartholomew, C., 200
Barton, L., 10
Barzillai, M., 227
Baynton, D.C., 7, 10
Bear, D.R., 234
Beers, Kylene, 212, 229, 233
Berg, Clara, 308
Bérubé, M., 5
Best, A.M., 165
Beyers, Erin, 69
Bigelow, B., 255, 257
Biggle, S.J., 90
Biklen, D., 9
Bingham, J., 288
Bissonnette, Larry, 17, 35
Blacksheare, Duane, 41
Bogdan, R., 8, 9, 14, 15
Boutte, G., 283
Bowers, B., 70
Bowman, Nancy Beth, 41
Brace, J., 26
Braddock, D., 5
Bresnahan, V., 186
Bricker, D., 71
Brightman, Alan, 141, 297
Bronfenbrenner, U., 66, 73
Brotherson, S.E., 85
Brown, Colleen, 180
Brown, Darlene, 41
Brown, Lou, 51
Brown, Oliver, 39, 41

Bruce, B.C., 223
Bruder, M.B., 67
Brueggemann, B.J., 8
Brunetto, C.F., 274
Bryant-Mole, K., 274
Bunn, K., 113
Burkley, E., 268
Burkley, M., 268
Buron, K.D., 305
Burrelli, J., 12
Bush, George H.W., 70
Buteau, G., 114
Butterfield, M., 288
Buysse, V., 71

Calabro, Tina, 146
Carlson, C., 24
Carlson, E.A., 7
Casey, A., 77
Chapman, C., 289
Charlton, J.I., 5, 9
Cheatham, G., 77
Childress, D., 71, 77
Church, E.B., 110
Clarket, T., 223
Clinton, Bill, 70
Codell, E., 234
Cohen, A.J., 64
Cole, C., 29
Collier-Bolkus, W.P., 78
Conderman, G., 186
Connell, B.R., 152
Cornbleth, C., 256
Cort, R.H., 15
Coutinho, M.J., 165
Cowhey, Mary, 111, 112, 185, 218, 300
Crandall, J., 318
Cregor, M., 120
Crockett, J., 71
Crovitz, D., 251
Curtis, M., 305

Danaher, Sheila, 269, 272, 273, 274, 275, 301
Daniel, J., 223
Davis, L.J., 9
DeVito, D., 5
DeVore, S., 70
Diaz, E.M., 115

Dickinson, Stewart, 272
Dingus-Eason, Jeannine, 54–55
Doben, Maggie, 16
Donahue, P., 228
Done, P., 248
Driscoll, Maggie, 206
DuFour, R., 186
Dye, H., 65

Eastwood, C., 5
Edom, H., 288
Eicher, L., 280, 284
Else-Quest, N.M., 268
Emmanuel, Sadie, 41
Emmerson, Margaret, 41
Erikson, Erik, 86

Fargo, J.D., 244
Feldman, R.S., 83, 84, 87, 89
Fialka, Janice, 67–68, 68–69
Field, C.T., 12
Fields, Marjika, 157
Fitzell, S., 270, 274, 275, 276, 285, 286, 289, 290, 291
Fleming, Shirla, 41
Fletcher, R., 248, 250
Flippo, R.F., 237
Florian, L., 66, 67
Flower, L.A., 24
Fountas, I.C., 245, 246

Gable, R.A., 109
Gable, S., 89
Gallagher, J., 65
Gallard, A.J., 281
Gamel-McCormick, M., 70
Gardner, H., 57, 97, 101, 245, 315
Gargiulo, R.M., 266, 271, 272, 285, 286, 287, 288, 290
Garland-Thomson, R., 8
Gartner, A., 70, 71
Gaston, Steven, 41
Gay, G., 281, 282
Gay, Geneva, 226
Gesell, Arnold, 65
Gibron, Bill, 17
Ginott, H., 206
Ginsburg, Ruth Bader, 13
Giordano, Matt, 135
Giuliani, G.A., 237
Glenn, H.S., 110
Godrej, D., 27
Goldman, Amy, 51
Graff-Mathis, M., 315
Graham, E., 86
Gray, C., 303
Greenberg, D., 274
Griffen, S., 317
Grigg, W., 228
Gutstein, E., 270, 274

Haager, D., 223, 224, 235
Habib, Dan, 16
Hadaway, N.L., 226

Halliburton, A., 89
Harbin, G., 78
Harper, Lena, 41
Haskins, J., 38
Hayman, R.L., Jr., 13
Hemmeter, M.L., 72
Henderson, Andrew, 41
Hester, P.H., 109
Hildenbrand, S.M., 319
Hill, R., 227, 228, 267
Hinkle, Stephen, 102
Hittie, M.M., 153
Hodison, Shirley, 41
Hoffman, C., 78
Holland, D.D., 237
Hook, J., 79
Horton, T. A., 262
Hosp, J.L., 165
Houston-Wilson, C., 313
Hudson, R.F., 236
Hughes, K.G., 109
Hyde, J.S., 268

Invernizzi, M., 234
Ipkeze, C., 227
Irujo, S., 268

Jackelen, Beth, 154
James, Jerome, 41
Janko-Summers, S., 78
Jarrett, D., 275, 286, 291
Jensen, E., 315
Jensen, W.R., 261
Jesien, G., 70, 78
Johnson, G.L., 283
Johnson, Harriet McBryde, 6
Johnson, J., 249
Johnson, Lyndon, 11, 66
Johnston, F., 234
Jones, C.D., 244
Joseph, G., 78
Jung, L.A., 77

Karuth, D., 14
Kauffman, J., 71
Kelley, W.L., 24
Kelly-Jackson, C., 283
Kennedy, John F., 65
Kennedy, Michael, 50
Keyes, L., 71
King, Janice, 41
King, Martin Luther, 260
Kingsley, Emily Perl, 98
Kirk, S., 65
Kirkebye, A., 314, 315
Klienhammer-Tramill, A., 26
Kliewer, C., 15, 25, 29, 101, 128, 129, 130, 131, 225, 300
Klingner, J.K., 223, 224, 235
Klinkbeil, C., 317
Kluth, Paula, 184, 193, 269, 272, 273, 274, 275, 301
Kohn, Alfie, 111, 115, 206

Konold, T.R., 236
Kosciw, J.G., 115
Kozol, J., 66
Kunc, Norm, 5

Ladson-Billings, Gloria, 184
Laman, T.T., 249
Lane, H.B., 236
Lavoie, Richard, 133, 298, 299, 305, 306, 308
Lawler, A., 12
Lawton, Richard, 41
Lee, C.D., 22
Lee, J., 228
LePatner, M., 274, 289
Levine, Mel, 85, 94, 95, 96, 97, 297, 298
Lewis, Alma, 41
Lewis, Jerry, 6, 9
Lewis, J.J., 12
Liddell, George, Jr., 41
Lieberman, L., 313
Liles, J., 255
Lincoln, Abraham, 11
Linehan, A., 70
Linton, S., 9, 13
Lipsky, D.K., 70, 71
Lott, L., 110
Lucchesi, G., 6
Lyon, G., 5

Majd, M., 29
Maples, Joellen, 238
Martin, E.W., 27
Martin, R., 27
Mayer, M., 233
McCarthy, M.T., 237
McCully, E.A., 283
McGregor, T., 230
McKenna, M.C., 222, 244
McLean, M.E., 72
McNeil, M., 31
McWilliam, R., 77
Meisels, S., 65, 66
Mertz, J.E., 268
Metcalf, D., 266, 271, 272, 285, 286, 287, 288,
    290
Michalko, L., 314
Milczarek-Desai, Shefali, 11
Miller, Alice Duer, 12
Miller, J., 243
Mills, K.A., 223
Mills, Peter, 41
Mock, Martha, 63, 70
Moore, M.T., 248
Morris, P., 73
Morris, W., 315
Muenchow, S., 66, 70
Myles, B.S., 299, 305

Nelsen, J., 110
Nelson, L.L., 261
Nevin, A.I., 117
Niles, R., 24

Norris, J., 274
Novak, G., 83, 87, 90, 96

O'Connor, Sandra Day, 13
O'Neal, D., 113
Oberti, Raphael, 50, 51
Odem, S., 70, 79
Ohlson, C., 70, 78
Oliver, M., 10
Ortenzi, Debra, 293
Oswald, D.P., 165
Ouellette, M., 223

Packer, L.E., 150
Parker, J., 268
Patterson, J.A., 24
Patton, J., 65
Payne, J., 65
Pedersen, T., 186
Peláez, M., 83, 87, 90, 96
Persky, H., 243
Peterson, B., 257, 270, 274
Peterson, J.M., 153
Peterson, N., 65, 66
Piaget, Jean, 82
Pierangelo, R., 237
Pinnell, G.S., 245, 246
Portalupi, J., 248, 250
Powell, J., 27
Provasnik, S., 22
Pullen, P.C., 236

Rapp, Sam, 133
Rapp, W.H., 270, 284
Regnier, M., 78
Reschly, D.J., 165
Reutzel, D.R., 244
Richardson, Iona, 41
Ringler, M., 113
Ro, Y.E., 77
Robinson, R.D., 222, 244
Robinson, T., 288
Rock, M.L., 109
Rodriguez, D., 113
Rosenberg, T., 6
Rostetter, David, 47–48
Rowley, Amy, 47–48
Rubin, S., 247
Ruddy, A.S., 6
Rutherford, P., 134, 258, 285, 290, 300

Saffron, J.R., 90
Safran, S.P., 5
Salahu-Din, D., 243
Sandall, S., 72
Santos, R.M., 77
Sapon-Shevin, M., 15, 111
Sapp, W., 260, 261
Saunders, J., 249
Scales, Vivian, 41
Schelvan, R.L., 299, 305
Schmidt, P.R., 283

Scieszka, J., 283
Scott, L., 200
Seider, S., 259
Seif, E., 256
Senechal, D., 229
Senghas, A., 90
Shackleford, J., 73
Shamberg, M., 5
Sher, S., 5
Shonkoff, J., 65, 66
Silverman, L.K., 266
Sims, J., 77
Singer, P., 259
Singh, N.N., 165
Skeels, H., 65
Smith, A., 288
Smith, B.J., 72
Smith, L., 283
Snyder, B.J., 8
Sotomayor, Sonia, 13
St. Croix, M., 319
Stainback, S., 70
Stainback, W., 70
Stanger, Megan, 180
Stanger, Sheri, 180
Stermer, P.S., 268
Sullivan, A.L., 165
Summers, J.A., 72
Swinning, E.A., 237
Switzer, Kathrine, 12

Tang, G., 269
Taylor, S., 4, 14, 15
Teale, W.H., 113
Templeton, S., 234
Terman, D.L., 27
Thoma, C., 200
Thomas, P., 243
Thompson, C.L., 250
Thomson, R.G., 5, 8, 14
Thousand, J.S., 117

Thurlow, M., 70
Todd, Lucinda, 41
Tomlinson, C.A., 275
Tompkins, G.E., 244, 248
Tramill, J., 26
Trautman, M.L., 299, 305
True, M., 114
Trueswell, J.C., 90
Turnbull, A.P., 72, 79

Urban, W.J., 21, 22, 23

Van der Klift, Emma, 5
Van Horn, G., 261
Villa, R.A., 117
Vygotsly, Lev, 30, 82, 84

Wagoner, J.L., Jr., 21, 22, 23
Waldron, N., 29
Wedman, J.M., 222, 244
Weicker, Lowell, 66, 67
Weigel, M., 245
Welch, Cady, 99
Wesley, P., 71
Westphal, L.E., 137, 138, 271
Whitcomb, Laura, 163, 177–178
White, J.W., 248
Williams, Michael, 41
Wilson, R., 303
Winter, J.A., 10
Wolf, M., 227
Wormeli, R., 30, 134, 141, 270, 273, 285, 287, 289
Wurzburg, G., 247

Yell, M.L., 71
Ysseldyke, J., 70

Zigler, E., 66, 70
Zindler, Rachel, 106
Zinn, H., 260

Subject Index

Tables and figures are indicated by *t* and *f*, respectively.

AAC, *see* Augmentative or alternative communication
Accommodation, in cognitive development, 83
Action
 multiple means of, 149–152
 universal design for learning and, 149–152
Active participants, 193
 in science, 281
Active processes
 definition of, 281
ADA, *see* Americans with Disabilities Act of 1990
Adaptations, 30, 31
Adaptive physical education (APE), 312–313
Advocacy, in transition to adult life, 193–194
Advocate, definition of, 42
Agencies, collaboration with, 187–188
Agenda, 209
Aliens, students as, 131
Alternate assessments, 119
Americans with Disabilities Act (ADA) of 1990, 49–50
Anchor activities
 in mathematics, 272–273
 in science, 287–288, 288*t*
Anecdotal records, 122
Antecedent, in behavior, 122
APE, *see* Adaptive physical education
Art
 mathematics and, 268–270
 science and, 282–283
Artifactual systems, 299
Assessment
 alternative, 119
 communication, 307, 307*t*
 formative, 162
 functional behavioral, 119, 120–123
 mathematics, 275–276
 nondiscriminatory, 45
 output and, 216–218
 performance-based, 292
 in planning-assessment-instruction cycle, 163–165, 164*f*
 product-based, 292
 reading, 237–238
 science, 291–292
 social skills, 307–308
 summative, 162–163
 writing, 242–243, 250–251
Assimilation, 83

Assistive technology (AT)
 communication and, 304
 cost of, 153
 definition of, 153
 high-tech, 153–154
 independence and, 154
 as investigation, 153
 low-tech, 153–154
 as product, 153
AT, *see* Assistive technology
At-risk children, 73
Attention control system, 94*t*
Attitude, about reading, 232–233, 232*t*
Auditory development, 85*t*
Augmentative or alternative communication (AAC),
 305–306
Authenticity
 definition of, 276
 in mathematics assessment, 276

Behavior chart, 121*f*
Behavior contract, 214, 214*f*
Behavioral intervention plan (BIP), 119, 120
Behavior-rating scales, 308
Beliefs
 in ability to think, 129
 community and, 107
 in individuality, 130
Bell curve, 8, 8*f*
Belton v. Gebhart, 40
"Better dead than disabled," 5–6
Bingo, social, 109
BIP, *see* Behavioral intervention plan
Blessings in a Backpack, 113
Bloom's taxonomy, 93–94, 94*t*, 263*t*
*Board of Education of the Hendrick Hudson Central School
 District, Westchester County, New York v. Amy Rowley*,
 48–49
Bolling v. Sharpe, 40
Brain development, 85*t*, *see also* Neurological
 development
Briggs v. Elliott, 40
Brown v. Board of Education, 23–24, 38–41, 44
Budget, differentiation and, 140–141
Bulah v. Gebhart, 40
Bullying, 216

Care, in identity development, 86t
Case conference, 67–68
Cedar Rapids Community School District v. Garret F., 52–53
Character, 212, 212t
Charity model, 9
Child find, 72, 171
Child support team (CST), 165
Citizenship, classroom, 129–131
Class covenant, 109–110
Class meetings, 110
Class puzzle, 108
Class rules, 109–110
Classifications, disability, 45, 45f
Classroom
    citizenship, 129–131
    fairness in, 133
    universal design for learning, 152–160, 156f
Classroom management, 115–123
    engagement and, 117–118
    expectations and, 116–117, 118–119
    feedback and, 117–118
    pyramid, 116f
    routines in, 116–117, 118–119
    special education and, 119–123
Code-switching, 247–248
Cognitive development, 82–84
    accommodation in, 83
    assimilation in, 83
    Bloom's taxonomy and, 93–94, 94t
    cultural tools and, 84
    disequilibrium in, 83
    education and, 93–94
    more knowledgeable other and, 84
    Piaget's theory of, 82–84
    scaffolding and, 84
    schemas and, 83
    Vygotsky's theory of, 84
    zone of proximal development and, 84
Collaboration
    asking for help and, 183
    best practices, 180–184
    common goals and, 183
    communication and, 181–183
    expertise and, 185
    flexibility and, 184
    home–school, 184–185
    interagency, 72–73
    risk taking and, 184
    within school, 186–187
    between school and agencies, 187–188
    student, 111
    subversive pedagogy and, 184
    between teachers and service professionals, 186–187
    teacher–teacher, 186
    with teaching assistants, 187
Common core state standards, 227–228, 267
Common goals, 183
Common school, 22
Communication
    alternative, 305–306
    assessment, 307, 307t
    assistive technology and, 304

    augmentative, 305–306
    board games for, 301, 302t
    collaboration and, 181–183
    of data, 217–218
    dramatic activities for, 301
    engagement and, 299–301, 302t
    expressive, 296, 305–306
    input and, 303–305
    Inside-Outside Circles activity for, 300
    multimodal, 306
    options for, 150
    output and, 305–307
    receptive, 296, 303–304
    road-map activity for, 300
    strategies, 297f
    see also Language
Community
    beliefs and, 107
    building, 106–115
    class covenant for, 109–110
    class meetings for, 110
    class puzzle for, 108
    class rules for, 109–110
    collaboration and, 111
    conflict management and, 110
    connections, 197–201
    engagement and, 208–209
    help and, 111
    social bingo for, 109
    social justice and, 111–112
    sustaining, 110–112
Competence
    in identity development, 86t, 96
    presuming, 20
Comprehension
    reading, 223, 236–237
    representation and, 149
    universal design for learning and, 149
Compulsory attendance laws, 22
Concept of normal, 7
Conceptual framework
    definition of, 128
    for differentiation, 128–134
Concrete operational stage, 83
Conference, case, 67–68
Conflict management, community and, 110
Conflict resolution, 214–215
Connections, community, 197–201
Consciousness, cultural, 184
Consequence, behavior, 122
Constructivism, social, 84
Continuum of services, 26, 174, 174f
Contract, behavior, 214, 214f
Coordinated set of activities, 194, 197
Coteaching, 186
Covenant, 109–110
Credo for Support (Kunc & Van der Klift), 5, 6
Critical life areas, 194
Critical thinking
    mathematics and, 266–267
    social studies and, 256, 263, 263t
Cross-curricular, 314

CST, *see* Child support team
Cultural consciousness, 184
Cultural considerations, early childhood interventions and, 78
Cultural relevance
    definition of, 24
    mathematics instruction and, 267–268
    reading instruction and, 226, 231–232
Cultural tools, 84
Curriculum
    formal, 281
    hidden, 299
    science, 281–282
    societal, 282
    standards, 227–228, 267
    symbolic, 281

Daniel R.R. v. State Board of Education, 51
Data
    anecdotal, 122
    collection, 217
    communication of, 217–218
    interview, 122
    observational, 121
Davis v. County School Board of Prince Edward County, 40
DEC, *see* Division for Early Childhood
Desegregation, 38–41
Development
    cognitive, 82–84
    in disability context, 98–99
    education and, impact of, 93–97
    identity, 86–87, 86t, 96–97
    language, 89–90, 97
    neurological, 84–86, 94–96
    physical, 90, 91f, 92f, 97
    social, 88–89, 97
    teachers and, 99–102
    theories of, 82–93
Developmental delay, definition of, 72
Developmental milestones, 90, 93t
Dichotomous needs, 139–140
Differentiation
    budget and, 140–141
    conceptual framework for, 128–134
    definition of, 30, 134
    dichotomous needs and, 139–140
    independence and, 141
    individualized education program and, 134
    of instruction, 134–139, 136f
    menus for, 137–138, 138f
    paradigm shifts and, 141–142
    ripple effect and, 139
    special education and, 30
    strategy selection, 141
Digital literacy, 223
Digital media
    reading and, 227
    writing and, 245
Disability
    as "bad," 5, 14
    as challenge, 15
    classifications, 45, 45f

concept of normal and, 7
development in context of, 98–99
as difference, 15
education and, 13–15
"freak" conception of, 8
in history, 5–10
identification of, 72–73
as inability, 14–15
industrialization and, 7
labeling and, 14–15
medical model of, 8–9
as opportunity, 15
pity/charity model of, 9
as scary, 14
social construction of, 13–15
social model of, 9–10
statistics and, 7–8
as worse than death, 5–6
Disability studies, definition of, 4
Disequilibrium, 83
Disproportionality, 43, 165
Division for Early Childhood (DEC), 72
Due process, procedural, 46

Early childhood intervention
    assessment in, 76–77
    at-risk children and, 73
    cultural considerations in, 78
    definition of, 66
    eligibility for, 73, 74t–76t
    family-centered practices in, 72
    major principles of, 71–79
    natural environment in, 77
    poverty and, 78–79
    routines-based intervention in, 77
    service coordination in, 73, 76
    service provision in, 76–77
    socioeconomic considerations in, 78
    transitions in, 78
Educate America Act, 70
Education
    Brown v. Board of Education and, 23–24
    cognitive development and, 93–94
    common school and, 22
    compulsory attendance laws and, 22
    cultural relevance and, 24
    desegregation in, 38–41
    developmental theories in, impact of, 93–97
    disability and, 13–15
    Enlightenment and, 21
    free appropriate public, 26, 45
    history of, 21
    identity development and, 96–97
    language development and, 97
    least dangerous assumption in, 20
    neurological development and, 94–96
    physical development and, 97
    postsecondary, 199–201
    presuming competence in, 20
    in the Progressive Era, 23
    race and, 22–24
    segregation in, 38–41

Education *(Continued)*
  social development and, 97
  in United States, 21–25
  see also Special education
Education for All Handicapped Children Act of 1975
    (EHC), 26, 27, 28, 44–46, 66
Education of the Handicapped Act Amendments of 1986,
    66–67
Effort, sustaining, 151
EHC, *see* Education for All Handicapped Children Act
Eligibility
  definition of, 45
  for early childhood intervention, 73, 74*t*–76*t*
  nondiscriminatory assessment and, 45
  for special education, 172–173
Emancipation Proclamation, 11
Emotional development, 85*t*
Enduring understandings, 256
Engagement
  catching interest and, 151
  classroom management and, 117–118
  communication and, 299–301, 302*t*
  community and, 208–209
  least dangerous assumption and, 225–226
  as management strategy, 207–210
  mathematics instruction and, 268–271
  multiple means of, 151–152
  reading instruction and, 225–226, 229–233
  routines and, 209, 210*t*
  science instruction and, 282–286
  social skills and, 299–301, 302*t*
  social studies instruction and, 256–269
  strategies, 229–233
  universal design for learning and, 151–152
  writing instruction and, 246–248
English for Speakers of Other Languages (ESOL)
    teachers, 318
English language learners, 113–114
  see also Special area classes
Enlightenment, 21
Environment
  least restrictive, 46, 46*f*
  natural, 71, 77
Equality, fairness *versus*, 132–133
ESOL, *see* English for Speakers of Other Languages
Executive functions
  definition of, 150
  expression and, 150
  scaffolding and, 150
Exit ticket, 210
Expectations, classroom management and, 116–117,
    118–119
Expertise, 185
Expository texts
  definition of, 281
  in science, 281
Expository writing, 243, *see also* Writing
Expression
  collaboration and, 182–183
  executive functions and, 150
  multiple means of, 149–152

  physical, 150
  universal design for learning and, 149–152
Expressive communication, 296, 305–306
Extrinsic motivators, 152

Fairness
  definition of, 132
  equality *versus*, 132–133
Families
  connecting with, 185*t*
  expertise of, 185
  in home–school collaboration, 184–185
  students and, 114–115
Family-centered practices, 67, 72
FAPE, *see* Free appropriate public education
FBA, *see* Functional behavioral assessment
Feedback
  classroom management and, 117–118
  for writing, 251
Fidelity, in identity development, 86*t*, 96
First Chance, 66
Flexibility, collaboration and, 184
Fluency, 223
Form, student at-risk referral, 169*f*
Formal curriculum, 281
Formal operational stage, 83
Formative assessment
  overview of, 162, 163
  in reading, 237
  see also Assessment
Freaks, 8
Free appropriate public education (FAPE), 26, 45
Full citizen, of classroom, 129–131
Functional behavioral assessment (FBA), 119, 120–123

Gardner's Multiple Intelligences, 182*t*
Gay students, 115
Gender, social construction of, 11–13
Goals
  definition of, 176
  sharing common, 183
Goals 2000, 70
Graphic organizers
  for mathematics, 271
  for writing, 250
Guided inquiry, 291

Handicapism, 9
Handicapped Children's Early Education Assistance Act
    (HCEEAA), 66
Handicapped Children's Early Education Programs
    (HCEEP), 66
Head Start, 66, 70
Hegemony, 24
Help
  asking for, 183
  community and, 111
Hidden curriculum, 299
Hierarchy of needs, 113*f*
Higher thinking system of school performance, 95*t*
Home–school collaboration, 184–185

Homosexual students, 115
Hope, in identity development, 86*t*
Howard University, 11

IDEA, *see* Individuals with Disabilities Education
    Improvement Act
Identification, of children with disabilities, 72–73, 171
Identity development, 86–87, 86*t*, 96–97
IEP, *see* Individualized education program
IFSP, *see* Individualized family service plan
Inclusion
    as attitude, 30, 31
    debate, 29
    in early childhood education, 70–71
Independence
    assistive technology and, 154
    differentiation and, 141
    increasing levels of, 141
Independent-living centers, 198
Individuality, belief in, 130
Individualized education program (IEP)
    background information and, 175
    definition of, 27, 46
    development of, 47
    differentiation and, 134
    Education for All Handicapped Children Act and, 46
    general education teacher in, 71
    meeting, 173–174
    placement and, 175–176
    present levels of performance and, 175–176
    recommended programs in, 176
    review of, 175
    special area classes and, 313, 314
    in special education process, 173–174
    teacher input in, 177–178
Individualized family service plan (IFSP)
    definition of, 71
    in family-centered practices, 72
    introduction of, 71
Individuals with Disabilities Education Improvement
    Act (IDEA), 28, 47
    assistive technology in, 153
    eligibility in, 74*t*–76*t*
    Part B, 64
    Part C, 64
    reauthorizations of, 53–54, 70–71
    response to intervention and, 165, 168
    transition services under, 194–195
Industrialization
    definition of, 7
    disability and, 7
    statistics and, 7–8
Informal reading inventories (IRIs), 237
Informative writing, 243, *see also* Writing
Input
    auditory, 271–272, 286
    communication and, 303–305
    in management, 210–216
    mathematics and, 271–273
    reading and, 233–236
    science and, 286–288

social skills and, 304–305
social studies and, 260–262
tactile, 271–272, 286
visual, 271–272, 286
writing and, 248–249
Inquiry
    definition of, 280
    guided, 291
    science as, 280–281
    structured, 291
    student-directed, 291
Instruction
    differentiation of, 134–139, 136*f*
    mathematics, 268–273
    in planning-assessment-instruction cycle, 163–165, 164*f*
    reading, 223–225
    science, 282–291
    social studies, 256–263
    writing, 245–246
Intelligence, traditional definitions of, 57
Interaction, observation of, 216
Interdisciplinary, 77
Interview data, 122
Interviews, 308
Intrinsic motivators, 152
iPad, 245
IRIs, *see* Informal reading inventories
Irving Independent School District v. Tatro, 52

Justice, social, 111–112

Kaleidoscope Profile, 182*t*
Kolb Learning Style Inventory, 182*t*

Labeling
    definition of, 14
    and disability in education, 14–15
    special education and, 27–29
Language
    development, 85*t*, 89–90, 97
    load, 226
    mathematical, 268, 272
    paralinguistics in, 299
    pragmatic, 296
    representation and, 147–149
    science, 286–287
    separatist, 57–58
    system of school performance, 95*t*
    see also Communication
Lanham Act, 64
Law, letter of *versus* spirit of, 56
Learning preferences, 182*t*
Least dangerous assumption, 20, 222, 225–226
Least restrictive environment (LRE), 46, 46*f*
Lesbian students, 115
Letter of law, 56
Letting go, 69
List menu, 137–138, 138*f*
Literacy
    balanced, 245
    digital, 223
    see also Reading

Literature
    mathematics and, 268–270
    science and, 282–283
Load, language, 226
Long-term adult outcomes, 195, 197
Love, in identity development, 86*t*
LRE, *see* Least restrictive environment

Mainstream, definition of, 51
Management strategies, 207–216, 208*f*
    engagement, 207–210
    input, 210–216
Manipulatives
    definition of, 273
    in mathematics instruction, 273–274
Marginalization, 131
Maslow's hierarchy of needs, 113*f*
Mathematical expressions, representation and,
        147–149
Mathematics
    anchor activities in, 272–273
    art and, 268–270
    assessment, 275–276
    auditory input and, 271–272
    choice in, 270
    common core state standards in, 267
    cultural relevance and, 267–268
    emotional connections in, 270
    engagement and, 268–271
    grading alternatives, 276
    graphic organizers for, 271
    importance of, 266–267
    input and, 271–273
    instruction, 268–273
    language in, 268, 272
    literature and, 268–270
    manipulatives in, 273–274
    mnemonics and, 271
    multiple intelligences and, 274, 274*t*
    music and, 268–270
    output and, 273–275
    real-life connections in, 270
    reproducibles in, 274
    self-regulation and, 271
    tactile input and, 271–272
    visual input and, 271–272
Media, digital, 227
Medical model, 8–9
Meetings
    class, 110
    individualized education program, 173–174
Memory, 94
Memory system of school performance, 95*t*
Mental Retardation Facilities and Community Mental
        Health Centers Construction Act of 1963, 65
Menus, for differentiation of instruction, 137–138, 138*f*
Milestones, developmental, 90, 93*t*
Mills v. Board of Education of District of Columbia, 42–43, 44
Mind profile, 86
Mnemonics, 271
Modality, 272

Modeling, 211
Modifications, 30, 31
More knowledgeable other, 84
Motor development, 85*t*
Motor system of school performance, 95*t*
Multidisciplinary, 77
Multimodal communication, 306
Multiple intelligences
    board games for, 302*t*
    mathematics and, 274, 274*t*
    science and, 288, 289*t*
Music
    mathematics and, 268–270
    science and, 282–283
Myers-Briggs Type Inventory, 181, 182*t*

Narrative writing, 243
    see also Writing
National Association for the Advancement of Colored
        People (NAACP), 39, 40
    see also Brown v. Board of Education
National Center on Educational Restructuring and
        Inclusion (NCERI), 70
National Committee on Science Education Standards and
        Assessment, 280
National Council of Teachers of Mathematics (NCTM),
        267
National Dissemination Center for Children with
        Disabilities, 170
National School Lunch Program, 112–113, 114*t*
Natural environment, 71, 77
Nature *versus* nurture, 7, 65
NCERI, *see* National Center on Educational
        Restructuring and Inclusion
NCLB, *see* No Child Left Behind Act
NCTM, *see* National Council of Teachers of
        Mathematics
Needs, dichotomous, 139–140
Neo2, 245
Neurological development, 84–86, 94–96
No Child Left Behind Act (NCLB), 31
    classroom management and, 119
    Goals 2000 and, 70
    response to intervention and, 165
Nondiscriminatory assessment, 45
Normal, concept of, 7

Oberti v. Board of Education, 50–52
Observation checklists, 308
Observational data, 121
Occupational therapists, 317
Old Deluder Satan Act, 21
Output
    communication and, 305–307
    in management, 216–218
    mathematics and, 273–275
    reading and, 236–237
    science and, 288–291
    social skills and, 306–307
    social studies and, 262–263
    writing and, 249–250

Paradigm shifts, differentiation and, 141–142
Paralinguistics, 299
Parents, participation of, 46
PBIS, *see* Positive behavioral interventions and supports
Pedagogical methods, 57
Pedagogy, subversive, 184
Pennsylvania Association of Retarded Citizens (PARC) v. Commonwealth of Pennsylvania, 41–42, 44
Perception
    definition of, 147
    representation and, 146–147
    in universal design for learning, 146–147
Performance-based assessment, 292
Permanent products, 122
Persistence, sustaining, 151
Personal Responsibility and Work Opportunity Reconciliation Act, 70
Person-centered planning, 194, 196
Persuasive writing, 243, *see also* Writing
Phonemic awareness, 223
Phonics, 223
Phonological awareness, 223
Physical development, 85*t*, 90, 91*f*, 92*f*, 97
Physical education, adaptive, 312–313
Physical expression, 150
Physical therapists, 317
Piaget's theory of cognitive development, 82–84
"Piss on pity," 27
Pity/charity model, 9
Planning-assessment-instruction cycle, 163–165, 164*f*
Plasticity, 86
Plessy v. Ferguson, 40
Policy development, 64–71
Positive behavioral interventions and supports (PBIS), 119–120, 168, 207
Postsecondary education programs, 199–201
Poverty
    early childhood interventions and, 78–79
    students and, 112–113
    war on, 66
PPMR, *see* President's Panel on Mental Retardation
Pragmatic language, 296
Preoperational stage, 83
President's Panel on Mental Retardation (PPMR), 65
Presuming competence, 20
Primary sources
    definition of, 260
    in social studies instruction, 260
Product-based assessment, 292
Progressive Era, 23
Proposed Program for National Action to Combat Mental Retardation, A (President's Panel on Mental Retardation), 65
Proximics, 299
Public Law 88-164, 65
Public Law 94-142, 66
Public Law 99-457, 66–67
Purpose, in identity development, 86*t*
Puzzle, class, 108

Qualification, classification and, 45

Race
    education and, 22–24
    hegemony and, 24
    social construction of, 10–11
Reading
    access to instruction in, 223–225
    assessment, 237–238
    common core state standards and, 227–228
    comprehension, 236–237
    cultural relevancy and, 226, 231–232
    daily, 236
    digital media and, 227
    engagement and, 225–226, 229–233
    importance of, 222
    independent levels, 231
    input and, 233–236
    instruction, 223–225
    language load and, 226
    least dangerous assumption concept and, 225–226
    output and, 236–237
    performance problems, 222
    positive attitude about, 232–233, 232*t*
    principles to support, 224*t*
    records, 236
    response to intervention and, 228–229
    skills, 223*t*
    strategies, 234–236
    whole-language approach to, 224
    writing and, 244–245
Real-life connections
    in mathematics, 270
    in science, 283–284
Receptive communication, 296, 303–304
Reciprocity
    definition of, 130
    in relationships, 130
Rehabilitation Act of 1973, 43–44
Related service professionals, 312, 316–319
Related services, 52
Relationships, reciprocity in, 130
Relevance, cultural
    definition of, 24
    mathematics instruction and, 267–268
    reading instruction and, 226, 231–232
Representation
    comprehension and, 149
    language and, 147–149
    mathematical expressions and, 147–149
    multiple means of, 146–149
    perception and, 146–147
    symbols and, 147–149
    in universal design for learning, 146–149
Reproducibles
    definition of, 274
    in mathematics instruction, 274
Respect, in conflict management, 110
Response to intervention (RTI)
    components of, 168
    definition of, 30, 163

Reproducibles *(Continued)*
  family guide brochure, 166*f*–167*f*
  Individuals with Disabilities Education Improvement
    Act and, 53, 165, 168
  No Child Left Behind and, 165
  pyramid, 170*f*
  reading instruction and, 228–229
  special education and, 30
Retro-fitting, universal design for learning *versus,* 145
Ripple effect
  definition of, 139
  differentiation and, 139
Risk taking, collaboration and, 184
Routines
  engagement and, 209, 210*t*
Routines, classroom management and, 116–117, 118–119
Routines-based intervention, 77
Rules, class, 109–110

Scaffolding
  cognitive development and, 84
  definition of, 150
  executive functions and, 150
  proactive behavior and, 210
SCANS Skills and Competencies, 296
Schema, 83
Science
  active processes in, 281
  anchor activities in, 287–288, 288*t*
  art and, 282–283
  assessment, 291–292
  auditory input in, 286
  choice in instruction, 284–285
  curriculum, 281–282
  engagement and, 282–286
  expository texts in, 281
  formal curriculum in, 281
  guided inquiry in, 291
  input and, 286–288
  as inquiry, 280–281
  instruction strategies, 282–291
  language, 286–287
  lesson planning ideas, 289
  literature and, 282–283
  multiple intelligences and, 288, 289*t*
  music and, 282–283
  output and, 288–291
  performance, 280
  performance-based assessment in, 292
  product-based assessment in, 292
  real-life connections in, 283–284
  self-regulation and, 285–286
  societal curriculum in, 282
  structured inquiry in, 291
  student-directed inquiry in, 291
  support strategies, 290–291
  symbolic curriculum in, 281
  tactile input in, 286
  visual input in, 286
Section 504 of Rehabilitation Act, 43–44
Segregation, 38–41
Self-advocacy, 193–194

Self-awareness, 87
Self-efficacy, 87
Self-monitoring, 213–214, 213*t*
Self-recognition, 87
Self-regulation, 151–152, 271, 285–286
Self-statements, 87
Sensorimotor stage, 83
Separatist language, 57–58
Sequential ordering system of school performance, 95*t*
Service coordination, 73, 76
Slavery, 10–11
SLPs, *see* Speech and language pathologists
Social bingo, 109
Social construction
  definition of, 10
  of disability, 13–15
  of gender, 11–13
  of race, 10–11
  of special education, 30
Social constructivism, 84
Social development, 85*t*, 88–89, 97
Social justice, 111–112
Social model, 9–10
Social place, shared, 130–131
Social Security Administration (SSA), 198
Social skills
  assessment, 307–308
  definition of, 296
  engagement and, 299–301, 302*t*
  input and, 304–305
  output and, 306–307
Social studies
  challenging in, 258–259
  concept diagrams in, 258, 259*f*
  critical thinking in, 256, 263, 263*t*
  demonstrating mastery in, 262–263
  digital resources in, 261
  enduring understandings in, 256
  engagement and, 256–269
  input and, 260–262
  local-global connections in, 257–258
  multiple perspectives in, 258
  output and, 262–263
  overview of, 254
  primary sources in, 260
  strategies for, 256–263
  thematic units in, 261–262
  themes in, 254, 255*f*
Social thinking system of school performance, 95*t*
Societal curriculum, 282
Socioeconomic considerations, early childhood
    interventions and, 78
Sociometric devices, 307–308
Spatial ordering system of school performance, 95*t*
Special area classes
  connecting in, 315–316
  definition of, 312
  individualized education programs and, 313, 314
  teachers in, 312–316
Special education
  classroom management and, 119–123
  continuum of services and, 26

development of, 25–29
early childhood, major principles of, 71–79
eligibility for, 172–173
evaluation for, 170–175
history of, 25–27
inclusion debate in, 29
labeling and, 27–29
process steps, 171*t*
social construction of, 30
success in, 31
supports in, 30–31
zone of proximal development and, 30
Speech and language pathologists (SLPs), 317
Spirit of law, 56
Squatters, 131
SSA, *see* Social Security Administration
Standardized, definition of, 136*f*
Standards, common core state, 227–228, 267
Statistics
definition of, 7
industrialization and, 7–8
Stigma, 58–59
Structured inquiry, 291
Student at-risk referral form, 169*f*
Student-directed inquiry, 291
Students
as aliens, 131
English language learner, 113–114
families and, 114–115
homosexual, 115
marginalization of, 131
poverty and, 112–113
as squatters, 131
transgendered, 115
Subversive pedagogy, 184
Success, traditional definitions of, 57
Summative assessment
overview of, 162–163
in reading, 237–238
see also Assessment
Supports, 30–31, 31–33
Symbolic curriculum, 281
Symbols, representation and, 147–149

Teacher-ranking systems, 308
Teachers
child development and, 99–102
English for Speakers of Other Languages, 318
power of, 206
service professionals and, collaboration among,
186–187
special area, 312–316
Teacher–teacher collaboration, 186
Teaching assistants, collaboration with, 187
Team, child support, 165
Technology
assistive
communication and, 304
cost of, 153
definition of, 153
high-tech, 153–154
independence and, 154

as investigation, 153
low-tech, 153–154
as product, 153
digital literacy and, 223
digital media and, 227
"Them" and "us," language of, 28*t*
Thematic units
definition of, 261
in social studies instruction, 261–262
Thinking, belief in ability for, 129
Tic-Tac-Toe menu, 138–139, 138*f*
Tourette syndrome, 135
Transdisciplinary, 77
Transgender students, 115
Transition to adult life
advocacy in, 193–194
community connections and, 197–201
as coordinated set of activities, 194, 197
critical life areas in, 194
early planning for, 192–193
inclusion in, 197
independent-living centers in, 198
in Individuals with Disabilities Education
Improvement Act, 194–195
issues in, 192–194
legislation in, 194–197
long-term adult outcomes in, 195, 197
person-centered planning in, 194, 196
postsecondary education programs in, 199–201
processes in, 194–197
self-advocacy in, 193–194
Social Security Administration in, 198
students as active participants in, 193
success in, 195–197
vocational rehabilitation agencies in, 198
Transitions, in early childhood intervention, 78
"Tweens," 89

UCEDD, *see* University Centers for Excellence in
Developmental Disabilities
United Nations Children's Fund (UNICEF), 30
Universal design for learning (UDL)
action in, 149–152
assistive technology in, 153–154
case example, 154–160
classroom, 152–160, 156*f*
comprehension and, 149
curriculum, 145
definition of, 144
effort and, 151
engagement and, 151–152
expression in, 149–152
language in, 147–149
mathematical expressions in, 147–149
perception in, 146–147
persistence and, 151
principles of, 145
reasons for, 145
representation in, 146–149
retro-fitting *versus*, 145
self-regulation and, 151–152
symbols in, 147–149

University Centers for Excellence in Developmental
     Disabilities (UCEDD), 65
"Us" and "them," language of, 28*t*

VARK Learning Profile Questionnaire, 182*t*
Virginia, 70
Visual development, 85*t*
Vocabulary, 223
Vocalics, 299
Vocational rehabilitation agencies, 198

War on Poverty, 66
Welfare reform, 70
Well-child visits, 73
Whole-language approach, to reading instruction, 224
Will, in identity development, 86*t*
Wisconsin, 70
Wisdom, in identity development, 86*t*
Workshop, writer's, 245
Writing
     assessment, 242–243, 250–251
     code-switching and, 247–248

components of, 243–245
digital media and, 245
engagement and, 246–248
expository, 243
feedback for, 251
graphic organizers for, 250
informative, 243
input and, 248–249
instruction models, 245–246
narrative, 243
output and, 249–250
persuasive, 243
process, 244
reading and, 244–245
six traits of, 245
stages of, 250
workshop, 245

Zero reject rule, 45
Zone of proximal development, 30, 84